Development and Underdevelopment

· · · · · · · · · ·

Development and Underdevelopment

The Political Economy of Inequality

edited by

Mitchell A. Seligson
John T Passé-Smith

Lynne Rienner Publishers　　•　　Boulder & London

For
Susan Berk-Seligson
and
Mary Sue Passé-Smith

Published in the United States of America in 1993 by
Lynne Rienner Publishers, Inc.
1800 30th Street, Boulder, Colorado 80301

and in the United Kingdom by
Lynne Rienner Publishers, Inc.
3 Henrietta Street, Covent Garden, London WC2E 8LU

Library of Congress Cataloging-in-Publication Data
Development and underdevelopment : the political economy of inequality
/ edited by Mitchell A. Seligson and John Passé-Smith.
    p.   cm.
    Includes bibliographical references and index.
    ISBN 1-55587-400-2 (pbk. : alk. paper)
    1. Developing countries—Economic conditions. 2. Economic
development. 3. Income distribution. 4. Capitalism. 5. Economic
history—1945–   6. Social history—1945–   I. Seligson, Mitchell A.
II. Passé-Smith, John T
HC59.7.D3945   1993
338.9—dc20   93-9796
                                                              CIP

British Cataloguing in Publication Data
A Cataloguing in Publication record for this book
is available from the British Library.

Printed and bound in the United States of America

 The paper used in this publication meets the requirements
of the American National Standard for Permanence of
Paper for Printed Library Materials Z39.48-1984.

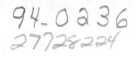

Contents

List of Tables and Figures   ix
Preface   xiii

PART 1   DEFINING THE GAP BETWEEN RICH AND POOR

1   The Dual Gaps: An Overview of Theory and Research
    Mitchell A. Seligson   3

2   The Gap Between Rich and Poor Countries
    David Morawetz   9

3   The Persistence of the Gap: Taking Stock of Economic Growth
    in the Post–World War II Era
    John T Passé-Smith   15

4   Income Inequality: Some Dimensions of the Problem
    Montek S. Ahluwalia   31

PART 2   THE CLASSIC THESIS REVISITED:
              LIMITS TO CONVERGENCE

5   Economic Growth and Income Inequality
    Simon Kuznets   43

v

6   Catching Up, Forging Ahead, and Falling Behind
     Moses Abramovitz   57

7   Productivity Growth, Convergence, and Welfare: What
     the Long-Run Data Show
     William J. Baumol   77

8   Productivity Growth, Convergence, and Welfare: Comment
     J. Bradford De Long   91

9   Could It Be That the Whole World Is Already Rich?
     A Comparison of RGDP/pc and GNP/pc Measures
     John T Passé-Smith   103

10   Basic Needs and Growth-Welfare Trade-Offs
     Bruce E. Moon and William J. Dixon   119

PART 3   CULTURE, MODERNIZATION, AND DEVELOPMENT

11   The Achievement Motive in Economic Growth
     David C. McClelland   141

12   Becoming Modern
     Alex Inkeles and David H. Smith   159

13   The Confucian Ethic and Economic Growth
     Herman Kahn   169

14   Underdevelopment Is a State of Mind
     Lawrence E. Harrison   173

15   On the Sociology of National Development:
     Theories and Issues
     Alejandro Portes   183

PART 4   DEPENDENCY AND WORLD-SYSTEM THEORY

16   The Structure of Dependence
     Theotonio dos Santos   193

17   Modernization and Dependency: Alternative Perspectives
     in the Study of Latin American Underdevelopment
     J. Samuel Valenzuela and Arturo Valenzuela   203

18 The Present State of the Debate on World Inequality
    Immanuel Wallerstein   217

19 Wallerstein's World Capitalist System: A Theoretical
    and Historical Critique
    Theda Skocpol   231

20 Transnational Penetration and Economic Growth
    Volker Bornschier and Christopher Chase-Dunn   239

21 Financial Dependence in the Capitalist World Economy
    and the Distribution of Income Within States
    Edward N. Muller   267

22 The Irish Case of Dependency: An Exception to the Exception?
    Denis O'Hearn   295

23 Inequality and Rebellion in Central America
    John A. Booth   315

PART 5   THE STATE, GROWTH, AND INEQUALITY:
         RENT-SEEKING, URBAN BIAS, AND DEMOCRACY

24 Governments and Agricultural Markets in Africa
    Robert H. Bates   333

25 Rent-Seeking or Dependency as Explanations of
    Why Poor People Stay Poor
    Erich Weede   347

26 Urban Bias and Inequality
    Michael Lipton   371

27 Urban Bias and Economic Growth in Cross-National Perspective
    Erich Weede   377

28 The Effects of Democracy on Economic Growth
    and Inequality
    Larry Sirowy and Alex Inkeles   389

29 Big Business and the State: Latin America and
    East Asia Compared
    Gary Gereffi   407

30 The Rise and Crisis of the Dragon Economies
    Walden Bello and Stephanie Rosenfeld   421

PART 6   CONCLUSION

31 Inequality in a Global Perspective: Directions
    for Further Research
    Mitchell A. Seligson   437

Index   449
About the Book and Editors   456

Tables and Figures

TABLES

2.1	The Relative and Absolute Gaps in GNP Per Capita, by Region, 1950–75	10
2.2	The Absolute Gap: When Might It Be Closed?	11
3.1	Economic Growth Rates by Income Group and Region	17
3.2	Economic and Population Growth Rates	18
3.3	The Relative and Absolute Gap by Income Group and Region	20
3.4	Income Groups' Percentage of World Population	21
3.5	Closing the Absolute Gap	23
3.6	Mobility Across Income Groups, 1962 and 1990	26
3.7	Mobility in Rankings of GNP/pc	27
4.1	Cross-classification of Countries by Income Level and Equality	36
6.1	Comparative Levels of Productivity, 1870–1979	62
6.2	The Association (Rank Correlation) Between Initial Levels and Subsequent Growth Rates of Labor Productivity	63
7.1	Total Growth from 1870 to 1979: Productivity, GDP Per Capita, and Exports, Sixteen Industrialized Countries	80
8.1	Regressions Using Maddison's Sixteen	93
8.2	Maximum Likelihood Estimation for the Once-Rich Twenty-Two, 1913–1979	95
8.3	Maximum Likelihood Estimation for the Once-Rich Twenty-Two, 1870–1979	96
8.4	Standard Deviations of Log Output for Maddison's Sixteen and the Once-Rich Twenty-Two	96
8.5	Democracy over 1950–1980 and Long-Run Growth for the Once-Rich Twenty-Two, 1870–1979	97

8.6   Democracy in 1870 and Long-Run Growth for the Once-Rich
        Twenty-Two, 1870–1979   97
8.7   Dominant Religion in 1870 and Long-Run Growth
        for the Once-Rich Twenty-Two, 1870–1979   98
9.1   Comparison of RGDP/pc and GNP/pc: Levels, Rank,
        and Growth Rates by Region   106
9.2   The Most Severe Changes in the Conversion from
        GNP/pc to RGDP/pc   112
9.3   Income Groups' Percentage of World Population   113
9.4   Growth Rates by Geographic Region,
        1962–1985, 1962–1975, 1975–1985   116
10.1   Regression of Real Product Growth Rate on Beginning
        Product Level, Domestic Investment, and Basic Needs
        Performance, 1960–1985   128
10.2   Regression of Real Product Growth Rate on Beginning
        Product Level, Domestic Investment, Basic Needs
        Performance, and Basic Needs Change, 1960–1985   129
10.3   Regression of Basic Needs Performance on Economic
        Growth, Lagged Basic Needs Performance, and Real
        GDP Per Capita, 1960–1985   131
10.4   Regression of Relative Basic Needs Performance on
        Economic Growth, Lagged Basic Needs Performance,
        and Real GDP Per Capita, 1960–1985   132
10.5   Regression of Relative Basic Needs Performance on
        Five-Year Growth Rates, Lagged Basic Needs Performance,
        and Real GDP Per Capita, 1960–1985   133
11.1   Rate of Growth in Electrical Output (1952–1958) and
        National n Achievement Levels in 1950   149
14.1   [no title]   174
20.1   Studies of the Effect of Transnational Corporations on
        Economic Growth Using Stock or Flow Measures,
        and Direction of Effects   243
20.2   Studies of the Effect of Transnational Corporate
        Penetration (Stocks) on Economic Growth by Country
        Composition and Direction of Effects   245
20.3   Regression of Average Annual Real Growth of Income
        Per Capita 1965–1977   252
20.4   Regressions for Peripheral and Semiperipheral Countries
        in Different Ranges of Internal Market Size and GNP
        Per Capita   256
20.5   Effects of Penetration and Flows of Foreign Investment
        in Larger and Smaller African Countries   257

20.6 Analysis of the Statistical Interactions Between Transnational
      Penetration and Dummy Variables for Core Countries and
      Countries Located in Africa, America, and Asia   258
21.1 Distribution of Scores on MNC Penetration and Share of
      National Income Accruing to the Upper Quintile: 50 Nations   277
21.2 Bivariate Correlation (r) for the General MNC Penetration
      Model   282
21.3 Regressions of the Income Received by the Highest Quintile
      on Logged MNC Penetration, Core Dummy, and
      MNC*CORE Interaction Term   282
22.1 Revenues from Customs Tariffs, and as Percentage of Total
      Net Government Receipts (million Irish punts)   298
22.2 Changes of Employment and Number of Firms in Domestic
      "Old" and "Adapted" Industry from 1973 to 1986, Ireland   298
22.3 Locally Purchased Materials as Percentage of Total Material
      Inputs in U.S. Affiliates Operating in Brazil, Mexico, and
      Ireland   301
22.4 Annual Percentage Rates of Growth of Gross Fixed Capital
      Formation (GFCF) and GNP during ELI, 1955–85   303
22.5 Distribution of Incomes and Tax Payments, by Decile, 1973
      and 1980   304
22.6 Profit Rates by Sector and Country of Ownership, Irish
      Manufacturing, 1983   307
22.7 Wages by Sector and Country of Ownership, Irish
      Manufacturing, 1983   309
23.1 Mean Annual Growth in Gross Domestic Products
      Per Capita in Central American Countries, 1950–1989   321
23.2 Real Working-Class Wage Indices for 1963–1984   322
23.3 Unemployment Trends, 1970–1989, in Percentages   323
23.4 Comparison of Central Government Expenditures
      as a Percentage of Budget   324
27.1 Results of Regressions of Economic Growth 1960–79
      on the Level of Economic Development, Gross Domestic
      Investment, Some Human Capital Variables, and Urban Bias   384
27.2 Regressions of Economic Growth 1960–79 on the Level
      of Economic Development, Gross Domestic Investment,
      Some Human Capital Variables, and Logged Urban Bias   385
28.1 [no title]   396
28.2 [no title]   397
28.3 Sets of Countries Examined in the Studies   400
29.1 The Ten Largest Companies in Mexico, Brazil, South Korea,
      and Taiwan, 1987   410
29.2 GDP Shares of the Ten Largest Companies, 1987   413

FIGURES

3.1	The Gap Between Rich, Middle, and Poor Countries	20
3.2	The Relative Gap Between Rich and Middle-Income Countries	24
3.3	The Relative Gap Between Rich and Poor Countries	25
7.1	Productivity Growth Rate	82
7.2	Growth Rate, 1950–80	85
9.1	Standard Deviations and Means of World RGDP/pc and GNP/pc	115
9.2	Variation from the World Mean RGDP/pc and GNP/pc	115
11.1	Average n Achievement Level	145
21.1	Relationship Between MNC Penetration and Top 20 Percent Income Share (Core)	279
21.2	Relationship Between MNC Penetration and Top 20 Percent Income Share (Periphery)	280
21.3	Time Series of Foreign Investment and Top 20 Percent Income Share	284
21.4	Relationship Between External Public Debt and Top 20 Percent Income Share (Periphery)	286

Preface

Most residents of industrialized nations have at some time been struck by the vast gap in wealth separating them from those who reside in the poor countries of the world. Whether they travel to those countries or visit them vicariously through television and film, the gap is probably the single most vivid impression that remains in their minds. There is a second gap, one that exists within the poor countries themselves, between the tiny affluent minority and the vast majority of the poor. This dichotomy can be observed in urban areas as well as in rural villages.

Two questions concern most social scientists who conduct research in the Third World, where they experience the gaps firsthand. First, what causes the gaps? Second, are they narrowing or widening? This book is an attempt to provide the clearest answers that these same social scientists have been able to offer to date.

This book is a substantially revised version of its predecessor, *The Gap Between Rich and Poor* (Westview Press, 1984). Lynne Rienner was editorial director at Westview when the idea for the first version emerged. She liked the concept and nursed it through the various stages of production. By the time the book had sold out, however, Lynne was the owner of her own academic press. She expressed interest in producing a revised version. We are deeply grateful for her faith in the enterprise.

The original volume grew out of a seminar taught by Mitchell Seligson at the University of Arizona. In preparing for the seminar while on sabbatical at the University of Essex in England, he recognized that there was a great deal of research addressing the two questions posed above, and he attempted to organize that material for his students. Although there were a number of collections that examined political and economic development, none directly addressed the questions he sought to answer. In addition, the most recent theoretical and empirical research on dependency and world systems was generally absent from these volumes.

When the seminar was taught for the first time, the students attending helped refine the thinking that went into its preparation. One of those students, John Passé-Smith, perused the subject matter presented in the seminar and wrote his doctoral dissertation on it. When Seligson was about to begin another sabbatical, this one at the Kellogg Institute at the University of Notre Dame, Passé-Smith suggested that a new edition of the volume be produced, incorporating the latest scholarship on the problem of the dual gaps between rich and poor. Hence this collaborative effort emerged, with Seligson and Passé-Smith serving as coeditors.

We have sought to retain the best of the old edition and so have included thirteen of the selections that made up that book. Much new material has emerged since the early 1980s, however, and as a result this volume contains eighteen new selections, reflecting the better, more extensive data bases now available on which to judge the magnitude and direction of the gaps between rich and poor. Economic historians have increased the historical data we have for national wealth statistics, and a study commissioned by the United Nations has provided new measures of contemporary wealth of nations based on purchasing power rather than exchange rate comparisons. As a result, there is new literature on the prospects of "convergence" among the economies of the world, a theme we treat in Part 2 of this new edition. There has also been a new focus on quality-of-life measures as a different and perhaps better way of measuring the gaps. This focus is also reflected in Part 2. On the other hand, dependency and world-system thinking have prospered less well, perhaps because of the fall of socialist systems throughout the world. Yet many of the concepts of those theories have been incorporated into our thinking, and therefore we have devoted Part 4 of the revised book to what we consider the best material on the subject. The newest and most dynamic area emerges in an entirely new section (Part 5), in which the focus of the causes of the gap moves back from the international system and lands squarely at the door of national governments. Some research seems to show convincingly that it is misdirected state policies that slow growth and increase the gap between rich and poor people. This research has grown into a school of thought called "rent-seeking," and another known as "urban bias." Some scholars have rejected these theses, arguing instead that the great successes of the East Asian newly industrializing countries (NICs) are due to historical factors that will not be repeated. Still other researchers have suggested that it is not government policies per se but the form of government that causes the gaps to become exacerbated. Hence, in Part 5 we also examine the impact of democracy on growth and inequality.

We have organized the volume so that it will be of maximum utility in the classroom. The six parts of the book are arranged to enable the instructor to assign any one part as a self-contained unit. The order in which the parts are presented makes a logical path that the student can easily follow. Part 1 provides the basic "facts" of the gap: the size of the gap between rich and poor countries and the size of the gap between rich and poor people. Part 2 deals with the dynamics question: Is the gap widening or narrowing? Part 3 presents the fascinating cultural explanations for the gaps. Part 4 covers dependency and world-system theories, with much empirical evidence and case study data supporting both sides of the debate. Part 5 covers the role of the state in stimulating or inhibiting growth and inequality. Finally, we offer some conclusions in Part 6.

We are indebted to numerous people for helping us get the book to press. In particular, we would like to thank Keith Miracle for his tireless work scanning the chapters. Also, Mary Sue Passé-Smith worked relentlessly and offered invaluable advice. This book would not have been completed without her help. Finally, we would like to thank the many authors and publishers who so kindly granted permission for their works to appear here.

Mitchell A. Seligson
John T Passé-Smith

PART 1

. . . .

Defining the Gap
Between Rich and Poor

. . . .

1

· · · · · · ·

The Dual Gaps: An Overview of Theory and Research

· · · · · · ·

MITCHELL A. SELIGSON

The income gap between rich and poor countries has grown dramatically since World War II. In 1950 the average per capita income (in 1980 U.S. dollars) of low-income countries was $164, whereas the per capita income of the industrialized countries averaged $3,841, yielding an absolute income gap of $3,677. Thirty years later, in 1980, incomes in the poor countries had risen to an average of only $245, whereas those in the industrialized countries had soared to $9,648; the absolute gap in 1980 stood at $9,403. For this period, then, there is clear evidence to support the old adage that "the rich get richer." It is not true, however, that the poor get poorer, but that would be a perverse way of looking at these data. A more realistic view of the increases in "wealth" in the poor countries would show that in this thirty-year period their citizens increased their incomes by an average of only $2.70 a year, less than what a North American might spend for lunch at a neighborhood fast-food stand. And in terms of relative wealth, the poor countries certainly did get poorer; the total income (gross national product, or GNP) of the low-income countries declined from 4.3 percent of the income earned by the industrialized countries in 1950 to a mere 2.5 percent by 1980.[1]

By 1990 the gap had grown even wider. In that year, the high-income countries earned a per capita average of $20,173, versus $353 in the low-income countries, for an absolute gap of $19,820 (1990 U.S. dollars). The relative gap had become even greater, with the income of the poor low-income countries equal to only 1.7 percent of that of the industrialized countries. Hence, since 1950 the relative gap between rich and poor countries had widened by 60 percent.[2]

One might suspect that these data do not reflect the general pattern of growth found throughout the world but are influenced by the disappointing performance of a few "basket case" nations. That suspicion is unfounded. The low-income countries comprise over half the world's population; more than three billion people live in countries with per capita incomes of less than $400 a year. It is also incorrect to speculate that because the growth rates of some poor countries have recently outperformed those of the industrialized countries that the gap will soon be narrowed. In Chapter 2, David Morawetz tells us that it could take China, which alone contains some one billion people, 2,900 years to close the gap. Even in the "miracle countries" such as South Korea and Taiwan, where growth rates have been twice as high as in the industrialized countries, the gap has doubled.

There is another gap separating rich from poor: Many developing nations are experiencing a growing gap between their own rich and poor citizens. Poor people who live in poor countries, therefore, are falling further behind not only the world's rich but also their more affluent countrymen. Moreover, precisely the opposite phenomenon has taken place within the richer countries, where the gap between rich and poor has narrowed. The world's poor, therefore, find themselves in double jeopardy.

The consequences of these widening gaps can be witnessed every day. In the international arena, tensions between the "haves" and "have-nots" dominate debate in the United Nations and other international forums. The poor countries demand a "New International Economic Order" (NIEO), which they hope will result in the transfer of wealth away from the rich countries. The industrialized countries have responded with foreign aid programs that, by all accounts, can only hope to make a small dent in the problem. Indeed, some argue that foreign aid actually exacerbates the gap.[3] Within the developing countries, domestic stability is frequently tenuous at best as victims of the yawning gap between rich and poor (along with their sympathizers) seek redress through violent means. The guerrilla fighting that spotted the globe during the Cold War may have been fueled by international conflict, but its root cause invariably can be traced to domestic inequality and deprivation, whether relative or absolute. This remains true in the post–Cold War era.

Thinking and research on the international and domestic gaps between rich and poor has been going through a protracted period of debate that can be traced back to the end of World War II. The war elevated the United States to the position of world leader, and in that position the nation found itself confronted with a Western Europe in ruins. The motivations behind the Marshall Plan for rebuilding Europe are debated to this day, but two things remain evident: Unprecedented amounts of aid were given, and the expected results were rapid in forthcoming. War-torn industries were rebuilt, new ones were begun, and economic growth quickly resumed.

The successful rebuilding of Europe encouraged many to believe that similar success would meet efforts to stimulate growth in the developing world. More often than not, however, such efforts have failed or fallen far below expectations. Even when programs have been effective and nations have seemed well on the way toward rapid growth, they nonetheless continued to fall further and further behind the wealthy countries. Moreover, growth almost inevitably seemed to be accompanied by a widening income gap within the developing countries.

The authors of this collection present a comprehensive treatment of the thinking that is evolving on the subject of the international and domestic gaps between rich and poor. Their studies are not confined to a single academic discipline or geographic area. Rather, their work reflects a variety of fields, including economics, political science, sociology, history, and psychology, and they have examined the problems from the viewpoint of a single country or region as well as with a macroanalytic approach. This diversity produced four major perspectives on the gap.

The first, what we label the "classic thesis," suggests that the gaps are temporal and will disappear over time. A number of economists, most notably Simon Kuznets (Chapter 5), have been associated with this school of thought, which sees domestic income inequality as an almost inevitable by-product of development. Kuznets traces a path that seems to have been followed quite closely by nations that have become industrialized. The process begins with relative domestic equality in the distribution of income. The onset of industrialization produces a significant shift in the direction of inequality and creates a widening gap. Once the industrialization process matures, however, the gap is again reduced. This view was certainly held by those who still regard the Marshall Plan as the model for the resolution of world poverty. Whereas Part 1 of the book presents the basic data on the extent of the dual gaps, Part 2 reexamines the classic thesis and suggests strongly that the gaps show few signs of narrowing, with or without a Marshall Plan for the Third World. Several of the authors show that convergence between rich and poor is an ever-receding dream.

In the second perspective, the widening gap between rich and poor nations is viewed as being principally a cultural problem (see Part 3). Specifically, the cultural values associated with industrialization are seen as foreign to many developing nations, which are deeply attached to more traditional cultural values. Yet punctuality, hard work, achievement, and other "industrial" values are the keys to unlocking the economic potential of poor countries, according to these scholars. Most adherents of this perspective believe that such values can be inculcated through deliberate effort (Chapter 11). Others argue that the values will emerge naturally as the result of a worldwide process of diffusion of values functional for development. This perspective has been incorporated into a more general school of thought focusing on the process called "modernization." Development occurs and the international gap is narrowed when a broad set of modern values *and* institutions is present (see Chapter 14). The success of the Asian economies in recent years has led some to speculate that there are cultural values found there that foster growth. This view, a variant on Max Weber's old notion of the value of the "Protestant ethic," is termed the "Confucian ethic."

In marked contrast to these two perspectives, which suggest that the phenomena of rich and poor disparity are transitory, a third, more recent school of thought comes to rather different conclusions (see Part 4). The scholars supporting this approach—known as *dependentistas*—observe that the economies of the developing nations have been shaped in response to forces and conditions established by the industrialized nations and that their development has been both delayed and dependent as a result. The *dependentistas* conclude that the failure of poor countries is a product of the distorted development brought on by dependency relations. A further elaboration on this thinking has emerged in recent years in the form of the "world-system" perspective developed by Immanuel Wallerstein and his followers. According to this group, since the sixteenth century a world capitalist economy has existed, divided geographically (rather than occupationally, as in the earlier system of empires) into three primary zones: core, semiperiphery, and periphery. The core dominates the system and drains the semiperiphery and periphery of their economic surplus. Both of these perspectives contend that the gaps will be perpetuated by the nature of the international system and cannot be narrowed unless a major restructuring of that system is undertaken.

The final and most recent explanation of the gaps focuses attention on the role of states within the Third World. As socialist economies throughout the world proved incapable of keeping up with the capitalist industrialized countries, international development agencies focused their attention on the need for policy reforms within the Third World. This attention brought with it a host of neoliberal policy prescriptions, including privatization, trade liberalization, and the ending of import substitution industrialization (ISI) policies. The collapse of the Soviet Union and the socialist states of Eastern Europe, along with increasing capitalist economics in China, has reinforced this tendency.

According to the perspective that focuses on the state, errors of state policy are largely responsible for the gaps. The growth of parastatal marketing boards in Africa is shown by Robert Bates (Chapter 24) to be a significant factor in slowing growth in those countries. These boards distort the prices paid to producers, ostensibly to provide income stability to them. But the primary purpose is actually to curry support among urban dwellers by guaranteeing low consumer prices for agricultural goods. In fact, the prices paid are so low that producers have no incentive to continue to grow their crops, and production falls. The Bates perspective is generalized by Erich Weede (Chapter 25) into what is called "rent-seeking," a situation in which government policy allows favored groups to charge prices above those that would have been set by the market. According to Weede, it is not dependency as imposed from abroad but domestic policies within the Third World that allow and indeed encourage rent-seeking behavior, which in turn explains slow growth and inequality in those countries. Another related manifestation of rent-seeking distortions is that of urban bias, suggested by Michael Lipton (Chapter 26) and tested by Erich Weede (Chapter 27). From this perspective, there are numerous policies in the Third World that favor the cities over the countryside, with the result that growth is slowed and the gap between rich and poor nations widens.

Because of the dramatic increase in the number of democratic governments in recent years, the focus on states has raised concerns over the connection between democracy on the one hand and growth and inequality on the other. Some have argued that democratic political systems are less capable than their authoritarian counterparts of setting a clear economic agenda, whereas others have argued that democracies not only are good for growth but also are inherently egalitarian in nature and hence help reduce the domestic gap between rich and poor. The paper by Larry Sirowy and Alex Inkeles (Chapter 28) presents the evidence in this debate.

Finally, the dramatic successes in both growth and equality in the so-called miracle economies of Asia, the "gang of four" and the "little tigers," have led to a careful examination of state policy in those countries. These economies have shown consistent growth that far exceeds that of the Third World and that of the industrialized countries. Moreover, this growth has been achieved in countries such as Taiwan, South Korea, and Japan at the same time as income inequality has been *reduced*. Some observers, such as Herman Kahn (Chapter 13), believe that the success can be largely explained by cultural factors, especially the "Confucian ethic." But others believe that it is state policies that have driven these successes (see Gary Gereffi, Chapter 29, and Walden Bello and Stephanie Rosenfeld, Chapter 30).

NOTES

1. These figures are based upon the World Bank's *World Development Report 1980* (New York: Oxford University Press, 1980), 34.

2. Data from World Bank, *World Development Report 1992* (New York: Oxford University Press, 1992), 218–219.

3. See Volker Bornschier, Christopher Chase-Dunn, and Richard Rubinson, 1978, "Cross-National Evidence of the Effects of Foreign Investment and Aid on Economic Growth and Inequality: A Survey of the Findings," *American Sociological Review*, vol. 84 (November 1978).

2

· · · · · · ·

The Gap Between
Rich and Poor Countries

· · · · · · ·

DAVID MORAWETZ

The enormity and persistence of the per capita income gap between rich and poor countries is the subject of this selection by David Morawetz. Using data gathered by the World Bank, Morawetz shows that there are two gaps, the relative and the absolute. Although some areas of the world (China, East Asia, and the Middle East) have narrowed the relative gap in the 1950–1975 period, others have seen it widen. For the developing countries as a whole, per capita income equalled only 7.6 percent of the per capita income of the industrialized nations. Even more distressing are the finding that only one country, Libya, was able to narrow the absolute gap during the twenty-five years of post–World War II development covered in this study and the projection that it will take anywhere from several hundred to more than three thousand years for developing countries to close the gap at present growth rates. Morawetz concludes by arguing that closing the relative and absolute gaps may be a goal that is neither attainable nor desirable.

Although during 1950–75 the per capita incomes (as conventionally measured) of the developing countries were growing faster than ever before, so too were those of the developed countries. As a result, the gap between the rich and the poor nations, which had been increasing for 100 to 150 years (Kuznets 1965), continued to widen.

Reprinted with permission from *Twenty-Five Years of Economic Development, 1950–1975*, David Morawetz, pp. 26–30. Published for the World Bank by Johns Hopkins University Press, Baltimore/London, 1977.

THE RELATIVE GAP

Since the developing and developed countries grew in per capita income at almost identical rates during 1950–75 (Table 2.1), the per capita income of the developing countries as a proportion of that of the developed countries stayed fairly constant, at around 7 to 8 percent. In China, East Asia, and particularly in the Middle East, the relative gap narrowed somewhat, whereas in South Asia, Africa, and Latin America it widened.

Table 2.1   The Relative and Absolute Gaps in GNP Per Capita, by Region, 1950–75

Region	Relative Gap[a] (percent)		Absolute Gap[b] (1974 U.S. dollars)	
	1950	1975	1950	1975
South Asia	3.6	2.5	2,293	5,106
Africa	7.1	5.9	2,208	4,930
East Asia	5.5	6.5[c]	2,248	4,897
China, People's Republic of	4.8	6.1[c]	2,265	4,918
Latin America	20.8	18.0	1,883	4,294
Middle East	19.3	31.7[c]	1,918	3,578
Developing countries	6.7	7.2[c]	2,218	4,863
Developing countries excluding China	7.9	7.6	2,191	4,837

   a. Relative gap is GNP per capita of region as percent of GNP per capita of the OECD countries.
   b. Absolute gap is GNP per capita of the OECD countries ($2,378 in 1950, $5,338 in 1975) less GNP per capita of the region.
   c. Relative gap decreased, 1950–75.
   Source: Computed from data tapes, *World Bank Atlas* (1977), and World Bank, *World Tables* 1976.

THE ABSOLUTE GAP

In 1950 the average GNP per capita of the OECD countries (in conventional 1974 dollars) was $2,191 greater than that of the developing countries.[1] By 1975 this difference had more than doubled, to $4,839 (Table 2.1). There is no single region in which the absolute gap did not at least double. Furthermore, apart from oil-rich Libya, not a single developing country for which data are available for 1950 managed to narrow the absolute gap even slightly during the full twenty-five-year period.[2] Even in fast-growing Korea and Taiwan the absolute gap doubled.

   This remarkable situation is the result of the simple algebra of gaps. In brief, a poor country growing faster than a rich one will not even begin to reduce the absolute gap between them until the ratio of their per capita

Table 2.2   The Absolute Gap: When Might It Be Closed?[a]

Country[b]	GNP Per Capita, 1975 (1974 U.S. dollars)	Annual growth rate, 1960–75 (percent)	Number of Years Until Gap Closed If 1960-75 Growth Rates Continue
OECD countries	5,238	3.7	—
Libyan Arab Republic	4,675	11.8	2
Saudi Arabia	2,767	8.6	14
Singapore	2,307	7.6	22
Israel	3,287	5.0	37
Iran	1,321	6.9	45
Hong Kong	1,584	6.3	48
Korea	504	7.3	69
China (Taiwan)	817	6.3	75
Iraq	1,180	4.4	223
Brazil	927	4.2	362
Thailand	319	4.5	365
Tunisia	695	4.2	422
Syrian Arab Republic	604	4.2	451
Lesoto	161	4.5	454
Turkey	793	4.0	675
Togo	245	4.1	807
Panama	977	3.8	1,866
Malawi	137	3.9	1,920
Malaysia	665	3.8	2,293
Papua New Guinea	412	3.8	2,826
China, People's Republic of	320	3.8	2,900
Mauritania	288	3.8	3,224

a. Absolute gap is GNP per capita of the OECD countries ($2,378 in 1950, $5,238 in 1975) less GNP per capita of the individual country.

b. All developing countries with population of 1 million or more whose growth rate of per capita income exceeded that of the OECD countries during 1960–75.

Source: Computed from data tapes, *World Bank Atlas* (1977).

incomes is equal to the inverse ratio of their growth rates. For example, even though Korea has been growing twice as fast as the OECD countries for the past fifteen years, the absolute gap between them will continue to widen until the per capita GNP of Korea reaches half that of the OECD countries. The proportion is currently not one-half but one-tenth.

Assuming for a moment that historical growth rates continue into the future and ignoring the fact that cross-country comparisons of conventional GNP per capita statistics are misleading, it is possible to calculate for each developing country the number of years that it would take until the absolute gap between it and the OECD countries would be closed (Table 2.2). For the large majority of developing countries containing most of the developing world's population, the gap would never be closed, for their measured rate of growth of per capita GNP has historically been slower than that of the

OECD countries. Even among the fastest-growing developing countries, only eight would close the gap within 100 years, and only sixteen would close it within 1,000 years.[3]

WELFARE IMPLICATIONS OF THE GAPS

It is not clear that "narrowing the relative gap" makes much sense as a development objective. To take a simple example, if the per capita income of Bangladesh as conventionally measured rises by $2 while that of the United States rises by $65, the relative gap would be narrowing—yet this hardly seems like a shining goal worth striving toward.[4] "Narrowing the absolute gap" appears to make more intuitive sense in welfare terms. But since it may take centuries before the absolute gap is narrowed—if it is ever narrowed—in most developing countries, to use this as a central goal of development is to guarantee long-term frustration.[5]

Fortunately, there are compelling reasons to believe that most developing countries will not place the closing of the gap at the center of their aspirations. First, not all of them regard the resource-wasting life style of the developed countries as an end toward which it is worth striving; at least some seem to prefer to create their own development patterns based on their own resources, and needs, and traditions.[6]

Second, when thinking of the per capita income that they would like to attain, most people (and governments) tend to think of the income of a close-by reference group. Thus, for example, despite the fact that within most countries there is a clear positive association between income and self-rated happiness, there is no observable tendency for people in poor countries to rate themselves as less happy on average than people in rich countries rate themselves (Easterlin 1974). There are several possible explanations of this apparent paradox (Abramovitz 1975). One of them is simply that most people in poor countries do not regard the rich foreigners as part of their reference group and hence are not overconcerned with the gap. They are more concerned, it seems, with their own internal income distributions and their own place within them.[7]

NOTES

1. OECD stands for the Organization for Economic Cooperation and Development, whose members include Australia, Austria, Belgium, Canada, Denmark, Finland, France, Germany, Greece, Iceland, Ireland, Italy, Japan, Luxembourg, the Netherlands, New Zealand, Norway, Portugal, Spain, Sweden, Switzerland, Turkey, the United Kingdom, and the United States.—*Eds.*

2. Intuitively, it seems that some of the other oil-exporting countries must surely have narrowed the absolute gap as well. This highlights a problem existing

throughout this and any other study that is based on *real* growth rates. In measuring a nation's increase in GNP, real growth rate—as they are usually calculated—abstract from price effects. The implicit assumption is that, in the long run, a country's consumption possibilities (and hence its economic welfare) are determined by its physical volume of production. Yet for some countries, and in particular for the oil exporters, the change over time in the relative prices of their principal products may be at least as important in determining national consumption possibilities as the change in physical output, if not more so. In such cases, the use of real growth rates to indicate growth in consumption possibilities may involve a serious bias. It certainly does involve such a bias for the oil-exporting countries during 1950–75, and the bias is clearly in a downward direction.

3. These time intervals may be quite different if purchasing-power parity GNP estimates are used, though the direction and magnitude of this difference will not be clear until it is established how growth rates calculated using purchasing-power parities differ from those rates calculated using conventional GNP statistics: see Bhagwati and Hansen (1972), Kravis, Heston, and Summers (1977 and 1977a), and Strout (1977). For an alternative formulation in which the gap is measured as the number of decades by which specific developing countries lag behind developed countries, see Chenery (1976).

4. In fact, each year's increase in measured GNP per capita in the United States is currently equal to about a century's increase in Bangladesh or India. This is more than a little misleading, however, since a 1 or 2 percent increase in per capita income probably does more to increase economic welfare in Bangladesh than a similar percentage increase does in the United States.

5. The 1974 U.N. General Assembly resolution on the New International Economic Order and the Leontief model (United Nations 1976) both place primary importance on reduction of the gap. Compare Lewis's concluding remarks to a special conference on the gap: "What will happen to the gap between the rich and the poor countries? . . . I do not know the answer and . . . since I think what matters is the absolute progress of the LDCS and not the size of the gap, I do not care" (1972, p. 420).

6. Compare Haq (1976, p. 2): "Similarly, the concept of catching up must be rejected. Catching up with what? Surely the Third World does not wish to imitate the life styles of the rich nations? It must meet its own basic human needs within the framework of its own cultural values, building development around people rather than people around development."

7. The multicountry study by Cantril (1965) indicates that the elite in developing countries tend to be more concerned with the international gap than poorer people. For some empirical evidence on the income distribution and self-rated happiness, see Morawetz and others (1977).

REFERENCES

Abramovitz, M. 1975. "Economic Growth and Its Discontents." Stanford, California: Stanford University. Typescript.

Bhagwati, J. and B. Hansen. 1972. "Should Growth Rates be Evaluated at International Prices?" In Jagdish Bhagwati and Richard Eckaus, eds., *Development and Planning: Essays in Honor of Paul Rosenstein-Rodan.* London: George Allen and Unwin.

Cantril, H. 1965. *The Pattern of Human Concerns.* New Brunswick, N.J.: Rutgers University Press.

Chenery, H. 1976. "Transitional Growth and World Industrialization." Paper presented at the Nobel Symposium on the International Allocation of Economic Activity. Stockholm. Typescript.

Easterlin, R. 1974. "Does Economic Growth Improve the Human Lot?" In David Paul and Melvin Reder, eds., *Nations and Households in Economic Growth: Essays in Honor of Moses Abramovitz*. New York: Academic Press.

Haq, M. 1976. "Concessions or Structural Change." Paper presented at a Special Meeting of the Club of Rome on the New International Order.

Kravis, I. B., A. Heston and R. Summers. 1977. "Real GDP Per Capita for 116 Countries, 1970 and 1974." Department of Economics Discussion Paper no. 391. Philadelphia: University of Pennsylvania.

————. 1977a. "International Comparisons of Real Product and Purchasing Power." United Nations International Comparison Project, Phase II. Washington D.C.: World Bank. Typescript.

Kuznets, S. 1965. *Economic Growth and Structure*. New York: W. W. Norton.

Lewis, W. A. 1972. "Objectives and Prognostications." In Gustav Ranis, ed., The *Gap Between Rich and Poor Nations*. London: Macmillan.

Morawetz, D. et al. 1977. "The Income Distribution and Self-rated Happiness: Some Empirical Evidence." *Economic Journal*. Forthcoming.

United Nations. 1976. "The Future of the World Economy." New York: United Nations Department of Economic and Social Affairs.

World Bank. 1976. *World Tables 1976*. Baltimore: Johns Hopkins University Press.

————. 1977. *World Bank Atlas, 1977*. Washington, D.C.: World Bank.

3

· · · · · · ·

The Persistence of the Gap:
Taking Stock of Economic Growth
in the Post–World War II Era

· · · · · · ·

JOHN T PASSÉ-SMITH

Following Western Europe's fast recovery after World War II, the governments of the industrialized countries turned their attention to aiding the Third World nations in their development efforts. In the 1950s and early 1960s, economic growth became the centerpiece of economists' development plans. To that end the United Nations declared the 1960s the "Development Decade" and set a goal of 6 percent annual growth as necessary to raise the poverty-stricken to a decent standard of living (Dube 1988, 2–3). Twenty-five years later David Morawetz (1977; see Chapter 2) was commissioned by the World Bank to take stock of what had been accomplished in the area of development. Morawetz evaluated the world's growth between 1950 and 1975, concluding that although the whole world had experienced relatively rapid growth, the gap between the rich and poor countries in terms of per capita GNP (GNP/pc) was growing wider.

Many events have occurred since 1975 that could have altered the character of world growth—events such as the two oil shocks (1974 and 1979), the extended world recession (1979–1982), the debt crisis of the eighties and nineties, a spreading of liberal economic views in nondeveloped countries, and so forth. Thus, this chapter seeks to discover if the characteristics of world growth established by Morawetz still prevail.

Since the 1950s it has become accepted that economic performance—as measured by GNP/pc growth—is only one of the factors defining development. As many scholars (Durning 1990, 135–153; Lipton 1977, 1989, and Chapter 26 of this volume; Morawetz 1977) have pointed out, some of the fastest-growing countries, such as Pakistan and Brazil, have also experienced very high levels of poverty and unemployment. It appears that poverty and hunger may have even worsened in some developing countries experiencing rapid economic growth (Lipton 1977, 30–32). Exactly how economic growth and other aspects of development—economic diversification, the distribution of income, the provision of basic needs, democracy—are related remains a subject of controversy (much of which is discussed elsewhere in this volume). Although this chapter focuses on an analysis of growth between 1962 and 1990, it is not meant to minimize the importance of the other components that make for development.

ECONOMIC GROWTH, 1962–1990

Data for the period 1962 to 1990 were obtained from the *World Tables 1992* (World Bank 1992) and the International Monetary Fund's *International Financial Statistics: Supplement on Output Statistics*, No. 8 (IMF 1984). Figures on GNP/pc are presented in constant 1980 U.S. dollars, and growth rates were computed from the constant per capita GNPs using the regression method described by the World Bank in the *World Development Report* (1988:288–289).[1] When income groupings are utilized in the analysis referring to the 1962–1990 period, the groups are defined by GNP/pc. Those countries with a GNP/pc of $4,000 or greater are considered rich; middle-income countries have a GNP/pc of $500 to $3,999; and the poor countries are those with a GNP/pc of less than $500.

Over the twenty-nine-year period 1962–1990, the annual average rate of GNP/pc growth for the world has been about 1.8 percent—down from 3.15 percent for the years 1962 to 1975 but still impressive (see Table 3.1). To put this achievement in perspective, we must realize that modern growth among those countries considered developed today began in the middle of the nineteenth century. During the hundred years prior to 1950, according to Simon Kuznets (1972:19), those countries experienced a century of unprecedented rates of growth (1.6 percent annual). Since 1962, the entire world—not just the fastest-growing countries—has surpassed the 1.6 percent mark. Both the 1.8 percent (1962–1990) and the 3.15 percent (1962–1975) growth rates hide considerable variation in economic expansion experienced by countries at different levels of growth, as well as by different regions of the world.

For the period as a whole, the richer countries had the highest growth rates. This fact is contrary to the expectation that nonrich countries with sufficient social capability have the highest growth potential (see Chapters 6, 7, and 8 in this volume). If the twenty-nine years are divided into periods of rapid growth and economic decline, the experience of the middle-income countries becomes clearer.

Until the early to mid-1970s, the world achieved annual average growth rates of 3.15 percent. During this era of rapid growth, the economic expansion of middle-income countries (3.83) surpassed that of the rich (3.58), while the poor grew at the slowest rate (1.99). When this pattern was found by Robert Jackman in his 1982 study of world growth, he labeled it the

Table 3.1   Economic Growth Rates by Income Group and Region

| | Annual Average Growth Rates (percent) | | |
	1962–1990	1962–1975	1975–1990
World	1.80	3.15	.58
Income Group			
Rich ($4,000 +)	2.46	3.58	1.45
Middle-Income ($500–$3,999)	2.11	3.83	.82
Poor ($500 and less)	1.19	1.99	-.03
Regions[a]			
Developed	2.58	3.92	1.95
Africa	.80	2.27	-.57
Asia	1.89	1.20	1.95
East Asia/Pacific	4.04	4.63	3.43
Middle East	2.14	4.91	-.75
Western Hemisphere	1.13	2.59	-.29

a. The regional divisions are those used in IMF publications (IMF 1984).
Source: Calculated from data in *The World Tables 1992* (World Bank), and *International Financial Statistics: Supplement on Output Statistics*, No. 8, 1984 (International Monetary Fund).

"modified Matthew effect" (1982:175). In the Bible, the Book of Matthew contains a reference to the continued accumulation of wealth by the rich and the further impoverishment of the poor; by "modified Matthew effect," Jackman meant that not only did the rich get richer, but so too did the middle-income countries.

During the 1975–1990 period, which captures much of the impact of the first oil shock, the second oil shock, the extended world recession, and the global debt crisis, the world growth rate dropped below 1 percent. All three income groups suffered during this period, and the relative fortunes of the income groups began to change. The era when the economic expansion of the middle-income countries surpassed that of the rich drew to a close, and the rich again grew the fastest. Whatever forces were modifying the Matthew effect were no longer dominant. It could be that middle-income countries have the highest potential for growth when global economic expansion is taking place but are not as able as the rich countries to protect themselves when economically difficult times arise.

As for regional economic growth, East Asia, containing the so-called Asian NICs (newly industrializing countries), has the fastest annual growth rate, 4.04 percent (see Table 3.1).[2] Between 1962 and 1975, the era of rapid growth, East Asia vied with the Middle East for the fastest growth rate. Unlike most of the other regions, East Asia was even able to maintain impressive growth during the global economic contraction of 1975–1985. Three of the regions during this period—Africa (-.57), the Middle East (-.75), and the Western Hemisphere (-.29)—experienced negative economic growth. It should be noted that the Middle East contains both oil-exporting and non-oil-exporting countries, so the rate of growth for the region is not as fast as would be expected if oil countries were in their own group.

The above analysis of groups masks the achievements of individual states. Table 3.2 remedies that problem by highlighting the ten fastest- and

Table 3.2   Economic and Population Growth Rates

	The Ten Fastest-Growing Countries, 1962–1990			
Income[a] Group 1962	Annual Average Growth Rates (percent) 1962–1990		Ranking Among the 118 Countries 1962–1990	
	GNP/pc	Population	GNP/pc	Population
P Botswana	7.48	1.56	1	70
M Singapore	7.24	1.03	2	79
M Malta	7.12	0.12	3	115
P Korea	7.00	1.68	4	64
M Hong Kong	6.65	1.69	5	63
M Oman	6.54	1.88	6	57
M Cyprus	5.65	0.25	7	105
M Japan	4.74	0.96	8	81
P Lesotho	4.73	1.33	9	74
P Thailand	4.51	2.40	10	33
	The Ten Slowest-Growing Countries, 1962–1990			
P Mozambique	-3.12	2.99	118	9
M Nicaragua	-2.61	2.48	117	26
P Niger	-2.09	2.44	116	29
M Zambia	-2.07	2.67	115	17
P Chad	-2.05	1.68	114	65
P Madagascar	-1.47	2.34	113	38
M Libya	-1.46	2.81	112	13
P Ghana	-1.37	2.44	111	30
P Zaire	-1.19	2.41	110	32
P Liberia	-0.94	1.93	109	54

	Annual Average Growth Rates					
	1962–1990		1962–1975		1975–1990	
	GNP/pc	Pop.	GNP/pc	Pop.	GNP/pc	Pop.
World	1.80	1.63	3.15	1.59	.58	1.67
Developed	2.58	.55	3.92	.77	1.95	.36
Africa	.80	2.19	2.27	1.95	-.57	2.35
Asia	1.89	2.46	1.20	2.43	1.95	2.50
East Asia/Pacific	4.04	1.70	4.63	1.83	3.43	1.59
Middle East	2.14	2.61	4.91	2.33	-.75	3.08
Western Hemisphere	1.13	1.49	2.59	1.53	-.29	1.50

a. P=poor; M=middle-income; R=rich
Source: Calculated from data in *The World Tables 1992* and *International Financial Statistics*, 1984.

slowest-growing countries. One of the more striking features of Table 3.2 is the fact that four of the ten fastest-growing countries in the world between 1962 and 1990—Botswana, Korea, Lesotho, and Thailand—started the period with GNP/pcs of less than $500. Indeed, a country that was categorized as poor in 1962, Botswana, maintained the world's fastest rate of economic growth rather than one of the Asian NICs.[3] Also, none of the ten fastest- or slowest-growing countries was in the rich category at the outset of the period. As might be expected, Africa dominates the list of the slowest-growing countries in the world.

The population factor is also introduced in Table 3.2. The mean annual average population growth rate for the ten fastest-growing countries is 1.29 percent, 2.42 percent for the ten slowest-growing countries. This gap appears to confirm the World Bank's concern about population levels and growth. Nevertheless, there does not appear to be a simple relationship between population and economic growth. If this were the case, it would be expected that Malta, with its population growing by .13 percent annually, would have achieved faster economic growth than Botswana, whose population increased by 1.56 percent annually.

As for the geographic regions, Africa attained a population growth rate of 2.19 percent, and its economic growth was only .8 percent for the 1962–1990 period; both Asia and the Middle East, however, increased their populations at a faster rate and still grew more quickly than Africa. Although the information in the table does not offer support for those who contend that rapid population growth spurs economic growth, it implies that the tie between the two is considerably more complex than some might think (see Kahn 1979).

THE ABSOLUTE GAP

The absolute gap, as defined by Morawetz (1977), is the difference between the mean GNP/pc of a set of rich countries and that of poorer countries or groups of countries. It indicates the increase that a country must achieve in order to have a GNP/pc equal to that of the rich countries.

In 1965 Simon Kuznets reported that the mean per capita GNP of the rich countries was $1,900, whereas that of the poor was $120.[4] One of the major trends over the previous 100 to 125 years, Kuznets argued, was that the absolute gap widened very slowly up until World War II and then began to accelerate. Kuznets stated, "[A] reasonable conjecture is that, in comparison with the quintupling of the per capita product of developed countries over the last century, the per capita product of the 'poor' LDCs rose two-thirds at most." (Kuznets 1972:19). It seems fair to say that the large disparity between the world's rich and poor countries is a relatively recent phenomenon.

Table 3.3   The Relative and Absolute Gap by Income Group and Region

	Relative Gap (percent)		Absolute Gap (1980 U.S. dollars)	
Income Group	1962	1990	1962	1990
Middle-Income	18.97	13.96	5,540	9,428
Poor	4.22	2.61	6,549	10,671
Region				
Africa	7.62	4.92	5,646	12,432
Asia	4.59	3.23	5,831	12,652
East Asia/Pacific	11.80	22.09[a]	5,390	10,186
Latin America/Caribbean	19.34	12.76	4,929	11,407

a. Closed the relative gap.
Source: Calculated from data in *The World Tables 1992* and *International Financial Statistics*, 1984.

Figure 3.1   The Gap Between Rich, Middle, and Poor Countries

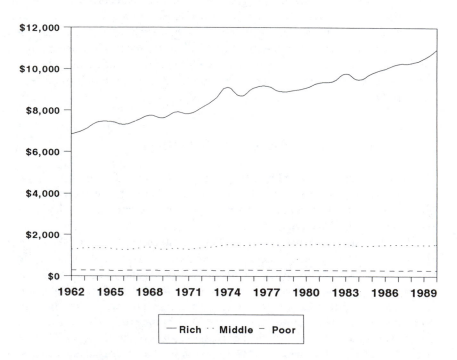

Source: Calculated from data in *The World Tables 1992* and *International Financial Statistics*, 1984.

Morawetz found that the absolute gap between the OECD and developing countries between 1950 and 1975 more than doubled (from $2,191 to $4,839 in 1975 U.S. dollars). The data presented in Table 3.3 show that the absolute gap has grown from $5,540 to $9,428 (in 1980 U.S. dollars) between the rich and middle-income countries and from $6,549 to $10,671 between the rich and poor countries for the 1962–1990 period. Figure 3.1 graphically illustrates GNP/pc for the three income groups; the absolute gap is the distance between the lines. The growth of the gap between the income groups is readily apparent.

If, over the twenty-nine years covered in this chapter, the number of people who lived in poor countries had dropped to a relatively small number, or even if the number of people was moderate but they lived in only a few countries, then interest in the gap would wane. But poverty remained a worldwide problem. Table 3.4 provides information on the population of the world, the number of countries in each income group, and each group's percentage of the world's population. Although there is not sufficient GNP data for China to include it in the analysis of GNP/pc, its population is too large to ignore. In 1990 the *World Development Report* listed China's GNP/pc as $330, so Table 3.4 reports data on world population by income group both with and without China. (The following analysis includes China.)

Table 3.4   Income Groups' Percentage of World Population

Year	World Population[a] (billions)	Rich percent	Rich number of countries	Middle-Income percent	Middle-Income number of countries	Poor percent	Poor number of countries	Oil percent	Oil number of countries
				Without China					
1962	1.980	21.73	17	30.61	57	47.31	41	.34	3
1965	2.105	21.93	18	32.19	60	46.26	37	.36	3
1970	2.322	27.12	23	27.88	60	44.62	32	.38	3
1975	2.568	27.21	25	27.58	56	44.80	34	.42	3
1980	2.830	26.15	28	34.24	57	39.22	30	.42	3
1985	3.119	24.47	29	34.44	53	40.55	33	.54	3
1990	3.430	23.00	29	38.11	53	38.38	33	.63	3
				China Included Among Poor Countries					
1962	2.663	16.20	17	22.80	57	60.80	42	.30	3
1965	2.839	15.70	18	23.90	60	60.20	38	.30	3
1970	3.165	19.90	23	20.50	60	59.40	33	.30	3
1975	3.515	19.90	25	20.20	56	59.70	35	.30	3
1980	3.847	19.20	28	25.20	57	55.30	31	.30	3
1985	4.197	18.20	29	25.60	53	55.80	34	.40	3
1990	4.564	17.20	29	28.60	53	53.70	34	.50	3

a. The world total reflects population data for the 118 countries for which there is also GNP/pc data. China is not included among the 118

As Table 3.4 shows, the number of countries in the rich category increased from seventeen to twenty-nine between 1962 and 1990, but their share of world population climbed by only one percentage point (from 16.2 to 17.2 percent). To a great extent, this disparity is explained by the very low birthrates in the rich countries versus the often very high fertility rates of nonrich countries. After increasing throughout the 1960s, the number of middle-income countries fell from fifty-seven in 1962 to fifty-three in 1990. These countries accounted for approximately 28.6 percent of the world's population in 1990, up from 22.8 percent in 1962. Throughout the period, the majority of the world's population has lived in countries with a GNP/pc of less than $500. A positive note is that their numbers dropped from about forty-one to thirty-four countries and their percentage of world population fell from about 61 percent in 1962 to 53.7 percent in 1990.

Unfortunately, this population distribution means that the gap between rich, middle-income, and poor countries is not insignificant. In 1962 there were almost 1.79 billion people living in countries having a GNP/pc of less than $500 (including China), and despite the declining percentage, the actual number of people living in poor countries grew to 2.5 billion by 1990.

At the aggregate level, then, the gap between the rich and the other two groups is growing. But does this prove the adage that "the rich get richer while the poor get poorer"? Figure 3.1 shows that although the gap is opening, the middle-income and poor countries as groups are not getting any poorer. The information provided in Figure 3.1 and Table 3.1 above thus lead to what are apparently incongruous conclusions: The absolute gap between the rich and nonrich is opening wider, even though growth rates for the middle-income countries for the first fourteen years are higher and over the entire period are quite close to those of the rich countries.

In order to eventually catch up with the rich countries' GNP/pc at some time in the future, nonrich countries must simply grow faster than the rich. But catching up could take hundreds if not thousands of years if the nonrich countries are relatively poor and their growth rates are only slightly faster than those of the rich. Indeed, in such a case the absolute gap will widen for years before it begins to shrink. A relatively simple way to determine if a nonrich country can close the absolute gap is to divide the growth rate of the rich country by the ratio of the nonrich country's GNP/pc to the rich country's GNP/pc. This equation yields the growth rate the nonrich country must exceed in order to begin closing the absolute gap. If, for example, the rich countries have a mean GNP/pc of $8,000 and a growth rate of 2 percent, a nonrich country with a GNP/pc of $1,000 must exceed a growth rate of 16 percent in order to begin closing the absolute gap that year. Very few countries are able to achieve or maintain such a rate of economic expansion for very long.

Can any country close the absolute gap? Replicating the projections of Morawetz (see Table 2.2 in Chapter 2), I have attempted to find out if there

Table 3.5   Closing the Absolute Gap

Country[a]	GNP/pc (1980 U.S. dollars)	Annual Growth Rate, 1962–1990 (percent)	Number of Years Until Gap Closes if 1962–1990 Growth Rates Continue
Rich[b]	11,046	3.01	—
Korea	3,452	7.00	31
Botswana	1,728	7.48	44
Thailand	1,264	4.51	150
Malaysia	2,279	3.99	167
Lesotho	533	4.73	184
Indonesia	774	4.49	186
Portugal	2,956	3.57	241
Hungary	2,218	3.68	246
Brazil	2,187	3.67	254
Tunisia	1,452	3.79	268
Egypt	756	3.86	328
Barbados	3,213	3.35	370
Belize	1,562	3.53	386
St. Lucia	1,306	3.40	568
Pakistan	559	3.43	734
Yugoslavia	2,366	3.09	2,007

a. The four "oil states"—Kuwait, Libya, Saudi Arabia, and Oman—have been excluded. The oil states are those identified in the *World Development Report, 1988.*

b. Australia, Austria, Bahamas, Belgium, Canada, Cyprus, Denmark, Finland, France, Germany, Greece, Hong Kong, Iceland, Ireland, Israel, Italy, Japan, Luxembourg, Malta, Netherlands, New Zealand, Norway, Singapore, Spain, Sweden, Switzerland, Trinidad and Tobago, United Kingdom, United States.

Source: Calculated from data in *The World Tables 1992* and *International Financial Statistics*, 1984.

exists any country capable of catching up to the rich. The results presented in Table 3.5 assume that countries will maintain the same growth rate as they achieved during the base period of 1962–1990. Given this assumption, the majority of countries cannot hope to close the gap. Only Korea, the richest of the hopefuls, and Botswana, the fastest-growing country for the base period, have any opportunity to catch up to the rich within a century.

THE RELATIVE GAP

The relative gap measures the GNP/pc of the poor or middle-income groups as a percentage of that of the developed countries. Morawetz reported in the previous chapter that the developing countries had narrowed the relative gap, their GNP/pc rising from 6.7 percent of the GNP/pc of the rich in 1950 to 7.2 percent in 1975. He added that it might be easier for nonrich countries to narrow the relative gap than the absolute gap, thereby making it a more accessible development goal.

However, my results, as shown in Table 3.3 above, indicate that the middle-income countries' GNP/pc expressed as a percentage of the GNP/pc of the rich has grown smaller over time. The same is true for the poor countries in relation to the rich. In other words, the relative gap between rich and middle-income countries and rich and poor countries widened between 1962 and 1990. In 1962 the GNP/pc of the middle-income countries was 19 percent that of the rich countries, slipping to about 14 percent in 1990. The poor dropped from 4.22 percent of the GNP/pc of the rich in 1962 to 2.61 percent in 1990. Only one of the geographic regions, East Asia/Pacific, has narrowed the relative gap. In 1962 the mean GNP/pc of the East Asia/Pacific region was almost 12 percent of the rich countries' GNP/pc, rising to just over 22 percent in 1990. Other than in this one region, even the relative gap is worsening for the nonrich groups.

As reported in Table 3.3, those countries that were middle-income in 1962 are not necessarily the same countries in the middle-income category in 1990. As countries surpassed or fell below the income level defining a group,

Figure 3.2   The Relative Gap Between Rich and Middle-Income Countries

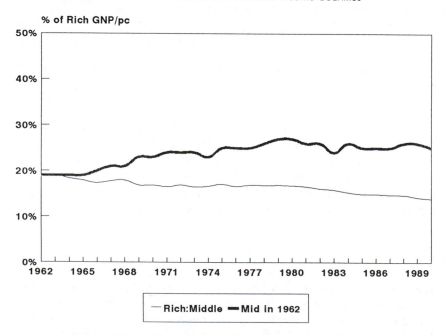

Source: Calculated from data in *The World Tables 1992* and *International Financial Statistics*, 1984.

they were incorporated into the higher or lower category. Thus, when Japan's GNP/pc surpassed $4,000, it was moved from the middle-income category to the rich. It could be, then, that the countries that were in the middle-income category in 1962 achieved growth sufficient to close the relative gap.

Figure 3.2 illustrates the relative gap between the middle-income and rich countries. The lighter line represents the middle-income countries as defined by their GNP/pc every year. The heavier line represents the fate of the countries that were in the middle-income category in 1962. The figure shows that the 1962 group did indeed improve the relative gap score slightly (from 19 to 25 percent). It should be kept in mind that Italy and Japan are included in this group. Without these two countries, the relative gap moves significantly closer to the lighter line.

Figure 3.3 illustrates the relative gap between the rich and poor countries. Again, the heavier line represents those countries defined as poor in 1962. The experience of the poor countries is similar to that of the middle-income countries. The group defined as poor in 1962 narrowed the relative gap from 4 percent in 1962 to 5 percent in 1990.

Figure 3.3   The Relative Gap Between Rich and Poor Countries

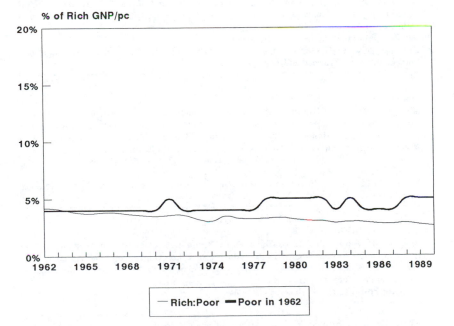

Source: Calculated from data in *The World Tables 1992* and *International Financial Statistics*, 1984.

MOBILITY

Can countries move from one income group to another or substantially improve their ranking within a grouping? In terms of upward mobility across income groups, the record has been unimpressive. Table 3.6 summarizes the movement of countries from one income group to another between 1962 and 1990. Of the 118 countries, 91 remained in the same category in 1990 that they occupied in 1962. Even though the number of upwardly mobile countries was small, only three countries—Guyana, Nicaragua, Zambia—moved down from one income group to the next, dropping from middle-income to poor. Thirteen countries were able to move up from the middle-income group to the rich, and eleven that started out poor became middle-income countries.

Although 77 percent of the countries in this sample remained within the same income group, Table 3.7 shows that there was quite a bit of movement within the ranks. Table 3.7 offers the ten countries that moved the most between 1962 and 1990, up or down, in terms of their GNP/pc rank. Botswana and South Korea made the most impressive jumps, up forty-five

Table 3.6   Mobility Across Income Groups, 1962 and 1990

Rich
Rich in 1962 and 1990
  Australia, Austria, Belgium, Canada, Denmark, Finland, France, Germany, Iceland, Luxembourg, Netherlands, New Zealand, Norway, Sweden, Switzerland, United Kingdom, United States
Joined Rich From the Middle-Income Category
  Bahamas, Cyprus, Greece, Hong Kong, Ireland, Israel, Italy, Japan, Malta, Oman, Singapore, Spain, Trinidad and Tobago

Middle-Income
Middle-Income in 1962 and 1990
  Algeria, Antigua and Barbuda, Argentina, Barbados, Belize, Brazil, Chile, Colombia, Congo, Costa Rica, Côte D'Ivoire, Dominica, Dominican Rep, Ecuador, El Salvador, Fiji, Gabon, Guatemala, Honduras, Hungary, Jamaica, Malaysia, Mauritius, Mexico, Morocco, Nigeria, Panama, Papua New Guinea, Paraguay, Peru, Portugal, South Africa, St. Lucia, Suriname, Syria, Tunisia, Turkey, Uruguay, Venezuela, Yugoslavia, Zimbabwe
Joined Middle-Income From the Poor Category
  Botswana, Cameroon, Egypt, Indonesia, Korea, Lesotho, Pakistan, Philippines, Solomon Islands, Swaziland, Thailand

Poor
Poor in 1962 and 1990
  Bangladesh, Benin, Bolivia, Burkina Faso, Burundi, Central African Republic, Chad, Ethiopia, The Gambia, Ghana, Haiti, India, Kenya, Liberia, Madagascar, Malawi, Mali, Mauritania, Mozambique, Nepal, Niger, Rwanda, Senegal, Sierra Leone, Somalia, Sri Lanka, Sudan, Tanzania, Togo, Zaire
Joined Poor From the Middle-Income Category
  Guyana, Nicaragua, Zambia

Source: Calculated from data in *The World Tables 1992* and *International Financial Statistics*, 1984.

Table 3.7   Mobility in Rankings of GNP/pc (difference from 1962 to 1990)

	Upwardly Mobile				Downwardly Mobile		
	GNP/pc Rank				GNP/pc Rank		
Country	1962	1990	Difference	Country	1962	1990	Difference
Botswana	97	52	+45	Nicaragua	51	86	-35
South Korea	78	33	+45	Peru	47	72	-25
Lesotho	113	84	+29	Mozambique	80	103	-23
Thailand	91	62	+29	Niger	89	110	-21
Malta	55	28	+27	Zambia	70	89	-19
Pakistan	106	83	+23	Argentina	29	45	-16
Indonesia	98	76	+22	Syria	53	68	-15
Swaziland	85	67	+18	Guyana	74	88	-14
Belize	71	54	+17	Jamaica	41	55	-14
Sri Lanka	109	92	+17	Liberia	82	96	-14

Source: Calculated from data in *The World Tables 1992* and *International Financial Statistics*, 1984.

places since 1962. Among the top ten movers, Lesotho was ranked the lowest in 1962 at 113, but was able to move up twenty-nine places. A third African country, Swaziland, also made the top ten, moving up eighteen places in the ranks. Other than Belize, Latin American (Western Hemisphere) countries did not move up in the rankings. However, five Latin American countries—Nicaragua, Peru, Argentina, Guyana, and Jamaica—were among the ten that *dropped* the most in the ranking of GNP/pc; four of the remaining five were African.

CONCLUSIONS

If scholars such as Simon Kuznets (1972) and Michael Lipton (1977) are correct, the worldwide economic growth experienced since World War II is unprecedented. Between 1850 and 1950, the countries considered rich in 1950 experienced economic expansion averaging 1.6 percent. Between 1962 and 1990, the entire world grew at 1.8 percent, and until 1975 the growth rate hovered at 3.15 percent. Morawetz (1977) informs us that this 3 percent rate goes back to 1950. Having grown accustomed to such rapid development, people have come to see very slow growth—less than 1 percent—as unusual, but historically it has been the norm. The research of Kuznets and others suggests that, over time, countries have likely experienced long periods of stagnation, or periods of economic expansion followed by periods of contraction.

Second, the data above indicate that not everyone has shared in the growth. The absolute gap between rich and middle-income and between rich and poor countries has grown steadily since 1962. For the middle-income countries, the absolute gap grew from $5,540 to $9,428, and the poor fell from a deficit of $6,549 to $10,671. On average, the absolute gap widened $134 for the middle-income countries and $142 for the poor countries every year. The mean annual expansion of the absolute gap for African countries was $232. In addition, neither the middle-income nor the poor group made significant improvement in the relative gap. The only region to increase its GNP/pc as a percentage of that of the rich was East Asia/Pacific, which includes the Asian NICs. This region cut the relative gap almost in half (from 12 to 22 percent). Although the relative gap may be easier to close than the absolute gap, as Morawetz indicated in the previous chapter, both groups failed to make significant progress. The relative gap was measured in two ways, one resulting in a slightly widening gap, the other a slightly narrowing gap.

Third, this analysis of income groups would have proven irrelevant if the percentage of the world's population in the lowest income group had fallen significantly. Unfortunately, such was not the case. The percentage of the world's population living in countries with a GNP/pc of less than $500 was 54 percent, or 2.5 billion people, in 1990. This figure does represent a percentage decline from 61 in 1962, but the number of people living in poor countries increased from 1.79 billion to 2.5 billion.

Fourth, the number of countries with a GNP/pc of greater than $4,000 (U.S. 1980 dollars) increased from seventeen in 1962 to twenty-nine in 1990. Twelve countries joined the rich, representing four different regions of the world: Europe, the Western Hemisphere, East Asia/Pacific, and the Middle East. In all, twenty-seven countries became mobile and crossed from one income category to another; only three of those countries moved down.

Finally, it appears that only two countries can close the gap with the rich within the next thirty to forty-five years: Korea and Botswana. Korea's position comes as no surprise, given the press the Asian NICs have received over the last few years. Botswana, however, has not received the notoriety that others have. It is one of the few countries in the world whose growth rates were not severely hurt by the global economic downturn of 1975–1990. If growth rates remain similar to those of the entire twenty-nine-year period or even those of the last sixteen years, Botswana will be the first African country to surpass the $4,000 per capita level and join the rich.

NOTES

1. The growth rates are calculated by the regression method described in the *World Development Report, 1988*. The least squares method finds the growth rate by fitting a least squares trend line to the log of the gross national product per capita. This takes the equation form of $X_t = a + bt + e_t$, where x equals the log of the GNP/pc, a is the intercept, b is the parameter to be estimated, t is time, and e is

the error term. The growth rate, r, is the [antilog (b)]-1. For further information, see *World Development Report 1988*, pp. 288–289. For a discussion of different methods of computing growth rates see Robert Jackman, "A Note on the Measurement of Growth Rates in Cross-National Research. *American Journal of Sociology*, 86:604–610.

2. The regional categories were drawn from distinctions made by the International Monetary Fund, except for the East Asian/Pacific category, which was drawn from the World Bank's *World Tables 1992*.

3. I verified my findings with growth rates published in the *World Development Report 1990*, for a similar growth era. In Table 1 (*WDR 1990*; 178–179) Botswana was shown to have the highest annual average growth rate in the world (8.6 percent) between 1965 and 1988, followed by Singapore (7.2 percent).

4. Kuznets defined the rich countries as those with a GNP/pc greater than $1,000 (1965 U.S. dollars). A "narrow" definition of the poor countries set the GNP/pc cutoff point at $120 or less. For his more broadly defined poor category, Kuznets raised the cutoff point to $300. The middle-income group varied according to Kuznets's choice of the narrowly or broadly defined poor group in any particular example. Kuwait and Qatar were excluded because of the fact that their growth had been dependent upon a single commodity and did not reflect diversified growth. Puerto Rico was excluded because its GNP/pc was so tightly connected to the United States. Japan was included in the rich group even though its GNP/pc was below the cutoff point because it had managed tremendous growth with very few natural resources. Thus its growth was achieved through diversified development of the economy. For further information on how Kuznets defined his income groups, see Ranis 1972.

REFERENCES

Dube, S. C. 1988. *Modernization and Development: The Search for Alternative Paradigms*. London and New Jersey: Zed Books Ltd.

Durning, A. B. 1990. "Ending Poverty," in L. Starke, ed., *State of The World, 1990*, New York and London: W. W. Norton.

International Monetary Fund. 1984. *International Financial Statistics: Supplement on Output Statistics*, No. 8. Washington, D.C.: IMF.

Jackman, R. W. 1982. "Dependence on Foreign Investment and Economic Growth in the Third World." *World Politics*, 34: 175-197.

———. 1980. "A Note on the Measurement of Growth Rates in Cross-National Research." *American Journal of Sociology* 86: 604–10.

Kahn, H. 1979. *World Economic Development: 1979 and Beyond*. Boulder, CO: Westview Press.

Kuznets, S. 1972. "The Gap: Concept, Measurement, Trends." In G. Ranis, ed., *The Gap Between Rich and Poor Nations*. London: The Macmillan Press, Ltd.

———. 1979. *Growth, Population, and Income Distribution*. New York: W. W. Norton.

———. 1984. "Economic Growth and Income Inequality." In M. A. Seligson, ed., *The Gap Between Rich and Poor*. Boulder, CO: Westview Press.

Lipton, M. 1977. *Why the Poor People Stay Poor: A Study of Urban Bias in World Development*. London: Temple Smith.

———. 1989. *New Seeds and Poor People*. London: Unwin Hyman.

Morawetz, D. 1977. *Twenty-Five Years of Economic Development: 1950–1975.* Washington, D.C.: World Bank.

World Bank. 1988, 1990. *World Development Report.* Oxford: Oxford University Press.

World Bank. 1992. *The World Tables 1992.* Washington, D.C.: The World Bank.

4

· · · · · · ·

Income Inequality:
Some Dimensions of the Problem

· · · · · · ·

MONTEK S. AHLUWALIA

This frequently cited study presents the data that have been used by many analysts to show that the gap between rich and poor is considerably wider within the developing economies than within the developed ones. The study notes a number of major limitations of the data upon which this conclusion is based but goes on to argue that these are "the only data we have" and that the conclusions drawn from such data can do more good than harm. Some critics of this view believe, however, that because large sums of development assistance funds are spent based upon the findings of studies such as this, faulty conclusions can do considerable harm—such funds will neither produce the desired result nor be available to projects that might truly benefit from them. Moreover, entire national development plans could fail if such conclusions were found to be unsupported by better data or better analysis.

Recent discussions of economic development reflect an increasing concern with widespread poverty in underdeveloped countries. The fact of poverty is not new: it was always self-evident to those familiar with economic realities. What *is* new is the suspicion that economic growth by itself may not solve or even alleviate the problem within any "reasonable" time period. Indeed it is often argued that the mechanisms which promote economic growth also promote economic concentration, and a worsening of the relative and perhaps

Reprinted by permission of Oxford University Press, Inc., from *Redistribution with Growth* by Hollis Chenery, Montek S. Ahluwalia, C. L. G. Bell, John H. Duloy, and Richard Jolly, pp. 3–10. Copyright © 1974 by the International Bank for Reconstruction and Development/The World Bank.

even absolute position of the lower-income groups. This pessimistic view has led to some questioning of growth-oriented development strategies which assume that the poverty problem would be solved without much difficulty if growth could be accelerated.

The empirical evidence underlying the new pessimism is limited but persuasive. Detailed studies of the nature and extent of poverty in particular countries show that the problem is of truly gigantic proportions. A study of poverty in India estimated that, in 1960, about 38 percent of the rural population and 50 percent of the urban population lived below a poverty level defined by consumption yielding 2,250 calories.[1] A recent study of Brazil showed that, also in 1960, about 30 percent of the total population lived below a poverty level defined by the minimum wage in northeast Brazil (the poorest region).[2] More importantly, both studies argued that the situation had worsened over the sixties, at least in terms of relative equality. Similarly pessimistic results on changes in relative equality over time were reported in a study of Argentina, Mexico, and Puerto Rico.[3] In addition to these case studies there is some evidence from cross-country analysis of distribution patterns which can be interpreted as showing that economic growth is associated with a worsening in the distribution of income, at least in the initial stages of development.

These studies raise important questions relevant to policy formulation. What is the extent of relative and absolute poverty in underdeveloped countries and does it vary systematically with the level of development? What evidence is there on the relationship between growth and inequality and how far can this relationship be affected by policy? What are the economic characteristics of the poor and what do they imply for distributional strategies? In this chapter we will attempt to sift the available evidence to provide qualitative answers to some of these questions. But first a general caveat is necessary. Analysis of income distribution problems is severely limited by the quality and reliability of the available data and a brief digression on this subject is desirable.

LIMITATIONS OF THE DATA

The primary sources of information on patterns of income distribution are sample surveys which provide data on income (and in some cases only consumption) and other socio-economic characteristics of the units sampled. Until recently, data of this type were available for only a few underdeveloped countries and generalizations about patterns of distribution were therefore based on very limited information. For example, Kuznets's (1963) study of cross-country patterns of income distribution included only eleven underdeveloped countries. The situation has changed considerably since then. A large number of surveys have been carried out in underdeveloped countries and results from these surveys are increasingly being used in analyses of income distribution problems.

Unfortunately, the increase in data availability has not been accompanied by an adequate improvement in statistical quality. In many cases the growing interest in the subject has simply led to the proliferation of crude estimates of income distribution for various countries, based on data sources which may be "the best available" but are simply not good enough. An exhaustive review of these problems is beyond the scope of this chapter, but some indication of their importance can be obtained by considering three major sources of error in this field.

First, the income concept used in many surveys falls far short of the comprehensive definition needed. For purposes of welfare measurement, the income concept should refer to "permanent income" and should include income from all sources whether accruing in the form of money income or income in kind (including production for own consumption and investment).[4] Furthermore, if it is to be a measure of welfare, the income concept should be adjusted for tax incidence and transfer payments. In practice, available surveys measure income over a short period—usually a month or at most a year. Frequently they cover only money income, and sometimes only wage income, giving a distorted picture of the true distribution of income in the economy.

Second, even if the income concept is properly defined, it may be difficult to measure in practice. Very different problems arise at the two ends of the income scale. In the highest income groups there is the ever present likelihood of deliberate understatement of income for fear of incurring a tax liability. At the other end of the income scale there is a genuine difficulty in valuing production for own consumption or investment in the subsistence sectors of the economy.[5] Closely related to the measurement problem is the difficulty in using relative money incomes as a measure of relative real incomes, given the wide variation in prices facing different consumers. Rural prices of some goods are typically much lower than urban prices, so that comparisons of urban-rural money incomes typically understate rural real income levels.

Third, there is the problem of accuracy in estimating the distribution of income in the population from the observed distribution in sample surveys. The accuracy of sample estimates depends upon a number of factors relating to the size of the sample and its representativeness. Many available estimates of income distribution are derived from samples that are statistically inadequate in these respects, with the result that sample estimates are both biased and have a large variance. In several cases the samples from which data are available were never originally intended to be representative of the population as a whole.[6] In other cases, despite an attempt at ensuring representativeness, the difficulties of sample design or implementation may have proved overwhelming. For example, no adequate sampling frame may exist from which to select a sample ensuring proportional coverage of different income groups. The existence of nomadic populations or inaccessible regions presents the most extreme form of this problem.

Because of these problems, available estimates of income distribution in most underdeveloped countries are, at best, approximations of the underlying distribution we wish to measure. Inaccuracy of measurement is not, of course, unique to income distribution; national accounts data are also subject to such errors. But the data limitations for income distribution are usually regarded as more serious. National accounts data are at least collected on a systematic basis and are therefore much more comparable over time and (although to a lesser extent) between countries. No such comparability can be claimed for data on income distribution. Estimates for different countries, and even for the same country at different points of time, are typically based on noncomparable data sources, making intercountry and intertemporal comparisons very hazardous.

These limitations present a familiar dilemma in empirical analysis. The data are very weak, but they are also the only data we have. An extreme response to the problem is to reject any use of most of the available data for analytical purposes. The approach adopted in this chapter is less puristic. We assume that until better data become available, cautious use of existing data—with all its limitations—provides some perspective on the nature of the problem. In common with Kuznets (1955), our excuse "for building an elaborate structure on such a shaky foundation" is the view that "speculation is an effective way of presenting a broad view of the field and . . . so long as it is recognized as a collection of hunches calling for further investigation, rather than a set of fully tested conclusions, little harm and much good may result."

THE EXTENT OF INEQUALITY

The first step in defining the dimensions of the problem with which this volume is concerned is to consider the extent of inequality in developed and underdeveloped countries. Cross-section data are particularly useful for this purpose because they reveal possible "uniform patterns" which characterize the problem in different countries. Identifying such uniformities helps to establish "averages" with which levels of inequality observed in particular countries can be compared. They also serve to determine reasonable "benchmarks" in terms of which targets and prospects for improvement can be defined. . . .

The conventional approach to income inequality is to define the problem in purely relative terms. A familiar technique for this purpose is to measure inequality by the extent to which the income share of groups of individuals or households differs from their population share. In this section, we will examine the problem in terms of income shares of the lowest 40 percent, the middle 40 percent, and the top 20 percent of households ordinally ranked by income.[7] For some countries, distribution estimates are available only for individuals in the workforce. We have included these estimates in our data set as the best available approximation to household income distribution.

The choice of income shares instead of one of the various conventional indexes of inequality calls for some explanation.[8] The conventional indexes are designed to provide summary measures of inequality over the entire range of the population and as such may be insensitive to the degree of inequality in particular ranges. Our treatment in terms of the income shares of ordinally ranked income groups enables us to concentrate on inequality at the lower end of the income range, which may be of special interest for policy.

Table 4.1 presents income share data for sixty-six countries cross-classified according to different levels of overall inequality and per capita income levels.[9] The table distinguishes between three inequality levels defined as high, moderate, and low (according to specified ranges of the share of the lowest 40 percent) and three income groupings defined as high, middle, and low (according to specified ranges of per capita GNP). The extent of inequality varies widely among countries but the following broad patterns can be identified.

The *socialist countries* have the highest degree of overall equality in the distribution of income. This is as we would expect, since income from the ownership of capital does not accrue as income to individuals.[10] The observed inequality in these countries is due mainly to inequality in wages between sectors and skill classes. Since the structural factors operating toward equality are the strongest in these countries, their average income share of the lowest 40 percent—amounting to about 25 percent of total income—may be taken as an upper limit for the target income share to which policymakers in underdeveloped countries can aspire.

The *developed countries* are evenly distributed between the categories of low and moderate inequality. The average income share of the bottom 40 percent amounts to about 16 percent, which is lower than the average for socialist countries but better than most of the underdeveloped countries. A major problem in comparing income distribution data between developed and underdeveloped countries is that pretax data does not reflect the equalizing impact of progressive taxes combined with welfare-oriented public transfer mechanisms. These fiscal corrections are generally more substantial and more egalitarian in developed countries. If this factor is taken into account, developed countries may be somewhat more egalitarian than appears from Table 4.1.

Most of the *underdeveloped countries* show markedly greater relative inequality than the developed countries. About half of the underdeveloped countries fall in the high inequality range with another third displaying moderate inequality. The average income share for the lowest 40 percent in

Table 4.1   Cross-classification of Countries by Income Level and Equality

High Inequality — Share of Lowest 40 Percent Less than 12 Percent

Country (Year)	GNP/pc US$	Low 40%	Middle 40%	Top 20%
Income up to U.S. $300				
Kenya (69)	136	10.0	22.0	68.0
Sierra Leone (68)	159	9.6	22.4	68.0
Philippines (71)	239	11.6	34.6	53.8
Iraq (56)	200	6.8	25.2	68.0
Senegal (60)	245	10.0	26.0	64.0
Ivory Coast (70)	247	10.8	32.1	57.1
Rhodesia (68)	252	8.2	22.8	69.0
Tunisia (70)	255	11.4	53.6	55.0
Honduras (68)	265	6.5	28.5	65.0
Ecuador (70)	277	6.5	20.0	73.5
Income U.S. $300–$750				
Malaysia (70)	330	11.6	32.4	56.0
Colombia (70)	358	9.0	30.0	61.0
Brazil (70)	390	10.0	28.4	61.5
Peru (71)	480	6.5	33.5	60.0
Gabon (68)	497	8.8	23.7	67.5
Jamaica (58)	510	8.2	30.3	61.5
Costa Rica (71)	521	11.5	30.0	58.5
Mexico (69)	645	10.5	25.5	64.0
South Africa (65)	669	6.2	35.8	58.0
Panama (69)	692	9.4	31.2	59.4

Moderate Inequality — Share of Lowest 40 Percent Between 12 Percent and 17 Percent

Country (Year)	GNP/pc US$	Low 40%	Middle 40%	Top 20%
Income up to U.S. $300				
Salvador (69)	295	11.2	36.4	52.4
Turkey (68)	282	9.3	29.9	60.8
Burma (58)	82	16.5	38.7	44.8
Dahomey (59)	87	15.5	34.5	50.0
Tanzania (67)	89	13.0	26.0	61.0
India (64)	99	16.0	32.0	52.0
Madagascar (60)	120	13.5	25.5	61.0
Zambia (59)	230	14.5	28.5	57.0
Income U.S. $300–$750				
Dominican Republic (69)	323	12.2	30.3	57.5
Iran (68)	332	12.5	33.0	54.5
Guyana (56)	550	14.0	40.3	45.7
Lebanon (60)	508	13.0	26.0	61.0
Uruguay (68)	618	16.5	35.5	48.0
Chile (68)	744	13.0	30.2	56.8

Low Inequality — Share of Lowest 40 Percent 17 Percent and Above

Country (Year)	GNP/pc US$	Low 40%	Middle 40%	Top 20%
Income up to U.S. $300				
Chad (58)	78	18.0	39.0	43.0
Sri Lanka (69)	95	17.0	37.0	46.0
Niger (60)	97	18.0	40.0	42.0
Pakistan (64)	100	17.5	37.5	30.0
Uganda (70)	126	17.1	35.8	47.1
Thailand (70)	180	17.0	37.5	45.5
Korea (70)	235	18.0	37.0	45.0
Taiwan (64)	241	20.4	39.5	40.1
Income U.S. $300–$750				
Surinam (62)	394	21.7	35.7	42.6
Greece (57)	500	21.0	29.5	49.5
Yugoslavia (68)	529	18.5	40.0	41.5
Bulgaria (62)	530	26.8	40.0	33.2
Spain (65)	750	17.6	36.7	45.7

Income Above U.S. $750

Country	GNP			
Venezuela (70)	1004	7.9	27.1	65.5
Finland (62)	1599	11.1	39.6	49.3
France (62)	1913	9.5	36.8	53.7
Argentina (70)	1079	16.5	36.1	47.4
Puerto Rico (68)	1100	13.7	35.7	50.6
Netherlands (67)	1990	13.6	37.9	48.5
Norway (68)	2010	16.6	42.9	40.5
Germany (64)	2144	15.4	31.7	52.9
Denmark (68)	2563	13.6	38.8	47.6
New Zealand (69)	2859	15.5	42.5	42.0
Sweden (63)	2949	14.0	42.0	44.0
Poland (64)	850	23.4	40.6	36.0
Japan (63)	950	20.7	39.3	40.0
U.K. (68)	2015	18.8	42.2	39.0
Hungary (69)	1140	24.0	42.5	33.5
Czechoslovakia (64)	1150	27.6	41.4	31.0
Australia (65)	2509	20.0	41.2	38.8
Canada (65)	2920	20.0	39.8	40.2
United States (70)	4850	19.7	41.5	38.8

Note: Sources for these data are listed in the Appendix [of the original article—*Eds.*]. The income shares of each percentile group were read off a free-hand Lorenz curve fitted to observe points in the cumulative distribution. The distributions are for pretax income. Per capita GNP figures are taken from the World Bank data files and refer to GNP at factor cost for the year indicated in constant 1971 U.S. dollars.

all underdeveloped countries as a group amounts to about 12.5 percent, but there is considerable variation around this average. Those of the underdeveloped countries classified in the low inequality category have income shares for the lowest 40 percent averaging 18 percent, as is the case with the most egalitarian of the developed countries. Against this, however, half the underdeveloped countries show income shares of the lowest 40 percent, averaging only 9 percent.

It is worth noting that overall income inequality in the underdeveloped countries is not particularly associated with relatively low income shares for the middle-income group rather than the poorest group. This view was originally put forward by Kuznets (1963) on the basis of data for eighteen countries in which it was observed that the shares of the lowest-income groups in underdeveloped countries were comparable with those in developed countries but the shares of upper-income groups were markedly larger. Kuznets suggested that higher income inequality in underdeveloped countries may be due to greater inequality between the top and middle group and speculated that the equalizing impact of development was perhaps based on a rising share of the middle. Table 4.1 suggests that this generalization is not valid when the sample is widened to include other countries. There are many underdeveloped countries which show high inequality in terms of low income shares for both the middle and the poorest group.

NOTES

1. Dandekar and Rath (1971). See also Bardhan (1970) and (1973).
2. Fishlow (1972).
3. Weisskoff (1970).
4. Permanent income takes account of variations over the lifetime of the individual arising from both the age profile of income and random fluctuations around this profile. Income differences due to age are an important element of observed inequality in most samples of individuals at different stages in their working life.
5. Even if the consumption items can be quantified in physical terms, there is the problem of determining the appropriate prices to use in obtaining a "money value" for this consumption. Producer prices (farm gate prices) differ from retail prices, especially in different seasons. The problem of valuing production for direct investment (i.e., various types of labor using farm improvements) is even more complex since there is typically no market for the capital good produced.
6. This is true, for example, of labor force surveys directed at determining the structure of wages, urban household surveys aimed at constructing cost-of-living indexes for particular socio-economic sections of the population and, of course, tax data which cover only a very small percentage of the population.
7. The choice of households rather than individuals as the basic income unit reflects the assumption that income within a household is equally distributed. Even so there are problems arising from variations in household size and age structure. An alternative is to rank the population according to household per capita income, but data on this basis are available only for a few countries.

8. The best known of the various indexes is the Gini coefficient, which is based on the Lorenz curve. Others include the variance of income, the variance of logarithms of income, the coefficient of variation, and also entropy measures borrowed from information theory such as the index developed by Theil (1967). Atkinson (1970) proposes a new measure of inequality which is explicitly related to an underlying social welfare function and therefore provides a more meaningful basis for comparing or ranking alternative distributions.

9. The data are taken from Jain and Tiemann (1974). The original sources for each country as reported in that document are listed in the Appendix to Chapter 1 [in the original work—Eds.].

10. Income distribution data for these countries may overstate income equality since they frequently refer to "workers," which may exclude workers outside the state system who are usually in the lower income ranges.

REFERENCES

Atkinson, A. B. 1970. "On the Measurement of Inequality." *Journal of Economic Theory*, 2(September):244–263.

Bardhan, P. K. 1970. "On the Minimum Level of Living and the Rural Poor." *Indian Economic Review*, 5(April):129–136.

———. 1973. "On the Incidence of Poverty in Rural India in the Sixties." *Economic and Political Weekly*, 8(February special number):245–254.

Dandekar, V. M. and N. R. Rath. 1971. "Poverty in India." *Economic and Political Weekly*, 6(January 2):25–48; (January 9): 106-146.

Fishlow, A. 1972. "Brazilian Size Distribution of Income." Papers and Proceedings of the American Economic Association, 62(May):391–402.

Jain, S. and Tiemann, A. 1974. "Size Distribution of Income: A Compilation of Data." Development Research Center Discussion Paper no. 4, mimeographed. Washington, D.C.: World Bank.

Kuznets, S. 1955. "Economic Growth and Income Inequality." *American Economic Review*, 45(March):1–28.

———. 1963. "Quantitative Aspects of Economic Growth of Nations: III, Distribution of Income by Size." *Economic Development and Cultural Change*, 11 (January):1–80.

Thiel, H. 1967. *Economics and Information Theory*. Amsterdam: North-Holland.

Weisskoff, R. 1970. "Income Distribution and Economic Growth in Puerto Rico, Argentina and Mexico." *Review of Income and Wealth*, 16(December):303–332.

PART 2

. . . .

The Classic Thesis Revisited: Limits to Convergence

. . . .

5

· · · · · · ·

Economic Growth and
Income Inequality

· · · · · · ·

SIMON KUZNETS

Most debate on the internal gap between rich and poor people in developing nations begins with this seminal presidential address delivered by Simon Kuznets to the American Economic Association in 1954. The address, portions of which are reprinted here, uses limited data from Germany, the United Kingdom, and the United States to show that since the 1920s, and perhaps even earlier, there has been a trend toward equalization in the distribution of income. Kuznets discusses in some detail the possible causes for this trend, examining those factors in the process of industrialization that tend to counteract the concentration of savings in the hands of the wealthy. That particular discussion is not included here, but the interested reader can consult the original piece. Our interest lies in Kuznets's conclusion that the central factor in equalizing income must have been the rising incomes of the poorer sectors outside of the traditional agricultural economy. Kuznets introduces the critically important notion of the "inverted U-curve" (although he does not label it as such in the address), arguing that there seems to be increasing inequality in the early phases of industrialization, followed by declines in the later phases only. Finally, Kuznets opens the debate over the relevance of these findings for the developing nations by examining data from India, Ceylon (Sri Lanka), and Puerto Rico. The findings that income inequality in the developing countries is greater than that in the advanced countries and that such inequality may be growing form the basis of virtually all subsequent research and debate on this subject.

Reprinted with permission from the *American Economic Review*, vol. 45 (March 1955):1, 3–6, 17–26.

The central theme of this chapter is the character and causes of long-term changes in the personal distribution of income. Does inequality in the distribution of income increase or decrease in the course of a country's economic growth? What factors determine the secular level and trends of income inequalities?

These are broad questions in a field of study that has been plagued by looseness in definitions, unusual scarcity of data, and pressures of strongly held opinions. . . .

TRENDS IN INCOME INEQUALITY

Forewarned of the difficulties, we turn now to the available data. These data, even when relating to complete populations, invariably classify units by income for a given year. From our standpoint, this is their major limitation. Because the data often do not permit many size groupings, and because the difference between annual income incidence and longer-term income status has less effect if the number of classes is small and the limits of each class are wide, we use a few wide classes. This does not resolve the difficulty; and there are others due to the scantiness of data for long periods, inadequacy of the unit used—which is, at best, a family and very often a reporting unit—errors in the data, and so on through a long list. Consequently, the trends in the income structure can be discerned but dimly, and the results considered as preliminary informed guesses.

The data are for the United States, England, and Germany—a scant sample, but at least a starting point for some inferences concerning long-term changes in the presently developed countries. The general conclusion suggested is that the relative distribution of income, as measured by annual income incidence in rather broad classes, has been moving toward equality—with these trends particularly noticeable since the 1920s but beginning perhaps in the period before the first world war.

Let me cite some figures, all for income before direct taxes, in support of this impression. In the United States, in the distribution of income among families (excluding single individuals), the shares of the two lowest quintiles rise from 13 ½ percent in 1929 to 18 percent in the years after the second world war (average of 1944, 1946, 1947, and 1950); whereas the share of the top quintile declines from 55 to 44 percent, and that of the top 5 percent from 31 to 20 percent. In the United Kingdom, the share of the top 5 percent of units declines from 46 percent in 1880 to 43 percent in 1910 or 1913, to 33 percent in 1929, to 31 percent in 1938, and to 24 percent in 1947; the share of the lower 85 percent remains fairly constant between 1880 and 1913, between 41 and 43 percent, but then rises to 46 percent in 1929 and 55 percent in 1947. In Prussia, income inequality increases slightly between 1875 and 1913—the shares of the top quintile rising from 48 to 50 percent, of the top 5 percent from 26 to 30 percent; the share of the lower 60 percent, however, remains about the same. In Saxony, the change between 1880 and 1913 is minor: the share of the two lowest quintiles declines from 15 to 14 $\frac{1}{2}$ percent; that of the third quintile rises from 12 to 13 percent, of the fourth quintile from 16 $\frac{1}{2}$ to about 18 percent; that of the top quintile declines from 56 $\frac{1}{2}$ to 54 $\frac{1}{2}$ percent, and of the top 5 percent from 34 to 33 percent. In Germany as a whole, relative income inequality drops fairly sharply from 1913 to the 1920s, apparently due to decimation of large fortunes and property incomes during the war and inflation, but then begins to return to prewar levels during the depression of the 1930s.[1]

Even for what they are assumed to represent, let alone as approximations to shares in distributions by secular income levels, the data are such that differences of two or three percentage points cannot be assigned significance. One must judge by the general weight and consensus of the evidence—which unfortunately is limited to a few countries. It justifies a tentative impression of constancy in the relative distribution of income before taxes, followed by some narrowing of relative income inequality after the first world war—or earlier.

Three aspects of this finding should be stressed. First, the data are for income before direct taxes and exclude contributions by government (e.g., relief and free assistance). It is fair to argue that both the proportion and progressivity of direct taxes and the proportion of total income of individuals accounted for by government assistance to the less privileged economic groups have grown during recent decades. This is certainly true of the United States and the United Kingdom, but in the case of Germany is subject to further examination. It follows that the distribution of income after direct taxes and including free contributions by government would show an even greater narrowing of inequality in developed countries with size distributions of pretax, ex-government-benefits income similar to those for the United States and the United Kingdom.

Second, such stability or reduction in the inequality of the percentage shares was accompanied by significant rises in real income per capita. The countries now classified as developed have enjoyed rising per capita incomes except during catastrophic periods such as years of active world conflict. Hence, if the shares of groups classified by their annual income position can be viewed as approximations to shares of groups classified by their secular income levels, a constant percentage share of a given group means that its per capita real income is rising at the same rate as the average for all units in the country; and a reduction in inequality of the shares means that the per capita income of the lower-income groups is rising at a more rapid rate than the per capita income of the upper-income groups.

The third point can be put in the form of a question. Do the distributions by annual incomes properly reflect trends in distribution by secular incomes? As technology and economic performance rise to higher levels, incomes are less subject to transient disturbances, not necessarily of the cyclical order that can be recognized and allowed for by reference to business cycle chronology, but of a more irregular type. If in the earlier years the economic fortunes of units were subject to greater vicissitudes—poor crops for some farmers, natural calamity losses for some nonfarm business units—if the over-all proportion of individual entrepreneurs whose incomes were subject to such calamities, more yesterday but some even today, was larger in earlier decades, these earlier distributions of income would be more affected by transient disturbances. In these earlier distributions the temporarily unfortunate might crowd the lower quintiles and depress their shares unduly, and the temporarily fortunate might dominate the top quintile and raise its share unduly—proportionately more than in the distributions for later years. If so, distributions by longer-term average incomes might show less reduction in inequality than do the distributions by annual incomes; they might even show an opposite trend.

One may doubt whether this qualification would upset a narrowing of inequality as marked as that for the United States, and in as short a period as twenty-five years. Nor is it likely to affect the persistent downward drift in the spread of the distributions in the United Kingdom. But I must admit a strong element of judgment in deciding how far this qualification modifies the finding of long-term stability followed by reduction in income inequality in the few developed countries for which it is observed or is likely to be revealed by existing data. The important point is that the qualification is relevant; it suggests need for further study if we are to learn much from the available data concerning the secular income structure; and such study is likely to yield results of interest in themselves in their bearing upon the problem of trends in temporal instability of income flows to individual units or to economically significant groups of units in different sectors of the national economy. . . .

Hence we may conclude that the major offset to the widening of income inequality associated with the shift from agriculture and the countryside to industry and the city must have been a rise in the income share of the lower groups within the nonagricultural sector of the population. This provides a lead for exploration in what seems to me a most promising direction: consideration of the pace and character of the economic growth of the urban population, with particular reference to the relative position of lower-income groups. Much is to be said for the notion that once the early turbulent phases of industrialization and urbanization had passed, a variety of forces converged to bolster the economic position of the lower-income groups within the urban population. The very fact that, after a while, an increasing proportion of the urban population was "native," i.e., born in cities rather than in the rural areas, and hence more able to take advantage of the possibilities of city life in preparation for the economic struggle, meant a better chance for organization and adaptation, a better basis for securing greater income shares than was possible for the newly "immigrant" population coming from the countryside or from abroad. The increasing efficiency of the older, established urban population should also be taken into account. Furthermore, in democratic societies the growing political power of the urban lower-income groups led to a variety of protective and supporting legislation, much of it aimed to counteract the worst effects of rapid industrialization and urbanization and to support the claims of the broad masses for more adequate shares of the growing income of the country. Space does not permit the discussion of demographic, political, and social considerations that could be brought to bear to explain the offsets to any declines in the shares of the lower groups, declines otherwise deducible from the trends suggested in the numerical illustration.

OTHER TRENDS RELATED
TO THOSE IN INCOME INEQUALITY

One aspect of the conjectural conclusion just reached deserves emphasis because of its possible interrelation with other important elements in the process and theory of economic growth. The scanty empirical evidence suggests that the narrowing of income inequality in the developed countries is relatively recent and probably did not characterize the earlier stages of their growth. Likewise, the various factors that have been suggested above would explain stability and narrowing in income inequality in the later rather than in the earlier phases of industrialization and urbanization. Indeed, they would suggest widening inequality in these early phases of economic growth, especially in the older countries where the emergence of the new industrial system had shattering effects on long-established pre-industrial economic and social institutions. This timing characteristic is particularly applicable to factors bearing upon the lower-income groups: the dislocating effects of the agricultural and industrial revolutions, combined with the "swarming" of population incident upon a rapid decline in death rates and the maintenance or even rise of birth rates, would be unfavorable to the relative economic position of lower-income groups. Furthermore, there may also have been a preponderance in the earlier periods of factors favoring maintenance or increase in the shares of top-income groups: in so far as their position was bolstered by gains arising out of new industries, by an unusually rapid rate of creation of new fortunes, we would expect these forces to be relatively stronger in the early phases of industrialization than in the later when the pace of industrial growth slackens.

One might thus assume a long swing in the inequality characterizing the secular income structure: widening in the early phases of economic growth when the transition from the pre-industrial to the industrial civilization was most rapid; becoming stabilized for a while; and then narrowing in the later phases. This long secular swing would be most pronounced for older countries where the dislocation effects of the earlier phases of modern economic growth were most conspicuous; but it might be found also in the "younger" countries like the United States if the period preceding marked industrialization could be compared with the early phases of industrialization, and if the latter could be compared with the subsequent phases of greater maturity.

If there is some evidence for assuming this long swing in relative inequality in the distribution of income before direct taxes and excluding free benefits from government, there is surely a stronger case for assuming a long swing in inequality of income net of direct taxes and including government benefits. Progressivity of income taxes and, indeed, their very importance characterize only the more recent phases of development of the presently developed countries; in narrowing income inequality they must have accentuated the downward phase of the long swing, contributing to the reversal of trend in the secular widening and narrowing of income inequality.

No adequate empirical evidence is available for checking this conjecture of a long secular swing in income inequality;[2] nor can the phases be dated precisely. However, to make it more specific, I would place the early phase in which income inequality might have been widening from about 1780 to 1850 in England; from about 1840 to 1890, and particularly from 1870 on in the United States; and from the 1840s to the 1890s in Germany. I would put the phase of narrowing income inequality somewhat later in the United States and Germany than in England—perhaps beginning with the first world war in the former and the last quarter of the nineteenth century in the latter.

Is there a possible relation between this secular swing in income inequality and the long swing in other important components of the growth process? For the older countries a long swing is observed in the rate of growth of population—the upward phase represented by acceleration in the rate of growth reflecting the early reduction in the death rate which was not offset by a decline in the birth rate (and in some cases was accompanied by a rise in the birth rate); and the downward phase represented by a shrinking in the rate of growth reflecting the more pronounced downward trend in the birth rate. Again, in the older countries, and also perhaps in the younger, there may have been a secular swing in the rate of urbanization, in the sense that the proportional additions to urban population and the measures of internal migration that produced this shift of population probably increased for a while—from the earlier much lower levels; but then tended to diminish as urban population came to dominate the country and as the rural reservoirs of migration became proportionally much smaller. For old, and perhaps for young countries also, there must have been a secular swing in the proportions of savings or capital formation to total economic product. Per capita product in pre-industrial times was not large enough to permit as high a nationwide rate of saving or capital formation as was attained in the course of industrial development: this is suggested by present comparisons between net capital formation rates of 3 to 5 percent of national product in underdeveloped countries and rates of 10 to 15 percent in developed countries. If then, at least in the older countries, and perhaps even in the younger ones—prior to initiation of the process of modern development—we begin with low secular levels in the savings proportions, there would be a rise in the early phases to appreciably higher levels. We also know that during recent periods the net capital formation proportion, and even the gross, failed to rise and perhaps even declined.

Other trends might be suggested that would possibly trace long swings similar to those for inequality in income structure, rate of growth of population, rate of urbanization and internal migration, and the proportion of savings or capital formation to national product. For example, such swings might be found in the ratio of foreign trade to domestic activities; in the aspects, if we could only measure them properly, of government activity that bear upon market forces (there must have been a phase of increasing freedom of market forces, giving way to greater intervention by government). But the suggestions already made suffice to indicate that the long swing in income inequality must be viewed as part of a wider process of economic growth, and interrelated with similar movements in other elements. The long alternation in the rate of growth of population can be seen partly as a cause, partly as an effect of the long swing in income inequality which was associated with a secular rise in real per capita income levels. The long swing in income inequality is also probably closely associated with the swing in capital formation proportions—in so far as wider inequality makes for higher, and narrower inequality for lower, countrywide savings proportions.

COMPARISON OF DEVELOPED AND UNDERDEVELOPED COUNTRIES

What is the bearing of the experience of the developed countries upon the economic growth of underdeveloped countries? Let us examine briefly the data on income distribution in the latter, and speculate upon some of the implications.

As might have been expected, such data for underdeveloped countries are scanty. For the present purpose, distributions of family income for India in 1949-50, for Ceylon in 1950, and for Puerto Rico in 1948 were used. While the coverage is narrow and the margin of error wide, the data show that income distribution in these underdeveloped countries is somewhat *more* unequal than in the developed countries during the period after the second world war. Thus the shares of the lower 3 quintiles are 28 percent in India, 30 percent in Ceylon, and 24 percent in Puerto Rico—compared with 34 percent in the United States and 36 percent in the United Kingdom. The shares of the top quintile are 55 percent in India, 50 percent in Ceylon, and 56 percent in Puerto Rico, compared with 44 percent in the United States and 45 percent in the United Kingdom.[3]

This comparison is for income before direct taxes and excluding free benefits from governments. Since the burden and progressivity of direct taxes are much greater in developed countries, and since it is in the latter that substantial volumes of free economic assistance are extended to the lower-income groups, a comparison in terms of income net of direct taxes and including government benefits would only accentuate the wider inequality of income distributions in the underdeveloped countries. Is this difference a reliable reflection of wider inequality also in the distribution of *secular* income levels in underdeveloped countries? Even disregarding the margins of error in the data, the possibility raised earlier in this chapter that transient disturbances in income levels may be more conspicuous under conditions of primitive material and economic technology would affect the comparison just made. Since the distributions cited reflect the annual income levels, a greater allowance should perhaps be made for transient disturbances in the distributions for the underdeveloped than in those for the developed countries. Whether such a correction would obliterate the difference is a matter on which I have no relevant evidence.

Another consideration might tend to support this qualification. Underdeveloped countries are characterized by low average levels of income per capita, low enough to raise the question of how the populations manage to survive. Let us assume that these countries represent fairly unified population groups, and exclude, for the moment, areas that combine large native populations with small enclaves of nonnative, privileged minorities, e.g., Kenya and Rhodesia, where income inequality, because of the excessively high income shares of the privileged minority, is appreciably wider than even in the underdeveloped countries cited above.[4] On this assumption, one may infer that in countries with low average income, the secular level of income in the lower brackets could not be below a fairly sizable proportion of average income—otherwise, the groups could not survive. This means, to use a purely hypothetical figure, that the secular level of the share of the lowest decile could not fall far short of 6 or 7 percent, i.e., the lowest decile could not have a per capita income less than six- or seven-tenths of the countrywide average. In more advanced countries, with higher average per capita incomes, even the *secular* share of the lowest bracket could easily be a smaller fraction of the countrywide average, say as small as 2 or 3 percent for the lowest decile, i.e., from a fifth to a third of the countrywide average—without implying a materially impossible economic position for that group. To be sure, there is in all countries continuous pressure to raise the relative position of the bottom-income groups; but the fact remains that the lower limit of the proportional share in the secular income structure is higher when the real countrywide per capita income is low than when it is high.

If the long-term share of the lower-income groups is larger in the underdeveloped than in the average countries, income inequality in the former should be narrower, not wider as we have found. However, if the lower brackets receive larger shares, and at the same time the very top brackets also receive larger shares—which would mean that the intermediate income classes would not show as great a progression from the bottom—the net effect may well be wider inequality. To illustrate, let us compare the distributions for India and the United States. The first quintile in India receives 8 percent of total income, more than the 6 percent share of the first quintile in the United States. But the second quintile in India receives only 9 percent, the third 11, and the fourth 16; whereas in the United States, the shares of these quintiles are 12, 16, and 22 respectively. This is a rough statistical reflection of a fairly common observation relating to income distributions in underdeveloped compared with developed countries. The former have no "middle" classes: there is a sharp contrast between the preponderant proportion of population whose average income is well below the generally low countrywide average, and a small top group with a very large relative income excess. The developed countries, on the other hand, are characterized by a much more gradual rise from low to high shares, with substantial groups receiving more than the high countrywide income average, and the top groups securing smaller shares than the comparable ordinal groups in underdeveloped countries.

It is, therefore, possible that even the distributions of secular income levels would be more unequal in underdeveloped than in developed countries—not in the sense that the shares of the lower brackets would be lower in the former than in the latter, but in the sense that the shares of the very top groups would be higher and that those of the groups below the top would all be significantly lower than a low countrywide income average. This is even more likely to be true of the distribution of income net of direct taxes and inclusive of free government benefits. But whether a high probability weight can be attached to this conjecture is a matter for further study.

In the absence of evidence to the contrary, I assume that it is true: that the secular income structure is somewhat more unequal in underdeveloped countries than in the more advanced—particularly in those of Western and Northern Europe and their economically developed descendants in the New World (the United States, Canada, Australia, and New Zealand). This conclusion has a variety of important implications and leads to some pregnant questions, of which only a few can be stated here.

In the first place, the wider inequality in the secular income structure of underdeveloped countries is associated with a much lower level of average income per capita. Two corollaries follow—and they would follow even if the income inequalities were of the same relative range in the two groups of countries. First, the impact is far sharper in the underdeveloped countries, where the failure to reach an already low countrywide average spells much greater material and psychological misery than similar proportional deviations from the average in the richer, more advanced countries. Second, positive savings are obviously possible only at much higher relative income levels in the underdeveloped countries: if in the more advanced countries some savings are possible in the fourth quintile, in the underdeveloped countries savings could be realized only at the very peak of the income pyramid, say by the top 5 or 3 percent. If so, the concentration of savings and of assets is even more pronounced than in the developed countries; and the effects of such concentration in the past may serve to explain the peculiar characteristics of the secular income structure in underdeveloped countries today.

The second implication is that this unequal income structure presumably coexisted with a low rate of growth of income per capita. The underdeveloped countries today have not always lagged behind the presently developed areas in level of economic performance; indeed, some of the former may have been the economic leaders of the world in the centuries preceding the last two. The countries of Latin America, Africa, and particularly those of Asia, are underdeveloped today because in the last two centuries, and even in recent decades, their rate of economic growth has been far lower than that in the Western World—and low indeed, if any growth there was, on a per capita basis. The underlying shifts in industrial structure, the opportunities for internal mobility and for economic improvement, were far more limited than in the more rapidly growing countries now in the developed category. There was no hope, within the lifetime of a generation, of a significantly perceptible rise in the level of real income, or even that the next generation might fare much better. It was this hope that served as an important and realistic compensation for the wide inequality in income distribution that characterized the presently developed countries during the earlier phases of their growth.

The third implication follows from the preceding two. It is quite possible that income inequality has not narrowed in the underdeveloped countries within recent decades. There is no empirical evidence to check this conjectural implication, but it is suggested by the absence, in these areas, of the dynamic forces associated with rapid growth that in the developed countries checked the upward trend of the upper-income shares that was due to the cumulative effect of continuous concentration of past savings; and it is also indicated by the failure of the political and social systems of underdeveloped countries to initiate the governmental or political practices that effectively bolster the weak positions of the lower-income classes. Indeed, there is a possibility that inequality in the secular income structure of underdeveloped countries may have widened in recent decades—the only qualification being that where there has been a recent shift from colonial to independent status, a privileged, *nonnative* minority may have been eliminated. But the implication, in terms of the income distribution among the *native* population proper, still remains plausible.

The somber picture just presented may be an oversimplified one. But I believe that it is sufficiently realistic to lend weight to the questions it poses—questions as to the bearing of the recent levels and trends in income inequality, and the factors that determine them, upon the future prospect of underdeveloped countries within the orbit of the free world.

The questions are difficult, but they must be faced unless we are willing completely to disregard past experience or to extrapolate mechanically oversimplified impressions of past development. The first question is: Is the pattern of the older developed countries likely to be repeated in the sense that in the early phases of industrialization in the underdeveloped countries income inequalities will tend to widen before the leveling forces become strong enough first to stabilize and then reduce income inequalities? While the future cannot be an exact repetition of the past, there are already certain elements in the present conditions of underdeveloped societies, e.g., "swarming" of population due to sharp cuts in death rates unaccompanied by declines in birth rates, that threaten to widen inequality by depressing the relative position of lower-income groups even further. Furthermore, if and when industrialization begins, the dislocating effects on these societies, in which there is often an old hardened crust of economic and social institutions, are likely to be quite sharp—so sharp as to destroy the positions of some of the lower groups more rapidly than opportunities elsewhere in the economy may be created for them.

The next question follows from an affirmative answer to the first. Can the political framework of the underdeveloped societies withstand the strain which further widening of income inequality is likely to generate? This query is pertinent if it is realized that the real per capita income level of many underdeveloped societies today is lower than the per capita income level of the presently developed societies before *their* initial phases of industrialization. And yet the stresses of the dislocations incident to early phases of industrialization in the developed countries were sufficiently acute to strain the political and social fabric of society, force major political reforms, and sometimes result in civil war.

The answer to the second question may be negative, even granted that industrialization may be accompanied by a rise in real per capita product. If, for many groups in society, the rise is even partly offset by a decline in their proportional share in total product; if, consequently, it is accompanied by widening of income inequality, the resulting pressures and conflicts may necessitate drastic changes in social and political organization. This gives rise to the next and crucial question: How can either the institutional and political framework of the underdeveloped societies or the processes of economic growth and industrialization be modified to favor a sustained rise to higher levels of economic performance and yet avoid the fatally simple remedy of an authoritarian regime that would use the population as cannon-fodder in the fight for economic achievement? How to minimize the cost of transition and avoid paying the heavy price—in internal tensions, in long-run inefficiency in providing means for satisfying wants of human beings as individuals—

which the inflation of political power represented by authoritarian regimes requires?

Facing these acute problems, one is cognizant of the dangers of taking an extreme position. One extreme—particularly tempting to us—is to favor repetition of past patterns of the now developed countries, patterns that, under the markedly different conditions of the presently underdeveloped countries, are almost bound to put a strain on the existing social and economic institutions and eventuate in revolutionary explosions and authoritarian regimes. There is danger in simple analogies; in arguing that because an unequal income distribution in Western Europe in the past led to accumulation of savings and financing of basic capital formation, the preservation or accentuation of present income inequalities in the underdeveloped countries is necessary to secure the same result. Even disregarding the implications for the lower-income groups, we may find that in at least some of these countries today the consumption propensities of upper-income groups are far higher and savings propensities far lower than were those of the more puritanical upper-income groups of the presently developed countries. Because they may have proved favorable in the past, it is dangerous to argue that completely free markets, lack of penalties implicit in progressive taxation, and the like are indispensable for the economic growth of the now underdeveloped countries. Under present conditions the results may be quite the opposite—withdrawal of accumulated assets to relatively "safe" channels, either by flight abroad or into real estate; and the inability of governments to serve as basic agents in the kind of capital formation that is indispensable to economic growth. It is dangerous to argue that, because in the past foreign investment provided capital resources to spark satisfactory economic growth in some of the smaller European countries or in Europe's descendants across the seas, similar effects can be expected today if only the underdeveloped countries can be convinced of the need of a "favorable climate." Yet, it is equally dangerous to take the opposite position and claim that the present problems are entirely new and that we must devise solutions that are the product of imagination unrestrained by knowledge of the past, and therefore full of romantic violence. What we need, and I am afraid it is but a truism, is a clear perception of past trends and of conditions under which they occurred, as well as knowledge of the conditions that characterize the underdeveloped countries today. With this as a beginning, we can then attempt to translate the elements of a properly understood past into the conditions of an adequately understood present.

NOTES

1. The following sources were used in calculating the figures cited: *United States*. For recent years we used *Income Distribution by Size, 1944–1950* (Washington, 1953) and Selma Goldsmith and others, "Size Distribution of

Income Since the Mid-Thirties," *Rev. Econ. Stat.*, Feb. 1954, XXXVI, 1–32; for 1929, the Brookings Institution data as adjusted in Simon Kuznets, *Shares of Upper Groups in Income and Savings* (New York, 1953), p. 220.

United Kingdom. For 1938 and 1947, Dudley Seers, *The Levelling of Income Since 1938* (Oxford, 1951) p. 39; for 1929, Colin Clark, *National Income and Outlay* (London, 1937) Table 47, p. 109; for 1880, 1910, and 1913, A. Bowley, *The Change in the Distribution of the National Income, 1880–1913* (Oxford, 1920).

Germany. For the constituent areas (Prussia, Saxony and others) for years before the first world war, based on S. Prokopovich, *National Income of Western European Countries* (published in Moscow in the 1920s). Some summary results are given in Prokopovich, "The Distribution of National Income," *Econ. Jour.,* March 1926, XXXVI, 69–82. See also, "Das Deutsche Volkseinkommen vor und nach dem Kriege," *Einzelschrift zur Stat. des Deutschen Reichs,* no. 24 (Berlin, 1932), and W. S. and E. S. Woytinsky, *World Population and Production* (New York, 1953) Table 192, p. 709.

2. Prokopovich's data on Prussia, from the source cited in footnote 1, indicate a substantial widening in income inequality in the early period. The share of the lower 90 percent of the population declines from 73 percent in 1854 to 65 percent in 1875; the share of the top 5 percent rises from 21 to 25 percent. But I do not know enough about the data for the early years to evaluate the reliability of the finding.

3. For sources of these data see "Regional Economic Trends and Levels of Living," submitted at the Norman Waite Harris Foundation Institute of the University of Chicago in November 1954 (in press in the volume of proceedings). This paper, and an earlier one, "Underdeveloped Countries and the Pre-industrial Phases in the Advanced Countries: An Attempt at Comparison," prepared for the World Population Meetings in Rome held in September 1954 (in press) discuss issues raised in this section.

4. In one year since the second world war, the non-African group in Southern Rhodesia, which accounted for only 5 percent of total population, received 57 percent of total income; in Kenya, the minority of only 2.9 percent of total population, received 51 percent of total income; in Northern Rhodesia, the minority of only 1.4 percent of total population, received 45 percent of total income. See United Nations, *National Income and Its Distribution in Underdeveloped Countries*, Statistical Paper, Ser. E, no. 3, 1951, Table 12, p. 19.

6

. . . .

Catching Up, Forging Ahead, and Falling Behind

. . . .

MOSES ABRAMOVITZ

In this chapter Moses Abramovitz explains convergence theory, the idea that there is an inverse relationship between the level and rate of productivity growth: Labor productivity in poor countries is thought to have a higher potential for rapid growth than in rich countries. The expectation is that over time the GNP/pc growth rates of poor countries will be more rapid than those of the rich, and thus the gap between rich and poor countries will close. However, not all poor countries have higher labor productivity rates than rich countries, according to Abramovitz, because they lack the "social capacity" to utilize modern technology. Recently there has been considerable discussion of how developed countries can remain "competitive" with developing countries, where labor costs are often a fraction of those in the developed countries. Abramovitz suggests that this is as much a political as an economic question.

Among the many explanations of the surge of productivity growth during the quarter century following World War II, the most prominent is the hypothesis that the countries of the industrialized "West" were able to bring into production a large backlog of unexploited technology. The principal part of this backlog is deemed to have consisted of methods of production and of industrial and commercial organization already in use in the United States at the end of the war, but not yet employed in the other countries of the West. In this hypothesis, the United States is viewed as the "leader," the other

Reprinted with permission from *Journal of Economic History*, Vol. XLVI, No. 2 (June 1986): 386–405. Copyright © 1986 The Economic History Association.

countries as "followers" who had the opportunity to "catch up." In conformity with this view, a waning of the opportunity for catching up is frequently advanced as an explanation of the retardation in productivity growth suffered by the same group of followers since 1973. Needless to say, the size of the initial backlog and its subsequent reduction are rarely offered as sole explanations of the speedup and slowdown, but they stand as important parts of the story.

These views about postwar following and catching up suggest a more general hypothesis that the productivity levels of countries tend to converge. And this in turn brings to mind old questions about the emergence of new leaders and the historical and theoretical puzzles that shifts in leadership and relative standing present—matters that in some respects fit only awkwardly with the convergence hypothesis. . . .

I. THE CATCH-UP HYPOTHESIS

The hypothesis asserts that being backward in level of productivity carries a *potential* for rapid advance. Stated more definitely the proposition is that in comparisons across countries the growth rates of productivity in any long period tend to be inversely related to the initial levels of productivity.

The central idea is simple enough. It has to do with the level of technology embodied in a country's capital stock. Imagine that the level of labor productivity were governed entirely by the level of technology embodied in capital stock. In a "leading country," to state things sharply, one may suppose that the technology embodied in each vintage of its stock was at the very frontier of technology at the time of investment. The *technological* age of the stock is, so to speak, the same as its *chronological* age. In an otherwise similar follower whose productivity level is lower, the technological age of the stock is high relative to its chronological age. The stock is obsolete even for its age. When a leader discards old stock and replaces it, the accompanying productivity increase is governed and limited by the advance of knowledge between the time when the old capital was installed and the time it is replaced. Those who are behind, however, have the potential to make a larger leap. New capital can embody the frontier of knowledge, but the capital it replaces was technologically superannuated. So—the larger the technological and, therefore, the productivity gap between leader and follower, the stronger the follower's potential for growth in productivity; and, other things being equal, the faster one expects the follower's growth rate to be. Followers tend to catch up faster if they are initially more backward.

Viewed in the same simple way, the catch-up process would be self-limiting because as a follower catches up, the possibility of making large leaps by replacing superannuated with best-practice technology becomes smaller and smaller. A follower's potential for growth weakens as its productivity level converges towards that of the leader.

This is the simple central idea. It needs extension and qualification. There are at least four extensions:

(1) The same technological opportunity that permits rapid progress by modernization encourages rapid growth of the capital stock partly because of the returns to modernization itself, and partly because technological progress reduces the price of capital goods relative to the price of labor. So—besides a reduction of technological age towards chronological age, the rate of rise of the capital-labor ratio tends to be higher. Productivity growth benefits on both counts. And if circumstances make for an acceleration in the growth of the capital stock its chronological age also falls.[1]

(2) Growth of productivity also makes for increase in aggregate output. A broader horizon of scale-dependent technological progress then comes into view.

(3) Backwardness carries an opportunity for modernization in disembodied, as well as in embodied, technology.

(4) If countries at relatively low levels of industrialization contain large numbers of redundant workers in farming and petty trade, as is normally the case, there is also an opportunity for productivity growth by improving the allocation of labor.

Besides extension, the simple hypothesis also needs qualification.

First, technological backwardness is not usually a mere accident. Tenacious societal characteristics normally account for a portion, perhaps a substantial portion, of a country's past failure to achieve as high a level of productivity as economically more advanced countries. The same deficiencies, perhaps in attenuated form, normally remain to keep a backward country from making the full technological leap envisaged by the simple hypothesis. I have a name for these characteristics. Following Kazushi Ohkawa and Henry Rosovsky, I call them "social capability."[2] One can summarize the matter in this way. Having regard to technological backwardness alone leads to the simple hypothesis about catch-up and convergence already advanced. Having regard to social capability, however, we expect that the developments anticipated by that hypothesis will be clearly displayed in cross-country comparisons only if countries' social capabilities are about the same. One should say, therefore, that a country's potential for rapid growth is strong not when it is backward without qualification, but rather when it is technologically backward but socially advanced.

The trouble with absorbing social capability into the catch-up hypothesis is that no one knows just what it means or how to measure it. In past work I identified a country's social capability with technical competence, for which—at least among Western countries—years of education may be a rough proxy, and with its political, commercial, industrial, and financial institutions, which I characterized in more qualitative ways.[3] I had in mind mainly experience with the organization and management of large-scale enterprise and with financial institutions and markets capable of mobilizing capital for individual firms on a similarly large scale. On some occasions the situation for a selection of countries may be sufficiently clear. In explaining postwar growth in Europe and Japan, for example, one may be able to say with some confidence that these countries were competent to absorb and exploit then existing best-practice technology. More generally, however, judgments about social capability remain highly problematic. A few comments may serve to suggest some of the considerations involved as well as the speculative nature of the subject.

One concerns the familiar notion of a trade-off between specialization and adaptability. The content of education in a country and the character of its industrial, commercial, and financial organizations may be well designed to exploit fully the power of an existing technology; they may be less well fitted to adapt to the requirements of change. Presumably, some capacity to adapt is present everywhere, but countries may differ from one another in this respect, and their capacities to adapt may change over time.

Next, the notion of adaptability suggests that there is an interaction between social capability and technological opportunity. The state of education embodied in a nation's population and its existing institutional arrangements constrains it in its choice of technology. But technological opportunity presses for change. So countries learn to modify their institutional arrangements and then to improve them as they gain experience. The constraints imposed by social capability on the successful adoption of a more advanced technology gradually weaken and permit its fuller exploitation. . . .

Social capability, finally, depends on more than the content of education and the organization of firms. Other aspects of economic systems count as well—their openness to competition, to the establishment and operation of new firms, and to the sale and purchase of new goods and services. Viewed from the other side, it is a question of the obstacles to change raised by vested interests, established positions, and customary relations among firms and between employers and employees. The view from this side is what led Mancur Olson to identify defeat in war and accompanying political convulsion as a radical ground-clearing experience opening the way for new men, new organizations, and new modes of operation and trade better fitted to technological potential.[4]

These considerations have a bearing on the notion that a follower's potential for rapid growth weakens as its technological level converges on the leader's. This is not necessarily the case if social capability is itself endogenous, becoming stronger—or perhaps weaker—as technological gaps close. In the one case, the evolution of social capability connected with catching up itself raises the possibility that followers may forge ahead of even progressive leaders. In the other, a leader may fall back or a follower's pursuit may be slowed.

There is a somewhat technical point that has a similar bearing. This is the fact, noticed by Kravis and Denison, that as followers' levels of per capita income converge on the leader's, so do their structures of consumption and prices.[5] R.C.O. Matthews then observed that the convergence of consumption and production patterns should make it easier, rather than more difficult, for followers to borrow technology with advantage as productivity gaps close.[6] This, therefore, stands as still another qualification to the idea that the catch-up process is steadily self-limiting.

The combination of technological gap and social capability defines a country's *potentiality* for productivity advance by way of catch-up. This, however, should be regarded as a potentiality in the long run. The pace at which the potentiality is realized depends on still another set of causes that are largely independent of those governing the potentiality itself. There is a long story to tell about the factors controlling the rate of realization of potential.[7] Its general plot, however, can be suggested by noting three principal chapter headings:

(1) The facilities for the diffusion of knowledge—for example, channels of international technical communication, multinational corporations, the state of international trade and of direct capital investment.

(2) Conditions facilitating or hindering structural change in the composition of output, in the occupational and industrial distribution of the workforce, and in the geographical location of industry and population. Among other factors, this is where conditions of labor supply, the existence of labor reserves in agriculture, and the factors controlling internal and international migration come in.

(3) Macroeconomic and monetary conditions encouraging and sustaining capital investment and the level and growth of effective demand.

Having considered the technological catch-up idea, with its several extensions and qualifications, I can summarize by proposing a restatement of the hypothesis as follows:

Countries that are technologically backward have a potentiality for generating growth more rapid than that of more advanced countries, provided their social capabilities are sufficiently developed to permit successful exploitation of technologies already employed by the technological leaders. The pace at which potential for catch-up is actually realized in a particular period depends on factors limiting the diffusion of knowledge, the rate of structural change, the accumulation of capital, and the expansion of demand. The process of catching up tends to be self-limiting, but the strength of the tendency may be weakened or overcome, at least for limited periods, by advantages connected with the convergence of production patterns as followers advance towards leaders or by an endogenous enlargement of social capabilities.

II. HISTORICAL EXPERIENCE WITH CATCHING UP

I go on now to review some evidence bearing on the catch-up process. The survey I make is limited to the 16 countries covered by the new Maddison estimates of product per worker-hour for nine key years from 1870 to 1979.[8] The estimates are consistently derived as regards gross domestic product and worker hours and are adjusted as regards levels of product per worker hour by the Kravis estimates of purchasing power parities for postwar years. I have compressed the message of these data into three measures (See Tables 6.1 and 6.2):

(1) Averages of the productivity levels of the various countries relative to that of the United States, which was the leading country for most of the period. (For 1870 and 1890, I have also calculated averages of relatives based on the United Kingdom.) I calculate these averages for each of the nine key years and use them to indicate whether productivity levels of followers, *as a group*, were tending to converge on that of the leader.[9]

(2) Measures of relative variance around the mean levels of relative productivity. These provide one sort of answer to the question of whether the countries that started at relatively low level of productivity tended to advance faster than those with initially higher levels.

Table 6.1   Comparative Levels of Productivity, 1870–1979: Means and Relative Variance of the Relatives of 15 Countries Compared with the United States (U.S. GDP per manhour = 100)[a]

	(1) Mean	(2) Coefficient of Variance[b]
1870	77 (66)	.51 (.51)
1890	68 (68)	.48 (.48)
1913	61	.33
1929	57	.29
1938	61	.22
1950	46	.36
1960	52	.29
1973	69	.14
1979	75	.15

a. 1870 and 1890. Figures in parentheses are based on relatives with the United Kingdom = 100.

b. Standard deviation divided by mean.

Source: Calculated from Angus Maddison, *Phases of Capitalist Development* (New York, 1982), Tables 5.2 and C.10.

Table 6.2   The Association (Rank Correlation) Between Initial Levels and Subsequent Growth Rates of Labor Productivity (GDP per manhour in 16 countries, 1870–1979)

Shorter Periods			Lengthening Periods Since 1870	
	(1)	(2)		(3)
1870–1913	−.59		1870–1890	−.32
1870–1890		−.32	−1913	−.59
1890–1913		−.56	−1929	−.72
			−1938	−.83
1913–1938	−.70		−1950	−.16
1913–29		−.35	−1960	−.66
1929–38		−.57	−1973	−.95
			−1979	−.97
1938–1950	+.48			
1950–1979	−.92			
1950–60		−.81		
1960–73		−.90		
1973–79		−.13		

Source of underlying data: Maddison, *Phases*, Tables 5.1, 5.2, and C.10.

(3) Rank correlations between initial levels of productivity and subsequent growth rates. If the potential supposedly inherent in technological backwardness is being realized, there is likely to be some inverse correlation; and if it works with enough strength to dominate other forces the coefficients will be high.

The data I use and the measures I make have a number of drawbacks. The data, of course, have the weaknesses that are inherent in any set of estimates of GDP and manhours, however ably contrived, that stretch back far into the nineteenth century. Beyond that, however, simple calculations such as I have made fail, in a number of respects, to isolate the influence of the catch-up hypothesis proper.

To begin with, my measures do not allow for variation in the richness of countries' natural resources in relation to their populations. Labor productivity levels, therefore, are not pure reflections of levels of technology. In the same way, these levels will also reflect past accumulations of reproducible capital, both physical and human, and these may also be independent of technological levels in one degree or another. Further, the measured growth rates of labor of productivity will be influenced by the pace of capital accumulation. As already said, differences in rates of accumulation may reflect countries' opportunities to make advances in technology, but rates of capital formation may also be independent, to some degree, of countries' potentials for technological advance. Finally, my measures make no allowance for countries' variant abilities to employ current best-practice technology for reasons other than the differences in social capability already discussed. Their access to economies of scale is perhaps the most important matter. If advanced technology at any time is heavily scale-dependent and if obstacles to trade across national frontiers, political or otherwise, are important, large countries will have a stronger potential for growth than smaller ones.

There are many reasons, therefore, why one cannot suppose that the expectations implied by the catch-up hypothesis will display themselves clearly in the measures I present. It will be something if the data show some systematic evidence of development consistent with the hypothesis. And it will be useful if this provides a chance to speculate about the reasons why the connections between productivity levels and growth rates appear to have been strong in some periods and weak in others.

Other countries, on the average, made no net gain on the United States in a period longer than a century (Table 6.1, col. 1). The indication of very limited, or even zero, convergence is really stronger than the figures suggest. This is because the productivity measures reflect more than gaps in technology and in reproducible capital intensity, with respect to which catch-up is presumably possible. As already said, they also reflect differences in natural resource availabilities which, of course, are generally favorable to America and were far more important to America and to all the other countries in 1870 than they are today. In 1870, the agricultural share of United States employment was 50 percent; in 1979, 3 $\frac{1}{2}$ percent. For the other 15 countries, the corresponding figures are 48 and 8 percent on the average. The declines were large in all the countries.[10] So the American advantage in 1870 depended much more on our favorable land-man ratio than it did in 1979. Putting it the other way, other countries on the average must have fallen back over the century in respect to the productivity determinants in respect to which catch-up is possible.

In other respects, however, one can see the influence of the potential for catching up clearly. The variance among the productivity levels of the 15 "follower" countries declines drastically over the century—from a coefficient of variation of 0.5 in 1870 to 0.15 in 1979. Not only that: the decline in variance was continuous from one key year to the next, with only one reversal—in the period across World War II. In the same way, the inverse rank correlation between the initial productivity levels in 1870 and subsequent growth rates over increasingly long periods becomes stronger and stronger, until we reach the correlation coefficient of -.97 across the entire 109 years.[11] (Again there was the single reversal across World War II when the association was actually—and presumably accidentally—positive.)

I believe the steadily declining variance measures and the steadily rising correlation coefficients should be interpreted to mean that initial productivity gaps did indeed constitute a potentiality for fast growth that had its effect later if not sooner. The effect of the potentiality became visible in a very limited degree very early. But if a country was incapable of, or prevented from, exploiting that opportunity promptly, the technological growth potential became strong, and the country's later rate of advance was all the faster. Though it may have taken a century for obstacles or inhibitions to be fully overcome, the net outcome was that levels of productivity tended steadily to even out—at least within the group of presently advanced countries in my sample.

This last phrase is important. Mine is a biased sample in that its members consist of countries all of whom have successfully entered into the process of modern economic growth. This implies that they have acquired the educational and institutional characteristics needed to make use of modern technologies to some advanced degree. It is by no means assured—indeed, it is unlikely—that a more comprehensive sample of countries would show the same tendency for levels of productivity to even out over the same period of time.[12]

This is the big picture. How do things look if we consider shorter periods? There are two matters to keep in mind: the tendency to converge *within* the group of followers; and the convergence—or lack of it—of the group of followers vis-à-vis the United States. I take up the second matter in Section III. As to the convergence *within* the follower group, the figures suggest that the process varied in strength markedly from period to period. The main difference was that before World War II it operated weakly or at best with moderate strength. For almost a quarter-century following the war it apparently worked with very great strength. Why?

Before World War II, it is useful to consider two periods, roughly the decades before 1913, and those that followed. In the years of relative peace before 1913 I suggest that the process left a weak mark on the record for two reasons, both connected with the still early state of industrialization in many of the countries. First, the impress of the process was masked because farming was still so very important; measured levels of productivity, therefore, depended heavily on the amount and quality of farmland in relation to population. Productivity levels, in consequence, were erratic indicators of gaps between existing and best-practice technology. Secondly, social competence for exploiting the then most advanced methods was still limited, particularly in the earlier years and in the more recent latecomers. As the pre-World War I decades wore on, however, both these qualifying circumstances became less important. One might therefore have expected a much stronger tendency to convergence after 1913. But this was frustrated by the irregular effects of the Great War and of the years of disturbed political and financial conditions that followed, by the uneven impacts of the Great Depression itself and of the restrictions on international trade.

The unfulfilled potential of the years 1913-1938 was then enormously enlarged by the effects of World War II. The average productivity gap behind the United States increased by 39 percent between 1938 and 1950; the poorer countries were hit harder than the richer. These were years of dispersion, not convergence.

The post-World War II decades then proved to be the period when—exceptionally—the three elements required for rapid growth by catching up came together.[13] The elements are large technological gaps; enlarged social competence, reflecting higher levels of education and greater experience with large-scale production, distribution, and finance; and conditions favoring rapid realization of potential. This last element refers to several matters. There was *on this occasion* (it was otherwise after World War I) a strong reaction to the experience of defeat in war, and a chance for political reconstruction. The postwar political and economic reorganization and reform weakened the power of monopolistic groupings, brought new men to the fore, and focused the attention of governments of the tasks of recovery and growth, as Mancur Olson has argued.[14] The facilities for the diffusion of technology improved. International markets were opened. Large labor reserves in home agriculture and immigration from Southern and Eastern Europe provided a flexible and mobile labor supply. Government support, technological opportunity, and an environment of stable international money favored heavy and sustained capital investment. The outcome was the great speed and strength of the postwar catch-up process.[15]

Looking back now on the record of more than a century, we can see that catching up was a powerful continuing element in the growth experience of the presently advanced industrial countries. The strength of the process varied from period to period. For decades it operated only erratically and with weakened force. The trouble at first lay in deficient social capability, a sluggish adaptation of education and of industrial and financial organization to the requirements of modern large-scale technology. Later, the process was checked and made irregular by the effects of the two world wars and the ensuing political and financial troubles and by the impact of the Great Depression. It was at last released after World War II. The results were the rapid growth rates of the postwar period, the close cross-country association between initial productivity levels and growth rates, and a marked reduction of differences in productivity levels, among the follower countries, and between them and the United States.

Looking to the future, it seems likely that this very success will have weakened the potentiality for growth by catching up among the group of presently advanced countries. The great opportunities carried by that potential now pass to the less developed countries of Latin America and Asia.

III. FORGING AHEAD AND FALLING BEHIND

The catch-up hypothesis in its simple form does not anticipate changes in leadership nor, indeed, any changes in the ranks of countries in their relative levels of productivity. It contemplates only a reduction among countries in productivity differentials. Yet there have been many changes in ranks since

1870 and, of course, the notable shift of leadership from Britain to America towards the end of the last century.[16] This was followed by the continuing decline of Britain's standing in the productivity scale. Today there is a widely held opinion that America is about to fall behind a new candidate for leadership, Japan, and that both Europe and America must contemplate serious injury from the rise of both Japan and a group of still newer industrializing countries. . . .

The Congruity of Technology and Resources: United States as Leader

Why did the gap between the United States and the average of other countries resist reduction so long? Indeed, why did it even appear to become larger between 1870 and 1929—before the impact of World War II made it larger still? I offer three reasons:

(1) The path of technological change which in those years offered the greatest opportunities for advance was at once heavily scale-dependent and biased in a labor-saving but capital- and resource-using direction. In both respects America enjoyed great advantages compared with Europe or Japan. Large-scale production was favored by a large, rapidly growing, and increasingly prosperous population. It was supported also by a striking homogeneity of tastes. This reflected the country's comparative youth, its rapid settlement by migration from a common base on the Atlantic, and the weakness and fluidity of its class divisions. . . .

(2) By comparison with America and Britain, many, though not all, of the "followers" were also latecomers in respect to social capability. In the decades following 1870, they lacked experience with large-scale production and commerce, and in one degree or another they needed to advance in levels of general and technical education.

(3) World War I was a serious setback for many countries but a stimulus to growth in the United States. European recovery and growth in the following years were delayed and slowed by financial disturbances and by the impact of territorial and political change. Protection, not unification, was the response to the new political map. The rise of social democratic electoral strength in Europe favored the expansion of union power, but failed to curb the development and activities of industrial cartels. Britain's ability to support and enforce stable monetary conditions had been weakened, but the United States was not yet able or, indeed, willing to assume the role of leadership that Britain was losing. In all these ways, the response to the challenge of war losses and defeat after the First World War stands in contrast to that after the Second.

Points (2) and (3) were anticipated in earlier argument, but Point (1) constitutes a qualification to the simple catch-up hypothesis. In that view, different countries, subject only to their social capability, are equally competent to exploit a leader's path of technological progress. That is not so, however, if that path is biased in resource intensity or if it is scale-dependent. Resource-rich countries will be favored in the first instance, large countries in the second. If the historical argument of this section is correct, the United States was favored on both counts for a long time; it may not be so favored in the future. Whether or not this interpretation of American experience is correct, the general proposition remains: countries have unequal abilities to pursue paths of progress that are resource-biased or scale-dependent.

Interaction between Followers and Leaders

The catch-up hypothesis in its simple form is concerned with only one aspect of the economic relations among countries: technological borrowing by followers. In this view, a one-way stream of benefits flows from leaders to followers. A moment's reflection, however, exposes the inadequacy of that idea. The rise of British factory-made cotton textiles in the first industrial revolution ruined the Irish linen industry. The attractions of British and American jobs denuded the Irish population of its young men. The beginnings of modern growth in Ireland suffered a protracted delay. This is an example of the negative effects of leadership on the economies of those who are behind. Besides technological borrowing, there are interactions by way of trade and its rivalries, capital flows, and population movements. Moreover, the knowledge flows are not solely from leader to followers. A satisfactory account of the catch-up process must take account of these multiple forms of interaction. Again, there is space only for brief comment.

Trade and its Rivalries. I have referred to the sometimes negative effects of leading-country exports on the economies of less developed countries. Countries in the course of catching up, however, exploit the possibilities of advanced scale-dependent technologies by import substitution and expansion of exports. When they are successful there are possible negative effects on the economies of leaders. This is an old historical theme. The successful competition of Germany, America, and other European countries is supposed to have retarded British growth from 1870 to 1913 and perhaps longer.[17] Analogous questions arise today. The expansion of exports from Japan and the newer industrializing countries has had a serious impact on the older industries of America and Europe, as well as some of the newer industries.

Is there a generalized effect on the productivity growth of the leaders? The effect is less than it may seem to be because some of the trade shifts are a reflection of overall productivity growth in the leader countries themselves. As the average level of productivity rises, so does the level of wages across industries generally. There are then relative increases in the product prices of those industries—usually older industries—in which productivity growth is lagging and relative declines in the product prices of those industries enjoying rapid productivity growth. The former must suffer a loss of comparative advantage, the latter a gain. One must keep an eye on both.

Other causes of trade shifts that are connected with the catch-up process itself may, however, carry real generalized productivity effects. There are changes that stem from the evolution of "product cycles," such as Raymond Vernon has made familiar. And perhaps most important, there is the achievement of higher levels of social capability. This permits followers to extend their borrowing and adaptation of more advanced methods, and enables them to compete in markets they could not contest earlier.

What difference does it make to the general prospects for the productivity growth of the leading industrial countries if they are losing markets to followers who are catching up?

There is an employment effect. Demand for the products of export- and import-competing industries is depressed. Failing a high degree of flexibility in exchange rates and wages and of occupational and geographical mobility, aggregate demand tends to be reduced. Unless macroeconomic policy is successful, there is general unemployment and underutilization of resources. Profits and the inducements to invest and innovate are reduced. And if this condition causes economies to succumb to protectionism, particularly to competitive protectionism, the difficulty is aggravated.

International trade theory assures us that these effects are transitory. Autonomous capital movements aside, trade must, in the end, balance. But the macroeconomic effects of the balancing process may be long drawn out, and while it is in progress, countries can suffer the repressive effects of restricted demand on investment and innovation.

There is also a Verdoorn effect. It is harder for an industry to push the technological frontier forward, or even to keep up with it, if its own rate of expansion slows down—and still harder if it is contracting. This is unavoidable but tolerable when the growth of old industries is restricted by the rise of newer, more progressive home industries. But when retardation of older home industries is due to the rise of competing industries abroad, a tendency to generalized slowdown may be present.

Interactions via Population Movements. Nineteenth-century migration ran in good part from the farms of Western and Southern Europe to the farms and cities of the New World and Australasia. In the early twentieth century, Eastern Europe joined in. These migrations responded in part to the impact on world markets of the cheap grains and animal products produced by the regions of recent settlement. Insofar they represent an additional but special effect of development in some members of the Atlantic community of industrializing countries on the economies of other members.

Productivity growth in the countries of destination was aided by migration in two respects. It helped them exploit scale economies; and by making labor supply more responsive to increase in demand, it helped sustain periods of rapid growth. Countries of origin were relieved of the presence of partly redundant and desperately poor people. On the other hand, the loss of population brought such scale disadvantages as accompany slower population growth, and it made labor supply less responsive to industrial demand.

Migration in the postwar growth boom presents a picture of largely similar design and significance. In this period the movement was from the poorer, more slowly growing countries of Southern Europe and North Africa to the richer and more rapidly growing countries of Western and Northern Europe.[18] There is, however, this difference: The movement in more recent decades was induced by actual and expected income differences that were largely independent of the market connections of countries of origin and destination. There is no evidence that the growth boom of the West itself contributed to the low incomes of the South.

Needless to say, migrations are influenced by considerations other than relative levels of income and changing comparative advantage. I stress these matters, however, because they help us understand the complexities of the process of catch-up and convergence within a group of connected countries.

Interaction via Capital Flows. A familiar generalization is that capital tends to flow from countries of high income and slow growth to those with opposite characteristics or, roughly speaking, from leaders to followers. One remembers, however, that that description applies to gross new investments. There are also reverse flows that reflect the maturing of past investments. So in the early stages of a great wave of investment, followers' rates of investment and productivity growth are supported by capital movement while those of leaders are retarded. Later however, this effect may become smaller or be reversed, as we see today in relations between Western leaders and Latin American followers.

Once more, I add that the true picture is far more complicated than this idealized summary. It will hardly accommodate such extraordinary developments as the huge American capital import of recent years, to say nothing of the Arabian-European flows of the 1970s and their reversal now underway.

Interactions via Flows of Applied Knowledge. The flow of knowledge from leader to followers is, of course, the very essence of the catch-up hypothesis. As the technological gaps narrow, however, the direction changes. Countries that are still a distance behind the leader in average productivity may move into the lead in particular branches and become sources of new knowledge for older leaders As they are surpassed in particular fields, old leaders can make gains by borrowing as well as by generating new knowledge. In this respect the growth potential of old leaders is enhanced as the pursuit draws closer. Moreover, competitive pressure can be a stimulus to research and innovation as well as an excuse for protection. It remains to be seen whether the newly rising economies will seek to guard a working knowledge of their operations more closely than American companies have done, and still more whether American and European firms will be as quick to discover, acquire, and adapt foreign methods as Japanese firms have been in the past.

Development as a Constraint on Change: Tangible Capital

The rise of followers in the course of catching up brings old leaders a mixed bag of injuries and potential benefits. Old leaders, however, or followers who have enjoyed a period of successful development, may come to suffer disabilities other than those caused by the burgeoning competitive power of new rivals. When Britain suffered her growth climacteric nearly a century ago, observers thought that her slowdown was itself due in part to her early lead. Thorstein Veblen was a pioneer proponent of this suggestion, and Charles Kindleberger and others have picked it up again.[19] One basis for this view is the idea that the capital stock of a country consists of an intricate web of interlocking elements. They are built to fit together, and it is difficult to replace one part of the complex with more modern and efficient elements without a costly rebuilding of other components. This may be handled efficiently if all the costs and benefits are internal to a firm. When they are divided among different firms and industries and between the private and public sectors, the adaptation of old capital structures to new technologies may be a difficult and halting process.

What this may have meant for Britain's climacteric is still unsettled. Whatever that may be, however, the problem needs study on a wider scale as it arises both historically and in a contemporaneous setting. After World War II, France undertook a great extension and modernization of its public transportation and power systems to provide a basis for later development of private industry and agriculture. Were the technological advances embodied in that investment program easier for France to carry out because its infrastructure was technically older, battered, and badly maintained? Or was it simply a heavy burden more in need of being borne? There is a widespread complaint today that the public capital structure of the United States stands in need of modernization and extension. Is this true, and, if it is, does it militate seriously against the installation of improved capital by private industry? One cannot now assume that such problems are the exclusive concern of a topmost productivity leader. All advanced industrial countries have large accumulations of capital, interdependent in use but divided in ownership among many firms and between private and public authorities. One may assume, however, that the problem so raised differs in its impact over time and among countries and, depending on its importance, might have some influence on the changes that occur in the productivity rankings of countries.

Development as a Constraint on Change: Intangible Capital and Political Institutions

Attention now returns to matters akin to social capability. In the simple catch-up hypothesis, that capability is viewed as either exogenously determined or else as adjusting steadily to the requirements of technological opportunity. The educational and institutional commitments induced by past development may, however, stand as an obstacle. That is a question that calls for study. The comments that follow are no more than brief indications of prominent possibilities.

The United States was the pioneer of mass production as embodied in the huge plant, the complex and rigid assembly line, the standardized product, and the long production run. It is also the pioneer and developer of the mammoth diversified conglomerate corporation. The vision of business carried on within such organizations, their highly indirect, statistical, and bureaucratic methods of consultation, planning and decision, the inevitable distractions of trading in assets rather than production of goods—these mental biases have sunk deep into the American business outlook and into the doctrine and training of young American managers. The necessary decentralization of operations into multiple profit centers directs the attention of managers and their superiors to the quarterly profit report and draws their energies away from the development of improved products and processes that require years of attention.[20] One may well ask how well this older vision of management and enterprise and the organizational scheme in which it is embodied will accommodate the problems and potentialities of the emerging computer and communications revolution. Or will that occur more easily in countries where educational systems, forms of corporate organization, and managerial outlook can better make a fresh start?

The long period of leadership and development enjoyed by the United States and the entire North Atlantic community meant, of course, a great increase of incomes. The rise of incomes, in turn, afforded a chance to satisfy latent desires for all sorts of non-market goods ranging from maintenance in old age to a safe-guarded natural environment. Satisfying these demands, largely by public action, has also afforded an ample opportunity for special interest groups to obtain privileges and protection in a process that Mancur Olson and others have generalized.

The outcome of this conjuncture of circumstances and forces is the Mixed Economy of the West, the complex system of transfers, taxes, regulations, and public activity, as well as organizations of union and business power, that had its roots long before the War, that expanded rapidly during the growth boom of the fifties and sixties, and that reached very high levels in the seventies. This trend is very broadly consistent with the suggestion that the elaboration of the mixed economy is a function of economic growth itself. To this one has to add the widely held idea advanced by Olson and many others that the system operates to reduce enterprise, work, saving, investment, and mobility and, therefore, to constrict the processes of innovation and change that productivity growth involves.

How much is there in all this? The answer turns only partly on a calculation of the direct effects of the system on economic incentives. These have proved difficult to pin down, and attempts to measure them have generally not yielded large numbers, at least for the United States.[21] The answer requires an equally difficult evaluation of the positive roles of government activity. These include not only the government's support of education, research, and information, and its provision of physical overhead capital and of the host of local functions required for urban life. We must remember also that the occupational and geographical adjustments needed to absorb new technology impose heavy costs on individuals. The accompanying changes alter the positions, prospects, and power of established groups, and they transform the structure of families and their roles in caring for children, the sick, and the old. Technical advance, therefore, engenders conflict and resistance; and the Welfare State with its transfers and regulations constitutes a mode of conflict resolution and a means of mitigating the costs of change that would otherwise induce resistance to growth. The existing empirical studies that bear on the economic responses to government intervention are, therefore, far from meeting the problem fully.

If the growth-inhibiting forces embodied in the Welfare State and in private expressions of market power were straightforward, positive functions of income levels, uniform across countries, that would be another reason for supposing that the catch-up process was self-limiting. The productivity levels of followers would, on this account, converge towards but not exceed the leader's. But these forces are clearly not simple, uniform functions of income. The institutions of the Welfare State have reached a higher degree of elaboration in Europe than in the United States. The objects of expenditure, the structures of transfers and taxes, and people's responses to both differ from country to country. These institutional developments, therefore, besides having some influence on growth rates generally, may constitute a wild card in the deck of growth forces. They will tend to produce changes in the ranks of countries in the productivity scale and these may include the top rank itself.

A sense that forces of institutional change are now acting to limit the growth of Western countries pervades the writings of many economists—and, of course, other observers. Olson, Fellner, Scitovsky, Kindleberger, Lindbeck, and Giersch are only a partial list of those who see these economies as afflicted by institutional arthritis or sclerosis or other metaphorical malady associated with age and wealth.

These are the suggestions of serious scholars, and they need to be taken seriously. One may ask, however, whether these views take account of still other, rejuvenating forces which, though they act slowly, may yet work effectively to limit and counter those of decay—at least for the calculable future. In the United States, interregional competition, supported by free movement of goods, people, and capital, is such a force. It limits the power of unions and checks the expansion of taxation, transfers, and regulation.[22] International competition, so long as it is permitted to operate, works in a similar direction for the United States and other countries as well, and it is strengthened by the development in recent years of a more highly integrated world capital market and by more vigorous international movements of corporate enterprise. . . .

Finally, it is widely recognized that the process of institutional aging, whatever its significance, is not one without limits. Powerful forces continue to push that way, and they are surely strong in resisting reversal. Yet it is also apparent that there is a drift of public opinion that works for modification both in Europe and North America. There is a fine balance to be struck between productivity growth and the material incomes it brings and the other dimensions of social welfare. Countries are now in the course of readjusting that balance in favor of productivity growth. How far they can go and, indeed, how far they should go are both still in question. . . .

NOTES

1. W.E.G. Salter, *Productivity and Technical Change* (Cambridge, 1960) provides a rigorous theoretical exposition of the factors determining rates of turnover and those governing the relation between productivity with capital embodying best practice and average (economically efficient) technology.

2. *Japanese Economic Growth: Trend Acceleration in the Twentieth Century* (Stanford, 1973), especially chap. 9.

3. Moses Abramovitz, "Rapid Growth Potential and its Realization: The Experience of Capitalist Economies in the Postwar Period," in Edmond Malinvaud, ed., *Economic Growth and Resources,* Proceedings of the Fifth World Congress of the International Economic Association, vol. 1 (London, 1979), pp. 1–30.

4. Mancur Olson, *The Rise and Fall of Nations: Economic Growth, Stagflation and Social Rigidities* (New Haven, 1982).

5. Kravis et al., *International Comparisons*; Edward F. Denison, assisted by Jean-Pierre Poullier, *Why Growth Rates Differ, Postwar Experience of Nine Western Countries* (Washington, D.C., 1967), pp. 239–45.

6. R.C.O. Matthews, Review of Denison (1967), *Economic Journal* (June 1969), pp. 261–68.

7. My paper cited earlier describes the operation of these factors in the 1950s and 1960s and tries to show how they worked to permit productivity growth to rise in so many countries rapidly, in concert and for such an extended period ("Rapid Growth Potential and Its Realization," pp. 18–30).

8. The countries are Australia, Austria, Belgium, Canada, Denmark, Finland,

France, Germany, Italy, Japan, Netherlands, Norway, Sweden, Switzerland, United Kingdom, and United States.

9. In these calculations I have treated either the United States or the United Kingdom as the productivity leader from 1870 to 1913. Literal acceptance of Maddison's estimates, however, make Australia the leader from 1870-1913. Moreover, Belgium and the Netherlands stand slightly higher than the United States in 1870. Here are Maddison's relatives for those years (from *Phases*, Table 5.2):

	1870	1890	1913
Australia	186	153	102
Belgium	106	96	75
Netherlands	106	92	74
United Kingdom	114	100	81
United States	100	100	100

Since Australia's high standing in this period mainly reflected an outstandingly favorable situation of natural resources relative to population, it would be misleading to regard that country as the technological leader or to treat the productivity changes in other countries relative to Australia's as indicators of the catch-up process. Similarly, the small size and specialized character of the Belgian and Dutch economies make them inappropriate benchmarks.

10. Maddison, *Phases*, Table C5.

11. Since growth rates are calculated as rates of change between standings at the terminal dates of periods, errors in the estimates of such standings will generate errors in the derived growth rates. If errors at both terminal dates were random, and if those at the end-year were independent of those at the initial year, there would be a tendency on that account for growth rates to be inversely correlated with initial-year standings. The inverse correlation coefficients would be biased upwards. Note, however, that if errors at terminal years were random and independent and of equal magnitude, there would be no tendency *on that account* for the variance of standings about the mean to decline between initial and end-year dates. The error bias would run against the marked decline in variance that we observe. Errors in late-year data, however, are unlikely to be so large, so an error bias is present.

12. See also William J. Baumol, "Productivity Growth, Convergence and Welfare: What the Long-run Data Show." C.V. Starr Center for Applied Economics, New York University, Research Report No. 85–27, August 1985.

13. See Abramovitz, "Rapid Growth Potential and its Realization."

14. Olson, *Rise and Fall*.

15. Some comments on the catch-up process after 1973 may be found in Abramovitz, "Catching Up and Falling Behind" (Stockholm, 1986), pp. 33–39.

16. If one follows Maddison's estimates (*Phases*, Table C. 19), the long period from 1870 to 1979 saw Australia fall by 8 places in the ranking of his 16 countries, Italy by $2\frac{1}{2}$, Switzerland by 8, and the United Kingdom by 10. Meanwhile the United States rose by 4, Germany by $4\frac{1}{2}$, Norway by 5, Sweden by 7, and France by 8.

17. See also R.C.O. Matthews, Charles Feinstein, and John Odling-Smee, *British Economic Growth, 1856-1973*, (Stanford, 1983), chaps. 14, 15, 17. Their analysis does not find a large effect on British productivity growth from 1870 to 1913.

18. The migration from East to West Germany in the 1950s was a special case. It brought to West Germany educated and skilled countrymen strongly motivated to rebuild their lives and restore their fortunes.

19. Charles P. Kindleberger, "Obsolescence and Technical Change." *Oxford Institute of Statistics Bulletin* (Aug. 1961), pp. 281–97).

20. These and similar questions are raised by experienced observers of American business. They are well summarized by Edward Denison, *Trends in American Economic Growth, 1929-1982*, (Washington, D.C., 1985), chap. 3.

21. Representative arguments supporting the idea that social capability has suffered, together with some quantitative evidence, may be found in Olson, *Rise and Fall*; William Fellner, "The Declining Growth of American Productivity: An Introductory Note," in W. Fellner, ed., *Contemporary Economic Problems, 1979* (Washington, D.C., 1979); and Assar Lindbeck, "Limits to the Welfare State," *Challenge* (Dec., 1985). For argument and evidence on the other side, see Sheldon Danzigar, Robert Haveman, and Robert Plotnick, "How Income Transfers Affect Work, Savings and Income Distribution," *Journal of Economic Literature* 19 (Sept. 1982), pp. 975–1028; and Edw. F. Denison, *Accounting for Slower Economic Growth* (Washington, D.C., 1979), pp. 127–38.

22. See R.D. Norton, "Regional Life Cycles and US Industrial Rejuvenation," in Herbert Giersch, ed., "Industrial Policy and American Renewal," *Journal of Economic Literature*, 24 (March 1986).

7

· · · · · · ·

Productivity Growth, Convergence, and Welfare: What the Long-Run Data Show

· · · · · · ·

WILLIAM J. BAUMOL

William Baumol provides empirical analysis of convergence theory and finds that for a sample of sixteen countries between 1870 and 1979 labor productivity and its growth are inversely related. In Chapter 6, Moses Abramovitz explained that not all countries will experience convergence because they lack the social capacity to utilize technology to achieve rapid growth. Baumol turns to the post–World War II era (1950–1980) to see if this relationship can be found for all countries. Using RGDP/pcs and growth rates as proxies for labor productivity, Baumol finds that the poorest countries have the slowest RGDP/pc growth, thus failing to converge with the rich. The rest of the countries belong to what Baumol calls a "convergence club." Hence, if Baumol is correct, convergence will take place but the poorest countries will be excluded from the process, meaning that the gap will widen between them and the rest of the world.

> No matter how refined and how elaborate the analysis, if it rests solely on the short view it will still be . . . a structure built on shifting sands.
> —Jacob Viner (1958, pp. 112–131)

Recent years have witnessed a reemergence of interest on the part of economists and the general public in issues relating to long-run economic growth. There has been a recurrence of doubts and fears for the future—aroused in this case by the protracted slowdown in productivity growth since the late 1960's, the seeming erosion of the competitiveness of U.S. industries in world markets, and the spectre of "deindustrialization" and

Reprinted with permission from the *American Economic Review*, vol. 76 (December 1986):1072–1084.

massive structural unemployment. These anxieties have succeeded in redirecting attention to long-run supply-side phenomena that formerly were a central preoccupation of economists in the industrializing West, before being pushed aside in the crisis of the Great Depression and the ensuing triumph of Keynesian ideas.

Anxiety may compel attention, but it is not necessarily an aid to clear thinking. For all the interest now expressed in the subject of long-run economic growth and policies ostensibly directed to its stimulation, it does not seem to be widely recognized that adequate economic analysis of such issues calls for the careful study of economic history—if only because it is there that the pertinent evidence is to be found. Economic historians have provided the necessary materials, in the form of brilliant insights, powerful analysis as well as a surprising profusion of long-period data. Yet none of these has received the full measure of attention they deserve from members of the economics profession at large.

To dramatize the sort of reorientation long-term information can suggest, imagine a convincing prediction that over the next century, U.S. productivity growth will permit a trebling of per capita GNP while cutting nearly by half the number of hours in the average work year, and that this will be accompanied by a sevenfold increase in exports. One might well consider this a very rosy forecast. But none of these figures is fictitious. For these developments in fact lay before the United Kingdom in 1870, just as its economic leadership began to erode.

This chapter outlines some implications of the available long-period data on productivity and related variables—some tentative, some previously noted by economic historians, and some throwing a somewhat surprising light on developments among industrialized nations since World War II. Among the main observations that will emerge here is the remarkable convergence of output per labor hour among industrialized nations. Almost all of the leading free enterprise economies have moved closer to the leader, and there is a strong inverse correlation between a country's productivity standing in 1870 and its average rate of productivity growth since then. Postwar data suggest that the convergence phenomenon also extends to both "intermediate" and centrally planned economies. Only the poorer less developed countries show no such trend.

It will also emerge that over the century, the U.S. productivity growth rate has been surprisingly steady, and despite frequently expressed fears, there is no sign recently of any *long-term* slowdown in growth of either total factor productivity or labor productivity in the United States. And while, except in wartime, *for the better part of a century*, U.S. productivity growth rates have been low relative to those of Germany, Japan, and a number of other countries, this may be no more than a manifestation of the convergence phenomenon which requires countries that were previously behind to grow more rapidly. Thus, the chapter will seek to dispel these and a number of other misapprehensions apparently widespread among those who have not studied economic history.

Nonspecialists may well be surprised at the remarkably long periods spanned in time-series contributed by Beveridge, Deane, Kuznets, Gallman, Kendrick, Abramovitz, David, and others. The Phelps Brown-Hopkins indices of prices and real wages extend over seven centuries. Maddison, Feinstein (and his colleagues), and Kendrick cover productivity, investment, and a number of other crucial variables for more than 100 years. Obviously, the magnitudes of the earlier figures are more than a little questionable, as their compilers never cease to warn us. Yet the general qualitative character of the time paths are persuasive, given the broad consistency of the statistics, their apparent internal logic and the care exercised in collecting them. In this chapter, the period used will vary with topic and data availability. In most cases, something near a century will be examined, using primarily data provided by Angus Maddison (1982) and R.C.O. Matthews, C. H. Feinstein, and J. C. Odling-Smee (1982—henceforth, M-F-O).

MAGNITUDE OF THE ACCOMPLISHMENT

The magnitude of the productivity achievement of the past 150 years resists intuitive grasp, and contrasts sharply with the preceding centuries. As the *Communist Manifesto* put the matter in 1848, with remarkable foresight, "The bourgeoisie, during its rule of scarce one hundred years, has created more massive and more colossal productive forces than have all preceding generations together." There obviously are no reliable measures of productivity in antiquity, but available descriptions of living standards in Ancient Rome suggest that they were in many respects higher than in eighteenth-century England (see Colin Clark, 1957, p. 677). This is probably true even for the lower classes—certainly for the free urban proletariat, and perhaps even with the inclusion of slaves. An upper-class household was served by sophisticated devices for heating and bathing not found in eighteenth-century homes of the rich. A wealthy Roman magically transported into an eighteenth-century English home would probably have been puzzled by the technology of only a few products—clocks, window panes, printed books and newspapers, and the musket over the fireplace.

It is true that even during the Middle Ages (see, for example, Carlo Cipolla, 1976), there was substantial technological change in the workplace and elsewhere. Ship design improved greatly. Lenses and, with them, the telescope and microscope appeared in the sixteenth century, and the eighteenth century brought the ship's chronometer which revolutionalized water transport by permitting calculation of longitude. Yet, none of this led to rates of productivity growth anywhere near those of the nineteenth and twentieth centuries.

Nonhistorians do not usually recognize that initially the Industrial Revolution was a fairly minor affair for the economy as a whole. At first, much of the new equipment was confined to textile production (though some progress in fields such as iron making had also occurred). And, as David Landes (1969) indicates, an entrepreneur could undertake the new types of textile operations with little capital, perhaps only a few hundred pounds, which (using the Phelps Brown-Hopkins data) translates into some 100,000 1980 dollars. Jeffrey Williamson (1983) tells us that in England during the first half-century of the Industrial Revolution, real per capita income grew only about 0.3 percent per annum,[1] in contrast with the nearly 3 percent achieved in the Third World in the 1970's (despite the decade's economic crises).

Table 7.1 shows the remarkable contrast of developments since 1870 for Maddison's 16 countries. We see (col. 1) that growth in output per work-hour ranged for the next 110 years from approximately 400 percent for Australia all the way to 2500 percent (in the case of Japan). The 1,100 percent increase of labor productivity in the United States placed it somewhat below the middle of the group, and even the United Kingdom managed a 600 percent rise. Thus, after not manifesting any substantial long-period increase for at least 15 centuries, in the course of 11 decades the median increase in productivity among the 16 industrialized leaders in Maddison's sample was about 1150 percent. The rise in productivity was sufficient to permit output per capita (col. 2) to increase more than 300 percent in the United Kingdom, 800 percent in West Germany, 1700 percent in Japan, and nearly 700 percent in France and the United States. Using Robert Summers and Alan Heston's

Table 7.1   Total Growth from 1870 to 1979[a]: Productivity, GDP Per Capita, and Exports, Sixteen Industrialized Countries[b]

	Real GDP per Work-Hour	Real GDP Per Capita	Volume of Exports
Australia	398	221	---
United Kingdom	585	310	930
Switzerland	830	471	4,400
Belgium	887	439	6,250
Netherlands	910	429	8,040
Canada	1,050	766	9,860
United States	1,080	693	9,240
Denmark	1,098	684	6,750
Italy	1,225	503	6,210
Austria	1,270	643	4,740
Germany	1,510	824	3,730
Norway	1,560	873	7,740
France	1,590	694	4,140
Finland	1,710	1,016	6,240
Sweden	2,060	1,083	5,070
Japan	2,480	1,661	293,060

Source: Angus Maddison (1982, pp. 8, 212, 248–53).
a. In 1970 U.S. dollars.
b. Shown in percent.

sophisticated international comparison data (1984), this implies that in 1870, U.S. output per capita was comparable to 1980 output per capita in Honduras and the Philippines, and slightly below that of China, Bolivia, and Egypt!

The growth rates of other pertinent variables were also remarkable. One more example will suffice to show this. Table 7.1, which also shows the rise in volume of exports from 1870 to 1979 (col. 3), indicates that the median increase was over 6,000 percent.

THE CONVERGENCE OF NATIONAL PRODUCTIVITY LEVELS

There is a long and reasonably illustrious tradition among economic historians centered on the phenomenon of convergence. While the literature devoted to the subject is complex and multifaceted, as revealed by the recent reconsideration of these ideas by Moses Abramovitz (1985), one central theme is that forces accelerating the growth of nations who were latecomers to industrialization and economic development give rise to a long-run tendency towards convergence of levels of per capita product or, alternatively, of per worker product. Such ideas found expression in the works of Alexander Gerschenkron (see, for example, 1952), who saw his own views on the advantages of "relative backwardness" as having been anticipated in important respects by Thorstein Veblen's writings on the penalties of being the industrial leader (1915). Although such propositions also have been challenged and qualified (for example, Edward Ames and Nathan Rosenberg, 1963), it is difficult to dismiss the idea of convergence on the basis of the historical experience of the industrialized world. (For more recent discussions, see also the paper by Robin Marris, with comments by Feinstein and Matthews in Matthews, 1982, pp. 12–13, 128–147, as well as Dennis Mueller, 1983.)

Using 1870–1973 data on gross domestic product (GDP) per work-year for 7 industrialized countries, M-F-O have shown graphically that those nations' productivity levels have tended to approach ever closer to one another. . . . [2]

The convergence toward the vanguard (led in the first decades by Australia—see Richard Caves and Laurence Krause, 1984—and the United Kingdom and, approximately since World War I, by the United States) is sharper than it may appear to the naked eye. In 1870, the ratio of output per work-hour in Australia, then the leader in Maddison's sample, was about eight times as great as Japan's (the laggard). By 1979, that ratio for the leader (the United States) to the laggard (still Japan) had fallen to about 2. The ratio of the standard deviation from the mean of GDP per work-hour for the 16 countries has also fallen quite steadily, except for a brief but sharp rise during World War II.

The convergence phenomenon and its pervasiveness is confirmed by Figure 7.1, on which my discussion will focus. The horizontal axis indicates each Maddison country's absolute level of GDP per work-hour in 1870. The vertical axis represents the growth rate of GDP per work-hour in the 110 years since 1870. The high inverse correlation between the two is evident. Indeed, we obtain an equation (subject to all sorts of statistical reservations)[3]

$$\textit{Growth Rate } (1870\text{--}1979) = 5.25 - 0.75\ln\,(\textit{GDP per WorkHr, } 1870),$$
$$R^2 = 0.88.$$

That is, with a very high correlation coefficient, the higher a country's productivity level in 1870 the more slowly that level grew in the following century.

IMPLICATIONS OF THE INVERSE CORRELATION: PUBLIC GOODS PROPERTY OF PRODUCTIVITY POLICY

The strong inverse correlation between the 1870 productivity levels of the 16 nations and their subsequent productivity growth record seems to have a startling implication. Of course, hindsight always permits "forecasts" of great accuracy—that itself is not surprising. Rather, what is striking is the

Figure 7.1   Productivity Growth Rate, 1870–1979 vs. 1870 Level (in percent)

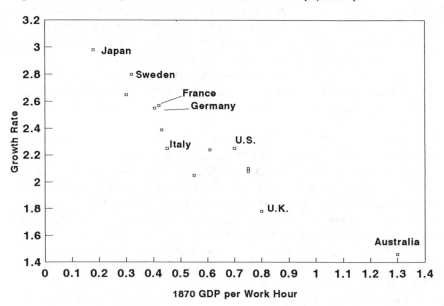

Source: Maddison (p. 212).

apparent implication that *only one variable*, a country's 1870 GDP per work-hour, or its relation to that of the productivity leader matters to any substantial degree, and that other variables have only a peripheral influence. It seems not to have mattered much whether or not a particular country had free markets, a high propensity to invest, or used policy to stimulate growth. Whatever its behavior, that nation was apparently fated to land close to its predestined position in Figure 7.1.

However, a plausible alternative interpretation is that while national policies and behavior patterns do substantially affect productivity growth, the spillovers from leader economies to followers are large—at least among the group of industrial nations. If country A's extraordinary investment level and superior record of innovation enhances its own productivity, it will almost automatically do the same in the long run for industrialized country B, though perhaps to a somewhat more limited extent. In other words, for such nations a successful productivity-enhancing measure has the nature of a public good. And because the fruits of each industrialized country's productivity-enhancement efforts are ultimately shared by others, each country remains in what appears to be its predestined *relative* place along the growth curve of Figure 7.1. I will note later some considerations which might lead one to doubt that the less developed countries will benefit comparably from this sharing process.

This sharing of productivity growth benefits by industrialized countries involves both innovation and investment. The innovation-sharing process is straightforward. If industry in country A benefits from a significant innovation, those industries in other countries which produce competing products will find themselves under pressure to obtain access to the innovation, or to an imitation or to some other substitute. Industrialized countries, whose product lines overlap substantially and which sell a good deal in markets where foreign producers of similar items are also present, will find themselves constantly running in this Schumpeterian race, while those less developed countries which supply few products competing with those of the industrialized economies will not participate to the same degree.

There is reason to suspect that the pressures for rapidity in imitation of innovation in industrial countries have been growing. The explosion in exports reported in Table 7.1 has given them a considerably larger share of gross national product than they had in 1870. This suggests that more of each nation's output faces the direct competition of foreign rivals. Thus, the penalties for failure to keep abreast of innovations *in other countries* and to imitate them where appropriate have grown.

Second, the means required for successful imitations have improved and expanded enormously. World communications are now practically instantaneous, but required weeks and even months at the birth of the Industrial Revolution. While today meetings of scientists and technicians are widely encouraged, earlier mercantilist practices entailed measures by each country to prevent other nations from learning its industrial techniques, and the emigration of specialized workers was often forbidden. Though figures in this arena are difficult to interpret, much less substantiate, one estimate claims that employment in "information activities" in the United States has grown from less than 1 percent of the labor force in 1830 to some 45 percent today (James Beniger, forthcoming, p. 364, leaning heavily on Marc Porat, 1977). Presumably, growth of the information sector in other industrialized nations has been similar. This must surely facilitate and speed the innovative, counterinnovative, and imitative tasks of the entrepreneur. The combination of direct U.S. manufacturing investment in Europe, and the technology transfer activities of multinational corporations in the postwar era were also of great significance (see, for example, David Teece, 1976). All of this, incidentally, suggests that as the forces making for convergence were stronger in the postwar era than previously, the rate of convergence should have been higher. The evidence assembled by Abramovitz (1985) on the basis of Maddison's data indicates that this is in fact what has happened.

The process that has just been described, then, provides mutual benefits, but it inherently helps productivity laggards more than leaders. For the laggards have more to learn from the leaders, and that is why the process makes for convergence.

Like innovation, investment, generally considered the second main source of growth in labor productivity, may also exhibit international public good properties. Suppose two industrialized countries, A and B, each produce two traded products: say automobiles and shoes, with the former more capital intensive. If A's investment rate is greater than B's then, with time, A's output mix will shift toward the cars while B's will move toward shoes. The increased demand for auto workers in A will raise their real wages, while A's increased demand for imports of B's shoes will raise real wages in B, and will raise the *value* of gross domestic product per labor hour in that country. Thus, even investment in country A automatically tends to have a spillover effect on value productivity and real wages *in those other countries that produce and trade in a similar array of goods.*

While, strictly speaking, the factor-price equalization theorem is not applicable to my discussion because it assumes, among other things, that technology is identical in all the countries involved, it does suggest why (for the reasons just discussed) a high investment rate may fail to bring a relative wage advantage to the investing country. In practice, the conditions of the theorem are not satisfied precisely, so countries in which investment rates are relatively high do seem to obtain increased relative real wages. Yet the analysis suggests that the absolute benefits are contagious—that one country's successful investment policy will also raise productivity and living standards in other industrialized countries.[4]

Thus, effective growth policy does contribute to a nation's living standards, but it may also help other industrialized countries and to almost the same degree; meaning that relative deviations from the patterns indicated in Figure 7.1 will be fairly small, just as the diagram shows. (However, see Abramovitz, 1985, for a discussion of the counterhypothesis, that growth of a leader creates "backwash" effects inhibiting growth of the followers.)

All this raises an obvious policy issue. If productivity growth does indeed have such public good properties, what will induce each country to invest the socially optimal effort and other resources in productivity growth, when it can instead hope to be a free rider? In part, the answer is that in Western capitalistic economies, investment is decentralized and individual firms can gain little by free riding on the actions of investors in other economies, so that the problem does not appear to be a serious one at the national policy level.

IS CONVERGENCE UBIQUITOUS?

Does convergence of productivity levels extend beyond the free-market industrialized countries? Or is the convergence "club" a very exclusive organization? While century-long data are not available for any large number

Figure 7.2   Growth Rate, 1950–80, GDP/pc vs. 1950 Level 72 Countries

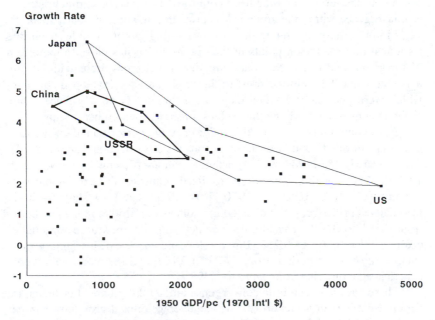

Source: Summers and Heston, 1984.

of countries, Summers and Heston provide pertinent figures for the 30-year period 1950–80 (data for more countries are available for briefer periods).[5] Instead of labor productivity figures, they give output per capita, whose trends can with considerable reservations be used as a rough proxy for those in productivity, as Maddison's figures confirm.

Figure 7.2 tells the story. Constructed just like Figure 7.1, it plots the 1950–80 real growth rate of GDP per capita for all 72 Summers-Heston countries against the initial (1950) level of this variable. The points form no tight relationship, and unlike those for the industrial countries, the dots show no negatively sloping pattern. Indeed, a regression yields a slightly positive slope. Thus, rather than sharing in convergence, some of the poorest countries have also been growing most slowly.

Figure 7.2 brings out the patterns more clearly by surrounding the set of points representing Maddison's 16 countries with a thin boundary and the centrally planned economy points[6] with a heavier boundary. We see that the Maddison country points lie near a sort of upper-right-hand boundary, meaning that most of them had the high incomes in 1950 (as was to be expected) and, for any given per capita income, the highest growth rates between 1950 and 1980. This region is very long, narrow, and negatively sloped, with the absolute slope declining toward the right. As in the Figure 7.1, productivity data for a 110-year period, this is exactly the shape one expects with convergence. Second, we see that the centrally planned economies are members of a convergence club of their own, forming a negatively sloping region lying below and to the left of the Maddison countries. The relationship is less tight, so convergence within the group is less pronounced, but it is clearly there.

Finally, there is the region of remaining points (aside from the rightmost non-Maddison points in the graph) which lies close to the origin of the graph and occupies something like a distorted circle without any apparent slope. The points closest to the origin are less developed countries which were poor in 1950, and have grown relatively slowly since. They show no convergence among themselves, much less with other groups.

A few numbers suggest the difference in performance of various subgroups of the 72 countries. Using a four-set classification Summers, I. B. Kravis and Heston (1984, p. 254) provide Gini coefficients by decade from 1950 to 1980. For their set of industrialized countries, this coefficient falls precipitously from 0.302 in 1950 to 0.129 in 1980—a sharp drop in inequality. For the centrally planned economies the drop is much smaller— from 0.381 to 0.301. The middle-income group exhibits an even smaller decline, from 0.269 to 0.258. But the low-income countries underwent a small *rise* over the period, from 0.103 to 0.112, and the world as a whole experienced a tiny rise from 0.493 to 0.498.

There has also been little convergence among the groups. For the entire period, Summers et al. report (p. 245) an average annual growth rate in per capita real GDP of 3.1 percent for industrialized countries 3.6 percent for centrally planned economies, 3.0 percent for middle-income market economies, and only 1.5 percent for the low-income group, with a world average growth rate of 2.7 percent.

This suggests that there is more than one convergence club. Rather, there are perhaps three, with the centrally planned and the intermediate groups somewhat inferior in performance to that of the free-market industrialized countries. It is also clear that the poorer less developed countries are still largely barred from the homogenization processes. Since any search for "the causes" of a complex economic phenomenon of reality is likely to prove fruitless, no attempt will be made here to explain systematically why poorer less developed countries have benefited to a relatively small degree from the public good properties of the innovations and investments of other nations. But part of the explanation may well be related to product mix and education. A less developed country that produces no cars cannot benefit from the invention and adoption of a better car-producing robot in Japan (though it does benefit to a lesser degree from new textile and rice-growing technology), nor can it benefit from the factor-price equalization effect of the accompanying Japanese investments, since it cannot shift labor force out of its (nonexistent) auto industry as the theorem's logic requires. Lack of education and the associated skills prevent both the presence of high-tech industries and the effective imitation (adoption) of the Japanese innovation. Obviously, there is much more to any reasonably fuller explanation of the exclusion of many less developed countries from the convergence process, but that is not my purpose here. . . .

NOTES

1. This observation does not quite seem to square with Charles Feinstein's estimates (1972, pp. 82–94) which indicate that while output per worker in the United Kingdom increased 0.2 percent per year between 1761 and 1800, between 1801 and 1830 the growth rate leaped up to 1.4 percent per annum. He estimates that total factor productivity behaved similarly. However, between 1801 and 1810, total annual investment fell to 10 percent of gross domestic product, in comparison with its 14 percent rate in the immediately preceding and succeeding periods.

2. Space prevents extensive consideration of Paul Romer's (1985) objection to the evidence offered for the convergence hypothesis provided here and elsewhere, i.e., that the sample of countries studied is an *ex post* selection of successful economies. Successes, by definition, are those which have done best relative to the leader. However, the Summers-Heston 1950–80 data for 72 countries represented in Figure 7.2 do permit an *ex ante* selection. Tests ranking countries both by 1950 and by 1960 GDP levels confirm that even an *ex ante* sample of the wealthiest countries yields a pattern of convergence which, less pronounced than that calculated from an *ex post* group, is still unambiguous.

3. The high correlation should not be taken too seriously. Aside from the reasons why its explanation may be misunderstood that are presently discussed in

the text, the tight fit of the data points is undoubtedly ascribable in good part to several biassing features of the underlying calculation. First, the 1870 figures were calculated by Maddison using backward extrapolation of growth rates, and hence their correlation is hardly surprising. Second, since growth rate, r, is calculated by solving $y_t = e^{rt}y_0$ for r, to obtain $r=(\ln y_t - \ln y_0)/t$, where $y_t = GDP$ per capita in period t, a regression equation $r=f(y_0)$ contains the same variable, y_0 on both sides of the equation, thus tending to produce a spurious appearance of close relationship. Indeed, if the convergence process were perfect, so that we would have $y_t=k$ with k the same for every country in the sample, every dot in the diagram would necessarily perfectly fit the curve $r=\ln k/t - \ln y_0/t$, and the r^2 would be unity, identically. The 72-country data depicted in Figure 7.2 hardly constitute a close fit (the R^2 is virtually zero), and do not even yield a negatively sloping regression line. Thus, a relationship such as that in Figure 7.1 is no tautology, nor even a foregone conclusion.

In addition, if the 1870 productivity levels are measured with considerable error, this must result in some significant downward bias in the regression coefficient on $ln(GDP$ per $WorkHr$, 1870). This is a point distinct from the one concerning the size of the correlation coefficient, although the latter is affected by the fact that relatively large measurement errors in the 1870 productivity levels enter as inversely correlated measurement errors in the 1870–1979 growth rate. The argument that this bias is not sufficient to induce a negative correlation in the 72-country sample may not be wholly germane, as the relative seriousness of the measurement errors in the initial and terminal observations may be much the same for observations confined to the period 1950–80.

4. It must be conceded that the longer-run data do not seem to offer impressive support for the hypothesis that the forces of factor-price equalization have, albeit imperfectly, extended the benefits of exceptional rates of investment from those economies that carried out the successful investment programs to other industrialized economies. Since we have estimates of relative real wages, capital stock, and other pertinent variables for the United Kingdom and Germany, these have been compared below:

	Period	Ratio: German Increase to U.K. Increase[b]
Real Wages	1860–1980	4.25
GDP per Labor Hour	1870–1979	2.35
Capital Stock[a]	1870–1979	6.26
Capital Stock per Worker	1870–1979	3.8
Capital Stock per Capita	1870–1979	5.4

Sources: Real wages, same as in Note 6 [in original]; all other data from Maddison.

a. Net nonresidential fixed tangible capital stock.

b. (German 1979 figure/German 1870 figure)/(U.K. 1979 figure/ U.K. 1987 figure) with appropriate modification of the dates for the wage figures.

If the public goods attribute hypothesis about the effects of investment in one country were valid and if factor-price equalization were an effective force, we would expect the relative rise in German real wages and in productivity to be small (on some criterion) in comparison with the relative increase in its capital stock. However, the figures do not seem to exhibit such a pattern.

5. There are at least two sources of such data: the World Bank and the University of Pennsylvania group. Here I report only data drawn from the latter, since their international comparisons have been carried out with unique sophistication and insight. Instead of translating the different currencies into one another using inadequate exchange rate comparisons, they use carefully constructed indices of relative purchasing power. I have also replicated my calculations using World Bank data and obtained exactly the same qualitative results.

6. The centrally planned economies are Bulgaria, China, Czechoslovakia, East Germany, Hungary, Poland, Romania, USSR, and Yugoslavia. The 5 countries with relatively high 1950 incomes included neither in Maddison's sample nor in the planned group are, in descending order of GDP per capita, Luxembourg, New Zealand, Iceland, Venezuela, and Argentina. The countries with negative growth rates are Uganda and Nigeria.

REFERENCES

Abramovitz, Moses. 1979. "Rapid Growth Potential and its Realization: The Experience of the Capitalist Economies in the Postwar Period," in Edmond Malinvaud, ed., *Economic Growth and Resources, Proceedings of the Fifth World Congress of the International Economic Association*, Vol. 1, London: Macmillan.

————. 1985. "Catching Up and Falling Behind," delivered at the Economic History Association, September 20, 1985.

Ames, Edward and Rosenberg, Nathan. 1963. "Changing Technological Leadership and Industrial Growth," *Economic Journal* 73 (March): 13–31.

Beniger, James R. Forthcoming. *The Control Revolution: Technological and Economic Origins of the Information Society*. Cambridge: Harvard University Press.

Caves, Richard E. and Krause, Lawrence B. 1984. *The Australian Economy: A View From the North*. Washington: The Brookings Institution.

Cipolla, Carlo M. 1976. *Before the Industrial Revolution: European Society and Economy, 1000–1700*. New York: W. W. Norton.

Clark, Colin. 1957. *The Conditions of Economic Progress*, 3rd ed. London: Macmillan.

Darby, Michael. 1984. "The U.S. Productivity Slowdown: A Case of Statistical Myopia," *American Economic Review*, 74 (June): 301–322.

David, Paul A. 1977. "Invention and Accumulation in America's Economic Growth: A Nineteenth-Century Parable," in K. Brunner and A. H. Meltzer, eds., *International Organization, National Policies and Economic Development*, pp. 179–228. Amsterdam: North-Holland.

Deane, Phyllis and Cole, W. A. 1962. *British Economic Growth 1688–1959*. Cambridge: Cambridge University Press.

Feinstein, Charles. 1972. *National Income, Expenditure and Output of the United Kingdom, 1855–1965*. Cambridge: Cambridge University Press.

Gerschenkron, Alexander. 1952. "Economic Backwardness in Historical Perspective," in Bert F. Hoselitz, ed., *The Progress of Underdeveloped Areas*. Chicago: University of Chicago Press.

Landes, David S. 1969. *The Unbound Prometheus*. Cambridge: Cambridge University Press.

Lawrence, Robert Z. 1984. *Can America Compete?* Washington: The Brookings Institution.

McCloskey, D. N. 1981. *Enterprise and Trade in Victorian Britain*. London: Allen & Unwin.

Maddison, Angus. 1982. *Phases of Capitalist Development*. New York: Oxford University Press.

Marx, Karl and Engels, Friedrich. 1946. *Manifesto of the Communist Party* (1848). London: Lawrence and Wishart.

Matthews, R.C.O. 1982. *Slower Growth in the Western World*. London: Heinemann.

————, Feinstein, C. H. and Odling-Smee, J. C. 1982. *British Economic Growth, 1856–1973*. Stanford: Stanford University Press.

Mueller, Dennis C. 1983. *The Political Economy of Growth*. New Haven: Yale University Press.

Phelps Brown, E. H. and Hopkins, S. V. 1955. "Seven Centuries of Building Wages," *Economica*, 22 (August): 195–206.

————. 1956. "Seven Centuries of the Prices of Consumables," *Economica*, 23 (November): 296–314.

Porat, Marc Uri. 1977. "The Information Economy, Definitions and Measurement," Office of Telecommunications, Special Publication, 77-12(1), U.S. Department of Commerce, Washington.

Romer, Paul M. 1985. "Increasing Returns and Long Run Growth," Working Paper No. 27. University of Rochester, October.

Summers, Robert, and Heston, Alan. 1984. "Improved International Comparisons of Real Product and its Composition, 1950–1980," *Review of Income and Wealth*, 30 (June): 207–262.

Summers, Robert, Kravis, I. B., and Heston, Alan. 1986. " Changes in World Income Distribution," *Journal of Policy Modeling*, 6 (May): 237–269.

Teece, David J. 1976. *The Multinational Corporation and the Resources Cost of International Technology Transfer*. Cambridge: Ballinger.

Veblen, Thorstein. 1915. *Imperial Germany and the Industrial Revolution*. New York: Macmillan.

Viner, Jacob. 1958. *The Long View and the Short*. Glencoe: Free Press.

Williamson, Jeffrey G. 1983. "Why was British Growth So Slow During the Industrial Revolution?" Unpublished, Harvard Institute of Economic Research.

U.S. Bureau of Census. 1973. *Long Term Economic Growth 1860–1970*. Washington, D.C., June.

8

· · · · · · ·

Productivity Growth, Convergence, and Welfare: Comment

· · · · · · ·

J. BRADFORD DE LONG

In the previous chapter, William Baumol confirmed the expectations of convergence theory by finding that between 1870 and 1979 productivity rates of poorer countries grew more rapidly than those of richer countries. In this chapter, J. Bradford De Long argues that because only countries that converged by 1979 were included in the data set used by Baumol, convergence was assured. When De Long corrects for this sample-selection bias, convergence disappears. De Long then analyzes other variables to determine if the pattern of growth that he found can be explained. He does not find an association between democracy in 1870 and subsequent growth. (For further research on the impact of democracy, see Chapter 28 of this volume.) De Long did find a significant relationship between religion and growth: Protestant cultures grew faster. But the author notes that the correlations will not hold for long given the growth rates of countries such as Japan and Italy. (See Chapter 14 for further thoughts on the issue of religion and development.) The optimistic view that there is a process of economic homogenization, a closing of the gap between rich and poor, is not sustained by the data. As the author concludes, "It pushes us away from the belief that even the nations of the now industrial West will have roughly equal standards of living in 2090 or 2190."

Economists have always expected the "convergence" of national productivity levels. The theoretical logic behind this belief is powerful. The per capita income edge of the West is based on its application of the

---

Reprinted with permission from the *American Economic Review*, vol. 78, 5 (1986):1038–1048.

storehouse of industrial and administrative technology of the Industrial Revolution. This storehouse is open: modern technology is a public good. The benefits of tapping this storehouse are great, and so nations will strain every nerve to assimilate modern technology and their incomes will converge to those of industrial nations.

William Baumol (1986) argues that convergence has shown itself strongly in the growth of industrial nations since 1870.[1] According to Baumol, those nations positioned to industrialize are much closer together in productivity now than a century ago. He bases this conclusion on a regression of growth since 1870 on 1870 productivity for sixteen countries covered by Angus Maddison (1982).[2]

Baumol's finding of convergence might—even though Baumol himself does not believe that it should—naturally be read to support two further conclusions. First, slow relative growth in the United States since World War II was inevitable: convergence implies that in the long run divergent national cultures, institutions, or policies cannot sustain significant productivity edges over the rest of the developed world. Second, one can be optimistic about future development. Maddison's sixteen all assimilated modern technology and converged; perhaps all developing nations will converge to Western living standards once they acquire a foundation of technological literacy.

But when properly interpreted Baumol's finding is less informative than one might think. For Baumol's regression uses an *ex post* sample of countries that are now rich and have successfully developed. By Maddison's choice, those nations that have not converged are excluded from his sample because of their resulting present relative poverty. Convergence is thus all but guaranteed in Baumol's regression, which tells us little about the strength of the forces making for convergence among national that in 1870 belonged to what Baumol calls the "convergence club."

Only a regression run on an *ex ante* sample, a sample not of nations that have converged but of nations that seemed in 1870 likely to converge, can tell us whether growth since 1870 exhibits "convergence." The answer to this *ex ante* question—have those nations that a century ago appeared well placed to appropriate and utilize industrial technology converged?—is no. . . .

Maddison (1982) compiles long-run national income and aggregate productivity data for sixteen successful capitalist nations.[3] Because he focuses on nations which (a) have a rich data base for the construction of historical national accounts and (b) have successfully developed, the nations in Maddison's sixteen are among the richest nations in the world today. Baumol regresses the average rate of annual labor productivity growth over 1870-1979 on a constant and on the log of labor productivity in 1870 for this sample. He finds the inverse relationship of the first line of Table 8.1. The slope is large enough to erase by 1979 almost all initial income gaps, and the residual variance is small.

Table 8.1   Regressions Using Maddison's Sixteen

Independent Variable	Dependent Variable	Constant	Slope Coefficient	Standard Error of Estimate	R^2
Natural Log of 1870 Productivity	Annual Percent Productivity Growth	5.251	-0.749 .075	.14	.87
Natural Log of 1870 Income	Log Difference of 1979 and 1870 Income	8.457	-0.995 .094	.15	.88

Source: Data from Maddison (1982).

Regressing the log difference in per capita income between 1870 and 1979 on a constant and the log of per capita income in 1870 provides a slightly stronger case for convergence, as detailed in the second line of Table 8.1. The logarithmic income specification offers two advantages. The slope has the intuitive interpretation that a value of minus one means that 1979 and 1870 relative incomes are uncorrelated, and extension of the sample to include additional nations becomes easier.

Baumol's regression line tells us little about the strength of forces making for convergence since 1870 among industrial nations. The sample suffers from selection bias, and the independent variable is unavoidably measured with error. Both of these create the appearance of convergence whether or not it exists in reality. Sample selection bias arises because any nations relatively rich in 1870 that have not converged fail to make it into Maddison's sixteen. Maddison's sixteen thus include Norway but not Spain, Canada but not Argentina, and Italy but not Ireland. . . .

The unbiased sample used here meets three criteria. First, it is made up of nations that had high potential for economic growth as of 1870, in which modern economic growth had begun to take hold by the middle of the nineteenth century. Second, inclusion in the sample is not conditional on subsequent rapid growth. Third, the sample matches Baumol's as closely as possible, both because the best data exist for Maddison's sixteen and because analyzing an unbiased sample close to Baumol's shows that different conclusions arise not from different estimates but from removing sample selection and errors in variables' biases.

Per capita income in 1870 is an obvious measure of whether a nation was sufficiently technologically literate and integrated into world trade in 1870 to be counted among the potential convergers. . . .

. . . The choice of cutoff level itself requires balancing three goals: including only nations which really did in 1870 possess the social capability for rapid industrialization; including as many nations in Baumol's sample as possible; and building as large a sample as possible. . . .

If the convergence club membership cutoff is set low enough to include all Maddison's sixteen, then nations with 1870 incomes above 300 1975 dollars are included. This sample covers half the world. All Europe including Russia, all of South America, and perhaps others (Mexico and Cuba?) were richer than Japan in 1870. This sample does not provide a fair test of convergence. The Japanese miracle is a miracle largely because there was little sign in 1870 that Japan—or any nation as poor as Japan—was a candidate for rapid industrialization.

The second poorest of Maddison's sixteen in 1870 was Finland. Taking Finland's 1870 income as a cutoff leads to a sample in which Japan is removed, while Argentina, Chile, East Germany,[4] Ireland, New Zealand, Portugal, and Spain are added. . . .

All the additional nations have strong claims to belong to the 1870 convergence club. All were well integrated into the Europe-based international economy. All had bright development prospects as of 1870. . . . Argentina, Chile, and New Zealand were grouped in the nineteenth century with Australia and Canada as countries with temperate climates, richly endowed with natural resources, attracting large-scale immigration and investment, and exporting large quantities of raw and processed agricultural commodities. They were all seen as natural candidates for the next wave of industrialization.

Ireland's economy was closely integrated with the most industrialized economy in the world. Spain and Portugal had been the technological leaders of Europe during the initial centuries of overseas expansion—their per capita incomes were still above the European mean in the 1830s (Paul Bairoch, 1981)—and had retained close trading links with the heart of industrial Europe. Coke was used to smelt iron in Asturias in the 1850s, and by 1877 3,950 miles of railroad had been built in Spain. It is difficult to see how one could exclude Portugal and Spain from the convergence club without also excluding nations like Sweden and Finland.

Baumol's sample failed to include those nations that should have belonged to any hypothetical convergence club but that nevertheless did not converge. The enlarged sample might include nations not in the 1870 convergence club. Consider Kuwait today: Kuwait is rich, yet few would take its failure to maintain its relative standard of living over the next fifty years as evidence against convergence. For Kuwait's present wealth does not necessarily carry with it the institutional capability to turn oil wealth into next generation's industrial wealth. . . .

The volume of overseas investment poured into the additional nations by investors from London and Paris between 1870 and 1913 tells us that investors thought these nation's development prospects good. Herbert Feis' (1930) standard estimates of French and British overseas investment [The interested reader should refer to Table 2, p. 1143 of the original article—*Eds.*] show the six non-European nations among the top ten[5] recipients of investment per capita from France and Britain, and four of the five top recipients of investment belong to the once-rich twenty-two.[6] Every pound or franc invested is an explicit bet that the recipient country's rate of profit will remain high and an implicit bet that its rate of economic growth will be rapid. The coincidence of the nations added on a per capita income basis and the nations that would have been added on a foreign investment basis is powerful evidence that these nations do belong in the potential convergence club.

Errors in estimating 1870 income are unavoidable and produce equal and opposite errors in 1870–1979 growth. These errors therefore create the appearance of convergence where it does not exist in reality. . . . [7]

From one point of view, the relatively poor quality of much of the nineteenth century data is not a severe liability for this chapter. Only if there is less measurement error than allowed for will the results be biased against convergence. A more direct check on the importance of measurement error can be performed by examining convergence starting at some later date for which income estimates are based on a firmer foundation. A natural such date is 1913.[8] The relationship between initial income and subsequent growth is examined for the period 1913–1979 in Table 8.2.

The longer 1870–1979 sample of Table 8.3 . . . is slightly more hospitable to convergence than is the 1913–1979 sample, but for neither sample do the regression lines reveal a significant inverse relationship between initial income and subsequent growth. When it is assumed that there is no measurement error in 1870 income, there is a large negative slope to the regression line. But even in this case the residual disturbance term is large. When measurement error variance is assumed equal to half disturbance variance, the slope is slightly but not significantly negative.

For the central case of equal variances growth since 1870 is unrelated to income in 1870. There is no convergence. Those countries with income edges have on average maintained them. If measurement error is assumed

Table 8.2   Maximum Likelihood Estimation for the Once-Rich Twenty-Two, 1913–1979

p	Slope Coefficient B	Standard Error of Slope	Standard Error of Regression	Standard Error in 1870 PCI
0.0	-.333	.116	.171	.000
0.5	-.140	.136	.151	.107
1.0	0.021	.158	.133	.133
2.0	0.206	.191	.106	.150
infinity	0.444	.238	.000	.167

Source: Data from Maddison (1982).

Table 8.3   Maximum Likelihood Estimation for the Once-Rich Twenty-Two, 1870–1979

p	Slope Coefficient B	Standard Error of Slope	Standard Error of Regression	Standard Error in 1870 PCI
0.0	-.566	.144	.207	.000
0.5	-.292	.192	.192	.136
1.0	0.110	.283	.170	.170
2.0	0.669	.463	.134	.190
infinity	1.381	.760	.000	.196

Source: Data from Maddison (1982).

larger than the regression disturbance there is not convergence but divergence. Nations rich in 1870 or 1913 have subsequently widened relative income gaps. The evidence can be presented in other ways. The standard deviations of log income are given in Table 8.4. Maddison's sixteen do converge: the standard deviation of log income in 1979 is only 35 percent of its 1870 value. But the appearance of convergence is due to selection bias: the once-rich twenty-two have as wide a spread of relative incomes today as in 1870.

The failure of convergence to emerge for nations rich in 1870 is due to the nations—Chile, Argentina, Spain, and Portugal. In the early 1970s none of these was a democracy. Perhaps only industrial nations with democratic political systems converge. A dummy variable for democracy over 1950–80 is significant in the central ($p = 1$) case in the once-rich twenty-two regression in a at the 1 percent level, as detailed in Table 8.5.

But whether a nation is a democracy over 1950-80 is not exogenous but is partly determined by growth over the preceding century. As of 1870 it was not at all clear which nations would become stable democracies. Of the once-rich twenty-two, France, Austria (including Czechoslovakia), and Germany were empires; Britain had a restricted franchise; Spain and Portugal were semiconstitutional monarchies; the United States had just undergone a civil war; and Ireland was under foreign occupation. That all of these countries would be stable democracies by 1950 seems *ex ante* unlikely. Table 8.6 shows that shifting to an *ex ante* measure of democracy[9] removes the

Table 8.4   Standard Deviations of Log Output for Maddison's Sixteen and the Once-Rich Twenty-Two

Sample	1870	1913	1979
Maddison's 16	.411	.355	.145
Once-Rich 22	.315	.324	.329

Source: Data from Maddison (1982).

Table 8.5.   Democracy over 1950–1980 and Long-Run Growth for the Once-Rich Twenty-Two, 1870–1979

p	Slope Coefficient B	Standard Error of Slope	Coefficient on Democracy Variable	Standard Error	Standard Error in 1870 PCI	Standard Error of Regression
0.0	-.817	.277	.495	.085	.155	.000
0.5	-.744	.203	.476	.084	.154	.109
1.0	-.599	.208	.437	.090	.150	.150
2.0	0.104	.227	.248	.071	.131	.185
Infinity	1.137	.019	.044	.003	.000	.198

Source: Data from Maddison (1982).

Table 8.6   Democracy in 1870 and Long-Run Growth for the Once-Rich Twenty-Two, 1870–1979

p	Slope Coefficient B	Standard Error of Slope	Coefficient on Democracy Variable	Standard Error	Standard Error in 1870 PCI	Standard Error of Regression
0.0	-.567	.342	.001	.091	.207	.000
0.5	-.272	.322	-.038	.094	.192	.136
1.0	0.164	.454	-.095	.115	.169	.169
2.0	0.742	.976	-.170	.180	.131	.155
Infinity	1.231	.167	-.195	.022	.000	.194

Source: Data from Maddison (1982).

correlation. Whether a nation's politics are democratic in 1870 has little to do with growth since. The elective affinity of democracy and opulence is not one way with democracy as cause and opulence as effect.

There is one striking *ex ante* association between growth over 1870-1979 and a predetermined variable: a nation's dominant religious establishment. As Table 8.7 shows, a religious establishment variable that is one for Protestant, one-half for mixed, and zero for Catholic nations is significantly correlated with growth as long as measurement error variance is not too high.[10]

This regression is very difficult to interpret.[11] It does serve as an example of how culture may be associated with substantial divergence in growth performance. But "Protestantism" is correlated with many things—early specialization in manufacturing (for a given level of income), a high investment ratio, and a northern latitude, to name three. Almost any view—except a belief in convergence—of what determines long-run growth is consistent with this correlation between growth and religious establishment. Moreover, this correlation will not last: neither fast grower Japan nor fast

Table 8.7   Dominant Religion in 1870 and Long-Run Growth for the Once-Rich Twenty-
Two, 1870–1979

p	Slope Coefficient B	Standard Error of Slope	Coefficient on Democracy Variable	Standard Error	Standard Error in 1870 PCI	Standard Error of Regression
0.0	-.789	.252	.429	.088	.166	.000
0.5	-.688	.225	.403	.088	.164	.116
1.0	-.470	.248	.347	.098	.158	.158
2.0	0.375	.232	.132	.061	.132	.187
Infinity	1.199	.021	-.003	.004	.000	.197

Source: Data from Maddison (1982).

grower Italy owes anything to the Protestant ethic. The main message of Table 8.7 is that, for the once-rich twenty-two, a country's religious establishment has been a surprisingly good proxy for the social capability to assimilate modern technology.

The long-run data do not show convergence on any but the most optimistic reading. They do not support the claim that those nations that should have been able to rapidly assimilate industrial technology have all converged. Nations rich among the once-rich twenty-two in 1870 have not grown more slowly than the average of the sample. And of the nations outside this sample, only Japan has joined the industrial leaders.

This is not to say that there are no forces pushing for convergence. Convergence does sometimes happen. Technology is a public good. Western Europe (except Iberia) and the British settlement colonies of Australia, Canada, and the United States are now all developed. Even Italy, which seemed outside the sphere of advanced capitalism two generations ago, is near the present income frontier reached by the richest nations. The convergence of Japan and Western Europe toward U.S. standards of productivity in the years after World War II is an amazing achievement, and this does suggest that those present at the creation of the post-World War II international order did a very good job. But others—Spain, Portugal, Ireland, Argentina, and Chile— that one would in 1870 have thought capable of equally sharing this prosperity have not done so.[12] The capability to assimilate industrial technology appears to be surprisingly hard to acquire, and it may be distressingly easy to lose.

The forces making for "convergence" even among industrial nations appear little stronger than the forces making for "divergence." The absence of convergence pushes us away from a belief that in the long run technology transfer both is inevitable and is the key factor in economic growth. It pushes us away from the belief that even the nations of the now industrial West will have roughly equal standards of living in 2090 or 2190. And the absence of convergence even among nations relatively rich in 1870 forces us to take seriously arguments like Romer's (1986) that the relative income gap between rich and poor may tend to widen.

NOTES

1. Consider Baumol (1986): "Among the main observations . . . is the remarkable convergence. . . . [T]here is a strong inverse correlation between a country's productivity . . . in 1870 and its . . . productivity growth since then," and Baumol (1987): "Even more remarkable . . . is the convergence in . . . living standards of the leading industrial countries. . . . In 1870 . . . productivity in Australia, the leader, was 8 times . . . Japan's (the laggard). By 1979, the ratio . . . had fallen to about two."

2. Moses Abramovitz (1986) follows the behavior or these sixteen over time and notes that even among these nations "convergence" is almost entirely a post–World War II phenomenon. Abramovitz' remarks on how the absence of the "social capability" to grasp the benefits of the Industrial Revolution may prevent even nations that could benefit greatly from industrializing are well worth reading. Also very good on the possible determinants of the social capability to assimilate technology are Irma Adelman and Cynthia Taft Morris (1980), Gregory Clark (1987), and Richard Easterlin (1981).

3. Maddison's focus on nations that have been economically successful is deliberate; his aim in (1964), (1982), and (1987) is to investigate the features of successful capitalist development. In works like Maddison (1970, 1983) he has analyzed the long-run growth and development of less successful nations.

4. Perhaps only nations that have remained capitalist should be included in the sample, for occupation by the Red Army and subsequent relative economic stagnation has no bearing on whether the forces making for convergence among industrial capitalist economies are strong. There is only one centrally planned economy in the unbiased sample, and its removal has negligible quantitative effects on the estimated degree of convergence.

5. The foreign investment figures do provide a powerful argument for adding other Latin American nations—Mexico, Brazil, and Cuba—to the sample of those that ought to have been in the convergence club. Inclusion of these nations would weigh heavily against convergence.

6. Japan would not merit inclusion in the 1870 convergence club on the basis of foreign investment before World War I, for Japanese industrialization was not financed by British capital. Foreign investors' taste for Japan was much less, investment being equal to about one pound sterling per head and far below investment in such nations as Venezuela, Russia, Turkey, and Egypt. Admittedly, Japan was far away and not well known. but who would have predicted that Japan would have five times the measured per capita GNP of Argentina by 1979?

7. By contrast, errors in measuring 1979 per capita income induce no systematic bias in the relationship between standard of living in 1870 and growth since, although they do diminish the precision of coefficient estimates.

8. The data for 1913 are much more plentiful and solid than for other years in the early years of the twentieth century because of the concentration of historians' efforts on obtaining a pre-World War I benchmark. Beginning the sample at 1913 does mean that changes in country's "social capability" for

development as a result of World War I appear in the error term in the regression. If those nations that suffered most badly in World War I were nations relatively poor in World War I, there would be cause for alarm that the choice of 1913 had biased the sample against finding convergence when it was really present. But the major battlefields of World War I lay in and the largest proportional casualties were suffered by relatively rich nations at the core of industrial Europe.

9. Defined as inclusion of the electorate of more than half the adult male population.

10. The once-rich twenty-two are split into nations that had Protestant religious establishments in 1870 (Australia, Denmark, Finland, E. Germany, Netherlands, New Zealand, Norway, Sweden, U.K., and United States), intermediate nations—nations that either were split in established religion in 1870 or that had undergone violent and prolonged religious wars between Protestant and Catholics in the centuries after the Protestant Reformation—(Belgium, Canada, France, West Germany, and Switzerland), and nations that had solid Catholic religious establishments in 1870 (Argentina, Austria, Chile, Ireland, Italy, Portugal, and Spain). This classification is judgmental and a matter of taste: are the Netherlands one of the heartlands of the Protestant Ethic or are they one of the few nations tolerant and pluralistic on matters of religion in the seventeenth century?

11. The easy explanation would begin with the medieval maxim *homo mercator vix aut numquam placere potest Deo*: the merchant's business can never please God. Medieval religious discipline was hostile to market capitalism, the Protestant Reformation broke this discipline down in some places, and capitalism flourished most and modern democratic growth took hold strongest where this breakdown of medieval discipline had been most complete.

But this easy explanation is at best incomplete. Initially the Reformation did not see a relaxation of religious control. Strong Protestantism—Calvin's Geneva or Cromwell's Republic of the Saints—saw theology and economy closely linked in a manner not unlike the Ayatollah's Iran. And religious fanaticism is not often thought of as a source of economic growth.

Nevertheless the disapproval of self-interested profit seeking by radical Protestantism went hand-in-hand with seventeenth century economic development. And by 1800 profit seeking and accumulation for accumulation's sake had become morally praiseworthy activities in many nations with Protestant religious establishments. How was the original Protestant disapproval for the market transformed? Accounting for the evolution of the economic ethic of the Protestant West from Jean Calvin to Cotton Mather to Benjamin Franklin to Andrew Carnegie is a deep puzzle in economic history. The best analysis may still be the psychological account given by Max Weber (1958). Originally published in 1905.

12. One can find good reasons—ranging from the Red Army to landlord political dominance to the legacy of imperialism—for the failure of each of the additional nations to have reached the world's achieved per capita income frontier in 1979. But the fact that there are good reasons for the relative economic failure of each of these seven nations casts substantial doubt on the claim that the future will see convergence, for "good reasons" for economic failure will always be widespread. It is a safe bet that in 2090 one will be able *ex post* to identify similar "good reasons" lying behind the relative economic decline of those nations that will have fallen out of the industrial core.

REFERENCES

Abramovitz, M. 1986. "Catching Up, Forging Ahead, and Falling Behind," *Journal of Economic History,* June, 46: 385–406.

Adelman, I. and C.T. Morris. 1980. "Patterns of Industrialization in the Nineteenth and Early Twentieth Centuries," in Paul Uselding, ed., *Research in Economic History*, Vol. 5, Greenwich: JAI Press, 217–46.

Bairoch, P. 1981. "The Main Trends in National Economic Disparities Since the Industrial Revolution," in P. Bairoch and M. Lévy-Leboyer, eds., *Disparities in Economic Development Since the Industrial Revolution*, New York: St. Martin's Press.

Baumol, W. 1986. "Productivity Growth, Convergence, and Welfare," *American Economic Review*, December, 76: 1072–85.

———. 1987. "America's Productivity 'Crisis'." *The New York Times*, February 15, 3:2.

Clark, G. 1987. "Why Isn't the Whole World Developed? Lessons from the Cotton Mills," *Journal of Economic History*, March, 47: 141–74.

Easterlin, R. 1981. "Why Isn't the Whole World Developed?," *Journal of Economic History*, March, 41: 1–19.

Feis, H. 1930. *Europe, The World's Banker*, New Haven: Yale.

Maddison, A. 1987. "Growth and Slowdown in Advanced Capitalist Economies," *Journal of Economic Literature*, June, 25: 649–98.

———. 1983. "A Comparison of Levels of GDP per Capita in Developed and Developing Countries, 1700–1980, *Journal of Economic History*, March, 43: 27–41.

———. 1982. *Phases of Capitalist Development*, Oxford: Oxford University Press.

———. 1970. *Economic Progress and Policy in Developing Countries*, London: Allen & Unwin.

———. 1964. *Economic Growth in the West*, New York: The Twentieth Century Fund.

Romer, P. 1986. "Increasing Returns and Long Run Growth," *Journal of Political Economy*, October, 94: 1002–37.

Weber, M. 1958. *The Protestant Ethic and the Spirit of Capitalism*, New York: Scribner's. Originally published in 1905.

9

. . . .

Could It Be That the Whole World Is Already Rich? A Comparison of RGDP/pc and GNP/pc Measures

. . . .

JOHN T PASSÉ-SMITH

Measuring growth is not an easy task. Although poverty and wealth are easily discernible to anyone traveling across the frontiers of rich and poor countries, they are not easy to quantify. Visitors to foreign lands are confronted with the "traveler's dilemma": After conversion from U.S. coin into foreign currency, one dollar does not necessarily yield the same buying power in India as it does in the United States, or Botswana, or France. The amount of cash it took to buy a feast in one country might purchase only a partial loaf of bread in the next. This dilemma alerted scholars to the need to replace exchange rates with a conversion factor that would better reflect purchasing power.

Few people argue over the existence of a gap between rich and poor countries, but the extent of the gap is often disputed, in part because of a lack of confidence in the accuracy of exchange rate conversions. Comparing the general conditions in Burkina Faso to those in Switzerland, one may be satisfied that the GNP/pc accurately reflects the difference in standards of living; however, some have argued that this is not the case. Many scholars (Ward 1985; Summers and Heston 1984; Morris 1979; Kravis, et al. 1975; Heston 1973; Kuznets 1972) have suggested that converting GNPs to a common currency utilizing official exchange rates overstates the poverty of poor countries.

Exchange rate conversions are said to distort the actual purchasing power of currencies because they fluctuate away from a hypothesized equilibrium value. The fluctuations may occur rapidly—because of inflation, changes in production techniques, import and export barriers (or perhaps the quick removal of present barriers), price shocks originating domestically or internationally, etc.—but the restoration of equilibrium occurs much more slowly. Thus, exchange rate fluctuations represent malalignments of currency prices that will ultimately move back toward a relative unity value (Katseli-

Papaefstratiou 1979:4). Morris (1979:10) pointed out that it is not uncommon for exchange rates to oscillate rather wildly in a relatively short time. For example, Brazil's official exchange rate during the first quarter of 1981 was 70.8 *cruzeiros* per U.S. dollar; the midyear rate climbed to 91.8; and by the end of the year the official rate stood at 118, a 60 percent shift.[1]

Some contend that the exchange rate/PPP difference involves more than a lag time for correction of an equilibrium-tending exchange rate. Simon Kuznets, for example, asserts that

> even if exchange rates are assumed to reflect purchasing power parities of goods entering foreign trade, the price structures of the latter do not fully represent the prices of the wider range of goods entering countrywide output and comprising gross domestic product; and more important, the degree of non-representation differs among countries at different levels of development and hence of per capita product . . . the overstatement . . . is apparently smaller for the country with the lower per capita product (Kuznets 1972: 8–9).[2]

The United Nations commissioned a series of related projects, beginning in 1968 and continuing today, dubbed the International Comparison Project (ICP).[3] The purpose of the ICP is to produce PPP conversion factors so that cross-national comparisons of national account statistics can be made. In 1984 Robert Summers and Alan Heston reported that the project had "develop[ed] a structural relationship between purchasing power parities and exchange rates . . . [that took] account of the variability of exchange rates" (1984:207–208). Using extensive research in thirty-four "benchmark" countries, this relationship was to be extrapolated to the remaining "nonbenchmark" countries of similar size, economic structure, and so on. In 1988 the sample of countries and the years of coverage were expanded to include 130 countries covering the period 1950–1985.

The following sections offer some simple comparisons of World Bank– and International Monetary Fund–produced GNP/pcs (*World Tables 1992*; IMF 1984) and the data produced by the ICP group. Only those countries present in both data sets and in every year are used. The merged sample includes 107 countries for the years 1962–1985. At least two questions are raised: First, how different is the data for individual countries?; second, how has the change in data altered the extent of the gap between rich and poor as illustrated in Chapter 3?

GNP/PC AND RGDP/PCS COMPARED

The gross national product of a country is equal to the gross domestic product less factor payments abroad, so in comparing the two one should expect a difference even if the GDPs are not "real" GDPs (RGDPs) produced with a purchasing power parity index. Although factor payments most often represent a negative flow, they are sometimes positive, so it cannot be readily assumed that the GNP will be smaller than the GDP. A quick glance at the International Monetary Fund's *International Financial Statistics, 1980 Yearbook* (IMF 1980) seems to show that the industrialized countries of Europe and the United States are more likely to experience an inflow of factor payments than developing countries, but this is impressionistic, not systematic, evidence.

The left-hand side of Table 9.1 lists RGDP/pcs (the ICP data) for 1962 and 1985, the rankings for both years, and the annual average growth rate.[4] The right-hand side of the table includes comparable GNP/pc data (World Bank/IMF data set). The countries are also broken down by geographic regions as defined by the International Monetary Fund (IMF 1984). The IMF classifications include one nonregionally defined group, the "developed countries"; the less developed countries were divided into geographic regions: Africa, Asia, East Asia/Pacific,[5] the Western Hemisphere, and Europe/Middle East.[6] Finally, the column running down the center offers the difference between RGDP/pc ranking and GNP/pc ranking for the year 1985.

Among the developed countries, only five differed by five or more places in the RGDP-GNP comparison, and only Canada (+5) ranked higher in RGDP/pc than it did in GNP/pc. The other four countries—Australia (-8), Iceland (-7), Luxembourg (-6), and Sweden (-5)—all moved downward in the RGDP rankings. Canada was also one of only five countries in the developed category whose GNP/pc ($12,173) was smaller—albeit very slightly—than its RGDP/pc ($12,196).

Proponents of PPPs have argued that exchange rate conversions overstate the poverty of poor countries. As might be expected, only three nondeveloped countries have exchange rate–converted GNP/pcs larger than their purchasing power–converted RGDP/pcs: Algeria, Côte D'Ivoire, and Mauritania. On average, however, a developed country's RGDP/pc was $1,878 *less* than its GNP/pc. Both Switzerland and Luxembourg's RGDP/pcs were over $6,000 less than their GNP/pcs. If these figures are accurate, then the ICP project is demonstrating not only that the poverty of the developing countries is exaggerated but also that the wealth of the rich is at least partially an illusion.

As for the regional groupings, the Asian countries—Bangladesh, India, Pakistan, Nepal, and Sri Lanka—experienced the largest apparent increase between GNP/pc and RGDP/pc. The mean GNP/pc for this region was $262 in 1985—ranging from $141 for Bangladesh to $398 for Pakistan—increasing to an RGDP/pc of $923. Here the GNP/pc is but 28 percent of the RGDP/pc. For every country in this group the change was very large. Indeed, Sri Lanka had a GNP/pc of $335 in 1985 but a purchasing power equivalence of $1,539. This disparity is either indicative of the type of

Table 9.1 Comparison of RGDP/pc and GNP/pc: Levels, Rank, and Growth Rates by Region

	Real Gross Domestic Product Per Capita					Difference Between RGDP/pc and GNP/pc	Gross National Product Per Capita (1980 U.S. dollars)				
	1962	1985	Rank 1962	Rank 1985	Annual Growth 1962–85	1985	1962	1985	Rank 1962	Rank 1985	Annual Growth 1962–85
						Developed Countries					
Norway	5,416	12,623	11	1	3.66	2	7,154	15,916	5	3	3.42
United States	7,726	12,552	1	2	1.88	3	8,475	13,348	3	5	1.89
Canada	6,411	12,196	3	3	2.78	5	6,471	12,173	10	8	2.70
Denmark	6,057	10,884	5	4	2.41	2	7,482	12,967	4	6	2.21
Germany	5,529	10,708	10	5	2.91	2	6,734	12,773	8	7	2.89
Switzerland	7,342	10,640	2	6	1.38	-4	11,292	17,200	1	2	1.63
Luxembourg	6,234	10,540	4	7	2.37	-6	7,077	17,724	6	1	4.26
France	4,881	9,918	15	8	3.35	3	5,763	11,315	14	11	3.15
Sweden	5,654	9,904	8	9	2.22	-5	8,600	14,455	2	4	2.08
Belgium	4,827	9,717	17	11	3.25	3	5,468	10,657	15	14	3.11
Japan	2,687	9,447	29	12	5.38	3	3,043	10,507	20	15	5.20
Finland	4,405	9,232	18	13	3.36	-1	5,310	11,305	16	12	3.39
Netherlands	4,896	9,092	14	15	2.89	-2	6,281	10,996	11	13	2.45
Iceland	4,877	9,037	16	16	2.82	-7	6,575	11,876	9	9	2.66
Austria	4,189	8,929	19	17	3.48	-1	4,570	9,982	17	16	3.62
Australia	5,336	8,850	12	18	1.95	-8	6,943	11,563	7	10	1.99
United Kingdom	5,104	8,665	13	19	2.32	-2	6,276	9,912	12	17	1.85
New Zealand	5,669	8,000	7	20	1.38	-2	5,764	7,828	13	18	1.12
Italy	3,660	7,425	20	21	3.32	-2	3,514	6,940	18	19	3.00
Spain	2,893	6,437	26	23	3.42	-1	2,571	5,284	23	22	3.13
Ireland	2,752	5,205	28	29	2.97	-4	2,981	4,701	22	25	2.34
Mean	5,074	9,523	13	12	2.83	-1	6,112	11,401	11	11	2.77

Africa

Country											
South Africa	2,754	3,885	27	33	1.65	1	1,862	2,332	29	34	1.20
Gabon	996	3,103	61	42	5.58	-10	2,284	2,376	25	32	1.44
Algeria	1,086	2,142	57	51	2.81	-18	977	2,334	44	33	3.56
Tunisia	825	2,050	65	53	4.41	-6	562	1,396	63	47	4.51
Mauritius	1,088	1,869	56	57	2.65	-4	834	1,270	49	53	2.23
Botswana	541	1,762	81	58	5.74	-1	263	1,201	88	57	7.95
Congo	773	1,338	67	65	1.76	-11	649	1,246	61	54	3.22
Morocco	740	1,221	71	68	2.23	-2	550	830	66	66	2.19
Swaziland	529	1,187	86	71	3.67	-11	430	1,008	76	60	3.23
Cameroon	560	1,095	80	73	2.91	-10	425	898	77	63	3.37
Zimbabwe	634	948	76	75	1.87	-11	680	844	60	64	1.09
Côte D'Ivoire	748	920	70	76	0.87	-14	715	956	56	62	1.17
Lesotho	277	771	104	78	4.68	-2	159	493	103	76	6.03
Senegal	777	754	66	79	-0.26	-1	457	442	75	78	-0.08
Kenya	429	598	94	83	1.73	1	225	349	92	84	2.23
Zambia	721	584	73	84	-0.42	-5	555	425	64	79	-1.41
Nigeria	532	581	84	85	1.55	-16	570	740	62	69	2.21
Mauritania	446	550	92	86	1.02	-3	319	379	81	83	0.67
Sudan	754	540	69	87	-0.83	-5	398	391	78	82	0.70
Mozambique	845	528	64	88	-2.45	10	482	249	71	98	-2.61
Gambia, The	402	526	97	90	1.33	-3	254	297	90	87	1.28
Benin	586	525	78	91	-0.69	1	239	272	91	92	0.46
Madagascar	660	497	75	92	-1.00	-2	382	282	79	90	-1.13
Liberia	406	491	96	93	0.38	-12	462	395	73	81	0.08
Togo	427	489	95	94	0.32	-5	217	291	93	89	1.06
Sierra Leone	334	443	101	95	1.24	-4	275	279	87	91	0.16
Central Africa	474	434	91	96	-0.14	-8	297	296	83	88	0.02
Niger	317	429	102	97	1.15	3	350	214	80	100	-1.90
Malawi	243	387	105	98	2.52	3	132	212	105	101	2.37
Tanzania	209	355	107	100	1.81	-4	206	255	95	96	1.03
Mali	381	355	98	99	0.10	5	135	158	104	104	0.96

(continues)

Table 9.1 (continued)

	Real Gross Domestic Product Per Capita					Difference Between RGDP/pc and GNP/pc 1985	Gross National Product Per Capita (1980 U.S. dollars)				
	1962	1985	Rank 1962	Rank 1985	Annual Growth 1962–85		1962	1985	Rank 1962	Rank 1985	Annual Growth 1962–85
					Africa (continued)						
Ghana	534	349	83	101	−1.89	−16	490	345	70	85	−1.76
Somalia	506	348	88	102	−0.64	−5	297	254	84	97	−0.16
Burundi	334	345	100	103	0.91	−10	163	269	101	93	2.22
Rwanda	211	341	106	104	3.53	−5	200	227	96	99	1.78
Ethiopia	294	310	103	105	0.06	2	103	120	107	107	0.93
Chad	539	254	82	106	−2.98	0	191	128	98	106	−2.63
Zaire	336	210	99	107	−2.20	−4	212	165	94	103	−1.28
Mean	612	882	83	83	1.18	−5	474	648	78	79	1.22
					Asia and East Asia/Pacific						
Sri Lanka	1,029	1,539	60	62	1.61	24	177	335	100	86	2.81
Pakistan	584	1,153	79	72	2.33	8	199	398	97	80	2.73
India	530	750	85	80	1.11	15	182	268	99	95	1.60
Bangladesh	444	647	93	81	1.08	24	117	141	106	105	0.67
Nepal	485	526	90	89	0.15	13	161	165	102	102	−0.22
Mean	614	923	81	77	1.25	17	167	262	101	94	1.52
Singapore	1,670	9,834	39	10	8.01	10	1,421	6,791	31	20	7.67
Hong Kong	1,984	9,093	33	14	6.81	7	1,337	5,694	33	21	6.75
Malaysia	1,194	3,415	52	40	5.56	5	758	1,789	53	45	4.28
Korea	704	3,056	74	43	7.14	−3	491	2,134	69	40	6.78

Fiji	1,795	2,893	37	46	2.72	0	1,122	1,656	37	46	2.53
Thailand	729	1,900	72	56	4.42	9	318	841	82	65	4.36
Papua New Guinea	1,168	1,374	54	63	0.49	4	550	765	65	67	1.30
Philippines	941	1,361	62	64	2.54	9	465	616	72	73	2.26
Indonesia	494	1,255	89	67	5.29	5	259	617	89	72	4.57
Mean	972	1,973	65	57	4.77	4	534	1,105	69	61	4.50

Western Hemisphere

Trinidad and Tobago	5,548	6,884	9	22	0.58	1	3,484	5,079	19	23	2.00
Barbados	1,996	5,212	32	28	4.14	1	1,352	2,889	32	29	3.85
Mexico	2,212	3,985	30	32	2.89	11	1,063	2,017	39	43	3.04
Venezuela	5,878	3,548	6	35	-2.63	-5	2,306	2,649	24	30	1.12
Suriname	1,605	3,522	41	36	3.99	1	1,193	2,256	34	37	3.91
Chile	3,128	3,486	25	38	0.49	4	2,020	2,092	27	42	0.07
Argentina	3,221	3,486	24	37	0.77	-1	2,021	2,269	26	36	0.82
Uruguay	1,421	3,462	22	39	1.13	2	1,986	2,118	28	41	1.17
Brazil	1,432	3,282	46	41	4.78	-3	1,012	2,180	41	38	4.40
Panama	1,726	2,912	45	44	3.25	0	1,030	1,990	40	44	2.96
Costa Rica	1,402	2,650	38	47	2.15	5	919	1,276	45	52	1.80
Colombia	1,134	2,599	47	48	3.32	2	808	1,359	51	50	2.95
Ecuador	1,940	2,387	55	50	4.12	8	702	1,119	58	58	2.96
Peru	1,039	2,114	34	52	0.58	7	1,011	1,014	42	59	0.19
Paraguay	1,804	1,996	59	54	3.54	-3	754	1,306	54	51	3.58
Nicaragua	1,069	1,989	36	55	-0.24	13	918	747	46	68	-1.17
Dominican Rep	1,556	1,753	58	59	3.04	-3	762	1,216	52	56	2.92
Jamaica	1,297	1,725	43	60	0.15	-5	1,172	1,224	36	55	-0.09
Guatemala	1,284	1,608	48	61	1.57	0	737	962	55	61	1.70
Guyana	1,182	1,259	49	66	0.51	9	537	515	67	75	0.48
El Salvador	926	1,198	53	69	0.05	1	701	716	59	70	0.07
Bolivia	755	1,089	63	74	1.40	3	458	480	74	77	0.59
Honduras		911	68	77	1.07	-3	533	596	68	74	0.59

(*continues*)

Table 9.1 (continued)

	Real Gross Domestic Product Per Capita					Difference Between RGDP/pc and GNP/pc 1985	Gross National Product Per Capita (1980 U.S. dollars)				
	1962	1985	Rank 1962	Rank 1985	Annual Growth 1962–85		1962	1985	Rank 1962	Rank 1985	Annual Growth 1962–85
	Western Hemisphere (continued)										
Haiti	598	631	77	82	0.77	12	277	268	86	94	0.54
Mean	1,970	2,654	42	50	1.72	2	1,157	1,597	46	53	1.69
	Europe and Middle East										
Israel	3,203	6,270	23	24	3.12	0	2,998	4,803	21	24	2.19
Hungary	3,485	5,765	21	25	2.18	14	888	2,174	47	39	4.36
Malta	1,214	5,319	51	26	7.71	2	812	3,619	50	28	7.99
Cyprus	2,089	5,310	31	27	3.93	-1	1,185	4,225	35	26	5.89
Yugoslavia	1,901	5,063	35	30	4.58	1	1,119	2,544	38	31	4.10
Greece	1,644	4,464	40	31	4.43	-4	1,616	4,151	30	27	4.20
Portugal	1,592	3,729	42	34	4.11	1	993	2,323	43	35	3.95
Syria	1,548	2,900	44	45	4.31	3	849	1,386	48	48	3.45
Turkey	1,255	2,533	50	49	3.16	0	708	1,382	57	49	2.99
Egypt	525	1,188	87	70	3.52	1	295	703	85	71	3.98
Mean	1,846	4,254	42	36	4.10	2	1,146	2,731	45	38	4.31

Sources: Calculated from data in *The World Tables 1992* (World Bank); *International Financial Statistics: Supplement on Output Statistics*, No. 8, 1984 (International Monetary Fund); Summers and Heston, 1988; and *Human Development Report*, 1990 (United Nations).

overestimation of poverty that PPP proponents were speaking of or an overstatement of the wealth of Sri Lanka. With these changes, the Asian countries ranked on average seventeen places higher than they did in GNP/pc.

For other regions the changes were less dramatic. In Africa, for instance, GNP/pc was about 73 percent of RGDP/pc, and the mean RGDP/pc rank (83) was four places lower than GNP/pc rank (79). The average RGDP/pc for Africa was only $234 higher than GNP/pc. The other regions, ranked by 1985 RGDP/pc and, in parentheses, the difference between RGDP/pc and GNP/pc, were: Europe/Middle East, $4,254 ($1,523); Western Hemisphere, $2,654 ($1,057); East Asia/Pacific, $1,973 ($868); Asia, $923 ($661); and Africa, $882 ($234). Every group other than the developed countries had a significantly higher mean RGDP/pc than GNP/pc.

Proponents of PPPs have therefore argued that the gap between rich and poor countries is swollen by exchange rate conversions. If this is the case, then a PPP conversion must either increase the apparent wealth of the poor, decrease the apparent wealth of the rich, or a combination of both. Both effects have been found using the ICP data: The developed countries' RGDP/pcs average $1,878 less than their exchange rate–converted GNP/pcs, whereas the non-developed countries' RGDP/pcs are approximately $870 dollars higher on the average.

Table 9.2 isolates the countries with the largest disparities between RGDP/pc and GNP/pc. The table also includes the income level designated by the World Bank in the *World Development Report 1990*. The most dramatic differences occur among the countries in the lower income group. For instance, Sri Lanka and Bangladesh move from GNP/pcs of $283 and $129 to RGDP/pcs of $1,199 and $540, respectively. Again, these differences either reflect that actual purchasing power in these two countries is greater than it seems or exaggerate their "wealth." At the very least, this ambiguity points to the need for further study.

Although this chapter does not address the issue of distribution of income or the provision of basic goods (see Chapter 10 in this volume for an extensive analysis of RGDP/pc and the provision of basic goods), Table 9.2 lists the human development index (HDI) to determine if the countries experiencing the greatest change from GNP/pc to RGDP/pc appear to more closely approximate the conditions of countries with similar RGDP/pcs or similar GNP/pcs. The countries with GNP/pcs similar to Sri Lanka's ($200–300) in Table 9.2—Benin, Haiti, India, Kenya, Madagascar, Mozambique, Pakistan, Sierra Leone, and Togo—score significantly lower on the HDI index (.343) than Sri Lanka (.789). In addition, many of the countries with significantly higher RGDP/pcs than Sri Lanka in Table 9.2 have HDI scores only slightly larger. For all 107 countries in the sample, the human development index varies (positively) with the RGDP/pc (.76) and GNP/pc (.68) and is statistically significant.

Table 9.2 The Most Severe Changes in the Conversion from GNP/pc to RGDP/pc

Country	World Development Report 1990 Grouping	Real GDP/pc 1980	GNP/pc 1980	Difference (RGDP/pc -GNP/pc)	GNP/pc as a percentage of RGDP/pc	Human Development Index
Mexico	Lower-Middle	4,333	2,133	2,200	49.23	.876
Chile	Lower-Middle	4,271	2,512	1,759	58.82	.931
Hungary	Upper-Middle	5,508	2,048	3,460	37.19	.915
Yugoslavia	Upper-Middle	4,733	2,703	2,030	57.11	.913
Uruguay	Upper-Middle	4,502	2,886	1,616	64.10	.916
Venezuela	Upper-Middle	4,424	3,306	1,118	74.73	.861
Argentina	Upper-Middle	4,342	2,823	1,519	65.02	.910
South Africa	Upper-Middle	4,286	2,558	1,728	59.68	.731
Sri Lanka	Low Income	1,199	283	916	23.64	.789
Pakistan	Low Income	989	341	648	34.49	.423
Senegal	Low Income	744	452	292	60.75	.273
Haiti	Low Income	696	308	388	44.31	.356
Lesotho	Low Income	694	453	241	65.27	.580
Kenya	Low Income	662	379	283	57.25	.481
Sudan	Low Income	652	415	237	63.65	.255
Mozambique	Low Income	637	366	271	57.46	.239
Togo	Low Income	625	339	286	54.24	.337
India	Low Income	614	234	380	38.14	.439
Madagascar	Low Income	589	366	223	62.14	.440
Mauritania	Low Income	576	409	167	71.01	.208
Bangladesh	Low Income	540	129	257	23.89	.318
Benin	Low Income	534	288	246	53.93	.224
Sierra Leone	Low Income	512	325	187	63.48	.150

Sources: Calculated from data in *The World Tables 1992*; *International Financial Statistics*, 1984; Summers and Heston, 1988; and *Human Development Report*, 1990

THE GAP BETWEEN RICH, MIDDLE-INCOME, AND POOR

If the income groups used in Chapter 3 were used here to analyze RGDP/pcs, the results would in many ways be quite different. These categories, similar to those defined by the World Bank in the *World Development Report 1990*, define low-income countries as those with per capita incomes of less than $500; $500 to $3,999, middle-income; and greater than $4,000, high-income. The most striking contrast is displayed in Table 9.3. Of the 107 countries, only 19 are considered low-income in 1962 using RGDP/pc. This figure further declines to 13 countries in 1970 before climbing back up to 16 by 1985. Among the countries in the sample, the portion of the population living in countries with an RGDP/pc of less than $500 never surpasses 13 percent and declines to only 5.7 percent by 1985 (40.5 percent using the GNP/pc figures). According to the ICP data, only 177 million people lived in impoverished countries in 1985, as opposed to 1.265 *billion* in the World Bank/IMF data.

Although RGDP/pc appears to be indicating that exchange rate–converted GNP/pcs overstate poverty to some degree, it is doubtful that only sixteen countries are impoverished. A much more in-depth study or series of studies that include all of the elements of development (elements such as the level of growth, economic diversity, income distribution, and basic needs provision) must be conducted to adequately define the world's poverty level.

Still, even without defining income groups, it is possible to determine if the gap between rich and poor is widening or narrowing. A simple method of detecting such a trend is to examine annual standard deviations. If the gap is closing, then the standard deviations should grow smaller, meaning that countries are moving closer to the world average RGDP/pc. Figure 9.1 shows the standard deviations of RGDP/pc and the GNP/pc for the world (N=107). The figure illustrates that both RGDP/pc and GNP/pc are growing

Table 9.3 Income Groups' Percentage of World Population

Year	World Population[a] (billions)	Rich percent	Rich number of counties	Middle-Income percent	Middle-Income number of countries	Poor percent	Poor number of countries
1962	1.980	22.3	19	64.9	69	12.8	19
1965	2.105	21.8	19	65.7	72	12.5	16
1970	2.322	30.7	25	62.2	69	7.1	13
1975	2.568	30.5	29	64.2	64	5.2	14
1980	2.830	33.0	37	61.6	57	5.4	13
1985	3.119	25.8	31	68.6	60	5.7	16

a. The world total reflects population data for the 107 countries for which there is also GNP/pc data. China is not included.
Source: The World Tables 1992.

larger over time. In fact, they move very similarly. In 1974 it appears that both measures point to a very slight closing—or at least slowing of the expansion of—the gap. The heavy line in Figure 9.1 shows the world mean RGDP/pc, and the lighter line is the average GNP/pc.[7] As might be expected, the standard deviation of the RGDP/pc is consistently smaller than that of the GNP/pc, yet still of considerable size.

The gap as illustrated in Figure 9.1, however, may be presenting a misleading picture. It would not be surprising that as the world grows richer, the increase in the standard deviation would also grow larger. The coefficient of variation adjusts the standard deviation for changing means; one can be relatively sure that an increase in the coefficient of variation is not merely a by-product of an increasing mean value.[8] Figure 9.2 displays the coefficient of variation for the RGDP/pc, the GNP/pc, presenting a slightly different picture of the world than appeared in the previous figure.

The coefficient of variation in both cases registers an increase from 1962 to 1985. However, after a brief rise, the measure for both the RGDP/pc and the GNP/pc slides downward until around 1977 and then begins to rise, accelerating in both cases in 1981. In terms of the gap, this pattern means that from around 1964 until 1977 countries were moving toward the world mean RGDP/pc and GNP/pc—the gap narrowed. This trend reversed, and the gap began to widen again in 1977. These movements may have been relatively small, but they were captured by both the RGDP/pc and GNP/pc measures. In fact, it is remarkable that with all the differences between the two measures, they show almost identical trends. The main difference between the two is that the RGDP/pc produces a slightly smaller gap. It would also appear that the difference between the two is slightly smaller in 1985 than it was in 1962.

Growth Rates

The world economy grew at an average annual rate of 2.21 percent as measured by both RGDP/pc and GNP/pc for the 107 countries in the sample (see Table 9.4). As explained in Chapter 3, this growth rate is quite impressive, yet the data from both methods of conversion showed an even faster rate for the 1962–1975 period. Both the RGDP/pc and the GNP/pc growth rates for the world slowed to under 1 percent between 1975 and 1985. Thus, both measures show very rapid growth in roughly the first half of the 1962–1985 period, slowing significantly in the second half. This pattern is replicated for all of the regions except Asia, which experienced slower first-half than second-half growth.

Except in a few instances, the RGDP/pc growth rates are very similar to the exchange rate–converted GNP/pc rates. The regions, however, change order when ranked by rate of growth. For the entire period, East Asia/Pacific grows the fastest in terms of RGDP/pc but is second on the GNP/pc list.

Figure 9.1   Standard Deviations and Means of World RGDP/pc and GNP/pc

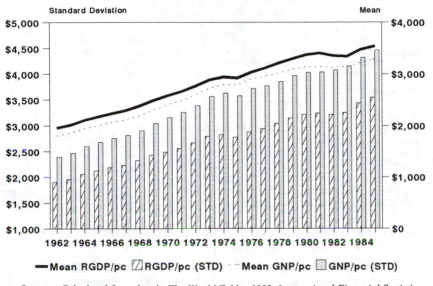

Sources: Calculated from data in *The World Tables 1992*; *International Financial Statistics*, 1984; Summers and Heston, 1988; and *Human Development Report*, 1990.

Figure 9.2   Variation from the World Mean RGDP/pc and GNP/pc

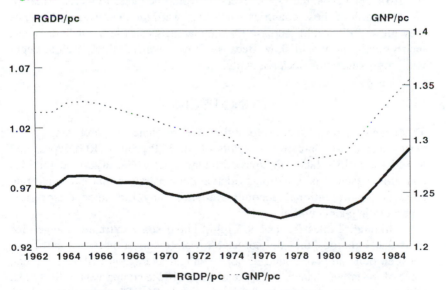

Note: Coefficient of variation is the standard deviation divided by the mean.
Sources: Calculated from data in *The World Tables 1992*; *International Financial Statistics*, 1984; Summers and Heston, 1988; and *Human Development Report*, 1990.

Table 9.4   Growth Rates by Geographic Region, 1962–1985, 1962–1975, 1975–1985

Region	Annual Growth (percentages) RGDP/pc			GNP/pc		
	1962–1985	1962–1975	1975–1985	1962–1985	1962–1975	1975–1985
World	2.21	3.02	.85	2.21	3.11	.49
Developed	2.83	3.70	1.87	2.77	3.77	1.66
East Asia/Pacific	4.77	5.09	3.74	4.50	5.01	3.38
Europe	4.30	5.19	2.77	4.78	5.98	2.59
Middle East	3.65	3.76	2.30	3.20	3.14	1.65
Western Hemisphere	1.72	2.73	-.23	1.69	2.76	-.86
Asia	1.25	.44	2.40	1.52	1.03	2.20
Africa	1.18	2.22	-.38	1.22	2.27	-.70

Sources: Calculated from data in *The World Tables 1992*; *International Financial Statistics*, 1984; Summers and Heston, 1988; and *Human Development Report*, 1990.

Three of the regional groupings have RGDP/pc growth rates lower than their GNP/pc rates—Asia, Africa, and Europe.

This comparison makes some sense for the two poorer regions because of the way the purchasing power conversions work. Proponents of the PPP conversion index argue that the gap between rich and poor is overstated. They claim that exchange rates do not adjust quickly enough to reflect distortions more likely to be present in developing countries and that more economic activity goes on outside of the capitalist monied economy in these countries. For Africa and Asia, the PPP conversion would be likely to increase the apparent wealth of those countries when they were the poorest, i.e., 1962; as they grew, PPP would increase their apparent wealth less and less. Thus, their growth rate would slow. Because Europe was relatively rich to begin with, this explanation does not apply.

CONCLUSIONS

This chapter had two foci: a) to outline the rationale for purchasing power parity; and b) to compare the results of the ICP project (RGDP/pcs) and World Bank/IMF data (GNP/pcs). Fundamentally, the argument for PPP conversion factors is based on evidence demonstrating that exchange rate conversions of national account statistics may introduce distortions, especially in poor countries.

Although Tables 9.1 and 9.2 highlighted some extreme changes for individual countries, they did not have a visible impact on *trends* in the gap between rich and poor countries nor in annual average growth rates. When some of the larger changes were examined, as in the comparison of Sri Lanka with other countries at similar levels of growth, RGDP/pc appeared, at least tentatively, to be more reliable.

Second, although RGDP/pcs did raise the level of growth of the regional groups, as PPP proponents suggested would be the case, they also *lowered* the apparent level of growth of the developed nations from $11,401 (GNP/pc 1985) to $9,523 (RGDP/pc 1985). Thus, the conversion factor did not leave the developed countries virtually unchanged, as its proponents predicted.

Third, analysis of standard deviations and coefficients of variation indicated that both PPP conversion factors and exchange rates show that the gap between rich and poor countries is growing wider. Upon closer scrutiny, the coefficient of variation showed the gap narrowing slightly between 1962 and 1977 (although not consistently every year), then widening for the rest of the period under examination.

Fourth, overall growth rates were very similar for the ICP and World Bank data. Both pointed to the 1962 to 1975 period as one of very rapid growth, with all of the regions except Asia witnessing a severe reversal of fortunes over the remaining years. This agreement suggests the possibility that contradictory findings in studies attempting to explain growth may be due to the period under study. Depending upon the research question, it would probably be useful not only to specify the longest possible period but also to be sensitive to crossing periods of rapid and slow growth.

Finally, more research needs to be done to define a poverty level for the ICP data. What does it mean to have an RGDP/pc of $1,000 or $3,000 in terms of economic diversity, distribution of income, and provision of basic needs? In other words, what constitutes poverty and wealth?

NOTES

1. The example follows the logic of that used by Morris (1979:10–11).

2. Kuznets also noted that if the currency of a rich country is used as the *numeraire* currency, the PPP conversion for richer countries is not affected by the conversion, and the poorer the country, the more the PPP conversion inflates the resulting figure. This means the PPP-converted GNP/pcs make the gap between rich and poor countries look smaller (1972: 9–10).

3. Other institutions making significant contributions to this work have been the University of Pennsylvania, the Ford Foundation, and the World Bank. For a more complete history of this project, see Irving Kravis, Zoltan Kenessey, Alan Heston, and Robert Summer, *A System of International Comparisons of Gross Product and Purchasing Power* (Baltimore and London: Johns Hopkins University Press, 1975).

4. The growth rates for both the RGDP/pcs and GNP/pcs are calculated by the regression method described in the *World Development Report 1988* (WDR 1988:288–289). The least squares method finds the growth rate by fitting a least squares trend line to the log of the gross national product per capita. This takes the equation form of $X_t=a+bt+e_t$, where x equals the log of the GNP/pc, t is time, and b is the parameter to be estimated. The growth rate, r, is the [antilog (b)]-1. For a discussion of different methods of computing growth rates see Robert Jackman, "A Note on the Measurement of Growth Rates in Cross-National Research," *American Journal of Sociology*, 86:604–610.

5. This region actually comes from the World Bank's *World Tables*. I included this category because it places the so-called "baby dragons" and the

proposed next generation of rapid industrializers in a group that is virtually their own (other than Papua New Guinea, and Fiji).

6. I merged these two categories because the Middle East only included three countries: Egypt, Israel, and Syria.

7. The minimum RGDP/pc for all of the years is $152 and the maximum is $12,623. The minimum and maximum figures for the GNP/pc are $93 and $17,724, respectively.

8. The coefficient of variation is the standard deviation divided by the mean.

REFERENCES

Bairoch, P. 1981. "The Main Trends in National Economic Disparities since the Industrial Revolution." In P. Bairoch and M. Lévy-Leboyer, eds., *Disparities in Economic Development Since the Industrial Revolution*. London: Macmillan Press Ltd.

Beckerman, W. 1966. *International Comparisons of Real Income*. Paris: OECD Development Center.

Gilbert, M., and I. Kravis. 1954. *An International Comparison of National Products and the Purchasing Power of Currencies*. Paris: Organization for European Economic Cooperation.

———. 1958. *An International Comparison of Comparative National Products and Price Levels: A Study of Western Europe and the United States*. Paris: Organization for European Economic Cooperation.

Heston, A. 1973. "A Comparison of Some Short-Cut Methods of Estimating Real Product per Capita," *Review of Income and Wealth* (March):79–104.

International Money Fund. 1980. *International Financial Statistics: Yearbook 1980*. Washington, D.C.: IMF.

———. 1984. *International Financial Statistics: Supplement on Output Statistics*, No. 8. Washington, D.C.: IMF.

Jackman, R. W. 1980. "A Note on the Measurement of Growth Rates in Cross-National Research," *American Journal of Sociology*, 86:604–610.

Kravis, I. B., Z. Kenessey, A. Heston, and R. Summers. 1975. *A System of International Comparisons of Gross Product and Purchasing Power*. Baltimore and London: Johns Hopkins University Press.

Kuznets, S. 1972. "The Gap: Concept, Measurement, Trends." In G. Ranis, ed., *The Gap Between Rich and Poor Nations*. London: Macmillan Press, Ltd.

Morris, M. D. 1979. *Measuring the Condition of the World's Poor: The Physical Quality of Life Index*. New York: Pergamon Press.

Summers, R. and A. Heston. 1984. "Improved International Comparisons of Real Product and its Composition: 1950–1980," *The Review of Income and Wealth* 3 (September):207–259.

Summers R., and A. Heston. 1988. "A New Set of International Comparisons of Real Product and Prices: Estimates for 130 Countries, 1950–1985," *The Review of Income and Wealth* (March):1–25.

United Nations. 1990. *Human Development Report*. New York: Oxford University Press.

Ward, M. 1985. *Purchasing Power Parities and Real Expenditures in the OECD*. Paris: OECD Press.

World Bank. 1988. *World Development Report*. Oxford: Oxford University Press.

World Bank. 1992. *The World Tables of Economic and Social Indicators, 1960–86*. Washington D.C.: The World Bank.

World Bank. 1992. *The World Tables 1992*. Washington, D.C.: The World Bank.

10

. . . .

Basic Needs and
Growth-Welfare Trade-Offs

. . . .

BRUCE E. MOON & WILLIAM J. DIXON

As we saw in Chapters 4 and 5, economic growth led to increasing inequality as money accrued to the new entrepreneurs of a developing society. Recent debate in development policy has revisited this issue, asking the questions: Can countries provide for the social welfare of their people and still achieve growth? And does growth erode the future welfare of individuals? In this chapter, Bruce Moon and William Dixon find that there is no evidence to support the orthodox view that the provision of basic needs derails growth. Furthermore, economic growth is found to have little bearing on future basic-needs improvements. (For the interested reader, an extensive methodological discussion is contained in the endnotes of the original work.)

VALUE TRADE-OFFS AND DEVELOPMENT CHOICES

Can nations achieve both growth and equity or must one value be sacrificed to attain the other? The controversy over such a trade-off lies at the heart of recent debates on development policy. Orthodox development planners have long counseled developing nations to maximize GNP growth, but over the last two decades an alternative "welfare-centric" school of theorists has emerged which urges the pursuit of a much broader range of goals (Seers, 1969; Griffin, 1981; Streeten et al., 1981; Dreze and Sen, 1989). They challenge the views of orthodox "growth-centric" strategies concerning the appropriate conceptualization and measurement of development as well as the

Reprinted with permission from Blackwell Publishers for the *International Studies Quarterly*, vol. 36 (June 1992):191–210.

policies that can bring it about. Growth-centric approaches are defined by the tenet that capital accumulation and rapid GNP growth should be the dominant short-term and medium-term goals. By contrast, the newer family of "welfare-centric" approaches has emphasized distributional and noneconomic components of development as significant near-term targets. Most prominent among these approaches are the so-called growth-with-equity and basic needs schools of development (Weaver and Jameson, 1981).

The two broad families of "growth-centric" and "welfare centric" approaches are divided by conflicting views of the competition between different values. In particular, the implications of their different short-term priorities have been highlighted in a much-publicized controversy concerning the existence of an empirical trade-off between "growth" and "equity" (Okun, 1976; Hicks, 1979; Wheeler, 1980). Although often conceived narrowly as a debate about income inequality, "equity" has been adopted as a short-hand term for a variety of concerns involving the welfare and physical quality of life of a nation's masses.

Advocates of growth-centric strategies typically argue that the direct pursuit of equity requires a sacrifice in growth due to the necessary diversion of resources away from their most efficient (i.e., growth-producing) use (Bauer, 1984; Lal, 1985). Because this argument underscores problems of inefficiency, in what follows we refer to "inefficiency effects" to denote the trade-off that is the chief concern of growth-centric theorists. By contrast, the theory underlying welfare-centric strategies contends that an emphasis upon rapid growth in GNP encourages distorted patterns of development that tend to diminish the welfare of the poor (Stewart, 1985). Because this interpretation of the trade-off emphasizes distorted development, we refer to "distortion effects" to capture the concerns of welfare-centric theorists.

The controversies surrounding these contending trade-offs pose enduring issues for scholars of development, although they have appeared in a different guise in the variety of policy contexts in which they have arisen. Further, the centrality of each trade-off has waxed and waned with the fortunes of the schools that emphasize it. Since the 1960s these trade-offs have informed discussions of specific development priorities and projects by international aid-givers, particularly the World Bank (Hoadley, 1981; Ayres, 1983). Growth-oriented theorists preferred infrastructural lending designed to speed industrialization, whereas welfare-oriented theorists, who came into prominence during McNamara's tenure at the Bank, emphasized rural development. The debate over the competitive or complementary nature of growth and equity has also been found at the core of nearly all subsequent debates concerning overall development strategies (Griffin, 1989). After a decade in which the dominance of liberalization strategies made avoidance of inefficiency effects the centerpiece of the World Bank program, a renewed emphasis on poverty alleviation has again projected concerns of distortion effects onto center stage (World Bank, 1990). These issues have also reappeared in the context of alternative stabilization and structural adjustment strategies, particularly for indebted nations seeking IMF assistance (Cornia, Jolly, and Stewart, 1987; Taylor, 1989).

This study seeks to adjudicate the controversies concerning the existence of these two variants of the growth-equity trade-offs. We do so by examining two empirical questions: (1) Does basic needs achievement compromise future economic growth? (2) Does rapid economic growth undermine future basic needs achievement?

GROWTH VERSUS EQUITY

Growth-centric theorists are quick to recognize inefficiency effects but deny the existence of distortion effects. Because they believe that aggregate growth produces basic needs improvements for the poor automatically through a "trickle-down" process, they contend that redistributive policy is both unwise and unnecessary. Welfare-centric theorists readily recognize distortion effects but deny the existence of inefficiency effects. Because they regard welfare improvements for the poor as an investment in "human capital" that speeds subsequent development, they contend that policies that emphasize equity accomplish growth as well.

Inefficiency Effects

Claims of inefficiency effects are deeply rooted in liberal economic theory. Nations marked by better than average provision of basic needs are expected to suffer slower future growth for at least three reasons. First, the pattern of resource allocation and factor ownership that maximizes relative basic needs provision is likely to yield too little investment and too little efficiency. One can think of diminishing inequality as an incremental process of shifting income from those above the income mean to those below it. Such an income shift—whether portrayed cross-sectionally or over time—has a characteristic impact on the pattern of consumption and investment. Following Engels' law, egalitarian income distributions will be marked by a higher proportion of income devoted to basic needs.[1] At the same time, because savings rates are much lower—indeed, often negative—among the poor, relatively egalitarian societies can be expected to have lower savings rates than more unequal ones. Further, lower savings rates are assumed to yield lower investment rates, which, in turn slows aggregate growth. Thus, when money is taken from those who would save it and given to those who will spend it on basic needs, investment levels will fall as basic needs levels will rise. Therefore, if growth follows from investment, basic needs fulfillment must come at the expense of economic growth.

Second, liberal theorists doubt that this kind of income shift can take place without some "dead weight" income loss (Bauer, 1972; Lal, 1985). For example, redistributive taxation is thought to distort the type as well as the level of investment. In particular, income is chased into black markets or tax shelters which yield little in future economic growth. Worse yet, many government policies designed to benefit the poor are seen by owners of capital—accurately or not—as harmful to their long-term interests. The result is a slowing or reversal of inflowing capital from foreigners and an acceleration of capital flight by nationals. Both sharply constrain growth.

Third, basic needs initiatives invariably imply a larger role for the state. Each of the forms this may take has been linked to diminished future growth by orthodox advocates of the stabilization and structural adjustment programs which have become the front line of development controversies in recent years. Direct welfare spending is always a chief target of austerity programs designed to balance government budgets and restrain the excess demand which the orthodox view identifies as the chief cause of destabilizing and growth-inhibiting inflation. The liberalization component of stabilization programs also attacks both the regulation of private actors because of its interference with the growth-maximizing operation of free markets and direct production by state-owned enterprises because of their notorious inefficiency (World Bank, 1987, 1988). Thus, this form of the trade-off should show up in especially dramatic form when state policy seeks rapid improvement in basic needs levels.

Proponents of basic needs development strategies conceptualize the process of targeting the welfare of the poor very differently. In particular, they deny that there is any inherent tension between investment and basic needs. Rather, they contend that expenditure to provide basic needs is *itself* investment, although it may take a different form than physical capital. By providing for enhanced education and improved health, investment in human capital increases the productivity of labor just as surely as does investment that provides additional tools to labor (Rao Maturu, 1979; World Bank, 1980; Psacharopoulos, 1985; Cornia, Jolly, and Stewart, 1987: chapter 6). Indeed, serious limitations of human capital and infrastructure are thought to be greater barriers to growth than overall investment levels in many poor countries, especially in the rural sector, because poor health and education are such a formidable bottleneck in achieving productivity gains in labor-intensive agriculture (Lipton, 1988). Because basic needs provision need not compromise overall productivity and output, it thus need not inhibit growth.

In fact, human capital theorists argue that systems providing superior basic needs have laid the groundwork for *faster* future growth.[2] Such arguments have a long history of theoretical support and policy advocacy (ILO, 1970, 1977; Chenery et al., 1974; Lipton, 1977; Hicks, 1979; Streeten et al., 1981; Adelman, 1986). Moreover, they are strongly supported empirically by the example of the most dramatic achievers of the postwar era: the Asian NICs (South Korea, Taiwan, Singapore, and Hong Kong) were—and remain—near the top of the list of nations ranked by basic needs attainment relative to GNP. Most commentators have regarded this attribute as a key to their developmental success (Fei, Ranis, and Kuo, 1979; Collins and Park, 1989; Griffin, 1989; Haggard, 1990). Apparently basic needs provision need not require state action which is inefficient or alarming to owners of capital. Indeed, many state actions designed to improve basic needs provision (e.g., land reform) may require very great political will but relatively small fiscal effort. Others have been shown to earn quite high rates of return, whether measured conventionally or with respect to welfare outcomes (Stewart, 1987).

Distortion Effects

The form of the trade-off emphasized by welfare-centric approaches assumes that development programs targeting aggregate growth while downplaying or ignoring distributional issues are likely to entail growth patterns containing little improvement in basic needs levels. This is especially so if plans call for rapid growth, which can be achieved only via development paths whose distortions necessarily compromise the interests of the poor.

The arguments proceed from the assumption that the average rate of per capita growth in a self-sustaining economy is relatively slow, seldom much more than 3–4% per year. Gains occur principally through capital accumulation (which is slow and incremental), technological progress (which tends to be sporadic and sectorally narrow), and improved efficiency (which is less frequent yet and even smaller in impact). This stability, along with other barriers to expansion such as the "low level equilibrium trap," suggests that rapid growth can be accomplished only by a significant shift in the allocation of endogenous resources or by a heavy reliance on external sources of capital, technology, and/or markets (Johnson, 1967).

For the relatively closed economy, the argument parallels the earlier discussion centering on consumption-investment trade-offs and the role of the state. Rapid growth requires high levels of investment, which in the absence of foreign sources must derive from high savings rates. Because this requires inegalitarian income distributions and a limited state, rapid GNP growth in a relatively closed economy is a strong clue that basic needs are receiving a lower than normal share of social resources. Moreover, there is also likely to be considerable dead-weight loss from policies designed to accelerate growth in this way. For example, because the savings rates of the rich are far below unity, any unit of income shifted from the poor will yield only a fraction of a unit increase in investment. Further, the resulting inequality and the policies that enforce it tend to generate domestic conflict which wastes resources (Muller, 1985; Dixon and Moon, 1989; Moon, 1991).

Although rapid GNP gains are *possible* through such "inward-looking" policies, they are historically rare. Far more frequently, the most rapidly growing economies have been driven by an external engine. And this external reliance is thought to be destructive of basic needs. The most common arguments concern the impact of foreign sources of capital, especially if introduced in the form of foreign direct investment by multinational corporations. Such investment is thought to exacerbate sectoral and class inequalities, introduce inappropriate technologies which increase capital-labor ratios and aggravate unemployment, weaken inter-sectoral linkages, foster regionally uneven growth, distort the social and political system, and bias state policy against the poor (Biersteker, 1978; Evans, 1979; Bornschier and Chase-Dunn, 1985). All of these hinder the promotion of basic needs.

Reliance upon foreign trade is another way to overcome the slow growth potential of entirely self-sustaining development. Bypassing the bottleneck of limited domestic demand, export-oriented development has frequently been espoused as an easy road to rapid GNP growth. Even this path, however, entails basic needs implications. De Janvry (1981) argues that replacing foreign with domestic demand undermines the social articulation which is key to egalitarian development. It is important to observe that when aggregate demand is largely domestic in origin, capitalists are torn between the two faces of high wage rates: the pain of paying higher wages is partially offset by the increase in market demand. As a result, largely indigenous development is more likely to feature a pattern of private sector wage bargaining favorable to labor. It is also more likely to feature state tolerance of worker organization and state actions to encourage equality, all of which are thought to be favorable to basic needs attainment. Furthermore, trade that is concentrated in primary products, a frequent specialization among poorer Third World nations, is widely thought to be especially damaging to egalitarian development.

Finally, rapid growth is biased against the poor in an even more fundamental way: aggregate GNP growth contains a built-in bias which weights more heavily the gains among the rich than those among the poor (Chenery et al., 1974). Consider, for example, a hypothetical country with an income distribution typical of poor nations—the top 20% of the population earns about 50% of the income while the bottom 40% of the population earns about 10% of the income. Mathematically, there are a variety of ways to divide any given annual per capita gain in GNP, but some are much more likely than others. Observe that a 5% increase in GNP can be achieved by a gain of 10% in the income of the wealthiest quintile and constant income among the remainder of the population. Alternatively, if the poorest 40% of the population were to wholly account for such an increase it would require that their income increase by an improbable 50% per year. As a consequence, rapid increases in GNP are very unlikely to be driven by welfare gains among the poor. Indeed, the most rapidly growing nations are much more likely to have achieved that growth through income gains among the already wealthy.

Against these arguments, proponents of growth-centric approaches offer a simple but powerful empirical observation: basic needs levels are highest in those countries with the highest GNP per capita.[3] Thus, growth is necessary to basic needs improvements. And, if some growth is good, more must be better. Whereas GNP may not map directly and immediately to the welfare of the poor, trickle-down processes operate to elevate basic needs levels. At worst, orthodox theorists would grant that the delay implicit in trickle-down processes could produce a lag between GNP growth and basic needs improvements that only appears to resemble the distortion effects so worrisome to welfare-centrists. Thus, many liberals advance a "grow now, redistribute later" strategy built upon the assumptions that any distortions produced by rapid growth are relatively short-lived and relatively easily reversible.

More structurally oriented theorists, however, doubt that such an optimistic scenario is likely because distributional factors are self-reinforcing and difficult to undo. Most obviously, unequal incomes become embodied in possessions which cannot be easily redistributed. One Mercedes cannot be made into a thousand bicycles (Weaver and Jameson, 1981). Nor, even if it were possible, is it likely. It is here that the political economy perspective of welfare-centric theorists clashes most pointedly with liberal assumptions. The former insist that the liberal view misunderstands the mechanisms responsible for trickle-down effects. Whereas markets may distribute some welfare gains, most trickle-down processes are either directly imposed by states or strongly conditioned by the economic and political structures they maintain. For example, labor legislation which heavily influences the bargaining power of unions and firms decisively shapes the distribution of any gains in productive output. Redistributive taxation, social welfare programs, and the public provision of health and educational infrastructure are all important state-centered mechanisms of trickle-down.

Thus, the nature of the political order and the relative power of the actors that compete within it must be significant components of any judgments concerning the efficacy of trickle-down processes and the longevity of the distortions engendered by rapid growth. For this reason, political economists advocating equity as an immediate goal emphasize that inegalitarian economies yield inegalitarian social structures and conservative political structures. Vested interests that are strengthened by growth-centric approaches are highly resistant to redistribution; the cycle creates greater inequalities and at the same time greater capacity to resist reducing them. Thus, they contend that the compromises on basic needs required to achieve rapid growth are likely to be relatively enduring.

Streeten (1979) argues that the lags involved in alternative development strategies are relatively predictable and yield characteristic patterns. For example, a simple shift of resources from investment to consumption by the poor might maximize the short-term welfare of the poor while compromising long-term growth prospects. Thus, by the medium-term, the pure growth strategy, which entails major sacrifice for the poor in the short-term, overtakes the welfare strategy in providing mass welfare. Finally, a basic needs strategy, which diverts resources to *investment in* rather than *consumption of* the poor, achieves middling success in the short-term, underperforms both alternatives in the mid-term, but by virtue of achieving the most rapid long-term growth after an initial lag, eventually outperforms both. Unfortunately, it is not clear that Streeten's formulation is correct, nor is it obvious what lags may be involved even if it is. To adjudicate the two general alternatives requires answers to the critical questions initially posed above. First, does basic needs provision sacrifice future growth or encourage it? Second, does rapid growth yield proportional benefits to the poor? Let us now turn to that empirical evidence.

AN EMPIRICAL EXAMINATION
OF THE GROWTH-EQUITY TRADE-OFF

As made clear in previous sections, our interest in the growth-welfare trade-off focuses on the physical well-being of a nation's citizens. From a basic needs perspective, social welfare involves maximizing the distribution of such minimal standards of living as access to food, potable water, medical care, and education. Accordingly, an appropriate measure of welfare must be an objective indicator of life chances that is sensitive to both distributional variations and the status of the very poor (Hicks and Streeten, 1979). For this purpose we rely on the two most commonly used measures of basic needs satisfaction: life expectancy at age one and infant mortality rate per 1,000 live births. Like many others, we are attracted to these indicators because they are very widely available on a comparable basis, they are relatively immune to distributional distortions, and they gauge actual achievements rather than merely the potential for achievement, which is true of measures like calorie consumption or hospital beds. Our measures of these two needs indicators come from the World Bank (1989). We combine them into a single scale, following the procedure developed by Morris (1979), to construct the well-known Physical Quality of Life Index.[4]

We measure growth using estimates of real GDP per capita based on purchasing power parities rather than nominal GNP figures. These estimates are expressed in 1980 international prices (dollars) and have been adjusted to overcome the comparability problems associated with exchange rate irregularities and inflation. For details of the estimation procedure and the tables from which we obtained these data, see Summers and Heston (1988).

In this study we employ a panel design that enables us to compare changes in our indicators of basic needs fulfillment and economic growth across various time intervals. We estimate equations representing the two manifestations of the growth-equity trade-off separately, using OLS regression.[5] We have elected to examine change over three different time periods. The main analysis spans the period 1960 to 1985, the longest time period permitted by available data for a large group of countries. We have augmented that main analysis with two other decade-long periods at either end of the quarter-century. This should enable us to identify any conclusions that apply only to particular eras in world development and to check the robustness of our general findings. In particular, the 1975 to 1985 decade may be rather different from the earlier period since growth rates were negative for a substantial number of Third World nations in the early 1980s, possibly leading to a different pattern of trade-offs. Our sample consists of all 104 nations for which data are available for all variables at all time points [see original article, Appendix A–*Eds.*].

Does Greater Equity Produce Slower Growth?

We begin our investigation with the first of our two central research questions: does successful provision of basic human needs compromise subsequent economic growth? Following our discussion above, we are concerned both with the effect on growth of the *levels* of basic needs achievement and also with *improvements* in those levels. It is well known that the most productive societies also enjoy the highest levels of education, health, and nutrition, but we must go beyond these transparent associations to probe the less obvious connection between *growth* and basic needs attainment. We do this with a simple model of economic growth which takes account of real income levels, real domestic investment as a percentage of GDP, and our indicator of needs achievement at the beginning of each period.[6]

Three percentage growth rate measures calculated over the 1960–1985, 1975–1985, and 1960–1970 periods serve as dependent variables in the analysis presented in Table 10.1. Each model is made up of two control variables known to affect growth rates—previous GDP level and GDP share in domestic investment—and the basic needs measure which is the focal point of our analysis.[7] Taken together the three sets of regression estimates reveal that better basic needs performance is very clearly related to more rapid growth rates in the subsequent period. As expected, the overall fit of the model is greatest and the causal dynamics clearest when the analysis is conducted over the longest available interval. Still, growth is enhanced by prior basic needs performance even for the 1975–1985 decade, during which average growth was the slowest and the most variable across nations. It is important to note that these are partial estimates that hold constant the considerable effects of domestic investment and beginning income level. However, Table 10.1 reveals that the positive effect of basic needs achievement on subsequent economic growth is fully comparable in magnitude to the well-established effect of investment on growth.

There can be little doubt that provision of basic needs is an investment in human capital that pays genuine dividends in the form of enhanced

Table 10.1   Regression of Real Product Growth Rate on Beginning Product Level, Domestic Investment, and Basic Needs Performance, 1960–1985

	1960–1985	1960–1970	1975–1985
Basic Needs Performance$_{t1}$	.05	.02	.10
	(5.6)	(1.8)	(4.9)
In Real GDP per capita$_{t1}$	−1.33	−.53	−1.81
	(−5.3)	(−1.6)	(−3.8)
Domestic Investment Share of Real GDP$_{t1}$	.15	.16	.11
	(7.2)	(5.5)	(3.2)
Constant	5.76	2.56	5.43
	(4.1)	(1.3)	(2.3)
Adjusted R^2	.554	.333	.314
Standard Error of Estimate	1.31	1.79	2.25
F–ratio	43.6	18.1	16.7

Note: Entries in parentheses are t–ratios.

economic growth rates. But to claim that satisfaction of basic needs promotes growth, other things being equal, is not necessarily to claim that basic needs *improvements* promote growth. This rather subtle distinction lies at the heart of the alleged trade-off since the inefficiency that critics have in mind would arise most clearly when resources are diverted away from growth-producing uses to basic needs improvements. We cannot test this argument in any definitive way because we are unable to directly measure the shift of societal resources to the purpose of raising basic needs levels. We can take a less direct approach, however, simply by examining how observed gains in needs satisfactions relate to rates of growth.[8]

Results of this analysis appear in Table 10.2 in a format identical to that of Table 10.1 except for the introduction of a raw basic needs improvement measure (i.e., the simple difference) to each equation. We would interpret an inverse relationship between basic needs improvement and concurrent economic growth as supportive of the inefficiency argument outlined above because this would indicate that more rapid progress in basic needs provision is associated with slower growth rates. Table 10.2 shows that this is clearly not the case. All three change estimates are positive, with that for the quarter-century panel revealing a strong and statistically significant relationship between improvement and economic growth. Once again, we find no evidence of inefficiency effects; indeed, quite the reverse.

Unfortunately, the direct relationship we find between progress and growth does not completely preclude inefficiency effects since the observed estimates may be merely an artifact of the trickle-down process. That is, basic needs improvements may be a *consequence*, not the *cause*, of economic

Table 10.2   Regression of Real Product Growth Rate on Beginning Product Level, Domestic Investment, Basic Needs Performance, and Basic Needs Change, 1960–1985

	1960–1985	1960–1970	1975–1985
Basic Needs Change$_{t1-t2}$	.06	.09	.04
	(2.8)	(1.8)	(0.5)
Basic Needs Performance$_{t1}$	.08	.04	.11
	(6.2)	(2.5)	(4.9)
In Real GDP per capita$_{t1}$	−1.57	−.74	−1.83
	(−6.2)	(−2.1)	(−3.8)
Domestic Investment Share of Real GDP$_{t1}$	.13	.15	.11
	(5.8)	(5.0)	(3.0)
Constant	5.33	2.65	5.02
	(3.9)	(1.4)	(2.3)
Adjusted R^2	.584	.347	.309
Standard Error of Estimate	1.27	1.77	2.26
F–ratio	37.1	14.7	12.5

Note: Entries in parentheses are t–ratios.

growth. Our further analyses give us considerable reason to doubt this, however. It is important to remember that the trickle-down of social benefits is not usually thought to be coterminous with the growth from which it derives. Even the most ardent advocates of the trickle-down thesis concede some temporal lag before an expanding economy can extend its benefits to the poorest elements of society. Although the ten- and twenty-five-year periods displayed in Table 10.2 may be lengthy enough for at least some trickle-down to obscure trade-offs in inefficiency, we also examined five-year periods and in every case still found either a positive or null relationship between needs improvement and growth. Finally, when we make the intended causal lag even more explicit by regressing five- and ten-year growth rates on *previous* five- and ten-year improvement scores, we still see no sign of trade-off effects. In sum, our empirical examinations, like those of others before us, have uncovered no evidence of a trade-off between rapid improvements in basic needs provisions and the pace of national economic expansion.

Does Rapid Growth Sacrifice Equity?

Our analysis in the previous section is not meant to be a rejection of the trickle-down thesis so much as a qualification of its effects, for as we turn our attention to the welfare implications of rapid macro-economic growth, the efficacy of the trickle-down process now assumes center stage. We expect that economic growth will entail some beneficial effect since the single most powerful influence on cross-national differences in basic needs achievement is the aggregate level of economic wealth (Morris, 1979). Even among theorists who argue that rapid growth paths involve a trade-off with equity, most argue merely that the welfare of the poor increases much less rapidly than the aggregates. The stronger form of the argument—that GNP growth causes the welfare of the poor to decline in absolute terms—is only occasionally advanced as a general principle. For example, the famous and very influential debate over the "Brazilian miracle" pitted the radical position that the poor were actually harmed by rapid growth against the more common contention that benefits accruing to the poor are not nearly proportional to GNP growth (Fishlow, 1972, 1980; Fields, 1977).[9] Thus, whereas we expect that growth will be positively associated with basic needs satisfaction through its definitional relationship to higher income levels, we pose the more subtle question of whether growth rates have any independent effect of their own apart from the resulting level of income.

We address this question in Table 10.3 by regressing our indicator of basic needs achievement on real GDP per capita growth rates and a set of control variables that includes beginning levels of the basic needs index, logged per capita GDP, and their squares. Inclusion of a lagged dependent variable in these regressions means that the parameter estimates no longer apply to levels of basic needs but rather to the changes occurring during the growth period. This is the standard linear panel model, and like most panel regressions, the proportion of explained variance is both very high and largely uninteresting. With these controls in place, we see that GNP growth rates do predict improvement in basic needs levels, although the parameter estimates are not particularly robust in relation to their standard errors. Indeed, the estimate fails to exceed twice its standard error during the 1975–1985 period. Still, it seems reasonably clear from Table 10.3 that faster growth does lead, on average, to improved basic needs performance.

Recall, however, our intention to assess the effects of growth independent of the closely related effect of income. In fact, the analyses of Table 10.3 manage only to control for *beginning* income. Owing to the functional collinearity between GDP levels at two points and the percentage rate of GDP growth, we are unable to control for both beginning and ending income in a single estimating equation. Our way around this restriction utilizes the residuals from a prior auxiliary regression of basic needs attainment on GNP as a new dependent variable. That is, we create new measures of *relative* basic needs achievement already purged of contemporaneous income effects.[10] When measures of basic needs achievement are purged of income effects in this way, any variation that remains will represent the deviation from a level of achievement expected purely on the basis of aggregate income. Conceptually, such a residual

Table 10.3   Regression of Basic Needs Performance on Economic Growth, Lagged Basic Needs Performance, and Real GDP Per Capita, 1960–1985

	1960–1985	1960–1970	1975–1985
Average Annual Growth In Real GDP per capita$_{t1-t2}$	1.24 (4.7)	.41 (2.9)	.16 (1.6)
Basic Needs Performance$_{t1}$	1.08 (11.2)	1.21 (18.9)	1.14 (14.0)
Basic Needs Performance$^2_{t1}$	−.005 (−5.8)	−.004 (−6.5)	−.002 (−3.8)
In Real GDP per capita$_{t1}$	32.69 (4.2)	11.55 (2.2)	10.85 (2.5)
In Real GDP per capita$^2_{t1}$	−1.82 (−3.4)	−.57 (−1.6)	−.61 (−2.1)
Constant	−108.05 (−4.1)	−43.09 (−2.4)	−36.60 (−2.5)
Adjusted R^2	.961	.986	.989
Standard Error of Estimate	4.21	2.86	2.26
F–ratio	509.0	1444.2	1815.1

Note: Entries in parentheses are t–ratios.

measure carries a strong distributional component in the sense that deviations above the expected achievement level indicate a relatively more equitable distribution of social benefits than the prevailing international average (i.e., the average at each income level).

This residualized measure of basic needs deviations serves as the dependent variable in Table 10.4, although in all other respects these regressions are identical to those in Table 10.3. Let us be clear about the distinction between Tables 10.3 and 10.4—in the former we purge basic needs of income effects at the beginning of the growth period; in the latter we also control for income at the end of the period. The most striking feature of Table 10.4 must surely be the huge negative estimates that now appear for economic growth. What are we to make of these negative effects? In the first place, we do not want to portray these results as linking rapid growth rates to an absolute decline in basic needs fulfillment, only to gains that are far from proportional to the pace of economic growth.

Still, we may be observing distortion effects if rapid growth rates are obtained at the cost of foregone opportunities to improve basic needs standards even further. This opportunity-cost argument advanced by welfare-centric theorists is difficult to demonstrate empirically, although we can

Table 10.4   Regression of Relative Basic Needs Performance on Economic Growth, Lagged Basic Needs Performance, and Real GDP Per Capita, 1960–1985

	1960–1985	1960–1970	1975–1985
Average Annual Growth In Real GDP per capita$_{t1-t2}$	−2.96 (−11.10)	−1.64 (−11.50)	−1.53 (−15.70)
Basic Needs Performance$_{t1}$	1.08 (11.2)	1.21 (19.0)	1.14 (14.0)
Basic Needs Performance$^2_{t1}$	−.005 (−5.8)	−.004 (−6.5)	−.002 (−3.8)
In Real GDP per capita$_{t1}$	15.88 (2.1)	−8.93 (−1.7)	−5.96 (−1.4)
In Real GDP per capita$^2_{t1}$	−1.82 (−3.4)	−.57 (−1.6)	−.61 (−2.1)
Constant	−52.71 (−2.0)	47.40 (2.6)	18.74 (1.3)
Adjusted R^2	.754	.941	.929
Standard Error of Estimate	4.21	2.86	2.26
F–ratio	64.0	327.2	270.5

Note: Entries in parentheses are t–ratios.

investigate the chief rival to this interpretation. That rival explanation, which is implied by growth-centric conceptions of the process, is based on extended trickle-down effects. According to this interpretation, the negative effects of growth apparently portrayed in Table 10.4 may be merely an artifact of aggregate growth overtaking the generally more sluggish basic needs measures, primarily due to the temporal lag that intervenes between growth and the eventual trickle-down of benefits. If this interpretation is correct, a model incorporating the proper lag structure should be able to detect a dampening of the effects over time.

We test this idea with the analyses in Table 10.5. Here we replicate the regressions in the first column of Table 10.4, except that we break apart the average twenty-five year growth rate into five half-decade growth rates. If the negative effects seen above are merely a reflection of a slow trickle-down process, we would expect negative parameter estimates to be largest for the most recent half-decade and smallest for the most distant one. For example, if the growth between 1960 and 1965 had "trickled down" to basic needs gains by 1985, the negative parameter estimate for growth during this earliest period should disappear. If, by contrast, the negative effect remains, we would be forced to doubt that the results of Table 10.4 could be attributed largely to a temporal lag.

Table 10.5   Regression of Relative Basic Needs Performance on Five-Year Growth Rates, Lagged Basic Needs Performance, and Real GDP Per Capita, 1960–1985

Average Annual Real Growth$_{1960-1965}$	−.37 (−2.6)
Average Annual Real Growth$_{1965-1970}$	−.63 (−3.5)
Average Annual Real Growth$_{1970-1975}$	−.72 (−4.9)
Average Annual Real Growth$_{1975-1980}$	−.45 (−2.9)
Average Annual Real Growth$_{1980-1985}$	−.81 (−5.4)
Basic Needs Performance$_{1960}$	1.12 (11.4)
Basic Needs Performance$^2{}_{1960}$	−.005 (−6.0)
In Real GDP per capita$_{1960}$	12.05 (1.5)
In Real GDP per capita$^2{}_{1960}$	−1.61 (−2.9)
Constant	−38.82 (−1.4)
Adjusted R^2	.756
Standard Error of Estimate	4.19
F–ratio	36.4

Note: Entries in parentheses are t–ratios.

Although the 1960–1965 growth effect in Table 10.5 is the smallest of those observed, the considerable fluctuation in the estimates belies any systematic trajectory of decline. Certainly, the estimates for the earliest periods do not appear to be moving toward zero. Indeed, an F test establishes that we cannot reject the null hypothesis that the true parameters representing each half-decade are identical to one another.[11] Thus, we must conclude either that the effects of trickle-down are even longer than the twenty-five-year period examined here, or that there exists a real trade-off between rapid growth rates and basic needs, perhaps attributable to distortion effects identified by welfare-centric theorists.

CONCLUSION

Let us now summarize our findings concerning the two alleged trade-offs. There is no evidence for the orthodox view that either basic needs fulfillment or improvements in basic needs provision compromise future growth. To the contrary, the contention originating in human capital theory that nations that provide for superior basic needs attainment will exhibit more rapid long-term growth is dramatically sustained. Thus, achieving basic needs successes does not preclude outstanding economic performance defined more conventionally; instead, there exists a complementarity in which the achievement of welfare goals helps in the later achievement of growth goals via the mechanism of human capital investment.

The reverse sequencing offers a more complex picture. Rapid growth rates do not so obviously produce basic needs benefits for the poor. It is clear that short-term growth does produce relatively modest improvements in basic needs levels overall, but the gains appear disproportional to income growth. Indeed, the basic needs performance relative to GDP of fast-growing nations is starkly poorer than that of their slower growing counterparts.

At a minimum, this implies that trickle-down processes are slow or incomplete, but our analysis suggests much more. Since there is no evidence that the relative underperformance of these nations diminishes at all during the quarter-century time period of our study, we must conclude that if trickle-down occurs, it must be very slow indeed. It seems likely that the explanation lies with the type of development that is capable of these large short-term GDP changes. What is involved is not merely the speed but the shape of development; that is, there appears to be a trade-off involving distortion effects. Unfortunately, it is beyond the capacity of this study to more fully elaborate or to more directly test this intriguing interpretation. It is especially interesting to us that the findings of this study are not contingent on the particular time period under examination. Despite marked changes in the global economy—overall growth rates, dominant paradigms of development, shifting rosters of successful and unsuccessful nations, etc.— the fundamental trade-offs and complementarities remain enduring patterns of development.

On the basis of these findings, then, what can we say about the desirability of alternative development plans? Even from the relatively narrow standpoint of basic needs provision, there are limits to our analysis. First, although basic needs attainment speeds subsequent growth, we are not in a position to evaluate choices between investment in human capital and investment in other forms of capital. We have no clear idea of what level of investment in human capital is required to raise basic needs levels, or even of what form it should take. Consequently, we cannot easily interpret the size of the coefficient that shows how large a growth gain follows from each unit of basic needs provision. Whether a basic needs focus will produce faster subsequent growth depends on the impact not only of basic needs attainment on growth but of basic needs effort on basic needs attainment. We have established only that a basic needs orientation is not self-defeating; we have not established that it is a preferred option.

Second, we do not know how long the distortion resulting from rapid economic growth lasts. If that distortion is very long-lasting, growth may yield permanent changes in the structure of the political economy that will doom a nation to perpetual underperformance in basic needs. Indeed, it is possible to construct a model in which rapid growth in the short-term implies slower long-term growth via diminished basic needs performance. That is, rapid growth strategies may be self-defeating even by their own standards. We cannot say whether this is likely or not, but we can say that the possibility demands much greater attention to potential distortion effects, even though the other half of our study suggests that inefficiency effects need not be regarded as a serious impediment to basic needs-oriented development.

NOTES

1. Engels' curves describe the relationship between income level and the percentage of income devoted to wage goods, especially food. The elasticity for food is around .8 for the poorest countries as a whole (Griffin and James, 1981:16) whereas among the poorest strata it is nearly unity. Generally consumption of wage goods—especially food—is thought to make a greater contribution to basic needs attainment than any alternative use of private income.

2. Furthermore, not only is growth more rapid when measured in GNP terms, it is also likely to be more conducive to further welfare improvements. Human capital investment that improves the quality and productivity of labor will encourage labor-intensive industrialization which typically increases employment levels and relative wage rates, both associated with basic needs improvements.

3. The cross-sectional correlation between measures of national product and measures of basic needs varies between about .5 and .75, depending on the measures, the sample, the year, and the study (Morris, 1979; Moon and Dixon, 1985; Stewart, 1985; Moon, 1991).

4. Each indicator is placed on a 0 to 100 scale, anchored on one end by the worst performance since 1950 (229 deaths per thousand for infant mortality and 39 for life expectancy) and on the other by the maximum thought feasible in this century (7 per thousand and 77, respectively). Our basic needs indicator is the arithmetic mean of the two scales. Alternative indicators and indexes are discussed at length in Moon (1991); no significant differences attributable to our choice of indicators have been found in any of the dozen of analyses of determinants of basic needs performance. All analyses performed with the index have been replicated using the raw indicators.

5. Possible violations of OLS assumptions and appropriate remedial measures are discussed in Moon and Dixon, 1992, Appendix B.

6. The data for real gross domestic investment is taken from Summers and Heston (1988). To minimize the impact of yearly fluctuations, it is computed as an average of the value over the first five years of each period.

7. Over the postwar period, GDP growth expressed as a percentage of previous GDP has been highest among nations at lower levels of income. Sometimes this relationship is slightly curvilinear, but in these analyses the squared term is not statistically significant and is thus omitted in the reported results.

8. By measuring change in both the independent and dependent variables over the same time period, this design risks simultaneity bias in the parameter estimates which might exaggerate the real effect. Worse yet, it could cause us to misunderstand the direction of causality implied by these results. See the discussion of the two-stage least squares estimation process in Moon and Dixon, 1992, Appendix B for the explanation of why we think that is not the case here.

9. Unfortunately, our method of operationalization cannot easily adjudicate these positions, although we can offer some evidence. The problem is that although our basic needs indicators are especially sensitive to the poor and strongly affected by distribution, they still remain aggregate measures. Improvements in average life expectancies, for example, need not imply that life expectancies among the poor are improving.

10. The auxiliary regression for 1985 produces a constant of -55.3 and a slope estimate on logged GDP per capita of 16.8 with an R^2 of .84; the comparable figures for 1970 are -90.5 and 20.5 with an R^2 of .76.

11. The same result obtains if the analysis covers only the 1960 to 1980 period. Thus, no time period effects appear to be responsible for this finding.

REFERENCES

Adelman, I. 1986. "A Poverty-Focused Approach to Development Policy." In *Development Strategies Reconsidered*, ed. J. P. Lewis and V. Kallab. New Brunswick, NJ: Transaction.

Ayres, R. I. 1983. *Banking on the Poor*. Cambridge, MA: MIT Press.

Bauer, P. T. 1972. *Dissent on Development: Studies and Debates on Development Economics*. Cambridge, MA: Harvard University Press.

———. 1984. *Reality and Rhetoric: Studies in the Economics of Development*. Cambridge, MA: Harvard University Press.

Biersteker, T. J. 1978. *Distortion or Development? Contending Perspectives on the Multinational Corporation*. Cambridge, MA: MIT Press.

Bornschier V. and C. Chase-Dunn, 1985. *Transnational Corporations and Underdevelopment*. New York: Praeger Publishers.

Chenery, H., et al., 1974. *Redistribution with Growth*. London: Oxford University Press.

Collins, S., and W. Park, 1989. "External Debt and Macroeconomic Performance in South Korea." In *Developing Country Debt and Economic Performance*, Vol. 3, ed. by J. Sachs and S. Collins. Chicago: University of Chicago Press.

Cornia, G., R. Jolly, and F. Stewart, 1987. *Adjustment with a Human Face*. Oxford: Clarendon Press.

De Janvry, A. 1981. *The Agrarian Question and Reformism in Latin America*. Baltimore: Johns Hopkins University Press.

Dixon W. and B. Moon. 1989. "Domestic Political Conflict and Basic Needs Outcomes: An Empirical Assessment." *Comparative Political Studies* 22: 178–198.

Dreze, J. and A. Sen, 1989. *Hunger and Public Action*. New York: Oxford University Press.

Evans, P. 1979. *Dependent Development: The Alliance of Multinational, State and Local Capital in Brazil*. Princeton, NJ: Princeton University Press.

Fei, J., G. Ranis, and S. Kuo, 1979. *Growth with Equity: The Taiwan Case*. New York: Oxford University Press.

Fields, G. S. 1977. "Who Benefits from Economic Development?: A Re-Examination of Brazilian Growth in the 1960s." *American Economic Review* 67:570–582.

Fishlow, A. 1972. "Brazilian Size Distribution of Income." *American Economic Review* 62:391-402.

———. 1980. "Who Benefits from Economic Development?: Comment." *American Economic Review* 70:250–259.

Griffin, K. 1981. *Land Concentration and World Poverty*. 2nd ed. New York: Holmes and Meier.

———. 1989. *Alternative Strategies for Economic Development*. London: MacMillan Press.

Griffin K., and J. James, 1981. *The Transition to Egalitarian Development: Economic Policies for Structural Change in the Third World*. New York: St. Martin's Press.

Haggard, S. 1990. *Pathways from the Periphery: The Politics of Growth in the Newly Industrializing Countries*. Ithaca, NY: Cornell University Press.

Hicks, N. 1979. "Growth versus Basic Needs: Is There a Trade-off?" *World Development* 7:985-994.

Hicks N. and P. Streeten, 1979. "Indicators of Development: The Search for a Basic Needs Yardstick." *World Development* 7:567–580.

Hoadley, J. S. 1981. "The Rise and Fall of the Basic Needs Approach." *Cooperation and Conflict* 16:149–164.

International Labour Office. 1970. *Towards Full Employment: A Programme for Colombia*. Geneva. New York: Praeger Publishers.

———. 1977. *Employment, Growth, and Basic Needs: A One-World Problem*. New York: Praeger.

Johnson, H. 1967. *Economic Policies Toward Less-Developed Countries*. Washington, D.C.: Brookings Institution.

Lal, D. 1985. *The Poverty of "Development Economics."* Cambridge, MA: Harvard University.

Lipton, M. 1977. *Why Poor People Stay Poor: Urban Bias in World Development*. London: Temple Smith.

———. 1988. "The Poor and the Poorest: Some Interim Findings." *World Bank Discussion Paper 25*.

Moon, B. 1991. *The Political Economy of Basic Human Needs*. Ithaca, NY: Cornell University Press.

Moon B., and W. Dixon, 1985. "Politics, the State, and Basic Human Needs: A Cross-National Study." *American Journal of Political Science* 29: 661–694.

Morris, M.D. 1979. *Measuring the Condition of the World's Poor: The Physical Quality of Life Index*. New York: Pergamon Press.

Muller, E. 1985. "Income Inequality, Regime Repressiveness, and Political Violence." *American Sociological Review* 50:47–61.

Okun, A. M. 1976. "Equality and Efficiency: The Big Trade-off." *New York Times Magazine*, July 4.

Psacharopoulos, G. 1985. *Returns to Education: A Further International Update and Implications*. Washington, D.C.: World Bank.

Rao Maturu, N. 1979. "Nutrition and Labour Productivity." *International Labour Review* 118, 1:1–12.

Seers, D. 1969. "The Meaning of Development." *International Development Review* 11:2–6.

Stewart, P. 1985. *Basic Needs in Developing Countries*. Baltimore: Johns Hopkins University Press.

————. 1987. "Supporting Productive Employment among Vulnerable Groups." In G. Cornia, R. Jolly, and F. Stewart, *Adjustment with a Human Face*. Oxford: Clarendon Press.

Streeten P. et al., 1979. "A Basic Needs Approach to Economic Development." In *Directions in Economic Development*, ed., K. Jameson and C. Wilber. Notre Dame, IN: University of Notre Dame Press.

————. 1981. *First Things First: Meeting Basic Needs in Developing Countries*. World Bank: Oxford University Press.

Summers R., and A. Heston. 1988. "A New Set of International Comparisons of Real Product and Prices: Estimates for 130 Countries, 1950–1985." *The Review of Income and Wealth* (March):1–25.

Taylor, L. 1989. *Varieties of Stabilization Experience*. Oxford: Clarendon Press.

Weaver, J. and K. Jameson, 1981. *Economic Development: Competing Paradigms*. Lanham, MD: University Press of America.

Wheeler, D. 1980. "Basic Needs Fulfillment and Economic Growth: A Simultaneous Model." *Journal of Development Economics* 7, 4:435–451.

World Bank. 1980, 1983, 1987, 1988, 1990. *World Development Report*. New York: Oxford University Press.

World Bank. 1988. *World Tables of Economic and Social Indicators, 1950–1987*. Baltimore: Johns Hopkins University Press.

PART 3

Culture, Modernization, and Development

11

·······

The Achievement Motive
in Economic Growth

·······

David C. McClelland

In this chapter, David C. McClelland, a psychologist, expands upon ideas developed by Max Weber, who examined the relationship between the Protestant ethic and the rise of capitalism. McClelland posits a more generalized psychological attribute he calls the "need for Achievement," or n Achievement. In this discussion, which is a summary of a book on the subject, McClelland presents some very interesting historical data he believes help explain the rise and decline of Athenian civilization. Turning to the present century, he produces data that show a close association between national levels of n Achievement and rates of economic growth. In seeking to determine what produces this psychological characteristic, McClelland finds that it is not hereditary but rather is instilled in people. It is therefore possible, he claims, to teach people how to increase their need to achieve and by so doing stimulate economic growth in developing countries. McClelland has been responsible for establishing training and management programs in developing countries in hopes that a change in the psychological orientation of public officials will help speed economic growth.

From the beginning of recorded history, men have been fascinated by the fact that civilizations rise and fall. Culture growth, as A. L. Kroeber has demonstrated, is episodic, and sometimes occurs in quite different fields.[1] For example, the people living in the Italian peninsula at the time of ancient Rome produced a great civilization of law, politics, and military conquest;

Reprinted with permission of UNESCO from *Industrialization and Society*, edited by Bert F. Hoselitz and Wilbert E. Moore, pp. 74–95. Paris: UNESCO, 1968.

and at another time, during the Renaissance, the inhabitants of Italy produced a great civilization of art, music, letters, and science. What can account for such cultural flowerings? In our time we have theorists like Ellsworth Huntington, who stresses the importance of climate, or Arnold J. Toynbee, who also feels the right amount of challenge from the environment is crucial though he conceives of the environment as including its psychic effects. Others, like Kroeber, have difficulty imagining any general explanation; they perforce must accept the notion that a particular culture happens to hit on a particularly happy mode of self-expression, which it then pursues until it becomes overspecialized and sterile.

My concern is not with all culture growth, but with economic growth. Some wealth or leisure may be essential to development in other fields—the arts, politics, science, or war—but we need not insist on it. However, the question of why some countries develop rapidly in the economic sphere at certain times and not at others is in itself of great interest, whatever its relation to other types of culture growth. Usually, rapid economic growth has been explained in terms of "external" factors—favorable opportunities for trade, unusual natural resources, or conquests that have opened up new markets or produced internal political stability. But I am interested in the *internal* factors—in the values and motives men have that lead them to exploit opportunities, to take advantage of favorable trade conditions; in short, to shape their own destiny. . . .

Whatever else one thinks of Freud and the other psychoanalysts, they performed one extremely important service for psychology: once and for all, they persuaded us, rightly or wrongly, that what people said about their motives was not a reliable basis for determining what those motives really were. In his analyses of the psychopathology of everyday life and of dreams and neurotic symptoms, Freud demonstrated repeatedly that the "obvious" motives—the motives that the people themselves thought they had or that a reasonable observer would attribute to them—were not, in fact, the real motives for their often strange behavior. By the same token, Freud also showed the way to a better method of learning what people's motives were. He analyzed dreams and free associations: in short, fantasy or imaginative behavior. Stripped of its air of mystery and the occult, psychoanalysis has taught us that one can learn a great deal about people's motives through observing the things about which they are spontaneously concerned in their dreams and waking fantasies. About ten or twelve years ago, the research group in America with which I was connected decided to take this insight quite seriously and to see what we could learn about human motivation by coding objectively what people spontaneously thought about in their waking fantasies.[2] Our method was to collect such free fantasy, in the form of brief stories written about pictures, and to count the frequency with which certain themes appeared—rather as a medical technician counts the frequency with which red or white corpuscles appear in a blood sample. We were able to demonstrate that the frequency with which certain "inner concerns" appeared in these fantasies varied systematically as a function of specific experimental conditions by which we aroused or induced motivational states in the subjects. Eventually we were able to isolate several of these inner concerns, or motives, which, if present in great frequency in the fantasies of a particular person, enabled us to know something about how he would behave in many other areas of life.

Chief among these motives was what we termed "the need for Achievement" (*n* Achievement)—a desire to do well, not so much for the sake of social recognition or prestige, but to attain an inner feeling of personal accomplishment. This motive is my particular concern in this chapter. Our early laboratory studies showed that people "high" in *n* Achievement tend to work harder at certain tasks; to learn faster; to do their best work when it counts for the record, and not when special incentives, like money prizes, are introduced; to choose experts over friends as working partners; etc. Obviously, we cannot here review the many, many studies in this area. About five years ago, we became especially interested in the problem of what would happen in a society if a large number of people with a high need for achievement should happen to be present in it at a particular time. In other words, we became interested in a social-psychological question: What effect would a concentration of people with high *n* Achievement have on a society?

It might be relevant to describe how we began wondering about this. I had always been greatly impressed by the very perceptive analysis of the connection between Protestantism and the spirit of capitalism made by the great German sociologist, Max Weber.[3] He argues that the distinguishing characteristic of Protestant business entrepreneurs and of workers, particularly from the pietistic sects, was not that they had in any sense invented the institutions of capitalism or good craftsmanship, but that they went about their jobs with a new perfectionist spirit. The Calvinistic doctrine of predestination had forced them to rationalize every aspect of their lives and to strive hard for perfection in the positions in this world to which they had been assigned by God. As I read Weber's description of the behavior of these people, I concluded that they must certainly have had a high level of *n* Achievement. Perhaps the new spirit of capitalism Weber describes was none other than a high need for achievement—if so, then *n* Achievement has been responsible, in part, for the extraordinary economic development of the West. Another factor served to confirm this hypothesis. A careful study by M. R. Winterbottom had shown that boys with high *n* Achievement usually came from families in which the mothers stressed early self-reliance and mastery.[4] The boys whose mothers did not encourage their early self-reliance, or did not set such high standards of excellence, tended to develop lower need for achievement. Obviously, one of the key characteristics of the Protestant Reformation was its emphasis on self-reliance. Luther stressed the "priesthood of all believers" and translated the Bible so that every man could have direct access to God and religious thought. Calvin accentuated a rationalized perfection in this life for everyone. Certainly, the character of the Reformation seems to have set the stage, historically, for parents to encourage their children to attain earlier self-reliance and achievement. If the parents did in fact do so, they very possibly unintentionally produced the higher level of *n* Achievement in their children that was, in turn, responsible for the new spirit of capitalism.

This was the hypothesis that initiated our research. It was, of course, only a promising idea; much work was necessary to determine its validity. Very early in our studies, we decided that the events Weber discusses were probably only a special case of a much more general phenomenon—that it was *n* Achievement as such that was connected with economic development, and that the Protestant Reformation was connected only indirectly in the extent to which it had influenced the average *n* Achievement level of its adherents. If this assumption is correct, then a high average level of *n* Achievement should be equally associated with economic development in ancient Greece, in modern Japan, or in a preliterate tribe being studied by anthropologists in the South Pacific. In other words, in its most general form, the hypothesis attempts to isolate one of the key factors in the economic development, at least, of all civilizations. What evidence do we have that this extremely broad generalization will obtain? By now, a great deal has been collected—far more than I can summarize here; but I shall try to give a few key examples of the different types of evidence.

First, we have made historical studies. To do so, we had to find a way to obtain a measure of *n* Achievement level during time periods other than our own, whose individuals can no longer be tested. We have done this—instead of coding the brief stories written by an individual for a test, we code imaginative literary documents: poetry, drama, funeral orations, letters written by sea captains, epics, etc. Ancient Greece, which we studied first, supplies a good illustration. We are able to find literary documents written during three different historical periods and dealing with similar themes: the period of economic growth, 900 B.C.–475 B.C. (largely Homer and Hesiod); the period of climax, 475 B.C.–362 B.C.; and the period of decline, 362 B.C.–100 B.C. Thus, Hesiod wrote on farm and estate management in the early period; Xenophon, in the middle period; and Aristotle, in the late period. We have defined the period of "climax" in economic, rather than in cultural, terms, because it would be presumptuous to claim, for example, that Aristotle in any sense represented a "decline" from Plato or Thales. The measure of economic growth was computed from information supplied by F. Heichelheim in his *Wirtschaftsgeschichte des Altertums*.[5] Heichelheim records in detail the locations throughout Europe where the remains of Greek vases from different centuries have been found. Of course, these vases were the principal instrument of Greek foreign trade, since they were the containers for olive oil and wine, which were the most important Greek exports.

Knowing where the vase fragments have been found, we could compute the trade area of Athenian Greece for different time periods. We purposely omitted any consideration of the later expansion of Hellenistic Greece, because this represents another civilization; our concern was Athenian Greece.

When all the documents had been coded, they demonstrated—as predicted—that the level of n Achievement was highest during the period of growth prior to the climax of economic development in Athenian Greece. (See Figure 11.1.) In other words, the maximum n Achievement level preceded the maximum economic level by at least a century. Furthermore, that high level had fallen off by the time of maximum prosperity, thus foreshadowing subsequent economic decline. A similar methodology was

Figure 11.1 Average n Achievement Level (plotted at midpoints of periods of growth, climax, and decline of Athenian civilization as reflected in the extent of her trade area)

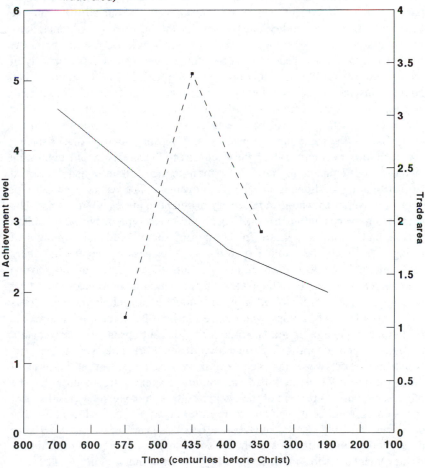

Note: Trade area measured for the sixth, fifth, and fourth centuries B.C. only.

applied, with the same results, to the economic development of Spain in the sixteenth century[6] and to two waves of economic development in the history of England (one in the late sixteenth century and the other at the beginning of the industrial revolution, around 1800).[7] The n Achievement level in English history (as determined on the basis of dramas, sea captains' letters, and street ballads) rose, between 1400–1800, *twice*, a generation or two before waves of accelerated economic growth (incidentally, at times of Protestant revival). This point is significant because it shows that there is no "necessary" steady decline in a civilization's entrepreneurial energy from its earlier to its later periods. In the Spanish and English cases, as in the Greek, high levels of n Achievement preceded economic decline. Unfortunately, space limitations preclude more detailed discussion of these studies here.

We also tested the hypothesis by applying it to preliterate cultures of the sort that anthropologists investigate. At Yale University, an organized effort has been made to collect everything that is known about all the primitive tribes that have been studied and to classify the information systematically for comparative purposes. We utilized this cross-cultural file to obtain the two measures that we needed to test our general hypothesis. For over fifty of these cultures, collections of folk tales existed that I. L. Child and others had coded,[8] just as we coded literary documents and individual imaginative stories, for n Achievement and other motives. These folk tales have the character of fantasy that we believe to be so essential for getting at "inner concerns." In the meantime, we were searching for a method of classifying the economic development of these cultures, so that we could determine whether those evincing high n Achievement in their folk tales had developed further than those showing lower n Achievement. The respective modes of gaining a livelihood were naturally very different in these cultures, since they came from every continent in the world and every type of physical habitat; yet we had to find a measure for comparing them. We finally thought of trying to estimate the number of full-time "business entrepreneurs" there were among the adults in each culture. We defined "entrepreneur" as "anyone who exercises control over the means of production and produces more than he can consume in order to sell it for individual or household income." Thus an entrepreneur was anyone who derived at least 75 percent of his income from such exchange or market practices. The entrepreneurs were mostly traders, independent artisans, or operators of small firms like stores, inns, etc. Nineteen cultures were classified as high in n Achievement on the basis of their folk tales; 74 percent of them contained some entrepreneurs. On the other hand, only 35 percent of the twenty cultures that were classified as low in n Achievement contained any entrepreneurs (as we defined it) at all. The difference is highly significant statistically (Chi square = 5.97, p<.02). Hence data about primitive tribes seem to confirm the hypothesis that high n Achievement leads to a more advanced type of economic activity.

But what about modern nations? Can we estimate their level of n

Achievement and relate it to their economic development? The question is obviously one of the greatest importance, but the technical problems of getting measures of our two variables proved to be really formidable. What type of literary document could we use that would be equally representative of the motivational levels of people in India, Japan, Portugal, Germany, the United States, and Italy? We had discovered in our historical studies that certain types of literature usually contain much more achievement imagery than others. This is not too serious as long as we are dealing with time changes within a given culture; but it is very serious if we want to compare two cultures, each of which may express its achievement motivation in a different literary form. At last, we decided to use children's stories, for several reasons. They exist in standard form in every modern nation, since all modern nations are involved in teaching their children to read and use brief stories for this purpose. Furthermore, the stories are imaginative; and, if selected from those used in the earliest grades, they are not often influenced by temporary political events. (We were most impressed by this when reading the stories that every Russian child reads. In general, they cannot be distinguished, in style and content, from the stories read in all the countries of the West.)

We collected children's readers for the second, third, and fourth grades from every country where they could be found for two time periods, which were roughly centered around 1925 and around 1950. We got some thirteen hundred stories, which were all translated into English. In all, we had twenty-one stories from each of twenty-three countries about 1925, and the same number from each of thirty-nine countries about 1950. Code was used on proper names, so that our scorers would not know the national origins of the stories. The tales were then mixed together, and coded for n Achievement (and certain other motives and values that I shall mention only briefly).

The next task was to find a measure of economic development. Again, the problem was to insure comparability. Some countries have much greater natural resources; some have developed industrially sooner than others; some concentrate in one area of production and some in another. Economists consider national income figures in per capita terms to be the best measure available; but they are difficult to obtain for all countries, and it is hard to translate them into equal purchasing power. Ultimately, we came to rely chiefly on the measure of electricity produced: the units of measurement are the same all over the world; the figures are available from the 1920s on; and electricity is the *form* of energy (regardless of how it is produced) that is essential to modern economic development. In fact, electricity produced per capita correlates with estimates of income per capita in the 1950s around .90 anyway. To equate for differences in natural resources, such as the amount of water power available, etc., we studied *gains* in kilowatt hours produced per capita between 1925 and 1950. The level of electrical production in 1925 is, as one would expect, highly correlated with the size of the gain between then and 1950. So it was necessary to resort to a regression analysis; that is, to calculate, from the average regression of gain on level for all countries, how much gain a particular country should have shown between 1925 and 1950. The actual gain could then be compared with the expected gain, and the country could be classified as gaining more or less rapidly than would have been expected on the basis of its 1925 performance. The procedure is directly comparable to what we do when we predict, on the basis of some measure of I.Q., what grades a child can be expected to get in school, and then classify him as an "under-" or "over-achiever."

The correlation between the n Achievement level in the children's readers in 1925 and the growth in electrical output between 1925 and 1950, as compared with expectation, is a quite substantial .53, which is highly significant statistically. It could hardly have arisen by chance. Furthermore, the correlation is also substantial with a measure of gain over the expected in per capita income, equated for purchasing power by Colin Clark. To check this result more definitively with the sample of forty countries for which we had reader estimates of n Achievement levels in 1950, we computed the equation for gains in electrical output in 1952–58 as a function of level in 1952. It turned out to be remarkably linear when translated into logarithmic units, as is so often the case with simple growth functions. Table 11.1 presents the performance of each of the countries, as compared with predictions from initial level in 1952, in standard score units and classified by high and low n Achievement in 1950. Once again we found that n Achievement levels predicted significantly ($r = .43$) the countries which would perform more or less rapidly than expected in terms of the average for all countries. The finding is more striking than the earlier one, because many Communist and underdeveloped countries are included in the sample. Apparently, n Achievement is a precursor of economic growth—and not only in the Western style of capitalism based on the small entrepreneur, but also in economies controlled and fostered largely by the state.

For those who believe in economic determinism, it is especially interesting that n Achievement level in 1950 is *not* correlated either with *previous* economic growth between 1925 and 1950, or with the level of prosperity in 1950. This strongly suggests that n Achievement is a *causative* factor— a change in the minds of men which produces economic growth rather than being produced by it. In a century dominated by economic determinism, in both Communist and Western thought, it is startling to find concrete evidence for psychological determinism, for psychological developments as preceding and presumably causing economic changes.

The many interesting results which our study of children's stories yielded have succeeded in convincing me that we chose the right material to analyze. Apparently, adults unconsciously flavor their stories for young children with the attitudes, the aspirations, the values, and the motives that they hold to be most important.

Table 11.1   Rate of Growth in Electrical Output (1952–1958) and National n Achievement Levels in 1950

Above Expectation Growth Rate			Below Expectation Growth Rate		
National n Achievement levels (1950)[1]	Country	Deviation From Expected Growth Rate[2]	National n Achievement Levels (1950)[1]	Country	Deviations From Expected Growth Rate[2]
High n Achievement Countries					
3.62	Turkey	+1.38			
2.71	India[3]	+1.12			
2.38	Australia	+0.42			
2.32	Israel	+1.18			
2.33	Spain	+0.01			
2.29	Pakistan[4]	+2.75			
2.29	Greece	+1.18	3.38	Argentina	−0.56
2.29	Canada	+0.08	2.71	Lebanon	−0.67
2.24	Bulgaria	+1.37	2.38	France	−0.24
2.24	U.S.A.	+0.47	2.33	South Africa	−0.06
2.14	West Germany	+0.53	2.29	Ireland	−0.41
2.10	U.S.S.R.	+1.61	2.14	Tunisia	−1.87
2.10	Portugal	+0.76	2.10	Syria	−0.25
Low n Achievement Countries					
1.95	Iraq	+0.29	2.05	New Zealand	−0.29
1.86	Austria	+0.38	1.86	Uruguay	−0.75
1.67	U.K.	+0.17	1.81	Hungary	−0.62
1.57	Mexico	+0.12	1.71	Norway	−0.77
0.86	Poland	+1.26	1.62	Sweden	−0.64
			1.52	Finland	−0.08
			1.48	Netherlands	−0.15
			1.33	Italy	−0.57
			1.29	Japan	−0.04
			1.20	Switzerland[5]	−1.92
			1.19	Chile	−1.81
			1.05	Denmark	−0.89
			0.57	Algeria	−0.83
			0.43	Belgium	−1.65

Note: Correlation of n Achievement level (1950) x deviations from expected growth rate = .43, $p < .01$.

1. Deviations in standard score units. The estimates are computed from the monthly average electrical production figures, in millions Kwh, for 1952 and 1958, from United Nations, *Monthly Bulletin of Statistics* (January, 1960), and *World Energy Supplies*, 1951–1954 and 1955–1958, (Statistical Papers, Series 3). The correlation between log level 1952 and log gain 1952–1958 is .976. The regression equation based on these thirty-nine countries, plus four others from the same climatic zone on which data are available (China-Taiwan, Czechoslovakia, Rumania, Yugoslavia), is: log gain (1952–1958) = .9229 log level (1952) + .0480. Standard scores deviations from mean gain predicted by the regression formula (M = -.01831) divided by the standard deviation of the deviations from the mean predicted gain (SD = .159).

2. Based on twenty-one children's stories from second-, third-, and fourth-grade readers in each country.

3. Based on six Hindi, seven Telegu, and eight Tamil stories.

4. Based on twelve Urdu and eleven Bengali stories.

5. Based on twenty-one German Swiss stories, mean = .91; twenty-one French Swiss stories, mean = 1.71; overall mean obtained by weighting German mean double to give approximately proportionate representation of the two main ethnic populations.

I want to mention briefly two other findings, one concerned with economic development, the other with totalitarianism. When the more and less rapidly developing economies are compared on all the other variables for which we scored the children's stories, one fact stands out. In stories from those countries which had developed more rapidly in both the earlier and later periods, there was a discernible tendency to emphasize, in 1925 and in 1950, what David Riesman has called "other-directedness"—namely, reliance on the opinion of particular others, rather than on tradition, for guidance in social behavior.[9] *Public opinion* had, in these countries, become a major source of guidance for the individual. Those countries which had developed the mass media further and faster—the press, the radio, the public-address system— were also the ones who were developing more rapidly economically. I think that "other-directedness" helped these countries to develop more rapidly because public opinion is basically more flexible than institutionalized moral or social traditions. Authorities can utilize it to inform people widely about the need for new ways of doing things. However, traditional institutionalized values may insist that people go on behaving in ways that are no longer adaptive to a changed social and economic order.

The other finding is not directly relevant to economic development, but it perhaps involves the means of achieving it. Quite unexpectedly, we discovered that every major dictatorial regime which came to power between the 1920s and 1950s (with the possible exception of Portugal's) was foreshadowed by a particular motive pattern in its stories for children: namely, a low need for affiliation (little interest in friendly relationships with people) and a high need for power (a great concern over controlling and influencing other people).

The German readers showed this pattern before Hitler; the Japanese readers, before Tojo; the Argentine readers, before Perón; the Spanish readers, before Franco; the South African readers, before the present authoritarian government in South Africa; etc. On the other hand, very few countries which did not have dictatorships manifested this particular motive combination. The difference was highly significant statistically, since there was only one exception in the first instance and very few in the second. Apparently, we stumbled on a psychological index of ruthlessness—i.e., the need to influence other people (n Power), unchecked by sufficient concern for their welfare (n Affiliation). It is interesting, and a little disturbing, to discover that the German readers of today still evince this particular combination of motives, just as they did in 1925. Let us hope that this is one case where a social science generalization will not be confirmed by the appearance of a totalitarian regime in Germany in the next ten years.

To return to our main theme—let us discuss the precise ways that higher n Achievement leads to more rapid economic development, and why it should lead to economic development rather than, for example, to military or artistic development. We must consider in more detail the mechanism by which the concentration of a particular type of human motive in a population leads to a complex social phenomenon like economic growth. The link between the two social phenomena is, obviously, the business entrepreneur. I am not using the term "entrepreneur" in the sense of "capitalist": in fact, I should like to divorce "entrepreneur" entirely from any connotations of ownership. An entrepreneur is someone who exercises control over production that is not just for his personal consumption. According to my definition, for example, an executive in a steel production unit in Russia is an entrepreneur.

It was Joseph Schumpeter who drew the attention of economists to the importance that the activity of these entrepreneurs had in creating industrialization in the West. Their vigorous endeavors put together firms and created productive units where there had been none before. In the beginning, at least, the entrepreneurs often collected material resources, organized a production unit to combine the resources into a new product, and sold the product. Until recently, nearly all economists—including not only Marx, but also Western classical economists—assumed that these men were moved primarily by the "profit motive." We are all familiar with the Marxian argument that they were so driven by their desire for profits that they exploited the workingman and ultimately forced him to revolt. Recently, economic historians have been studying the actual lives of such entrepreneurs and finding—certainly to the surprise of some of the investigators—that many of them seemingly were not interested in making money as such. In psychological terms, at least, Marx's picture is slightly out of focus. Had these entrepreneurs been above all interested in money, many more of them would have quit working as soon as they had made all the money that they could possibly use. They would not have continued to risk their money in further entrepreneurial ventures. Many of them, in fact, came from pietistic sects, like the Quakers in England, that prohibited the enjoyment of wealth in any of the ways cultivated so successfully by some members of the European nobility. However, the entrepreneurs often seemed consciously to be greatly concerned with expanding their businesses, with getting a greater share of the market, with "conquering brute nature," or even with altruistic schemes for bettering the lot of mankind or bringing about the kingdom of God on earth more rapidly. Such desires have frequently enough been labeled as hypocritical. However, if we assume that these men were really motivated by a desire for achievement rather than by a desire for money as such, the label no longer fits. This assumption also simplifies further matters considerably. It provides an explanation for the fact that these entrepreneurs were interested in money without wanting it for its own sake, namely, that money served as a ready quantitative index of how well they were doing—e.g., of how much they had achieved by their efforts over the past year. The need to achieve can never be satisfied by money; but estimates of profitability in money terms can supply direct knowledge of how well one is doing one's job.

The brief consideration of the lives of business entrepreneurs of the past suggested that their chief motive may well have been a high *n* Achievement. What evidence have we found in support of this? We made two approaches to the problem. First, we attempted to determine whether individuals with high *n* Achievement behave like entrepreneurs; and second, we investigated to learn whether actual entrepreneurs, particularly the more successful ones, in a number of countries, have higher *n* Achievement than do other people of roughly the same status. Of course, we had to establish what we meant by "behave like entrepreneurs"—what precisely distinguishes the way an entrepreneur behaves from the way other people behave?

The adequate answers to these questions would entail a long discussion of the sociology of occupations, involving the distinction originally made by Max Weber between capitalists and bureaucrats. Since this cannot be done here, a very brief report on our extensive investigations in this area will have to suffice. First, one of the defining characteristics of an entrepreneur is *taking risks* and/or innovating. A person who adds up a column of figures is not an entrepreneur—however carefully, efficiently, or correctly he adds them. He is simply following established rules. However, a man who decides to add a new line to his business is an entrepreneur, in that he cannot know in advance whether this decision will be correct. Nevertheless, he does not feel that he is in the position of a gambler who places some money on the turn of a card. Knowledge, judgment, and skill enter into his decision making; and, if his choice is justified by future developments, he can certainly feel a sense of personal achievement from having made a successful move.

Therefore, if people with high *n* Achievement are to behave in an entrepreneurial way, they must seek out and perform in situations in which there is some moderate risk of failure—a risk which can, presumably, be reduced by increased effort or skill. They should not work harder than other people at routine tasks, or perform functions which they are certain to do well simply by doing what everyone accepts as the correct traditional thing to do. On the other hand, they should avoid gambling situations, because, even if they win, they can receive no sense of personal achievement, since it was not skill but luck that produced the results. (And, of course, most of the time they would lose, which would be highly unpleasant to them.) The data on this point are very clear-cut. We have repeatedly found, for example, that boys with high *n* Achievement choose to play games of skill that incorporate a moderate risk of failure. . . .

Another quality that the entrepreneur seeks in his work is that his job be a kind that ordinarily provides him with accurate knowledge of the results of his decisions. As a rule, growth in sales, in output, or in profit margins tells him very precisely whether he has made the correct choice under uncertainty or not. Thus, the concern for profit enters in—profit is a measure of success. We have repeatedly found that boys with a high *n* Achievement work more efficiently when they know how well they are doing. Also, they will not work harder for money rewards; but if they are asked, they state that greater money rewards should be awarded for accomplishing more difficult things in games of skill. In the ring-toss game, subjects were asked how much money they thought should be awarded for successful throws from different distances. Subjects with high n Achievement and those with low n Achievement agreed substantially about the amounts for throws made close to the peg. However, as the distance from the peg increased, the amounts awarded for successful throws by the subjects with high n Achievement rose more rapidly than did the rewards by those with low n Achievement. Here, as elsewhere, individuals with high n Achievement behaved as they must if they are to be the successful entrepreneurs of society. They believed that greater achievement should be recognized by quantitatively larger reward.

What produces high n Achievement? Why do some societies produce a large number of people with this motive, while other societies produce so many fewer? We conducted long series of researches into this question. I can present only a few here.

One very important finding is essentially a negative one: n Achievement cannot be hereditary. Popular psychology has long maintained that some races are more energetic than others. Our data clearly contradict this in connection with n Achievement. The changes in n Achievement level within a given population are too rapid to be attributed to heredity. For example, the correlation between respective n Achievement levels in the 1925 and 1950 samples of readers is substantially zero. Many of the countries that were high in n Achievement at one or both times may be low or moderate in n Achievement now, and vice versa. Germany was low in 1925 and is high now; and certainly the hereditary makeup of the German nation has not changed in a generation.

However, there is substantiating evidence that n Achievement is a motive which a child can acquire quite early in life, say, by the age of eight or ten, as a result of the way his parents have brought him up. . . . The principal results . . . indicate the differences between the parents of the "high n Achievement boys" and the parents of boys with low n Achievement. In general, the mothers and the fathers of the first group set higher levels of aspiration in a number of tasks for their sons. They were also much warmer, showing positive emotion in reacting to their sons' performances. In the area of authority or dominance, the data are quite interesting. The mothers of the "highs" were more domineering than the mothers of the "lows," but the *fathers* of the "highs" were significantly *less* domineering than the fathers of the "lows." In other words, the fathers of the "highs" set high standards and are warmly interested in their sons' performances, but they do not directly interfere. This gives the boys the chance to develop initiative and self-reliance.

What factors cause parents to behave in this way? Their behavior certainly is involved with their values and, possibly, ultimately with their religion or their general world view. At present, we cannot be sure that Protestant parents are more likely to behave this way than Catholic parents— there are too many subgroup variations within each religious portion of the community: the Lutheran father is probably as likely to be authoritarian as the Catholic father. However, there does seem to be one crucial variable discernible: the extent to which the religion of the family emphasizes individual, as contrasted with ritual, contact with God. The preliterate tribes that we studied in which the religion was the kind that stressed the individual contact had higher n Achievement; and in general, mystical sects in which this kind of religious self-reliance dominates have had higher n Achievement.

The extent to which the authoritarian father is away from the home while the boy is growing up may prove to be another crucial variable. If so, then one incidental consequence of prolonged wars may be an increase in n Achievement, because the fathers are away too much to interfere with their sons' development of it. And in Turkey, N. M. Bradburn found that those boys tended to have higher n Achievement who had left home early or whose fathers had died before they were eighteen.[10] Slavery was another factor which played an important role in the past. It probably lowered n Achievement—in the slaves, for whom obedience and responsibility, but not achievement, were obvious virtues; and in the slave-owners, because household slaves were often disposed to spoil the owner's children as a means for improving their own positions. This is both a plausible and a probable reason for the drop in n Achievement level in ancient Greece that occurred at about the time the middle-class entrepreneur was first able to afford, and obtain by conquest, as many as two slaves for each child. The idea also clarifies the slow economic development of the South in the United States by attributing its dilatoriness to a lack of n Achievement in its elite; and it also indicates why lower-class American Negroes, who are closest to the slave tradition, possess very low n Achievement.[11]

I have outlined our research findings. Do they indicate ways of accelerating economic development? Increasing the level of n Achievement in a country suggests itself as an obvious first possibility. If n Achievement is so important, so specifically adapted to the business role, then it certainly should be raised in level, so that more young men have an "entrepreneurial drive." The difficulty in this excellent plan is that our studies of how n Achievement originates indicate that the family is the key formative influence; and it is very hard to change on a really large scale. To be sure, major historical events like wars have taken authoritarian fathers out of the home; and religious reform movements have sometimes converted the parents to a new achievement-oriented ideology. However, such matters are not ordinarily within the policymaking province of the agencies charged with speeding economic development.

Such agencies can, perhaps, effect the general acceptance of an achievement-oriented ideology as an absolute *sine qua non* of economic development. Furthermore, this ideology should be diffused not only in business and governmental circles, but throughout the nation, and in ways that will influence the thinking of all parents as they bring up their children. As B. C. Rosen and R. G. D'Andrade found, parents must, above all, set high standards for their children. The campaign to spread achievement-oriented ideology, if possible, could also incorporate an attack on the extreme authoritarianism in fathers that impedes or prevents the development of self-reliance in their sons. This is, however, a more delicate point, and attacking this, in many countries, would be to threaten values at the very center of social life. I believe that a more indirect approach would be more successful. One approach would be to take the boys out of the home and to camps. A more significant method would be to promote the rights of women, both legally and socially—one of the ways to undermine the absolute dominance of the male is to strengthen the rights of the female! Another reason for concentrating particularly on women is that they play the leading role in rearing the next generation. Yet, while men in underdeveloped countries come in contact with new achievement-oriented values and standards through their work, women may be left almost untouched by such influences. But if the sons are to have high n Achievement, the mothers must first be reached.

It may seem strange that a chapter on economic development should discuss the importance of feminism and the way children are reared; but this is precisely where a psychological analysis leads. If the motives of men are the agents that influence the speed with which the economic machine operates, then the speed can be increased only through affecting the factors that create the motives. Furthermore—to state this point less theoretically—I cannot think of evinced substantial, rapid long-term economic development where women have not been somewhat freed from their traditional setting of "Kinder, Kuche und Kirche" and allowed to play a more powerful role in society, specifically as part of the working force. This generalization applies not only to the Western democracies like the United States, Sweden, or England, but also to the USSR, Japan, and now China.

In the present state of our knowledge, we can conceive of trying to raise n Achievement levels only in the next generation—although new research findings may soon indicate n Achievement in adults can be increased. Most economic planners, while accepting the long-range desirability of raising n Achievement in future generations, want to know what can be done during the next five to ten years. This immediacy inevitably focuses attention on the process or processes by which executives or entrepreneurs are selected. Foreigners with proved entrepreneurial drive can be hired, but at best this is a temporary and unsatisfactory solution. In most underdeveloped countries where government is playing a leading role in promoting economic development, it is clearly necessary for the government to adopt rigid achievement-oriented standards of performance like those in the USSR.[12] A government manager or, for that matter, a private entrepreneur, should have to produce "or else." Production targets must be set, as they are in most economic plans; and individuals must be held responsible for achieving them, even at the plant level. The philosophy should be one of "no excuses accepted." It is common for government officials or economic theorists in underdeveloped countries to be weighed down by all the difficulties which face the economy and render its rapid development difficult or impossible. They note that there is too rapid population growth, too little capital, too few technically competent people, etc. Such obstacles to growth are prevalent, and in many cases they are immensely hard to overcome; but talking about them can provide merely a comfortable rationalization for mediocre performance. It is difficult to fire an administrator, no matter how poor his performance, if so many objective reasons exist for his doing badly. Even worse, such rationalization permits, in the private sector, the continued employment of incompetent family members as executives. If these private firms were afraid of being penalized for poor performance, they might be impelled to find more able professional mangers a little more quickly. I am not an expert in the field, and the mechanisms I am suggesting may be far from appropriate. Still, they may serve to illustrate my main point: if a country short in entrepreneurial talent wants to advance rapidly, it must find ways and means of insuring that only the most competent retain positions of responsibility. One of the obvious methods of doing so is to judge people in terms of their *performance*—and not according to their family or political connections, their skill in explaining why their unit failed to produce as expected, or their conscientiousness in following the rules. I would suggest the use of psychological tests as a means of selecting people with high *n* Achievement; but, to be perfectly frank, I think this approach is at present somewhat impractical on a large enough scale in most underdeveloped countries.

Finally, there is another approach which I think is promising for recruiting and developing more competent business leadership. It is the one called, in some circles, the "professionalization of management." Frederick Harbison and Charles A. Myers have recently completed a worldwide survey of the efforts made to develop professional schools of high-level management. They have concluded that, in most countries, progress in this direction is slow.[13] Professional management is important for three reasons: (1) It may endow a business career with higher prestige (as a kind of profession), so that business will attract more of the young men with high *n* Achievement from the elite groups in backward countries; (2) It stresses *performance* criteria of excellence in the management area—i.e., what a man can do and not what he is; (3) Advanced management schools can themselves be so achievement-oriented in their instruction that they are able to raise the *n* Achievement of those who attend them.

Applied toward explaining historical events, the results of our researches clearly shift attention away from external factors and to man—in particular, to his motives and values. That about which he thinks and dreams determines what will happen. The emphasis is quite different from the Darwinian or Marxist view of man as a creature who *adapts* to his environment. It is even different from the Freudian view of civilization as the sublimation of man's primitive urges. Civilization, at least in its economic aspects, is neither adaptation nor sublimation; it is a positive creation by a people made dynamic by a high level of *n* Achievement. Nor can we agree with Toynbee, who recognizes the importance of psychological factors as "the very forces which actually decide the issue when an encounter takes place," when he states that these factors "inherently are impossible to weigh and measure, and therefore to estimate scientifically in advance."[14] It is a measure of the pace at which the behavioral sciences are developing that even within Toynbee's lifetime we can demonstrate that he was mistaken. The psychological factor responsible for a civilization's rising to a challenge is so far from being "inherently impossible to weigh and measure" that it has been weighed and measured and scientifically estimated in advance; and, so far as we can now tell, this factor is the achievement motive.

NOTES

1. A. L. Kroeber, *Configurations of Culture Growth* (Berkeley, California, 1944).

2. J. W. Atkinson (Ed.), *Motives in Fantasy, Action, and Society* (Princeton, N.J., 1958).

3. Max Weber, *The Protestant Ethic and the Spirit of Capitalism*, trans. Talcott Parsons (New York, 1930).

4. M. R. Winterbottom, "The Relation of Need for Achievement to Learning and Experiences in Independence and Mastery," in Atkinson, *op. cit.,* pp. 453–478.

5. F. Heichelheim, *Wirtschaftsgeschichte des Altertums* (Leiden, 1938).

6. J. B. Cortés, "The Achievement Motive in the Spanish Economy between the Thirteenth and the Eighteenth Centuries," *Economic Development and Cultural Change*, IX (1960), 144–163.

7. N. M. Bradburn and D. E. Berlew, "Need for Achievement and English Economic Growth," *Economic Development and Cultural Change*, 1961.

8. I. L. Child, T. Storm, and J. Veroff, "Achievement Themes in Folk Tales Related to Socialization Practices," in Atkinson, *op. cit.,* pp. 479–492.

9. David Riesman, with the assistance of Nathan Glazer and Reuel Denney, *The Lonely Crowd* (New Haven, Conn., 1950).

10. N. M. Bradburn, "The Managerial Role in Turkey" (unpublished Ph.D. dissertation, Harvard University, 1960).

11. B. C. Rosen, "Race, Ethnicity, and Achievement Syndrome," *American Sociological Review*, XXIV (1959), 47–60.

12. David Granick, *The Red Executive*, (New York, 1960).

13. Frederick Harbison and Charles A. Myers, *Management in the Industrial World* (New York, 1959).

14. Arnold J. Toynbee, *A Study of History* (abridgment by D. C. Somervell; Vol. I; New York, 1947).

12

. . . .

Becoming Modern

. . . .

ALEX INKELES & DAVID H. SMITH

This chapter reports on what is perhaps the most extensive investigation ever undertaken to explore the psychocultural factors influencing development. Using interview data from some 6,000 young men in six developing countries (Argentina, Chile, India, Israel, Nigeria, and East Pakistan), the authors and their fellow researchers devised an overall measure of modernization they call their "OM scale." The characteristics of the "modern man" are described in the portions of their work that follow; the interested reader may consult the original book for the methodological details of the study. The authors discuss the developmental implications of the presence or absence of such modern men in a given society and argue that modern attitudes produce modern behaviors that are essential to development. Moreover, without modern men, modern institutions are bound to fail. In sum, for these researchers "underdevelopment is a state of mind." The reader should compare the qualities of n Achievement discussed by McClelland (Chapter 11) with the qualities of OM discussed in this chapter. In what ways are they similar, and how persuasive is the argument that attitudes are, as Inkeles and Smith state, "the essence of national development itself"?

The main purpose of economic development is to permit the achievement of a decent level of living for all people, everywhere. But almost no one will argue that the progress of a nation and a people should be measured solely in terms of gross national product and per capita income. Development assumes, as well, a high degree of political maturation, as expressed in stable and orderly processes of government resting on the expressed will of the people. And it also includes the attainment of popular education, the burgeoning of the arts, the efflorescence of architecture, the growth of the means of communication, and the enrichment of leisure. Indeed, in the end, development requires a transformation in the very nature of man, a transformation that is both a means to yet greater growth and at the same time one of the great ends of the development process.

We have described this transformation as the shift from traditionalism to individual modernity. The object of our research was to delineate the elements of such personal change, to measure its degree, to explain its causes, and to throw some light on its observed and probable future consequences. It is time for us to sum up the progress we made in that task, taking the opportunity, in so doing, to deal briefly with some of the issues we earlier may have left unresolved.

DEFINING AND MEASURING INDIVIDUAL MODERNITY

One who sets out to define and to measure individual modernity is like the animal trainer whose new act requires he learn to ride on the back of his tiger. He may emerge alive, but the chances are very great he will have been knocked about quite a bit in the process. Nevertheless, we accepted as a critical element in the structure of our whole intellectual and scientific enterprise the construction of a reliable, cross-national measure of individual modernity.

We do not claim to have invented the idea of the modern man. The concept was already there when we began our work, even though its content was vague. Inventing types of men has, after all, always been a fundamental preoccupation of sociologists: Karl Marx described the consciousness of the bourgeoisie and the proletariat; Robert Redfield defined the contrasting attributes of the folk and urban types; Everett V. Stonequist gave us the marginal man; David Riesman the inner-, outer-, and other-directed man. These "ideal types" people the pages of almost every well-known sociologist's work. Yet it has been the rare instance, indeed, in which any systematic attempt has been undertaken to measure whether there are real people in the world who, in their own persons, actually incorporate the qualities identified by these ideal types.[1] We were determined to break with this sociological tradition, and firmly committed ourselves to testing how far the set of qualities by which we defined the modern man actually cohered as a psychosocial syndrome in real men.

Our results provide definitive evidence that living individuals do indeed conform to our model of the modern man, that they do so in substantial numbers, and that essentially the same basic qualities which define a man as modern in one country and culture also delineate the modern man in other places. The modern man is not just a construct in the mind of sociological theorists. He exists and can be identified with fair reliability within any population where our test can be applied.

The modern man's character, as it emerges from our study, may be summed up under four major headings. He is an informed participant citizen; he has a marked sense of personal efficacy; he is highly independent and autonomous in his relations to traditional sources of influence, especially when he is making basic decisions about how to conduct his personal affairs; and he is ready for new experiences and ideas, that is, he is relatively open-minded and cognitively flexible.

As an informed participant citizen, the modern man identifies with the newer, larger entities of region and state, takes an interest in public affairs, national and international as well as local, joins organizations, keeps himself informed about major events in the news, and votes or otherwise takes some part in the political process. The modern man's sense of efficacy is reflected in his belief that, either alone or in concert with others, he may take actions which can affect the course of his life and that of his community; in his active efforts to improve his own condition and that of his family; and in his rejection of passivity, resignation, and fatalism toward the course of life's events. His independence of traditional sources of authority is manifested in public issues by his following the advice of public officials or trade-union leaders rather than priests and village elders, and in personal matters by his choosing the job and the bride he prefers even if his parents prefer some other position or some other person. The modern man's openness to new experience is reflected in his interest in technical innovation, his support of scientific exploration of hitherto sacred or taboo subjects, his readiness to meet strangers, and his willingness to allow women to take advantage of opportunities outside the confines of the household.

These *main* elements of individual modernity seem to have in common a thrust toward more instrumental kinds of attitudes and behavior. The more expressive and interpersonal aspects of overall modernization or OM syndrome tended to be less important, by and large, although still significantly involved in the syndrome. This fits well with the relative emphasis on new and more effective ways of doing things as central to the modernization process, with changes in ways of relating to other people coming largely as side effects. The Japanese case is a good example of how the instrumental aspects of OM can be present with, we would judge, many fewer of the expressive elements.

Although these are the principal components, they by no means exhaust the list of qualities which cohere as part of the modernity syndrome. The modern man is also different in his approach to time, to personal and social planning, to the rights of persons dependent on or subordinate to him, and to the use of formal rules as a basis for running things. In other words, psychological modernity emerges as a quite complex, multifaceted, and multidimensional syndrome. . . .

Considering that the modernization process seems to work so consistently in so many different cultural settings, is there then no choice? Must everyone become modern, and to the same degree?

This issue seems to generate the greatest misunderstanding, and satisfying people with regard to it is most difficult. Dispassionate discussion becomes overshadowed by lurid images of modern science turning out a race of automatons, machine-produced golems who are as uniform and unfeeling as are the products of Detroit's massive assembly lines.

Our image of man's nature is not that of a sponge which must soak up everything with which it comes in contact. In our view individual change toward modernization is a process of interaction between the individual and his social setting. Quite contrary to the conception of men as putty passively taking on whatever shape their environment imposes on them, we see the process of individual modernization as one requiring a basic personal engagement between the individual and his milieu. In this engagement the individual must first selectively perceive the lessons the environment has to teach, and then must willingly undertake to learn them, before any personal change can come about.

If the qualities of industrial organization are truly alien to a man, he will not incorporate them. Moreover, even if he finds an organization to be unthreatening or, better, congenial, a man will not necessarily learn new ways unless he personally has the readiness and the capacity to learn. And even if the environment is benign and the individuals are ready to learn, the process will not work if the environment itself is confusing and the messages it conveys are unclear or even contradictory.

In brief, if the process of modernization were at all like the situation described in Aldous Huxley's *Brave New World*, the outcome of our study should have yielded a perfect correlation rather than the much more modest figure it attained. Moreover, *all* the men in our samples should have changed, and all should have become completely modern in short order. Instead, as we know, many did not change at all and most only changed to some degree, so that after years of exposure to the modernizing influences only a modest proportion qualified as truly modern. And these, like all others, became modern with some degree of selectivity, changing fully in some respects but holding to divergent and even traditional views in others. . . .

THE SOCIAL SIGNIFICANCE
OF INDIVIDUAL MODERNIZATION

To a social psychologist, it is gratifying, indeed it is an activity sufficient unto itself, to be able to measure individual modernity, and to show how far and in what ways schooling and jobs bring about increased modernity scores. But the more pragmatic among our readers, and not only those from the developing countries, are likely to ask: "Is this purely an academic exercise? In particular, does it have any practical contribution to make to national development? Are not attitude and value changes rather ephemeral and peripheral? Can you give us any evidence that all this has much to do with the real problem of underdevelopment?"

In response, we affirm that our research has produced ample evidence that the attitude and value changes defining individual modernity are accompanied by changes in behavior precisely of the sort which we believe give meaning to, and support, those changes in political and economic institutions which lead to the modernization of nations.

We were able to document most extensively those behavioral changes accompanying attitudinal modernization in the realm of political and civic action. The modern man more often took an interest in political affairs, he kept informed and could identify important political events and personalities, he often contacted governmental and political agencies, more often joined organizations, more often voted—and all these by large margins. He was in every way a more active participant citizen of his society.[2]

It seems obvious to us that these are precisely the qualities one needs in the citizen of a modern polity. The introduction of modern political institutions imported from outside, or imposed from above by elites, tends to be an empty gesture unless there are active, interested, informed citizens who can make the institutions really work. And, as we have seen, such citizens are the more modern men shaped by the modernizing institutions we have identified, namely, the school, the newspaper, and the factory.

Beyond politics, the modern man showed himself to perform differently from the more traditional man in many realms of action having practical bearing on the process of societal modernization. The more modern man is quicker to adopt technical innovation, and more ready to implement birth-control measures; he urges his son to go as far as he can in school, and, if it pays better, encourages him to accept industrial work rather than to follow the more traditional penchant for office jobs; he informs himself about the goods produced in the more modern sector of the economy, and makes an effort to acquire them; and he permits his wife and daughter to leave the home for more active participation in economic life. In these and a host of other ways, only some of which we have documented, the man who is more modern in attitude and values acts to support modern institutions and to facilitate the general modernization of society.

While it was important to show that men who were more modern in attitude and value also acted in more modern ways, we feel it even more important to challenge the assumption that a "mere" change in attitudes and values cannot in itself be a truly important factor in the process of national development.

In saying this we are not espousing some form of naive psychological determinism. We are not unaware that a modern psychology cannot alone make a nation modern. We fully understand that to be modern a nation must have modern institutions, effective government, efficient production, and adequate social services. And we recognize full well that there may be structural obstacles to such development stemming not only from nature, but from social, political, and economic causes as well. Narrow class interests, colonial oppression, rapacious great powers, international cartels, domestic monopolies, archaic and corrupted governments, tribal antagonisms, and religious and ethnic prejudices, to name but a few, are among the many objective forces which we know may act to impede modernization.

Nevertheless, we believe a change in attitudes and values to be one of the most essential preconditions for substantial and effective functioning of those modern institutions which most of the more "practical" programs of development hope to establish. Our experience leads us to agree with many of the intellectual leaders of the Third World who argue that, in good part, underdevelopment is a state of mind.[3] It is admittedly difficult with presently available techniques and information to establish the case scientifically, but we are convinced that mental barriers and psychic factors are key obstacles to more effective economic and social development in many countries.

The technology which is, perhaps, the most distinctive ingredient of modernity can be borrowed by and established in developing countries with relative ease. Machinery is influenced by temperature and humidity, but it is otherwise immune to culture shock. Although they travel less well, political, economic, and cultural institutions can also be relatively easily imitated in their totality. Systems of taxation and of voter registration, and even political party systems, are regularly copied from the more advanced countries by those in the earlier stages of development. Patterns of factory management, forms of administration for business and government, new faculties, research institutions, indeed whole universities are being created every day in the developing countries as copies of institutions and procedures originating in the more developed countries.

How many of these transplanted institutions actually take root and bear fruit in their new setting is not precisely known. But the experience of almost everyone who has worked extensively on problems of development is replete with examples of the failure of such transplantation. The disappointment of high hopes and aspirations is endemic among those who have attempted such transplanting, and the hollow shells of the institutions, sometimes transformed into grotesque caricatures of their original design, sometimes barely functioning, often standing altogether abandoned, can be found strewn about in almost any developing country in which one chooses to travel.

In the explanations which are offered for this situation, one hears again and again the echo of one basic refrain: "The people were not ready for it yet." When one probes this generalization, it quickly becomes apparent that the material resources, the manuals for repair and maintenance, the charts and tables for organization, and the guidelines for administration which accompanied the transplanted institutions were meaningless without the support of an underlying and widespread pattern of culture and personality which could breathe life into the otherwise sterile forms and give human meaning and continuity to their activity.

In the last analysis, the successful functioning of these institutions was critically dependent on the availability of individuals who could bring to the job certain special personal qualities. These new institutions required people who could accept and discharge responsibility without constant close supervision, could manifest mutual trust and confidence in co-workers which extended beyond the situations in which one could keep them under direct surveillance, could subordinate the special interests of one's clique or parochial group to the goals of the larger organization, could be flexible and imaginative in the interpretation of rules, could show sympathetic consideration for the feelings of subordinates and openness to their ideas and other potential contributions. These, and a host of other personal qualities requisite to running a complex modern institution effectively, are not in excess supply in any society. In many of the developing countries, moreover, people possessed of the requisite qualities are actually scarce. And in some cases, the small set of individuals who possess the qualities necessary for effectively running the new institutions are either not called upon, or may even be socially ineligible, for service in those roles in which they could be most useful.

Such conditions in the institutions of national standing have their precise analogue in the more commonplace situation of individuals engaged in very modest pursuits, within purely local and parochial settings. In such settings we find most widely diffused the qualities our research has identified as characteristic of the traditional man: passive acceptance of fate and a general lack of efficacy; fear of innovation and distrust of the new; isolation from the outside world and lack of interest in what goes on in it; dependence on traditional authority and the received wisdom of elders and religious and customary leaders; preoccupation with personal and especially family affairs to the exclusion of community concerns; exclusive identification with purely local and parochial primary groups, coupled to feelings of isolation from and fear of larger regional and national entities; the shaping and damping of ambition to fit narrow goals, and the cultivation of humble sentiments of gratitude for what little one has; rigid, hierarchical relations with subordinates and others of low social status; and undervaluing of education, learning, research, and other concerns not obviously related to the practical business of earning one's daily bread.

Of course, not all these qualities are prevalent in all traditional settings, and they are unequally distributed among the men in them. Yet they are extremely common in individuals, and exceptionally pervasive across cultures and settings, in the countries of the less-developed world.

We must acknowledge that some of these qualities of the traditional man facilitate his adaptation to life. Such qualities help men to make a successful adjustment to the real conditions which exist in, and indeed pervade, their life space. But those qualities also tend to freeze people into the situations and positions in which they find themselves, and this, in turn, serves to preserve the outmoded, indeed archaic, and often oppressive institutions which hold the people in their grip. To break out of that iron grip requires, among other things, that people become modern in spirit, that they adopt and incorporate into their personalities the attitudes, values, and modes of acting which we have identified with the modern man. Without this ingredient neither foreign aid nor domestic revolution can hope successfully to bring an underdeveloped nation into the ranks of those capable of self-sustained growth.

Economists define modernity in terms of gross national product per capita, and political scientists in terms of effective institutions for governance. We are of the opinion that neither rapid economic growth nor effective government can develop, or, if introduced, will be long sustained, without the widespread diffusion in the rank and file of the population of those qualities we have identified as those of the modern man. In the conditions of the contemporary world, the qualities of individual modernity are not a luxury, they are a necessity. They are not a marginal gain, derived from the process of institutional modernization, but are rather a precondition for the long-term success of those institutions. Diffusion through the population of the qualities of the modern man is not incidental to the process of social development; it is the essence of national development itself.

NOTES

1. There are, of course, some notable exceptions. The most important early example was the effort by Gordon Allport to test Spranger's belief that men could be classified according to the predominance in their personality of "theoretical," "religious," "social," or "economic-and-political" values. See Gordon Allport, Philip Vernon, and Gardner Lindzey, *Study of Values: A Scale for Measuring the Dominant Interests in Personality*, 3rd ed. (Boston: Houghton-Mifflin, 1959). Probably the best-known and most widely studied syndrome is that first proposed by Erich Fromm under the rubric "the authoritarian personality" in *Escape From Freedom* (New York: Farrar and Rinhart, 1941) and later built into the famous "F scale." See Theodor W. Adorno et al., *The Authoritarian Personality* (New York: Harper, 1950).

2. The evidence concerning these differences in political behavior is built into the OM scale, and may be observed by checking the list of questions in Appendix A. [Not reproduced here—*Ed.*] A full account of the 39 items dealing with political orientations and behavior covered by our questionnaire, the scales

those items yielded, and their relation to the independent variables is given in Alex Inkeles, "Participant Citizenship in Six Developing Countries," *American Political Science Review*, 63 (December 1969):1120–1141.

3. In his unpublished contribution to the conference on Alternatives in Development sponsored by the Vienna Institute for Development in June 1971, Dr. Salazar Bondy, a leading intellectual of Peru, wrote as follows: "Underdevelopment is not just a collection of statistical indices which enable a socio-economic picture to be drawn. It is also a state of mind, a way of expression, a form of outlook and a collective personality marked by chronic infirmities and forms of maladjustment."

13

· · · · · · ·

The Confucian Ethic
and Economic Growth

· · · · · · ·

HERMAN KAHN

The most recent theory on the cultural origins of economic growth derives from the observation that a group of countries that have made spectacular strides since World War II (e.g., Japan, South Korea, Taiwan) are Confucian societies. Until his recent death, Herman Kahn was director of the Hudson Institute think tank and was well known as a futurist. In this contribution, Kahn says that much of the success of these nations can be attributed directly to their cultures. It is interesting to compare the attributes of Confucianism that Kahn suggests are important for development with the attributes of n Achievement and OM discussed in Chapters 11 and 12. It is also worth considering the implication of Kahn's argument for those nations in Latin America, Africa, and elsewhere that have dramatically different traditions. Has the absence of a "Confucian ethic" held back the development of these nations? If so, is it likely to make closing the gap between them and the developed nations an impossible dream?

Most readers of this book are familiar with the argument of Max Weber that the Protestant ethic was extremely useful in promoting the rise and spread of modernization.[1] Most readers, however, will be much less familiar with the notion that has gradually emerged in the last two decades that societies based upon the Confucian ethic may in many ways be superior to the West in the pursuit of industrialization, affluence, and modernization. Let us see what some of the strengths of the Confucian ethic are in the modern world.

Reprinted with permission from Mrs. Jane Kahn. *World Economic Development: 1979 and Beyond*, by Herman Kahn (Boulder, CO: Westview Press, 1979).

THE CONFUCIAN ETHIC

The Confucian ethic includes two quite different but connected sets of issues. First and perhaps foremost, Confucian societies uniformly promote in the individual and the family sobriety, a high value on education, a desire for accomplishment in various skills (particularly academic and cultural), and seriousness about tasks, job, family, and obligations. A properly trained member of a Confucian culture will be hard working, responsible, skillful, and (within the assigned or understood limits) ambitious and creative in helping the group (extended family, community, or company). There is much less emphasis on advancing individual (selfish) interests.

In some ways, the capacity for purposive and efficient communal and organizational activities and efforts is even more important in the modern world than the personal qualities, although both are important. Smoothly fitting, harmonious human relations in an organization are greatly encouraged in most neo-Confucian societies. This is partly because of a sense of hierarchy but even more because of a sense of complementarity of relations that is much stronger in Confucian than in Western societies.

The anthropologist Chie Nakane has pointed out that in Western societies there is a great tendency for "like to join like" in unions, student federations, women's groups, men's clubs, youth movements, economic classes, and so on.[2] This tends to set one group in society against another: students against teachers, employees against employers, youths against parents, and so on. In the Confucian hierarchic society, the emphasis is on cooperation among complementary elements, much as in the family (which is in fact the usual paradigm or model in a Confucian culture). The husband and wife work together and cooperate in raising the children; each has different assigned duties and responsibilities, as do the older and younger siblings and the grandparents. There is emphasis on fairness and equity, but it is fairness and equity in the institutional context, not for the individual as an individual. Synergism—complementarity and cooperation among parts of a whole—are emphasized, not equality and interchangeability. The major identification is with one's role in the organization or other institutional structure, whether it be the family, the business firm, or a bureau in the government.

Since the crucial issues in a modern society increasingly revolve around these equity issues and on making organizations work well, the neo-Confucian cultures have great advantages. As opposed to the earlier Protestant ethic, the modern Confucian ethic is superbly designed to create and foster loyalty, dedication, responsibility, and commitment and to intensify identification with the organization and one's role in the organization. All this makes the economy and society operate much more smoothly than one whose principles of identification and association tend to lead to egalitarianism, to disunity, to confrontation, and to excessive compensation or repression.

A society that emphasizes a like-to-like type of identification works out reasonably well as long as there is enough hierarchy, discipline, control, or motivation within the society to restrain excessive tendencies to egalitarianism, anarchy, self-indulgence, and so on. But as the society becomes more affluent and secular, there is less motivation, reduced commitment, more privatization, and increasingly impersonal and automatic welfare. Interest in group politics, group and individual selfishness, egoism, intergroup antagonisms, and perhaps even intergroup warfare all tend to increase. It becomes the old versus the young, insiders versus outsiders, men versus women, students versus teachers, and—most important of all— employees against employers. The tendencies toward anarchy, rivalry, and payoffs to the politically powerful or the organized militants become excessive and out of control.

For all these reasons we believe that both aspects of the Confucian ethic—the creation of dedicated, motivated, responsible, and educated individuals and the enhanced sense of commitment, organizational identity, and loyalty to various institutions—will result in all the neo-Confucian societies having at least potentially higher growth rates than other cultures. . . .

Whether or not one accepts our analysis of *why* neo-Confucian cultures are so competent in industrialization, the impressive data that support the final thesis are overwhelming. The performance of the People's Republic of China; of both North and South Korea; of Japan, Taiwan, Hong Kong, and Singapore; and of the various Chinese ethnic groups in Malaysia, Thailand, Indonesia, and the Philippines, discloses extraordinary talent (at least in the last twenty-five years) for economic development and for learning about and using modern technology. For example, the North Vietnamese operated one of the most complicated air defense networks in history more or less by themselves (once instructed by the Soviets), and the American army found that the South Vietnamese, if properly motivated, often went through training school in about half the time required by Americans. We do not gloss over the enormous differences among these neo-Confucian cultures. They vary almost as much as do European cultures. But all of them seem amenable to modernization under current conditions.

NOTES

1. Max Weber, *The Protestant Ethic and the Spirit of Capitalism*, translated by Talcott Parsons (New York: Charles Scribner's Sons, 1930).
2. Chie Nakane, *Japanese Society* (Berkeley, Calif.: University of California Press, 1970).

14

· · · · · · ·

Underdevelopment Is a
State of Mind

· · · · · · ·

LAWRENCE E. HARRISON

*After twenty years of working for the United States Agency for
International Development (USAID), Lawrence Harrison has concluded that Latin America's culture explains its lack of development. As
should be clear by now, the cultural approach blames the poor for
their poverty. According to Harrison, Latin Americans have become so
preoccupied with a belief in the self-defeating "myths" of dependency and imperialism that they are paralyzed to the point that they
do not use the resources they have to develop. At its heart, the process of development is one of human creative capacity, the ability to
imagine, conceptualize, and so on. If a country is to tap the creative
energy of its people, the government must establish an environment
that encourages and uses all of its people's abilities.*

WHAT MAKES DEVELOPMENT HAPPEN?

Development, most simply, is improvement in human well-being.[1] Most
people today aspire to higher standards of living, longer lives, and fewer
health problems; education for themselves and their children that will increase
their earning capacity and leave them more in control of their lives; a
measure of stability and tranquility; and the opportunity to do the things

Reprinted with permission from *Underdevelopment Is a State of Mind: The Latin
American Case*, by Lawrence E. Harrison (Cambridge, MA: The Center for
International Affairs, Harvard University), pp. 1–9. © 1985 by the President and
Fellows of Harvard College.

Table 14.1

	Low-income Countries	Industrialized Countries
Total population (mid–1980)	2.2 billion	671 million
Annual average population growth rate (1970–80)	2.1 percent	.8 percent
Average per capita gross national product (1980)	$260	$10,320
Average life expectancy at birth (1980)	57 years	74 years
Average adult literacy (1977)	50 percent	99 percent

that give them pleasure and satisfaction. A small minority will take exception to one or more of these aspirations. Some others may wish to add one or more. For the purposes of this chapter, however, I think the list is adequate.

The enormous gap in well-being between the low-income and the industrialized countries is apparent from the above summary table, the source of which is the World Bank's *World Development Report* 1982. . . .

What explains the gap? What have the industrialized countries done that the low-income countries have not? Why was the Marshall Plan a monumental success, the Alliance for Progress much less successful? What makes development happen or not happen?

There are those who will say that what the industrialized countries have done that the low-income countries have not is to exploit the low-income countries; that development is a zero-sum game; that the rich countries are rich because the poor countries are poor. This is doctrine for Marxist-Leninists and it has wide currency throughout the Third World. To be sure, colonial powers often did derive great economic advantage from their colonies, and U.S. companies have made a lot of money in Latin America and elsewhere in the Third World, particularly during the first half of this century. But the almost exclusive focus on "imperialism" and "dependency" to explain underdevelopment has encouraged the evolution of a paralyzing and self-defeating mythology. The thesis of this chapter is in diametrical contrast. It looks inward rather than outward to explain a society's condition.

I believe that the creative capacity of human beings is at the heart of the development process. What makes development happen is our ability to imagine, theorize, conceptualize, experiment, invent, articulate, organize, manage, solve problems, and do a hundred other things with our minds and hands that contribute to the progress of the individual and of human-kind. Natural resources, climate, geography, history, market size, governmental policies, and many other factors influence the direction and pace of progress. But the engine is human creative capacity.

The economist Joseph Schumpeter (1883–1950) singled out the

entrepreneurial geniuses—the Henry Fords of the world—as the real creators of wealth and progress, as indeed they must have appeared in the early years of Schumpeter's life. Economist and political scientist Everett Hagen was less elitist: "The discussion of creativity refers . . . not merely to the limiting case of genius but to the quality of creativity in general, in whatever degree it may be found in a given individual."[2]

My *own* belief is that the society that is most successful at helping its people—*all* its people—realize their creative potential is the society that will progress the fastest.

It is not just the entrepreneur who creates progress, even if we are talking narrowly about material—economic—progress. The inventor of the machine employed by the entrepreneur; the scientist who conceived the theory that the inventor turned to practical use; the engineer who designed the system to mass-produce the machine; the farmer who uses special care in producing a uniform raw material to be processed by the machine; the machine operator who suggests some helpful modifications to the machine on the basis of long experience in operating it—all are contributing to growth. So is the salesman who expands demand for the product by conceiving a new use for it. So, too, are the teachers who got the scientist, the inventor, and the engineer interested in their professions and who taught the farmer agronomy.[3]

Production takes place within a broader society, and the way that society functions affects the productive process. Good government can assure stability and continuity, without which investment and production will falter. Good government can provide a variety of services that facilitate production. And the policies government pursues, e.g., with respect to taxation, interest rates, support prices for agricultural products, will importantly affect producer decisions. Thus, the creativity and skill of government officials play a key role in economic development. It can be argued, in fact, that an effective government policymaker—e.g., a Treasury Secretary—is worth many Henry Fords.[4] W. Arthur Lewis observes, "The behaviour of government plays as important a role in stimulating or discouraging economic activity as does the behaviour of entrepreneurs, or parents, or scientists, or priests."[5]

But our definition of development is far broader than just the productive dimension of human existence. It also embraces the social dimension, particularly health, education, and welfare. It is government that bears the principal responsibility for progress in these sectors, and, as with economic progress, innovation and creativity are at the root of social progress. The people who conceive the policies that expand and improve social services are thus comparable in their developmental impact to industrial entrepreneurs, as are public-sector planners, administrators, technicians, and blue-collar workers to their private-sector counterparts.

It is not difficult to see how this view of what makes development happen can be extended to virtually all forms of work, intellectual and physical, performed within a society. While it is obvious that the contribution of some will be greater than that of others, and while the role of gifted people can be enormously important, all can contribute. It is thus probably more accurate, at least in the contemporary world, to think of development as a process of millions of small breakthroughs than as a few monumental innovations, the work of geniuses. A society that smooths the way for these breakthroughs is a society that will progress.

How does a society encourage the expression of human creative capacity? Basically, in seven ways:

1. Through creation of an environment in which people expect and receive fair treatment.
2. Through an effective and accessible education system: one that provides basic intellectual and vocational tools; nurtures inquisitiveness, critical faculties, dissent, and creativity; and equips people to solve problems.
3. Through a health system that protects people from diseases that debilitate and kill.
4. Through creation of an environment that encourages experimentation and criticism (which is often at the root of experimentation).
5. Through creation of an environment that helps people both discover their talents and interests and mesh them with the right jobs.
6. Through a system of incentives that rewards merit and achievement (and, conversely, discourages nepotism and "pull").
7. Through creation of the stability and continuity that make it possible to plan ahead with confidence. Progress is made enormously more difficult by instability and discontinuity.

TWO EXAMPLES IN NICARAGUA

My recent experience in Nicaragua provides two examples that symbolize what societies can do to nurture or frustrate human creative capacity.

The United States ambassador to Nicaragua during my two years there was Lawrence A. Pezzullo. Larry Pezzullo grew up in the Bronx, the son of an immigrant Italian butcher. His mother, also an immigrant, was illiterate. He attended public schools in New York City, served in the U.S. Army in Europe during World War II, and returned to New York to attend Columbia University under the GI bill. Following graduation, he taught in a public high school on Long Island for six years, then joined the Foreign Service. He rose steadily through the ranks, served as deputy assistant secretary of state for congressional affairs from 1975 to 1977, and was named ambassador to Uruguay in 1977. He became ambassador to Nicaragua in July 1979, simultaneous with the installation of the revolutionary Government of National Reconstruction.

Larry Pezzullo is a person of extraordinary talent. He has great capacity for understanding complicated political processes. But he also has a flair for conceiving and orchestrating responses to the circumstances he faces, and an unerring sense of timing. He is a diplomatic entrepreneur who, in Nicaragua, was the right man in the right place at the right time. (He has since become executive director of Catholic Relief Services.)

Rosa Carballo was born into similar humble circumstances, but in Nicaragua. She is a woman in her sixties, highly intelligent, dignified, and self-disciplined. She has a profound understanding of human nature and sees well below the surface of the political process in her country. With those qualities, she might well have been a successful professional in another society. In Nicaragua she is a domestic servant. She is effectively illiterate.

I want to note in passing that, today, there are few countries that could not virtually eradicate illiteracy within a generation if the will to do so existed.

VALUES AND ATTITUDES THAT FOSTER PROGRESS

We now have to ask what values and attitudes foster the conditions that facilitate the expression of human creative capacity—and development. . . .

The society's world view is the source of its value and attitude systems. The world view is formed by a complex of influences, including geography, economic organization, and the vagaries of history. The world view and its related value and attitude systems are constantly changing, but usually at a very slow pace, measurable in decades or generations. The world view is expressed at least in part through religion.

Of crucial importance for development are: (1) the world view's time focus—past, present, or future; (2) the extent to which the world view encourages rationality; and (3) the concepts of equality and authority it propagates.

If a society's major focus is on the past—on the glory of earlier times or in reverence of ancestors—or if it is absorbed with today's problems of survival, the planning, organizing, saving, and investment that are the warp and woof of development are not likely to be encouraged. Orientation toward the future implies the possibility of change and progress. And that possibility, as Max Weber stressed in his landmark work *The Protestant Ethic and the Spirit of Capitalism*, must be realizable in this life. The Calvinist concepts of "calling" and "election" force the eyes of the faithful toward the future. So do the basic tenets of Judaism: "Judaism clings to the idea of Progress. The Golden Age of Humanity is not in the past, but in the future."[6]

If the society's world view encourages the belief that humans have the capacity to know and understand the world around them, that the universe operates according to a largely decipherable pattern of laws, and that the scientific method can unlock many secrets of the unknown, it is clearly imparting a set of attitudes tightly linked to the ideas of progress and change. If the world view explains worldly phenomena by supernatural forces, often in the form of numerous capricious gods and goddesses who demand obeisance from humans, there is little room for reason, education, planning, or progress.

Many world views propagate the idea of human equality, particularly in the theme of the Golden Rule and its variations. The idea is stressed more in some ethical systems than in others. It is obviously present in both the Protestant and Catholic ethical systems. But Weber argues that the traditional Catholic focus on the afterlife, in contrast to the Protestant (and Jewish) focus on life in this world, vitiates the force of the ethical system, particularly when that focus is accompanied by the cycle of transgression/confession/absolution.[7] One possible consequence may be a relatively stronger Protestant orientation toward equality and the community, and a relatively stronger Catholic orientation toward hierarchy and the individual.

Directly related to the idea of equality is the concept of authority. Subsequent chapters [in the original book—*Eds.*] observe repeatedly the negative consequences of authoritarianism for growth of individuals and societies. There may well be truth in the belief of Weber and others that traditional Catholicism, with its focus on the afterlife and the crucial role of the church hierarchy and the priest, encouraged a dependency mindset among its adherents that was an obstacle to entrepreneurial activity. Martin Luther by contrast, preached "the priesthood of all believers;"[8] every Christian had to be a monk all his life."[9]

But there are also some religions—including, to be sure, some Protestant denominations—whose basic tenets embrace the idea of inequality. Traditional Hinduism comes immediately to mind, as do Gunnar Myrdal's comments on South Asia:

> . . . Social and economic stratification is accorded the sanction of religion. . . . The inherited stratification implies low social and spatial mobility, little free competition in its wider sense, and great inequalities.[10]
>
> It should be an hypothesis for further study that people in this region are not inherently different from people elsewhere, but that they live and have lived for a long time under conditions very different from those in the Western world, and that this has left its mark upon their bodies and minds. Religion has, then, become the emotional container of this whole way of life and work and by its sanction has rendered it rigid and resistant to change.[11]

The fundamental questions of future versus past and present orientation, encouragement or discouragement of rationality, and emphasis on equality versus emphasis on authority strongly influence three other cultural factors that play an important role in the way a society develops: (1) the extent of identification with others, (2) the rigor of the ethical system, and (3) attitudes about work.

Several of the people whose works are discussed . . . (e.g., Weber, Myrdal, David McClelland) have emphasized the importance for progress of a radius of identification and trust that embraces an entire society. There is evidence that the extended family is an effective institution for survival but an obstacle to development.[12] Weber observes, "The great achievement of ethical religions, above all of the ethical and ascetistic sects of Protestantism, was to shatter the fetters of the sib [i.e., the extended family]."[13]

The social consequences of widespread mistrust can be grave. Samuel Huntington makes the point:

> . . . the absence of trust in the culture of the society provides formidable obstacles to the creation of public institutions. Those societies deficient in stable and effective government are also deficient in mutual trust among their citizens, in national and public loyalties, and in organization skills and capacity. Their political cultures are often said to be marked by suspicion, jealousy, and latent or actual hostility toward everyone who is not a member of the family, the village, or, perhaps, the tribe. These characteristics are found in many cultures, their most extensive manifestation perhaps being in the Arab world and in Latin America. . . . In Latin America . . . traditions of self-centered individualism and of distrust and hatred for other groups in society have prevailed.[14]

A whole set of possibilities opens up when trust is extended beyond the family, possibilities that are likely to be reflected in both economic and social development. Myrdal observes, ". . . a more inclusive nationalism then becomes a force for progress. . . a vehicle for rationalism and for the ideals of planning, equality, social welfare, and perhaps democracy."[15] In such an environment, the idea of cooperation will be strengthened, with all that implies for modern production techniques, community problem-solving, and political stability. The idea of compromise, which is central to the working of a pluralistic system, is also reinforced.[16] When the idea of compromise—i.e., that a relationship is important enough to warrant seeking to avoid confrontation, even if some concession is necessary—is weak, the likelihood of confrontation is increased. Constant confrontation undermines stability and continuity, which, as noted earlier, are crucial to development.

There is a gap in all societies between the stated ethical system and the extent to which that system is honored in practice. Religions' treatment of ethical issues obviously has something to do with the size of the gap. Broad identification among the members of a society will strengthen the impact of the ethical system. Where the radius of identification and trust is small, there may effectively be no operative ethical system.

The rigor of the effective ethical system will shape attitudes about justice, which are central to several major development issues. If the members of a society expect injustice, the ideas of cooperation, compromise, stability, and continuity will be undermined. Corruption and nepotism will be encouraged. And the self-discipline necessary to keep a society working well (e.g., payment of taxes, resistance to the temptation to steal) will be weakened. The system of criminal and civil jurisprudence will be politicized and corrupted and will not be taken seriously by the citizenry. The idea of justice is also central to crucial social issues: the fairness of income distribution, availability of educational opportunities and health services, and promotion by merit.

Another link to these questions of radius of identification, rigor of the effective ethical system, and justice is the idea of dissent.[17] Its acceptance is fundamental to a functioning pluralistic political system, and it is clearly related to the idea of compromise. But it is also an important idea for creativity: what the inventor and the entrepreneur do is a kind of creative dissent.

Attitudes about work link back to several of these ideas, but particularly to future orientation. If the idea of progress is well established in the culture, there is a presumption that planning and hard work will be rewarded by increased income and improved living conditions. When the focus is on the present, on day-to-day survival, the ceiling on work may be the amount necessary to survive.

This brings us back to the seven conditions that encourage the expression of human creative capacity:

1. The expectation of fair play
2. Availability of educational opportunities
3. Availability of health services
4. Encouragement of experimentation and criticism
5. Matching of skills and jobs
6. Rewards for merit and achievement
7. Stability and continuity

Taken together, the seven conditions describe a functional modern democratic capitalist society. The extent to which countries realize their potential is determined, I believe, by the extent to which these conditions exist . . . [T]he seven conditions substantially exist in the fifteen countries whose per-capita gross national product (GNP) is the highest in the world (excluding four oil-rich Arab countries). These same fifteen countries accounted for 83 percent of the Nobel Prize winners from 1945 to 1981. . . .

NOTES

1. "Development" and "progress" are used synonymously in this chapter.
2. Everett E. Hagen, *On the Theory of Social Change: How Economic Growth Begins*, p. 88.
3. Hagen makes similar points on p. 11 of *On the Theory of Social Change*.
4. This point is elaborated in Lawrence E. Harrison, "Some Hidden Costs of the Public Investment Fixation," pp. 20–23.
5. W. Arthur Lewis, *The Theory of Economic Growth*, p. 376.
6. The words of a former Chief Rabbi of Great Britain in J. H. Hertz (ed.), *The Pentateuch and Haftorahs*, p. 196.
7. Clearly, contemporary Catholicism is moving toward the Protestant and Jewish focus on this life, particularly since Pope John XXIII.
8. Quoted in David C. McClelland, *The Achieving Society*, p. 48.
9. Max Weber, *The Protestant Ethic and the Spirit of Capitalism*, p. 121.
10. Gunnar Myrdal, *Asian Drama: An Inquiry into the Poverty of Nations*, p. 104.
11. *Ibid.*, p. 112.
12. The conditions for human progress and happiness are still worse where trust extends no further than the nuclear family, as in Banfield's "Montegrano." In that case, both development and survival are threatened.
13. Max Weber, *The Religion of China*, p. 237.
14. Samuel P. Huntington, *Political Order in Changing Societies*, p. 28.
15. Myrdal, *Asian Drama*, p. 122.
16. It is, I believe, significant that there is no truly apt Spanish word for "compromise."
17. It also seems significant that there is no truly apt Spanish word for "dissent."

REFERENCES

Hagen, E. E. 1962. *On the Theory of Social Change: How Economic Growth Begins*. Homewood, IL: Dorsey Press.
Harrison, L. E. 1970. "Some Hidden Costs of the Public Investment Fixation." *International Development Review* 12.
Hertz, J. H. (ed.) 1961. *The Pentateuch and Haftorahs*. London: Soncino Press.
Huntington, S. P. 1968. *Political Order in Changing Societies*. New York and London: Yale University Press.
Lewis, W. A. 1955. *The Theory of Economic Growth*. Homewood, IL: Richard D. Irwin, Inc.
McClelland, D. C. 1961. *The Achieving Society*. Princeton: D. Van Nostrand Co., Inc.
Myrdal, G. 1968. *Asian Drama: An Inquiry into the Poverty of Nations*. New York: Pantheon.
Weber, M. 1950. *The Protestant Ethic and the Spirit of Capitalism*. New York: Charles Scribner's Sons.
Weber, M. 1951. *The Religion of China*. New York: Macmillan.
World Bank. 1982. *World Development Report*. 1982.

15

········

On the Sociology of National Development: Theories and Issues

········

ALEJANDRO PORTES

In this chapter, sociologist Alejandro Portes calls into question the value of the cultural explanations of development and underdevelopment that were the subject of Chapters 11 through 14. He begins by criticizing the proponents of this view for having misunderstood Max Weber's explanation of the importance of the Protestant ethic for the rise of capitalism. Portes then enumerates three major flaws in the logic of the culturalists: (1) the failure to consider the importance of structural constraints on development; (2) the antidevelopmental role that so-called modern values can have; and (3) the "historical fiction" of development. Structural constraints will be elaborated on in greater detail in later chapters of this book dealing with dependency and the world system.

Myron Weiner (1966) notes that, for many scholars, the starting point of any definition of development is not the character of the society but the character of individuals. The same author observes that "although there are differences among social scientists as to how values and attitudes can be changed, it is possible to speak of one school of thought that believes that attitudinal and value changes are prerequisites to creating a modern society, economy, and political system" (Weiner 1966, p. 9).

For Szymon Chodak (1973, p. 11), writers of this school do not ask, "What is development?" or "What happens in its course?" but rather why it happened and what specifically caused the breakthrough from traditional into

Reprinted with permission from the *American Journal of Sociology*, vol. 82 (July 1976):68–74.

modern societies. Where such factors were present, development happens; where they are absent, stagnation prevails. The distinctive factor is then sought in the sphere of value orientation. . . .

The search in this case is for those "mental viruses" (McClelland 1967) changing the "spirit" (Inkeles 1969) of men so that they come to adapt and promote a modern society. This perspective derives its impetus from the general emphasis in United States sociology on value-normative complexes (Parsons 1964a) as opposed to the structure of material interests in society (Mills 1956). More specifically, the value approach to the problem of development lays claim to, and often labels itself as a direct continuation of, the thesis Max Weber developed in *The Protestant Ethic and the Spirit of Capitalism* (1958).

Weber's argument was, however, securely embedded in a body of research which clearly brought forth the importance of structural forms and the politico-economic interests of groups and classes. Emergence of an urban burgher class out of the feudal "oikos" and the relative vulnerability of feudalism, as opposed for example to the "prebendary" system of China, are subjects examined at length in his work (Weber 1951). The combined effects of the political assault by the central state and the economic assault by rising urban classes on the weakened feudal order meant an increasingly "open" structure for capitalist expansion (Weber 1958; Bendix 1962). Only because of the growing predicament of a lordly class incapable of defending its position by enforcing old prerogatives could the Protestant "spirit" of capitalism, or any other spirit for that matter, transform the economic order to its own advantage (Wallerstein 1974).

Psychological theories of development, such as those proposed by David G. McClelland (1967) and Everett E. Hagen (1962), have chosen to ignore the Weberian treatment of historico-structural issues and concentrate on the primacy of ideas in society: "This is just one more piece of evidence to support the growing conviction among social scientists that it is values, motives, or psychological forces that determine ultimately the rate of economic and social development. . . . *The Achieving Society* suggests that ideas are in fact more important in shaping history than purely materialistic arrangements" (McClelland 1963, p. 17).

Since ideas inhere in individuals, these theories result in an "additive" image of societal development in which the larger the number of people "infected" by the strategic psychological ingredient, the greater the economic growth of the country. This arithmetic approach is concerned neither with differences in positions in the stratification system nor with existing arrangements of economic and political power. Theorists of this persuasion subscribe to the proverb "Where there is a will, there is a way"; their voluntarism is, in turn, predicated on the creation of sufficiently high levels of motivation. In the best known of these theories, the factor responsible for this result is labeled "*n* Achievement": "The mental virus received the odd name of n-Ach (short for 'need for Achievement') because it was identified in a sample of a person's thoughts by whether the thoughts had to do with 'doing something well' or 'doing something better' than it had been done before: more efficiently, more quickly, with less labor, with a better result and so on" (McClelland 1966, p. 29). Extrapolating the result to national development, McClelland (1966, p. 30) reports: ". . . a country that was high in n-Ach level in its children's texts around 1925 was more likely to develop rapidly from 1929 to 1950 than one that was low in n-Ach in 1925. The same result was obtained when 1950 n-Ach levels were related to rates of economic development in the late nineteen-fifties." Apart from "n-Ach," McClelland prescribes a series of additional psychological ingredients making for societal development. Sense of collective responsibility and feelings of superiority over others are the most important ones.

Hagen's (1962) theory of "withdrawal of status respect" is more complex, in a psychoanalytic sense, than McClelland's. It comes, however, to the same formal conclusion. Again, a psychological motor, present in sufficiently large numbers of people, provides the strategic impulse for economic development. In this case, however, the "virus" is not transmitted by children's texts but instead has a gestation period of several generations. Humiliations resulting from status withdrawal among parents have certain psychic consequences for their sons who, in turn, transmit them to their own children. After a complicated evolution of complexes and stages, the "virus" finally matures and is ready to do its work in society. Whether the society is ready for the actions of the new entrepreneurial group is not of major importance to the theory.

More recent, and perhaps more accepted among sociologists, is the theory of "modernity" as a psychosocial complex of values. "Modern man" is characterized, internally, by a certain mental flexibility in dealing with new situations and, externally, by similarity to the value orientations dominant in industrial Western societies (see Lerner 1965). The spirit of modernity is regarded by these writers both as a precondition for societal modernization and as a major consequence of it: "Indeed, in the end, the ideal of development requires the transformation of the nature of man—a transformation that is both a *means* to the end of yet greater growth and at the same time one of the great *ends* itself of the development process" (Inkeles 1966, p. 138).

Alex Inkeles identifies nine major attitudes and values distinguishing modern man: (1) readiness for new experience and openness to innovation, (2) disposition to form and hold opinions, (3) democratic orientation, (4) planning habits, (5) belief in human and personal efficacy, (6) belief that the world is calculable, (7) stress on personal and human dignity, (8) faith in science and technology, and (9) belief in distributive justice.

This list is not complemented by a similar description of "traditional man." The latter tends to be defined by default: whatever is not properly modern must be traditional. It is difficult to understand, however, why "traditional man" does not stress "personal and human dignity" or believe in distributive justice.

The list of what goes on to make "modern man" tends to vary from author to author. This is not surprising, since much of what enters into the definition appears to come from introspection. Theorists of this persuasion vie with each other in developing ever more elaborate descriptions of what modern man is like. In doing so, they tend to contradict one another. While, for some, individualism and self-reliance are clearly modern traits, for others the ability to subordinate personal goals to the welfare of the collectivity and the ability to work with others toward its common pursuits constitute the mark of modernity (see Kahl 1968). As seen above, dichotomies between "traditional" and "modern" man are then built by extrapolation, through attributing to the former the reverse of characteristics assigned to the latter (Gusfield 1967).

In addition to the dimensions quoted above, the following are frequently encountered in characterizations of modern man: (1) participation: motivation and ability to take part in organizations and electoral processes; (2) ambition: high mobility aspirations for self and children and willingness to take risks; (3) secularism: limited religious attachments and low receptivity to religious and ideological appeals; (4) information: frequent contact with news media and knowledge of national and international affairs; (5) consumption orientation: desire to own new goods and technologically advanced recreation and labor-saving appliances; (6) urban preference: desire to move to or remain in urban areas; (7) geographic mobility: experience of moving and or willingness to move from original residence in search of better opportunities (Lerner 1965; Kahl 1968; Schnaiberg 1970; Horowitz 1970; Portes 1974). . . .

DISCUSSION

Discussion of this . . . sociology of development must consider, however, several important aspects. A systematic presentation of these will cover three major points: structural constraints, consumption-oriented values, and historical fiction.

Structural Constraints

No matter how compelling the image of highly motivated entrepreneurs racing to break the barriers of stagnation, the fact remains that individual action is highly conditioned by external social arrangements. Despite the frequent application of "tribal" imagery to underdeveloped nations, the reality of such societies is not one of an open frontier awaiting conquest by an entrepreneurial elite. Indeed, a complex structure of economic and political interests penetrates every aspect of them. To think that more modernity, achievement motivation, or status withdrawal will automatically transform these structures is, at best, naive. Regardless of what psychologists may think, societies are not the simple "additive" sum of individual members.

An active set of individuals, motivated by whatever psychological mechanism one may wish to posit, must still cope with existing economic and political arrangements. One way of doing so is to attempt to transform them, in which case "entrepreneurs" must organize themselves and enter the political arena in conflict with entrenched interest groups. The transformation of "modernity" or "*n* Achievement" into potential rebellion and ideologically committed elites is a possibility seldom contemplated in these theories.

A second alternative is that "entrepreneurs" may attempt to work through established channels. This alternative, the most likely one in view of the costs involved, may explain the embracement by established power groups of this perspective as their sociology of development. Highly motivated modern individuals may be extremely functional for maintenance of existing power structures. They may be hired, for example, as highly paid managers of foreign corporations, as has been increasingly the practice of multinational companies (see Blair 1974). They may also be brought into preexisting civilian and military bureaucracies. There are indeed many opportunities for entrepreneurial fulfillment within the existing social order. Altruistic motivations of "moderns" may even be employed in melioristic welfare activities, irrelevant for the structural task of development but functional for legitimizing the existing politico-economic system.

Individual motivations for achievement can be absorbed, fulfilled, and utilized without changing a basic situation of economic subordination and social maldistribution. The issue is not how much individual motivation there is, or what its sources are, but rather to what goals it is directed. The fundamental individualism apparent in theories of achievement and entrepreneurial motivation may be either irrelevant or inimical to struggles for national transformation. Elites committed to the task of development are not formed by "moderns" but by "modernizers"—individuals committed to achievement of collective economic and social change (Kerr et al. 1960).

Consumption-Oriented Values

A second, related aspect has to do with some of the values defined as "modern." That most modern of traits, "empathy," is usually described as ability to comprehend and place oneself symbolically in the midst of urban-industrial life (see Lerner 1965). This, in turn, is directly linked with a "demonstration effect" which raises demands for consumption beyond what a poor country can realistically afford. Excessive, media-promoted demand is a problem faced by both status quo and development-oriented governments in the Third World. For the latter, however, it presents a major difficulty, for it exercises pressure on scarce resources required for long-term investment. The dilemma of choosing between "political" and "economic" strategies (immediate consumption and resulting mass political loyalty versus consumption restrictions and long-term planning) emerges here as a major developmental issue (Malloy 1971).

Communications experts agree that modern values are diffused through the mass media. Some argue that advertisements in the commercial media are effective carriers of the "modern" message: "Advertising itself may also be a powerful instrument of development. It is a way of facilitating the distribution of commodities, broadening the market, and making people aware of possibilities with which they would not otherwise be familiar" (Pool 1966, p. 108).

The market is certainly broadened, often for the benefit of multinational enterprises, strains are placed on the country's capacity to import, and new "possibilities" are taught which often bear no relationship to local conditions. Such modern values—premature wants, imported needs and tastes, excessive consumption—are not the values of development. Historical experiences of national development in this century show consistently the necessity for restriction of consumption and for an orientation which places as much emphasis on achievement of national goals as on personal gratification. "Mobilization systems" in the Third World have evolved precisely as attempts to diffuse these "nonmodern" values (Apter 1967).

Finally, much-derided "traditional" cultures have often furnished value legitimations necessary in periods of rapid national change. Secular modernity lacks sufficient cultural depth to match the force of great national traditions. Japanese ideology during the Meiji period furnishes perhaps the best known, but not the only, example of the uses of tradition for development (Bellah 1965; Gusfield 1967; Walton 1976).

Historical Fiction

Theories of modernity share with those of evolutionary differentiation the belief that development proceeds from an early traditional stage toward a terminal "advanced" one. It is proper at this time to complete analysis of the character of this analogy.

As seen above, tradition is described in terms which are only logical counterparts to those embodied in modernity. There is no existing nation in the Third World which can be labeled "traditional" in this sense. The fictional character of the initial stage of the process is due to the fact that it is not based on observation of actual societies but on reflection on the features of the "terminal" stage. Modernity creates tradition very much as in Owen Lattimore's (1962) words, "Civilization gave birth to barbarism."

At the other extreme, as seen above, the current stage of development in industrial societies is unlikely to be replicated in underdeveloped countries.

While providing points of reference for developmental efforts, features of currently industrialized nations are products of unique historical processes which already belong to mankind's past. The concrete features of advanced societies of today cannot be reproduced exactly in the future, nor is this the goal of most Third World nations (Illich 1969).

Sociologies of development dominant in the West thus come to posit a transition from a fictional stage to an impossible one. By concentrating on current characteristics of industrial societies, they neglect the fact that these traits, as well as those of underdeveloped societies, are themselves evolving and that social change in each type of society occurs in interaction with the other type. As a contemporary Latin American sociologist states: "A science of development is only science when it abandons the assumption of a formal goal to be reached and attempts instead to comprehend development as a historical process. . . . The object of [such] a theory cannot be to describe the passage from a society that is not really known to one that is not going to exist" (Dos Santos 1970a, p. 174).

REFERENCES

Apter, D. 1967. *The Politics of Modernization*. Chicago: University of Chicago Press.

Bellah, R. N. 1965. *Religion and Progress in Modern Asia*. New York: Free Press.

Bendix, R. 1962. *Max Weber: An Intellectual Portrait*. Garden City, N.Y.: Doubleday.

———. 1967. "Tradition and Modernity Reconsidered." *Comparative Studies in Society and History* 9 (April):292–346.

Blair, C. P. 1974. "Las Empresas multinacionales en el comercio Latino-americano: Una Mirada hacia el futuro." Mimeographed. Austin: University of Texas.

Chodak, S. 1973. *Societal Development*. New York: Oxford University Press.

Dos Santos, T. 1970a. "La Crisis de la teoria del desarrollo y las relaciones de dependencia en America Latina." Pp. 147–87 in *La Dependencia politico-economica de America Latina*. Mexico, D.F.: Siglo Veintiuno.

———. 1970b. "The Structure of Dependence." *American Economic Review* 60 (May):231–36.

Gusfield, J. R. 1967. "Tradition and Modernity: Misplaced Polarities in the Study of Social Change." *American Journal of Sociology* 72 (January): 351–62.

Hagen, E. E. 1962. *On the Theory of Social Change*. Homewood, Ill.: Dorsey.

Horowitz, I. L. 1966. *Three Worlds of Development*. New York: Oxford University Press.

———. 1970. "Personality and Structural Dimensions in Comparative International Development." *Social Science Quarterly* 51 (December): 494–513.

Illich, I. 1969. *Celebration of Awareness*. New York: Doubleday.

Inkeles, A. 1966. "The Modernization of Man." Pp. 138–50 in *Modernization: The Dynamics of Growth*, edited by Myron Weiner. New York: Basic.

———. 1969. "Making Men Modern: On the Causes and Consequences of

Individual Change in Six Countries." *American Journal of Sociology* 75 (September):208-25.

Kahl, J. A. 1968. *The Measurement of Modernism*. Austin: University of Texas Press.

Kerr, C., J. T. Dunlop, F. Harbison, and C. A. Myers. 1960. *Industrialism and Industrial Man: The Problems of Labor and Management in Economic Growth*. New York: Oxford University Press.

Lattimore, O. 1962. "La Civilisation, mère de barbarie." *Annales* E.S.C. 17 (January–February):99.

Lerner, D. 1965. *The Passing of Traditional Society: Modernizing the Middle East*. New York: Free Press.

McClelland, D. G. 1963. "Motivational Patterns in Southeast Asia with Special Reference to the Chinese Case." *Journal of Social Issues* 29 (January):17.

———. 1966. "The Impulse of Modernization." Pp. 28–39 in *Modernization: The Dynamics of Growth*, edited by Myron Weiner. New York: Basic.

———. 1967. *The Achieving Society*. New York: Free Press.

Malloy, J. M. 1971. "Generation of Political Support and Allocation of Costs." Pp. 23–42 in *Revolutionary Change in Cuba*, edited by C. Mesa-Lago. Pittsburgh: University of Pittsburgh Press.

Mills, C. W. 1956. *The Power Elite*. New York: Oxford University Press.

Parsons, T. 1964a. *The Social System*. New York: Free Press.

———. 1964b. "Evolutionary Universals in Society." *American Sociological Review* 29 (June):339–57.

Pool, I. S. 1966. "Communications and Development." Pp. 98–109 in *Modernization: The Dynamics of Growth*, edited by Myron Weiner. New York: Basic.

Portes, A. 1974. "Modernity and Development: A Critique." *Studies in Comparative International Development* 9 (Spring):247–79.

Schnaiberg, A. 1970. "Measuring Modernism: Theoretical and Empirical Explorations." *American Journal of Sociology* 76 (December):399–425.

Wallerstein, I. 1974. *The Modern World-System—Capitalist Agriculture and the Origins of the European World-Economy in the Sixteenth Century*. New York: Academic Press.

Walton, J. 1974. "Urban Hierarchies and Patterns of Dependence in Latin America." Paper presented at the May 1974 Seminar on New Directions of Urban Research in Latin America, Institute of Latin American Studies, University of Texas at Austin.

———. 1976. "Elites and the Politics of Urban Development." In *Urban Latin America: The Political Condition from Above and Below*, by A. Portes and J. Walton. Austin: University of Texas Press.

Weber, M. 1951. *The Religion of China*. New York: Free Press.

———. 1958. *The City*. New York: Free Press.

Weiner, M. 1966. "Introduction." Pp. 1–14 in *Modernization: The Dynamics of Growth*, edited by M. Weiner. New York: Basic.

PART 4

. . . .

Dependency and World-System Theory

. . . .

16

· · · · · · ·

The Structure of Dependence

· · · · · · ·

THEOTONIO DOS SANTOS

In Part 3 of this book we examined internal causes of slow growth among the poor countries. In Part 4 we examine external causes, starting with dependency. In this chapter, Theotonio dos Santos, a Brazilian economist, provides a classical definition of dependency. Dos Santos is a member of what has been called the "dependentista school" of development thinkers, the great majority of whom are Latin American intellectuals. Dependency theory comes in many varieties; indeed, some argue that there is no such thing as dependency "theory." Nonetheless, there is a body of thinking common to many of those in the dependista school, and in this chapter dos Santos presents a concise statement of some of its fundamental tenets. He definnes dependence and shows its linkages to Marxian theory, then goes on to elaborate three basic forms of dependence: (1) colonial, (2) financial-industrial, and (3) multinational. This latter form, arising out of the power of the large multinational corporations that maintain operations in developing countries, is of greatest concern to dos Santos because he sees it as limiting the developmental potential of newly industrializing nations. This new form of dependence restricts the size of the local market and thus contributes to income inequality in developing nations. Ultimately, according to dos Santos, dependent development must culminate in revolutionary movements of the left or right.

This chapter attempts to demonstrate that the dependence of Latin American countries on other countries cannot be overcome without a qualitative change

Reprinted with permission from *The American Economic Review*, vol. 60 (May 1970):231–236.

in their internal structures and external relations. We shall attempt to show that the relations of dependence to which these countries are subjected conform to a type of international and internal structure which leads them to underdevelopment or more precisely to a dependent structure that deepens and aggravates the fundamental problems of their peoples.

I. WHAT IS DEPENDENCE?

By dependence we mean a situation in which the economy of certain countries is conditioned by the development and expansion of another economy to which the former is subjected. The relation of interdependence between two or more economies, and between these and world trade, assumes the form of dependence when some countries (the dominant ones) can expand and can be self-sustaining, while other countries (the dependent ones) can do this only as a reflection of that expansion, which can have either a positive or a negative effect on their immediate development [see reference no. 7, p. 6].

The concept of dependence permits us to see the internal situation of these countries as part of world economy. In the Marxian tradition, the theory of imperialism has been developed as a study of the process of expansion of the imperialist centers and of their world domination. In the epoch of the revolutionary movement of the Third World, we have to develop the theory of laws of internal development in those countries that are the object of such expansion and are governed by them. This theoretical step transcends the theory of development which seeks to explain the situation of the underdeveloped countries as a product of their slowness or failure to adopt the patterns of efficiency characteristic of developed countries (or to "modernize" or "develop" themselves). Although capitalist development theory admits the existence of an "external" dependence, it is unable to perceive underdevelopment in the way our present theory perceives it, as a consequence and part of the process of the world expansion of capitalism—a part that is necessary to and integrally linked with it.

In analyzing the process of constituting a world economy that integrates the so-called "national economies" in a world market of commodities, capital, and even of labor power, we see that the relations produced by this market are unequal and combined—unequal because development of parts of the system occurs at the expense of other parts. Trade relations are based on monopolistic control of the market, which leads to the transfer of surplus generated in the dependent countries to the dominant countries; financial relations are, from the viewpoint of the dominant powers, based on loans and the export of capital, which permit them to receive interest and profits, thus increasing their domestic surplus and strengthening their control over the economies of the other countries. For the dependent countries these relations represent an export of profits and interest which carries off part of the surplus generated domestically and leads to a loss of control over their productive resources. In order to permit these disadvantageous relations, the dependent countries must generate large surpluses, not in such a way as to create higher levels of technology but rather creating superexploited manpower. The result is to limit the development of their internal market and their technical and cultural capacity, as well as the moral and physical health of their people. We call this combined development because it is the combination of these inequalities and the transfer of resources from the most backward and dependent sectors to the most advanced and dominant ones which explains the inequality, deepens it, and transforms it into a necessary and structural element of the world economy.

II. HISTORIC FORMS OF DEPENDENCE

Historic forms of dependence are conditioned by: (1) the basic forms of this world economy which has its own laws of development; (2) the type of economic relations dominant in the capitalist centers and the ways in which the latter expand outward; and (3) the types of economic relations existing inside the peripheral countries which are incorporated into the situation of dependence within the network of international economic relations generated by capitalist expansion. It is not within the purview of this chapter to study these forms in detail but only to distinguish broad characteristics of development.

Drawing on an earlier study, we may distinguish: (1) Colonial dependence, trade export in nature, in which commercial and financial capital in alliance with the colonialist state dominated the economic relations of the Europeans and the colonies by means of a trade monopoly, complemented by a colonial monopoly of land, mines, and manpower (self or slave) in the colonized countries. (2) Financial-industrial dependence, which consolidated itself at the end of the nineteenth century, characterized by the domination of big capital in the hegemonic centers, and its expansion abroad through investment in the production of raw materials and agricultural products for consumption in the hegemonic centers. A productive structure grew up in the dependent countries devoted to the export of these products (which I.V. Levin labeled export economies [11]; other analysis in other regions [12] [13]), producing what the Economic Commission for Latin America (ECLA) has called "foreign-oriented development" (*desarrollo hacia afuera*) [4]. (3) In the postwar period a new type of dependence has been consolidated, based on multinational corporations which began to invest in industries geared to the internal market of underdeveloped countries. This form of dependence is basically technological-industrial dependence [6].

Each of these forms of dependence corresponds to a situation which conditioned not only the international relations of these countries but also their internal structures: the orientation of production, the forms of capital accumulation, the reproduction of the economy, and, simultaneously, their social and political structure.

III. THE EXPORT ECONOMIES

In forms (1) and (2) of dependence, production is geared to those products destined for export (gold, silver, and tropical products in the colonial epoch; raw materials and agricultural products in the epoch of industrial-financial dependence); i.e., production is determined by demand from the hegemonic centers. The internal productive structure is characterized by rigid specialization and monoculture in entire regions (the Caribbean, the Brazilian Northeast, etc.). Alongside these export sectors there grew up certain complementary economic activities (cattle-raising and some manufacturing, for example) which were dependent, in general, on the export sector to which they sell their products. There was a third, subsistence economy which provided manpower for the export sector under favorable conditions and toward which excess population shifted during periods unfavorable to international trade.

Under these conditions, the existing internal market was restricted by four factors: (1) Most of the national income was derived from export, which was used to purchase the inputs required by export production (slaves, for example) or luxury goods consumed by the hacienda- and mine-owners, and by the more prosperous employees. (2) The available manpower was subject to very arduous forms of superexploitation, which limited its consumption. (3) Part of the consumption of these workers was provided by the subsistence economy, which served as a complement to their income and as a refuge during periods of depression. (4) A fourth factor was to be found in those countries in which land and mines were in the hands of foreigners (cases of an enclave economy): a great part of the accumulated surplus was destined to be sent abroad in the form of profits, limiting not only internal consumption but also possibilities of reinvestment [1]. In the case of enclave economies the relations of the foreign companies with the hegemonic center were even more exploitative and were complemented by the fact that purchases by the enclave were made directly abroad.

IV. THE NEW DEPENDENCE

The new form of dependence, (3) above, is in process of developing and is conditioned by the exigencies of the international commodity and capital markets. The possibility of generating new investments depends on the existence of financial resources in foreign currency for the purchase of machinery and processed raw materials not produced domestically. Such purchases are subject to two limitations: the limit of resources generated by the export sector (reflected in the balance of payments, which includes not only trade but also service relations); and the limitations of monopoly on patents which leads monopolistic firms to prefer to transfer their machines in the form of capital rather than as commodities for sale. It is necessary to analyze these relations of dependence if we are to understand the fundamental structural limits they place on the development of these economies.

1. Industrial development is dependent on an export sector for the foreign currency to buy the inputs utilized by the industrial sector. The first consequence of this dependence is the need to preserve the traditional export sector, which limits economically the development of the internal market by the conservation of backward relations of production and signifies, politically, the maintenance of power by traditional decadent oligarchies. In the countries where these sectors are controlled by foreign capital, it signifies the remittance abroad of high profits, and political dependence on those interests. Only in rare instances does foreign capital not control at least the marketing of these products. In response to these limitations, dependent countries in the 1930s and 1940s developed a policy of exchange restrictions and taxes on the national and foreign export sector; today they tend toward the gradual nationalization of production and toward the imposition of certain timid limitations on foreign control of the marketing of exported products. Furthermore, they seek, still somewhat timidly, to obtain better terms for the sale of their products. In recent decades, they have created mechanisms for international price agreements, and today the United Nations Conference on Trade and Development (UNCTAD) and ECLA press to obtain more favorable tariff conditions for these products on the part of the hegemonic centers. It is important to point out that the industrial development of these countries is dependent on the situation of the export sector, the continued existence of which they are obliged to accept.

2. Industrial development is, then, strongly conditioned by fluctuations in the balance of payments. This leads toward deficit due to the relations of dependence themselves. The causes of the deficit are three:

a. Trade relations take place in a highly monopolized international market, which tends to lower the price of raw materials and to raise the prices of industrial products, particularly inputs. In the second place, there is a tendency in modern technology to replace various primary products with synthetic raw materials. Consequently, the balance of trade in these countries tends to be less favorable (even though they show a general surplus). The overall Latin American balance of trade from 1946 to 1968 shows a surplus for each of those years. The same thing happens in almost every underdeveloped country. However, the losses due to deterioration of the terms of trade (on the basis of data from ECLA and the International Monetary Fund), excluding Cuba, were $26,383 million for the 1951-66 period, taking 1950 prices as a base. If Cuba and Venezuela are excluded, the total is $15,925 million.

b. For the reasons already given, foreign capital retains control over the most dynamic sectors of the economy and repatriates a high volume of profit; consequently, capital accounts are highly unfavorable to dependent countries. The data show that the amount of capital leaving the country is much greater than the amount entering; this produces an enslaving deficit in capital accounts. To this must be added the deficit in certain services which are virtually under total foreign control—such as freight transport, royalty payments, technical aid, etc. Consequently, an important deficit is produced in the total balance of payments; thus limiting the possibility of importation of inputs for industrialization.

c. The result is that "foreign financing" becomes necessary, in two forms: to cover the existing deficit, and to "finance" development by means of loans for the stimulation of investments and to "supply" an internal economic surplus which was decapitalized to a large extent by the remittance of part of the surplus generated domestically and sent abroad as profits.

Foreign capital and foreign "aid" thus fill up the holes that they themselves created. The real value of this aid, however, is doubtful. If overcharges resulting from the restrictive terms of the aid are subtracted from the total amount of the grants, the average net flow, according to calculations of the Inter-American Economic and Social Council, is approximately 54 percent of the gross flow [5].

If we take account of certain further facts—that a high proportion of aid is paid in local currencies, that Latin American countries make contributions to international financial institutions, and that credits are often "tied"—we find a "real component of foreign aid" of 42.2 percent on a very favorable hypothesis and of 38.3 percent on a more realistic one [5, II, p. 33]. The gravity of the situation becomes even clearer if we consider that these credits are used in large part to finance North American investments, to subsidize foreign imports which compete with national products, to introduce technology not adapted to the needs of underdeveloped countries, and to invest in low-priority sectors of the national economies. The hard truth is that the underdeveloped countries have to pay for all of the "aid" they receive. This situation is generating an enormous protest movement by Latin American governments seeking at least partial relief from such negative relations.

3. Finally, industrial development is strongly conditioned by the technological monopoly exercised by imperialist centers. We have seen that the underdeveloped countries depend on the importation of machinery and raw materials for the development of their industries. However, these goods are not freely available in the international market; they are patented and usually belong to the big companies. The big companies do not sell machinery and processed raw materials as simple merchandise: they demand either the payment of royalties, etc., for their utilization or, in most cases, they convert these goods into capital and introduce them in the form of their own investments. This is how machinery which is replaced in the hegemonic centers by more advanced technology is sent to dependent countries as capital

for the installation of affiliates. Let us pause and examine these relations in order to understand their oppressive and exploitative character.

The dependent countries do not have sufficient foreign currency, for the reasons given. Local businessmen have financing difficulties, and they must pay for the utilization of certain patented techniques. These factors oblige the national bourgeois governments to facilitate the entry of foreign capital in order to supply the restricted national market, which is strongly protected by high tariffs in order to promote industrialization. Thus, foreign capital enters with all the advantages: in many cases, it is given exemption from exchange controls for the importation of machinery; financing of sites for installation of industries is provided; government financing agencies facilitate industrialization; loans are available from foreign and domestic banks, which prefer such clients; foreign aid often subsidizes such investments and finances complementary public investments; after installation, high profits obtained in such favorable circumstances can be reinvested freely. Thus it is not surprising that the data of the U.S. Department of Commerce reveal that the percentage of capital brought in from abroad by these companies is but a part of the total amount of invested capital. These data show that in the period from 1946 to 1967 the new entries of capital into Latin America for direct investment amounted to $5,415 million, while the sum of reinvested profits was $4,424 million. On the other hand, the transfers of profits from Latin America to the United States amounted to $14,775 million. If we estimate total profits as approximately equal to transfers plus reinvestments we have the sum of $18,983 million. In spite of enormous transfers of profits to the United States, the book value of the United States's direct investment in Latin America went from $3,045 million in 1946 to $10,213 million in 1967. From these data it is clear that: (1) Of the new investments made by U.S. companies in Latin America for the period 1946–67, 55 percent corresponds to new entries of capital and 45 percent to reinvestment of profits; in recent years, the trend is more marked, with reinvestments between 1960 and 1966 representing more than 60 percent of new investments. (2) Remittances remained at about 10 percent of book value throughout the period. (3) The ratio of remitted capital to new flow is around 2.7 for the period 1946–67; that is, for each dollar that enters $2.70 leaves. In the 1960s this ratio roughly doubled, and in some years was considerably higher.

The *Survey of Current Business* data on sources and uses of funds for direct North American investment in Latin America in the period 1957–64 show that, of the total sources of direct investment in Latin America, only 11.8 percent came from the United States. The remainder is, in large part, the result of the activities of North American firms in Latin America (46.4 percent net income, 27.7 percent under the heading of depreciation), and from "sources located abroad" (14.1 percent). It is significant that the funds obtained abroad that are external to the companies are greater than the funds originating in the United States.

V. EFFECTS ON THE PRODUCTIVE STRUCTURE

It is easy to grasp, even if only superficially, the effects that this dependent structure has on the productive system itself in these countries and the role of this structure in determining a specified type of development, characterized by its dependent nature.

The productive system in the underdeveloped countries is essentially determined by these international relations. In the first place, the need to conserve the agrarian or mining export structure generates a combination between more advanced economic centers that extract surplus value from the more backward sectors and internal "metropolitan" centers on the one hand, and internal interdependent "colonial" centers on the other [10]. The unequal and combined character of capitalist development at the international level is reproduced internally in an acute form. In the second place the industrial and technological structure responds more closely to the interests of the multi-national corporations than to internal developmental needs (conceived of not only in terms of the overall interests of the population, but also from the point of view of the interests of a national capitalist development). In the third place, the same technological and economic-financial concentration of the hegemonic economies is transferred without substantial alteration to very different economies and societies, giving rise to a highly unequal productive structure, a high concentration of incomes, underutilization of installed capacity, intensive exploitation of existing markets concentrated in large cities, etc.

The accumulation of capital in such circumstances assumes its own characteristics. In the first place, it is characterized by profound differences among domestic wage-levels, in the context of a local cheap labor market, combined with a capital-intensive technology. The result, from the point of view of relative surplus value, is a high rate of exploitation of labor power. (On measurements of forms of exploitation, see [3].)

This exploitation is further aggravated by the high prices of industrial products enforced by protectionism, exemptions and subsidies given by the national governments, and "aid" from hegemonic centers. Furthermore, since dependent accumulation is necessarily tied into the international economy, it is profoundly conditioned by the unequal and combined character of international capitalist economic relations, by the technological and financial control of the imperialist centers by the realities of the balance of payments, by the economic policies of the state, etc. The role of the state in the growth of national and foreign capital merits a much fuller analysis than can be made here.

Using the analysis offered here as a point of departure, it is possible to understand the limits that this productive system imposes on the growth of the internal markets of these countries. The survival of traditional relations in the countryside is a serious limitation on the size of the market, since industrialization does not offer hopeful prospects. The productive structure created by dependent industrialization limits the growth of the internal market.

First, it subjects the labor force to highly exploitative relations which limit its purchasing power. Second, in adopting a technology of intensive capital use, it creates very few jobs in comparison with population growth, and limits the generation of new sources of income. These two limitations affect the growth of the consumer goods market. Third, the remittance abroad of profits carries away part of the economic surplus generated within the country. In all these ways limits are put on the possible creation of basic national industries which could provide a market for the capital goods this surplus would make possible if it were not remitted abroad.

From this cursory analysis we see that the alleged backwardness of these economies is not due to a lack of integration with capitalism but that, to the contrary, the most powerful obstacles to their full development come from the way in which they are joined to this international system and its laws of development.

VI. SOME CONCLUSIONS: DEPENDENT REPRODUCTION

In order to understand the system of dependent reproduction and the socio-economic institutions created by it, we must see it as part of a system of world economic relations based on monopolistic control of large-scale capital, on control of certain economic and financial centers over others, on a monopoly of complex technology that leads to unequal and combined development at a national and international level. Attempts to analyze backwardness as a failure to assimilate more advanced models of production or to modernize are nothing more than ideology disguised as science. The same is true of the attempts to analyze this international economy in terms of relations among elements in free competition, such as the theory of comparative costs which seeks to justify the inequalities of the world economic system and to conceal the relations of exploitation on which it is based [14].

In reality we can understand what is happening in the underdeveloped countries only when we see that they develop within the framework of a process of dependent production and reproduction. This system is a dependent one because it reproduces a productive system whose development is limited by those world relations which necessarily lead to: the development of only certain economic sectors, to trade under unequal conditions [9], to domestic competition with international capital under unequal conditions, to the imposition of relations of superexploitation of the domestic labor force with a view to dividing the economic surplus thus generated between internal and external forces of domination. (On economic surplus and its utilization in the dependent countries, see [1].)

In reproducing such a productive system and such international relations, the development of dependent capitalism reproduces the factors that prevent it from reaching a nationally and internationally advantageous situation; and it thus reproduces backwardness, misery, and social marginalization within its borders. The development that it produces benefits very narrow sectors, encounters unyielding domestic obstacles to its continued economic growth (with respect to both internal and foreign markets), and leads to the progressive accumulation of balance-of-payments deficits, which in turn generate more dependence and more superexploitation.

The political measures proposed by the developmentalists of ECLA, UNCTAD, Inter-American Development Bank (BID), etc., do not appear to permit destruction of these terrible chains imposed by dependent development. We have examined the alternative forms of development presented for Latin America and the dependent countries under such conditions elsewhere [8]. Everything now indicates that what can be expected is a long process of sharp political and military confrontations and of profound social radicalization which will lead these countries to a dilemma: governments of force, which open the way to fascism, or popular revolutionary governments, which open the way to socialism. Intermediate solutions have proved to be, in such a contradictory reality, empty and utopian.

REFERENCES

1. Paul Baran, *Political Economy of Growth* (Monthly Review Press, 1967).

2. Thomas Balogh, *Unequal Partners* (Basil Blackwell, 1963).

3. Pablo Gonzalez Casanova, *Sociología de la explotación, Siglo XXI* (México, 1969).

4. Cepal, *La CEPAL y el Análisis del Desarrollo Latinoamericano* (1968, Santiago, Chile).

5. Consejo Interamericano Economico Social (CIES) O.A.S., Interamerican Economic and Social Council, External Financing for Development in L.A. *El Financiamiento Externo para el Desarrollo de América Latina* (Pan-American Union, Washington,1969).

6. Theotonio Dos Santos, *El nuevo carácter de la dependencia*, CESO (Santiago de Chile, 1968).

7. ———, *La crisis de la teoría del desarrollo y las relaciones de dependencia en América Latina*, Boletin del CESO, 3 (Santiago, Chile, 1968).

8. ———, *La dependencia económica y las alternotivas de cambio en América Latina*, Ponencia al IX Congreso Latinoamericano de Sociología (México, Nov., 1969).

9. A. Emmanuel, *L'Echange Inégal* (Maspero, Paris, 1969).

10. Andre G. Frank, *Development and Underdevelopment in Latin America* (Monthly Review Press, 1968).

11. I. V. Levin, *The Export Economies* (Harvard Univ. Press, 1964).

12. Gunnar Myrdal, *Asian Drama* (Pantheon, 1968).

13. K. Nkrumah, *Neocolonialismo, última etapa del imperialismo* (Siglo XXI, México, 1966).

14. Cristian Palloix, *Problemes de la Croissance en Economie Ouverte* (Maspero, Paris, 1969).

17

· · · · · · ·

Modernization and Dependency: Alternative Perspectives in the Study of Latin American Underdevelopment

· · · · · · ·

J. SAMUEL VALENZUELA & ARTURO VALENZUELA

This chapter contrasts the modernization and dependency perspectives. Because the main notions of modernization theory have been covered in the previous chapters, only those portions of the Valenzuelas' discussion that elaborate on dependency theory are included here. The Valenzuelas enumerate the principal assumptions held by dependency thinkers and present some of the supporting evidence for the theory's validity, drawing upon the Latin American experience. After evaluating the relative merits of the two perspectives, they conclude that dependency is the superior framework primarily because it is firmly grounded in historical reality.

THE DEPENDENCY PERSPECTIVE

Like the modernization perspective, the dependency perspective resulted from the work of many different scholars in different branches of the social sciences. Much of the work proceeded in an inductive fashion. This was the case with economists working in the Economic Commission for Latin America (ECLA) who first sought to explain the underdevelopment of Latin America by focusing on the unequal terms of trade between exporters of raw materials and exporters of manufactured goods. ECLA "doctrine" called for a concerted effort to diversify the export base of Latin American countries and

Reprinted with permission from *Comparative Politics*, vol. 10 (July 1978), pp. 543-557.

accelerate industrialization efforts through import substitution. However, the continued difficulties with that model of development soon led to a focus on the internal constraints to industrialization, with an emphasis on factors such as the distorting effects of unequal land tenure patterns and the corrosive results of an inflation best explained by structural rather than monetary variables. Soon these two trends came together when scholars, such as Osvaldo Sunkel, combined the early emphasis on external variables with the internal constraints to development.[1]

But this dependency perspective was anticipated by Latin American historians who had been working for years on various aspects of economic history. Studies such as those of Sergio Bagú stressed the close interrelation of domestic developments in Latin America and developments in metropolitan countries. And in Brazil, sociologists such as Florestan Fernandes, Octávio Ianni, Fernando Henrique Cardoso, and Theotonio dos Santos also turned to broad structural analyses of the factors of underdevelopment. The fact that many of these scholars found themselves in Santiago in the 1960s only contributed to further development of the perspective.

In its emphasis on the expansive nature of capitalism and in its structural analysis of society, the dependency literature draws on Marxist insights and is related to the Marxist theory of imperialism. However, its examination of processes in Latin America imply important revisions in classical Leninist formulations, both historically and in light of recent trends. The focus is on explaining Latin American underdevelopment, and not on the functioning of capitalism, though some authors argue that their efforts will contribute to an understanding of capitalism and its contradictions.

Assumptions

The dependency perspective rejects the assumption made by modernization writers that the unit of analysis in studying underdevelopment is the national society. The domestic cultural and institutional features of Latin America are in themselves simply not the key variables accounting for the relative backwardness of the area, though, as will be seen below, domestic structures are certainly critical intervening factors. The relative presence of traditional and modern features may, or may not, help to differentiate societies; but it does not in itself explain the origins of modernity in some contexts and the lack of modernity in others. As such, the tradition-modernity polarity is of little value as a fundamental working concept. The dependency perspective assumes that the development of a national or regional unit can only be understood in connection with its historical insertion into the worldwide political-economic system which emerged with the wave of European colonizations of the world. This global system is thought to be characterized by the unequal but combined development of its different components. As Sunkel and Pedro Paz put it:

> Both underdevelopment and development are aspects of the same phenomenon, both are historically simultaneous, both are linked functionally and, therefore, interact and condition each other mutually. This results ... in the division of the world between industrial, advanced or "central" countries, and underdeveloped, backward or "peripheral" countries. ... [2]

The center is viewed as capable of dynamic development responsive to internal needs, and as the main beneficiary of the global links. On the other hand, the periphery is seen as having a reflex type of development; one which is both constrained by its incorporation into the global system and which results from its adaptation to the requirements of the expansion of the center. As dos Santos indicates:

> Dependency is a situation in which a certain number of countries have their economy conditioned by the development and expansion of another ... placing the dependent countries in a backward position exploited by the dominant countries.[3]

It is important to stress that the process can be understood only by reference to its historical dimension and by focusing on the total network of social relations as they evolve in different contexts over time. For this reason dependence is characterized as "structural, historical and totalizing" or an "integral analysis of development."[4] It is meaningless to develop, as some social scientists have, a series of synchronic statistical indicators to establish relative levels of dependence or independence among different national units to test the "validity" of the model.[5] The unequal development of the world goes back to the sixteenth century with the formation of a capitalist world economy in which some countries in the center were able to specialize in industrial production of manufactured goods because the peripheral areas of the world which they colonized provided the necessary primary goods, agricultural and mineral, for consumption in the center. Contrary to some assumptions in economic theory, the international division of labor did not lead to parallel development through comparative advantage. The center states gained at the expense of the periphery. But, just as significantly, the different functions of center and peripheral societies had a profound effect on the evolution of internal social and political structures. Those which evolved in the periphery reinforced economies with a narrow range of primary exports. The interdependent nature of the world capitalist system and the qualitative transformations in that system over time make it inconceivable to think that individual nations on the periphery could somehow replicate the evolutionary experience of the now developed nations.[6]

It follows from an emphasis on global structural processes and variations in internal structural arrangements that contextual variables, at least in the long run, shape and guide the behavior of groups and individuals. It is not inappropriate attitudes which contribute to the absence of entrepreneurial behavior or to institutional arrangements reinforcing underdevelopment. Dependent, peripheral development produces an opportunity structure such that personal gain for dominant groups and entrepreneurial elements is not conducive to the collective gain of balanced development. This is a fundamental difference with much of the modernization literature. It implies that dependence analysts, though they do not articulate the point explicitly, share the classical economic theorists' view of human nature. They assume that individuals in widely different societies are capable of pursuing rational patterns of behavior; able to assess information objectively in the pursuit of utilitarian goals. What varies is not the degree of rationality, but the structural foundations of the incentive systems which, in turn, produce different forms of behavior given the same process of rational calculus. It was not attitudinal transformations which generated the rapid industrialization which developed after the Great Depression, but the need to replace imports with domestic products. Or, as Cardoso points out in his studies of entrepreneurs, it is not values which condition their behavior as much as technological dependence, state intervention in the economy, and their political weakness vis-à-vis domestic and foreign actors.[7] What appear as anomalies in the modernization literature can be accounted for by a focus on contextual processes in the dependence literature.

It is necessary to underscore the fact that dependency writers stress the importance of the "way internal and external structural components are connected" in elaborating the structural context of underdevelopment. As such, underdevelopment is not simply the result of "external constraints" on peripheral societies, nor can dependency be operationalized solely with reference to clusters of external variables.[8] Dependency in any given society is a complex set of associations in which the external dimensions are determinative in varying degrees and, indeed, internal variables may very well reinforce the pattern of external linkages. Historically, it has been rare for local interests to develop on the periphery which are capable of charting a successful policy of self-sustained development. Dominant local interests, given the nature of class arrangements emerging from the characteristics of peripheral economies, have tended to favor the preservation of rearticulation of patterns of dependency in their interests.

It is also important to note that while relations of dependency viewed historically help to explain underdevelopment, it does not follow that dependent relations today necessarily perpetuate across the board underdevelopment. With the evolution of the world system, the impact of dependent relations can change in particular contexts. This is why Cardoso, in studying contemporary Brazil, stresses the possibility of "associated-dependent development," and Sunkel and Edmundo Fuenzalida are able to envision sharp economic growth among countries most tied into the contemporary transnational system.[9] Because external-internal relations are complex, and because changes in the world system over time introduce new realities, it is indispensable to study comparatively concrete national and historical situations. As Aníbal Quijano says, "The relationships of dependency. . . take on many forms. The national societies in Latin America are dependent, as is the case with the majority of the Asian, African and some European countries. However, each case does not present identical dependency relations."[10] The dependency perspective has thus concentrated on a careful historical evaluation of the similarities and differences in the "situations of dependency" of the various Latin American countries over time implying careful attention to "preexisting conditions" in different contexts.[11]

The description of various phases in the world system and differing configurations of external-internal linkages, follow from this insistence on diachronic analysis and its application to concrete cases. The dependency perspective is primarily a historical model with no claim to "universal validity." This is why it has paid less attention to the formulation of precise theoretical constructs, such as those found in the modernization literature, and more attention to the specification of historical phases which are an integral part of the framework.

The dependency literature distinguishes between the "mercantilistic" colonial period (1500–1750), the period of "outward growth" dependent on primary exports (1750–1914), the period of the crisis of the "liberal model" (1914–1950), and the current period of "transnational capitalism."

As already noted, because of the need for raw materials and foodstuffs for the growing industrialization of England, Germany, the United States, and France, Latin American productive structures were aimed from the outset at the export market. During the colonial period, the economic specialization was imposed by the Iberian monarchies. As Bagú notes in his classic study, "Colonial production was not directed by the needs of national consumers, and not even by the interests of local producers. The lines of production were structured and transformed to conform to an order determined by the imperial metropolis. The colonial economy was consequently shaped by its complementary character. The products that did not compete with those of Spain or Portugal in the metropolitan, international or colonial markets, found tolerance or stimulus. . . ."[12] During the nineteenth century, exports were actively pursued by the politically dominant groups. The independence movement did not attempt to transform internal productive structures; it was aimed at eliminating Iberian interference in the commercialization of products to and from England and northern Europe. The logic of the productive system in this period of "outwardly directed development," in ECLA's terms, was not conducive to the creation of a large industrial sector. Economic rationality, not only of individual entrepreneurs but also of the system, dictated payments in kind and/or extremely low wages and/or the use of slavery, thus markedly limiting the internal market. At the same time, the accumulation of foreign exchange made relatively easy the acquisition of imported industrial products. Any expansion of exports was due more to political than economic factors and depended on a saleable export commodity, and plenty of land and labor, for its success.

There were, however, important differences among regions and countries. During the colonial period these are attributable to differences in colonial administrations, natural resources, and types of production. During the nineteenth century a key difference was the degree of local elite control over productive activities for export. Though in all countries elites controlled export production initially (external commercialization was mainly under foreign control), toward the end of the century in some countries control was largely relinquished to foreign exploitation. Where this occurred, the economic role of local elites was reduced considerably, though the importance of this reduction varied depending both on the degree to which the foreign enclave displaced the local elite from the export sector and the extent to which its economic activities were diversified. Concurrently, the state bureaucracy expanded and acquired increasing importance through regulations and taxation of the enclave sector. The state thus became the principal intermediary between the local economy and the enclave, which generally had little *direct* internal secondary impact. Other differences, especially at the turn of the century, are the varying importance of incipient industrialization, the size and importance of middle- and working-class groups, variations in export products, natural resources, and so on.[13]

The world wars and the depression produced a crisis in the export-oriented economies through the collapse of external demand, and therefore of the capacity to import. The adoption of fiscal and monetary policies aimed at supporting the internal market and avoiding the negative effects of the external disequilibrium produced a favorable climate for the growth of an industrial sector under national auspices. The available foreign exchange was employed to acquire capital goods to substitute imports of consumer articles.[14] The early successes of the transition to what ECLA calls "inwardly directed development" depended to a large extent on the different political alliances which emerged in the various national settings, and on the characteristics of the social and political structures inherited from the precrisis period.

Thus, in the enclave situations the earliest developments were attained in Mexico and Chile, where middle- and lower-class groups allied in supporting state development policies, ultimately strengthening the urban bourgeoisie. The alliance was successful in Chile because of the importance of middle-class parties which emerged during the final period of export-oriented development, and the early consolidation of a trade union movement. The antecedents of the Mexican situation are to be found in the destruction of agricultural elites during the revolution. Such structural conditions were absent in other enclave situations (Bolivia, Perú, Venezuela, and Central America) where the internal development phase began later under new conditions of dependence, though in some cases with similar political alliances (Bolivia, Venezuela, Guatemala, Costa Rica). Throughout the crisis period agrarian-based and largely nonexporting groups were able to remain in power, appealing in some cases to military governments, and preserving the political scheme that characterized the export-oriented period.

In the nonenclave situations, considerable industrial growth was attained in Argentina and Brazil. In the former, export-oriented entrepreneurs had invested considerably in production for the internal market and the contraction of the export sector only accentuated this trend. In Brazil the export-oriented agrarian groups collapsed with the crisis and the state, as in Chile and Mexico, assumed a major developmental role with the support of a complex alliance of urban entrepreneurs, nonexport agrarian elites, popular sectors, and middle-class groups. In Colombia the export-oriented agrarian elites remained in power and did not foster significant internal industrialization until the fifties.[15]

The import substituting industrialization attained greatest growth in Argentina, Brazil, and Mexico. It soon, however, reached its limits, given the parameters under which it was realized. Since capital goods for the establishment of industrial parks were acquired in the central nations, the success of the policy ultimately depended on adequate foreign exchange supplies. After reaching maximum growth through the accumulation of foreign exchange during World War II, the industrialization programs could only continue—given the available political options—on the basis of an increased external debt and further reliance on foreign investments. This accumulation of foreign reserves permitted the success of the national-populist alliances in Argentina and Brazil which gave the workers greater welfare while maintaining investments. The downfall of Perón and the suicide of Vargas symbolized the end of this easy period of import substitution.

But the final blow to "import substitution" industrialization came not from difficulties in the periphery but further transformations in the center which have led, in Sunkel's term, to the creation of a new "transnational" system. With rapid economic recovery the growing multinational corporations sought new markets and cheaper production sites for their increasingly technological manufacturing process. Dependency consequently acquired a "new character" as dos Santos noted, which would have a profound effect on Latin America. Several processes were involved resulting in (1) the investment of centrally based corporations in manufactures within the periphery for sales in its internal market or, as Cardoso and Enzo Faletto note, the "internationalisation of the internal market"; (2) a new international division of labor in which the periphery acquires capital goods, technology, and raw materials from the central nations, and export profits, along with its traditional raw materials and a few manufactured items produced by multinational subsidiaries; and (3) a denationalization of the older import substituting industries established originally.[16] Although the "new dependence" is in evidence throughout the continent, the process has asserted itself more clearly in the largest internal markets such as Brazil, where the weakness of the trade-union movement (the comparison with Argentina in this respect is instructive) coupled with authoritarian political structures has created a singularly favorable investment climate.

In subsequent and more recent works writers in the dependency framework have pursued different strategies of research. Generally speaking, the early phases of the historical process have received less attention, though the contribution of Immanuel Wallerstein to an understanding of the origins of the world system is a major addition to the literature.[17] Most writers have preferred to focus on the current "new situation" of dependence. Some have devoted more attention to an effort at elaborating the place of dependent capitalism as a contribution to the Marxist analysis of capitalist society. Scholars in this vein tend to argue more forcefully than others that dependent capitalism is impossible and that socialism provides the only historically viable alternative.[18] Others have focused more on the analysis of concrete cases of dependence, elaborating in some detail the various interconnections between domestic and foreign forces, and noting the possibility of different kinds of dependent development.[19] Still others have turned their attention to characterizing the nature of the new capitalist system, with particular emphasis on the emergence of a "transnational system" which is rendering more complex and problematic the old distinctions of center and periphery.[20] Particularly for the last two tendencies, the emphasis is on the design of new empirical studies while attempting to systematize further some of the propositions implicit in the conceptual framework.

SUMMARY AND CONCLUSIONS

Modernization and dependency are two different perspectives each claiming to provide conceptual and analytical tools capable of explaining the relative underdevelopment of Latin America. The object of inquiry is practically the only thing that these two competing "visions" have in common, as they differ substantially not only on fundamental assumptions, but also on methodological implications and strategies for research.

Though there are variations in the literature, the *level of analysis* of a substantial tradition in the modernization perspective, and the one which informs most reflections on Latin America, is behavioral or microsociological. The primary focus is on individuals or aggregates of individuals, their values, attitudes, and beliefs. The dependency perspective, by contrast, is structural or macrosociological. Its focus is on the mode of production, patterns of international trade, political and economic linkages between elites in peripheral and central countries, group and class alliances and conflicts, and so on. Both perspectives are concerned with the process of development in national societies. However, for the modernization writer the national society is the basic *unit of analysis*, while the writer in a dependence framework considers the global system and its various forms of interaction with national societies as the primary object of inquiry.

For the dependency perspective, the *time dimension* is a crucial aspect of what is fundamentally a historical model. Individual societies cannot be presumed to be able to replicate the evolution of other societies because the very transformation of an interrelated world system may preclude such an option. The modernization potential of individual societies must be seen in light of changes over time in the interactions between external and internal variables. The modernization perspective is obviously concerned about the origins of traditional and modern values; but, the time dimension is not fundamental to the explanatory pretensions of a model which claims "universal validity." Without knowing the source of modernity-inhibiting characteristics, it is still possible to identify them by reference to their counterparts in developing contexts.

At the root of the differences between the two perspectives is a fundamentally different *perception of human nature*. Dependency assumes that human behavior in economic matters is a "constant." Individuals will behave differently in different contexts not because they are different but because the contexts are different. The insistence on structures and, in the final analysis, on the broadest structural category of all, the world system, follows logically from the view that opportunity structures condition human behavior. Modernizationists, on the other hand, attribute the lack of certain behavioral patterns to the "relativity" of human behavior; to the fact that cultural values and beliefs, regardless of opportunity structures, underlie the patterns of economic action. Thus, the *conception of change* in the modernization perspective is a product of innovations which result from the adoption of modern attitudes among elites, and eventually followers. Though some modernization theorists are now more pessimistic about the development potential of such changes, modernizing beliefs are a prerequisite for development. For dependency analysts the conception of change is different. Change results from the realignment of dependency relations over time. Whether or not development occurs and how it occurs is subject to controversy. Given the rapid evolution of the world system, dependent development is possible in certain contexts, not in others. Autonomy, through a break in relations of dependency, may not lead to development of the kind already arrived at in the developed countries because of the inability to recreate the same historical conditions, but it might lead to a different kind of development stressing different values. Thus, the *prescription for change* varies substantially in the dependency perspective depending on the ideological outlook of particular authors. It is not a logical consequence of the historical model. In the modernization perspective the prescription for change follows more automatically from the assumptions of the model, implying greater consensus.

From a methodological point of view the modernization perspective is much more parsimonious than its counterpart. And the focus of much of the literature on the microsociological level makes it amenable to the elaboration of precise explanatory propositions such as those of David McClelland or Everett Hagen. Dependency, by contrast, is more descriptive and its macrosociological formulations are much less subject to translation into a simple set of explanatory propositions. Many aspects of dependency, and particularly the linkages between external phenomena and internal class and power relations are unclear and need to be studied with more precision and care. For this reason the dependency perspective is an "approach" to the study of underdevelopment rather than a "theory." And yet, precisely because modernization theory relies on a simple conceptual framework and a reductionist approach, it is far less useful for the study of a complex phenomenon such as development or underdevelopment.

But the strengths of the dependency perspective lie not only in its consideration of a richer body of evidence and a broader range of phenomena, it is also more promising from a methodological point of view. The modernization perspective has fundamental flaws which make it difficult to provide for a fair test of its own assumptions. It will be recalled that the modernization perspective draws on a model with "universal validity" which assumes that traditional values are not conducive to modern behavioral patterns of action. Given that underdevelopment, on the basis of various economic and social indicators, is an objective datum, the research task becomes one of identifying modernizing values and searching for their opposites in underdeveloped contexts.

In actual research efforts, the modernity-inhibiting characteristics are often "deduced" from impressionistic observation. This is the case with much of the political science literature on Latin America. However, more "rigorous" methods, such as survey research, have also been employed, particularly in studies of entrepreneurial activity. Invariably, whether through deduction or survey research, less appropriate values for modernization such as "arielismo" (a concern for transcendental as opposed to material values) or "low-achievement" (lack of risk-taking attitudes) have been identified thus "confirming" the hypothesis that traditional values contribute to underdevelopment. If by chance the use of control groups should establish little or no difference in attitudes in a developed and underdeveloped context, the research instrument can be considered to be either faulty or the characteristics tapped not the appropriate ones for identifying traditional attitudes. The latter alternative might lead to the "discovery" of a new "modernity of tradition" literature or of greater flexibility than anticipated in traditional norms or of traditional residuals in the developed country.

The problem with the model and its behavioral level of analysis is that the explanation for underdevelopment is part of the preestablished conceptual framework. It is already "known" that in backward areas the modernity-inhibiting characteristics play the dominant role, otherwise the areas would not be backward. As such, the test of the hypothesis involves a priori acceptance of the very hypothesis up for verification, with empirical evidence gathered solely in an illustrative manner. The focus on individuals simply does not permit consideration of a broader range of contextual variables which might lead to invalidating the assumptions. Indeed, the modernity of tradition literature, which has pointed to anomalies in the use of the tradition modernity "polarities," is evidence of how such a perspective can fall victim to the "and so" fallacy. Discrepancies are accounted for not by a reformulation, but by adding a new definition or a new corollary to the preexisting conceptual framework.

Much work needs to be done within a dependency perspective to clarify its concepts and causal interrelationships, as well as to assess its capacity to explain social processes in various parts of peripheral societies. And yet the dependency approach appears to have a fundamental advantage over the modernization perspective: It is open to historically grounded conceptualization in underdeveloped contexts, while modernization is locked into an illustrative methodological style by virtue of its very assumptions.

NOTES

1. See Osvaldo Sunkel, "Politica nacional de desarrollo y dependencia externa," *Estudios Internacionales*, I (April 1967). For reviews of the dependency literature see Norman Girvan, "The Development of Dependency Economics in the Caribbean and Latin America: Review and Comparison," *Social and Economic Studies*, XXII (March 1973); Ronald H. Chilcote, "A Critical Synthesis of the Dependency Literature," *Latin American Perspectives*, I (Spring 1974); and Phillip O'Brien, "A Critique of Latin American Theories of Dependence," in I. Oxaal, et al., eds. *Beyond the Sociology of Development* (London, 1975).

2. Osvaldo Sunkel and Pedro Paz, *El subdesarrollo latinoamericano y la teoría del desarrollo* (Mexico, 1970), p. 6.

3. Theotonio dos Santos, "La crisis del desarrollo y las relaciones de dependencia en América Latina," in H. Jaguaribe, et al., eds. *La dependencia político-económica de América Latina* (Mexico, 1970), p. 180. See also his *Dependencia y cambio social* (Santiago, 1970) and *Socialismo o Fascismo: El nuevo carácter de la dependencia y el dilema latinoamericano* (Buenos Aires, 1972).

4. Sunkel and Paz, p. 39; Fernando Henrique Cardoso and Enzo Faletto, *Dependencia y desarrollo en América Latina* (Mexico, 1969).

5. This is the problem with the studies by Robert Kaufman, et al., "A Preliminary Test of the Theory of Dependency," *Comparative Politics*, VII (April 1975), 303–30, and C. Chase-Dunn, "The Effects of International Economic Dependence on Development and Inequality: A Cross National Study," *American Sociological Review*, XL (December 1975). It is interesting to note that Marxist scholars make the same mistake. They point to features in the dependency literature such as unemployment, marginalization etc., noting that they are not peculiar to peripheral countries but characterize capitalist countries in general.

Thus "dependence" is said to have no explanatory value beyond a Marxist theory of capitalist society. See Sanyaya Lall, "Is Dependence a Useful Concept in Analyzing Underdevelopment?," *World Development*, III (November 1975) and Theodore Weisscopf, "Dependence as an Explanation of Underdevelopment: A Critique," (paper presented at the Sixth Annual Latin American Studies Association Meeting, Atlanta, Georgia, 1976). The point of dependency analysis is not the relative mix at one point in time of certain identifiable factors but the evolution over time of structural relations which help to explain the differential development of capitalism in different parts of the world. As a historical model it cannot be tested with cross national data. For an attempt to differentiate conceptually contemporary capitalism of the core and peripheral countries, and thus more amenable to such criticism, see Samir Amin, *Accumulation on a World Scale* (New York, 1974).

6. Some authors have criticized the focus of the literature on the evolution of the world capitalist system. David Ray, for example, has argued that "soviet satellites" are also in a dependent and unequal relationship vis-à-vis the Soviet Union and that the key variable should not be capitalism but "political power." Robert Packenham has also argued that the most important critique of the dependency literature is that it does not consider the implications of "power." See Ray, "The Dependency Model of Latin American Underdevelopment: Three Basic Fallacies," *Journal of Interamerican Studies and World Affairs*, XV (February 1973) and Packenham, "Latin American Dependency Theories: Strengths and Weaknesses," (paper presented to the Harvard-MIT Joint Seminar on Political Development, February 1974), especially pp. 16–17, 54. This criticism misses the point completely. It is not power relations today which cause underdevelopment, but the historical evolution of a world economic system which led to economic specialization more favorable to some than others. It is precisely this concern with the evolution of world capitalism which has led to the preoccupation in the dependency literature with rejecting interpretations stressing the "feudal" rather than "capitalist" nature of colonial and postcolonial Latin American agriculture. On this point see Sergio Bagú, *Económia de la Sociedad Colonial* (Buenos Aires, 1949); Luis Vitale, "América Latina: Feudal o Capitalista?," *Revista Estrategia*, III (1966) and *Interpretación Marxista de la historia de Chile* (Santiago, 1967); and E. Laclau, "Feudalism and Capitalism in Latin America," *New Left Review*, LXVII (May–July 1971). A brilliant recent exposition of the importance of studying the evolution of the capitalist world system in order to understand underdevelopment which focuses more on the center states than on the periphery is Immanuel Wallerstein, *The Modern World System: Capitalist Agriculture and the Origins of the European World Economy in the Sixteenth Century* (New York, 1974).

7. Cardoso, *Empresário industrial e desenvolvimento económico no Brazil* (São Paulo, 1964) and *Ideologías de la burguesia industrial en sociedades dependientes* (Mexico, 1971).

8. Cardoso and Faletto, *Dependencia y desarrollo*, p. 20. Indeed, Cardoso argues that the distinction between external and internal is "metaphysical." See his "Teoría de la dependencia o análisis de situaciones concretas de dependencia?," *Revista Latinoamericana de Ciencia Política*, I (December 1970), 404. The ontology implicit in such an analysis is the one of "internal relations." See Bertell Ollman, *Alienation: Marx's Conception of Man in Capitalist Society* (London, 1971). This point is important because both André Gunder Frank and the early ECLA literature was criticized for their almost mechanistic relationship between external and internal variables. Frank acknowledges this problem and tries to answer his critics in *Lumpenbourgeoisie and Lumpendevelopment* (New

York, 1967). "Tests" of dependency theory also attribute an excessively mechanical dimension to the relationship. See Kaufman, et al., "A Preliminary Test of the Theory of Dependency."

9. Cardoso, "Associated Dependent Development: Theoretical Implications," in Alfred Stepan, ed. *Authoritarian Brazil* (New Haven, 1973), and Sunkel and Edmundo Fuenzalida, "Transnational Capitalism and National Development," in José J. Villamil, ed. *Transnational Capitalism and National Development* (London, forthcoming). It is thus incorrect to argue that dependency analysts ignore the evidence of certain kinds of economic growth. For fallacies in the dependency literature see Cardoso "Las contradicciones del desarrollo asociado," *Desarrollo Económico*, IV (April-June 1974).

10. Aníbal Quijano, "Dependencia, Cambio Social y Urbanización en América Latina," in Cardoso and F. Weffort, eds. *América Latina: Ensayos de interpretación sociológico político* (Santiago, 1970).

11. Cardoso and Faletto, *Dependencia y desarrollo*, pp. 19–20; Sunkel and Paz, *El subdesarrollo latinoamericano*, pp. 5, 9.

12. Bagú, Economía de la Sociedad Colonial, pp. 122–23.

13. On industrialization see A. Dorfman, *La industrialisación en América Latina y las políticas de fomento* (Mexico, 1967).

14. See M. de C. Tavares, "El proceso de sustitución de importaciones como modelo de desarrollo reciente en América Latina," in Andres Bianchi, ed. *América Latina: Ensayos de interpretación económica* (Santiago, 1969).

15. For detailed discussions of nonenclave versus enclave situations see Cardoso and Faletto, and Sunkel and Paz.

16. Sunkel "Capitalismo transnacional y desintegración nacional en América Latina," *Estudios Internacionales*, IV (January–March 1971) and "Big Business and Dependencia: A Latin American View," *Foreign Affairs*, L (April 1972); Cardoso and Faletto; Dos Santos, *El nuevo carácter de la dependencia* (Santiago, 1966).

17. Wallerstein, *The Modern World System*.

18. V. Bambirra. *Capitalismo dependiente latinoamericano* (Santiago, 1973); R. M. Marini, *Subdesarrollo y revolución* (Mexico, 1969); F. Hinkelammert, *El subdesarrollo latinoamericano: un caso de desarrollo capitalista* (Santiago, 1970).

19. Cardoso, "Teoría de la dependencia." A recent trend in dependency writings attempts to explain the current wave of authoritarianism in Latin America as a result of economic difficulties created by the exhaustion of the easy import substituting industrialization. The new situation leads to a process of development led by the state and the multinational corporations which concentrates income toward the top, increases the levels of capital accumulation, and expands heavy industry; the old populist alliances can therefore no longer be maintained. See Dos Santos, *Socialismo o fascismo: el nuevo carácter de la dependencia y el dilema latinoamericano* (Buenos Aires, 1972); Guillermo O'Donnell, *Modernization and Bureaucratic Authoritarianism: Studies in Latin American Politics* (Berkeley, 1973); Atilio Borón, "El fascismo como categoría histórica: en torno al problema de las dictaduras en América Latina," *Revista Mexicana de Sociología*, XXXIV (April–June 1977); the effects of this situation on labor are explored in Kenneth P. Erickson and Patrick Peppe, "Dependent Capitalist Development, U.S. Foreign Policy, and Repression of the Working Class in Chile and Brazil," *Latin American Perspectives*, III (Winter 1976). However, in the postscript to their 1968 book, Cardoso and Faletto caution against adopting an excessively mechanistic view on this point, against letting "economism kill history": Cardoso and Faletto, "Estado y proceso político en

América Latina," *Revista Mexicana de Sociología*, XXXIV (April–June 1977), 383. Articles with dependency perspective appear frequently in the *Revista Mexicana de Sociología* as well as in *Latin American Perspectives*.

20. Sunkel, "Capitalismo transnacional y desintegración nacional en América Latina," and Sunkel and Fuenzalida, "Transnational Capitalism and National Development."

18

. . . .

The Present State of the
Debate on World Inequality

. . . .

IMMANUEL WALLERSTEIN

*Immanuel Wallerstein is generally considered the driving intellectual
force behind the "world-system" school of thought. He has articulated
his view of development in a series of books and articles, perhaps the
best known of which is* The Modern World-System: Capitalist Agriculture
and the Origins of the European World-Economy in the Sixteenth
Century *(Academic Press, 1974). Wallerstein sees dependency theory
as a subset of his broader world-system perspective. In this chapter, he
argues that all states form part of a capitalist world economy in which
the existence of differences in wealth is not an anomaly but rather a
natural outcome of the fundamental processes driving that economy.
According to this perspective, the gap between rich and poor
ultimately will disappear, but only when the capitalist world system that
has been in place since the sixteenth century itself disappears.*

It has never been a secret from anyone that some have more than others. And
in the modern world at least, it is no secret that some countries have more
than other countries. In short, world inequality is a phenomenon about which
most men and most groups are quite conscious.

I do not believe that there has ever been a time when these inequalities
were unquestioned. That is to say, people or groups who have more have
always felt the need to justify this fact, if for no other reason than to try to
convince those who have less that they should accept this fact with relative
docility. These ideologies of the advantaged have had varying degrees of

---

Reprinted with permission from *World Inequality: Origins and Perspectives on
the World System*, edited by Immanuel Wallerstein (Montreal: Black Rose Books,
1975).

success over time. The history of the world is one of a constant series of revolts against inequality—whether that of one people or nation vis-à-vis another or of one class within a geographical area against another.

This statement is probably true of all of recorded history, indeed of all historical events, at least since the Neolithic Revolution. What has changed with the advent of the modern world in the sixteenth century is neither the existence of inequalities nor of the felt need to justify them by means of ideological constructs. What has changed is that even those who defend the "inevitability" of inequalities in the present feel the need to argue that eventually, over time, these inequalities will disappear, or at the very least diminish considerably in scope. Another way of saying this is that of the three dominant ideological currents of the modern world—conservatism, liberalism, and Marxism—two at least (liberalism and Marxism) are committed in theory and the abstract to egalitarianism as a principle. The third, conservatism, is not, but conservatism is an ideology that has been very much on the defensive ever since the French Revolution. The proof of this is that most conservatives decline to fly the banner openly but hide their conservative ideas under the mantle of liberalism or occasionally even Marxism.

Surely it is true that in the universities of the world in the twentieth century, and in other expressions of intellectuals, the contending ideologies have been one variant or another of liberalism and Marxism. (Remember at this point we are talking of ideologies and not of political movements. Both "liberal" parties and social democratic parties in the twentieth century have drawn on liberal ideologies.)

One of the most powerful thrusts of the eighteenth-century Enlightenment, picked up by most nineteenth- and twentieth-century thought-systems, was the assumption of progress, reformulated later as evolution. In the context of the question of equality, evolution was interpreted as the process of moving from an imperfect, unequal allocation of privileges and resources to some version of equality. There was considerable argument about how to define equality. (Reflect on the different meanings of "equality of opportunity" and "to each according to his needs.") There was considerable disagreement about who or what were the obstacles to this desired state of equality. And there was fundamental discord about how to transform the world from its present imperfection to the desired future, primarily between the advocates of gradualism based on education to advocates of revolution based on the use at some point in time of violence.

I review this well-known history of modern ideas simply to underline where I think our current debates are simply the latest variant of now classic debates and where I think some new issues have been raised which make these older formulations outdated.

If one takes the period 1945–1960, both politically and intellectually, we have in many ways the apogee of the liberal-Marxist debate. The world was politically polarized in the so-called cold war. There were two camps. One called itself the "free world" and argued that it and it alone upheld the first part of the French Revolution's trilogy, that of "liberty." It argued that its economic system offered the hope over time of approximating "equality" through a path which it came to call "economic development" or sometimes just "development." It argued too that it was gradually achieving "fraternity" by means of education and political reform (such as the 1954 Supreme Court decision in the United States, ending the legality of segregation).

The other camp called itself the "socialist world" and argued that it and it alone represented the three objectives of the French Revolution and hence the interests of the people of the world. It argued that when movements inspired by these ideas would come to power in all non-"socialist" countries, (and however they came to power,) each would enact legislation along the same lines and by this process the whole world would become "socialist" and the objective would be achieved.

These somewhat simplistic ideological statements were of course developed in much more elaborate form by the intellectuals. It has become almost traditional (but I think nonetheless just) to cite W. W. Rostow's *The Stages of Economic Growth* as a succinct, sophisticated, and relatively pure expression of the dominant liberal ideology which informed the thinking of the political leadership of the United States and its Western allies. Rostow showed no modesty in his subtitle, which was "a non-Communist Manifesto."

His basic thesis is no doubt familiar to most persons interested in these problems. Rostow saw the process of change as a series of stages through which each national unit had to go. They were the stages through which Rostow felt Great Britain had gone, and Great Britain was the crucial example since it was defined as being the first state to embark on the evolutionary path of the modern industrial world. The inference, quite overtly drawn, was that this path was a model, to be copied by other states. One could then analyze what it took to move from one stage to another, why some nations took longer than others, and could prescribe (like a physician) what a nation must do to hurry along its process of "growth." I will not review what ideological function such a formulation served. This has been done repeatedly and well. Nonetheless, this viewpoint, somewhat retouched, still informs the developmentalist ideas of the major Western governments as well as that of international agencies. I consider Lester Pearson's "Partners in Progress" report in the direct line of this analytic framework.

In the socialist world in this period there was no book quite the match of Rostow's. What there was instead was an encrusted version of evolutionary Marxism which also saw rigid stages through which every state or geographical entity had to go. The differences were that the stages covered longer historical time and the model country was the USSR. These are the stages known as slavery-feudalism-capitalism-socialism. The absurdities of the rigid formulation which dates from the 1930s and the inappropriateness of applying this on a *national* level have been well argued recently by an Indian Marxist intellectual, Irfan Habib, who argues not only the meaningfulness of the concept of the "Asiatic mode of production" but also the illogic of insisting that the various historical modes of extracting a surplus must each, necessarily, occur in all countries and follow in a specific order. Habib argues:

> The materialist conception of history need not necessarily prescribe a set universal periodisation, since what it essentially does is to formulate an analytic method for the development of class societies, and any periodisation, theoretically, serves as no more than the illustration of the application of such a method. . . .The crucial thing is the definition of principal contradiction (i.e., class-contradictions) in a society, the marking out of factors responsible for intensifying them, and the delineation of the shaping of the social order, when a particular contradiction is resolved. It is possible that release from the set P-S-F-C pattern [primitive communism-slavery-feudalism-capitalism] may lead Marxists to apply themselves better to this task, since they would no longer be obliged to look for the same "fundamental laws of the epoch" (a favorite Soviet term), or "prime mover," as premised for the supposedly corresponding European epoch.[1]

I give this excerpt from Habib because I very much agree with his fundamental point that this version of Marxist thought, so prevalent between 1945 and 1965, is a sort of "mechanical copying" of liberal views. Basically, the analysis is the same as that represented by Rostow except that the names of the stages are changed and the model country has shifted from Great Britain to the USSR. I will call this approach the developmentalist perspective, as espoused either by liberals or Marxists.

There is another perspective that has slowly pushed its way into public view during the 1960s. It has no commonly accepted name, in part because the early formulations of this point of view have often been confused, partial, or unclear. It was first widely noticed in the thinking of the Latin American structuralists (such as Raúl Prebisch and Celso Furtado) and those allied to them elsewhere (such as Dudley Sears). It later took the form of arguments such as the "development of underdevelopment" (A.G. Frank, in the heritage of Paul Baran's *The Political Economy of Growth*), the "structure of dependence" (Theotonio Dos Santos), "unequal exchange" (Arghiri Emmanuel), "accumulation of world capital" (Samir Amin), "sub-imperialism" (Ruy Mauro Marini). It also surfaced in the Chinese Cultural Revolution as Mao's concept of the continuity of the class struggle under socialist regimes in single countries.[2]

What all these concepts have in common is a critique of the developmentalist perspective. Usually they make it from a Marxist tradition but it should be noted that some of the critics, such as Furtado, come from a liberal heritage. It is no accident that this point of view has been expressed largely by persons from Asia, Africa and Latin America or by those others particularly interested in these regions (such as Umberto Melotti of *Terzo Mondo*).[3]

I would like to designate this point of view the "world-system perspective." I mean by that term that it is based on the assumption, explicitly or implicitly, that the modern world comprises a single capitalist world-economy, which has emerged historically since the sixteenth century and which still exists today. It follows from such a premise that national states are *not* societies that have separate, parallel histories, but parts of a whole reflecting that whole. To the extent that stages exist, they exist for the system as a whole. To be sure, since different parts of the world play and have played differing roles in the capitalist world-economy, they have dramatically different internal socio-economic profiles and hence distinctive politics. But to understand the internal class contradictions and political struggles of a particular state, we must first situate it in the world-economy. We can then understand the ways in which various political and cultural thrusts may be efforts to alter or preserve a position within this world-economy which is to the advantage or disadvantage of particular groups located within a particular state.[4]

What thus distinguishes the developmentalist and the world-system perspective is not liberalism versus Marxism nor evolutionism vs. something else (since both are essentially evolutionary). Rather I would locate the distinction in two places. One is in mode of thought. To put it in Hegelian terms, the developmentalist perspective is mechanical, whereas the world-system perspective is dialectical. I mean by the latter term that at every point in the analysis, one asks not what is the formal structure but what is the consequence for both the whole and the parts of maintaining or changing a certain structure at that particular point in time, given the totality of particular positions of that moment in time. Intelligent analysis demands knowledge of the complex texture of social reality (historical concreteness) within a long-range perspective that observes trends and forces of the world-system, which can explain what underlies and informs the diverse historically concrete phenomena. If synchronic comparisons and abstracted generalizations are utilized, it is only as heuristic devices in search of a truth that is ever contemporary and hence ever-changing.

This distinction of scientific methodology is matched by a distinction of praxis, of the politics of the real world. For what comes through as the second great difference between the two perspectives (the developmentalist and the world-system) is the prognosis for action. This is the reason why the latter perspective has emerged primarily from the intellectuals of the Third World. The developmentalist perspective not only insists that the model is to be found in the old developed countries (whether Great Britain, USA, or USSR) but also that the fundamental international political issues revolve around the relations among the hegemonic powers of the world. From a world-system perspective, there are no "models" (a mechanical notion) and the relations of the hegemonic powers are only one of many issues that confront the world-system.

The emergence of the world-system perspective is a consequence of the dramatic challenge to European political domination of the world which has called into question all Europo-centric constructions of social reality. But intellectual evolution itself is seldom dramatic. The restructuring of the allocation of power in the world has made itself felt in the realm of ideas, particularly in the hegemonic areas of the world, via a growing malaise that intellectuals in Europe (including of course North America) have increasingly felt about the validity of their answers to a series of "smaller" questions— smaller, that is, than the nature of the world-system as such.

Let us review successively six knotty questions to which answers from a developmentalist perspective have increasingly seemed inadequate.

Why have certain world-historical events of the last two centuries taken place where and when they have? The most striking "surprise," at the moment it occurred and ever since, is the Russian Revolution. As we all know, neither Marx nor Lenin nor anyone else thought that a "socialist revolution" would occur in Russia earlier than anywhere else. Marx had more or less predicted Great Britain as the likely candidate, and after Marx's death, the consensus of expectation in the international socialist movement was that it would occur in Germany. We know that even after 1917 almost all the leading figures of the Communist Party of the Soviet Union (CPSU) expected that the "revolution" would have to occur quickly in Germany if the Soviet regime was to survive. There was however no socialist revolution in Germany and nonetheless the Soviet regime did survive.

We do not want for explanations of this phenomenon, but we do lack convincing answers. Of course, there exists an explanation that turns Marx on his head and argues that socialist revolutions occur not in the so-called "advanced capitalist" countries but precisely in "backward" countries. But this is in such blatant contradiction with other parts of the developmentalist perspective that its proponents are seldom willing to state it baldly, even less defend it openly.

Nor is the Russian Revolution the only anomaly. There is a long-standing debate about the "exceptionalism" of the United States. How can we explain that the USA replaced Great Britain as the hegemonic industrial power of the world, and in the process managed to avoid giving birth to a serious internal socialist movement? And if the USA could avoid socialism, why could not Brazil or Russia or Canada? Seen from the perspective of 1800, it would have been a bold social scientist who would have predicted the particular success of the USA.

Again there have been many explanations. There is the "frontier" theory. There is the theory that underlines the absence of a previously entrenched "feudal" class. There is the theory of the USA as Britain's "junior partner" who overtook the senior. But all of these theories are precisely "exceptionalist" theories, contradicting the developmentalist paradigm. And furthermore, some of these variables apply to other countries where they did not seem to have the same consequences.

We could go on. I will mention two more briefly. For a long time, Great Britain's primacy (the "first" industrial power) has been unquestioned. But was Britain the "first" and if so why was she? This is a question that only recently has been seriously adumbrated. In April 1974 at an international colloquium held here in Montreal on the theme of "Failed Transitions to Industrialism: The Case of 17th Century Netherlands and Renaissance Italy," one view put forward quite strongly was that neither Italy nor the Netherlands was the locus of the Industrial Revolution precisely because they were too far *advanced* economically. What a striking blow to a developmentalist paradigm.

And lastly one should mention the anomaly of Canada: a country which economically falls into a category below that of the world's leading industrial producers in structural terms, yet nonetheless is near the very top of the list in per capita income. This cannot be plausibly explained from a developmentalist perspective.

If the world has been "developing" or "progressing" over the past few centuries, how do we explain the fact that in many areas things seem to have gotten worse, not better? Worse in many ways, ranging from standard of living, to the physical environment, to the quality of life. And more to the point, worse in some places but better in others. I refer not merely to such contemporary phenomena as the so-called "growing gap" between the industrialized countries and the Third World, but also to such earlier phenomena as the deindustrialization of many areas of the world (starting with the widely known example of the Indian textile industry in the late eighteenth and early nineteenth century).

You may say that this contradicts the liberal version of the developmentalist perspective but not its Marxist version, since "polarization" was seen as part of the process of change. True enough, except that "polarization" was presumably within countries and not between them. Furthermore, it is not clear that it is "polarization" that has occurred. While the rich have gotten richer and the poor have gotten poorer, there is surely a fairly large group of countries now somewhere in between on many economic criteria, to cite such politically diverse examples as Mexico, Italy, Czechoslovakia, Iran, and South Africa.

Furthermore, we witness in the 1970s a dramatic shift in the distribution of the profit and the international terms of trade of oil (and possibly other raw materials). You may say it is because of the increased political sophistication and strength of the Arab world. No doubt this has occurred, but is this an explanation? I remind this group that the last moment of time in which there was a dramatic amelioration of world terms of trade of primary products was in the period 1897–1913, a moment which represented in political terms the apogee of European colonial control of the world.

Once again it is not that there are not a large number of explanations for the rise in oil prices. It is rather that I find these explanations, for what they're worth, in contradiction with a developmentalist perspective.

Why are there "regressions"? In 1964, S. N. Eisenstadt published an article entitled "Breakdowns of Modernization," in which he discussed the fact that there seemed to be cases of "reversal" of regimes to "a lower, less flexible level of political and social differentiation. . . ."[5]

In seeking to explain the origins of such "reversals," Eisenstadt restricted himself to hesitant hypotheses:

> The problem of why in Turkey, Japan, Mexico, and Russia there emerge in the initial stages of modernization elites with orientations to change and ability to implement relatively effective policies, while they did not develop in these initial phases in Indonesia, Pakistan, or Burma, or why elites with similar differences tended to develop also in later stages of modernization, is an extremely difficult one and constitutes one of the most baffling problems in comparative sociological analysis. There are but four available indications to deal with this problem. Very tentatively, it may perhaps be suggested that to some extent it has to do with the placement of these elites in the preceding social structure, with the extent of their internal cohesiveness, and of the internal transformation of their own value orientation.[6]

As is clear, Eisenstadt's tentative explanation is to be found in anterior factors operating internally in the state. This calls into question the concept of stages through which all not only must pass but all *can* pass, but it leaves intact the state framework as the focus of analysis and explanation. This of course leads us logically to ask how these anterior factors developed. Are they pure historical accident?

Similarly, after the political rebellion of Tito's Yugoslavia against the USSR, the latter began to accuse Yugoslavia of "revisionism" and of returning to capitalism. Later, China took up the same theme against the USSR.

But how can we explain how this happens? There are really two varieties of explanation from a developmentalist perspective. One is to say that "regression" seems to have occurred, but that in fact "progress" had never taken place. The leaders of a movement, whether a nationalist movement or a socialist movement, only pretended to favor change. In fact they were really always "neocolonialist" stooges or "revisionists" at heart. Such an explanation has partial truth, but it seems to me to place too much on "false consciousness" and to fail to analyze movements in their immediate and continuing historical contexts.

The second explanation of "regression" is a change of heart—"betrayal." Yes, but once again, how come sometimes, but not always? Are we to explain large-scale social phenomena on the basis of the accident of the biographic histories of the particular leaders involved? I cannot accept this, for leaders remain leaders in the long run only if their personal choices reflect wider social pressures.

If the fundamental paradigm of modern history is a series of parallel national processes, how do we explain the persistence of nationalism, indeed quite often its primacy, as a political force in the modern world? Developmentalists who are liberals deplore nationalism or explain it away as a transitional "integrating" phenomenon. Marxists who are developmentalists are even more embarrassed. If the class struggle is primary—that is, implicitly the intra-national class struggle—how do we explain the fact that the slogan of the Cuban revolution is "Patria o muerte—venceremos?" And how could we explain this even more astonishing quotation from Kim Il Sung, the leader of the Democratic People's Republic of Korea:

> The homeland is a veritable mother for everyone. We cannot live nor be happy outside of our homeland. Only the flourishing and prosperity of our homeland will permit us to go down the path to happiness. The best sons and daughters of our people, all without exception, were first of all ardent patriots. It was to recover their homeland that Korean Communists struggled, before the Liberation, against Japanese imperialism despite every difficulty and obstacle.[7]

And if internal processes are so fundamental, why has not the reality of international workers' solidarity been greater? Remember World War I.

As before, there are many explanations for the persistence of nationalism. I merely observe that all these explanations have to *explain away* the primacy of internal national processes. Or to put it another way, for developmentalists nationalism is sometimes good, sometimes bad. But when it is the one or the other, it is ultimately explained by developmentalists in an ad hoc manner, adverting to its meaning for the world-system.

An even more difficult problem for the developmentalists has been the recrudescence of nationalist movements in areas smaller than that of existing states. And it is not Biafra or Bangladesh that is an intellectual problem, because the usual manner of accounting for secessionist movements in Third World countries has been the failure to attain the stage of "national integration."

No, the surprise has been in the industrialized world: Blacks in the USA, Québec in Canada, Occitania in France, the Celts in Great Britain, and lurking in the background the nationalities question in the USSR. It is not that any of these "nationalisms" is new. They are all long-standing themes of political and cultural conflict in all these countries. The surprise has been that, as of say 1945 or even 1960, most persons in these countries, using a developmentalist paradigm, regarded these movements or claims as remnants of a dying past, destined to diminish still further in vitality. And lo, a phoenix reborn.

The explanations are there. Some cry, anachronism—but if so, then the question remains, how come such a flourishing anachronism? Some say, loud shouting but little substance, a last bubble of national integration. Perhaps, but the intellectual and organizational development of these ethno-national movements seem to have moved rapidly and ever more firmly in a direction quite opposite to national integration. In any case, what in the developmentalist paradigm explains this phenomenon?

One last question, which is perhaps only a reformulation of the previous five. How is it that the "ideal types" of the different versions of the developmentalist perspective all seem so far from empirical reality? Who has not had the experience of not being quite certain which party represents the "industrial proletariat" or the "modernizing elite" in Nigeria, or in France of the Second Empire for that matter? Let us be honest. Each of us, to the extent that he has ever used a developmentalist paradigm, has stretched empirical reality to a very Procrustean bed indeed.

Can the world-system perspective answer these questions better? We cannot yet be sure. This point of view has not yet been fully thought through. But let me indicate some possible lines of argument.

If the world-system is the focus of analysis, and if in particular we are talking of the capitalist world-economy, then divergent historical patterns are precisely to be expected. They are not an anomaly but the essence of the system. If the world-economy is the basic economic entity comprising a single division of labor, then it is natural that different areas perform different economic tasks. Anyway, it is natural under capitalism, and we may talk of the core, the periphery and the semiperiphery of the world-economy. Since, however, political boundaries (states) are smaller than the economic whole, they will each reflect different groupings of economic tasks and strengths in the world-market. Over time, some of these differences may be accentuated rather than diminished—the basic inequalities which are our theme of discussion.

It is also clear that over time the loci of economic activities keep changing. This is due to many factors—ecological exhaustion, the impact of new technology, climate changes, and the socio-economic consequences of these "natural" phenomena. Hence, some areas "progress" and others "regress." But the fact that particular states change their position in the world-economy, from semi-periphery to core say, or vice versa, does not in itself change the nature of the system. These shifts will be registered for individual states as "development" or "regression." The key factor to note is that within a capitalist world-economy, all states cannot "develop" simultaneously *by definition*, since the system functions by virtue of having unequal core and peripheral regions.[8]

Within a world-economy, the state structures function as ways for particular groups to affect and distort the functioning of the market. The stronger the state machinery, the more its ability to distort the world-market in favor of the interests it represents. Core states have stronger state machineries than peripheral states.

This role of the state machineries in a capitalist world-economy explains the persistence of nationalism, since the primary social conflicts are quite often between groups located in different states rather than between groups located within the same state boundaries. Furthermore, this explains the ambiguity of class as a concept, since class refers to the economy which is worldwide, but class consciousness is a political, hence primarily national, phenomenon. Within this context, one can see the recrudescence of ethno-nationalisms in industrialized states as an expression of class consciousness of lower caste-class groups in societies where the class terminology has been preempted by nationwide middle strata organized around the dominant ethnic group.

If then the world-system is the focus of analysis rather than the individual states, it is the natural history of this system at which we must look. Like all systems, the capitalist world-economy has both cyclical and secular trends, and it is important to distinguish them.

On the one hand, the capitalist world-economy seems to go through long cycles of "expansion" and "contraction." I cannot at this point go into the long discussion this would require. I will limit myself to the very brief suggestion that "expansion" occurs when the totality of world production is less than world effective demand, as permitted by the existing social distribution of world purchasing power, and that "contraction" occurs when total world production exceeds world effective demand. These are cycles of 75–100 years in length in my view and the downward cycle is only resolved by a political reallocation of world income that effectively expands world demand. I believe we have just ended an expansionary cycle and we are in the beginning of a contractual one.

These cycles occur within a secular trend that has involved the physical expansion and politico-structural consolidation of the capitalist world-economy as such, but has also given birth to forces and movements which are eating away at these same structural supports of the existing world-system. In particular, these forces which we call revolutionary forces are calling into question the phenomenon of inequality so intrinsic to the existing world-system.

The trend toward structural consolidation of the system over the past four centuries has included three basic developments:

The first has been the capitalization of world agriculture, meaning the ever more efficient use of the world's land and sea resources in large productive units with larger and larger components of fixed capital. Over time, this has encompassed more and more of the earth's surface, and at the present we are probably about to witness the last major physical expansion, the elimination of all remaining plots restricted to small-scale, so-called "subsistence" production. The counterpart of this process has been the steady concentration of the world's population as salaried workers in small, dense pockets—that is, proletarianization and urbanization. The initial impact of this entire process has been to render large populations more exploitable and controllable.

The second major structural change has been the development of technology that maximizes the ability to transform the resources of the earth into usable commodities at "reasonable" cost levels. This is what we call industrialization, and the story is far from over. The next century should see the spread of industrial activity from the temperate core areas in which it has hitherto been largely concentrated to the tropical and semi-tropical peripheral areas. Industrialization too has hitherto tended to consolidate the system in providing a large part of the profit that makes the system worth the while of those who are on top of it, with a large enough surplus to sustain and appease the world's middle strata. Mere extension of industrial activity will not change a peripheral area into a core area, for the core areas will concentrate on ever newer, specialized activities.

The third major development, at once technological and social, has been the strengthening of all organizational structures—the states, the economic corporate structures, and even the cultural institutions—vis-à-vis both individuals and groups. This is the process of bureaucratization, and while it has been uneven (the core states are still stronger than the peripheral states, for example), all structures are stronger today than previously. Prime ministers of contemporary states have the power today that Louis XIV sought in vain to achieve. This too has been stabilizing because the ability of these bureaucracies physically to repress opposition is far greater than in the past.

But there is the other side of each of these coins. The displacement of the world's population into urban areas has made it easier ultimately to organize forces against the power structures. This is all the more so since the ever-expanding market-dependent, property-less groups are simultaneously more educated, more in communication with each other, and hence *potentially* more politically conscious.

The steady industrialization of the world has eaten away at the political and hence economic justifications for differentials in rewards. The technological advances, while still unevenly distributed, have created a new military equality of destructive potential. It is true that one nation may have 1000 times the fire power of another, but if the weaker one has sufficient to incur grievous damage, of how much good is it for the stronger to have 1000 times as much strength? Consider not merely the power of a weaker state with a few nuclear rockets but the military power of urban guerrillas. It is the kind of problem Louis XIV precisely did *not* need to worry about.

Finally, the growth of bureaucracies in the long run has created the weakness of top-heaviness. The ability of the presumed decision makers to control not the populace but the bureaucracies has effectively diminished, which again creates a weakness in the ability to enforce politico-economic will.

Where then in this picture do the forces of change, the movements of liberation, come in? They come in precisely as not totally coherent pressures of groups which arise out of the structural contradictions of the capitalist world-economy. These groups seem to take organizational form as movements, as parties, and sometimes as regimes. But when the movements become regimes, they are caught in the dilemma of becoming part of the machinery of the capitalist world-economy they are presuming to change. Hence the so-called "betrayals." It is important neither to adulate blindly these regimes, for inevitably they "betray" in part their stated goals, nor to be cynical and despairing, for the movements which give birth to such regimes represent real forces, and the creation of such regimes is part of a long-run process of social transformation.

What we need to put in the forefront of our consciousness is that both the party of order and the party of movement are currently strong. We have not yet reached the peak of the political consolidation of the capitalist world-economy. We are already in the phase of its political decline. If your outlook is developmentalist and mechanical, this pair of statements is an absurdity. From a world-system perspective, and using a dialectical mode of analysis, it is quite precise and intelligible.

This struggle takes place on all fronts—political, economic, and cultural—and in all arenas of the world, in the core states, in the periphery (largely in the Third World), and in the semi-periphery (many but not all of which states have collective ownership of basic property and are hence often called "socialist" states).

Take a struggle like that of Vietnam, or Algeria, or Angola. They were wars of national liberation. They united peoples in these areas. Ultimately, the forces of national liberation won or are winning political change. How may we evaluate its effect? On the one hand, these colonial wars fundamentally weakened the internal supports of the regimes of the USA, France and Portugal. They sapped the dominant forces of world capitalism. These wars made many changes possible in the countries of struggle, the metropolises, and in third countries. And yet, and yet—one can ask if the net result has not been in part further to integrate these countries, even their regimes, into the capitalist world-economy. It did both of course. We gain nothing by hiding this from ourselves. On the other hand, we gain nothing by showing Olympian neutrality in the form of equal disdain for unequal combatants.

The process of analysis and the process of social transformation are not separate. They are obverse sides of one coin. Our praxis informs, indeed makes possible, our analytic frameworks. But the work of analysis is itself a central part of the praxis of change. The perspectives for the future of inequality in the world-system are fairly clear in the long run. In the long run the inequalities will disappear as the result of a fundamental transformation of the world-system. But we all live in the short run, not in the long run. And in the short run, within the constraints of our respective social locations and our social heritages, we labor in the vineyards as we wish, toward what ends we choose. . . .

NOTES

1. Irfan Habib, "Problems of Marxist Historical Analysis in India," *Enquiry*, Monsoon, 1969, reprinted in S. A. Shah, ed., *Towards National Liberation: Essays on the Political Economy of India* (Montreal: n.p., 1973), 8–9.

2. See my "Class Struggle in China?", *Monthly Review*, XXV, 4, Sept. 1973, 55–58.

3. See U. Melotti, "Marx e il Terzo Mondo," *Terzo Mondo*, No. 13–14, sett. dict. 1971. Melotti subtitles the work: "towards a multilinear schema of the Marxist conception of historical development."

4. I have developed this argument at length elsewhere. See *The Modern World-System: Capitalist Agriculture and the Origins of the European World-Economy.* (New York and London: Academic Press, 1974) and "The Rise and Future Demise of the World Capitalist System: Concepts for Comparative Analysis," *Comparative Studies in Society and History*, XVI, Oct. 1974, 387–415.

5. S. N. Eisenstadt, "Breakdowns of Modernization," *Economic Development and Cultural Change*, XII, 4, July 1964, 367.

6. *Ibid.*, pp. 365-366.

7. *Activité Révolutionnaire du Camarade Kim Il Sung* (Pyongyang: Ed. en langues étrangères, 1970). Livre illustré, 52nd page (edition unpaginated). Translation mine—I. W.

8. As to how particular states can change their position, I have tried to furnish an explanation in "Dependence in an Interdependent World: The Limited Possibilities of Transformation Within the Capitalist World-Economy," *African Studies Review*, XVII, 1, April 1974, 1–26.

19

·······

Wallerstein's World Capitalist System: A Theoretical and Historical Critique

·······

THEDA SKOCPOL

In order to gain acceptance, a new paradigm must first offer an effective critique of accepted ideas, then propose a plausible alternative approach that explains all that the old one did and some of what the old one could not. Theda Skocpol states that Immanuel Wallerstein has made a thorough critique of modernization theory in The Modern World-System *but that his alternative approach falls prey to the "mirror image" trap. That is, world-system theory may not offer new answers because it suffers from many of the same weaknesses of modernization theory, having arisen in polemic opposition to modernization theory rather than as a clean break with past analysis.*

Immanuel Wallerstein's *The Modern World-System* aims to achieve a clean conceptual break with theories of "modernization" and thus provide a new theoretical paradigm to guide our investigations of the emergence and development of capitalism, industrialism, and national states. This splendid undertaking could hardly be more appropriately timed and aimed. For quite some time, modernization approaches have been subjected to telling critical attacks (e.g., Gusfield 1967; Frank 1966; Bendix 1967; Tipps 1973; Smith 1973; Tilly 1975, chap. 9). They have been called to task for reifying the nation-state as the sole unit of analysis, for assuming that all countries can potentially follow a single path (or parallel and converging paths) of evolutionary development from "tradition" to "modernity," and, concomitantly, for disregarding the world-historical development of transnational

———————

Reprinted with permission from the *American Journal of Sociology*, vol. 82 (March 1977):1075–1091.

structures that constrain and prompt national and local developments along
diverse as well as parallel paths. Moreover, modernization theorists have been
criticized for the method of explanation they frequently employ: ahistorical
ideal types of "tradition" versus "modernity" are elaborated and then applied to
national cases; if the evidence seems to fit, one assumes that a particular
historical instance is adequately explained; if not, one looks for the "chance"
factors that account for its deviation. . . .

Despite his avowed desire to avoid "abstract model building," Wallerstein
in fact deals with historical evidence primarily in terms of a preconceived
model of the capitalist world economy. I shall, therefore, start by describing
and discussing this model, before proceeding to consider its adequacy for
explaining historical developments in early modern Europe.[1]

Wallerstein insists that any theory of social change must refer to a
"social system"—that is, a "largely self-contained" entity whose developmental dynamics are "largely internal" (p. 347). For self-containment to
obtain, he reasons, the entity in question must be based upon a complete
economic division of labor. Leaving aside small-scale, isolated subsistence
societies, there have been, he says, only two kinds of large-scale social
systems: (1) empires, in which a functional economic division of labor,
occupationally not geographically based, is subsumed under an overarching,
tribute-collecting imperial state, and (2) world economies, in which there are
multiple political sovereignties, no one of which can subsume and control
the entire economic system. A world economy should be, in Wallerstein's
view, more able than a world empire to experience sustained economic
development precisely because economic actors have more freedom to
maneuver and to appropriate and reinvest surpluses.

Such a world economy—of which capitalism from the sixteenth century
to the present has been (according to Wallerstein) the only long-lasting
historical instance—is based upon a geographically differentiated division of
labor, featuring three main zones—core, semiperiphery, and periphery—tied
together by world market trade in bulk commodities that are necessities for
everyday consumption. Each major zone of the world economy has an
economic structure based upon its particular mixture of economic activities
(e.g., industry plus differentiated agriculture in the core; monoculture in the
periphery) and its characteristic form of "labor control" (e.g., skilled wage
labor and tenantry in the core; sharecropping in the semiperiphery; and
slavery or "coerced cash-crop labor" in the periphery). The different zones are
differentially rewarded by the world economy, with surplus flowing
disproportionately to the core areas. Moreover, the economic structure of each
zone supports a given sort of dominant class oriented toward the world
market, as well as states of a certain strength (strongest in the core and
weakest in the periphery) that operate in the interests of that class. Finally,
according to Wallerstein, the differential strength of the multiple states
within the world capitalist economy is crucial for maintaining the system as

a whole, for the strong states reinforce and increase the differential flow of surplus to the core zone. This happens because strong states can provide "extra-economic" assistance to allow their capitalist classes to manipulate and enforce terms of trade in their favor on the world market. . . .

Taking our cue from his emphases, then, let us take a close critical look at the ideas about determinants of socioeconomic and political structures that are built into Wallerstein's model of the world capitalist system. We can most readily pinpoint the problematic points, I suggest, if we see that the model is based on a two-step reduction: first, a reduction of socioeconomic structure to determination by world market opportunities and technological production possibilities; and second, a reduction of state structures and policies to determination by dominant class interests.

The ways in which Wallerstein tries to make sense of the differences of economic structure among his three major zones of core, semiperiphery, and periphery lead him to make the first reduction. The crux of the differences is the "mode of labor control" "adopted" in each zone by the dominant classes oriented to the world market. In his theoretical passages addressed to this issue (see esp. chap. 2, pp. 87–116), Wallerstein repeatedly implies that the dominant classes choose freely among alternative strategies of labor control by assessing rationally the best means for maximizing profits, given the geographical, demographic, technological, and labor-skill conditions in which they find themselves, and given the profitable possibilities they face for selling particular kinds of products on the world market. Now the curious thing here is that, despite the fact that Wallerstein seems to be placing a great deal of stress on the class structures of the major zones of world capitalism, actually (as far as I can see) he is explaining the fundamental economic dynamics of the system in terms of exactly the variables usually stressed by liberal economists, while ignoring the basic Marxist insight that the social relations of production and surplus appropriation are the sociological key to the functioning and development of any economic system. For this Marxist idea demands that one pay attention to institutionalized *relationships* between producing and surplus-appropriating classes and allow for the ever-present potential of collective resistance from below. Instead, Wallerstein treats "labor control" primarily as a market-optimizing strategy of the dominant class alone.

One major theoretical effect of his reliance on liberal economics is a nonexploitative picture of the process of income distribution within the world system. To be sure, he argues that the forces of the marketplace tend to maintain established differences of "occupational" structure among regions (p. 350). But notice the reason offered: "a capitalist world-economy essentially rewards accumulated capital, including human capital, at a higher rate than 'raw' labor power. . . " (p. 350). Would a liberal economist say anything different, since all that is being argued here is that regions with the scarcer factors of production are differentially rewarded by the market?

Yet, of course, Wallerstein does argue theoretically that the structure and functioning of the world capitalist economy are inherently exploitative. He does so by assigning the international hierarchy of dominating and dominated states (especially core vs. periphery) a crucial mediating role in exacerbating and sustaining overall inequalities in the system as a whole. Thus he writes, "Once we get a difference in the strength of state-machineries, we get the operation of 'unequal exchange' which is enforced by strong states on weak ones, by core states on peripheral areas. Thus capitalism involves not only appropriation of surplus-value by an owner from a laborer, but an appropriation of surplus of the whole world-economy by core areas" (1974, p. 401).

But, then, how are degrees of state strength and kinds of state economic policies to be explained? Here we arrive at the second reduction built into Wallerstein's model. For in his theory, differences of state strength and policies among states located in different major zones of the world system are explained as the result of differences in regional rates of surplus appropriation and, above all, as the expressions of the different world market interests of the dominant classes within the national political arenas that happen to be located in each major zone (chap. 3, passim). Thus the core area ends up with strong states primarily because there are more plentiful surpluses to tax and because the dominant capitalist classes want state protection for industry and their control of international trade; on the other hand, the periphery ends up with weak or nonexistent states because it reaps less from world trade and because its dominant capitalist classes are interested in profiting from direct dealings with merchants from the core areas. In short, to explain differences in state strength, Wallerstein relies upon arguments about economic conditions and world market interests, largely ignoring other potentially important variables such as historically preexisting institutional patterns, threats of rebellion from below, and geopolitical pressures and constraints.

Given that the economic structure and functioning of the world system have (logically speaking) already been explained in market-technological rather than class terms, Wallerstein *must* make this second reduction, of politics to world market-oriented class interest, in order to be able to assert that the system will be exploitative, and stably so over the long run. For as he points out, if states were equally strong (or potentially equally strong across the major regions), "they would be in the position of blocking the effective operation of transnational economic entities whose locus [*sic*] were in another state. It would then follow that the world division of labor would be impeded, the world-economy decline, and eventually the world-system fall apart" (p. 355). Without a hierarchy of dominating and dominated states corresponding to the existing pattern of economic differentiation, there is no worldwide "unequal exchange" in this theory. Ironically, then, Wallerstein has managed to create a model that simultaneously gives a decisive role to international political domination (curiously enough for a theory that set out to deemphasize the nation-state!) and deprives politics of any independent efficacy, reducing it to the vulgar expression of market-class interests.

Well, so what? Do these theoretical peculiarities matter? Certainly some quite implausible assumptions have to be made to make the model internally consistent. Since everything is directly or indirectly an expression of capitalist class interests (under given technical conditions), we are forced to assume that these classes always get what they want, reshaping institutions and their relations to producing classes to suit their current world market opportunities. At the same time, we must assume that, although all of the variously situated dominant capitalist classes want and are able to maximize their world market trading advantages, nevertheless *only* the core-area capitalists want, need, and get the extra-economic assistance of strong states, while peripheral capitalists do not. . . .

Finally, aside from this substantive critique of Wallerstein's approach, two methodological criticisms need to be made. The first has to do with the way Wallerstein handles historical evidence in relation to his theory-building enterprise. In many of the arguments cited in this essay, we have witnessed the major method of argumentation to which Wallerstein resorts: the teleological assertion. Repeatedly he argues that things at a certain time and place had to be a certain way in order to bring about later states or developments that accord (or seem to accord) with what his system model of the world capitalist economy requires or predicts. If the actual causal patterns suggested by historical accounts or comparative-historical analyses happen to correspond with the a posteriori reasoning, Wallerstein considers them to be adequately explained in terms of his model, which is, in turn, held to be supported historically. But if obvious pieces of historical evidence or typically asserted causal patterns do not fit, either they are not mentioned, or (more frequently) they are discussed, perhaps at length, only to be explained in ad hoc ways and/or treated as "accidental" in relation to the supposedly more fundamental connections emphasized by the world-system theory.[2] Frankly, I find this aspect of Wallerstein's approach very disturbing because it has the effect of creating an impenetrable abyss between historical findings and social science theorizing. For, through his a posteriori style of argument, deviant historical cases do not force one to modify or replace one's theory, while even a very inappropriate model can be illustrated historically without being put to the rigorous test of making real sense of actual patterns and causal processes in history. This has been exactly the methodological shortcoming of modernization theories, and it needs badly to be overcome in any new paradigm for development studies!

Which brings me to my second and final methodological point. At the beginning of this review essay I pointed out that Wallerstein hoped to overcome the worst faults of modernization theories by breaking with their overemphasis on national states and their tendency toward ahistorical model building. Ironically, though, he himself ends up reproducing the old difficulties in new ways. Thus strong states and inter*national* political domination assume crucial roles in his theory—though, just like the developmentalists, he reduces politics to economic conditions and to the expression of the will of the dominant groups within each national arena! Moreover, as we have just seen, Wallerstein creates an opposition between a formalistic theoretical model of universal reference, on the one hand, and the particularities and "accidents" of history, on the other hand—an opposition that uncannily resembles the relationship between theory and history in the ideal type method of the modernization approach.

How could these things happen, given Wallerstein's original intentions? The answer, I suggest, is the "mirror image" trap that plagues any attempt to create a new paradigm through direct, polemic opposition to an old one. Social science may, as it is often said, grow through polemics. But it can also stagnate through them, if innovators uncritically carry over outmoded theoretical categories (e.g., "system") and if they define new ones mainly by searching for the seemingly direct opposite of the old ones (e.g., "world system" vs. "national system"). For what seems like a direct opposite may rest on similar assumptions, or may lead one (through the attempt to work with an artificial, too extreme opposition) around full circle to the thing originally opposed. The better way to proceed is to ask what new units of analysis—probably not only one, but several, perhaps changing with historical points of reference—can allow one to cut into the evidence in new ways in order to investigate exactly the problems or relationships that the older approaches have neglected.

This review essay has obviously been a very critical one. In it I have grappled with a monumental and difficult book, trying to pinpoint and critically examine the theoretical essentials of its argument. No one should suppose, however, that I am suggesting that we dismiss or ignore Wallerstein's on-going study (for this is just the first of four projected volumes). On the contrary, I can think of no intellectual project in the social sciences that is of greater interest and importance. Even if Wallerstein has so far given imperfect answers about the historical development of capitalism, still he has had the unparalleled boldness to raise all the important issues. Even the shortcomings of his effort, therefore, can be far more fruitful for the social sciences than many minute successes by others who attempt much less. No book could have been more deserving of the Sorokin Award than *The Modern World-System*—and no book is more worthy of continued attention and debate.

NOTES

1. This essay does not pretend to present an adequate overview of *The Modern World-System*. A good sense of the scope and richness of the work is conveyed in the reviews by Hechter (1975), Lenzer (1974), and Thomas (1975).

2. Why does Wallerstein resort to this a posteriori style of argument? In his "Introduction" he argues that astronomers use this mode of argument to explain

the evolution of the universe--a unique system supposedly like the world capitalist system (pp. 7–8). But as Friedmann (1976) points out in a brilliant critique of Wallerstein, astronomers do not have historical evidence (not much, anyway) to test their hypotheses, whereas social scientists do. Yet I suggest that the very content of Wallerstein's theory makes it awkward for him to use historical evidence effectively. For historians stress chronologically ordered causal processes, while Wallerstein's world market approach prompts him to stress synchronic interdependencies (see 1974, p. 403) and anticipatory acts on the part of profit-maximizing capitalists and "entrepreneur-like" (p. 60) nation-states.

REFERENCES

Bendix, R. 1967. "Tradition and Modernity Reconsidered." *Comparative Studies in Society and History* 9 (June):292–346.

Frank, A. G. 1966. "Sociology of Development and Underdevelopment of Sociology." *Catalyst* 2 (Summer):20–73.

Friedmann, H. 1976. "Approaches to the Conceptualization of a World System." Unpublished manuscript, Department of Sociology, Harvard University.

Gusfield, J. R. 1967. "Tradition and Modernity: Misplaced Polarities in the Study of Social Change." *American Journal of Sociology* 72 (January):351–62.

Hechter, M. 1975. Review Essay on *The Modern World-System. Contemporary Sociology* 4 (May):217–22.

Lenzer, G. 1974. Review of *The Modern World-System. New York Times Book Review* (December 29):17–18.

Smith, A. D. 1973. *The Concept of Social Change.* London and Boston: Routledge & Kegan Paul.

Thomas, K. 1975. "Jumbo History." *New York Review of Books* (April 17), pp. 26–28.

Tilly, C., ed. 1975. "Modernization Theory and the Comparative Study of Societies: A Critical Perspective." *Comparative Studies in Society and History* 15 (March):199–226.

20

·······

Transnational Penetration
and Economic Growth

·······

VOLKER BORNSCHIER & CHRISTOPHER CHASE-DUNN

Volker Bornschier and Christopher Chase-Dunn are notable among world-system theorists in that they have broken with proponents of world-system/dependency theory who deny the applicability of quantitative analysis of hypotheses generated by the approach. They have also made great strides in identifying, defining, and measuring pertinent variables. In this chapter, Bornschier and Chase-Dunn explain the impact of transnational corporations (TNCs) on economic growth. They find support for their contention that TNCs have a positive short-term impact on economic growth but that over the long term the inflow of investment reverses, slowing growth. Earlier in their book, the authors seemed to make a concession to those criticizing world-system theory for minimizing, if not denying, the importance of the state in devising development policy. State officials can make mistakes that undermine growth, the authors said, but in the concluding sections of this chapter Bornschier and Chase-Dunn see little hope that the state can over-come the negative impact of TNCs. Nevertheless, their concession could open the way for new research on the role of the state in development policy within world systems theory.

. . . The question at issue here is, what are the effects of transnational corporate penetration on economic growth? We are only concerned here with the observed overall relationships and not with mediating variables. This chapter examines the consequences of overall transnational penetration; that

Reprinted with permission from *Transnational Corporations and Underdevelopment* by Volker Bornschier and Christopher Chase-Dunn, pp. 80–101, Praeger Publishers, an imprint of Greenwood Publishing Group, Inc.

is, the level of national dependence on foreign capital in all economic sectors combined. . . .

ECONOMIC THEORY AND LONG-RUN CONSEQUENCES OF TRANSNATIONAL INVESTMENT

. . . Economic theory maintains that investment results in income growth. This is not at all at variance with our theory. Rather, we have specified the long-term consequences that take into account institutional and structural features of the world-system. These crucial elements, which are indispensable for reaching sound long-term predictions, are neglected by neo-classical economics.

The potential for investment by transnational corporations results from high profits due to their monopolistic or oligopolistic advantages. These advantages are based on sheer market power and on technological and organizational knowledge (Hymer, 1960; Bornschier, 1976). This investment potential need not logically result in an average social loss for the host country. It *could* allow a higher accumulation rate and therefore a higher economic growth rate, since national income growth is dependent on capital formation. This neglects, however, the capacity aspect as well as the "realization problem" in a capitalist economy. And it neglects the transnational corporation seen as an institution.

Considering the transnational firm as a substantive institution, a predictable social loss seems inevitable in the long run for peripheral countries. Since the capital and knowledge of transnational corporations are sector specific, there is a reluctance to move to other sectors within the same country. This is because such sectors do not offer monopolistic advantages and higher profitability. Thus, the continuous reinvestment of the comparatively high profits of transnational firms in their own sectors would result in overcapacity and/or overproduction relative to market demand—the realization problem. This is especially the case for manufacturing investment for the domestic market in peripheral countries, since the unequal distribution of income prevents mass consumption. In order to avoid overcapacities transnational corporations are unlikely to make investments in a particular country that will severely affect the accumulation process of higher profits within that country. The transnational corporation, as a private growth and profit-seeking institution, will look for new investment opportunities within its worldwide operations. The investment of these resources in less penetrated countries and in research and development in core countries can postpone the realization problem on the level of the world-economy as a whole.

Transnational corporations, after facing potential or actual overcapacities, start to take surplus out of the penetrated country. This means that their efforts to generate higher income for themselves affect the growth potential of the penetrated country adversely. As can be shown, such behavior results in disturbances with respect to steady growth conditions, analyzed by the Domar model in the post-Keynesian tradition. Domar's model (1946, 1948) is an abstract analysis of the *conditions* of steady growth.[1]

We deduce from the above argument that the penetration of a modern sector of a national economy generally starts with large increases of net-investment by transnational corporations and that the relative increase of net-investment slows down in the course of time and may even become negative (capital repatriation). This is because transnational corporations have expanded their activities within a particular country to a point where (1) market saturation is approached and/or (2) political risks increase due to high penetration and visibility. It follows from these considerations that from a certain point the transnational corporation is likely to start taking more money out of the penetrated country than it has ever brought into the country due to its investments. If this is true, the host country would lose money that is not compensated by prior inflows. More specifically, it loses resources for accumulation, which implies a negative investment multiplier (since "autonomous" investment is negative).

Let us assume, furthermore, that transnational corporations generally operate under monopolistic conditions and these are even more pronounced in peripheral countries. This allows for higher than "normal" profits, and also lowers the "normal" profit of other local enterprises or local competitors. Then it is, on the average, *unlikely* that the long-term decrease in transnational net-investment and the outflow of money can be compensated by indigenous capital formation. This is because indigenous capital has a lower profitability and thus a lower investment potential. And, for an abstract deduction, if we ignore imports and exports for a while (a closed system), then the long-term investment cycle of transnational corporations results in a distortion with respect to the equilibrium conditions of steady growth in Domar's model.

In an extension of Keynes, Domar analyzes not only the income, but also the capacity effect of investment. Distortions, according to his approach, can only be avoided if the additional production capacity, which is a function of net-investment of one period, is fully employed. And this can only be the case if the whole demand (income) expands by the same amount. Given a certain marginal propensity to consume, additional income is generated according to the investment multiplier and it is a function of the *relative increase* of net-investment. If it should hold that the increase in production (capacity) is equal to the increase in income, then the *relative* increase in net-investment must be equal to the coefficient of capital productivity times the investment multiplier (share of savings in total income).[2] This is the equilibrium condition for steady growth along the so-called "growth trajectory."[3] On the basis of the simplifying model assumptions (linear-homogeneous relationships) all variables grow, then, at the same constant growth rate.[4]

From a slowing down in the *relative* increase of net investment due to the long-term investment cycle of transnational corporations it follows that a new "equilibrium" has to be found on a lower growth rate level. Either the propensity to save has to decrease, or capital productivity, or both at the same time.[5] The first means that consumption as a share of total income has to increase, but this is limited by high income inequality. And a reduced capital coefficient, in reality, means that the degree of capital utilization becomes smaller, implying underemployment.

The conclusion of this digression into the formal economic model is that income growth is adversely affected by transnational corporations *in the long run*. Such a long-term distortion with regard to steady growth will be greater the more net investment relies on foreign capital inputs (i.e., the higher the penetration by transnational corporations, *and* the more these corporations slow down their relative increase in net investment in the course of time).[6] Given the assumptions of increasing monopoly and the threat of overcapacity, and thus reduction of profitability, this is unavoidable. Following this line of argument we can make different predictions for short- and long-term consequences of transnational penetration.

SHORT-TERM CONSEQUENCES

In a first phase, when there is a large increase in net investment of transnational corporations, the average growth of income should be affected positively. This effect is the stronger the higher the net investment of the transnational firms. At the same time, already in this phase, growth is expected to be uneven:

- with respect to sectors (modern versus traditional and, within the modern, monopolistic versus competitive sector)
- with respect to regions (enclaves where transnationals invest versus the others)
- with respect to labor income, which is higher in the monopolistic and foreign-dominated sectors than in the competitive and traditional sectors

LONG-TERM CONSEQUENCES

In a second phase, when the increase of the net investment slows down, or tends to stagnate, or even becomes negative, the average income growth is adversely affected. Again this will be more the case as more total investment depends on foreign corporations which slow down their investment (i.e., the higher the penetration). In this second phase the strains already produced by uneven growth in the first phase will add to the adverse growth effects. However, the growth-reducing consequence of high penetration is mitigated or compensated if net investment of the corporations remains very high.

The results in Table 20.1 suggest support for the hypotheses with regard to short- and long-term consequences of transnational penetration. The table lists the studies according to whether they find positive or negative associations with economic growth and whether they measure the short-term effect (flow of investments) or the long-term effect (accumulated stock of capital). With only one exception the studies with flow measures find positive effects, and of the 25 studies using a stock measure, 16 find a negative association. The exceptions will be discussed below.

Table 20.1   Studies of the Effect of Transnational Corporations on Economic Growth Using Stock or Flow Measures, and Direction of Effects

Measurement of Foreign Capital Dependency	Direction of Effects	
	Positive	Negative
Stocks	Kaufman et al. (1975)	Alschuler (1976)
	McGowan and Smith (1978)	*Berweger and Hoby (1978)
	Ray and Webster (1978)	*Bornschier (1975, 1980, 1981)
	Szymanski (1976)	*Bornschier and Ballmer-Cao
	*Jackman (1982)	(1978)
		Chase-Dunn (1975a)
		Delacroix and Ragin (1981)
		*Dolan and Tomlin (1980)
		Evans (1972)
		Gobalet and Diamond (1979)
		*Meyer-Fehr (1978, 1979)
		Rubinson (1977)
		*Stoneman (1975)
		Timberlake and Kentor (1983)
		*van Puijenbroek (1984)
		Weede (1981a, 1981b)
		Weede and Tiefenbach (1981b)
Flows	*Berweger and Hoby (1978)	Stevenson (1972)
	*Bornschier (1975, 1980, 1981)	
	*Dolan and Tomlin (1979)	
	*Jackman (1982)	
	Kaufman, et al. (1975)	
	*Meyer-Fehr (1978, 1979)	
	Papanek (1973)	
	Ray and Webster (1978)	
	*Stoneman (1975)	
	*van Puijenbroek (1984)	

*Studies which test for the effect of transnational penetration (stocks) and which control for new investment by transnational corporations (flows) in the same analysis. Bornschier and Ballmer-Cao control for the ratio of later and earlier stocks instead of flows.

With one exception, discussed below, the studies using both flow and stock measures in the same analysis report that high transnational penetration has the consequence of lowering the economic growth rate of the host country. And high flows of new foreign investment have a positive consequence for growth, even when penetration is high. This means that new investment of transnational corporations can mitigate and compensate the effect of penetration. This is supported by the fact that most of these studies report stronger negative effects of penetration once new investment is controlled. Such a compensation is, however, on the average not very relevant since the empirical association between transnational penetration and new investment is only moderate.[7] This supports our argument about the investment cycle of transnational corporations.

There is also other evidence in these studies that indicates the importance of the long- versus short-term distinction. Stoneman (1975) reports that lagging the stock measure (using a penetration indicator measured earlier than the dependent variable) increases the significance of the negative effect. Chase-Dunn (1975b) reports a series of panel analyses that show that stock measures tend to have zero effects on growth over short time lags but increasingly negative ones over longer and longer lag periods. That is, the immediate effect of stocks tends to be zero, but the longer-term effect is negative.

The same result is shown by Bornschier (1975) with a different measure for transnational penetration. He also shows a similar result in analyses that include both the level of penetration and change in the level of penetration. He finds that increases in penetration, which are due to inflows of new investment, have positive effects on growth but become zero and then negative as the lag period is lengthened.

The above results in a good overall support for our hypotheses. But there are a few studies in Table 20.1 that report results that seem to contradict what we have said. Stevenson's (1972) study is the only one that does not find positive effects due to a flow measure. His finding is not an important contradiction because he uses a poor measure of economic growth. He analyzes simple rank correlations of yearly GNP per capita figures that are pooled over a seven year period, and his analyses include only seven Latin American countries. Thus, this one exception does not strongly contradict the mass of other evidence, and we can conclude that flows of new foreign investment do indeed cause economic growth.

Of the 25 studies employing capital stock measures, however, five find positive associations with economic growth. Three of these (Kaufman et al., Ray and Webster and Szymanski) study countries in Latin America and one (McGowan and Smith) studies only African countries. A common element of these studies is that they investigate only countries of a specific geographical region. There are, however, two studies in Table 20.1 which analyze only Latin American countries and which report negative associations (Alschuler,

Evans). Furthermore, there are studies which present their results separately for geographical subsamples, namely the studies of Stoneman, and Dolan and Tomlin. They find negative associations for Latin America, positive associations for Africa, and a positive and negative one for Asian countries. In the following we discuss the contradictory findings that appear in studies of separate geographic regions.

Table 20.2 shows those studies which use stock measures by the countries they include and their findings. We note first that 16 of the 17 studies which include countries unrestricted by geographic region find negative effects. These studies investigate either all countries for which data are available or all peripheral countries. They report stronger negative effects for peripheral countries when they exclude core countries from the analyses, and no or only small and insignificant effects for core countries analyzed separately.

The only study which fails to find a negative effect of penetration while studying a larger number of countries from all continents is that by Jackman (1980). Jackman's finding is negative but statistically insignificant. The study by Jackman uses both stock and flow measures similar to the ones we employ in our reanalysis. This study, unlike the five other studies in Table

Table 20.2 Studies of the Effect of Transnational Corporate Penetration (Stocks) on Economic Growth by Country Composition and Direction of Effects

Country Composition	Effect of Transnational Penetration	
	Positive	Negative
Unrestricted		Berweger and Hoby (1978)
		Bornschier (1975, 1980, 1981)
		Bornschier and Ballmer-Cao (1978)
		Chase-Dunn (1975a)
		Delacroix and Ragin (1981)
		Dolan and Tomlin (1980)
		Gobalet and Diamond (1979)
		Jackman (1982)
		Meyer-Fehr (1978, 1979)
		Rubinson (1977)
		Stoneman (1975)
		van Puijenbroek (1984)
		Weede (1981a, 1981b)
		Weede and Tiefenbach (1981b)
America, peripheral countries	Kaufman et al. (1975)	Alschuler (1976)
	Ray and Webster (1978)	Dolan and Tomlin (1980)
	Szymanski (1976)	Evans (1972)
		Stoneman (1975)
Asia	Stoneman (1975)	Dolan and Tomlin (1980)
Africa	Dolan and Tomlin (1980)	
	McGowan and Smith (1978)	
	Stoneman (1975)	

20.1 that use both flow and stock measures, finds no effects of transnational penetration in a sample of 72 "Third World" countries. This is inconsistent with our reanalysis below and we suspect the inconsistency is due to one or a combination of the following three factors:

1. Jackman's measure of stocks may be extremely skewed, and thus not appropriate for linear regression analysis. Most studies either recode the extreme outliers or log the measure to normalize distribution.
2. Jackman does not effectively control the earlier relationship between the level of economic development and the degree of transnational penetration. Since higher levels of development attract greater amounts of foreign investment, this confuses the effect of penetration on growth.
3. Jackman's use of the time dimension is sloppy. He looks at the effect of penetration in 1967 on growth from 1960 to 1978. Obviously penetration in 1967 could not have effected growth between 1960 and 1967. In many cases this misuse of the time dimension would not be crucial, but in this case it is. Fresh foreign investment is associated with growth and it adds to foreign capital stocks. Thus, the inaccurate use of the time dimensions suppresses the negative effect of accumulated stocks of transnational capital.

Also Weede (1981a, 1981b) and Weede and Tiefenbach report, for some of their tests, insignificant negative effects of penetration in 1967 on growth from 1960 to 1977. They vary the penetration measure, the treatment of outliers on that measure, and the control variables in order to estimate the robustness of the earlier findings. These studies report that:

1. The negative effect on GDP growth is smaller than the one on GNP per capita growth (Weede 1981a). Unfortunately the two growth measures do not cover the same period.
2. Some weights for the stock of foreign capital (used in the penetration measure) produce more significant effects than others (Weede 1981a).
3. A log transformation in order to solve the problem of outliers on the penetration variable results in negative, but insignificant effects (Weede 1981b).
4. The effect is only significant for the world sample but not for a sample of less developed countries (Weede and Tiefenbach 1981b). This is clearly opposite to the bulk of other findings which either find the same effect or a somewhat more negative effect in a sample of less developed countries.

Weede and Tiefenbach conclude from the various reanalyses that the reported finding of a negative effect of penetration on growth lacks robustness and that the capital dependency approach "fails to explain why some LDCs do so much better or worse than others" (Weede and Tiefenbach, 1981b, 391). Following these reanalyses a controversy has evolved that includes a dispute over many technical details.[8] Beside these details we would like to stress the following points:

1. The reanalyses by Weede and Tiefenbach have generally revealed negative effects which in some cases do not reach statistical significance.
2. Unlike Jackman, these researchers to not try to test different effects of stocks of foreign investment and flows of foreign direct investment.
3. They have an inappropriate specification of the time dimension (as does Jackman) since they are analyzing the effect of penetration in 1967 on growth from 1960 to 1977.

Thus, studies unrestricted by geographic region unanimously find negative effects of penetration on growth. In those discrepant cases where the effect does not reach statistical significance there are shortcomings in the test design which are the likely reasons for failing to obtain significant results.

Contrary to the nearly unanimous results of studies including countries unrestricted by geographical region, those that study particular regions are inconsistent. Of the seven studies of peripheral countries in the Americas, four report a negative association and three find a positive one. One study of Asia finds a positive and one a negative association. All three studies of African countries report positive associations.

In comparing the three studies of peripheral countries in Latin America and the Caribbean that find positive effects with the four that find negative ones, it is not easy to discover any systematic reason that could explain the discrepant results. The studies include basically the same countries, with the exclusion or inclusion of Venezuela being the main difference. Ray and Webster (1978) show, however, that this has little effect on estimates. The measurement of transnational penetration, however, suffers from shortcomings in all studies except the ones by Stoneman, and Dolan and Tomlin. Evans, Kaufman et al., Ray and Webster, and Szymanski use figures for the stock of United States capital as a proxy for the total foreign stock. This is a problematic proxy.[9]

We should point out, however, that none of the findings is very large in a statistical sense.[10] Also, the number of countries analyzed ranges from 17 to 19 cases, the 22 cases in the Dolan and Tomlin analysis being an exception. Such small numbers of observations are rather problematic for correlation and regression analysis, since differences in one or two cases can affect the magnitude and direction of estimates. It should be noted that the two studies without shortcomings in the measurement of penetration and with larger samples (i.e., Dolan and Tomlin, and the study of Stoneman [who pools observations]), find consistently negative effects.

Thus, our comparison of the different studies reveals no systematic explanation of the different findings in the studies of peripheral countries in the Americas. Similarly, the positive effects found in the studies of the African and Asian subsamples are problematic. McGowan and Smith's findings of a positive effect of transnational penetration on growth may be due to the fact that they use a very short time lag. As noted above, it is the longer-term effects that are negative. Stoneman's as well as Dolan and Tomlin's findings, do not suffer to the same extent from this drawback. The problem, then, is to explain why the findings in separate geographic regions diverge from those with larger numbers of countries unrestricted by region.

Thinking about the pattern in Table 20.2, we can offer five hypotheses to explain these different findings from the study of geographic regions.

Hypothesis 1. The discrepant results in geographical regions might indicate that the relationship between transnational penetration and economic growth actually varies by geographic region. Although the researchers who use only regional subsamples of countries do not offer any theoretical reason why it should vary by region, the possibility still exists.

Hypothesis 2. Another explanation may be that variables that should be controlled on theoretical grounds are not associated with foreign capital penetration in world comparisons, but are in regional subsamples. Therefore, a more specified, but spurious "geographical-region effect" may be operating. To test such a hypothesis requires that the same set of variables be used in each equation that tests the effects of foreign capital penetration in regional subsamples.

Hypothesis 3. The discrepant findings in subsamples could mean that the relationship between foreign capital penetration and economic growth varies with the size of the market (or the modernized segment of the economy) or with the level of economic development. Most of the African countries are very small with respect to market size and are the poorest in the world. This applies also to several countries in Asia, whereas market size, as well as per capita income, in peripheral America are, on the average, much greater. The hypothesis that the effect might vary with level of development is suggested by McGowan and Smith, as well as by Stoneman; Bornschier and Ballmer-Cao (1978) argue that the effect is less strong in smaller peripheral countries.

Hypothesis 4. Another explanation is suggested by the fact that in regional subsamples there is an accumulation of *special cases* that affect the relationship. Such theoretically suggested special cases for the analysis of economic growth are war regions, city-states, and countries that are extremely specialized in the export of petroleum. Asia is especially characterized by an accumulation of such special cases.

Hypothesis 5. The last hypothesis assumes that the results may be a "statistical artifact" produced by the limited range of variation and small samples sizes that naturally characterize any such subsample analysis. Since all the studies that use larger numbers of countries with greater variation find negative effects, it is possible that the studies that use smaller samples with limited variation are subject to greater sampling error. That is, if we imagine that the true regression line relating foreign capital penetration to economic growth is negative, it is possible that any limited subset of points along that line shows a smaller or even different relationship among the variables under study than the entire set of points. Stoneman suggests this explanation to account for why African and Asian subsamples differ from his much larger sample of all peripheral countries. This hypothesis can be tested by employing an analysis of covariance that analyzes all cases simultaneously and looks for statistical interaction effects for subsamples.

The method of comparing and contrasting existing studies does not allow us to choose among the five alternative hypotheses. The effect of level of development, market size, geographical region, and limited variation are all confounded in those studies that use only countries from a single region. Therefore, we have done new analyses in order to resolve the contradictory findings of earlier research.

NEW ANALYSES

The new analyses that we present in this section are intended to reconcile the discrepant findings in some of the earlier research, and incorporate a number of improvements over results presented earlier. The breadth of countries studied has been extended by the inclusion of cases formerly left out either because of missing data or sampling criteria. Our 103 cases include all nations with a population greater than one million, except that most centrally planned countries are not included.[11] In line with our discussion of the world-economy as a whole we have included all possible countries, even those formerly excluded because of special circumstances such as current involvement in war, exceptional oil producers, or city-states.

We have also improved our measures, added data for more recent years and included control variables that increase the amount of variance explained by the overall model to better specify the effects of penetration by transnational corporations. Our measure of penetration is the total book value of the stock of foreign direct investment at the end of 1967 (the first year for which these data are available), weighted by the amount of domestic capital stock of the country and the size of the population. The measure of penetration has been improved over that used in earlier studies (Bornschier et al. 1978) by weighting it by an improved estimate of the total stock of capital. The estimation procedure for the weight used is described in Ballmer-

Cao and Scheidegger (1979). There, all data can be found that are employed in the analyses, except for income growth (see below). The measure of transnational penetration we now use weights the total stock of FDI in million U.S. dollars as follows:

$$PEN = \frac{\text{Total Stock FDI}_{67}}{\sqrt{\text{Capital Stock * Labor Force}}}$$

We take total population as a proxy for the labor force. The estimated total stock of capital in billion U.S. dollars is multiplied by the country's population in millions (and the square root taken) in order to correct for differences in average capital intensity. We consider a country to be highly penetrated if the stock of foreign capital is high relative to both major productive forces, capital and labor. . . . [12]

The dependent variable in our new analyses is the average annual real growth rate of GNP per capita (in percentage units) for the period between 1965 and 1977. The source is the World Bank.[13] This differs from earlier analyses (Bornschier et al. 1978) by including data for 1976 and 1977.

As in earlier analyses we control for flows of foreign direct investment in order to separate the effects of recent flows from the effects of accumulated stocks. The flow variable (FDI) is measured by the difference between the stock of foreign direct investment in 1973 and in 1967 divided by the average total Gross Domestic Product for the years 1965 to 1970. We use the flows only for the first part of the time studied because we do not want to confuse the effects of the new flows with those of accumulated stocks. Cumulating over a long period comes eventually to the point of equivalence with stocks because of the depreciation of capital.[14]

We also control the level of domestic capital formation because this is thought to be related to both prior flows of foreign direct investment and economic growth. Our measure is the Gross Domestic Investment divided by Gross Domestic Product, averaged for 1965, 1970, and 1973 (GDI).

In addition we control for the logged level of economic development (YN) in 1965 and the square of this ($YN)^2$. The squared term, which has only been included in two earlier analyses, is necessary to take into account the nonlinear shape of the relationship between level of development and penetration. Penetration is not evenly distributed among countries at different levels of development, but rather is more pronounced in those at middle levels. The squared term takes this into account and controls for the "ceiling effect" which produced smaller percentage increases in growth for countries at high levels of development—a situation in which socially determined processes of saturation are likely to be at work (Bornschier 1980).

We also control for the relative level of exports in order to separate out the effects of penetration on exports from its effects on income growth.

Exports are positively related both to natural resources and overall penetration by foreign capital.[15] In a growing world-economy access to the world market has, in general, favorable consequences for economic growth due to returns for scarce mineral resources and/or due to enlarging the scale of the market and the scale of production for industrial products. Therefore, to the extent that penetration by transnational corporations goes together with exports, it should have a smaller adverse effect on growth.[16]

Controlling for the level of exports shows the income growth effect of penetration independently of the access to the world market.[17] Our measure of EXPORT is the total value of exports divided by the Gross Domestic Product, averaged for the years 1965, 1970, and 1973.

The size of the domestic market is also included as a variable in our complete model. Size indicates a growth potential which is allowed to develop more independently from the international market. Since this variable is empirically not linearly related either to penetration by transnational corporations, exports or relative importance of raw materials, it does not affect the other variables in linear regression. It is introduced in order to reach at a more complete specification of potential growth factors. Size can, however, be thought of as interacting with penetration in the following way. The fact that size of the domestic market is not linearly related to penetration can be seen to result from its contradictory implications for development. Market size can be either a resource for independent national development, or a factor that attracts more foreign industrial capital because of the larger domestic markets. In either case it is a resource which may help a country attain semiperipheral status and upward mobility within the core/periphery division of labor. We propose that political action is more crucial for countries with larger size in order to further either of the two development paths. Moreover, state strength is also likely to be greater in these countries so that the economic policy options mentioned are more feasible than in smaller peripheral countries.

We measure SIZE with the logged total energy consumption in 1967 in thousand tons of coal equivalent. This measure is preferred to total GDP or GNP because it estimates the absolute size of the monetized part of the economy, not the subsistence sector, which contributes only minimally to domestic market demand.

The results which will allow us to choose among the five hypotheses listed above are presented in the following way. First, following the form of the earlier studies cited in Table 20.2, we present analyses separately by the different regions, levels of development, and market sizes. In a next step we perform more detailed tests with regard to the effect of penetration by transnational corporations in countries with different market sizes and different levels of economic development. Finally, we use the whole sample of 103 countries in an analysis of covariance model which allows us to test for interactions between regions and penetration. This analysis of a large number of countries allows us to overcome the problems of small sample

Table 20.3 Regression of Average Annual Real Growth of Income Per Capita 1965–1977 (unstandardized regression estimates. F values in parentheses)

Equation	Sample	PEN	FDI	YN	$(YN)^2$	GDI	Export	Size	Constant	R^2 (adjusted)
1) N=103	World sample	-.0262‡ (16.15)	.0076† (9.27)	13.81† (14.48)	-2.49† (16.68)	.0664* (3.92)	.0444* (8.17)	.8856† (11.00)	-20.48	.39
2) N=15	Rich countries	.0012 (0.00)	-.0055 (0.11)	259.9 (2.94)	-35.37 (2.97)	.1773 (1.97)	.0538 (0.46)	1.1739 (0.85)	-485.64	.45
3) N=88	Less developed countries (LDCs)	-.0310 (15.61)	.0082† (9.10)	9.92 (2.56)	-1.69 (2.56)	.0606 (8.23)	.0510† (0.46)	.9137† (8.77)	-15.76	.40
4) N=37	LDCs in Africa	-.0065 (0.28)	.0067 (3.76)	-1.20 (0.01)	.13 (0.01)	.1211 (3.51)	-.0097 (0.14)	.2146 (0.16)	0.96	.05
5) N=21	LDCs in the Americas	-.0104 (0.45)	.0054 (2.15)	5.40 (0.03)	-1.32 (0.10)	.1782 (2.39)	-.0785 (1.66)	.1977 (0.00)	-3.68	.18
6) N=23	LDCs in Asia	-.0182 (0.74)	.0162 (3.26)	4.01 (0.10)	-0.32 (0.02)	-.0200 (0.06)	.0518 (1.03)	1.2546* (5.77)	-9.94	.60
7) N=23	LDCs in Asia (w/o special cases)	-.0421* (3.96)	.0180 (3.39)	20.50 (1.38)	-3.23 (0.96)	.0129 (0.03)	.0338 (0.34)	.7353 (1.88)	-30.22	.65
8) N=41	Larger LDCs (above 1.5 million t)	-.0447 (18.70)	.0072* (3.97)	26.88 (3.61)	-4.73 (3.42)	.0454 (0.58)	.0885† (10.92)	1.6433* (4.47)	-41.72	.37
9) N=47	Small LDCs (below 1.5 million t)	-.0103 (0.68)	.0102* (4.84)	3.50 (0.25)	-0.57 (0.19)	-.0378 (0.53)	.0156 (0.33)	.5361 (0.88)	-5.99	.17
10) N=46	Wealthier LDCs (above $400)	-.0413† (15.80)	.0075* (4.57)	17.29 (0.52)	-3.16 (0.65)	.0624 (1.12)	.0899† (13.86)	1.4706* (6.67)	-26.99	.36
11) N=42	Poor LDCs (below $400)	-.0222 (3.80)	.0167* (13.82)	-78.87* (6.66)	17.87* (6.95)	.0033 (0.01)	.0041 (0.02)	.9157* (7.77)	85.52	.41

Notes: Figures that are two, three, or four times as large as the standard error of the estimate are indicated by *, †, and ‡, respectively. Figures are given for data collected on penetration by transnational corporations in 1967 (PEN), flows of foreign direct investment (FDI), logged income per capita 1965 (YN), gross domestic investment (GDI), exports, and size of the internal market for a world sample of 103 countries and subsamples.

size and restricted variation that occur in the separate analyses by region. Tables 20.3, 20.4, and 20.5 report the results of our new analyses.

Table 20.3 presents the regression estimates and F statistics for our basic model estimated for all the countries and also for subsamples. First, a subsample of the 15 richest countries is analyzed separately. These are the countries which have been, since World War II and before 1965, a stable group at the top of the world stratification structure. There has been a natural break in the distribution of income values between these 15 and the other countries. Most of the richest countries, 10 of the 15, are important headquarter countries of transnational corporations, both in absolute and relative terms.[18] We expect no significant negative impact of penetration by transnational corporations in these countries since the relations among them are relatively symmetrical, and they are all core states in the world economy.

The remaining 88 peripheral and semiperipheral countries are also analyzed separately. It should be kept in mid that this group, which is called "less developed," is rather heterogeneous with regard to wealth and size. It covers, on the one hand, countries like, for example, Burundi and India (both poor but different in size) and, on the other hand, countries like Ireland and Argentina (both wealthier, but different in size).

Earlier research (Bornschier et al. 1978, Gobalet and Diamond, and Dolan and Tomlin) has reported different magnitudes of the effect of penetration by transnational corporations for countries at different levels of development and different sizes of the internal market. In our research we have split the subsample of less developed countries in a number of different ways in order to evaluate the idea that penetration effects interact with size and level of development. In Table 20.3 we present the results of separately analyzing very small and very poor countries. The very small countries are those with less than 1.5 million tons of coal equivalent of total energy consumption in 1967. The very poor countries are those with less than $400 per capita GNP in 1965.

We also divide the sample of less developed countries into regional subsamples in order to reanalyze the contradictory findings for such regional subsamples in earlier research. We use, within the 88 less developed countries, regional samples for Africa, Asia and America. The Asian subsample is also analyzed excluding six countries that are thought to be special cases.[19]

Equation 1 in Table 20.3 shows the estimates of the variables in our basic model for the 103 countries of the world. This equation shows that penetration by transnational corporations (PEN) has an overall negative effect on economic growth which is statistically extremely unlikely to be by chance. This replicates the findings of previous research using large numbers of countries unrestricted by geographical region. The effect of flows of foreign direct investments (FDI) is in the predicted positive direction and also is statistically significant. This is further evidence of the conclusion drawn from our comparison of earlier studies that stocks and flows have opposite effects on economic growth.[20] The effect of the level of development is curvilinear. The term YN is positive and the effect of squared GNP per capita $(YN)^2$ is negative, showing the ceiling and/or saturation process discussed above. The turning point of the curvilinear function is at $600 per capita GNP.

The level of gross domestic capital formation (GDI) is positive and significant, as all economic theories would predict. The effects of exports is also positive and significant.[21] The effect of the world market position with regard to important raw commodities has been tested but this variable is not included in the model since its initial positive effect on growth vanishes once the level of exports is controlled. Equation 1 strongly supports our theory of development in the capitalist world-economy and the conclusions we have drawn from comparisons of earlier studies.

Equation 2 shows that penetration by transnational corporations does not have negative effects on the economic development of the 15 richest countries. This supports our contention that penetration of core countries by the corporations of other core countries result in a different process of development than asymmetrical penetration of the periphery by the core.

Equation 3, excluding the richest countries, shows the same basic patterns of effects as Equation 1 except that the estimated effect of penetration is larger because it is not diluted by the inclusion of the richer countries.[22] The penetration by transnational corporations is the most significant single predictor of the economic growth of the peripheral countries.[23] The other growth predictors have the same direction of influence as in the whole sample, but only market size and exports are significant, whereas capital formation is not.

This suggests that capital formation is of less importance for peripheral countries than it is generally assumed. This indirectly supports the proposition that many of the problems of the peripheral countries are due to lack of *effective* demand, which is a long-term consequence of the unequal distribution of income. This puts into question some conventional "wisdoms" in development theory that advocate more transfers of investment capital from rich to poor countries. The share of capital formation in total product, in general, does not seem to be a crucial variable for economic growth within peripheral countries in the world-economy, and more specifically, while fresh capital formation by transnational corporations (PDI) has a positive effect, accumulated prior capital formation (PEN) has clearly disadvantageous consequences for economic growth.

The effects in regional subsamples (Equations 4–7 of Table 20.3) are consistently negative, but small. This is consistent with earlier studies of regional subsamples, and as we have hypothesized above could be due to a number of different possibilities: sample size, restricted variation, interaction with size and level of economic development, or real regional differences in the operation of dependency processes.

The effect for the Asian subsample is small until the six special case nations (*see* note 19) are excluded from the subsample. Then, as shown in

Equation 7, the estimated effect of penetration is large and statistically significant. Thus, we can support Hypothesis 4 as an explanation of the small or inconsistent effects of transnational corporate penetration on economic growth found in studies that do not control for special case countries in Asia. However, special cases (defined in the same way as for Asia) do not play an important role in the other regions.[24] Before examining the other hypotheses in order to find an explanation for the small negative effects in American and African subsamples, we shall first discuss the interaction with size and wealth.

Equations 8 and 9 show the consequences of splitting the less developed sample to separate those countries with a small internal market from the rest of peripheral countries. In Equation 8 the estimated effect of penetration is larger and more significant than in the whole sample of peripheral countries analyzed in Equation 3. In Equation 9, including only the small countries, the effect of penetration is much smaller. This supports the idea that the effects of penetration are different for countries depending on market size. Similarly, Equations 10 and 11 show the results of separating the very poor from the rest of the less developed countries. Among the countries with higher and middle levels of economic development the effects of penetration remain large, but among the poor countries the effects are clearly smaller.

These results, by splitting the sample according to the size and wealth are similar to those of earlier research.[25] [26] Our empirical research for the true shape of the interaction between penetration, market size and level of development led us to split the subsamples in several different ways.[27] We performed more analyses (1) in order to try to locate a natural breaking point or step-function in the interaction effect, and (2) in order to discover whether both interaction effects are of the same importance or whether one is spurious, since market size and level of economic development are substantially correlated for less developed countries. This detailed analysis leads to new insights with regard to the shape of the interaction. The results will be reported in Table 20.4 before we try to explain the smaller effect for African countries on the basis of many small countries in that region (Hypothesis 3).

Table 20.4 shows that by employing various splitting points for internal market size the relationship between penetration and economic growth is of similar strength and negative for all less developed countries in the range between 0.5 and 226 million tons of coal equivalent, the latter being the maximum value among less developed countries. In this broad range the association is therefore practically independent of size. In the range between 0.03 and 0.5 million tons a discontinuity can be detected. The relationship, which is independent of size above this range, changes direction from negative to positive for countries below 0.5, and especially below 0.2, million tons. Below 0.5 million tons there are 26 countries, 19 of which are located in Africa. We refer to these 26 countries as very small with regard to

Table 20.4 Regressions for Peripheral and Semiperipheral Countries in Different Ranges of Internal Market Size and GNP per Capita

Market Size in Million Tons (ranges schematically)

0.03	0.2	0.5	1.5	2.5	5	20	226	N	PEN	(F)
								88	-.0310†	(15.61)
								11	-.0347	(1.03)
								27	-.0438†	(10.07)
								30	-.0369†	(9.82)
								35	-.0274	(3.30)
								28	-.0342*	(4.67)
								34	-.0457‡	(16.10)
								41	-.0447‡	(18.70)
								62	-.0401‡	(20.63)
								72	-.0359‡	(20.17)
								47	-.0103	(0.68)
								26	.0045	(0.11)
								16	.0262	(1.46)

GNP Per Capita in U.S. Dollars (ranges schematically)

88	150	200	300	400	2,450	N	PEN	(F)
						46	-.0413†	(15.80)
						52	-.0384‡	(17.27)
						65	-.0341‡	(16.04)
						42	-.0222	(3.80)
						36	-.0154	(0.91)
						23	-.0138	(0.72)
						14	-.0217	(0.15)

Note: For explanations of significance levels, see Table 20.3. The same control variables have been used in Table 20.3. Total energy consumption figured in million tons of coal equivalent.

internal market size. And below 0.2 million tons there are 16 countries, which we call extremely small countries. Of these, 13 are located in Africa.

A similar detailed subsample analysis is performed in Table 20.4 according to various ranges of income per capita of less developed countries. It is revealed that the effect of penetration on growth becomes smaller in samples below $300 per capita GNP, but also for countries below this limit the association is always negative, even for the 14 very poor countries with a per capita of GNP of below $150. The explanation for this different pattern is that poorer peripheral countries are frequently very or extremely small, and this is the reason that they show smaller effects. For example, among the 23 countries below $200 GNP per capita there are 11 which are extremely small and another three are very small.

According to these new results the interaction effect of wealth with penetration is spurious. It is thus not the level of economic development that acts as a decisive variable, but the size of the internal market. This interaction with size occurs, however, only in the sense of a threshold variable. Very poor countries, for example India and Indonesia, are well above this threshold size due to their vast population. This means that a monetized sector, although it might be small in relative terms, is still considerable in absolute terms. Such large poor countries can be heavily integrated into the world-economy, whereas extremely small, poor countries like Rwanda and Mali do not have a similar potential for integration into the world-economy. They can be considered, therefore, as territories which are on the edge of the periphery of the world-economy.

Even though the very or extremely small countries do not stand completely outside the world-economy, their average level of penetration by transnational corporations is far below the average for all less developed countries. We assume that for these countries on the edge of the periphery every contact with the world-economy increases money circulation and thus the relative size of the monetized sector. Statistically, this could well lead to a spurious association between intensity of contact with the world-economy and economic growth expressed in money terms. The empirical finding that penetration by transnational corporations has a small positive effect on economic growth (not statistically significant) within this special group of countries may thus be explained.

The findings in Table 20.4 provide an explanation for the smaller negative effect of penetration found for African countries in Table 20.3. Out of 16 extremely small countries, 13 are located in Africa. The African sample is large enough to repeat the analysis excluding the 13 extremely small countries (below 0.2 million tons). Table 20.5 shows a substantial and statistically significant negative association between penetration by transnational corporations and economic growth for other than extremely small African countries. Also the positive effect of fresh foreign direct investment becomes more significant if the extremely small countries are excluded.

Thus, we can conclude that the small negative effect for the sample in Africa can be explained with Hypothesis 3. This hypothesis about threshold size cannot be used for the explanation of the small effect found for the

Table 20.5 Effects of Penetration and Flows of Foreign Investment in Larger and Smaller African Countries

	N	PEN (F-value)	FDI (F-value)	R^2 (adjusted)
Without extremely small countries	24	−.0318 (5.29)	.0086 (5.81)	.28
Results for all African countries	37	−.0065 (0.28)	.0067 (3.76)	.05

Americas sample since only one out of 21 countries in the Americas, Haiti, falls into the extremely small category. Even if Haiti is excluded, the effect of penetration does not become stronger. In the case of the Asian sample the exclusion of the six special case countries (Hypothesis 4) demonstrates significant results (see Table 20.3, Equation 7). The additional exclusion of the two extremely small countries in Asia does not make the relationship larger.

For an explanation of the small effect in the Americas sample, Hypothesis 5 should be considered. Before exploring this possibility, we shall test for Hypothesis 1 in Table 20.6. Hypothesis 1 proposes that there are different effects of penetration in subsamples.

The analysis of covariance in Table 20.6 tests for statistical interaction with region by using the world sample of 103 cases. Therefore, the problem of analyzing small samples is removed. The equations contain, besides the statistical interactions, the same control variables as in Table 20.3. The dummy variables used for the interactions take values one (1) or zero (0). The interactions with regional dummy variables (for example PEN times AFRICA) take either the value of penetration for those countries which are located in that region or the value zero for countries outside the region.

Equation 1 in Table 20.6 is the same as Equation 1 in Table 20.3 and is included for purposes of comparison with the other equations. The effects of FDI and the other variables in the model are similar to those shown in Table 20.3 and so they are not presented in the analysis of covariance results in Table 20.6, although they were included in each equation. Equation 2 adds to the model for the interaction between PEN and the richest countries to

Table 20.6   Analysis of the Statistical Interactions Between Transnational Penetration and Dummy Variables for Core Countries and Countries Located in Africa, America, and Asia

Equations	PEN	PEN Core Country Dummy	PEN Africa Dummy	PEN America Dummy	PEN Asia Dummy	R^2 (adjusted)
(1)	−.0262‡					.39
	(16.15)					
(2)	−.0301‡	.0205				.39
	(17.81)	(1.52)				
(3)	−.0259†	.0172	−.0025			.43
	(10.56)	(1.07)	(0.06)			
(4)	−.0267†	.0170		−.0098		.38
	(10.50)	(0.97)		(0.42)		
(5)	−.0282†	.0186			.0023	.40
	(13.97)	(1.22)			(0.02)	

Notes: For the estimation of the regression the same control variables as in Table 20.3 have been used (results not shown). The main effect of the various dummy variables has been included in the equations (results not shown in order to simplify presentation). Number of Cases = 103 in all equations.

control for the different consequences of the operations of transnational corporations in the richest countries of the world-economy. As can be seen, this interaction term is positive although not statistically significant, and its inclusion results in an increase in the estimated negative direct effect of PEN. This is consistent with the subsample analysis presented in Table 20.3.[28]

Equations 3 through 5 show the effects of interaction between geographical regions and penetration. It can be seen that all the regional interactions are extremely small and insignificant while the main effects remain large. This can be interpreted to mean that there are no interactions between geographical location and penetration which are independent of the other variables included in our model. Therefore, we can dismiss Hypothesis 1 which suggests such interactions. The rather more negative estimate for the interaction between PEN and location in the Americas is evidence against the possibility that the small effect in less developed America can be attributed to different relationships in these countries.

Hypothesis 5 remains a plausible explanation for the small effect of penetration in less developed American countries. Among all the regional subsamples, the Americas have the highest average value of penetration and the lowest coefficient of variation (i.e., all American countries in our sample of peripheral countries tend to be penetrated rather substantially).[29] Without being able to compare situations of higher and lower degrees of penetration in this subsample, the effects of penetration are not revealed. The absence of a significant positive interaction between penetration and location in America (Table 20.6) indicates that these countries lie on the line within the overall pattern, but have too small a variation among them to detect the effect in the regional subsample. This is support for Hypothesis 5.

We have thus found the explanation of the contradictory results from geographical regions in earlier studies. Our new analyses find only small effects of penetration by transnational corporations on economic growth in regional subsamples (Table 20.3). Detailed analyses show that this is, however, a spurious finding. Out of the five hypotheses which were proposed, the first one can be dismissed on the basis of the results of Table 20.6. Also, the second hypothesis is disproven since we use the same control variables for all subsamples in Table 20.3. The third hypothesis is supported in the sense that there exists a significant negative effect of penetration on economic growth only for countries above a threshold level of the size of the international market. This accounts for the results of studies of Africa. The larger African countries show the same significant association as all less developed countries. The fourth hypothesis is applicable to Asia; here special cases dilute the pattern. Without these special cases the negative effect for Asia is as strong as for all peripheral countries. The fifth hypothesis explains earlier findings based on studies of countries in the Americas. The peripheral American countries fit into the overall negative pattern which holds for all peripheral countries, but they have among them too low a variation, which hinders the detection of a substantial association when this region is analyzed separately.

NOTES

1. Contrary to neoclassical analysis, Domar's model does not assume that the growth trajectory is inherently stable. In this it is similar to Harrod's knife-edge theorem.

2. The formal deduction is as follows:

$$\Delta P = \sigma I$$

the increase in production is a function of social average capital productivity and net investment.

$$\Delta Y = \frac{1}{dS / dy} \Delta I,$$

the increase in national income, is a function of the "investment multiplier" and *increase* of net investment. With regard to the multiplier theory, Domar (1946, 140) states that it is "too familiar to need any comment, except for an emphasis on the obvious but often forgotten fact that with any given marginal propensity to save, dy/dt is a function not of I, but of dI/dt." If it should hold that $\Delta P = \sigma Y$, then $\Delta I / I = \sigma dS / dy$.

3. The growth trajectory is $Y_t = Y_0 E^s \sigma^t$, income as a function of time, where s denotes the propensity to save, (dS/dY) and E the base of the natural logarithm.

4. This growth rate would be: $g = s\sigma$. The maintenance of full employment requires investment to grow at a constant compound-growth rate.

5. Cross-national evidence seems to support this deduction. There is empirical support for the proposition that foreign capital inflows are inversely related to domestic savings (Weisskopf 1971; Papanek 1972; Stoneman 1975).

6. $\Delta I / I$, see above, note 2, can be split up in: $\Delta I^d + \Delta I^f / I^d + I^f$, where d denotes domestic and f foreign.

7. According to our own results the correlation in the world sample of 103 cases is $r = .40$. For 15 core countries the correlation is somewhat higher than in larger peripheral countries since the limits to growth are less important due to comparatively low income inequality which allows high mass consumption ($r = .43$).

In the larger peripheral countries the correlation is very low ($r = .19$). Here a large part of the foreign capital can be assumed to be producing for the domestic market. The great income inequality in these countries limits the size of the market and thus they suffer from unfavorable long-term investment opportunities.

In smaller peripheral countries, where most of the foreign capital produces for export to the international market, internal growth constraints are less important and, consistent with this, the correlation is higher ($r = .65$).

8. For replies and rejoinders in that controversy see Bornschier (1981b, 1982c).

9. This can be shown with the following figures. According to the

Organization for Economic Cooperation and Development (OECD-DAC 1972) estimates of the book value of the stock of foreign direct investment in 1967 in peripheral countries, $17.4 billion was controlled by U.S. companies and $17.7 by companies in other D.A.C. (core) countries. The U.S. share was not the same across regions. For example, in Africa the U.S. share was $1.4 billion and the non-U.S. share $5.2 billion. In peripheral America the U.S. share was $7.4 billion and the non-U.S. share $4.7 billion. Nor are the relative shares of U.S. and non-U.S. stocks the same across countries within regions. Within peripheral America, for example, the U.S. share in Argentina was 56 percent in 1967, in Brazil 35 percent, in Colombia 86 percent, and in Venezuela 73 percent. These figures strongly suggest that the U.S. stocks of foreign direct investment are not good proxies for the total stocks.

10. Only Ray and Webster, using data on on U.S. investment, find large and significant positive effects of foreign capital stocks on economic growth in Latin America. But in reanalyses of their results and those of the other Latin American studies, we found their unusually large effects resulted from their use of the GNP per capita figures compiled by the United States Agency for International Development (USAID). The use of the GNP per capita data compiled by either the World Bank or the United Nations produces small positive effects similar to the findings of Kaufman et al., and Szymanski. Given the extreme care with which the World Bank compiles GNP data, we suspect that its data are superior to those provided by USAID.

11. We include only Yugoslavia and Romania in our comparison because the World Bank presents growth data for these countries. We would want to include the other "socialist" countries in our analysis because of the contention that they are part of the larger capitalist world-economy, but growth data for these countries are contradictory between United Nations and World Bank sources. These countries have no penetration by transnational corporations during the time period studied, and their growth rates are relatively high. This would produce even larger negative results if these countries were included in our analyses.

12. This variable is fairly evenly distributed except for 18 outliers. These we have recoded, maintaining the rank order of the recoded cases . . . to make the variable useful for linear regression. Other researchers have employed log scores or rank scores to obtain a more even distribution, but recoding the outliers preserves the metric of the measure for the great majority of cases.

13. The measure is constructed in the following way:

$$[(\sqrt[12]{YN_{1977} / YN_{1965}} - 1) * 100]$$

The data are from a series of GNP per capita (YN) figures in constant market prices and U.S. dollars of the base period 1975–1977 provided by the Economic Analysis and Projections Department of the World Bank, computer run April 12, 1977, Washington (D.C.), mimeo. All the income per capita data used in the new analyses are from this source.

14. For our estimate of the total stock of capital we argue that cumulated domestic investment over a period of 18 years (times a correction factor for partial depreciation or loss of capital) is equivalent to total stock (Ballmer-Cao and Scheidegger 1979). This is to assume that the average time in which capital stock depreciates is 18 years or less. With regard to FDI we should note, in addition, that 12 outliers have been recoded maintaining their rank order. As with the penetration measure, this is done to normalize the distribution, a requirement of linear regression.

15. This is somewhat similar to earlier studies (Chase-Dunn 1975; Gobalet and Diamond 1979) that controlled for specialization in production of mineral resources (percentage of GDP in mining and petroleum production) to separate the effects of penetration from the effects of endowment with natural resources. Developing nations with high levels of exports are most often those that have natural resources that attract foreign capital. We want to know the effect of penetration by transnational corporations net of the effect of having these natural resources.

16. Stepwise regression substantiates this expectation. Without controlling for exports, penetration by transnational corporations has a significant negative effect on economic growth which becomes even more substantial after controlling for exports.

17. Albert Szymanski (1983) argues that controlling for the level of exports is misleading because one of the ways foreign investment positively affects economic development is by increasing exports. Our response to his criticism demonstrates that transnational penetration does not cause the growth of exports and thus exports are not an intervening variable between investment dependence and growth (Bornschier and Chase-Dunn 1983).

18. Absolute and relative criteria that make sense are based on data reported by the Kommission der Europaeischen Gemeinschaften (1976, 43) for 1973. Important headquarter countries (Belgium, Denmark, France, West Germany, Netherlands, Norway, Sweden, Switzerland, United Kingdom, United States) are those having more than 100 transnational corporations and those having more than 100 foreign links (subsidiaries and direct or indirect participation abroad) per million inhabitants. We should remark that Japan, which is often thought of as a core country, is not in the group of 15 richest countries before 1965 and it does not qualify for being an important headquarter country according to the above criteria. In 1973 Japan had 211 transnational corporations (as compared to an average of 799 for the ten important headquarter countries) and had only 11 subsidiaries abroad per million inhabitants (the range for the ten important headquarter countries varies from 119 for the U.S. to 645 for Switzerland). The other countries belonging to the group of 15 richest countries before 1965 which do not qualify as important transnational headquarters are: Australia, Austria, Canada, Finland, and New Zealand.

19. The six cases excluded from the Asian subsample are Hong Kong, Singapore, Israel, Jordan, Syria, and Saudi Arabia. These were all excluded from earlier analyses because they were considered special cases outside the scope conditions of the theoretical model (Bornschier and Ballmer-Cao 1978). Hong Kong and Singapore are city-states playing a specialized entrepôt role in the world-economy. As such they are unlikely to have the same type of development processes as countries that include hinterland regions within their political boundaries. Israel, Jordan and Syria composed a war zone during the period we are studying. Vietnam and Cambodia are not in our world sample because of missing data. While we do not wish to exclude warfare as a "normal" process for restructuring political relations in the evolution of the world-economy, it does disrupt the economic growth processes we are studying in this book. Saudi Arabia is a special case due to its extreme specialization in the export of oil. This commodity is not only a natural resource, but in the period under study it exhibits incredible price inelasticity combined with rising prices due to cartelization. The exclusion of these six cases from the Asian subsample changes the estimate of the effect of penetration on growth from a small and insignificant negative one to a large and significant negative estimate (Table 20.3). This illustrates the dangers inherent in small sample analyses such as those employed by studies focusing on

a single geographical region. The six cases are included in the world sample and the larger subsamples but in these the less restricted variance does not allow them to mask the overall pattern of effects.

20. In order to make sure that the results are not affected by the recodings for PEN and FDI, the same equation has been estimated *excluding* the 23 cases where either PEN and/or FDI have been recoded. The coefficients for the remaining eighty cases are as follows. PEN: $b = -.0245$ ($F = 8.07$), FDI: $b = .0097$ ($F = 8.12$). It is noteworthy that the exclusion of 18 countries with the highest values for penetration does not change the coefficient for PEN substantially. This means that the unfavorable impact of penetration on growth is a continuous one that does not rely on extreme cases.

21. Note that this measure for the level of exports does not consider the trade composition. Measures of trade composition like the one proposed by Galtung (1971) which are interpreted as trade dependency have been found by various researchers to affect economic growth in the following way. An unfavorable position with regard to "vertical trade" is negatively related to growth. The same is reported in the literature for trade commodity and trade partner concentration. However, the detailed reanalysis of most of the trade dependency studies by Bornschier and Hartlieb (1981) does not find support for earlier findings regarding trade effects on long-term economic growth (1965 to 1977) within large samples (up to 100 cases).

22. We have also tested whether the strong negative effect of penetration is mainly due to including Romania and Yugoslavia, which did not show any penetration in 1967 and which were growing rapidly during the period under study. The results without these two countries (i.e., with the remaining 78 LDCs) are much the same: PEN: $b = -.0285$ ($F = 12.82$), FDI: $b = .0084$ ($F = 9.99$), $R^2 = .37$.

23. Stepwise regression shows that the control of FDI (flows) increases the negative weight of PEN (stocks). Such an increase also occurs when the level of income is controlled and applies both to the linear and the squared term. Furthermore, the already significant negative effect of PEN gets more substantial when level of exports are controlled. Exports, however, enter as a positive predictor into the equation only after penetration is controlled. For a discussion of trade variables, see Bornschier and Hartlieb (1981).

24. In peripheral America there is no country which could be excluded due to the same criteria. Venezuela, although being highly specialized in oil exports, is not comparable to the extreme specialization exhibited by Saudi Arabia. And in Africa, there are only two cases, namely Egypt (war region) and Libya (oil exports), which could be excluded. These two cases are, however, unlikely to affect the result of the large African sample which contains 37 countries.

25. The cutting point was in both cases the mean of the logged values for SIZE and YN.

26. Bornschier, et al. (1978), Bornschier and Ballmer-Cao (1978) and Dolan and Tomlin (1980) report similar findings, whereas the findings of Gobalet and Diamond (1979) are inconsistent.

27. This led us also to consider the possibility that penetration effects may be relatively greatest among the semiperipheral countries. We identified 15 countries from our sample of less developed countries that are deemed to be semiperipheral in the contemporary world-economy (Wallerstein 1979) and performed a separate analysis with these, most of which were relatively large in terms of internal market size. The comparison between this subsample and the sample of remaining less developed countries revealed that there is a somewhat larger estimated effect for semiperipheral countries. This larger effect is, however, very similar to the one which results if only small countries are excluded. Thus,

we conclude that there is no special interaction effect for semiperipheral countries.

28. We have also tested the interaction between SIZE and PEN but the results are not presented here. This analysis shows a negative effect of the interaction term, indicating support for the subsample results in Tables 20.3 and 20.4, but the interaction effect is not statistically significant, indicating that, in the range of the world sample, this interaction between level of development and penetration reveals a similar small effect in the analysis of the whole sample. In order to further substantiate the conclusion in Table 20.4 that the interaction effect is with SIZE and not with level of development (YN), we entered both of them in the same analysis. This supports the earlier conclusion: the far more important interaction effect is with the size of the domestic market rather than the level of income. The latter interaction becomes zero when the interaction with SIZE is controlled.

29. Here are the mean values for penetration by transnational corporations in the whole sample of less developed countries and in the regional subsamples, and also the coefficients of variation. As can be seen the mean value for the American subsample is the highest and the coefficient of variation is the lowest.

Sample	N	Mean for PEN	Coefficient of Variation
All less developed	88	49.04	.72
Africa	37	50.00	.72
Asia	23	34.89	1.04
Asia without special cases	17	26.61	1.16
Europe	7	36.25	.90
America	21	67.24	.42

REFERENCES

Alschuler, L. R. 1976. "Satellization and Stagnation in Latin America." *International Studies Quarterly* 20(1):39–82.

Ballmer-Cao, T.-H. and J. Scheidegger. 1979. Compendium Data for World System Analysis. *Bulletin of the Sociological Institute of the University of Zurich*, March.

Berweger, G. and J.-P. Hoby. 1978. Wirtschaftspolitik gegenuber Auslandskapital. *Bulletin des Soziologischen Instituts der Universitat Zurich* Nr. 35:1–136.

Bornschier, V. 1975. "Abhaengige Industrialisierung und Einkommensentwicklung." *Schweizerische Zeitschrift für Soziologie* 1(1):67-105.

———. *Wachstum, Konzentration und Multinationalisierung von Industrieunternehmen*. Frauenfeld und Stuttgart: Verlag Huber.

———. 1980. "Multinational Corporations and Economic Growth: A Cross-National Test of the Decapitalization Thesis." *Journal of Development Economics* 7 (June):191–210.

———. 1981a. "Dependent Industrialization in the World Economy: Some Comments and Results Concerning a Recent Debate." *Journal of Conflict Resolution* 25 (3):371–400.

———. 1981b. "Weltwirtschaft, Wachstum und Verteilung: Eine Replik zur Arbeit von Erich Weede." *Schweizerische Zeitschrift für Soziologie* 7(1):129–36.

————. 1982c. "Dependence on Foreign Capital and Economic Growth: A Reply to Weede and Tiefenbach's Critique." *European Journal of Political Research* 10 (4):445–450.

————, C. Chase-Dunn, and R. Rubinson. 1978. "Cross-National Evidence of the Effects of Foreign Investment and Aid on Economic Growth and Inequality: A Survey of Findings and a Reanalysis." *American Journal of Sociology* 84 (3):651–683.

Bornschier, V. and T.-H. Ballmer-Cao. 1978. "Multinational Corporations in the World Economy and National Development. An Empirical Study of Income Per Capita Growth 1960–1975." *Bulletin of the Sociological Institute of the University of Zurich* no. 32:1–169.

Bornschier, V. and O. Hartlieb. 1981. "Weltmarktabhaengigkeit und Entwicklung: Uebersich ueber die Evidenzen und Reanalyse," [Structure and Income Distribution.] *Bulletin of the Sociological Institute of the University of Zurich* no. 39.

Bornschier, V. and C. Chase-Dunn. 1983. "Reply to Szymanski." *American Journal of Sociology* 89 (3):694–699.

Chase-Dunn, C. 1975a. "The Effects of International Economic Dependence on Development and Inequality: A Cross-National Study." *American Sociological Review* 40 (6):720–738.

————. 1975b. *International Economic Dependence in the World-System.* Dissertation, Department of Sociology, Stanford University.

Delacroix, J. and Ragin, C. C. 1981. "Structural Blockage: A Cross-national Study of Economic Dependency, State Efficiency, and Underdevelopment." *American Journal of Sociology* 86:1311–1347.

Dolan, M. B. and B. W. Tomlin. 1980. "First World-Third World Linkages: External Relations and Economic Development." *International Organization* 34 (1):41–63.

Domar, E. D. 1946. "Capital Expansion, Rate of Growth, and Employment." *Econometrica* 14:137–147.

————. 1948. "The Problem of Capital Accumulation." *American Economic Review* 38 (5):777–794.

Evans, P. 1980. "The Developmental Effects of Direct Investment." Paper read at the Annual Meeting of the American Sociological Association, New Orleans, August.

Galtung, J. 1971. "A Structural Theory of Imperialism." Journal of Peace Research 8 (2):81–117.

Gobalet, J. G. and Diamond, L. J. 1979. "Effects of Investment Dependence on Economic Growth: The Role of Internal Structural Characteristics and Periods in the World Economy," *International Studies Quarterly* 23:412–444.

Hymer, S. H. 1972. "The Multinational Corporation and the Law of Uneven Development." In J. N. Bhagwati (ed.), *Economics and the World Order.* New York: Macmillan.

Jackman, R. W. 1982. "Dependence on Foreign Investment and Economic Growth in the Third World," *World Politics* 34:175–196.

Kaufman, R. R., Chernotsky, H. I. and Geller, D. S. 1975. "A Preliminary Test of the Theory of Dependency," *Comparative Politics* 7:303–330.

McGowan, P. and D. Smith. 1978. "Economic Dependency in Black Africa: A Causal Analysis of Competing Theories," *International Organization* 32 (Winter):179–235.

Meyer-Fehr, P. 1978. "Bestimmungsfaktoren des Wirtschaftswachstums von Nationen. Komparative Analyse unter Berucksichtigung Multinationaler

Konzerne." *Bulletin des Soziologischen Instituts der Universitat Zurich* Nr. 34:1–105.

―――. 1980. "Technologische Kontrolle durch Multinationale Konzerne und Wirtschaftswachstum." In V. Bornschier (ed.), *Multinationale Konzerne, Wirtschaftspolitik un Nationale Entwicklung im Weltsystem*, pp. 106–28. Frankfurt: Campus Verlag.

OECD (Organization for Economic Cooperation and Development). 1972. Stock of Private Direct Investments by D.A.C. Countries in Developing Countries, End 1967. Paris: Development Assistance Directorate.

Papanek, G. 1972. "The Effect of Aid and Other Resource Transfers on Savings and Growth in Less Developed Countries." *Economic Journal* 82 (September):934–950.

Ray, J. L. and Webster, T. 1978. "Dependency and Economic Growth in Latin America." *International Studies Quarterly* 22:409–434.

Rubinson, R. 1976. "Reply to Bach and Irwin," *American Sociological Review* 42 (5):817–821.

Stevenson, P. 1972. "External Economic Variables Influencing the Economic Growth Rate of Seven Major Latin American Nations," *Canadian Review of Sociology and Anthropology* 9:347–356.

Stoneman, C. 1975. "Foreign Capital and Economic Growth." *World Development* 3 (1):11–26.

Szymanski, A. 1976. "Dependence, Exploitation, and Development." *Journal of Military and Political Sociology* 4 (Spring):53–65.

―――. 1983. "Comment on Bornschier, Chase-Dunn, and Rubinson." American Journal of Sociology 89 (3):690–694.

Timberlake, M. and Kentor, J. 1983. "Economic Dependence, Overurbanization, and Economic Growth: A Study of Less Developed Countries." *Sociological Quarterly* 24 (4):489–508.

van Puijenbroek, R.A.G. 1984. "Enkele politieke en economische determinanten van economische groei." Doctoral thesis, Katholieke Universiteit, Nijmegen (Netherlands).

Wallerstein, I. 1979. *The Capitalist World Economy*. Cambridge: Cambridge University Press.

Weede, E. 1981a. "Militar, Multis und Wirtschaft. Eine international vergleichende Studie unter besonderer Beruksichtigung der Entwicklungslander. *Schweizerische Zeitschrift für Soziologie* 7:113–27.

―――. 1981. "Dependenztheorie und Wirtschaftswachstum." *Kölner Zeitschrift für Soziologie und Sozialpsychologie* 33 (4): 690-707. Weede, E. and Tiefenbach, H. 1981a. "Some Recent Explanations of Income Inequality." *International Studies Quarterly* 25 (2):255–282.

―――. 1981b. "Three Dependency Explanations of Economic Growth." *European Journal of Political Research* 9:391–406.

Weisskopf, T. E. 1971. "The Impact of Foreign Capital Inflow on Domestic Savings in Underdeveloped Countries." Summary in *Econometrica* 39 (Appendix of abstracts of the papers presented at the Second World Congress of the Econometric Society, Cambridge, England): 109.

21

· · · · · · ·

Financial Dependence in the Capitalist World Economy and the Distribution of Income Within States

· · · · · · ·

EDWARD N. MULLER

In this contribution, Edward N. Muller seeks to test the hypothesis derived from the dependency/world-system perspective that the financial dependence of developing countries increases income inequality within them. His approach is to examine the hypothesis alongside the contrary view that the distribution of income within states is largely the result of internal noneconomic forces. Muller reviews the cases of Canada and Taiwan and finds evidence refuting the dependency/world-system perspective. He then turns to the cross-national income inequality data and finds four serious flaws with the figures employed in virtually all previous studies. He corrects for three of those and seeks again to determine the influence of financial dependence on income distribution. Using transnational corporation penetration and the size of a country's external public debt as measures of financial dependence, he finds that there is little support for the dependency/world-system perspective and suggests that future research concentrate on the autonomous role of the state.

The developed "core" countries in the capitalist world economy are not only much wealthier than the less developed countries of the "periphery," they are also much more egalitarian. Data on income distribution from the most recent *World Development Report* (World Bank, 1982) show that during the 1970s the upper quintile of households in 14 countries of the core

Reprinted with permission of author from *The Gap Between Rich and Poor: Contending Perspectives on the Political Economy of Development*, edited by Mitchell A. Seligson (Boulder, CO: Westview Press 1984).

(industrial market economies) received, on the average, 40.5 percent of total household income, with a range of 36.8 (Finland) to 45.8 (France). By contrast, among 23 countries of the periphery, the average income share of the upper quintile was 52.6 percent, and the range was 38.7 (Yugoslavia) to 66.6 (Brazil).

The highly unequal distribution of income that prevails in many countries of the periphery is explained by dependency theory as a result in large part of the fact that the accumulation and expansion of capitalism is controlled by powerful foreign economic actors (for general reviews of dependency theory see, e.g., O'Brien, 1975; Portes, 1976). The few (employers and workers alike) who become linked with the international sector of the economy are thought to profit from the infusion of foreign capital at the expense of the majority of the population, which remains or becomes increasingly "marginalized," since the superior resources of transnational corporations retard the emergence of a national industrial bourgeoisie, while the advanced capital intensive technology that is imported from abroad fails to absorb labor surpluses, and in some sectors increases them.

The *bête noire* of contemporary dependency theorists—whether they stem from the Economic Commission for Latin America (ECLA) structuralist perspective, the Marxist perspective, or straddle both (see O'Brien, 1975:10–16)—is the transnational corporation (TNC), which is regarded as the fundamental causal mechanism of dependency in the post-World War II period. The core-headquartered TNC fosters dependence in the periphery: (1) indirectly, by causing a net outflow of capital from the periphery to the core, thus creating balance of payments deficits that must be financed by foreign loans, which in turn entail a loss of national political autonomy since core financial institutions gain the right to participate in the policymaking process of debtor countries; and (2) directly, by using its advantages of capital and technology to acquire a position of dominance among medium and large firms within the most dynamic sectors of private economic activity, thereby, in Sunkel's (1972:526) phrase, seizing "control of the commanding heights of the economy."

Dependency theorists postulate a variety of specific mechanisms to relate TNC penetration to income inequality (representative writings in English are Dos Santos, 1970; Sunkel, 1972; Cardoso, 1973; Furtado, 1973). The general argument, as stated by one of the more prolific empirical theorists of dependency, Volker Bornschier,[1] runs as follows:

> Due to the links with the world economy [through the presence of transnational corporations] one may argue that the political actor of a dependent country is less likely to be willing or able to act in favor of income equilibration via the redistribution of incomes. . . . The socio-political basis of such an inaptitude of the peripheral State is a specific class composition underlying the social formation process, namely a

class coalition within the integrated [into the world economy] segment against the marginalized majority of the population. . . . The integrated segment strives after the bourgeois life style of this reference system [the bourgeois lifestyle that exists in the core countries]. This is likely to contribute to income privileges with regard to the average life situation in their specific less developed countries. A higher income gap and a more intense marginalization in poor countries than in richer ones is thus likely to occur.

In the rich countries, however, affluence acts as a break on such a mechanism. Also multinational corporations in the wealthy countries are not interested in income inequality. Their market chances—given a very high average income in these countries—are larger the higher the mass incomes. . . . [Thus] the degree of penetration by multinational corporations as a central aspect for the structural position within the world economy is expected to go together with higher income inequality within peripheral countries and tends to have an opposite effect for core countries. [Bornschier 1983:12–13.]

The essence of the argument is: (1) that the interest of transnational corporations is inequality in the periphery (since elite demand is thought to be the only effective market for TNC-produced goods) but (2) equality in the core (where the wealthier masses can afford to purchase TNC-produced goods); (3) that the peripheral state is powerless to control the behavior of TNCs (the power of the core state vis-à-vis TNCs is a moot point, since core states, as headquarters of TNCs, benefit from their global economic activities); and (4) that inequality is in the interest of the dominant social class formation in the periphery (the workers and elements of the bourgeoisie who benefit from the presence of TNCs); with the logical result that the political elite in peripheral countries is unable (due to assumptions 1 and 3) and unwilling (due to assumption 4) to carry out egalitarian policies, whereas the political elite in core countries is encouraged or at least not discouraged by TNCs to pursue egalitarian policies (due to assumption 2).

Bornschier (1983: 12) places his version of dependency theory within the world-system paradigm, which asserts that the transnational corporation is the central institution of the modern capitalist world economy, structuring the world division of labor such that distinctions between core and periphery (the core specializing in technologically sophisticated industrial production and control over capital; the periphery specializing in production of raw materials and routinized industrial production) "reflect the organizational domination of the multinational corporation." Thus, in the world-system paradigm, as in Marxist analyses, economic processes of northern capitalism, currently manifested through the institution of the transnational corporation headquartered in the core, are history's locomotive.

The most compelling counter hypothesis is certainly not the "modernization" approach (often taken to include neoclassical economics), which posits an inverse relationship between foreign investment and income inequality (Chase-Dunn, 1975:724–726, gives a review of the literature).

Rather, it is an approach sensitive to the possibility that internal often noneconomic forces, instead of external economic variables representing the logic of capitalist imperialism, may decisively shape social and economic development—including the distribution of income—not only in the periphery but in the core as well.

Consider Canada. Of all countries for which data are available, Canada's economy is the most highly penetrated by transnational corporations (see Ballmer-Cao and Scheidegger, 1979, Table 3.2.5). Yet Canada ranks among the most egalitarian capitalist countries in the world. How is it that Canada can be at once so extraordinarily dependent on foreign capital and yet have such an egalitarian distribution of income? According to Bornschier's world economy model, transnational corporations are interested in promoting equality of income in rich core countries like Canada; therefore, Canada's egalitarian income distribution is explained by its wealth and high penetration by TNC-controlled capital.

However, it would appear that Canada's egalitarian income distribution predated the "quantum leap" in foreign investment (mostly by U.S.-headquartered TNCs) that occurred after World War II. Thus, the income share of the upper quintile was 42.9 percent in 1951 (Sawyer, 1976:26), while U.S. direct investment was increasing from $2.6 billion in 1945 to $8.5 billion in 1957 (Watkins, 1975:84). By 1967 total TNC-controlled capital stood at $10.6 billion and the total of foreign direct investment was $20.7 billion (Ballmer-Cao and Scheidegger, 1979, Tables 3.2.2 and 3.2.1). But during this massive build-up of foreign investment in Canada, income distribution showed virtually no change.[2] From a longitudinal time-series perspective, then, the postulated inverse relationship between degree of TNC economic penetration and income inequality does not appear to hold in the case of Canada. One cannot help but suspect that the real causes of Canada's income distribution have much more to do with the form of her government, the nature of land tenure, the size of her population, not to mention the quality of her "human resources" (with respect to tangibles such as education, as well as intangibles such as achievement motivation), than with the force of capitalist imperialism (even in reverse!).

Indeed, Bornschier's novel twist to the standard imperialism argument, standing it, so to speak, on its head for core countries, is theoretically plausible only if one assumes that the transnational corporation is the *primum mobile* (to borrow a phrase from Tony Smith, 1981b) of the post-World War II First and Third World. Such an extreme emphasis on the power of transnational corporations is not unique to Bornschier,[3] but he is the first to propose TNC economic penetration as a *cause* of greater income equality in the core countries of the First World.

With respect to the periphery, the criticism made by Smith (1981b; also see Smith, 1979; 1981a) of dependency theory in general is relevant to the world economy model of Bornschier.

Too much emphasis is placed on the dynamic, molding power of capital-ist imperialism and the socioeconomic forces in league with it locally; too little attention is paid to political motives behind imperialism or to the autonomous power of local political circumstances in influencing the course of change in Africa, Asia, and Latin America. . . . Nowhere in this literature do we find, for example, recognition that local physical, social, or political forces might for their own autonomous reasons have been simply unable to generate industrial development, so that imperialism is only partially and secondarily, if indeed at all, respon-sible for the present predicaments of many countries in the Third World. By contrast, nowhere do we find any recognition of . . . the positive, substantial uses these countries can make and have made of their contacts with the international system. [Smith, 1981b:757.]

A contemporary case in point is Taiwan. As a dependent territory of Japan, Taiwan before the end of World War II was subject to relations of traditional colonial economic dependency. From 1945 until the early 1960s, Taiwan was highly dependent on foreign economic aid, ranking fourteenth in the world in U.S. economic aid per capita during 1958–65 (Taylor and Hudson, 1972, Table 6.4). Direct foreign investment in Taiwan accelerated rapidly in the 1960s, but while the penetration of Taiwan's economy by TNCs was "taking off," income distribution was becoming markedly more egalitarian. The share of the richest quintile in national income declined from 61.8 percent in 1953 to 51.8 percent in 1961 (Jain, 1975, Table 70); and by 1971 the income share of the upper quintile had dropped to below the 40 percent mark, rendering it comparable in size to that of Denmark, Norway, Sweden, and the United Kingdom—the most egalitarian countries of the core. On the basis of a detailed case study of the Taiwan experience, Barrett and Whyte (1982: 1086) observe that "the presence in Taiwan of a strong state bureaucracy able to maintain separation from, and dominance over, powerful economic interests seems to have been a major determinant of the form development took on that island." Thus the assumption of dependency theory that domestic governments are pawns of *comprador* elites allied with transnational corporations does not hold for Taiwan.

Nor is Taiwan merely a deviant case. Among other semi-industrial countries of the periphery, the income share of the upper quintile in Spain is similar to that in Taiwan, despite an even higher degree of TNC penetration of the Spanish economy; and Argentina registers a moderately egalitarian income distribution (the income share of the upper quintile in 1970 was 50.3), which has remained virtually unchanged since the early 1950s (the upper quintile income share was 50.1 percent in 1953 and 51.6 percent in 1961 according to data from Table 1 of Figueroa and Weisskoff, 1980), despite a quite high degree of TNC economic penetration. As in Taiwan, so would it seem in Spain and Argentina that autonomous domestic political forces (the Franco regime in Spain; Perón's rule in Argentina from 1946 to

1955) had far more influence on the distribution of income than the force of international capitalist imperialism operating through the guise of the transnational corporation.

The prototype of inegalitarian dependent development is, of course, Brazil, which *dependencistas* such as Cardoso, Dos Santos, Furtado, and Sunkel had prominently in mind during the initial flourishing of the dependency school in the late 1960s. Brazil indeed has a very high level of TNC penetration, and as foreign investment poured into Brazil in the 1960s—encouraged mightily by the military-dominated authoritarian regime that was established in 1964—the distribution of personal income became increasingly concentrated in the hands of the few (the income share of the upper quintile rose from 56.9 1960 to 66.6 in 1970—see Table 1 of Figueroa and Weisskoff, 1980). But in generalizing from a particular country such as Brazil, the student of economic development in the periphery risks the fallacy of the special case (see Seers, 1963). Is inegalitarian dependent development an inevitable consequence of the "laws of motion" of capitalist imperialism or does the Brazilian case reflect the operation of internal possibly idiosyncratic forces?

Previous cross-national research purports to have shown that inegalitarian dependent development is a general phenomenon. These studies, however, have been subject to flaws of research design, compounded by unreliable measurement of income distribution. As I will show in the next section, they cannot be regarded as at all conclusive. In this chapter, I will correct these flaws and perform a reliable test of the dependency world-system hypothesis. If the null hypothesis cannot be confidently rejected, I will interpret this as support for the rival "internal dynamics" hypothesis.

PREVIOUS RESEARCH

The initial cross-national investigation of the association between financial dependence and the distribution of personal income was performed by Chase-Dunn (1975), who reported positive but nonsignificant relationships between inequality and two indicators of financial dependence, debits on investment income per capita and external public debt per capita, for a sample of 31 less developed countries (LDCs). This was followed by a global analysis of 41 countries by Rubinson (1976), who reported a positive, statistically significant effect of investment dependence on inequality and a positive but nonsignificant effect of debt dependence on inequality. For an expanded global sample (N = 50), Bornschier and Ballmer-Cao (1979) also found a positive, statistically significant relationship between investment dependence and inequality, while Evans and Timberlake (1980) found such a relationship in their analysis of an expanded sample of less developed countries (N = 49). (The latter two studies further investigated intervening mechanisms between investment dependence and income inequality: indicators of the distribution of power and growth of the service sector of the labor force.)

Weede and Tiefenbach (1981) challenged the growing consensus on the existence of a cross-nationally valid, positive relationship between investment dependence and income inequality (see the review article by Bornschier, Chase-Dunn, and Rubinson, 1978). They pointed out that all previous investigations except that of Bornschier and Ballmer-Cao had failed to control for the correct specification of the relationship between income inequality and economic development, a nonmonotonic quadratic polynomial function (see Ahluwalia, 1974, 1976). Upon controlling for the nonmonotonic economic development relationship, Weede and Tiefenbach 1981: 273) showed that across three different data sets (Paukert, 1973; Ahluwalia, 1974; Ballmer-Cao and Scheidegger, 1979) investment dependence as measured by a variable constructed by Bornschier (1978) called multinational corporation (MNC) penetration was estimated consistently to have a nonsignificant effect on inequality. Although Bornschier and Ballmer-Cao (1979) had taken the nonmonotonic economic development relationship into account, Weede and Tiefenbach were unable to replicate the statistically significant positive result reported by Bornschier and Ballmer-Cao, even for Bornschier and Ballmer-Cao's own data (Bornschier and Ballmer-Cao had analyzed only 50 cases of their data; Weede and Tiefenbach used the full sample of 64 cases with information on both income distribution and MNC penetration).

The response of Bornschier (1981) to the results of the Weede and Tiefenbach analysis entailed two points, one related to research design, the other to measurement. In regard to research design, Bornschier (1981:283–284) claimed that Weede and Tiefenbach had misunderstood his argument:

> The key point of the argument [of a positive relationship between MNC penetration and inequality] is that this relationship holds for LDC's only. For the group of richest countries, which are the headquarter countries of MNC's, there is a tendency toward an opposite association between MNC's and income inequality. . . . When this was combined with the positive relationship between MNC penetration for peripheral countries, one effect cancels out the other, and hence Weede and Tiefenbach find no effect in their particular world sample.

Bornschier (1981:284) also stated that he had in the meantime developed an improved MNC penetration indicator. Theoretically, the ideal measure of the concept of penetration of an economy by transnational (or "multinational" in Bornschier's terminology)[4] corporations would be a ratio of the stock of capital controlled by transnationals to the total stock of domestically owned capital and the size of the labor force. Bornschier's first MNC penetration indicator (used in Bornschier and Ballmer-Cao, 1979) had employed proxies for all terms, i.e., TNC-controlled capital was estimated by

the stock of foreign direct investment, domestic capital was estimated by total energy consumption, and the size of the labor force was estimated by total
population. Bornschier's theoretically more appropriate MNC Penetration indicator drew upon recently available data on the stock of capital invested by
the world's largest transnationals in order to measure TNC-controlled capital
directly. A much more direct estimate of the total stock of capital was constructed (see Bornschier, 1980:197), and total population was retained as a
proxy for size of labor force. MNC penetration then is defined as the ratio of
TNC-controlled capital to the geometric mean of total domestic capital and
population.

On the one hand, it is indisputable that the research design and
measurement points raised by Bornschier represent significant improvements
upon much of the earlier empirical work. A basic characteristic of dependency
theory is rejection of what Hirschman (1981:3–5) calls the *monoeconomics
claim* of orthodox economic theory. The monoeconomics claim is simply the
belief in the existence of universal economic laws. In rejecting this claim,
dependency theorists draw a fundamental distinction between countries that
occupy a central or "core" position in the capitalist world economy and those
on the periphery. The economic "laws of motion" of countries on the
periphery are regarded as being substantially different from those of core
countries. With respect to income distribution, dependency theory predicts
only that within countries of the periphery, the greater the financial
dependence on the core, the greater the inequality in the distribution of
income. Therefore, correct specification of the financial dependency
hypothesis requires explicit differentiation between core and periphery.

Operational definition of the concept of TNC economic penetration has
been problematic in all previous research. More or less indirect proxies have
been used as indicators of the stock of TNC-controlled capital; but the most
serious limitation has been failure to measure the stock of TNC-controlled
capital as a proportion of the total stock of domestic capital—a procedure
essential to accurate representation of the degree to which TNC-controlled
capital "penetrates" the economy.

However, on the other hand, Weede and Tiefenbach should not be faulted
for failing to correct problems of research design measurement present in the
Bornschier and Ballmer-Cao analysis of 1979. In any event, the corrected
reanalysis of Bornschier (1981; also see Bornschier, 1983) reports a
statistically significant positive effect of MNC penetration on income
inequality in LDCs and a statistically significant negative effect of MNC
penetration on income inequality in developed countries, independent of the
nonmonotonic relationship between income inequality and level of economic
development.

Although Bornschier's current results are more convincing than those of
previous analyses, they nevertheless still are subject to certain flaws of
research design and measurement. The remaining research design problem is

that of temporal ordering between presumed cause and effect variables. MNC penetration scores are for 1967. In order not to violate the logic of causal inference, income distribution should be observed at least circa 1967 and preferably somewhat later. Among the developed countries income distribution scores are for various years between 1967 and 1973 (except Denmark, which is 1966), so the temporal ordering of MNC penetration and income distribution is appropriate. But in the sample of LDCs, of which there are 48, income distribution in 18 instances (38 percent of the total) is measured before 1967, and in 12 LDCs the measurement of income distribution is very old, i.e., 1960 or earlier. Thus, in a nonnegligible number of LDCs, Bornschier is correlating MNC penetration with income distributions that existed well before the observation of penetration of the economy by TNC-controlled capital. Moreover, 7 of the 12 very old measurements are for African countries before (or during the year of) independence. It requires a considerable leap of faith (and logic) to assume that an MNC penetration score assessed nearly a decade after a dependent territory has become a self-governing state could have been a major cause of the distribution of income that prevailed under colonial status.[5]

To further exacerbate the temporal ordering problem, 4 of the 12 very old measurements (Burma, 1958; Chad, 1958; Niger, 1960; Nigeria, 1959) and 1 of the 6 measurements between 1961–65 (Morocco, 1965) were considered by their compiler (Paukert, 1973:125), in a note of caution to the user, to be of "rather doubtful value." Another very old measurement, the 1957 income distribution for Greece, appears to be for urban areas only, which is not a reliable basis for estimating country-wide distribution. Consequently, the likelihood of measurement error is correlated with inappropriate temporal ordering.

In light of these potential sources of error, one's confidence in Bornschier's current findings is reduced. A reinvestigation sensitive to the temporal ordering of cause and effect observations and to the quality of measurement of income distribution obviously is called for.

DATA

Information on income distribution and on the extent to which the economy is penetrated by capital controlled by transnational corporations is available in Ballmer-Cao and Scheidegger (1979: Tables 3.2.5 and 5.3) for 64 countries. MNC penetration scores are for 1967, derived from the formula:

$$\text{MNC Penetration} = \frac{\text{Stock of Capital Invested by MNCs}}{\sqrt{\text{Stock of Capital * Population}}} \quad (1)$$

MNC penetration thus is defined as the ratio of capital controlled by transnational corporations to the geometric mean of domestic capital and population, a procedure that affords an indicator of the relative weight (or penetration) of TNC-controlled capital in an economy.

With respect to the data on income distribution, I have where necessary updated, revised, or deleted information as follows:

1. data for Argentina, Denmark, Spain, and Trinidad and Tobago have been updated from pre-1967 to post-1967 measurements;
2. data for Brazil, Canada, Chile, Ecuador, Honduras, Ivory Coast, Japan, Kenya, Malawi, Netherlands, Norway, Panama, Peru, Sweden, Taiwan, Tanzania, United States, and Venezuela have been revised according to more recent calculations;[6]
3. data for Sierra Leone (1968) have been deleted because they do not cover the Western Province;
4. data for Greece (1957) have been deleted because they do not include rural areas and are too old;
5. data for Austria (1967) have been deleted because they were judged unreliable by Sawyer (1976: 22);
6. data for Burma (1958), Chad (1958), Morocco (1965), Niger (1960), and Nigeria (1959) have been deleted because they were judged unreliable by Paukert (1973: 125) and, except for Morocco, are too old;
7. data for Benin (1959), Iraq (1956), Jamaica (1958), Madagascar (1960), Senegal (1960), and Zambia (1959) have been deleted because they are too old.

The result of these emendations and deletions is the data listed in Table 21.1, which I divide into a restricted sample of 45 countries and an extended sample of 50. The extended sample allows income distribution measurements up to five years prior to observation of MNC penetration and includes data from a "secondary source" (Roberti, 1974) used by Ballmer-Cao and Scheidegger (1979).

The income share accruing to the highest 20 percent of recipients is a standard measure of inequality, often used in preference to the Gini coefficient (see, for example, the discussion in Ahluwalia, 1976), which is unduly sensitive to the middle of the distribution (e.g., Allison, 1978: 868). The dependency hypothesis predicts a concentration of income at the upper end of the distribution as a result of MNC penetration (or other indicators of financial dependence) in peripheral economies; therefore, the income share of the upper quintile is the most appropriate inequality measure.

Countries are grouped in Table 21.1 by core versus peripheral status in the world capitalist economy and, within the periphery, by their trade structure (following the classification in World Bank, 1981, Table 6.1). Core

Table 21.1 Distribution of Scores on MNC Penetration and Share of National Income Accruing to the Upper Quintile: 50 Nations

Core

Country	1967 MNC Penetration	Income Share of Upper Quintile c. 1970, percent	(Source/Year)
Australia	186.4	38.8	(W:67)
Canada	215.7	41.0	(W:69)
Denmark	34.2	37.5	(W:76)
Finland	5.4	49.1*	(R:67)
France	61.5	46.9	(W:70)
Germany (FRG)	51.8	45.6	(S:70)
Italy	38.1	46.5	(W:69)
Japan	12.8	41.0	(W:69)
Netherlands	71.6	42.9	(W:67)
New Zealand	58.3	41.0	(A:71)
Norway	34.1	37.3	(W:70)
Sweden	57.9	37.0	(W:72)
Switzerland	92.5	45.9	(B:68)
U.K.	73.1	39.4	(S:72)
U.S.	18.0	42.8	(W:72)
Mean	*67.4*	*42.2*	

Periphery: Semi-Industrial

Country	1967 MNC Penetration	Income Share of Upper Quintile c. 1970, percent	(Source/Year)
Argentina	63.0	50.3	(W:70)
Brazil	64.4	66.6	(W:72)
Colombia	56.4	59.4	(A:70)
India	11.3	53.1	(J:68)
Mexico	45.8	64.0	(A:69)
Pakistan	16.2	41.5	(J:71)
Philippines	24.7	53.9	(W:71)
S. Africa	107.7	62.0*	(J:65)
S. Korea	3.5	43.4	(J:71)
Spain	56.8	42.2	(W:74)
Taiwan	41.5	39.2	(W:71)
Turkey	38.6	60.6	(A:68)
Uruguay	26.3	47.4	(A:67)
Yugoslavia	0.4	41.5	(A:68)
Mean	*39.8*	*51.8*	

Periphery: Primary Producing and Least Developed

Country	1967 MNC Penetration	Income Share of Upper Quintile c. 1970, percent	(Source/Year)
Oil Exporters			
Ecuador	28.3	73.5	(A:70)
Indonesia	9.9	52.0	(J:71)
Trinidad	69.4	50.0	(W:75)
Venezuela	98.6	54.0	(W:70)
Mean	*51.6*	*57.4*	
Other Primary			
Bolivia	8.1	61.0	(P:68)
Chile	27.2	51.4	(W:68)
Costa Rica	26.6	50.6	(A:71)
El Salvador	31.8	61.4*	(J:61)
Ghana	64.4	47.8*	(R:68)
Honduras	4.9	67.8	(W:67)
Ivory Coast	32.2	57.2	(A:70)
Kenya	49.7	68.0	(A:69)
Malaysia	48.9	56.6	(W:70)
Panama	185.6	61.8	(W:70)
Peru	47.8	61.0	(W:72)
Sri Lanka	9.4	43.4	(W:70)
Thailand	11.1	57.7*	(A:62)
Tunisia	18.5	55.0	(A:70)
Zimbabwe	91.9	69.1	(J:68)
Mean	*43.9*	*58.0*	
Least Developed			
Malawi	14.8	50.6	(W:68)
Tanzania	20.0	50.4	(W:69)

*Extended sample.
Sources: A-Ahluwalia, 1976; B-Ballmer-Cao and Scheidegger, 1979; J-Jain, 1975; P-Paukert, 1973; R-Roberti, 1974; S-Sawyer, 1976; W-World Bank, 1979, 1980, 1981, 1982

countries are defined as the 17 members of the Development Assistance Committee (DAC) of the Organization for Economic Cooperation and Development (OECD). Coverage of this group is comprehensive (only Austria and Belgium are missing). Among countries of the periphery, the sample contains 70 percent of the semi-industrialized group;[7] 40 percent of the capital-deficit oil exporters (but none of the capital surplus oil exporters); 41 percent of the primary producing (other than oil) group; and 8 percent of the least developed group.

The economies of the core countries are by far the most highly penetrated by TNC-controlled capital; but they also, as noted previously, have the lowest mean inequality. In the periphery, the economies of primary producing countries are on the average more highly penetrated by TNC-controlled capital than the semi-industrialized group, and the former also have higher mean inequality than the latter. One cannot generalize about the least developed countries of the periphery on the basis of this sample.

MNC PENETRATION

A general model for testing the dependency/world-system explanation of variation in income distribution within nations can be stated as:

$$\text{Income Share}_{T20} = a + b_1 \text{ MNC Penetration} + b_2 \text{ Core} + b_3 \text{ (MNC*Core)} + b_4 Z_i + E \qquad (2)$$

where:

Income Share$_{T20}$ is the share of personal income accruing to the upper quintile of recipients;

MNC Penetration is given by (1);

Core is a dummy variable scored "1" for DAC countries of OECD, "0" otherwise;

MNC*Core is the product of MNC Penetration and Core;

Z_i represents other possible determinants of Income Share$_{T20}$, e.g., level of economic development;

E is an error term.

Bornschier's world-system version of dependency theory predicts a positive b_1 parameter estimate and a negative b_3 parameter estimate. Versions of modernization theory or neoclassical economics might be construed as predicting a negative b_1 parameter estimate and estimates approximately equal to zero for the b_2 and b_3 parameters.[8] The argument of the internal dynamics approach is, in regard to indicators of financial dependence, the null hypothesis. The internal dynamics prediction thus is for estimates of b_1 and

b_3 to be approximately zero, while b_2 should be negative simply because of the known fact that core countries are on the average more egalitarian for whatever reasons than countries of the periphery.

Prior to full-sample estimation of the parameters of (2) it is useful to examine scatterplots of the relationship between MNC Penetration and Income Share$_{T20}$ within core and periphery subsamples. Given the presence of extreme MNC penetration scores for Canada and Australia in the core and for Panama in the periphery, it is not surprising that Income Share$_{T20}$ scores show a better fit to a natural log (increment of "1" added to Yugoslavia) function of MNC penetration ($r = -.317$ and $.323$ in core and periphery, respectively) than a linear function ($r = -.223$ and $.283$ in core and periphery, respectively); therefore the abscissa of the plots shown in Figures 21.1 and 21.2 is lnMNC Penetration.

From Figure 21.1 it is apparent that no systematic relationship of any form exists between lnMNC penetration and Income Share$_{T20}$ in the restricted sample of the core, which does not include Finland. The Finnish data are excluded from the restricted sample because they are based only on tax statistics. As Sawyer (1976:23) observes, this results in:

Figure 21.1   Relationship Between MNC Penetration and Top 20 Percent Income Share (extended sample of the core)

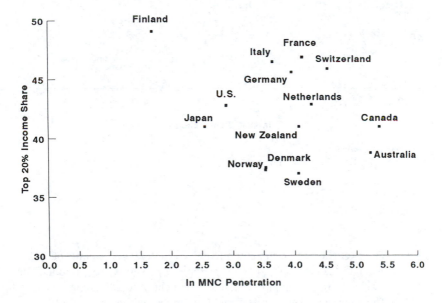

$r = -.317$; $N = 15$. Excluding Finland, $r = -.013$.

Figure 21.2 Relationship Between MNC Penetration and Top 20 Percent Income Share
(extended sample of the periphery)

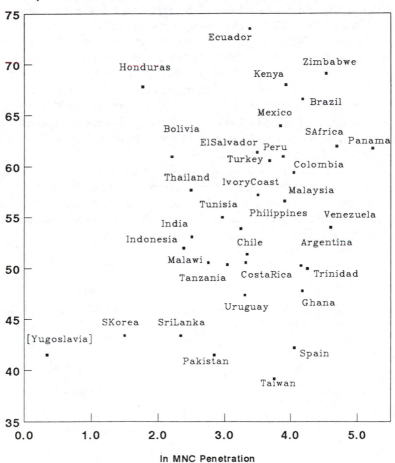

Top 20% Income Share

In MNC Penetration

[ ] Communist Regime
$r = .322$; $N = 35$. Excluding Yugoslavia, $r = .223$.

1. The exclusion of nontaxable income from the income concept. Thus
"social" (as opposed to "occupational") pensions are excluded. In
1969 they represented as much as 6 percent of total income.
2. The separate assessment of many young people who are still living
with their parents. Thus, nearly 20 percent of individuals receiving

an income of less than 2,000 markkaa (the boundary of the lowest income class) were in this category.

The Finnish data consequently are not considered by Sawyer to be comparable with the income data for the other core countries because the distribution is downwardly biased among lower percentiles and upwardly biased among higher percentiles. Data for 1977, prepared to conform with the standards of the Conference of European Statisticians, show an income share of 36.8 percent accruing to the upper quintile of households (World Bank, 1982, Table 25); this amount is 12.3 percentage points less than that calculated by Roberti (1974, Appendix Table II) from 1967 tax statistics. Thus, the negative correlation of −.317 in the extended sample is due entirely to the presence of noncomparable data for Finland.

A slight positive trend is discernible in the plot of Income Share$_{T20}$ by lnMNC Penetration for the extended sample of the periphery (Figure 21.2), but the correlation of .322 is not significant at the .05 level (two-tailed test with 33 degrees of freedom). The magnitude of the correlation is also quite sensitive to the presence of a single case, Yugoslavia, the only country under communist rule. Presumably, the ideology of Yugoslavia's political system has had far more influence on income distribution than the absence of TNC economic penetration. If the absence of TNC economic penetration is indeed the relevant factor, instead of the presence of communist rule, then one should observe at least a slight rise in inequality following any substantial rise in the stock of foreign investment. Between 1967 and 1973 the stock of foreign investment in Yugoslavia registered a sharp increase, growing from zero to $70 million; yet five years later, the income share of the upper quintile stood at 38.7 percent (World Bank, 1982, Table 25) a *decrease* of 2.8 percentage points from 1967. In light of this trend, there seems to be no firm basis for asserting a causal connection between Yugoslavia's extremely low 1967 MNC penetration score and the highly egalitarian distribution of income that prevails there (and in other countries under communist rule).

If Yugoslavia is excluded on the grounds of being a special case because of its type of regime, the relationship between lnMNC Penetration and Income Share$_{T20}$ in the periphery is reduced to a randomly distributed cloud of data points. Moreover, these results do not change for the restricted sample of 31 cases, where $r = .341$—a value again not significant at the .05 level—and drops to .241 upon exclusion of Yugoslavia.

Bivariate correlations for the variables in the general model of TNC economic penetration given by (2) are listed in Table 21.2. One should note, first, the very strong correlation—almost unity—between the Core dummy variable and the MNC*Core interaction term and, second, the correlation of almost exactly zero between lnMNC Penetration and Income Share$_{T20}$.

OLS (ordinary least squares) regression estimates of the parameters of the general model are given in Table 21.3 for the extended and restricted samples

Table 21.2   Bivariate Correlation (r) for the General MNC Penetration Model: Extended Sample (*N*=49) Below Diagonal; Restricted Sample (*N*=45) Above Diagonal

	Income Share$_{T20}$	lnMNC Penetration	CORE	MNC*CORE
Income share$_{T20}$:	—	.007	-.627	-.612
lnMNC penetration:	.013	—	.336	.418
Core:	-.630	.310	—	.976
MNC*core:	-.616	.388	.978	—

Table 21.3   Regressions[a] of the Income Received by the Highest Quintile on Logged MNC Penetration, Core Dummy, and MNC*CORE Interaction Term

	Intercept	lnMNC Penetration	Core	MNC*CORE	R^2	F
I. *Extended Sample*:						
(1) Income Share$_{T20}$	46.19**	+2.71*	-4.27	-2.77	.42	12.58**
	(10.82)	(2.20)	(-0.37)	(-0.94)	(*N* = 49)	
(2) Income Share$_{T20}$	47.80**	+2.23	-15.02**		.42	18.47**
	(12.23)	(1.99)	(-6.08)		(*N* = 49)	
(Excluding Yugoslavia)						
(3) Income Share$_{T20}$	48.48**	+2.09	-6.56	-2.14	.42	12.18**
	(9.67)	(1.46)	(0.55)	(-0.71)	(*N* = 48)	
(4) Income Share$_{T20}$	50.09**	+1.61*	-14.86**		.42	18.23**
	(11.28)	(1.29)	(-6.01)		(*N* = 48)	
II. *Restricted Sample*:						
(5) Income Share$_{T20}$	45.31**	+2.94*	-3.39	-3.00	.42	11.59**
	(10.09)	(2.24)	(-0.29)	(-1.00)	(*N* = 45)	
(6) Income Share$_{T20}$	47.18**	+2.37	-14.96**		.42	16.89**
	(11.55)	(2.00)	(-5.81)		(*N* = 45)	
(Excluding Yugoslavia)						
(7) Income Share$_{T20}$	47.50**	+2.34	-5.58	-2.39	.41	11.41**
	(8.85)	(1.52)	(-0.45)	(-0.78)	(*N* = 44)	
(8) Income Share$_{T20}$	49.46**	+1.75	-14.79**		.42	16.59**
	(10.54)	(1.32)	(-5.73)		(*N* = 44)	

[a]t ratio in parenthesis.
*p < .05   **p < .01

with and without Yugoslavia. The F test for the first equation indicates statistical significance at a high level of confidence, but of the explanatory variables, only the parameter estimate for lnMNC Penetration is significant at better than .05. The implication is that Core and MNC*Core are irrelevant variables and can be deleted from the equation; yet, if they are deleted, Income Share$_{T20}$ becomes a function only of lnMNC Penetration, with which it is uncorrelated. This nonsensical result reflects the presence of extreme multicollinearity between Core and MNC*Core, a condition that typically prevents the calculation of reliable parameter estimates. The third, fifth, and seventh equations also have relatively high R^2s, but unreliable parameter estimates, due to the problem of multicollinearity.

The additive equations, I(2), I(4), II(6), and II(8) afford as high a level of predictive accuracy as the interactive equations, I(1), I(3), II(5), and II(7). Since the additive equations are not affected by multicollinearity and are more parsimonious without loss of predictive accuracy, they are to be preferred to the interactive specification.

The t ratios for equations I(2), I(4), II(6), and II(8) show that the Core parameter estimates are significantly different from zero at a high level of confidence, whereas one cannot confidently reject the null hypothesis in the case of the parameter estimates for lnMNC Penetration. Also, with respect to accuracy of prediction, there is little to be gained from including the MNC Penetration variable, since Core alone can account for 40 percent of the variance of Income Share$_{T20}$. Moreover, inclusion of the MNC Penetration variable in the additive specification implies a positive *global* effect on inequality, which is a misrepresentation of the world economy paradigm and an empirical misrepresentation to boot.

The results of bivariate scatterplots and multivariate regression thus support the internal dynamics argument, at least with respect to cross-sectional variation in income inequality. It is possible to further investigate the dependency thesis from the perspective of longitudinal variation, using short-duration time series data that are available for a limited but heterogeneous sample of countries of the periphery.

Change in the income share of the upper quintile between c. 1970 and c. 1976 (data from World Bank, 1982, Table 25) is plotted in Figure 21.3 by change in the stock of foreign direct investment between 1967 and 1973 (data from Ballmer-Cao and Scheidegger, 1979, Table 3.2.1) for five peripheral countries from the semi-industrial group (ranging from relatively poor India to relatively rich Spain) and two from the primary producing group. In every case but one, the income share of the upper quintile declined by a not insubstantial margin (from 2.6 to 6.3 percentage points) subsequent to sizable (especially in terms of percentage change) increases in the stock of foreign investment. In South Korea, the exceptional case of an income distribution becoming less egalitarian after an increase in the stock of foreign investment, the gain in the upper quintile income share was less than 2 percentage points. These longitudinal data thus run counter to the prediction of dependency theory; and in conjunction with the support for the null hypothesis from the cross-sectional analysis, it would seem to be correct to infer that economic penetration of the periphery by the core, through the institution of the transnational corporation, is not a systematic or general cause of inequality in the distribution of income within peripheral countries.

Figure 21.3   Time Series of Foreign Investment and Top 20 Percent Income Share

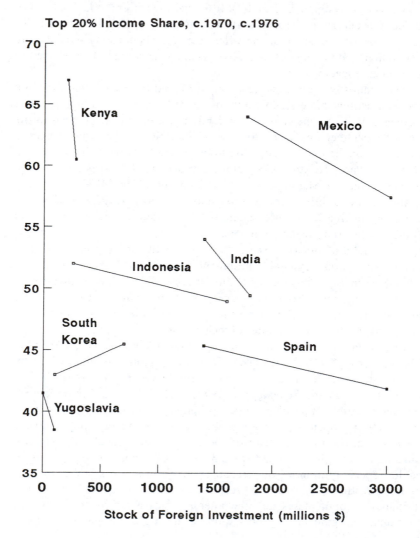

Top 20% Income Share, c.1970, c.1976

Stock of Foreign Investment (millions $)

DEBT DEPENDENCE

An alternative indicator of financial dependence within the capitalist world economy is a country's level of external public indebtedness. Dependency theorists regard debt dependence as a result of TNC economic penetration. Thus, Dos Santos (1970:234) writes:

> Foreign capital retains control over the most dynamic sectors of the economy and repatriates a high volume of profit; consequently, capital accounts are highly unfavorable to dependent countries. . . . An important deficit is produced in the total balance of payments. . . . The result is that "foreign financing" becomes necessary, in two forms: to cover the existing deficit and to "finance" development by means of loans for the stimulation of investments and to "supply" an internal economic surplus which was decapitalized to a large extent by the remittance of part of the surplus generated domestically and sent abroad as profits.

And Bornschier (1982:51) reiterates and expands upon this argument:

> The acute infrastructure requirements in the periphery for the capital-intensive mode of core corporation production are likely to increase the external debt of the state. . . . Moreover, the class coalition which is favored by the operatives of core corporations is likely to increase social cleavages and thus the sharpness of social conflict, the state will consequently need increasing resources to control and suppress such conflict. . . . Furthermore, at the level of the system as a whole, the World Bank also acts like a "fire brigade" to stave off bankruptcy: highly indebted governments are therefore likely to receive World Bank support.

The core-headquartered TNC is considered by Bornschier (1982:52) to be the "backbone in the entire system of economic dependencies"; variation in TNC economic penetration is postulated to cause variation both in external public debt and in World Bank debt/aid, and variation in external public debt is postulated to cause variation in World Bank debt/aid. A panel regression analysis of mid-1960s to mid-1970s data from 66 peripheral countries is cited as empirical support for the postulated causal linkages.

Since debt dependence is thought to be a result of TNC economic penetration, its causal status logically is that of an intervening variable between TNC economic penetration and income inequality. Therefore, one should investigate the possibility that debt dependence, because it is a more direct antecedent, might have a stronger effect on income inequality than TNC economic penetration.

Data on external public debt as a percentage of GNP in 1970 are available from the World Bank (1980, Table 15) for countries of the periphery only.[9] When 1970 scores on the External Debt variable are correlated with 1967 lnMNC Penetration, the positive relationship expected from dependency theory does not appear. For the extended sample the correlation between lnMNC Penetration and External Debt is -.281 (not significant at the .05 level); excluding Yugoslavia raises the correlation to -.409 (significant at .05). The respective correlations for the restricted sample are -.310 (not significant at .05) and -.467 (significant at .01). The reason for the inverse relationship is that countries with high External Debt scores such as Bolivia, Malawi, and Tunisia have low MNC penetration scores, while many countries with low External Debt scores, e.g., Argentina, Brazil, South Africa, Spain, and Venezuela, have high scores on MNC penetration.

Since the expected positive relationship between MNC Penetration and External Debt is not present in these data, it is not surprising to find that Income Share$_{T20}$ is uncorrelated with External Debt, as can be seen from the scatterplot in Figure 21.4. The correlation is quite close to zero in the extended sample, with and without Yugoslavia, and the same is true for the restricted sample ($r = .012$ and $-.033$, with and without Yugoslavia).

Figure 21.4 Relationship Between External Public Debt and Top 20 Percent Income Share (extended sample of the periphery)

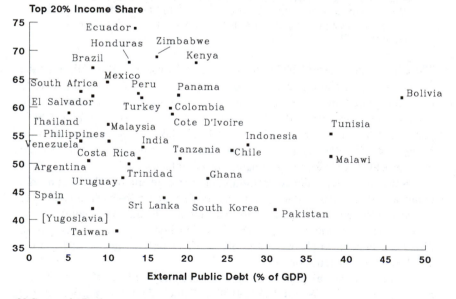

[ ] Communist Regime
$r = -.049$; $N = 35$. Excluding Yugoslavia, $r = -0.98$.

CONCLUSION

A basic tenet of dependency theory is the proposition that among less developed countries on the periphery of the capitalist world economy, international relations of financial dependence on the core are a major cause of intranational inequality within the periphery. Core-headquartered transnational corporations are assumed to control the "commanding heights" of peripheral economies in an alliance with local elites and a small "labor aristocracy" of workers that favors concentration of income in the hands of the few. Confronted with the overwhelming economic power of this unholy alliance, national political elites are unwilling and/or unable to act in favor of income redistribution. Penetration of the peripheral economy by transnational corporations thus reduces the peripheral state to the role of willing captive or helpless pawn in a process of uneven exchange that results in economic development and relative equality in the core and underdevelopment and extreme inequality in the periphery.

Generally sympathetic reviews of the writing of dependency theorists in the late 1960s and early 1970s called attention to certain empirical weaknesses such as the overlooking of countries like Australia and Canada, which, in the description of Portes (1976:78), "are profoundly 'dependent,' in the sense of penetration of their economies by foreign-owned subsidiaries, and yet exhibit a much higher per capita income, a better distribution of wealth, and more efficient health and educational services than most 'Third World' countries." And O'Brien (1975:19) cautioned that, in general, "the empirical evidence offered in support of these hypotheses is admittedly somewhat casual."

The challenge of empirical verification of dependence theory has been taken up since the mid-1970s by scholars who have sought to cast dependency hypotheses into scientifically testable propositions subject to cross-national falsification. The culmination of this endeavor is a global model formulated by Bornschier, based on the world-system paradigm, which assumes that the driving force or "backbone" of the capitalist world economy is the transnational corporation, an economic actor whose interest is continued or enhanced concentration of income in the poorer countries of the periphery, where elite demand is presumed to be the only effective market for the products of TNCs, but less concentration of income in the rich countries of the core, where mass consumption constitutes the effective market. Thus does Bornschier's world-system approach explain the anomaly of egalitarian income distribution in financially dependent countries such as Australia and Canada, while preserving the dependency theory hypothesis of a positive relationship between financial dependency and inequality in the periphery, all within the context of a global model sensitive to the general dependency claim that the "laws of motion" in the periphery are fundamentally different from those in the core.

The major counter hypothesis to dependency theory and the world-system paradigm stems from an "internal dynamics" approach to explanation of income distribution. This approach does not necessarily reject the claim of different laws of motion for core and periphery, but it emphatically rejects the claim that the laws of motion are those of capitalist imperialism operating as an international economic force that determines the distribution of income within nations. In rejecting the economic determinism of the dependency/world-system paradigm, the internal dynamics approach counters with the specific prediction that the cross-national relationship between indicators of financial dependence in the capitalist world economy and distribution of income within nations will conform to the null hypothesis.

It should be stressed here that the internal dynamics perspective is not an argument for historical uniqueness. The distribution of income within nations is not *necessarily* considered to be the result of *idiosyncratic* internal forces; quite to the contrary, internal characteristics of an economic, political, sociological, or psychological nature certainly could exert a systematic effect, cross-nationally on income distribution. But it is assumed that any such general determinants, should they exist, are not externally conditioned.

In this analysis of mostly cross-sectional data on international financial dependence and intranational income distribution, I have sought to perform a methodologically rigorous test of predictions from the dependency/world-system model. In this regard, I have rejected data on the distribution of income that suffer from one or more of the following limitations:

1.   only partial coverage of income distribution;
2.   unreliable coverage of income distribution;
3.   measurement of income distribution that predates the observation of financial dependence by a substantial margin;
4.   measurement of income distribution for dependent territories.

These problems affect, by my estimation, about 30 percent of the observations of income distribution from Ballmer-Cao and Scheidegger (1979, Table 5.3) used in the various analyses of Bornschier; about 40 percent of the observations of income distribution used by Evans and Timberlake (1980, Appendix A, Column 1b); and about 50 percent of the observations of income distribution used by Rubinson (1976, Appendix 3). Therefore, the results of previous research, which claim to show support for the dependency/world-system approach to explanation of income distribution, are open to question. The data on income distribution that I use obviously are not flawless; but they are not subject to the first, third, and fourth problems mentioned above; and as for their reliability, they are the best currently available information from World Bank sources, given the caveat that the monitoring of income distribution data according to standardized procedures has not yet been integrated into the official statistical accounting system in many countries.

The most straightforward way to approach the empirical question of a relationship between international financial dependence and intranational income distribution, given a relatively reliable data base, is to begin by inspecting scatterplots, an elementary procedure that has been bypassed in previous research (which rarely even reports bivariate correlations). A scatterplot reveals that the negative relationship between MNC penetration and income inequality in the core, previously reported by Bornschier, is not strong and, more importantly, is almost completely an artifact of an unreliable observation of income distribution for Finland. For the sample of countries of the periphery, which includes reasonably comprehensive coverage only of those in the middle income range, a positive relationship between MNC penetration and income inequality is indeed observed, but it again is not very strong and in this instance is quite sensitive to the special case of Yugoslavia, where there is good reason to believe that the *political* factor of communist rule is responsible for the egalitarian distribution of income. Short-duration time-series data reinforce the speculation about the irrelevance of MNC penetration (specifically, the lack thereof in 1967) for income distribution in Yugoslavia; and they more generally do not support the prediction of dependency theory, although the sample of countries is very small. Finally, an alternative indicator of international financial dependence, the size of a country's external public debt, shows a virtually zero correlation with income inequality in a cross-sectional analysis of the periphery. These findings indicate that it is pointless to carry the investigation further, introducing additional control variables, since the basic bivariate results (and a multivariate test of a core-periphery interaction specification) point consistently in the direction of the null hypothesis.

It is possible to boost the correlation between MNC penetration and income inequality to statistical significance by including more countries under communist rule in the periphery (and arbitrarily assuming approximately zero MNC penetration, in the absence of actual data) and/or by introducing very old income distribution data from dependent territories into the analysis. The former procedure does not "save" dependency theory, however, because the alternative political hypothesis is so obvious, and the simple inclusion of a dummy communist rule variable reduces the MNC penetration effect to statistical nonsignificance. The latter procedure is not justifiable methodologically; but if more comprehensive data on income distribution become available for the group of least developed countries, and if they raise the MNC penetration effect beyond that observed currently for predominantly middle-income countries of the periphery, then the income inequality hypothesis of dependency theory might be saved (with a twist of irony, since it was not formulated with the poverty-stricken countries of Africa and Asia in mind).

In global comparative perspective, then, the Brazilian "model," a major source of inspiration for the hypothesis that dependence on TNC-controlled capital leads to income inequality in the periphery, does not appear to be representative of any general trend characteristic of middle-income developing countries as a group. And even in the case of Brazil, an argument can be made that it was not dependence on foreign capital which caused the income-concentrating policies of the late 1960s and 1970s, but rather decisions taken independently by the Brazilian military rulers, after the *golpe de estado* of 1964, to follow the "wisdom" of neoclassical economics that redistributive policies would retard economic growth and that, in accordance with the "law" of the Kuznets inverted U curve of inequality and development, the best way to benefit all classes of society would be to pursue short-run income-concentrating policies in order to stimulate rapid economic growth, which would lead automatically to greater income equality in the long run (see the discussion in Wright, 1978: 63–66). Thus, with respect to future cross-national investigation of the causes of income inequality within nations, the more promising avenue of approach would seem to be one that leads away from external "world-system" economic determinism and toward the consideration of internal dynamics, with particular attention to the autonomous role of the state.

NOTES

1. I describe Bornschier as an *empirical* theorist because he states concepts and propositions in testable form and confronts them with data.

2. The income share of the upper quintile hovered at about the 41 percent mark during the 1950s and 1960s (see Sawyer, 1976: 26).

3. For example, Sunkel (1972:523) cites approvingly the following passage from a 1969 Harvard University Division of Research paper by Vaupel and Curham:

> The international corporation is acting and planning in terms that are far in advance of the political concepts of the nation-state. As the Renaissance of the fifteenth century brought an end to feudalism, aristocracy and the dominant role of the Church, the twentieth-century Renaissance is bringing an end to middle-class society and the dominance of the nation-state. The heart of the new power structure is the international organization and the technocrats who guide it. Power is shifting away from the nation-state to international institutions, public and private.

And Cardoso (1973:149) describes the transnational corporation as the "moving force" behind his model of associated dependent development.

4. "Transnational" corporation is the usage adopted by the United Nations in order to avoid confusion about the ownership of these enterprises, which is not in any sense multinational. Their operations are across political frontiers; hence the term "transnational."

5. Arrighi (1970:223–225) observes that since decolonization in Africa a new pattern of foreign investment, in which transnational ("oligopolistic") corporations play a major role, has replaced the small-scale enterprises of colonial capitalism. Therefore, it would be a mistake to attribute long-term retroactive temporal stability to 1967 MNC Penetration scores for newly independent African nations.

6. The upper quintile income share for these countries differs from that reported in Ballmer-Cao and Scheidegger (1979) by more than 1 percentage point; trivial revisions of less than a single point also have been made for other countries.

7. Unlike the World Bank (1981, Table 6.1), which excludes Taiwan from all consideration, I include it in the semi-industrialized group; I also place Ireland in this group, as well as India and Pakistan, which are considered to be partially industrialized by the World Bank, despite having low per capita income. Countries under communist rule and dependent territories are not included.

8. The negative effect on inequality presumably would occur as the result of a positive relationship between foreign investment and economic growth, the benefits of which would eventually "trickle down" through the mass of the population, increasing the size and wealth of the middle class.

9. The World Bank does not collect data on external debt for other than developing countries; also, according to the World Bank (1980:161), comparable data do not exist for other countries.

REFERENCES

Ahluwalia, M.S. 1974. "Income Inequality: Some Dimensions of the Problem." Pp. 3–37 in H. Chenery et al. (eds.), *Redistribution with Growth*. New York: Oxford University Press.

———. 1976. "Inequality, Poverty, and Development." *Journal of Development Economics* 3:307–342.

Allison, P. D. 1978. "Measures of Inequality." *American Sociological Review* 43:865–879.

Arrighi, G. 1970. "International Corporations, Labor Aristocracies, and Economic Development in Tropical Africa." Pp. 220–267 in R.I. Rhodes (ed.), *Imperialism and Underdevelopment*. New York: Monthly Review Press.

Ballmer-Cao, T.-H. and J. Scheidegger. 1979. *Compendium Data for World System Analysis*. Zurich: Soziologisches Institut der Universitat.

Barrett, R. E. and M .K. Whyte. 1982. "Dependency Theory and Taiwan: Analysis of a Deviant Case." *American Journal of Sociology* 87:1064–1089.

Bornschier, V. 1978. "Einkommensungleichheit innerhalb von Laendern in komparativer Sicht," *Schweizerische Zeitschrift fuer Soziologie* 1 (November):67–105.

———. 1980. "Multinational Corporations and Economic Growth." *Journal of Development Economics* 7:191–210.

———. 1981. "Comment." *International Studies Quarterly* 25:283–288.

———. 1982. "The World Economy in the World-System: Structure, Dependence and Change." *International Social Science Journal* 34:37–59.

———. 1983. "World Economy, Level Development and Income Distribution: An Integration of Different Approaches to the Explanation of Income Inequality." *World Development* 11:11–20.

Bornschier, V. and T.-H. Ballmer-Cao. 1979. "Income Inequality: A Cross-

National Study of Relationships between MNC-Penetration, Dimensions of the Power Structure and Income Distribution." *American Sociological Review* 44:487–506.

Bornschier, V., C. Chase-Dunn, and R. Rubinson. 1978. "Cross-National Evidence of the Effects of Foreign Investment and Aid on Economic Growth and Inequality." *American Journal of Sociology* 84:651–683.

Cardoso, F. H. 1973. "Associated Dependent Development: Theoretical and Practical Implications." Pp. 142–176 in A. Stepan (ed.), *Authoritarian Brazil*. New Haven: Yale University Press.

Chase-Dunn, C. 1975. "The Effects of International Economic Dependence on Development and Inequality: A Cross-National Study." *American Sociological Review* 40:720–738.

Dos Santos, T. 1970. "The Structure of Dependence." *American Economic Review* 60:231–236.

Evans, P. and M. Timberlake. 1980. "Dependence, Inequality, and Growth in Less Developed Countries." *American Sociological Review* 45:531–552.

Figueroa, A. and R. Weiskoff. 1980. "Viewing Social Pyramids: Income Distribution in Latin America." Pp. 257–294 in R. Ferber (ed.), *Consumption and Distribution in Latin America*. Organization of American States, ECIEL.

Furtado, C. 1973. "The Post-1964 Brazilian 'Model' of Development." *Studies in Comparative International Development*, 115–127.

Hirschman, A. O. 1981. *Essays in Trespassing*. New York: Cambridge University Press.

Jain, S. 1975. *Size Distribution of Income*. Washington, D.C.: World Bank.

O'Brien, P.J. 1975. "A Critique of Latin American Theories of Dependency." Pp. 7–27 in I. Oxaal et al. (eds.), *Beyond the Sociology of Development*. Boston: Routledge & Kegan Paul.

Paukert, F. 1973. "Income Distribution at Different Levels of Development." *National Labor Review* 108:97–125.

Portes, A. 1976. "On the Sociology of National Development: Theories and Issues." *American Journal of Sociology* 82:55–85.

Roberti, P. 1974. "Income Distribution: A Time Series and a Cross-Section Survey." *The Economic Journal* 84:629–638.

Rubinson, R. 1976. "The World Economy and the Distribution of Income Within States: A Cross-National Study." *American Sociological Review* 41:638–659.

Sawyer, M. 1976. "Income Distribution in OECD Countries." *OECD Economic Outlook*, 3–36.

Seers, D. 1963. "The Limitations of the Special Case." *The Bulletin of the Institute of Economics and Statistics, Oxford* 25:77–98.

Smith, T. 1979. "The Underdevelopment of Development Literature." *World Politics* 31:247–288.

———. 1981a. *The Pattern of Imperialism*. New York: Cambridge University Press.

———. 1981b. "The Logic of Dependency Theory Revisited." *International Organization* 35:755–761.

Sunkel, O. 1972. "Big Business and 'Dependencia.'" *Foreign Affairs* 50:517–531.

Taylor, C. L. and M. C. Hudson. 1972. *World Handbook of Political and Social Indicators*, 2nd ed. New Haven: Yale University Press.

Watkins, M. 1975. "Economic Development in Canada." Pp. 72–96 in I. Wallerstein (ed.), *World Inequality*. Montreal: Black Rose Books.

Weede, E. and H. Tiefenbach. 1981. "Some Recent Explanations of Income Inequality." *International Studies Quarterly* 25:255–282.

World Bank. 1979. *World Development Report 1979*. New York: Oxford University Press.

———. 1980. *World Development Report 1980*. New York: Oxford University Press.

———. 1981. *World Development Report 1981*. New York: Oxford University Press.

———. 1982. *World Development Report 1982*. New York: Oxford University Press.

Wright, C. L. 1978. "Income Inequality and Economic Growth: Examining the Evidence." *The Journal of Developing Areas* 13:49–66.

22

. . . .

The Irish Case of Dependency: An Exception to the Exception?

. . . .

DENIS O'HEARN

*According to dependency/world-system theory, transnational corpo-
ration (TNC) penetration depresses growth and worsens income inequality. In the previous chapter, Edward Muller pointed to the relatively high degree of TNC penetration and income equality in Canada,
questioning why TNC investment has one outcome in developing
countries but another in penetrated developed countries. In this
chapter, Denis O'Hearn addresses Ireland's dependency and its
record of economic growth and income inequality. Unlike Walden
Bello and Stephanie Rosenfeld in Chapter 30, who think the growth of
the Asian NICs is attributable to cold war politics and a special relationship with Japan, O'Hearn argues that some countries have regimes
that make them vulnerable to dependency relations whereas others
do not. He reports that Ireland's growth was undermined by the type of
decapitalization described by Volker Bornschier and Christopher
Chase-Dunn in Chapter 20 and further notes that radical free-trade
policies in Ireland are also related to rising income inequality.*

For the past 20 years, the approach loosely termed as *dependency* enjoyed
popularity in development studies, particularly among radical scholars. Many
studies concentrated on the connections between foreign penetration,
economic growth, and income distribution. Baran (1957) and others emphasized the *tendencies* of foreign-penetration to limit economic growth in the
LDCs. Later works (Frank 1969) implied "laws" of development, relating
proximity to the "metropole" with underdevelopment in the periphery. A

Reprinted with permission from the *American Sociological Review*, vol. 54
(August 1989): 578–596.

series of analysts then attempted to "test" the hypotheses that foreign penetration caused (1) low growth rates and (2) inequality in LDCs (Chase-Dunn 1975; Bornschier 1980; Biersteker 1978; Bornschier and Ballmer-Cao 1979; Evans and Timberlake 1980).

Within the past few years some scholars have strongly challenged the dependency approach. A number of empirical analyses concentrated on "exceptions" to dependency, particularly from East Asia (for a review, see Chakravarty 1987). In place of dependency, these analysts propose a return to orthodox principles of neoclassical development economics and modernization theory. . . .

In place of dependency, a series of trade theorists give the following reasons for the "gang of four's" [Taiwan, South Korea, Singapore, and Hong Kong—*Eds.*] success:

(a) maintenance of an outward-looking orientation throughout the rapid growth phase of these countries;
(b) maintenance of a very hospitable climate for foreign investment;
(c) and finally, "keeping the prices right," by which they imply a relatively low real price of labour, a relatively high real rate of interest and "realistic" exchange rates (Chakravarty 1987).

Sociological and political accounts of the success in East Asia concentrate less on openness to foreign penetration than on political and class variables—the nature of the colonial and post-colonial relationship with Japan, the emphasis on labor-intensive enterprises, and the absence of an entrenched bourgeoisie. In fairness, many of these "non-economic" analyses have taken great pains to point out that South Korea and Taiwan are special or deviant cases and, therefore, do not in themselves constitute a threat to the dependency approach. Barrett and Whyte, for example, argue that Taiwan is a "deviant case" of dependency theory because foreign penetration was linked neither to stagnation nor inequality (Barrett and Whyte 1982; see also Cummings 1984).

In the present chapter, I will challenge the new modernizationism in development studies by presenting the case study of Ireland (i.e., the 26 southern counties). Ireland represents not only an "exception" to the "exceptions" in the so-called gang of four. It is in many ways a truer representation of the open, foreign-dominated, free-enterprise regime that the new modernizationists prescribe. In development terms, it is also an abject failure. This is especially significant because Ireland has for 30 years been in the heart of European economic integration. For 15 years, Ireland has "enjoyed" full membership in the European Economic Community, one of the dominant economic powers of the "modern industrial West." Indeed, this close relationship to the core, in classical "dependency" terms, directly contributed to Ireland's development problems.

SPECIFICITY OF IRISH DEPENDENCY

Ireland is an island about the size of the state of Maine, lying 30–60 miles from the British mainland. Its population is about four and a half million, well below its mid-19th century population of eight million. Its modern history is dominated by British occupation, four major waves of emigration, and several famines, including the famous mid-19th century "potato famine." In the 19th-century, Irish peasants won limited ownership of farms and limited rights against British landlords. Ireland's traditional industrial area, around Belfast, was based on shipbuilding and linen-making for the British empire. Industry in the rest of the island was impeded by British laws, which removed Irish tariffs on industrial goods and outlawed certain lines of industry and exports.

Ireland was partitioned in 1921, at the end of a war of independence. Britain retained six of the nine counties of the province of Ulster, which included industrial Belfast and the largest adjoining area with a built-in settler majority. The southern state of today, therefore, comprises an area of about four-fifths of the island, with a population of about 3 million.

The new postcolonial state in 1932 embarked on an attempt to build native industry through a classical program of import-substituting industrialization (ISI), with high levels of tariff protection. Despite an economic war waged by Britain against Ireland, this program was quite successful: between 1931 and 1947 the number of manufacturing establishments employing more than 10 grew by 63 percent, and those employing over a hundred more than doubled. In the same period, industrial employment grew by about 80 percent, from 110,588 to 197,605 (O'Hearn 1988, pp. 82, 89). But in the mid-1950s, because of rising dollar trade deficits, external political pressures tied to Marshall Aid and European integration, and economic recession, the Irish regime changed the industrialization program from ISI to export-led industrialization (ELI). The new ELI regime had three distinguishing characteristics: (1) radical free trade, (2) radical free enterprises, and (3) foreign industrial domination.

Radical Free Trade

Unlike many developing countries, which followed a "stop-and-go" pattern of deprotection and reprotection, Ireland was forced to free its trade rapidly and totally. The removal of protection began after Ireland joined the Organisation for European Economic Cooperation (OEEC) in the 1950s—a prerequisite for receiving Marshall Aid—and ended when Ireland joined the EEC in 1972. Table 22.1 clearly shows the fall of tariff receipts during ELI, beginning in 1959 when OEEC free trade pressures became severe. In 1972, tariff revenues as a percentage of total Irish government revenues fell by almost 6 percent. Four years later, as a result of Ireland's terms of accession to the EEC, tariff revenues fell to practically nil.[1]

Table 22.1 Revenues from Customs Tariffs, and as Percentage of Total Net Government Receipts (million Irish punts[a])

Year	(1) Tariff Revenue	(2) Total Revenue	(1) as a Percentage of (2)	Year	(1) Tariff Revenue	(2) Total Revenue	(1) as a Percentage of (2)
1954	37	83	44.6	1970	88	338	26.0
1955	37	85	43.5	1971	92	398	27.2
1956	39	89	43.8	1972	101	469	21.5
1957	45	94	47.9	1973	117	540	21.7
1958	47	97	48.5	1974	139	665	20.8
1959	48	98	49.0	1975	176	901	19.5
1960	45	103	43.7	1976	25	1,222	2.0
1961	41	107	38.3	1977	29	1,445	2.0
1962	45	119	37.8	1978	35	1,709	2.0
1963	47	129	36.4	1979	39	1,991	2.0
1964	50	145	34.5	1980	46	2,584	1.8
1965	56	177	31.6	1981	58	3,274	1.8
1966	58	194	29.9	1982	62	4,014	1.5
1967	68	222	30.6	1983	77	4,503	1.7
1968	70	248	28.2	1984	94	5,115	1.8
1969	76	282	27.0				

a. The punt is the Irish currency. Its value was tied to the British pound until Ireland joined the European Monetary System in 1979.
Source: Irish Revenue Commissioners (various years).

As a result, the Irish market was penetrated by competing imports. Between 1960 and 1980, imports took over the Irish market in nearly every category of manufactured goods. In footwear and clothing, imports rose from 8 percent of domestic consumption in 1960, to 70–80 percent in 1980. In

Table 22.2 Changes of Employment and Number of Firms in Domestic "Old" and "Adapted" Industry from 1973 to 1986, Ireland

Sector	Employment 1973	1986	Percent Change	Number of Firms 1973	1986	Percent Change
Food	27,601	17,330	–37.2	598	448	–25.1
Drink	3,804	3,197	–16.0	77	56	–27.3
Textiles	8,561	894	–89.6	120	43	–64.2
Clothing	8,084	1,231	–84.8	213	78	–63.4
Wood	5,186	2,769	–46.6	361	284	–21.3
Paper	8,446	4,453	–47.3	218	176	–19.3
Clay	9,861	7,519	–23.8	211	161	–23.7
Chemical	2,245	1,047	–53.4	64	28	–56.3
Metals	12,148	5,172	–57.4	354	239	–32.5
Other mfg.	3,267	766	–76.6	132	71	–46.2
Nonfood	58,825	23,851	–59.5	1,673	1,080	–35.4
Total	90,230	44,378	–50.8	2,348	1,584	–32.5

Source: Author's calculations from IDA Employment Surveys.

nonelectrical machinery, the share of imports during the same period rose from 55 to 98 percent.

The results for Irish-owned industry were disastrous (Table 22.2). Between 1973 and 1986, 85 to 90 percent of the jobs in pre-1955 clothing and textiles firms were lost. Three-fourths of the jobs in domestic miscellaneous manufacturing and over half of the jobs in domestic chemicals and metals were lost. In the pre-ELI Irish manufacturing sector as a whole, half of the jobs held in 1973 were lost by 1986 (60 percent in the nonfood sector). Of course, this demolition of protected nationalist industry *could* be viewed as "restructuring"—that is, clearing out inefficient and unprofitable sectors to make way for more profitable "modern" sectors. To validate the dependency approach, therefore, we must show that the new industry which replaced domestic manufacturing was not conducive to economic growth.

Radical Free Enterprise

From its inception, the ISI regime was based strictly on principles of "private enterprise." Interventions by the state into the "business of business" were few, and state industry was limited (in 1945 there were three infrastructural and two industrial state companies). These principles were intensified under ELI. The state's role was to market Ireland as a profitable location for business—to provide incentives for industry to locate in Ireland and to find firms that would respond to the incentives. After that, new foreign firms could avoid any kind of scrutiny. The disposition of profits is left entirely in the hands of the firm. No profits taxes are paid on most manufactured exports, and profits may be freely repatriated. Means of production are freely imported, and output is freely exported. The regime does not pressure TNCs to use Irish inputs or to create other linkages. In the words of an Irish Minister for Industry and Commerce at the beginning of ELI, "we aim to convince [U.S. industrialists] that Ireland is the best possible location because of its attitude to private enterprise. . . . the more profits they make the better we will like it" (Dail Eireann 1958).

Foreign Domination

The Irish regime perceives foreign industry as a substitute for—not a complement to—domestic industry. An early and influential proponent of ELI captured the Irish attitude, saying, "By far the most hopeful means of getting good management, technical knowledge, and capital all at once is from subsidiaries of large foreign companies. . . . a plant which is paid for by foreign capital is a great deal better than one which has to be paid for from the scanty saving of the Republic" (Carter 1957). Since the inception of ELI, the regime relies *first and foremost* on the attraction of new foreign capital for industrial expansion. . . .

. . . During the first half of the 1960s, TNCs created more than half of the new manufacturing jobs. After 1965, at least 70 to 80 percent of the new manufacturing jobs were in TNCs (O'Hearn 1987).

Ireland's adherence to free trade, free enterprise, and foreign industrial domination sets it apart from "exceptional" cases, such as South Korea and Taiwan. Regimes in these countries are characterized by strong state intervention in business, widespread use of selective protection and import-substitution, and a definite preference for domestic industry. The "free market" in Singapore, another high-growth East Asian economy, has been described as a "myth" (Lim 1983; see also Rodan 1985; Islam and Kirkpatrick 1986). . . .[2]

RESULTS I: SLOW ECONOMIC GROWTH

How do the specificities of the Irish case affect the relation of foreign penetration to economic growth and inequality? Are the relations of "dependency" at work in Ireland? . . .

Linkages

Even if the resources for investment and expansion are available, productive outlets for investment must be found. For many years, orthodox development theorists stressed the desirability of balanced growth among economic sectors, to avoid bottlenecks and realization problems (see Nurkse 1953; Lewis 1955). Albert Hirschman (1958) challenged this orthodoxy in his seminal work *The Strategy of Economic Development*. According to Hirschman, investment opportunities are created by the imbalanced development of the economy. Bottlenecks and gaps induce productive investment to correct or fill them.

Hirschman lists three kinds of linkages, or investment inducements. (1) If a firm buys inputs locally, it induces someone to produce them (*backward linkages*). (2) If a firm makes a product which may be processed further, it may induce a local firm to make a new product (*forward linkages*). (3) If a firm's activities contribute to the state's economic resources (through taxes and import duties), it creates *fiscal linkages*. Hirschman's analysis of linkages is behind more recent concepts such as *disarticulation* between "modern" and "traditional" economic sectors (Amin 1974) and *economic dualism* (Myint 1970; Singer 1970).

Fiscal linkages are probably negative in Ireland because (1) the typical TNC pays no taxes due to "free enterprise" tax provisions and pays no import duties due to free trade, and (2) large incentives and infrastructural costs are incurred by the state to attract foreign investment. Since TNCs in Ireland export nearly all of their product, forward linkages are few. The only possible significant linkages from TNC operations in Ireland are *backward* linkages.

Irish data on backward linkages are sparse. There were surveys of industrial firms in 1966, 1971, 1974, and 1983 (Survey Team 1967; O hUiginn 1972; McAleese 1977). Unfortunately, the coverage and classification of firms differ among the surveys, so longitudinal comparisons are awkward. But it is still possible to construct a fairly good picture of TNCs' backward linkages. Buckley (1974) found that TNCs in 1971 purchased only 31.5 percent of their material inputs from Irish sources, while Irish firms purchased 68.3 percent locally. McAleese and McDonald (1978) found that new (post-1955) nonfood TNCs purchased 11.2 percent of their inputs in Ireland, while new domestic firms purchased 22.2 percent locally. Thus, we can conclude that (a) the rate of TNC-related linkages is very low, (b) domestic firms have twice as many linkages as TNCs, and (c) the rate of linkages created by new domestic industry is also low. It is important to note that linkages were reduced in Ireland not only by the predominance of TNCs in new industry, but also because free trade encouraged (or forced) *domestic* firms to turn to foreign sources of supply. . . .

TNCs' backward linkages in Ireland are also extremely low relative to other dependent countries. Table 22.3 compares the proportions of material inputs that are locally purchased by manufacturing subsidiaries of U.S. TNCs in Ireland, Brazil, and Mexico. TNCs' local purchases are uniformly lower in Ireland, particularly in the "modern" sectors. In manufacturing as a whole,

Table 22.3   Locally Purchased Materials as Percentage of Total Material Inputs in U.S. Affiliates Operating in Brazil, Mexico, and Ireland

Sector	Brazil	Mexico	Ireland U.S. TNCs	Ireland All TNCs
Food	89.5	96.8	73.0	70.7
Textiles	*	94.1	13.8	18.1
Paper	91.4	93.5	33.3	55.3
Chemicals	44.7	54.8	19.3	18.2
Rubber	92.7	88.5	3.1	1.5
Clay/cement	81.7	66.7	15.3	49.6
Metals	83.8	90.8	7.0	15.4
Nonelectric machinery	63.6	45.7	12.6	15.4
Electric machinery	60.0	61.6	10.9	11.2
Transport	97.1	60.7	8.9	18.6
Instruments	11.2	44.7	21.9	18.9
Other	74.0	97.6	19.2	19.2
Total	76.4	68.5	19.7	27.7

Note: Irish data are for 1983; Brazilian and Mexican data are for 1972.
Source: IDA Components of Sales Survey data, Connor (1977).

U.S. affiliates purchased 76.4 percent of their material inputs locally in Brazil and 68.5 percent in Mexico, but less than 20 percent in Ireland. While this confirms the extremely low level of TNC-induced linkages in Ireland by comparison with other semiperipheral countries, it also indicates the importance of specificities of Irish development. In particular, the most important causes of low linkages in Ireland—unlike Mexico and Brazil—are (1) the predominance of TNC production for export rather than for local markets, and (2) the degree of free enterprise (absence of local-content regulations).

In an economy such as Ireland's, where the regime emphasizes the attraction of new foreign capital, and where imports have swamped the domestic consumer market, *linkages* are an important source of investment opportunities. The scarcity of linkages between TNCs and the local Irish economy means that the contribution of new TNCs to growth is practically restricted to the activities of the TNCs themselves. Foreign investment creates few multipliers that lead to the growth of domestic investment.

Foreign Penetration and Growth

The logic of the Irish development regime is deceptively simple, as is the logic of modernizationist analysis in general: attract as much foreign investment as possible, the foreign investors will export a lot, exports will bring new resources into the country, and economic development will surely follow, along with jobs and prosperity.

Irish ELI was *spectacularly* successful at attracting foreign investment and increasing exports. Real foreign investment grew at an annual rate of 25 percent between 1955 and 1983. Real exports grew by 7.5 percent annually between 1955 and 1985 (8.3 percent after 1972), and manufactured exports by more than 10 percent (calculated from OECD 1987). If foreign investments and exports are the key to growth, the Irish economy should have expanded especially rapidly during the 1970s and 1980s.

The actual Irish growth experience was very different (Table 22.4). Throughout ELI, gross fixed capital formation (GFCF) grew annually by only 5 percent. Since 1972 (when Ireland joined the EEC) per capita GFCF grew by less than 2 percent. Annual rates of growth of per capita GNP were even slower. At its highest, per capita GNP grew at an annual rate of 3.4 percent (1965–1970). During ELI as a whole, the annual growth rate of per capita GNP was a mere 2.3 percent. Most significantly, the annual per capita economic growth rate fell to 0.4 percent during the post-EEC period, and was negative (-1.25 percent) in the 1980s.

These rates of growth are strikingly low compared to rates of growth in other countries. Ireland's annual rate of economic growth over the 30 years of ELI was the lowest in Europe, well below rates of growth in the European periphery (4–6 percent) and the average rates of growth for upper-income

Table 22.4   Annual Percentage Rates of Growth of Gross Fixed Capital Formation (GFCF)
and GNP during ELI, 1955–85 (constant 1958 Irish punts)

Years	GFCF	Per Capita GFCF	GFCF (mfg.)	GNP	Per Capita GNP	Net Output (mfg.)
1955–60	–3.91	–3.31	3.60	1.22	1.83	4.40
1960–65	11.88	11.59	14.64	3.41	3.14	7.75
1965–70	6.34	5.87	7.82	3.90	3.41	8.23
1970–75	3.48	1.98	6.51	3.33	1.81	5.61
1975–80	6.89	5.34	6.61	3.53	2.16	6.99
1980–85	–0.39	–1.02	–6.12	–0.45	–1.25	6.88
1955–72	6.73	6.53	11.30	3.40	3.19	7.44
1972–85	3.24	1.97	1.61	1.65	0.38	5.90
1955–85	5.83	5.02	7.74	3.15	2.34	6.92

Note: Five-year rates of growth for each variable x are calculated according to the following formula:

$$[\log x(t+5) - \log x(t)] / 5.$$

Rates of growth for longer periods are calculated by least square regression of the log of the variable on time in years.
Source: Central Statistics Office (various years); OECD (1987).

LDCs (about 5 percent), and far below the "exceptional" East Asian economies (6–8 percent). Even in its so-called "miracle years" of the 1960s, Ireland's annual growth rate of per capita GNP never reached 4 percent over any five-year period. Can this poor growth performance be associated with foreign penetration, free trade, and free enterprise?[3]

Growth of output and investment became slower as foreign penetration became higher, and growth rates became particularly low (and finally negative) after Ireland joined the EEC and was forced into full-fledged free trade. *Every industrial sector except chemicals and metals experienced significantly lower rates of growth of net output after Ireland's accession to the EEC than in the pre-EEC period of ELI* (O'Hearn 1988, chap. 14). Textiles and clothing experienced negative post-EEC growth rates. Food, drink, wood, paper, and clay were stagnant after 1972. Only metals, chemicals, and other manufacturing experienced annual growth rates of more than 5 percent after Ireland entered the EEC and embarked on full free trade. . . .

RESULTS II: INCOME DISTRIBUTION

The second major claim of dependency is that foreign penetration either increases inequality or prevents its decrease. Here again most of the existing evidence is from cross-sectional studies, which do not adequately explain how the effects of dependency may unfold over time (for a review of findings, see Bornschier 1980b). Dependency posits three major types of arguments about foreign penetration and inequality: (1) arguments about structural unemployment and poverty, (2) arguments about class inequality, and (3) arguments about wage inequality.

Structural Unemployment and Poverty

Foreign penetration may cause unemployment for several reasons, two of which are particularly relevant in the Irish case. (*a*) Radical free trade and discrimination in favor of foreign industry may cause widescale displacement of domestic industry. To this may be added the migration of farmers to the cities and towns, which may further swell the ranks of the unemployed. (*b*) If new foreign industry is more capital-intensive than domestic industry, or is concentrated in capital- (or materials-) intensive sectors, the employment created per unit of foreign investment may be too low to offset employment *losses* associated with foreign-penetration (Rubinson 1976; Bornschier and Ballmer-Cao 1979).

Although Irish income distribution data are scarce,[4] structural unemployment has certainly been a major cause of inequality since Ireland joined the EEC. In Table 22.5 I show the distribution of direct incomes in 1973 and 1980. Unemployment is the source of the major differences between the two distributions. In 1973, the lowest 10 percent of Irish households received less than 1 percent of direct incomes, while the next decile received 1.7 percent. By 1980, the lowest decile received no direct income, while the next decile received a mere 0.7 percent of total incomes. Today, with unemployment exceeding 20 percent, the lowest *two* deciles

Table 22.5   Distribution of Incomes and Tax Payments, by Decile, 1973 and 1980

Decile	Direct Income		Gross Income		Indirect Tax
	1973	1980	1973	1980	1980
1	*	Nil	2.9	2.6	10.0
2	1.7	0.7	4.4	4.2	10.0
3	4.4	3.5	5.3	5.1	6.7
4	6.1	5.7	6.5	6.2	7.2
5	7.6	7.5	7.5	7.4	8.3
6	9.0	9.3	8.8	8.8	9.6
7	11.0	11.2	10.3	10.4	11.1
8	13.5	13.9	12.4	12.7	12.5
9	17.0	18.0	15.5	16.1	14.6
10	29.6	30.1	26.3	26.5	20.1
	99.9	99.9	99.9	100.0	100.1

Source: Roche (1984); Revenue Commissioners (1985).

receive no direct income. To the extent the ELI regime caused unemployment in Ireland, it unquestionably *caused* higher inequality of direct incomes.

Apart from industrial closures, rising capital intensity is the major cause of unemployment. Assets per hour of labor expended in Irish industry grew during ELI (1955–82) at an annual rate of 5.3 percent (O'Hearn 1988). Not only did highly capital-intensive foreign operations penetrate Irish industry, but the regime's generous capital grants encouraged local firms to replace labor with machines. These factors added considerably to unemployment in the 1970s and 1980s.

An important difference between the Irish case and other situations of dependency, however, is the degree to which popular demands for social welfare have been met. Ireland's proximity to England, its claim to full European membership and "modernity," and its national aspirations to regain its northern territory all contributed to pressures on the regime to keep its social welfare benefits roughly in line with Britain's. At the same time, Britain's claim over the North of Ireland necessitated the introduction of social welfare benefits there at the same level as existed in England. Thus, when postwar welfare reforms were introduced in Britain, Ireland followed with a similar, if slightly less "grandiose" scheme. As a result, the distribution of *gross* incomes in Ireland is more equitable than direct incomes (Table 22.5), although the share of the bottom 20 percent of families is still falling. Unfortunately, data more recent than 1980 are not available. Social welfare cutbacks have increased dramatically in the 1980s because of severe public and foreign debt crisis in Ireland. When the effects of these cutbacks on gross income distribution are accounted, it will surely be shown that inequality rose significantly.

Finally, the introduction of free trade in Ireland led to a massive loss of tariff revenues for the state. As a result, highly regressive value-added taxes were introduced in 1964, and the rates were rapidly increased during the 1970s and 1980s. Indirect (value-added and excise) taxes now account for more than half of government revenues. As shown in Table 22.5, the proportion of *indirect* taxes paid by low-income receivers is much greater than the proportion of income they receive. Since indirect taxes have risen considerably during ELI—they made up 19.8 percent of government revenues in 1955 and 50.5 percent of revenues in 1985—they have added considerably to inequality over time. Thus, free trade is responsible for yet another dimension of income inequality in terms of spending power.

Class Inequality

Explanations of inequality that concentrate on income differences among *classes* emphasize the aspects of foreign penetration that increase elite power and decrease working-class power. Some analysts concentrate on the tendency of local elites to use their alliances with foreign capital in order to resist popular demands for income redistribution (Rubinson 1976; Bornschier and Ballmer-Cao 1979). Others concentrate on the power of TNCs to resist labor demands and weaken labor organization. A structural argument emphasizes that the high proportion of unskilled workers in TNC subsidiaries increases the number of the lowest industrial wage earners, while the failure to locate skilled work in subsidiaries leaves a gap in the middle ranges of the income scale. At the same time, foreign penetration may encourage the expansion of low-paying service jobs (Evans and Timberlake 1980).

Certain specific characteristics of the Irish case tend to make some of these effects inoperable. The most obvious is the difference between the Irish political system—where overt authoritarianism is largely avoided—and regimes in other developing countries. A related difference is the degree to which the very rich elites in pre-independence Ireland were *absentee* elites, since England was so close. Very rich landlords and very rich capitalists in Ireland tended to remove their incomes to England, where they do not figure in Irish income distribution statistics. Therefore, 20th-century Ireland never developed the kind of measurable elite-mass inequality that is observed throughout the developing world.

These special Irish characteristics are reflected in the movement of upper income shares between 1973 and 1980 (Table 22.5). The increases of higher-income shares that are associated with falling low-income shares are spread throughout the top 50 percent of income earners. The share of the top 20 percent of income receivers grew only a little, from 46.6 percent to 48.1 percent of total incomes. No identifiable small elite in Ireland appeared to benefit greatly from the worsening position of the lowest-income receivers. This is because the lost income of the lowest 20 percent was due less to lower wages than to the complete loss of wages. Wage earners who remained employed may not be better off absolutely but still moved up to higher income deciles as the unemployed filled up lower deciles.

The lack of significant "bunching" of income shares in the higher deciles is also consistent with the structural argument that there are few new high-salaried professionals and managers in TNC subsidiaries. Evidence in support of this conclusion comes from studies of the skill structure of TNCs in Ireland. In the electronics industry, for example, Wickham (1986) finds a large concentration of employees in assembly operations, and a particular preponderance of women in these occupations.

The most significant change of class inequality to come out of dependent Irish industrialization is absent from Irish income distribution statistics. This change involves the large-scale movement of incomes from wages to profits, and within profits from domestic industry to the TNCs. The high levels of profit repatriations simply reflect the rapid rise of TNC profits, and the duality of profit rates between foreign and domestic industry. During TNC-penetration (1955–85), the surplus-share of incomes rose by 2 percent a year in manufacturing as a whole, and by 3.5 percent annually in electronics and 6.4 percent in pharmaceuticals (O'Hearn 1988, chap. 16).

The level of *international* inequality that is engendered by dependency is clearly shown in Table 22.6, where I report profit rates in 1981 by economic sector and nationality of ownership. The duality of profit rates is particularly large in the "modern" sectors—electronics, pharmaceuticals, and other manufacturing— and a few "traditional" sectors such as drink, wood, and clay. Profits in certain foreign sectors—soft drinks, pharmaceuticals, healthcare, computers, instrument engineering, and others—were well in excess of 25 percent of sales and in some cases as high as *60 percent*. Overall, non-British TNCs' profit rates in Ireland averaged 22 percent, while domestic firms' profit rates averaged less than 2 percent. It is clearly possible, therefore, that the effects of dependency on inequality *among countries* are much greater than its effects on local inequality.

Finally, the relationship between elites, TNCs, and trade union power may differ significantly in Ireland from many other cases of dependency. The Irish working class developed in close proximity to the highly-unionized British working class. Trade unionists were involved in the struggle for national liberation, and their support for early nationalist governments was very important. By 1958, 92 percent of Irish industrial workers were unionized (Registrar of Friendly Societies 1959). At the same time, the uneasy alliance between governments and trade unions, which is an important factor that neutralizes working class opposition to foreign penetration, led most unions to become nonmilitant. For many years, the IDA advised TNCs who located in Ireland to recognize trade unions. An incoming TNC

Table 22.6   Profit Rates by Sector and Country of Ownership, Irish Manufacturing, 1983

Sector	(a) Irish	(b) British	(c) Other Foreign	$\frac{c}{a}$
Food	2.26	3.01	5.23	2.31
Drink	9.29	18.60	26.95	2.90
Textiles	0.90	7.23	2.09	2.32
Clothing	−1.88	6.71	1.33	—
Wood	0.98	1.55	27.68	28.24
Paper	0.95	1.63	8.12	8.55
Clay	4.13	−8.90	27.32	6.62
Chemicals	−12.04	3.04	5.34	—
Pharmaceutical	10.15	22.02	48.66	4.79
Metals	1.09	5.52	10.25	9.40
Electric	−1.47	−196.00	22.65	—
Other	3.74	5.62	25.09	6.70
Total	1.82	7.03	22.09	12.14

Note: Profits rate refers to pretax profits as percentage of total sales.
Source: Author's calculations from IDA Components of Sales Survey.

commonly made a "sweetheart" agreement with an Irish trade union, giving it sole organizing rights in return for guarantees of labor peace. Recently, however, as the Irish regime became desperate for new TNC investments, they acceded to the wishes of the latest wave of entrants—the "yuppie" U.S. electronic firms—and dropped their pressure for unionization of TNC subsidiaries. The first major TNC to "go nonunion" was the computer firm Digital, which is now one of the largest employers in the country. The consequences on interclass income distribution of these successes of TNC power over Irish trade unions have yet to be worked out.

Wage Inequality

The effects of foreign penetration on wage differentials have probably been the most widely discussed aspect of dependency and inequality. Much has been written about *dualism*, where a thriving foreign-dominated "modern" sector exists alongside a stagnant "traditional" sector (Myint 1970; Singer 1970). According to this approach, wages in the "modern" sectors are expected to be higher than in the "traditional" sectors, and this encourages *wage* inequality.

On the other hand, the expectation that subsidiaries' employment structures are weighted toward unskilled jobs, with the more skilled and professional positions kept in the parent country, contradicts the *dualism* argument. If TNCs concentrate their employment in unskilled assembly trades, they *decrease* wage inequality, even if their unskilled workers are paid more than unskilled workers in domestic firms. Finally, in a labor-rich economy, with high unemployment—and particularly with a highly educated working class as in Ireland—there may be little reason to expect the TNCs to pay higher wages than local firms. This is particularly true where centralized wage-setting or wage-bargaining structures exist, as they do not only in Ireland, but also in some of the East Asian economies (e.g., Singapore).

There is little evidence that foreign penetration caused significant *wage* inequality in Ireland. Average wage rates within industrial sectors in 1983 were quite similar among Irish, British, and other foreign firms (Table 22.7). Neither are wage rates particularly high in the "modern" sectors. Wages in electronics, metals, and "other manufacturing" are at or below the average for industry. Among foreign sectors, only chemicals and pharmaceuticals have relatively high average wages. Clearly, the sectoral differentials in wage rates are tied to the structure of the labor force within those sectors. Electronics, healthcare products, textiles, and clothing have a high proportion of female assembly-type workers. The drink and chemicals industries are highly capital-intensive and have a higher proportion of technical and other skilled workers.

Specific local factors are more important than foreign penetration or "duality" in determining the Irish wage distribution. The Irish wage bargaining structure—where wages are negotiated in a series of centralized

Table 22.7   Wages by Sector and Country of Ownership, Irish Manufacturing, 1983 (annual wage per capita in Irish punts)

Sector	Irish	British	Other Foreign
Food	9,445	10,822	9,600
Drink	12,694	15,840	12,652
Textiles	6,545	7,025	9,208
Clothing	5,619	5,567	4,838
Wood	7,114	10,383	4,039
Paper	12,787	9,276	9,781
Clay	12,424	13,821	15,561
Chemicals	15,455	10,191	12,925
Pharmaceutical	9,720	10,675	13,830
Metals	8,967	10,520	9,139
Electronics	7,861	10,202	9,867
Other	7,664	9,251	8,837
Total	9,502	9,235	9,307

Source: Author's calculations from IDA Components of Sales Survey.

"wage rounds" with tripartite participation of capital, trade unions, and the state—is the most important determinant of wage distribution. It is in the area of wage determination that the specificities of dependent cases, rather than any general "laws" of dependency, are likely to be most important.

Still, there are important dependency-related trends—economic decline, capital intensity, and unemployment—which have a strong influence in favor of *income* (as opposed to wage) inequality. These "pure dependency" effects of foreign penetration on income distribution differ significantly from other developing regimes, where localized political factors—often connected with authoritarian regimes—play a more important role in determining inequality.

CONCLUSIONS

The "dependency" approach to development studies has come under fire in recent years because of the seemingly "deviant" cases of East Asia. Proponents of modernization cite Taiwan and South Korea as instances where foreign penetration was *not* accompanied by either slow growth or rising inequality. They imply that other developing countries may also achieve rapid growth *with* equality by following a radical regime of free trade, free enterprise, and openness to foreign enterprise.

Unfortunately for the new modernizationists, neither South Korea nor Taiwan is really characterized by these traits. Both regimes intervene strongly in business, use selective protection and import-substitution, and have a definite preference for domestic industry. If South Korea, Taiwan, and even Singapore are "getting the prices right," it is because of their regimes' extensive intervention, not their reliance on "the market."

Ireland, on the other hand, has closely followed the prescriptions of the modernizationists. Since the 1950s, it has been highly penetrated by foreign industry, in preference to domestic industry; it removed its protective barriers and allows free movement of goods and profits in and out of the country; it disdained any form of control of business, including the use of indirect economic instruments such as credit and foreign exchange manipulations.

Ireland has also grown at a snail's pace and, recently, experienced negative economic growth. While the level of inequality has been reduced by social welfare policies—a remnant of the country's proximity to Europe— there is an underlying trend toward rising inequality, resulting from slow growth and tax policies that are forced by free trade and free enterprise. Since Ireland is among the top five debtor countries in the world (foreign debt as a percentage of GNP), the regime has already begun social welfare cutbacks that will drive it toward greater inequality. It is a classic case of "dependent" relations: slow growth and inequality caused by foreign penetration.[5]

There are other countries that are like Ireland in many respects, although the *specific* nature of dependent relations always differs significantly from country to country. The present analysis of Ireland does not resolve the problems of using dependency as a general approach to the study of development. Rather, it demonstrates how dependency-type mechanisms may thrive in a liberal, open atmosphere. Liberalness and openness, however, do not predominate in the periphery today—deviations from liberal regimes reinforce the need to rigorously examine the specificity of dependent situations. Thus, the Peruvian case of export-led "bonanza development"— where the state tries to maximize its share of TNC profits—is quite different from Irish ELI, where the state tries to maximize TNC investment and depend on trickle-down. The Brazilian case, where the state attempts to maximize linkages of TNCs with local capital, differs from the Irish regime, where linkages are simply hoped for.

Still, there are strong pressures afoot for liberalization, as proposed by the new modernizationists. These pressures are seen less in East Asia, however, than in places like Mexico and in the conditional lending of the IMF. The experience of foreign penetration, limited growth, and inequality— despite the exceptional cases of East Asia—is still much more common among developing countries than so-called "success." Students of development may have a lot to learn from the "exceptions"— particularly about ways to bring about economic development while avoiding the extreme authoritarianism of the East Asian cases. They have still more to learn from careful comparative historical analyses of specific cases of dependent development. The route of free trade, free enterprise, foreign penetration, and the new modernizationism is *not* the way to go.

NOTES

1. Care should be taken not to confuse tariff revenues with categories such as "taxes on international trade and transactions" (e.g., in *World Development Report*). For Ireland, the latter is primarily excise taxes on alcohol and tobacco, a consumption tax which has partly replaced tariffs as a source of government revenues. Excise taxes are not a form of protection because locally produced alcoholic drinks and tobacco products are taxed at the same rate as imports. In addition, because excise taxes are placed on goods that are highly price inelastic, they have a limited effect on consumption of taxed items.

2. Apart from the level of state intervention in Singapore, its special characteristics as a city-state—like Hong Kong—reduce its usefulness as a "model of development" (Rodan 1985, pp. 9–10).

3. Critics of the present approach may suggest that Ireland's poor per capita growth performance is caused by its high rate of population growth. This is not the case. It is true that Ireland has the highest rate of natural increase in Western Europe, and that population grew more rapidly in the 1960s and 1970s than in previous periods (when it actually declined, because of emigration). Thus, population growth did exacerbate the slow growth of the 1970s. In the 1980s, however, Irish population is again declining—emigration is reaching its highest levels ever (see Irish Census of Population 1986). Most experts agree that emigration and population decline will continue at a rapid rate for some years to come, barring an unforeseen economic recovery. While there is some reciprocity Irish population growth rates (which change according to emigration rates) clearly respond to economic growth rates more than they "cause" them.

4. The Irish census contains no questions about income. There are a few tax-based surveys of income distribution, but these have gaps in coverage, because many people pay no income taxes. A few household budget surveys were conducted (in 1951/52, 1965/66, 1973, and 1981) and these seem to provide the best information on income distribution. For existing studies of Irish income distribution, see Stark (1977) and Roche (1984).

5. A similar analysis could be made regarding the North of Ireland. It has also experienced severe economic decline and inequality during the postwar period. The reasons for stagnation and inequality in the North, however, are quite different from the South. Stagnation is mainly a result of the decline in importance to England of shipbuilding and natural fibers. The North has been allowed to decline as part of a British regional policy which favors Southern England at the expense of the so-called "Celtic fringe" and the old industrial regions of Northern England. In other words, Britain has largely withdrawn economically from its Northern Irish colony, although it refuses to withdraw militarily and politically. Inequality in the North of Ireland, unlike the South, is affected not only by class relations and economic decline, but also by sectarianism. The unemployment rate among the settler ("Protestant") population, for example, remains below the British average, at the expense of the native ("Catholic") population, which suffers unemployment averaging over 35 percent (above 80 percent in some Catholic areas).

REFERENCES

Amin, S. 1974. *Accumulation on a World Scale.* New York: Monthly Review.

Baran, P. 1957. *The Political Economy of Growth.* New York: Monthly Review.

Barrett, R. E. and M. K. Whyte. 1982. "Dependency Theory and Taiwan: Analysis of a Deviant Case." *American Journal of Sociology* 87:1064–89.

Biersteker, T. 1978. *Distortion or Development? Contending Perspectives on the Multinational Corporation.* Cambridge, MA: MIT Press.

Bornschier, V. 1980a. "Multinational Corporations and Economic Growth: A Cross-National Test of the Decapitalization Thesis." *Journal of Development Economics* 7:191–210.

———. 1980b. "Multinational Corporations, Economic Policy and National Development in the World System." *International Social Sciences* 32:158–71 .

Bornschier, V. and T.-H. Ballmer-Cao. 1978. "Income Inequality: A Cross-National Study of the Relationships between MNC-Penetration, Dimensions of the Power Structure and Income Distribution." *American Sociological Review* 44:487–506.

Buckley, P. J. 1974. "Some Aspects of Foreign Private Investment in the Manufacturing Sector of the Economy of the Irish Republic." *Economic and Social Review* 5:301–21.

Carter, C. 1957. "The Irish Economy Viewed from Without." *Studies* 46:137–43.

Central Statistics Office. Various years. *National Income Accountants.* Dublin: Stationery Office.

Chakravarty, S. 1987. "Marxist Economics and Contemporary Developing Economies." *Cambridge Journal of Economics* 11:3–22.

Chase-Dunn, C. 1975. "The Effects of International Economic Dependence on Development and Inequality." *American Sociological Review* 40:720–38.

Connor, J. M. 1977. *The Market Power of Multinationals: A Quantitative Analysis of U.S. Corporations in Brazil and Mexico.* New York: Praeger.

Cummings, B. 1983. "The Origins and Development of the Northeast Asian Political Economy: Industrial Sectors, Product Cycles, and Political Consequences." *International Organization* 38:1–40.

Dail Eireann. 1958. Parliamentary Debates 165. Dublin: Stationery Office.

Evans, P. and M. Timberlake. 1980. "Dependence, Inequality, and Growth in Less Developed Countries." *American Sociological Review* 45:531–52.

Frank, A. G. 1969. *Latin America: Underdevelopment or Revolution.* New York: Monthly Review.

Hirschman, A. O. 1958. *The Strategy of Economic Development.* New York: Norton.

Islam, I. and C. Kirkpatrick. 1986. "Export-Led Development, Labour-Market Conditions and the Distribution of Income: The Case of Singapore." *Cambridge Journal of Economics.* 10:113–27.

Lewis, W. A. 1955. *Theory of Economic Growth.* Homewood, IL: Irwin.

Lim, L. 1983. "Singapore's Success: The Myth of the Free Market Economy." *Asian Survey* 23:752–64.

McAleese, D. 1977. *A Profile of Grant-Aided Industry in Ireland.* Dublin: Institute of Public Administration.

——— and D. McDonald. 1978. "Employment Growth and the Development of Linkages in Foreign-Owned and Domestic Manufacturing Enterprises." *Oxford Bulletin of Economics and Statistics* 40:321–39.

Myint, H. 1970. "Dualism and the International Integration of the

Underdeveloped Economies." *Banca Nazionale del Lavoro Quarterly Review* 93:128–56.

Nurkse, R. 1953. *Problems of Capital Formation in Underdeveloped Countries*. Oxford: Oxford University Press.

O'Hearn, Denis. 1987. "Estimates of New Foreign Manufacturing Employment in Ireland (1956–1972)." *Economic and Social Review* 18:173–88.

———. 1988. *Export-led Industrialization in Ireland: A Specific Case of Dependent Development*. Ph.D. diss., University of Michigan.

O hUiginn, P. 1972. *Regional Development and Industrial Location in Ireland. Volume 1, Locational Decisions and Experiences of New Industrial Establishments 1960–1970*. Dublin: An Foras Forbartha.

Organization for Economic Cooperation and Development (OECD). 1987. *National Accounts: Main Aggregates 1960–1985*. Paris: OECD.

Registrar of Friendly Societies (Ireland). 1959. Annual Report. Dublin: Stationery Office.

Revenue Commissioners (Ireland). Various years. Annual Report. Dublin: Stationery Office.

Roche, J. D. 1984. *Poverty and Income Maintenance Policies in Ireland*. Dublin: Institute of Public Administration.

Rodan, G. 1985. *Singapore's "Second Industrial Revolution": State Intervention and Foreign Investment*. Kuala Lumpur: ASEAN-Australian Joint Research Project.

Rubinson, R. 1976. "The World Economy and the Distribution of Income within States: A Cross-National Study," *American Sociological Review* 41:638–50.

Singer, H. 1970. "Dualism Revisited: A New Approach to the Problems of the Dual Society in Developing Countries." *Journal of Development Studies* 7:60–75.

Stark, T. 1977. *The Distribution of Income in Eight Countries*. London: HMSO.

Survey Team. 1967. *Survey of Grant-Aided Industry, 1967*. Dublin: Stationery Office.

U.S. Department of Commerce. 1980. "U.S. Direct Investment Abroad." *Survey of Current Business* 60:16 38.

Wickham, J. 1986. *Trends in Employment and Skill in the Irish Electronics Industry*. Report to National Board for Science and Technology, Dublin.

World Bank. 1981. *World Development Report 1981*. Washington, D.C.: World Bank.

23

· · · · · · ·

Inequality and Rebellion
in Central America

· · · · · · ·

JOHN A. BOOTH

Inequality in the distribution of wealth can have serious consequences for domestic stability, which in turn can slow or even reverse economic growth, thus further widening the income gap between rich and poor countries. Dependency theory argues that small agroexport countries are likely to suffer internal distortions in their labor markets. In this chapter, John Booth makes the case that rapid economic growth in Central America has created the conditions for political violence. The point is not just that Central America has grown but rather the way in which it has grown. The author contends that the expansion of speculative export agriculture and rapid capital-intensive industrialization has created or enlarged a number of subclasses, among them landless agricultural wage laborers and an urban proletariat. In the absence of government policies that could have mitigated the exacerbation of inequalities that arose from rapid economic growth, these groups began mobilizing.

Since the mid-1970s, tens of thousands of persons in three out of the five Central American countries have revolted against their governments or fought to repress such rebellions. These conflicts have cost more than a quarter of a million lives and created more than two million internal and external refugees. In 1979 a bloody insurrection toppled Nicaragua's Somoza regime. El Salvador's crippling civil war lasted some twelve years and cost 75,000 lives. In Guatemala since 1980, brutal counterinsurgency warfare, pro-regime

Reprinted with permission from *Latin American Research Review*, vol. 26, 1 (1991):33–43, 48–49, 52–53, 59–62.

terror, and political reform have failed to eliminate a resurgent guerrilla rebellion. Yet while these countries have rent themselves with political violence, their neighbors Honduras and Costa Rica have in general remained politically peaceful.

This chapter draws on theories of sociopolitical violence and revolution in an attempt to explain the origin of the widespread popular political mobilization that has played a major part in Central America's recent rebellions. The study employs aggregate data from the 1950s through the 1980s as well as descriptive data to explore how differences in the rate and nature of economic growth, income and wealth distribution, and governmental response to unrest may have contributed to rebellions in Somoza's Nicaragua (1977–1979), El Salvador (since 1979), and Guatemala (since 1978) and to the lack of rebellions in Honduras and Costa Rica.

These violent upheavals exhibit many common features but also important differences. All of them cannot be classified as revolutions because only Nicaragua's Sandinistas won power and attempted a full-scale social revolution. In this context, John Walton's concept of national revolt, which is broader than revolution, provides a useful common framework for studying all three cases.[1] The national revolt concept also permits comparing these cases with the Central American countries that have not experienced such revolts.

SCHOLARSHIP ON CENTRAL AMERICA'S NATIONAL REVOLTS

The study of Central American conflict, violence, and revolution has grown rapidly over the last decade. Although little of the resulting literature is explicitly theoretical,[2] several distinct approaches emphasize the following causes of rebellion in the isthmus: the development of production and evolving class relations;[3] domestic political factors such as elites, pressure groups, and the breakdown of the state or traditional systems of dominance;[4] "communist subversion";[5] religion and religious groups;[6] and other domestic and external actors.[7]

It has become increasingly common to treat Central America's recent national revolts as having been produced by a complicated combination of developmental changes and internal and external political processes. According to what may be the most promising theories,[8] recent economic development trends worsened the region's historically extreme maldistribution of wealth and income, intensifying grievances among negatively affected class groups. These grievances escalated in the 1970s with the rapid expansion of Central America's rural and industrial proletariats, declining urban and rural real incomes, and increasing concentration of wealth (especially agricultural land). Such problems led the aggrieved to demand change and sparked growing opposition to incumbent regimes by political parties, labor unions, religious community organizers, and revolutionary groups. Violent repression of opposition demands for reform in Nicaragua, El Salvador, and Guatemala not only failed to suppress mobilization for change but actually helped forge revolutionary coalitions that fought for control of the state.

This approach to the nearly simultaneous rebellions in three Central American nations has by no means become an explanatory paradigm, but it enjoys growing currency. Moreover, it manifests important parallels with more general recent theories on the origin and development of revolutions and major national revolts.

GENERAL THEORIES ON REBELLION AND REVOLUTION

When individuals join rebel movements, some basic source of strong grievances must exist (Kriesberg 1982, 29). Recent theories regard economic factors, especially evolving class relations, as a fundamental source of grievance in great social revolutions (Skocpol 1979, 13), national revolts (Walton 1984), and peasant rebellions (Paige 1975; Wolf 1969). In particular, the entry of agrarian societies into the world capitalist economy by becoming heavily dependent on export agriculture is viewed as a major source of social transformation and grievances. As Walton has observed, "The penetration of global capitalism into precapitalist societies [fosters] export agriculture and an internal market for the consumption of imports [so that] the peripheral economy is unevenly developed, . . . [eventually producing] a massive transformation of the indigenous economy" (Walton 1984, 161–62). Such changes harm large sectors of the peasantry, urban poor, and middle classes and leave many citizens angry.

Political factors also play key roles. The mere existence of aggrieved citizens will not generate overt political conflict, however (Kriesberg 1982, 66–106). Popular mobilization must occur: aggrieved groups must first become aware of their own opposition and then focus their struggle on some target, typically the state or incumbent regime. Popular mobilization alone, however, may be too diffuse or too weak to challenge the state. Effective organization for opposition also requires mobilizing such resources as cadres, cash, arms, communication, and allies (Aya 1979, 41–44; Tilly 1981, 21–23).

Contrary to economically deterministic theories of revolution, recent approaches emphasize the importance of the state in the political process of rebellion. Skocpol (1979) and Walton (1984) concur with Aya and Tilly that the state plays two key roles. First, governments implement public policy and bring about social change in the course of governing. For example, governments often repress their opponents, which may both generate and focus popular mobilization. Governments represent much more than mere reflections of economic systems—they become actors in the political arena. Second, the state ultimately becomes the target of the organized aggrieved. A widespread and violent contest for sovereignty is the essence of rebellion against an established regime.

The congruencies between these more general theories about revolution and rebellion and the arguments advanced by many Central Americanists suggest several propositions around which the following discussion will be organized. First, expansion of speculative export agriculture (from the 1950s through the 1970s) and rapid capital-intensive industrialization (in the 1960s and 1970s) in Central America created or expanded classes or subclasses of landless agricultural wage laborers, urban subproletarians, proletarians, and white-collar sectors such as commercial and public employees. In the absence of state efforts to mitigate inequity and poverty in society through agrarian reform or wage policies, the nature and rapid rate of Central American economic growth from the 1950s to the 1970s exacerbated inequalities in wealth and real income and reduced the real wages of agricultural and urban wage laborers. Rapidly escalating oil prices and the resulting inflation combined with the deterioration of the Central American Common Market (in the middle and late 1970s) and natural or economic catastrophes to reduce real income and employment sharply among working-class and some white-collar sectors.

Second, the grievances caused by declining income or wealth, catastrophes, and political dissatisfaction among would-be competing elites led to protests against public policy. These grievances also fostered popular mobilization in the forms of agrarian, labor, neighborhood, community self-help, and opposition-party organizations as well as reformist demands on the state.

Third, differing regime responses to organization and protest determined whether national revolts (or revolution in the case of Nicaragua) would occur. Where regimes responded to demands with policies designed to reduce inequalities of wealth and to permit recovery of real wages and with low or modest levels of force or repression, popular mobilization and protests subsided. But where regimes did not pursue ameliorative policies and sharply escalated repression by public security forces, protests and opposition organization increased and national revolts ensued.

COMMON FEATURES OF CENTRAL AMERICAN NATIONS

The nearly simultaneous outbreak of a revolution in Nicaragua and national revolts in El Salvador and Guatemala (three of the five Central American nations) was not coincidental. It stemmed from many common factors of history, economics, and geopolitics.[9] These shared factors should be reviewed before examining the data relevant to the theories under discussion.

When Mexico became independent in 1821, Central America's six former colonies briefly joined the Mexican Empire. But when the empire collapsed in 1823, all but Chiapas withdrew and formed the federated Central American Republic. By 1838, however, economic and political conflict destroyed the federation. Throughout most of the isthmus, the military's political role was strengthened by a combination of liberal-conservative factionalism, extensive mineral or agricultural wealth, plentiful indigenous communities for coerced labor, and the emergent hacienda system. Civil institutions developed slowly and weakly while military rule and political violence became the norm. Except in Costa Rica, Central American nations experienced mostly dictatorships between 1840 and 1945. Costa Rica suffered relatively less conflict and less military involvement in politics because of an early conservative victory, scarce mineral wealth, a paucity of Indians who could be subjugated, and few great haciendas.

International pressures on Central America grew after 1850. First Britain and then the United States pursued economic, political, and security objectives in the region, especially the construction of a canal across the isthmus. Direct foreign intervention in Central America increased and exacerbated the propensity of the region's nations to meddle in each other's politics. By 1900 the United States had become the dominant foreign power in Central America. The Panama Canal and U.S. business interests led to extensive direct U.S. military and political intervention through the mid-1930s. After 1945 the United States shifted its emphasis in Central America to containing communism, a goal implemented by aiding anticommunist regimes and engineering the overthrow of Guatemalan President Jacobo Arbenz in 1954 with Central American assistance. The Cuban Revolution reinforced the U.S. preoccupation with containing communism and prompted U.S. support for the Central American Common Market (CACM) through the Alliance for Progress.

In the economic arena, Central American societies have specialized in exporting agricultural commodities since the colonial era. After 1850 coffee dominated regional exports, with bananas, cacao, cotton, and sugar assuming importance in the twentieth century. Each of these products experienced cyclical price swings that spawned periodic severe recessions. The spread of coffee production concentrated landownership and established coffee growers, millers, and exporters as dominant national economic and political elites.[10] Industrialization, in contrast, proceeded slowly. Agroexport elites in most countries used the state so tenaciously to oppose socioeconomic reform that one critic has labeled them "reactionary despots" (Baloyra 1983).

Beginning in the 1950s, socioeconomic change accelerated in Central America. National populations doubled between 1960 and 1983, and the proportion of urban-dwellers grew by half or more. Literacy increased notably in Honduras, El Salvador, and Nicaragua, although it remained low everywhere except in Costa Rica. Employment increasingly shifted away from agriculture into services and manufacturing. Middle sectors of the population grew with the expansion of education, industry, commerce, and government.[11]

Underlying such rapid social changes were important shifts in Central American economies and deliberate governmental efforts to promote growth. Two new waves of agroexport production occurred: the intensive cultivation of grains and cotton in the 1950s and 1960s, and extensive cattle-raising in the 1960s and 1970s. Except in Honduras,[12] these trends reduced the small-holding and subsistence agricultural sector of each Central American nation while expanding migrant wage-labor forces. Landownership and agricultural production became increasingly concentrated in the hands of the agroexport sector. Rural labor surpluses developed, swelling migration to cities by un-employable campesinos. Domestic food production shrank and food imports rose, afflicting more and more citizens directly with imported inflation.

Public policy helped accelerate socioeconomic change in the 1960s, following Castro's rise to power in Cuba and political turmoil in the isthmus. Central American governments in 1960 formed the Central American Common Market, which sought to promote regional economic integration, intraregional trade, foreign investment, and industrialization. It was hoped that the CACM would increase demand and production in the capitalist mode, thus creating new jobs and a better distribution of income. This anticipated trickling down of income was intended to reduce poverty and to undercut the appeal of revolutionary politics as exemplified by Cuba. The Alliance for Progress shared these objectives and together with the CACM greatly increased public investment in Central America. This development in turn stimulated a surge in new private investment. Domestic and foreign investment concentrated in the capital-intensive production of consumer goods that were manufactured mainly with imported raw materials and fuel. Gross domestic products (GDPs) and GDPs per capita grew rapidly into the early 1970s during a period marked by stable input prices and booming industrial production and productivity.

The CACM-induced industrial boom did not absorb the rapidly growing labor supply, however, and rural and urban unemployment rose simultaneously throughout the region. During the 1970s, the CACM's import-substitution model began to exhaust its growth potential. Industrial input prices soared while investment and productivity lagged. Markets contracted with higher consumer prices, which led to further unemployment and further shrinkage of demand. In Nicaragua, El Salvador, and Guatemala, the industrial sector's share of exports declined markedly (averaging about 6 percent) between 1970–1974 and 1975–1979. Growth slowed from a regional mean annual rate of 2.2 percent per capita for 1970–1974 to a mere 0.4 percent for 1975–1979, with Nicaragua's performance the worst in the region (see Table 23.1). The region's mean annual per capita growth rate for 1980–1984 fell further to -2.9 percent. Declining terms of trade, higher

Table 23.1   Mean Annual Growth in Gross Domestic Products Per Capita in Central American Countries, 1950–1989

Period	Costa Rica (percent)	El Salvador (percent)	Guatemala (percent)	Honduras (percent)	Nicaragua (percent)	Region[a] (percent)
1950–1959	1.9	1.9	0.3	0.9	3.9	1.5
1960–1969	3.5	2.2	2.6	1.8	4.3	2.7
1970–1974	3.0	1.8	3.2	0.6	2.0	2.2
1975–1979	1.6	0.4	2.4	1.0	−6.8	0.4
1980–1984	−2.3	−5.5	−3.1	−2.4	0.2	−2.9
1985–1989	1.0	−0.7	−0.7	0.1	−6.6	−1.2

a. Weighted mean for period.
Sources: CEPAL (1985, t. 2; 1986, t. 3; 1989, t. 3); and Wilkie and Haber (1981, t. 22-3).

interest rates, falling commodity prices, and a world recession together caused a severe imbalance of payments. These problems aggravated internal imbalances within the CACM, causing it effectively to collapse by the end of the 1970s (Weeks 1985a). Guatemala, El Salvador, and Nicaragua suffered further economic contraction during the late 1980s.

Central American nations in the 1970s shared many trends, the most important being a growing concentration of wealth. National bourgeoisies were prospering greatly, while the middle classes were growing and their living standards were improving. This trend contrasted markedly with increased rural and urban lower-class unemployment and decreased agricultural self-sufficiency among the rural poor. . . .

SOCIOECONOMIC ROOTS OF CLASS CONFLICT

To what extent did the expansion of export-led agriculture and the CACM-driven boom of the 1960s and 1970s create new classes and class relations, increase inequalities in wealth and income, and reduce working-class living standards in Central America? As the CACM boom began to wane in the 1970s, relative and absolute income, employment, and relative wealth eroded among working-class groups in all five Central American nations. Such trends reversed late in the decade in Honduras and Costa Rica, but the problems worsened in Nicaragua, El Salvador, and Guatemala.

Workers' Real Wages

After a decade of industrialization and rapid growth in general production, the 1973 OPEC oil embargo and subsequent rapid escalation of oil prices drove up consumer prices for the rest of the decade. In Guatemala, for example, the average annual change in the consumer price index (CPI) for 1963–1972 was only 0.7 percent, but it jumped to 12.3 percent for 1973–1979. Similar or even more severe CPI increases also hit the other four nations.[13]

The impact of such inflation on workers' real wages varied markedly within the region.[14] Despite momentary corrections, estimated real wages in each Central American country either began to slide with the mid-1970s inflation or continued downward trends begun in the late 1960s (see Table 23.2). In Honduras and Costa Rica, however, wages recovered much of their purchasing power in the late 1970s. Real wages fell again in Costa Rica in the early 1980s but recovered once more. In sharp contrast, real wages in Nicaragua, El Salvador, and Guatemala continued to decline through 1980. Indeed, in El Salvador real wages generally continued to fall through 1984. In Guatemala real wages apparently stabilized somewhat in the early 1980s, although they remained well below levels of the early 1970s. This evidence

Table 23.2   Real Working-Class Wage Indices for 1963-1984 (1972 = 100)

Year	Costa Rica	El Salvador[a]	Guatemala[b]	Honduras[c]	Nicaragua[d]
1963	78	96	—	—	81
1965	—	98	102	—	110[e]
1967	91[e]	99	107	—	120
1970	93	98	102	—	106
1971	104	99	102	—	104
1972	100	100	100	100	100
1973	97	106	93	104	88
1974	105	104	90	98	88
1975	88	96	89	95	93
1976	100	101	91	106	93
1977	110	90	76	99	85
1978	119[e]	93	79	105	77
1979	124	89	79[e]	107	66[e]
1980	125[e]	87	79[e]	101	56[e]
1981	111[e]	81[f]	80[e]	97[f]	56[e]
1982	89[e]	72[f]	86[e]	105[f]	49[e]
1983	99[e]	64[f]	79[e]	96[f]	43[e]
1984	107[e]	61[f]	79[e]	93[f]	40[e]

Note: Values of the indices represent an unweighted average of wages in manufacturing, construction, transport, storage, and communication, and in agriculture, corrected for consumer price changes except for items under note e, which are wages only for persons included in national social-security systems.

a. Excludes construction (after 1974); data drawn from Wilkie and Perkal (1984, t. 1405).

b. Unweighted average of all sectors reported in Wilkie and Perkal (1984, t. 1405).

c. Unweighted average wages in manufacturing, construction, and agriculture (agricultural wages not included in 1972 and 1973 figures).

d. Includes wages in manufacturing, transportation (only), and construction.

e. Data drawn from Wilkie and Lorey (1987, t. 1413).

f. Data drawn from Gallardo and López (1986, 168).

Sources: Based on Wilkie and Haber (1981, tt. 1400, 1401, 1402, 1403), Wilkie and Perkal (1984, t. 1405), and consumer price data in Table 23.3. The 1978 and 1979 data for Nicaragua come from Mayorga (1985, 65).

strongly suggests that grievances among affected classes in Nicaragua, El Salvador, and Guatemala probably intensified steadily throughout the middle and late 1970s while in Costa Rica and Honduras, workers' recovery of their purchasing power probably attenuated such grievances.[15]

Employment

Employment failed to keep up with the growth of the work force in Central America during the CACM boom (Camacho et al. 1979). For the region, unemployment is estimated to have increased from 8.1 percent in 1960 to 14.5 percent in 1980 (IICA 1982, 256), and it has risen further since 1980 (Gallardo and López 1986, 189). Experts also believe that underemployment affects from one to five times as much of Central America's economically active population as does unemployment, depending on the country.[16]

Table 23.3 presents unemployment levels for 1970, 1980, and 1984 (note that computational methods vary from country to country, so that cross-national comparisons of raw data should not be made; however, trends within nations are disclosed). Between 1970 and 1980, unemployment rose in every country in Central America except in Honduras, where agrarian reform provided many jobs. In Nicaragua from 1970 through 1978 (the year the insurrection began), unemployment almost tripled from 3.7 percent to 14.5 percent.[17] Overall, by 1984 unemployment had risen only a modest 22 percent in Honduras but had increased by 86 percent in Costa Rica, 88 percent in El Salvador, 89 percent in Guatemala, and a whopping 440 percent in Nicaragua. Costa Rican unemployment surged sharply between 1981 and 1983 during a recession but returned to pre-1980 levels by 1989. . . . [18]

Table 23.3 Unemployment Trends, 1970-1989, in Percentages

Year	Costa Rica	El Salvador	Guatemala	Honduras	Nicaragua
1970	3.5	16.0[a]	4.8[b]	8.8[c]	3.7
1980	5.9	24.0	5.5	8.8	17.8
1984	6.6	30.0	9.1	10.7	16.3
1989	5.5	—	7.2	9.4	—

a. The Salvadoran figure for 1970 is an estimate based on Central American mean unemployment trends (IICA 1982, 256); Salvadoran datum for 1984 from U.S. Department of State data from the Office of Regional Economic Policy, Bureau of Inter-American Affairs.

b. Guatemalan data for 1970 and 1980 from Wilkie and Haber (1981, t. 1308). Figures for 1984 and 1989 from CEPAL (1989, t. 4).

c. Value for 1970 is an estimate projected from economically active population from base years of 1974 and 1977 (Wilkie and Haber 1981, t. 1301). Value is the number of unemployed as a percent of economically active population. Data from 1980 on is taken from CEPAL (1989, t. 4).

Sources: Wilkie and Haber (1981, t. 1308); Gallardo and López (1986, 189); CEPAL (1985, t. 4; 1989, t. 4); and DGEC–Costa Rica (1980, t. 196).

Throughout Central America, the rapid growth of extensive, export-oriented agriculture and the CACM industrialization boom produced sharp and fairly quick deterioration of real wages among urban and rural workers and certain middle-sector groups during the 1970s. In Nicaragua, El Salvador, and Guatemala, these factors (aided by natural and economic disasters) compounded growing unemployment, redistributed wealth and income away from the poor and toward the wealthy, and lowered living standards for a majority of citizens. Late in the 1970s, a recession began to erode the security and return on investments of the upper classes of these three countries. In marked contrast, despite rapid inflation in the mid-1970s, redistributive public policies in Honduras and Costa Rica permitted the wages of working-class citizens to recover and appeared to make income distribution either slightly less inequitable or at least not sharply worse (see Table 23.4). Although much of the specific evidence presented is not strictly comparable cross-nationally, strikingly similar changes appear to have taken place in Nicaragua, El Salvador, and Guatemala, in marked contrast with the cases of Honduras and Costa Rica.

Popular Mobilization

As the theoretical discussion has suggested, did declining income and wealth, natural catastrophes, and dissatisfactions among competing elites contribute to popular mobilization, reformist demands on Central American governments, and protests of public policies in the 1970s? As the ranks of the aggrieved in Central America increased due to socioeconomic conditions, the number of organizations and their activities multiplied. Ordinary citizens typically first attempted easier, more acceptable actions (community self-help, petitioning government, organizing) before turning to more

Table 23.4   Comparison of Central Government Expenditures as a Percentage of Budget

Year	Costa Rica 1978	Costa Rica 1983	El Salvador 1984	Guatemala 1978	Guatemala 1984	Honduras 1976	Nicaragua 1976
Defense	2.7	3.0	24.6	11.0	13.7	10.5	12.8
Total percent on education, health, and social security/ welfare	56.3	56.3	27.3	24.2	24.1	40.1	40.9
Ratio of human services to defense	21:1	19:1	1:1	2:1	2:1	4:1	3:1

Sources: Inforpress Centroamericana (1985a, 5); Wilkie and Haber (1981, t. 2323); and Wilkie and Lorey (1987, t. 3010).

confrontational, higher-risk actions like protests, strikes, or support for armed resistance. . . .[19]

As expected, all five Central American nations experienced increased mobilization by working-class and middle-class groups in the 1960s and 1970s, an era of great economic change and shifting distribution of income and wealth. Political parties remained fairly stable in Costa Rica and Honduras while major new parties formed, factions split off, and coalitions developed among extant parties in Nicaragua, El Salvador, and Guatemala. The Catholic Church played a much less important role in mobilization in Costa Rica and Honduras than in the other three nations.

Government Response to
Popular Mobilization and Its Effect on Opposition

Central American regimes responded to popular mobilization in the 1970s in distinctive ways. . . .

The findings generally confirm the predictions about ameliorative policies and repression. As expected, where the Nicaraguan, Salvadoran, and Guatemalan regimes responded to popular mobilization with heavy repression, opposition organization grew and progressively broader coalitions formed. In Guatemala the 1985 elections, restoration of nominal civilian rule, and partial abatement of urban political repression have at least interrupted opposition unification. Whether Guatemala's recent reformism will arrest opposition mobilization and unification permanently or only momentarily in the presence of continuing high levels of repression is one of the most interesting empirical questions regarding Central American politics.

CONCLUSIONS

The evidence strongly suggests that Central America's rapid growth of export agriculture after 1950 and industrialization after 1960 markedly reduced the relative and absolute living standards of many members of the working class, who then mobilized to demand redress of their grievances. Where the state responded accommodatingly and with limited repression (in Costa Rica and Honduras), opposition mobilization stagnated or subsided. Where the state did not ameliorate growing inequality and employed heavy repression (in Nicaragua, El Salvador, and Guatemala), opposition mobilization and unity increased and led to a broad, rebellious challenge to regime sovereignty.

These findings, examined in light of both general theories of revolution and rebellion and Central Americanists' explanations of regional turmoil, suggest five related hypotheses for future research.

First, the expansion of speculative export agriculture (from the 1950s through the 1970s) and rapid capital-intensive industrialization (in the 1960s and 1970s) in Central America created or expanded classes or subclasses of landless agricultural wage laborers, urban subproletarians, proletarians, and white-collar sectors such as commercial and public employees.

Second, in the absence of concerted state efforts to ameliorate inequalities within society (by such means as agrarian reform or wage policies), Central America's rapid economic growth during the 1950s and 1970s increased inequalities in wealth and real income and reduced the real wages of agricultural and urban wage laborers.

Third, rapidly escalating oil prices and resultant inflation, the deterioration of the Central American Common Market (in the middle and late 1970s), and natural or economic catastrophes sharply reduced real income and employment among working-class and some white-collar sectors.

Fourth, grievances caused by declining income or wealth, catastrophes, and political dissatisfaction among would-be competing elites fostered popular mobilization in the form of agrarian, labor, neighborhood, community self-help, and opposition-party organizations as well as reformist demands on the state and protests against public policy.

Fifth, differing regime responses to organization and protest determined whether national revolts would occur. Where regimes responded to demands with ameliorative policies (for reducing inequalities of wealth and permitting recovery of real wages) and with low or modest levels of force or repression, popular mobilization and protests subsided. Where regimes did not implement ameliorative policies and sharply escalated repression by public security forces, protests and opposition organization increased and national revolts occurred. . . .

NOTES

1. Walton defines national revolts as "protracted, intermittently violent, nonlocal struggles [with extensive] mobilization of classes and status groups that become recognized claimants of rival sovereignty and engage the state" (1984, 13). He argues that national revolts ultimately affect policy and social development in the incumbent regime. Most national revolts, however, never lead to a revolutionary program because they fail to wrest power from the regime.

2. See, for instance, Schulz (1984b).

3. For examples, see Brockett (1988), Bulmer-Thomas (1987), Castillo Rivas (1983), Durham (1979), Graham (1984), Pérez Brignoli and Baíres Martínez (1983), Chinchilla (1980), and Weeks (1985a).

4. For example, Aguilera Peralta (1983), Arnson (1984), Baloyra (1982, 1983), Castellano Cambranes (1984), Jung (1984), Millett (1984a), and Schulz (1984a).

5. See, for instance, Cruz Sequeira (1984), Enders (1982, 9), U.S. Department of State (1981a), U.S. Department of State–U.S. Department of Defense (1984a, 1984b), Kirkpatrick (1984,167–72), and Leiken, ed. (1984).

6. See, for example, Berryman (1984), Bonpane (1985), Cáceres Prendes et al. (1983), Crahan (1982, 1984), Dodson and Montgomery (1982), Dodson and O'Shaughnessy (1990), Lernoux (1984), Montgomery (1984), O'Shaughnessy and Serra (1986), and Richard and Meléndez (1982).

7. For example, Chavarría (1983), Gleijeses (1984), Gorman (1984), Krumwiede (1984), McClintock (1985), Millett (1984a), and Wiarda (1982).

8. For promising theories, see T. Anderson (1982), Berryman (1983), Black (1981), Booth (1984a, 1984b), Booth and Walker (1989), Bowen (1984), Castillo Rivas (1983, 1984), Chamorro (1983), Cohen and Rosenthal (1983), Davis (1983), Dunkerley (1982, 1988), Hoeffel (1984), Kurth (1982), LaFeber (1983), López et al. (1979), Meléndez (1982), Molina Chocano (1983), Montgomery (1982), Schoultz (1983), Smith (1986), Stone (1979, 1983), Torres Rivas (1981, 1983, 1984), Vilas (1986), Villagrán Kramer (1982), Vuskovic (1983), Walker (1981), Walker, ed. (1982a), and Williams (1986).

9. This section draws mainly on Brockett (1988), Camacho et al. (1979), Cardoso and Pérez Brignoli (1977), CSUCA (1978), Delgado (1981), Gudmundson (1986), Menjívar (1974), Pérez Brignoli (1985), Pérez Brignoli and Baíres Martínez (1983), Torres Rivas (1971), Weeks (1985a), Williams (1986), and Woodward (1985).

10. Honduras never developed a national landowning aristocracy like those in the other countries. Instead, regional hacendados and later urban commercial, financial, and industrial entrepreneurs retained economic and political power (Morris 1984b, 193).

11. Data drawn from IADB (1984, tt. 1, 2, 3, and 1–4), Torres Rivas (1982, t. 4), Pérez Brignoli and Baíres Martínez (1983, t. 9), Castillo Rivas (1983, t. 1), Ropp and Morris (1984, t. 1.6), and Nicaragua–Ministerio de Educacíon (1979, 140–41, 147).

12. In Honduras, agrarian colonization and expanding employment in the modern capitalist sector of agriculture continued to absorb much of the growth of the rural labor force.

13. Data from Wilkie and Haber (1981, tt. 2505, 2508, 2509, 2511, 2513), IADB (1983, country profile tables), U.S. Department of State (1985), CEPAL (1986, t. 5; 1989, t. 5); see also Booth (1985, t. 5).

14. Wage indices vary for each nation and do not represent all wages and salaries within any nation (see Table 23.2 for details). Central American countries report wage data differently, so that no precise equivalency between nations can be assumed. Reported or legal wage rates often overstate actual wages paid, especially in agriculture, making any error in the conservative direction—that is, real disposable income would be lower than estimated.

15. Since 1985, Costa Rican real-wage indices have continued to rise to an index value of 113 for 1989 (with 1972 equaling 100). Data are not yet available on the other Central American countries (CEPAL 1989, t. 5).

16. Underemployment is typically defined as being unable to find full-time work or having to perform wage labor because of insufficient land for family subsistence (Camacho et al. 1979; Inforpress Centroamericana 1985d, 18; Gallardo and López 1986, 189).

17. Booth and Walker (1989, 52).

18. *Ibid*. For additional analysis and data on Central American unemployment, see these sources: for El Salvador, Molina (1979, 245, 254), Orellana (1985, 5–9), and Russell (1984, 76–78); and in general, Gallardo and López (1986, 188–90).

19. See Chaffee (1979, 12–17).

REFERENCES

Aya, R. 1979. "Theories of Revolution Reconsidered: Contrasting Models of Collective Violence." *Theory and Society* 8 (June–Dec.):39–100.

Baloyra, E. A. 1982. *El Salvador in Transition*. Chapel Hill: University of North Carolina Press.

———. 1983 "Reactionary Despotism in Central America." *Journal of Latin American Studies* 15, pt. 2 (Nov.):295–319.

Booth, J.A. 1985. *The End and the Beginning: The Nicaraguan Revolution*. 2d ed. Boulder, Colo.: Westview.

Booth, J. A. and T. W. Walker. 1989. *Understanding Central America*. Boulder, Colo.: Westview.

Brockett, C. D. 1988. *Land, Power, and Poverty: Agrarian Transformation and Political Conflict in Central America*. Boston, Mass.: Unwin Hyman.

Bulmer-Thomas, V. 1987. *The Political Economy of Central America since 1920*. Cambridge: Cambridge University Press.

Camacho, D. et al. 1979. *El fracaso social de la integración centroamericana*. San José, Costa Rica: Editorial Universitaria Centroamericana.

Cardoso, C.F.S. and H. Pérez Brignoli. 1977. *Centroamérica y la economía occidental (1520–1930)*. San José: Editorial Universidad de Costa Rica.

Castillo Rivas, D. 1983. "Modelos de acumulación, agricultura y agroindustria en Centroamérica." In Castillo Rivas, ed., 1983, *Centroamérica: más allá de la crisis*, pp. 183–216. Mexico City: Ediciones SIAP.

CEPAL (Comision Economica Para America Latina y El Caribe). 1985. *Preliminary Overview of the Latin American Economy, 1985*. Santiago, Chile: United Nations.

———. 1986. *Preliminary Overview of the Latin American Economy, 1986*. Santiago, Chile: United Nations.

———. 1989. *Balance preliminar de la economía de América Latina y el Caribe, 1989*. Santiago, Chile: United Nations.

Chaffee, W. 1979. "Let Jorge Do It: A Rational Choice Model of Political Participation." In Seligson and Booth (eds.) *Politics and the Poor: Political Participation in Latin America*, vol. 2, pp. 18–34. New York: Holmes and Meier.

CSUCA (Consejo Superior Universitaria Centroamericana). 1978. *Estructura agraria, dinámica de población y desarrollo capitalista en Centroamérica*. San José, Costa Rica: Editorial Universitaria Centroamericana.

Delgado, E. 1981. *Evolución del Mercado Común Centroamericano y desarrollo equilibrado*. San José, Costa Rica: Editorial Universitaria Centroamericana.

DGEC-Costa Rica (Direccion General De Estadistica y Censos). 1980. *Anuario Estadístico de Costa Rica, 1977*. San José: DGEC.

Gallardo, M. E. and J. R. López. 1986. *Centroamérica: la crisis en cifras*. San José, Costa Rica: Instituto Interamericano de Cooperación con la Agricultura (IICA) and Facultad Latinoamericano de Ciencias Sociales (FLACSO).

Gudmundson, L. 1986. *Costa Rica before Coffee*. Baton Rouge: Louisiana State University Press.

IADB (Inter-American Development Bank). 1983. *Economic and Social Progress in Latin America: Natural Resources, 1983 Report*. Washington, D.C.: IADB.

———. 1984. *Economic and Social Progress in Latin America: Economic Integration, 1984 Report*. Washington, D.C.: IADB.

IICA (Instituto Interamerican De Cooperacion Para La Agricultura). 1982. "América Central frente a la década de los años ochenta." In *América Central frente a la década de los años de los 80.* Heredia: Escuela de Relaciones Internacionales, Universidad Nacional Autónoma de Costa Rica.

Inforpress Centroamericana. 1985a. "1985 Budget Has Few Surprises," *Central America Report*, 11 Jan., 4–5.

————. 1985d. *Guatemala: Elections 1985.* Guatemala City: Inforpress Centroamericana.

Kriesberg, L. 1982. *Social Conflicts.* 2nd ed. Englewood Cliffs, N.J.: Prentice-Hall.

Menjívar, R., ed. 1974. *La inversión extranjera en Centroamérica.* San José, Costa Rica: Editorial Universitaria Centroamericana.

Molina, H. 1979. "Las bases económicas del desarrollo industrial y la absorción de fuerza de trabajo en El Salvador. In Camacho, et al. (eds.) *El fracaso social de la integración centroamericana,* 218–75. San José, Costa Rica: Editorial Universitaria Centroamericana.

Morris, J. A. 1984a. "Government and Politics. " In Rudolph (ed.) *Honduras: A Country Study,* pp. 147–206. Washington, D.C.: Foreign Area Studies, American University, and the U.S. Department of the Army.

Nicaragua, Ministerio de Educación. 1979. *Situación del sistema educativo después de 45 años de dictadura militar somocista y perspectivas que plantea la revolución sandinista.* Managua: Ministerio de Educación.

Orellana, V. A. 1985. *El Salvador: Crisis and Structural Change.* Occasional Paper no. 13. Miami: Latin American and Caribbean Center. Florida International University.

Paige, J. M. 1975. *Agrarian Revolution; Social Movements and Export Agriculture in the Underdeveloped World.* New York: Free Press.

Pérez Brignoli, H. 1985. *Breve historia de Centroamérica.* Madrid: Alianza Editorial.

————. with Y. Baíres Martínez. 1983. "Growth and Crisis in the Central American Economies, 1950–1980." *Journal of Latin American Studies* 15, pt. 2 (Nov.):365–98.

Ropp, S. C. and J. Morris, eds. 1984. *Central America: Crisis and Adaptation.* Albuquerque: University of New Mexico Press.

Russell, P. L. 1984. *El Salvador in Crisis.* Austin, Tex.: Colorado River Press.

Schulz, D. E. 1984a. "El Salvador: Revolution and Counterrevolution in the Living Museum." In Schulz and Graham (eds.), *Revolution and Counterrevolution in Central America and the Caribbean,* pp. 189–268. Boulder, Colo.: Westview.

————. 1984b. "Ten Theories in Search of Central American Reality" In Schulz and Graham (eds.), *Revolution and Counterrevolution in Central America and the Caribbean,* pp. 3–64. Boulder, Colo.: Westview.

Skocpol, T. 1979. *States and Revolutions.* Cambridge: Cambridge University Press.

Tilly, C. 1981. "Introduction," In Tilly and Tilly (eds.), *Class Conflict and Collective Action,* pp. 13–25. Beverly Hills, Calif.: Sage.

Torres Rivas, E. 1971. *Interpretación del desarrollo social centroamericano.* San José, Costa Rica: Editorial Universitaria Centroamericano.

————. 1982. "Cambio social y crisis en la década de los años ochenta." In *América Central frente a la década de los años de los 80.* Heredia: Escuela de Relaciones Internacionales, Universidad Nacional Autónoma de Costa Rica.

Walton, J. 1984. *Reluctant Rebels: Comparative Studies in Revolution and Underdevelopment.* New York: Columbia University Press.

Weeks, J. 1985a. *The Economies of Central America.* New York: Holmes and Meier.

Wilkie, J. W. and S. Haber, eds. 1981. *Statistical Abstract of Latin America 21*. Los Angeles: University of California Latin America Center Publications.

Wilkie, J. W. and D. Lorey, eds. 1987. *Statistical Abstract of Latin America 25*. Los Angeles: University of California Latin America Center Publications.

Wilkie, J. W. and A. Perkal, eds. 1984. *Statistical Abstract of Latin America 23*. Los Angeles: University of California Latin America Center Publications.

Williams, R. G. 1986. *Export Agriculture and the Crisis in Central America*. Chapel Hill: University of North Carolina Press.

Wolf, Eric. 1969. *Peasant Revolts of the Twentieth Century*. New York: Harper and Row.

Woodward, R. L., Jr. 1985. *Central America: A Nation Divided*, 2nd ed. New York: Oxford University Press.

PART 5

. . . .

The State, Growth, and Inequality: Rent-Seeking, Urban Bias, and Democracy

. . . .

24

· · · · · · ·

Governments and
Agricultural Markets in Africa

· · · · · · ·

ROBERT H. BATES

*The focus of Part 5 of this book shifts from external causes of the gaps
to domestic causes. Flawed policies of governments in the Third World
are viewed as being largely responsible for slowed growth and
domestic inequality. The negative consequences of interference with
the market is a central theme in much of this research. In this chapter,
Robert Bates focuses on, among other things, the pernicious effect in
Africa of state-controlled "marketing boards" for export crops and
government monopsonies for the purchase of food crops. Given that
these programs are notorious failures, why do governments maintain
them? Bates describes farm and industrial policies and presents two
different explanations for why governments act as they do: They act
as agents of private interests and as agencies that seek to retain
power. In his analysis of government actions, the author attempts to
provide a theory of government that is so often lacking in economic
analysis.*

Governments in Africa intervene in agricultural markets in characteristic
ways: they tend to lower the prices offered for agricultural commodities, and
they tend to increase the prices that farmers must pay for the goods they buy
for consumption. And although African governments do subsidize the prices
farmers pay for the goods they use in farming, the benefits of these subsidies
are appropriated by the rich few: the small minority of large-scale farmers.

Reprinted with permission from Regents of the University of California and the
University of California Press. *Toward a Political Economy of Development*,
Robert H. Bates, ed. (Berkeley: University of California Press, 1988), pp. 331–
332, 334–343, 345–354, 356–358.

Other patterns, too, are characteristic of government market intervention. Insofar as African governments seek increased farm production, their policies are project-based rather than price-based. Insofar as they employ prices to strengthen production incentives, they tend to encourage production by lowering the prices of inputs (that is, by lowering costs) rather than by increasing the prices of products (that is, by increasing revenues). A last characteristic is that governments intervene in ways that promote economic inefficiency: they alter market prices, reduce market competition, and invest in poorly conceived agricultural projects. In all of these actions, it should be stressed, the conduct of African governments resembles the conduct of governments in other parts of the developing world.

One purpose of this paper is to describe more fully these patterns of government intervention. A second is to examine a variety of explanations for this behavior.

THE REGULATION OF COMMODITY MARKETS

It is useful to distinguish between two kinds of agricultural commodities: food crops, many of which can be directly consumed on the farm, and cash crops, few of which are directly consumable and which are instead marketed as a source of cash income. Many cash crops are in fact exported; they provide not only cash incomes for farm families but also foreign exchange for the national economies of Africa.

Export Crops

An important feature of the African economies is the nature of the marketing systems employed for the purchase and export of cash crops. The crops are grown by private farm families, but they are then sold through official, state-controlled marketing channels. At the local level, these channels may take the form of licensed agents or registered private buyers; they may also take the form of cooperative societies or farmers' associations. But the regulated nature of the marketing system is clearly revealed in the fact that these primary purchasing agencies can in most cases only sell to one purchaser: a state-owned body, commonly known as the marketing board. . . .

Government Taxation. Initially, the revenues accumulated by the marketing boards were to be used for the benefit of the farmers, in the form of price assistance funds. At times of low international prices, these funds were to be employed to support domestic prices and so to shelter the farmers from the vagaries of the world market. For example, 70 percent of the western Nigerian marketing board's revenues were to be retained for such purposes. But commitments to employ the funds for the benefit of the farmers proved short-lived. They were overborne by ambitions to implement development programs and by political pressures on governments from nonagricultural sectors of the economy. . . .

Food Crops

African governments also intervene in the market for food crops. And, once again, they tend to do so in ways that lower the prices of agricultural commodities.

One way African governments attempt to secure food cheaply is by constructing bureaucracies to purchase food crops at government-mandated prices. A recent study by the United States Department of Agriculture examined the marketing systems for food crops in Africa and discovered a high incidence of government market intervention. In the case of three of the food crops studied, in over 50 percent of the countries in which the crop was grown the government had imposed a system of producer price controls, and in over 20 percent the government maintained an official monopsony for the purchase of that food crop; in these instances, the government was by law the sole buyer of the crop.

Regulation of food markets entails policing the purchase and movement of food stocks and controlling the storage, processing, and retail marketing of food. An illustration is offered by the maize industry of Kenya; according to subsection 1 of section 15 of the Maize Marketing Act, "All maize grown in Kenya shall, subject to the provision of this Act, be purchased by and sold to the Board, and shall, without prejudice to the Board's liability for the price payable in accordance with section 18 of this Act, rest in the Board as soon as it has been harvested. . . ."

More directly relevant to the concerns of this chapter, however, is the impact of food marketing controls on food prices. For insight into this subject we can turn to Doris Jansen Dodge's study of NAMBoard, the food marketing bureaucracy in Zambia. Over the years studied by Dodge (1966–1967 to 1974–1975) NAMBoard depressed the price of maize by as much as 85 percent; that is, in the absence of government controls over maize movements, the farmers could have gotten up to 85 percent higher prices for their maize than they were able to secure under the market controls imposed by NAMBoard. Gerrard extends Dodge's finding for Zambia to Kenya, Tanzania, and Malawi; Dodge herself extends them to eight other African countries.[1] The result is a weakening of incentives to produce food.

Projects. In order to keep food prices low, governments take additional measures. In particular, they attempt to increase food supplies. This can be done either by importing food or by investing in food production projects. Foreign exchange, however, is scarce; especially since the rise of petroleum prices, the cost of imports is high. So as to conserve foreign exchange, then, African governments attempt to become self-sufficient in food. To keep prices low, they invest in projects that will yield increased food production.

In some cases, governments turn public institutions into food production units: youth-league farms and prison farms provide illustrative cases. In other instances, they attempt to provide factors of production. In Africa, water is commonly scarce and governments invest heavily in river-basin development schemes and irrigation projects. Capital equipment is also scarce; by purchasing and operating farm machinery, governments attempt to promote farm production. Some governments invest in projects to provide particular crops: rice in Kenya, for example, or wheat in Tanzania. In other instances, governments divert large portions of their capital budgets to the financing of food production schemes. Western Nigeria, for example, spent over 50 percent of the Ministry of Agriculture's capital budget on state farms over the period of the 1962–1968 development program.[2]

Nonbureaucratic Forms of Intervention

Thus far I have emphasized direct forms of government intervention. But there is an equally important, less direct form of intervention: the over-valuation of the domestic currency.

Most governments in Africa maintain an overvalued currency.[3] Foreign money therefore exchanges for fewer units of local currency. A result is to lower the prices received by the exporters of cash crops. For a given sum earned abroad, the exporters of cash crops receive fewer units of the domestic currency. In part, overvaluation inflicts losses on governments; deriving a portion of their revenues from taxes levied by the marketing boards, the governments command less domestic purchasing power as a result of overvaluation. But because their instruments of taxation are monopolistic agencies, African governments are able to transfer much of the burden of overvaluation: they pass it on to farmers, in the form of lower prices.

In addition to lowering the earnings of export agriculture, overvaluation lowers the prices paid for foreign imports. This is, of course, part of the rationale for a policy of overvaluation: it cheapens the costs of importing plant, machinery, and other capital equipment needed to build an industrial sector. But items other than plant and equipment can be imported, and among these other commodities is food. As a consequence of overvaluation, African food producers face higher levels of competition from foreign foodstuffs. And in search of low-price food, African governments do little to protect their domestic food markets from foreign products—products whose prices have artificially been lowered as a consequence of public policies.

Industrial Goods

In the markets for the crops they produce, African farmers face a variety of government policies that serve to lower farm prices. In the markets for the goods that they consume, however, they face a highly contrasting situation: they confront prices for consumers that are supported by government policy.

In promoting industrial development, African governments adopt commercial policies that shelter local industries from foreign competition. To some degree they impose tariff barriers between the local and the international markets. To an even greater extent, they employ quantitative restrictions. Quotas, import licenses, and permits to acquire and use foreign exchange are all employed to conserve foreign exchange, on the one hand, while, on the other, protecting the domestic market for local industries. In connection with the maintenance of overvalued currencies, these trade barriers create incentives for investors to import capital equipment and to manufacture domestically goods that formerly had been imported from abroad.[4]

Not only do government policies shelter industries from low cost foreign competition, they shelter them from domestic competition as well. In part, protection from domestic competition is a by-product of protection from foreign competition. The policy of allocating licenses to import in conformity with historic market shares provides an example of such a measure. The limitation of competition results from other policies as well. In exchange for commitments to invest, governments guarantee periods of freedom from competition. Moreover, governments tend to favor larger projects; seeking infusions of scarce capital, they tend to back the proposals that promise the largest capital investments. With the small markets typical of most African nations, the result is that investors create plants whose output represents a very large fraction of the domestic market; a small number of firms thus come to dominate the market. Finally, particularly where state enterprises are concerned, governments sometimes confer virtual monopoly rights upon particular enterprises. The consequence of all these measures is to shelter industries from domestic competition.

One result is that inefficient firms survive. Estimates of the use of industrial capacity range as low as one-fifth of the single-shift capacity of installed plant.[5] Another consequence is that prices rise. Protected from foreign competition and operating in noncompetitive market settings, firms are able to charge prices that enable them to survive despite operating at very high levels of cost.

Farm Inputs

By depressing the prices offered farmers for the goods they sell, government policies lower the revenues of farmers. By raising the prices that consumers—including farmers—must pay, governments reduce the real value of farm revenues still further. As a consequence of these interventions by governments, then, African farmers are taxed. Oddly enough, while taxing farmers in the market for products, governments subsidize them in the market for farm outputs.

Attempts to lower input prices take various forms. Governments provide subsidies for seeds and fertilizers, the level of the latter running from 30 percent, in Kenya, to 80 percent, in Nigeria. They provide tractor-hire services at subsidized rates—up to 50 percent of the real costs in Ghana in the mid-1970s.[6] They provide loans at subsidized rates of interest for the purchase and rental of inputs. And they provide highly favorable tax treatment for major investors in commercial farming ventures.[7] Moreover, through their power over property rights African governments have released land and water to commercial farmers at costs that lie below the value they would generate in alternative uses. The diversion of land to large-scale farmers and of water to private tenants on government irrigation schemes, without paying compensation to those who had employed these resources in subsistence farming, pastoral production, fishing or other ventures, represents the conferring of a subsidy on the commercial farmer—and one that is paid at the expense of the small-scale, traditional producer. . . .

In the case of land and water use, then, a major effect of government intervention in the market for inputs is to augment the fortunes of large-scale farmers at the expense of small-scale farmers. . . . Because the large farmers have the same social background as those who staff the public services, the public servants feel they can work most congenially and productively with these people.[8] Moreover, to favor the large farmer is politically productive. I will elaborate this argument below.

DISCUSSION

Governments intervene in the market for products in an effort to lower prices. They adopt policies which tend to raise the price of the goods farmers buy. And while they attempt to lower the costs of farm inputs, the benefits of this policy are reaped only by a small minority of the richer farmers. Agricultural policies in Africa thus tend to be adverse to the interests of most producers.

Studies in other areas suggest that this configuration of pricing decisions is common in the developing nations.[9] Indeed, it is argued by some that the principal problems bedeviling agriculture in the developing areas originate from bad public policies. . . . In the remaining sections, I will advance several explanations for their choices. . . .

GOVERNMENTS AS AGENTS OF PRIVATE INTERESTS

Put bluntly, food policy in Africa appears to represent a form of political settlement, one designed to bring about peaceful relations between African governments and their urban constituents. And it is a settlement in which the costs tend to be borne by the mass of the unorganized: the small-scale farmers. . . .

Urban consumers in Africa constitute a vigilant and potent pressure group demanding low-priced food. Because they are poor, much of their income goes for food; some studies suggest that urban consumers in Africa spend between 50 and 60 percent of their incomes on food.[10] Since changes in the price of food have a major impact on the economic well-being of urban dwellers in Africa, they pay close attention to the issue of food prices.

Urban consumers are potent because they are geographically concentrated and strategically located. Because of their geographic concentration, they can be organized quickly; and because they control transport, communications, and other public services, they can impose deprivations on others. They are therefore influential. Urban unrest frequently heralds a change of government in Africa, and the cost and availability of food supplies are major factors promoting urban unrest.

It should be noted that it is not only the workers who care about food prices. It is also the employers. Employers care about food prices because food is a wage good; with higher food prices, wages rise and, all else being equal, profits fall. Governments care about food prices not only because they are employers in their own right but also because as owners of industries and promoters of industrial development programs they seek to protect industrial profits. Indicative of the significance of these interests is that the unit that sets agricultural prices often resides not in the Ministry of Agriculture but in the Ministry of Commerce or of Finance.

When urban unrest begins among food consumers, the political discontent often spreads rapidly to upper echelons of the polity: to those whose incomes come from profits, not wages, and to those in charge of major bureaucracies. Political regimes that are unable to supply low-cost food are seen as dangerously incompetent and as failing to protect the interests of key elements of the social order. At times of high prices, influential elites are likely to ally with the urban masses, to shift their political loyalties and replace those in power. Thus it was that protests over food shortages and rising prices formed a critical prelude to the coups and coup attempts in Ghana, Liberia, Kenya, and Guinea.

It is ironic but true that among those governments most committed to low-cost food are the "radical" governments in Africa. Despite their stress on economic equality, they impose lower prices on the commodity from which the poorest of the poor, the peasant farmers, derive their income. A major reason for their behavior is that they are deeply committed to rapid industrialization; moreover, they are deeply committed to higher real wages for urban workers and have deep institutional ties to organized labor.

We can thus understand the demand for low-cost food. Its origins lie in the urban areas. It is supported by governments, both out of political necessity and, on the part of more radical ones, out of ideological preference. Food is a major staple and higher prices for such staples threaten the real value of wages *and* profits. . . .

There are thus fundamental political reasons for governments to seek to lower the price of food. There are also real limitations on their ability to do so. One limitation is political: insofar as farmers themselves are powerful, they are likely to resist the efforts of governments to lower agricultural prices. Only occasionally, however, are farmers powerful. In West Africa, urban/bureaucratic elites have entered rice farming; and where they have done so, they have won protected commodity prices and subsidized prices for farm inputs.[11] In East Africa, similar elites maintain large-scale wheat farms; they too have employed their political influence to avoid adverse pricing policies. But most farms are owned by members of the peasantry, not the elite; they are small-scale, not large-scale; and the farmers are politically weak, not strong. Rarely, then, are farmers powerful; and most often they are taxed.

Political power on the part of farmers thus occasionally influences the pricing decisions of governments. A more common influence is the limitation of governmental resources. When lower price levels are imposed on farmers, consumers may face shortages; indeed, food production tends to be highly price-elastic. A necessary corollary to low-food-price policies in Africa is thus the use of public resources to produce or to import food. But most African governments are poor and have little foreign exchange. Governments therefore lack the resources with which to make up the shortfalls resulting from their pricing policies, and this places a major limitation on the degree to which they can lower agricultural prices. . . .

Pressure groups form only one component of a pluralist model of politics.[12] A second is competitive elections. Clearly, were competitive elections contested by rival parties in Africa, agricultural policy could not be so strongly biased against rural dwellers. With less than 10 percent of their population in cities, most nations would contain electoral majorities composed of farm families; and electoral incentives would almost inevitably lead politicians to advocate pro-agrarian platforms in their efforts to secure votes and to win power.

Evidence of the significance of electoral incentives is to be found in Zambia. From 1964 to 1972, the government of Zambia devoted on average over 70 percent of its capital budget to expenditures in the urban areas. In the years prior to national elections, however, the government reallocated its capital program: over 40 percent of the capital budget was then spent in the rural districts. Moreover, it was in the years prior to elections that major rural development programs were announced: the creation of zones of intensive rural development, new credit programs, mechanization schemes, the decentralization of rural administration. The commitment to rural development was thus tied to the electoral cycle. Having periodically to face a rural constituency, the government periodically recommitted itself to the enhancement of their fortunes.[13]

There is thus a tension between the two components of the pluralist model. In the African context, the impact of organized interest groups works to the detriment of agrarian interests, whereas competitive elections work to their advantage. In recent years the frequency of the return to democratic forms of government among the African states has been more than matched by the frequency of the demise of competitive party systems. Electoral incentives have little opportunity to counter the biases produced by interest-group politics.

GOVERNMENTS AS AGENCIES THAT SEEK TO RETAIN POWER

The interest-group model thus accounts for major elements of the food policies maintained by African governments. It explains the political pressures for low food prices and thus helps to explain why, when governments want more food, they prefer to secure it by building more projects rather than offering higher prices. By the same token, it helps to account for the governments' preference for production subsidies rather than higher food prices as incentives for food production.

Nonetheless, an interest-group explanation too is incomplete. Its primary virtue is that it helps to account for the essentially draconian pricing policies adopted by African governments. Its primary limitation is that it fails to explain how governments get away with such policies. How, in nations where the majority of the population are farmers and the majority of the resources are held in agriculture, are governments able to succeed in implementing policies that violate the interests of most farmers? In search of answers to this question, a third approach is needed, one that looks at agricultural programs as part of a repertoire of devices employed by African governments in their efforts to secure political control over their rural populations and thus to remain in power.

Organizing a Rural Constituency

We have already seen that adopting policies in support of higher prices for agricultural commodities would be politically costly to African governments. It is also important to note that such a stance would generate few political benefits. From a political point of view, conferring higher prices offers few attractions for politicians, for the benefits of the measure could be enjoyed by rural opponents and supporters alike. The benefits could not be restricted to the faithful or withheld from the politically disloyal. Pricing policies therefore cannot be employed by politicians to organize political followings.

Project-based policies suffer less from this liability. Officials can exercise discretion in locating projects; they can also exercise discretion in staffing them. Such discretion allows them to bestow benefits selectively on those whose political support they desire. Politicians are therefore more likely to be attracted to project-based policies as a measure of rural development.

The relative political utility of projects explains several otherwise puzzling features of government agricultural investments. One is the tendency to construct too many projects, given the budgetary resources available. A reason for this proliferation is that governments often wish to ensure that officials in each administrative district or electoral constituency have access to resources with which to secure a political backing.[14] Another tendency is to hire too large a staff or a staff that is technically untrained, thus undercutting the viability of the projects. A reason for this is that jobs on projects—and jobs in many of the bureaucracies involved with agricultural programs, for that matter—represent political plums, given by those in charge of the programs to their political followers. State farms in Ghana were staffed by the youth brigade of the ruling Convention People's Party, and the cooperative societies in Zambia were formed and operated by the local and constituency level units of the governing party, to offer just two examples of the link between staffing and political organization. . . .

Disorganizing the Rural Opposition

We have seen that government policies are often aimed at establishing low prices for agricultural products. Particularly in the market for cash crops, governments maintain monopsonistic agencies and use their market power to lower product prices. They therefore impose deprivations on all producers. What is interesting, however, is that they return to selected members of the farm community a portion of the resources which they thus exact. Some of the earnings taxed from farmers are returned to a privileged few, in the form of subsidies for farm inputs. While imposing collective deprivations, governments thus confer selective benefits.

These benefits serve as side-payments: they compensate selected members of the rural sector for the losses they sustain as a consequence of the government's programs. They thereby make it in the private interests of particular members of the rural sector to abide by policies that are harmful to rural dwellers as a whole. By so doing, they secure the defection of favored farmers from a potential rural opposition and their adherence to the governing coalition, which implements agricultural programs that are harmful to farming as a whole. . . .

It should be noted, incidentally, that the bestowal of privileged access to farm inputs was a technique employed by the colonial governments as well. And the exchange of political loyalty for access to these inputs was widely recognized to be part of the bargain. In Northern and Southern Rhodesia, for example, the colonial governments used revenues secured by their monopsonistic maize marketing agency to subsidize the costs of inputs, which they then lavished upon a relatively small number of so-called improved or progressive farmers. The nationalist movements presciently labeled these farmers stooges of the colonial regimes. They saw that the apportionment of the inputs had been employed to separate the interests of these privileged farmers from the interests of the mass of rural producers and to detach their political loyalties from those of their fellow Africans.

By conferring selective benefits in the markets for farm inputs while imposing collective deprivations in the markets for products, governments secure the deference of a privileged few to programs that are harmful to the interests of most farmers. By politicizing farm-input programs and making access to their benefits contingent upon political loyalty, the governments secure acquiescence to those in power and compliance with their policies. The political efficacy of these measures is underscored by the fact that they are targeted to the large producers, who have the most to gain from a change in pricing policy and who might otherwise provide the leadership for efforts on the part of farmers to alter the agricultural policies of their governments. . . .

CONCLUSION

Governments in Africa, like governments elsewhere in the developing world, intervene in agricultural markets in ways that violate the interests of most farmers. They tend to adopt low-price policies for farm products; they tend to increase the prices farmers must pay for the goods they consume. And while they subsidize the prices of goods that farmers use in production, the benefits of these subsidies are appropriated by the richer few. In addition, the farm policies of African governments are characterized by a stress on projects rather than prices; when price policies are used, by a preference for lowering farm costs rather than increasing farm revenues; and by widespread economic inefficiency.

I have examined several political explanations for this configuration of agricultural policies. I conclude by commenting on their durability.

The pattern of price interventions, I have argued, represents the terms of a political pact among organized political interests, the costs of which are transferred to unorganized interests who are excluded from the price-setting coalition. Members of the pact are labor, industry, and government; small-scale farmers constitute its victims; and large-scale farmers stand as passive allies, politically neutralized through subsidy programs.

No member of the winning coalition possesses an incentive to alter its political demands unilaterally. Organized labor, for example, will not unilaterally alter its demand for cheap food. Nor will industry call for reforms that raise food prices, and thus wages, unless other members of the coalition make credible commitments to offsetting concessions. In the short term, then, the coalition and the price structure that supports it appear stable.

Over the longer run, however, the structure of the payoffs achieved by the coalition changes. Farmers adjust; in response to pricing policies, they produce less. The result in food markets is lower supplies at higher prices. The result in export markets is fewer exports and less foreign exchange. The costs which once were externalized upon the unorganized agrarian sector are now internalized, through the operation of markets, onto the dominant coalition. The farmers have transferred the costs of the political settlement to the intended beneficiaries. And as these costs mount, the pact among them becomes less stable.

As the payoffs from this basis for governance in Africa erode, opportunities arise for the introduction of new pricing policies. And as the costs of the present policies are disproportionately borne by one of the more influential of the coalition partners, the governments themselves, the likelihood of policy changes is enhanced. To support low food prices, governments must provide additional supplies, either by subsidizing local production or by financing imports from abroad. But, throughout Africa, states are undergoing a fiscal crisis; they lack both revenues and foreign exchange. One consequence is that governments are less willing or able to bear the costs of current agricultural policies. Another is the reallocation of political power. At moments of fiscal crisis, finance ministers and directors of the central banks gain greater influence over public policy. Moreover, they find allies among foreign donors and international creditors, who pressure governments to make adjustments that will lessen their burden of debt. In league with international agencies, these figures have assumed greater influence over public policy.

The set of public policies described in this paper have thus formed the basis for a political pact among organized interests. But they have set in motion economic forces which erode their economic and political value. Moreover, the fiscal crisis in contemporary Africa has restructured power relations within African governments and has brought new players into the policymaking process. The result is that the commitment to these policies may not be stable and they may in fact be subject to change.

NOTES

1. See Doris J. Jansen, "Agricultural Pricing Policy in Sub-Saharan Africa of the 1970s," unpublished paper, 1980 (mimeo.); Christopher David (Gerrard, "Economic Development, Government Controlled Markets, and External Trade in Food Grains: The Case of Four Countries in East Africa," Ph.D. dissertation, University of Minnesota, 1981; and Doris Jansen Dodge,

Agricultural Policy and Performance in Zambia (Berkeley: Institute of International Studies, 1977).

2. Frances Hill, "Experiments with a Public Sector Peasantry," *African Studies Review* 20 (1977):25–41; and Werner Roider, *Farm Settlements for Socio-Economic Development: The Western Nigerian Case* (Munich: Weltforum, 1971).

3. International Bank for Reconstruction and Development, *Accelerated Development in Sub-Saharan Africa: An Agenda for Action* (Washington, D.C.: IBRD, 1981); and Franz Pick, *Pick's Currency Yearbook, 1976–1977* (New York: Pick Publishing, 1978).

4. J. Dirck Stryker, "Ghana Agriculture," paper for the West African Regional Project, 1975 (mimeo.); Scott R. Pearson, Gerald C. Nelson, and J. Dirck Stryker, "Incentives and Comparative Advantage in Ghanaian Industry and Agriculture," paper for the West African Regional Project, 1976 (mimeo.); International Bank for Reconstruction and Development, *Kenya: Into the Second Decade* (Washington, D.C.: IBRD, 1975); and International Bank for Reconstruction and Development, *Ivory Coast: The Challenge of Success* (Washington, D.C.: IBRD, 1978).

5. Ghana, *Report of the Commission of Enquiry into the Local Purchasing of Cocoa* (Accra: Government Printer, 1967); and Tony Killick, *Development Economics in Action: A Study of Economic Policies in Ghana* (New York: St. Martin's Press, 1978), p. 171.

6. Stryker, "Ghana Agriculture"; C. K. Kline, D. A. G. Green, Roy L. Donahue, and B. A. Stout, *Industrialization in an Open Economy: Nigeria 1945–1966* (Cambridge, England: Cambridge University Press).

7. See, for example, David Onaburekhale Ekhomu, "National Food Policies and Bureaucracies in Nigeria: Legitimization, Implementation, and Evaluation," paper presented at the African Studies Association Convention, Baltimore, Maryland, 1978 (mimeo.).

8. See David M. Leonard, *Reaching the Peasant Farmer: Organization Theory and Practice in Kenya* (Chicago: University of Chicago Press, 1977); and H. U. E. Van Velzen, "Staff, Kulaks and Peasants:" in Lionel Cliffe and John Saul, eds., *Socialism in Africa*, vol. 2 (Dar es Salaam: East African Publishing House, 1973).

9. Raj Krishna, "Agricultural Price Policy and Economic Development" in M. Southworth and Bruce F. Johnston, eds., *Agricultural Development and Economic Growth* (Ithaca: Cornell University Press); U.S. General Accounting Office, *Disincentives to Agricultural Production in Developing Countries* (Washington, D.C.: Government Printer 1975); Carl Gotsch and Gilbert Brow, "Prices, Taxes and Subsidies in Pakistan Agriculture, 1960–1976:" World Bank Staff Working Paper no. 387 (Washington, D.C.: World Bank, 1980); Keith Griffin, *The Green Revolution: An Economic Analysis* (Geneva: United Nations Research Institute, 1972); Michael Lipton, *Why Poor People Stay Poor: Urban Bias in World Development* (Cambridge, Mass.: Harvard University Press, 1977).

10. Hiromitsu Kaneda and Bruce F. Johnston, "Urban Food Expenditure Patterns in Tropical Africa," *Food Research Institute Studies* 2 (1961):229–75.

11. Scott R. Pearson, J. Dirck Stryker, and Charles P. Humphreys, *Rice in West Africa* (Stanford: Stanford University Press, 1981).

12. A more systematic analysis of pressure-group politics, based on more rigorous microeconomic foundations, is contained in Robert H. Bates and William P. Rogerson, "Agriculture in Development: A Coalitional Analysis," *Public Choice* 35 (1980): 513–27; and Bates, *Markets and States*. The first deals primarily with the demand for price intervention; the second, with the supply. Both attempt to explain the relative inefficacy of farmers in pressure-group

politics in the developing areas. A major source of relevant theorizing for this portion of the analysis is the capture-theory approach to industrial regulation. See George Stigler, "The Theory of Economic Regulation, *Bell Journal of Economics and Management Science* 3 (1971):3–21; Sam Peltzman, "Toward a More General Theory of Regulation," *Journal of Law and Economics* 19 (1976):211–40.

13. See Robert H. Bates, *Rural Responses to Industrialization: A Study of Village Zambia* (New Haven: Yale University Press, 1978).

14. See Bates, *Rural Responses*; Jerome C. Wells, *Agricultural Policy and Economic Growth in Nigeria, 1962–1968* (Ibadan: Oxford University Press for the Nigerian Institute of Social Science and Economic Research, 1974); Alfred John Dadson, "Socialized Agriculture in Ghana, 1962–1965," Ph.D. dissertation, Harvard University, 1970.

25

· · · · · · ·

Rent-Seeking or Dependency
as Explanations of
Why Poor People Stay Poor

· · · · · · ·

ERICH WEEDE

In this chapter, Erich Weede argues that although dependency theory seems to be popular because it blames the privileged for making or keeping poor people poor, perhaps a more valid reason lies in the price distortion caused by rent-seeking. Weede explains that rent-seeking is an attempt to distort markets and avoid competition. Monopolists will try to maximize their profits by selling products or services at prices above what would be found in a competitive market. Governments tolerate the distortions because they derive benefits (political, economic, and social) from them. Weede further explains that in this struggle over distributional benefits, the poor most often lose. The quickest path to ending rent-seeking, according to the author, is to remove trade impediments and let the market system set prices. Weede argues that open borders will undermine rent-seeking because most monopolies involved in this distributional struggle are national, not international. Using different terminology, proponents of world-system theory argue that simply opening borders would result in the replacement of domestic rent-seeking corporations with transnational rent-seeking organizations. This chapter presents an alternative paradigm to dependency theory (Part 4 in this volume), but Weede concludes that there have not been sufficient cross-national studies to judge the rent-seeking approach.

According to the World Bank (1981:18), "in 1980 about 750 million people lived in absolute poverty in the developing world, about 33 per cent of its population (these estimates exclude China)." In a more optimistic scenario

---

Reprinted with permission *International Sociology*, 1, 4 (1986):421–441.

the World Bank hopes for a reduction of this number to 630 million in two decades or 18 per cent of the LDC population outside of China; in a more pessimistic scenario the Bank conceives of 850 million living in absolute poverty in the year 2000. Whether optimistic or pessimistic scenarios become true, the absolute number of poor people is likely to remain terribly high. Optimism amounts to hoping for a falling proportion of mankind suffering from absolute poverty and hardly at all to hoping for a reduction in numbers. Many truly poor people do stay poor. Why?

For some time dependency theorists have suggested that the persistence of Third World poverty is not accidental, that somebody makes or keeps poor people poor, that Northern affluence and Southern poverty are just two faces of a single coin. While dependency theorists disagree among themselves on exactly which mechanisms maintain Third World poverty, they tend to shift responsibility for poverty from the poor to the privileged. Since the general idea that the privileged make or keep poor people poor is so plausible, criticism of dependency theories—all of which (like dependency theory) comes from more or less privileged persons—sounds implausible, self-serving and even immoral. That is why I cannot imagine that dependency theories will lose their grip on the minds of people because of anomalies, falsification, or destructive criticism. Pointing to evidence which is incompatible with dependency theories is important, because it forces dependency theorists to withdraw on this or on that intellectual front, but it does not suffice to overcome the paradigm. Only a competing paradigm can do so.

The theory of the rent-seeking society offers such a competing paradigm. Moreover, adherents of rent-seeking and dependency theories do agree on the general notion that the privileged make or keep poor people poor. Therefore the rent-seeking approach looks as plausible as the dependency paradigm. Of course, dependency theories and the rent-seeking approach do differ in many important respects. At best, dependency theorists demonstrate "benign neglect" for micro-economic theory despite the fact that economists find it easier to agree on micro-economic theory than on macro-economic theory (see Bell and Kristol 1981), and despite the widespread feeling that economics is the "queen of the social sciences." By contrast, the rent-seeking approach is not only compatible with micro-economic theory, but should be conceived of as a broadening and deepening of this theory.

In the next sections I shall outline what dependency and rent-seeking theories do assert, what evidence is available for a preliminary evaluation of these theories, what the policy implications of these theories are, and why I believe rent-seeking theory to be superior to dependency theories. Wherever possible, I shall give special attention to cross-national analyses of economic growth rates or income distribution. Given the scope and urgency of the global poverty problem there is little hope in reducing it without more economic growth in poor countries (Ahluwalia, Carter and Chenery 1979) or without equalising size distributions of income in many or most of them.

Since I compare an older and—albeit only outside of the discipline of economics!—more established paradigm, dependency, with a younger or even still nascent one, rent-seeking, the reader should not be surprised that there is more quantitative and cross-national evidence on dependency theories than on rent-seeking, that dependency theories tend to suffer from anomalies while the rent-seeking approach tends to suffer from a dearth of evidence. Such a state of affairs is typical when a new paradigm aspires to replace an older one (see Kuhn 1962).

DEPENDENCY, GROWTH, AND INEQUALITY

Dependency theorists agree with one another that poor people stay poor because privileged people contribute to and maintain their poverty, because privileged nations somehow benefit from the international economic order at the expense of poor nations. But they disagree with each other on exactly how worldwide inequity is created and maintained. I shall restrict myself to a discussion of those three dependency theories[1] which so far have received most scrutiny in quantitative and cross-national research on economic growth and income inequality: Galtungs's (1971) "structural theory of imperialism," Wallerstein's (1974, 1979, 1980) world-system approach which has been translated into quantitative research designs by an adherent of the theory (Rubinson 1976, 1977), and Bornschier's (1980a, 1980b; Bornschier and Ballmer-Cao 1979) view that investment dependence and penetration of LDCs by multinational corporations contribute to stagnation and inequality.

According to Galtung (1971), developing countries suffer from vertical trade and feudal interaction patterns. Vertical trade refers to the fact that most rich, industrialised and powerful countries tend to import raw materials, but to export processed goods, while LDCs demonstrate the reverse pattern. In Galtung's view, the production of raw materials in LDCs creates few positive spill-overs; sometimes the eventual exhaustion of mineral deposits will leave nothing behind but a hole in the ground. But production of sophisticated processed goods in the top-dog nations necessarily contributes to human capital formation. Workers and management learn new skills which tend to remain useful even when production is shifted from one good to another. In essence, the worldwide division of labour, which concentrates manufacturing and processing, and in particular sophisticated processing, in some nations and extraction and agricultural raw material production in others is the root cause of more privileged standards of living in wealthy industrial societies and of deprivation in LDCs. The need for a broad human capital base in sophisticated industrial economies exerts some equalising pressure in these countries. Since raw material extraction or production favours landed property owners, the global division of labour permits a very unequal distribution of income in LDCs.

Galtung's mechanism of vertical trade is supplemented by feudal interaction patterns. By and large, export earnings of many less developed countries derive from a very small number of products; sometimes a single product accounts for most export earnings. Moreover, commodity concentration often is accompanied by partner concentration. For example, some Central American "banana republics" do not only depend on the export of bananas, but also suffer from exporting most of them to the US market where they also buy most of their imports. Comparable degrees of dependency characterise the relationship between some former French colonies in Africa and France. Even where the pattern is less obvious, commodity concentration and partner concentration create opportunities for privileged nations to keep poor peoples poor.

This crude sketch of Galtung's theory suffices to raise a number of questions. Countries like Australia or Canada, and most important of all, the United States, do not really fit the theory. Australia, Canada and even the US do too well on exporting raw materials or agricultural products. So do some sparsely populated OPEC nations, which even enjoy (close to) tax-free welfare states. But I do not want to evaluate Galtung's "structural theory of imperialism" by pointing to a couple of anomalies. After all, "all theories are born refuted" (Kuhn 1962; Lakatos 1968:163). More important than the existence of anomalies is whether the independent variables of his theory, which Galtung already operationalised himself, do or do not contribute to the explanation of cross-national patterns of economic growth or income inequality. Does the import of (sophisticated) processed goods and the export of raw materials reduce the growth prospects of LDCs and simultaneously contribute to income inequality? Do export commodity concentration and partner concentration in trade decrease economic growth rates, but increase income inequality?

Before I attempt to summarise the empirical evidence on Galtung's theory, I want to continue my sketch or various lines of reasoning within a dependency paradigm. According to Wallerstein (1974:406), "the functioning of a capitalist world economy requires that groups pursue their economic interests within a single world market while seeking to distort this market for their benefit by organising to exert influence on states, some of which are more powerful than others but none of which controls the market in its entirety." In this view, some groups and nations succeed in distorting markets and rigging prices to their own benefit and at the expense of other groups and nations.[2]

In his effort to translate this general idea into quantitative research designs, Rubinson (1977:7) argued that a strong state "is able to control the activities of the population within its boundaries . . . one indicator of state strength is the government revenues of a state as a proportion of GNP. . . This indicator measures the degree to which the total economic resources of the country are available to the state." In addition to a domestic dimension of state strength, there is an international dimension of it. While Rubinson (1976, 1977) discusses and applies a variety of indicators, some of the most potent ones are trade, i.e., import and/or export shares of GNP. To summarize the Wallerstein/Rubinson perspective: states are most likely and able to promote economic growth and income equalisation, if they exercise much control of economic activities within their borders, as indicated by government revenue to GDP or GNP proportions, and if they depend little on the vicissitudes of the world market, as indicated by low trade to GNP shares.

Finally, there is a third perspective. According to Bornschier (1980a, 1980b; Bornschier and Ballmer-Cao 1979), multinational corporations (henceforth abbreviated MNCs) are the main culprits for Third World poverty. LDCs heavily depend on foreign investment, most of which is supplied by MNCs. In the short run, the inflow of MNC-capital contributes to investment and growth. In the long run, however, MNCs succeed in getting more out of LDCs than they put in, i.e., in decapitalising Third World economies. Rigging of the terms of trade in *intra*-MNC, but simultaneously *inter*national trade is one of the mechanisms whereby such decapitalisation can be achieved. The more powerful MNCs are in a less developed economy, the worse its growth prospects become. But MNCs do even more harm than that in LDCs. Since MNCs apply capital-intensive production technologies, which do not need much local and unskilled labour input, since they tend to produce for the more privileged classes in LDCs only and ally themselves with them politically, MNC penetration reinforces income inequality too.

This crude sketch of three dependency explanations of why poor people stay poor has yielded a list of six independent variables: vertical trade (or export of raw materials and import of processed goods), export commodity concentration, trade partner concentration, low government revenues as a proportion of GNP, high trade to GNP proportions, and strong MNC penetration. According to the above discussed dependency theories, all of these variables should simultaneously decrease growth and increase inequality and thereby hurt the poor. Do they?

Adherents and opponents of dependency theories did a lot of cross-national and cross-sectional work. So, there is *some* evidence that LDCs, which are extraordinarily dependent on exporting raw materials and importing processed goods or which suffer from severe export commodity concentration and trade partner concentration, do indeed demonstrate greater income inequality and/or grow more slowly than other nations (Alschuler 1976: Galtung 1971; Rubinson 1977; Stokes and Jafree 1982; Walleri 1978a, 1978b). But there are also studies which cast a much less favourable light on Galtung's (1971) "structural theory of imperialism" (Bradshaw 1985a;[3] Delacroix 1977; Delacroix and Ragin 1978, 1981;[4] Kaufmann et al 1975; Ray and Webster 1978; Weede 1981, 1982; Weede and Tiefenbach 1981a, 1981b). Similarly, there is *some* evidence for a relationship between low government revenue/GDP or high trade/GNP ratios, on the one hand, and less economic growth and more income inequality, on the other (Bornschier 1980a; Bornschier, Chase-Dunn and Rubinson 1978; Meyer and Hannan 1979; Rubinson 1976, 1977; Rubinson and Quinlan 1977). But there are also other studies which call these findings, and thereby the Wallerstein-Rubinson line of reasoning, into question (Landau 1983; Marsden 1983; Weede 1980, 1981, 1982; Weede and Tiefenbach 1981a, 1981b). Finally, there is *some* evidence for a negative impact of investment dependence, or MNC penetration, on economic growth and income equality (Bornschier 1980a, 1980b, 1981a, 1982; Bornschier and Ballmer-Cao 1979; Chase-Dunn 1975; Gobalet and Diamond 1979). But again there are studies which do not support these contentions (Bradshaw 1985a:202, 1985b:93–94; Delacroix and Ragin 1981; Jackman 1982; Muller 1984; Weede 1981, 1982; Weede and Tiefenbach 1981a, 1981b). Even a recent study by Bornschier (1985) himself concedes that the negative effects of MNC penetration on economic growth are no longer significant in the late 1970s.

Since these studies differ in sample size, period of observation, operationalisation of variables, and specification of regression equations, it is difficult to explain their inconsistent findings. In my view, it is not essential to do so for the purposes of this paper. The mere fact of contradictory findings, instead of robust support in favour of dependency theories, justifies some doubt. Moreover, most studies neglect competing explanations of cross-national differences of growth rates or income inequality and thereby risk some specification error. If one takes into account that income inequality and economic growth demonstrate curvilinear and non-monotonic relationships with the level of economic development, that human capital formation (as assessed by literacy, school enrolment ratios or even military participation ratios) contributes to growth and equality, that investment contributes to growth, then empirical support for dependency theories tends to wither away (Weede 1981, 1982; Weede and Tiefenbach 1981a, 1981b).[5] While the research strategy outlined above suffices to call dependency theories into question, this strategy is not necessary in order to arrive at similar conclusions (see Delacroix 1977; Muller 1984; Ray and Webster 1978). Although it is always conceivable that a research programme in trouble—as dependency currently is—may recover and score better and more lasting explanatory success in the future than in the past, looking for alternative and possibly better explanations of why poor people stay poor seems justified.

RENT-SEEKING, GROWTH AND INEQUALITY

Economists (Buchanan, Tollison and Tullock 1980; Tollison 1982: 577) define rent as "a payment to a resource owner above the amount his resources could command in their next best alternative use." In a truly competitive market where everyone is a price-taker rents do not exist. Therefore rent-seeking is an attempt to distort markets and to evade competition. Where rent-seeking is on the rampage, we refer to rent-seeking societies. The fundamental problem of rent-seeking societies is that they suffer from a serious distortion of incentives. There are strong incentives to engage in distributional struggles and to seek contrived transfers, but comparatively weak incentives to engage in productive and growth-promoting activities. While rent-seeking decreases growth, there is no reason to expect the poor to be particularly successful in distributional struggles.

In order to elaborate on rent-seeking, let us look to monopolies. Typically, monopolists maximise their profits by supplying smaller quantities at higher prices than a competitive market would do. Buyers pay more than they should and the monopolist enjoys his rent. The monopoly implies three important effects. First, there is a transfer of income from buyers or consumers to the monopolist. Since buyers or consumers are often poorer than the monopolist, this transfer of income tends to be regressive. Second, some people will suffer a welfare loss because of the monopoly without a corresponding improvement for someone else. Some people who would have bought a product at competitive prices simply stop buying it at higher monopoly prices. While these people suffer a welfare loss— technically labelled deadweight loss—not even the monopolist gains from it. He is unable to exploit those who stop buying. Finally, there is the third and probably worst effect of monopolies. Since monopolies are profitable for those who can gain them, many would-be monopolists invest resources in attempts to become monopolists. Most of these attempts must be in vain. Still, even unsuccessful attempts to become a monopolist consume resources which thereafter are no longer available for productive purposes. The fiercer the fight among monopoly contenders, the more resources are wasted for the only purpose of neutralising the efforts of other contenders.[6]

Cartels are little better than monopolies. The purpose remains the same: to maximise profits by selling (lower quantities) at higher prices. In general, there still is the regressive transfer from poorer buyers or consumers to richer cartel members. The consumer surplus of those who are ready to pay competitive prices, but not cartel prices, still disappears. In particular if illegal, cartelisation still requires resources. But, in contrast to monopolies, cartels require collective action. Seen from the perspective of a group of producers of a particular good, a cartel provides a collective good. If higher prices can be imposed on consumers, every producer receives some rental income. For simplicity's sake, let us assume that cartelisation is illegal and requires bribing politicians and bureaucrats into looking the other way.[7] Then there is a freeriding tendency. Every producer would like to benefit from the cartel, but to make other producers pay for it. According to Olson (1965, 1982), the prospects for the provision of collective goods and for overcoming free-riding tendencies are much better in small groups than in large groups.[8] That is why oligopolists should find cartelisation easier than a multitude of small and scattered producers. Elitist interests always enjoy a headstart in the cartelisation game. Equalisation by cartelisation is extremely unlikely. Since cartelisation consumes resources and interferes with an efficient allocation and growth, it is a collective bad for society as a whole.

Trade unions are a special type of distributional coalition or cartel. Since workers belong to large groups, there are strong free-riding tendencies. Therefore workers need skilful political entrepreneurs (Frohlich, Oppenheimer and Young 1971) to guide them[9] and the application of selective incentives and coercion. Moreover, it takes time to organise a union (Olson 1965, 1982). But explaining how trade unions come into existence is not the purpose of this paper. Here the concern is to understand their effects.

Trade unions try to increase the wages or salaries of their members. Since workers are usually poorer than their employers, a transfer of income from employers to workers is progressive. In this respect, unions seem better than most other cartels. In other respects they are not. If workers succeed in obtaining higher wages than they could in a competitive situation, then employers are likely to offer less jobs. Would-be employees in the unionised sector of the economy are thereby driven into the informal sector or even into involuntary unemployment (Hayek 1960; McKenzie and Tullock 1978:256; Olson 1982:201). In order to obtain wages which are inflated by the inclusion of a rental component, workers need to invest resources, ie. they organise themselves, prepare for strikes and prevent their employer from maintaining production with the assistance of non-unionised and possibly previously unemployed labour. Since employers dislike excessive wages and a profit squeeze, employers are likely to invest some resources in cancelling out the effects of workers' efforts. Whoever wins this struggle, some resources will simply be wasted.

Rent-seeking requires government acquiesence or, "better" still, support. Most monopolies or cartels are organised at the national level, not on a global scale. Therefore national governments could easily restore competition by abolishing all tariffs and non-tariff barriers to international trade. Foreign producers could and would sell below monopoly or cartel prices and cause these prices to collapse and corresponding rents to disappear. Similarly, wide open borders for foreign labour would contribute to undermining union power. While governments *could* decrease rent-seeking, they often contribute to it by granting monopolies, by organising cartels, by helping trade unions, by subsidising some activities and applying discriminatory taxation against others, by interfering with international trade and migration. That is why Tullock (1980:211) deplores: "One or the major activities of modern governments is the granting of special privileges to various groups of politically influential people." Similarly, Buchanan (1980:9) claims: "Rent-seeking activity is directly related to the scope and range of government activity in the economy, to the relative size of the public sector."

Rent-seeking is not only wasteful. It is contagious. Imagine that there is a monopoly or cartel in some sector of the economy which produces goods, like steel, which serve as important inputs to the production of other goods, say cars or trucks. Expensive inputs tend to make domestic industries uncompetitive compared with foreign rivals. If the government has condoned a monopoly or cartel of steel producers, it is likely to come under pressure from steel-consuming industries to protect domestic markets and/or to subsidise exports. In granting protection, the government makes it easier or more worthwhile for the industries concerned to become cartelised too. So the evil spreads.

The fundamental problem in rent-seeking societies is that economic actors and groups invest too many resources in capturing rents and too little in productive activities. While rent-seeking is obviously harmful to growth and prosperity, there is no reason to expect it to contribute to equity or equality. For small, elitist, privileged groups enjoy a headstart in the game. The strong are likely to win distributional struggles and the poor are likely to lose them. Olson (1982:175) puts this proposition in these words: "There is greater inequality . . . in the opportunity to create distributional coalitions"—whose purpose is rent-seeking (author's comment)—"than there is in the inherent productive abilities of people."

So far the discussion of rent-seeking has been rather abstract and removed from the problems of less developed countries. This need not be so. Without using the term rent-seeking, Lipton (1977) in his seminal book *Why Poor People Stay Poor* nevertheless analyses the phenomenon. In his view, there is a conflict of interest between urban and rural populations in LDCs which urban dwellers tend to decide in their favour. In a conflict of interest between groups the recipe for successful collective action and overcoming resistance is to generate concentrated gains for a relatively small group and diffused and preferably invisible losses for a much larger group (Olson 1965). In most LDCs, by far the largest group is the rural population tilling the land. In general, this rural-agrarian population is poorer than the urban population. If the smaller, relatively more privileged, urban population could succeed in rigging the urban-rural terms of trade, the recipe of concentrated gains and diffused losses would be realised.[10] That is why an incentive for urban exploitation of their rural brethren exists.

It is much easier for urban people to organise themselves for the promotion of their collective interests than for scattered rural-agrarian people. Karl Marx (1852, 1969) knew it long ago. Urban interests are concentrated in small, but densely populated, areas. Rural interests in LDCs are widely scattered and often suffer from poor transportation and communication facilities. The higher cost of collective action in the underdeveloped countryside makes a rural defence of agrarian interest less likely.

A comparatively small number of urban producers in the LDCs finds little difficulty in creating an informal cartel if the law should not permit a formal one. It is much easier for urban factory workers to unionise than for scattered rural people, some of whom may be tenants or sharecroppers. Nevertheless, these different rural people do share an interest in high prices for whatever they sell. Finally, the largely urban public sector with its bureaucratic structure tends to be born organised for collective action. Aggregation of these somewhat organised urban interests is relatively easy. Urban employers and manufacturers, urban workers and largely urban civil servants and politicians do share an interest in cheap food to be supplied from the rural hinterland to the cities. Obviously, distorted urban-rural terms of trade—i.e. artificially low prices for food and artificially high prices for urban products—depend on governmental policies and some degree of state interference with international trade. If farmers were free to sell their products to highest bidding buyers from anywhere inside or outside the country, then food prices could not be distorted downwards. But prohibition of exports or state-buying monopolies may prevent such harmful getting in the way of urban interests. Differential degrees of unionisation and corresponding urban-rural wage differentials also contribute to the distortion of urban-rural terms of trade and simultaneously decrease the labour absorption capacity of unionised, urban sectors.

Why should ruling politicians contribute to or at least tolerate some distortion of urban-rural terms of trade in LDCs? There are a number of reasons. First, but possibly least important, such a distortion benefits themselves by reducing their cost of living. Second, it is much easier for a political entrepreneur to build a power base from better organised groups than from amorphous groups. The costs of resource mobilisation for political action can be dramatically cut by assembling a coalition of previously existing interest groups or organisations compared with calling them into existence in the first place (Oberschall 1973). Third, most rulers prefer poverty, disorder and violence to occur out of sight, if they cannot prevent it. They prefer starvation in remote villages to an urban riot in front of the presidential palace. Fourth, since unorganised rural-agrarian groups in remote parts of the country cannot effectively fight back (short of guerilla war, which probably requires some foreign help; see Gurr 1968; Gurr and Duvall 1973), it may even be politically stabilising to redistribute from the rural poor to the somewhat better-off urban dwellers.

Sometimes low food prices and government action to achieve them are rationalised by state support for agriculture such as subsidising pesticides or fertilisers. In theory this is fine. In practice it often is not. Subsidisation makes inputs appear cheaper than they are. So demand is bound to increase. In LDCs it usually cannot be met. Then somebody has to decide which farmers obtain the subsidised inputs and which ones do not. This somebody is likely to be a bureaucrat or local politician. Even if honest—and that is a big if—allocation is likely to be discriminatory. Bureaucrats want to be properly approached. They like written applications or might even be legally required to insist on them. The smallest and poorest farmers in the remotest areas are least likely to pass this hurdle. Richer and bigger farmers are more likely to find somebody in their family or among their personal friends who is able to write an application or to fill out a form. Since Third World bureaucrats or local politicians rarely enjoy affluence, even if their incomes are *much* higher than those of ordinary peasants, tenants or share-croppers, there must be a strong temptation to accept gifts or bribes for allocations of subsidised fertilisers or pesticides. If the worst comes to the worst, what has been intended as a subsidy for agriculture turns into a subsidy for bureaucrats and/or politicians and into an incentive for corruption.

Overvaluation of the domestic currency is a useful tool for rigging urban-rural terms of trade. It automatically reduces farmers' export prospects and simultaneously benefits mostly urban consumers of imported goods. Since overvaluation necessarily reduces the competitiveness of urban industries and tends to suck in imports, a poor country with an overvalued currency is likely to experience some balance of payments problems. To handle it and to protect domestic industry, what an Indian newspaper once termed "permit, license, quota Raj" is created. Such regulations boost bureaucratic employment and promotion opportunities to the benefit of some urban people. They provide gratifying rents for those who obtain them. Take an import licence, for example. Even after illegal payments to bureaucrats or politicians, such a licence may still be a source of nice profits. The licensed importer and bureaucrats or politicians in regulatory agencies share the rent which has been created by the regulation of foreign trade.

As Lipton (1977, 1984) pointed out, distorting the urban-rural terms of trade in LDCs is closely related to inefficient development strategies. Often investment is characterised by an urban bias which neglects factor scarcities in LDCs. Except for capital surplus oil exporters, most LDCs suffer from a scarcity of capital, but command an ample supply of unskilled or even semiskilled labour. Urban investments often outperform rural investments in raising labour productivity. But rural investments generally outperform urban ones in capital productivity. Where capital is scarce and labour is not, it is more important to maximise productivity per unit of capital than per unit of labour. Nevertheless, many LDCs prefer urban investments as a matter of principle and neglect rural ones. Therefore, they get lower rates of growth than they could.

While a capital-intensive strategy of industrialisation retards development, it pleases some industrialists and unionised urban labour aristocracies, who succeed in obtaining higher wages. Simultaneously, such higher wages slow down the labour absorption capacity of the modern industrial sector and thereby condemn those not yet employed there to remain in the agricultural or in the urban-informal sector, both of which contain the bulk of absolutely poor people in LDCs.

Rent-seeking is bad for society and growth since it distorts incentives and interferes with efficient resource allocation. In LDCs most rents benefit urban groups and harm rural-agrarian ones because the latter find it hard to organise themselves for collective action and to become included in prevailing distributional coalitions. In rent-seeking societies there is a protracted distributional struggle where the poorest rural groups are destined to become losers. Equity loses alongside efficiency.

In my view, all societies are to some degree afflicted by rent-seeking. After all the generation and distribution of rents is what makes politics and government attractive for many (or most?) active participants.[11] But societies differ in the degree to which they tolerate or encourage rent-seeking. Is there any quantitative evidence that those LDCs, which permit more rent-seeking, grow more slowly than others without at least generating a more equal distribution of income? While there is not much evidence, the existing evidence is fairly strong.

There is no rent-seeking without price distortion. Therefore an index of price distortion is simultaneously an index of rent-seeking. For the 1970s and 31 LDCs the World Bank (1983:57–63) provides such an index. The Bank's price distortion index "concentrates on distortions in the prices of foreign exchange, capital, labour, and infrastructural services (particularly power)." If the trade-weighted exchange rate of an LDC currency appreciates or does not depreciate despite higher inflation at home than abroad, if competitiveness is thereby eroded, this is simultaneously a cue to the presence of price distortions and a cause for interfering with international trade, which is another cue to the existence of price distortions. Distortion of capital prices is assumed to exist wherever real interest rates are negative. Minimum wage laws, high social security taxes and cheap provision of infrastructural services by state agencies are further indications of price distortions and rent-seeking.

In the 1970s the World Bank's (1983:57–63) price distortion index alone explains about one third of the variance in GDP growth rates. But price distortion is *not* significantly correlated with income inequality. While certainly in need of replication in larger samples and for different periods of observation,[12] the reported correlation is much stronger than what dependency theory can offer. Moreover, if one introduces those control variables, which make effects hypothesised by dependency theorists wither away, then the negative impact of price distortions on growth remains essentially as it was in bivariate analysis and the relationship between price distortions and equality remains close to zero and insignificant (Weede 1986a).

All societies are likely to be somewhat afflicted by rent-seeking, but not to an equal degree. Political system characteristics should be expected to influence the amount of rent-seeking in societies. Political democracy offers civil liberties and political rights to everyone. Necessarily this includes the right to create distributional coalitions or to participate in them. Because of its egalitarianism and liberty, democracy *may* increase the number of players in the rent-seeking game. But I do not want to argue that democracy *per se* retards economic growth and development in LDCs, as many previous writers have argued (Adelman and Morris 1967:202; Andreski 1969:266; Huntington and Dominguez 1975:61; Huntington and Nelson 1975:23; Marsh 1979: 240). If one properly controls for the level of economic development, for investment and human capital formation, then democracy is not significantly related to economic growth rates (Weede 1983a, 1983b), nor to income inequality (Weede and Tiefenbach 1981a).[13]

If political democracy *enables* more people to participate in the rent-seeking game than authoritarian or totalitarian systems do, how can democracies avoid retarding growth? The answer must be that many people even in democracies resist the temptation to join distributional coalitions and to seek contrived transfers. But there might be important differences among democracies in this respect. While democracy *per se* need not retard growth, democracy in combination with some other characteristic, which reinforces rent-seeking, still might do so.

The incentive to seek rents does not only depend on governmental tolerance for interest groups and their activities, but also on the degree of state interference in the economy (Buchanan 1980:9). By and large, capturing rents needs some governmental assistance by establishing barriers to entry for domestic or, probably more often, foreign competitors. That is why rent-seeking requires not only a permissive environment for the formation of distributional coalitions, but simultaneously strong government control of and interference in the economy. Among those nations or LDCs where government revenues exceed 20 per cent of GDP and thereby indicate an economically strong state, democracy does slow down growth (Weede 1983a, 1983b). This is another piece of quantitative and cross-national evidence which fits a rent-seeking approach. Finally, Singh (1985) reports some cross-national regressions of economic growth rates on a general state intervention index and concludes that state intervention in the economy significantly reduces growth rates.

RENT-SEEKING IN A GLOBAL PERSPECTIVE

Even where a discussion of rent-seeking focuses on the domestic context, it is unavoidable to refer to the world economy as a whole. The deadliest blow to the rent-seeking society, which I can imagine, is to open wide the doors to foreign competition. In essence, rent-seeking requires barriers to entry in order to avoid competition. While international borders are not the only conceivable barriers to entry, they constitute probably the most powerful and persistent ones that actually exist. International borders do not only enable some domestic distributional coalitions to capture rents at the expense of other groups *at home*, but also at the expense of other groups *abroad*. Moreover, the winning group at home may be fairly inclusive, and the losers or losses may be scattered worldwide or nearly so.

Some core insights which have been first developed by a dependency theorist, Emmanuel (1972), may be retained, if one replaces his Marxist or theory of value assumptions, with a rent-seeking perspective. Emmanuel makes four major observations. First, wages in industrialised democracies are much higher than in the Third World, even when different skill levels or work intensities are accounted for. Second, capital is fairly mobile from country to country. That is why capital yields similar returns everywhere, leaving out risk premiums in some politically unstable places. Third, labour is much less mobile than capital is, despite Mexicans pouring into the United States, Algerians into France, Indians or Pakistanis into Britain and Turks into West Germany. Fourth, labour is much better organised in the more developed countries than in the less developed countries. As Emmanuel claimed, these facts are interdependent.

One may improve one's understanding of worldwide rent-seeking, if one applies a similar line of reasoning to Emmanuel's major observations as Becker (1971) did in his work on the economics of discrimination or as Krauss (1983) did more recently. From a global perspective the best solution would be to overlook the Northern (or OECD) or Southern (or Third World) origin of capital and labour; i.e. no nation-state would interfere with movements of capital or labour and newly arrived labour could compete on an equal footing with others.[14] Capital and labour would move to places where the outlook for high returns is best. Obviously, much Southern labour would move to the North and some Northern capital would move to the South. These movements of capital and labour would exert globally equalising pressures on capital and labour returns. In this scenario, some people would gain and others would lose compared with the current status quo. By and large, unskilled and semi-skilled Northern labour would suffer great losses and Southern labour would score major gains. Just imagine the pain in Chicago or Paris and the joy in Calcutta or Lagos, if the gap in wages for, say, garbage collection, started to close, since no one any longer prevented garbage collectors from poor countries from threatening the job security of garbage collectors in rich countries.

Whether the Southern capital would lose and the Northern capital would win depends on one's assessment of the effectiveness of current restrictions on international capital movements. I am inclined to accept Emmanuel's (1972) belief that current restrictions on capital movements are by and large ineffective. Consequently, dismantling them would not make much of a difference. Thus it is evident that the overriding effect of abolishing all state interference with capital and labour movements would be beneficial to Southern labour (or parts of it) and quite harmful to Northern labour.[15]

The above sketched scenario, if it ever came true, would do much more to fight absolute poverty on a global scale than the welfare states in industrialised democracies. As Tullock (1983:64) and Krauss (1983) observed, Northern welfare states cater for, or redistribute within, the most privileged decile or quintile of mankind and simultaneously their redistributive efforts depend on keeping the less fortunate majority of mankind out. But the above sketched scenario is unlikely ever to become true for the obvious reason that relatively well organised and unionised rental income receivers in the North will prevent it from happening.[16]

A brief look at South Africa may clarify the general issue. In South Africa there is job reservation for white citizens and tight control over the influx of blacks and others. Undoubtedly unskilled and semi-skilled whites gain from this at the expense of comparably skilled, but much poorer, blacks. While the South African economy grows more slowly than it conceivably could without discrimination, a bigger slice of the cake easily compensates white rental income receivers for the slower expansion of the cake. OECD citizens may be more like their white South African brethren than most care to think.

OECD welfare states do little to help the poor in LDCs. The efficiency of their aid is questionable (Bauer 1981: Bornschier, Chase-Dunn and Rubinson 1978: Krauss 1983; Singh 1985). The biggest economies (USA and Japan) are niggardly donors. Moreover, they do not concentrate their aid on the poorest countries. On top of this one may even argue with Krauss (1983) that OECD welfare states slow down LDC growth rates *by being welfare states:* first, the welfare state distorts incentives and reduces allocative efficiency and growth (Bernholz 1982; Weede 1984, 1986b). Less growth in rich countries simultaneously impedes the growth prospects of poor countries. Second, the transformation of a capitalist country into a welfare state affects the structure of demand. Public demand partially replaces private demand. Public demand is less likely than private demand to improve the export prospects of LDCs. It is possible that American and Japanese hesitation to become full welfare states according to the Scandinavian model helps LDCs more than generous Scandinavian aid does.

The very existence of a multitude of states on the globe and state interference in the world economy is closely related to the problem of why poor people stay poor. State-supported or state-tolerated price distortions within domestic economies are supplemented by state-generated price distortions within the world economy. Both kinds of distortion keep poor people poor. Now I find myself in partial agreement with a dependency theorist whom I critically evaluated above. Therefore I quote Wallerstein once more:

> The functioning of the capitalist world economy requires that groups pursue their economic interests within a single world market while seeking to distort this market for their benefit by organising to exert influence on states, some of which are more powerful than others but none of which controls the market in its entirety (Wallerstein 1974:406).

I agree with Wallerstein on the harmful impact of price distortions and on the state's role in generating these distortions, although I do not classify these observable aberrations as functional requisites of a capitalist world economy. Nor can I conceive of avoiding the negative effects of price distortions by manipulating these distortions to the benefit of the poor, as Wallerstein (1974, 1979, 1980) seems to imagine.

"POLICY IMPLICATIONS" AND CONCLUSION

Recently, Olson deplored that:

> in these days it takes an enormous amount of stupid policies or bad or unstable institutions to prevent economic development. Unfortunately growth-retarding regimes, policies, and institutions are the rule rather than the exception, and the majority of the world's population lives in poverty (Olson, 1982:175).

From a global perspective, rent-seeking at the expense of other groups at home or abroad is indeed incredibly wasteful and—if one wants to call it so— stupid. Losers always lose much more than winners gain. Still the game looks gratifying to those who win it. The "stupidity" of the game serves winners well. Privileged people keep poor people poor, and must do so if they want to protect their rental incomes because rents rest on barriers to entry. Of course, even without rent-seeking, inequality and poverty would persist, but probably less inequality and almost certainly less poverty.

What can be done about it? In theory, providing a list of policy recommendations is deceptively simple. LDC governments should stop distorting prices for domestic currencies, for food, for capital and for labour. They should open their economies and be less tolerant of the efforts of monopolies and distributional coalitions to distort prices than they are. Industrialised democracies should improve the prospects of the poor by eliminating agrarian and industrial protectionism and discrimination against low wage exporters, by interfering less with worldwide capital and labour flows than they do, by eliminating discrimination between citizens and foreign labour and discrimination between those who already hold some job for some time and new, and possibly foreign and usually poor, applicants. While such reforms are incompatible with welfare states for the most privileged quintile of humanity (Krauss 1983; Tullock 1983), they could help the truly poor, almost all of whom live in the Third World.

But I am aware that provision of *this* list of "policy recommendations" comes close to implying a pessimistic prediction: the poor will not get the help they need. It is possible that there will be some marginal improvements but no wholesale renunciation of rent-seeking. If economic man is a self-interested utility-maximiser, he will always prefer competition among others and rents for himself. The general fulfilment of such human desires is inconceivable. But our uncoordinated efforts do maintain domestic and global rent-seeking societies.

While I do not know how to overcome the rent-seeking society, how to achieve the equivalent of general disarmament in distributional struggles, I do think that an obvious strategy does not work. The poor cannot as easily unite, exert political pressure or compel revolutionary change and obtain a better deal as more privileged groups can.[17] As Bauer (1981:138–150) has elaborated in somewhat different words, such a strategy may serve the rent-seeking purposes of some already privileged persons better than those of the poor. Politics, and the price distortions thereby created, is at least as much, if not more, closely related to the causes of poverty than to their cure. If the poor only unite, they have no chance to prevail. If *some* poor groups receive an offer to participate in some winning coalitions, they will accept it. The winning coalition will aim at concentrated gains for their members including previously poor ones and dispersed and preferably invisible losses for others who cannot fight back—for example, because they are not yet organised and still poor.

It is possible that the true heroes of human history and improvement are those who aim for minor but useful reforms, who never get tired in an uphill struggle against rent-seeking. But to ask for this is to ask for a kind of altruism. The trouble with altruism is that it is so rare that we should not trust some self-confident group to enforce it on others. Most guardians of morality are likely to defect and look for rents.

NOTES

1. There are other dependency approaches. One of them is incompatible with rent-seeking theory in its economic foundations, but is similar to it in its analysis of distributional conflicts (Emmanuel 1972). This approach is discussed later.

2. Wallerstein's (1974, 1979, 1980) focus on government-sponsored distortion of markets is compatible with rent-seeking theory. Much of his theorising and Rubinson's (1976, 1977) interpretation of it is not.

3. Bradshaw (1985a:202) does not even refer to Galtung or his theory. But he reports a weak *positive* effect of primary product specialisation on growth and an equally weak *negative* effect of commodity concentration on growth in black Africa. While the former result flatly contradicts Galtung's expectations, the latter provides some extremely weak support for it.

4. Some readers may object to my listing of the studies by Delacroix and Ragin (1978, 1981) among those who call Galtung's ideas into question. The *older* study was mainly concerned with different issues. But it did control for human capital formation, ie., secondary school enrolment. In my view, this is useful and other studies should have done so, too. Therefore, one should note that the older study does *not* find a negative effect of primary product exports and manufactured imports. The more recent study maintains that the export or primary

products and commodity concentration obstructs development in "advanced peripheral countries." Most LDCs are not classified by Delacroix and Ragin with this category, but countries like Japan, Israel, Italy, Austria, the Soviet Union, Poland, Czechoslovakia, East Germany and some true LDCs are. Given the heterogeneity of the 'advanced' category, the important result seems to be that neither the export or primary products nor commodity concentration hurts the growth prospects of the so-called 'poor periphery', which still contains nations like Brazil, Turkey or South Korea among its members.

5. The relationship between military participation and human capital formation is discussed in Weede (1983c). By and large, negative findings on dependency propositions do *not* depend on inclusion or exclusion or military participation ratios as control variables. Still, *some* results are fairly sensitive to one's point of view on a number or technical issues. See the debate between Bornschier (1981b, 1982), on the one hand, and Weede and Tiefenbach (1981a, 1981b, 1982), on the other.

6. With Schumpeter (1942) one may argue that this treatment of monopolies rests on oversimplification. Monopolies may produce positive rather than negative effects because they permit economies of scale or provide incentives for innovation. The hope to achieve a temporary monopoly may provide one of the most important incentives to innovate. Therefore innovators deserve and receive legal protection, although such protection limits competition. While I admit the validity of these arguments, I contend that *on balance* the negative effects of monopolies which are described in the main text predominate. Whether competition among would-be monopolies is harmful or not, depends on how they compete. Price and quality competition may be desirable. Competition for political influence and legal protection or monopoly rights is always undesirable. Unfortunately, monopolists *must* aim at such protection because otherwise monopoly profits will be limited by the fear that fat profits attract challengers and renew competition.

7. It may be that reality is sometimes even worse where there are *no* bribes. Lobbying, dining with bureaucrats, entertaining legislators and offering electoral support may be even more costly than outright bribes (and do some recipients less good) and still result in similar policies.

8. Unequal size of group members also makes the provision of collective goods more likely. Simultaneously it may create the interesting phenomenon of the exploitation of the strong by the weak.

9. While workers need political entrepreneurs and leadership, leaders are likely to exact a price which Michels (1910, 1962) has described in his iron law of oligarchy.

10. By and large we can observe a mirror-image phenomenon in contemporary industrialised democracies. Here rural-agrarian minorities succeed in distorting the urban-rural terms of trade in their favour and at the expense of urban consumers and taxpayers. Again, the recipe of concentrated gains and dispersed losses is met.

11. One may dispute this statement in so far as rich industrialised democracies are concerned. In the United States, entering public service or politics often implies major income losses. Not so in LDCs, where politics or state employment come close to being the only available paths to personal advancement. That is why politics in poor countries without vigorous private enterprise so easily degenerates into what Andreski (1969:64) aptly termed "kleptocracy." Possibly one may minimise (not abolish) 'kleptocracy' by limiting government revenues or governmental control of the economy.

12. In some respects, Bradshaw's (1985b, 1986) cross-national studies pre-

sent an alternative approach to the World Bank's index of price distortions and studies based on it. Bradshaw focuses on 'urban bias' only, i.e., on the disparity (ratio) between output per worker outside and inside agriculture. He thereby captures a much narrower range of rent-seeking phenomena than the World Bank does in its index of price distortions. But data are more easily available, thereby permitting different and larger samples. Unfortunately Bradshaw's work has been focused on urbanisation rather than on growth or inequality. While the direct effect of urban bias on growth appears weak and sometimes insignificant in Bradshaw's regressions, he does support a positive effect of urban bias on overurbanisation which indirectly contributes to lower growth rates. For the purposes of my paper, a summary measure of direct *and* indirect effects of urban bias on growth rates would be more interesting than the information Bradshaw provides.

13. *All* results reported on the democracy-inequality relationship should be treated with caution. The quality or inequality data leaves much to be desired. Results may depend on the data set used (see Weede and Tiefenbach 1981a for a demonstration).

14. In this scenario nobody would enjoy job security or tenure. Such privileges are inherently discriminatory.

15. As Emmanuel (1972) claimed, worldwide unity of labour movements is unrealistic. Whatever the declared policy of Northern unions is, their actual policy must aim at defending their privileges against Southern competition, whether by protectionism, migration control or by impeding the outflow of capital and technology. For a more recent treatment, see Krauss (1983).

16. It is hard to imagine how one can make a humanitarian case for local welfare states in rich countries without implicit or explicit recourse to ethnocentric or racist arguments. Why should rich people in OECD countries be taxed in order to enable their less fortunate *fellow citizens* to buy used cars or to enjoy Mediterranean holidays instead of saving truly poor *fellow men and women* in LDCs from abject poverty and starvation?

17. For a systematic treatment of revolutions from an economic perspective, see Tullock (1974).

REFERENCES

Adelman, I. and Morris, C. T. 1967. *Society, Politics, and Economic Development*. Baltimore: Johns Hopkins University Press.

Ahluwalia, M. S., Carter, N. G. and Chenery, H. B. 1979. "Growth and Poverty in Developing Countries." *Journal of Development Economics* 6:299–341.

Alschuler, L. R. 1976. "Satellization and Stagnation in Latin America." *International Studies Quarterly* 20(1):39–82.

Andreski, S. 1969. *Parasitism and Subversion: The Case of Latin America*. New York: Schocken.

Bauer, P. T. 1981. *Equality, the Third World and Economic Delusion*. London: Weidenfeld and Nicholson.

Becker, G. S. 1971. *The Economics of Discrimination*. Second ed. Chicago: Chicago University Press.

Bell, D. and Kristol, I. 1981. *The Crisis in Economic Theory*. New York: Basic Books.

Bernholz, P. 1982. "Expanding Welfare State, Democracy and Free Market Economy: Are they Compatible?" *Zeitschrift für die gesamte Staatswissenschaft* 138:583–598.

Bornschier, V. 1980a. *Multinationale Konzerne, Wirtschaftspolitik und nationale Entwicklung im Weltsystem*. Frankfurt/Main: Campus.

————. 1980b. "Multinational Corporations and Economic Growth." *Journal of Development Economics* 7:191–210.

————. 1981a. "Dependent Industrialization in the World Economy." *Journal of Conflict Resolution* 25(3):371–400.

————. 1981b. "Comment" (on Weede and Tiefenbach 1981a). *International Studies Quarterly* 25:283–288.

————. 1982. "Dependence on Foreign Capital and Economic Growth." *European Journal of Political Research* 10(4):445–450.

————. 1985. "World Social Structure in the Long Economic Wave." Paper delivered at the 26th Annual Meeting of the International Studies Association, Washington, DC.

Bornschier, V. and Ballmer-Cao, T.H. 1979. "Income Inequality: A Cross-National Study of the Relationships between MNC-Penetration, Dimensions of the Power Structure and Income Distribution." *American Sociological Review* 44:487–506.

Bornschier, V., Chase-Dunn, C. and Rubinson, R. 1978. "Cross-National Evidence of the Effects of Foreign Investment and Aid on Economic Growth and Inequality: A Survey of Findings and a Reanalysis." *American Journal of Sociology* 84:651–683.

Bradshaw, Y. W. 1985a. "Dependent Development in Black Africa." *American Sociological Review* 50:195–207.

————. 1985b. "Overurbanization and Underdevelopment in Subsaharan Africa." *Studies in Comparative International Development* 20(3):74–101.

————. 1986. "Urbanization and Underdevelopment: A Global Study of Modernization, Urban Bias and Economic Dependency." Paper delivered at the 27th Annual Meeting of the International Studies Association, Anaheim, CA.

Buchanan, J. M. 1980. "Rent-Seeking and Profit Seeking", in Buchanan, J. M., Tollison, R. D. and Tullock, G.(eds.), *Toward a Theory of the Rent-Seeking Society*. College Station: Texas A and M University Press, pp. 3–15.

Buchanan, J. M., Tollison, R. D. and Tullock, G. 1980. *Toward a Theory of the Rent-Seeking Society*. College Station: Texas A and M University Press.

Chase-Dunn, C. 1975. "The Effects of International Economic Dependence on Development and Inequality." *American Sociological Review* 40:720–738.

Delacroix, J. 1977. "Export of Raw Materials and Economic Growth." *American Sociological Review* 42:795–808.

Delacroix, J. and Ragin, C. C. 1978. "Modernizing Institutions, Mobilization, and Third World Development: A Cross-national Study." *American Journal of Sociology* 84:123–150.

Delacroix, J. and Ragin. C. C. 1981. "Structural Blockage: A Cross-national Study of Economic Dependency, State Efficiency, and Underdevelopment." *American Journal of Sociology* 86:1311–1347.

Emmanuel, A. 1972. *Unequal Exchange: A Study of the Imperialism of Trade*. New York: Monthly Review Press.

Frohlich, N., Oppenheimer, J.A. and Young, O. R. 1971. *Political Leadership and Collective Goods*. Princeton: Princeton University Press.

Galtung, J. 1971. "A Structural Theory of Imperialism." *Journal of Peace Research* 8:81–117 .

Gobalet. J. G. and Diamond, L. J. 1979. "Effects of Investment Dependence on Economic Growth: The Role of Internal Structural Characteristics and Periods in the World Economy." *International Studies Quarterly* 23:412–444.

Gurr, T. R. 1968. "A Causal Model Of Civil Strife." *American Political Science Review* 62:1104–1124.

Gurr, T. R. and Duvall, R. 1973. "Civil Conflict in the 1960s." *Comparative Political Studies* 6:135–169.

Hayek, F. A. von. 1960. *The Constitution of Liberty*. Chicago: Chicago University Press.

Huntington, S. P. and Dominguez, J. I. 1975. "Political Development," in Greenstein, F. I. and Polsby, N. W. (eds.), *Handbook of Political Science. Vol. 3. Macropolitical Theory*. Reading, Mass.: Addison-Wesley.

Huntington, S. P. and Nelson, J. M. 1976. "No Easy Choice: Political Participation in Developing Countries." Cambridge, Mass.: Harvard University Press.

Jackman, R. W. 1982. "Dependence on Foreign Investment and Economic Growth in the Third World." *World Politics* 34:175–196.

Kaufman, R. R., Chernotsky, H. I. and Geller, D. S. 1975. "A Preliminary Test of the Theory of Dependency." *Comparative Politics* 7:303–330.

Krauss, M. B. 1983. *Development Without Aid: Growth, Poverty and Government*. New York: New Press (McGraw-Hill).

Kuhn, T. S. 1962. The Structure of Scientific Revolutions. Chicago: Chicago University Press.

Lakatos, I. 1968/69. "Criticism and the Methodology of Scientific Research Programmes." *Proceedings of the Aristotelian Society* LXIX:149–186.

Landau, D. 1983. "Government Expenditure and Economic Growth." *Southern Economic Journal* 49:783–792.

Lipton, M. 1977. *Why Poor People Stay Poor*. London: Temple Smith.

Lipton, M. 1984. "Urban Bias Revisited." *Journal of Development Studies* 20 (3):139–166.

Marsden, K. 1983. "Steuern und Wachstum." *Finanzierung und Entwicklung* (HWWA–Institut für Wirtschaftsforschung, Hamburg) 20(3):40–43.

Marsh, R. M. 1979. "Does Democracy Hinder Economic Development in the Latecomer Developing Nations?" *Comparative Social Research* 2:215–248.

Marx, K. 1852 (1969). "The Eighteenth Brumaire of Louis Bonaparte," in Marx, K. and Engels, F., *Selected Works*. 2 vols. London: Lawrence and Wishart.

McKenzie, R. B. and Tullock, G. 1978. *Modern Political Economy*. Tokyo: McGraw-Hill Kogakusha.

Meyer, J. W, and Hannan, M. T. eds. 1979. *National Development and the World System: Educational, Economic and Political Change*. Chicago: Chicago University Press.

Michels, R. 1910 (1962). *Political Parties*. New York: Collier.

Muller, E. N. 1984. "Financial Dependence in the Capitalist World Economy and Distribution of Income within Nations," in Seligson, M. A. (ed.), *The Gap Between Rich and Poor*. Boulder, Colorado: Westview, pp. 256–282.

Oberschall, A. 1973. *Social Conflict and Social Movements*. Englewood Cliffs, N.J.: Prentice-Hall.

Olson, M. 1965. *The Logic of Collective Action*. Cambridge, Mass.: Harvard University Press.

———. 1982. *The Rise and Decline of Nations: Economic Growth, Stagflation and Social Rigidities*. New Haven: Yale University Press.

Ray, J. L. and Webster, T. 1978. "Dependency and Economic Growth in Latin America." *International Studies Quarterly* 22:409–434.

Rubinson, R. 1976. "The World Economy and the Distribution of Income Within States." *American Sociological Review* 41:638–659.

Rubinson, R. 1977. "Dependence, Government Revenue, and Economic Growth, 1955–1970." *Studies in Comparative International Development* 12:3–28.

Rubinson, R. and Quinlan, D. 1977. "Democracy and Social Inequality." *American Sociological Review* 42:611–623.

Schumpeter, J. A. 1942. *Capitalism, Socialism and Democracy*. New York: Harper.

Singh, R. D. 1985. "State Intervention, Foreign Economic Aid Savings and Growth in LDCs." *Kyklos* 38(2):216–232.

Stokes, R. and Jaffee, D. 1982. "The Export of Raw Materials and Economic Growth." *American Sociological Review* 47(3):402–407.

Tollison, R. D. 1982. "Rent-Seeking: A Survey." *Kyklos* 35(4):575–602.

Tullock, G. 1974. The Social Dilemma: The Economics of War and Revolution. Blacksburg, Va.: University Publications.

———. 1980. "Rent-Seeking as a Negative-Sum Game," in Buchanan, J. B., Tollison, R. D., and Tullock. G. (eds.) *Toward a Theory of the Rent-Seeking Society*. College Station: Texas A and M University Press.

———. 1983. *Economics of Income Redistribution*. Boston/The Hague/London: Kluwer-Nijhoff.

Walleri, R. D. 1978a. "The Political Economy Literature on North-South Relations: Alternative Approaches and Empirical Evidence." *International Studies Quarterly* 22:587–624.

Walleri, R. D. 1978b. "Trade Dependence and Underdevelopment." *Comparative Political Studies* 11:94–127.

Wallerstein, I. 1974. *The Modern World System: Capitalist Agriculture and the Origins of the European World Economy in the Sixteenth Century*. New York: Academic Press.

———. 1979. *The Capitalist World Economy (Essays)*. Cambridge: Cambridge University Press.

———. 1980. *The Modern World System II: Mercantilism and the Consolidation of the European World Economy, 1600–1750*. New York: Academic Press.

Weede, E. 1980. "Beyond Misspecification in Sociological Analyses of Income Inequality." *American Sociological Review* 45:497–501.

———. 1981. "Dependenztheorie und Wirtschaftswachstum." *Kölner Zeitschrift für Soziologie und Sozialpsychologie* 33(4):690–707.

———. 1982. "Dependenztheorie und Einkommensverteilung." *Zeitschrift für die gesamte Staatswissenschaft* 138(2):241–261.

———. 1983a. "The Impact of Democracy on Economic Growth." *Kyklos* 36(1):21–39.

———. 1983b. "Das Verhältnis von Demokratisierung und Wirtschaftswachstum in Entwicklungsländern," in Hartwich, H. H. (ed.). *Gesellschaftliche Probleme als Anstoss und Folge von Politik*. Opladen: Westdeutscher Verlag, pp. 154–168.

———. 1983c. "Military Participation Ratios, Human Capital Formation and Economic Growth." *Journal of Political and Military Sociology* 11:11–19.

——— 1984. "Democracy, Creeping Socialism, and Ideological Socialism in Rent-Seeking Societies." *Public Choice* 44(2):349–366.

———. 1986a. "Rent-Seeking, Military Participation, and Economic Performance in LDCs," *Journal of Conflict Resolution* 3(2):291–314.

———. 1986b. "Catch-up Distributional Coalitions and Government as Determinants of Economic Growth or Decline in Industrialized Democracies." *British Journal of Sociology* 37(2):194–220.

Weede, E. and Tiefenbach, H. 1981a. "Some Recent Explanations of Income Inequality," *International Studies Quarterly* 25(2):255–282 and 289–293.

————. 1981b. "Three Dependency Explanations of Economic Growth." *European Journal of Political Research* 9(4):391–406.

————. 1982. "A Reply to Volker Bornschier." *European Journal of Political Research* 10(4):451–454.

World Bank. 1981. *World Development Report 1981*. London: Oxford University Press.

World Bank. 1983. *World Development Report 1983*. London: Oxford University Press.

26

Urban Bias and Inequality

MICHAEL LIPTON

Michael Lipton is the principal advocate of the thesis that the primary explanation for the internal gap between rich and poor is "urban bias." He argues that even though leaders of developing countries sympathize with the plight of the rural poor, they consistently concentrate scarce development resources in the urban sector. The result is that the urban sectors, which are already well-off in a comparative sense, get an increasing share of national income, which exacerbates the inequalities. In the book from which this chapter is drawn, Lipton tries to show that it is in the interests of the elites of developing countries to maintain this urban bias because they benefit directly from it. Critics of Lipton's thesis claim that historically there has been a rural bias in development and that much political power continues to reside in the hands of the rural elite. One might also ask if there is anything about the cultures found in developing nations that encourages policies favoring one sector over another; rural or urban biases (if they truly exist) might be a function of conditions established by the international environment.

The most important class conflict in the poor countries of the world today is not between labor and capital. Nor is it between foreign and national interests. It is between the rural classes and the urban classes. The rural sector contains most of the poverty, and most of the low-cost sources of potential advance; but the urban sector contains most of the articulateness, organization, and power. So the urban classes have been able to "win" most of the rounds of the struggle with the countryside; but in so doing they have made the development process needlessly slow and unfair. Scarce land, which might grow millets and beansprouts for hungry villagers, instead produces a trickle of costly calories from meat and milk, which few except the urban rich (who have ample protein anyway) can afford. Scarce investment, instead of going into water-pumps to grow rice, is wasted on urban motorways. Scarce human skills design and administer, not village wells and agricultural extension services, but world boxing championships in showpiece stadia. Resource allocations, within the city and the village as well as between them, reflect urban priorities rather than equity or efficiency. The damage has been increased by misguided ideological imports, liberal and Marxian, and by the town's success in buying off part of the rural elite, thus transferring most of the costs of the process to the rural poor.

But is this urban bias really damaging? After all, since 1945 output per person in the poor countries has doubled; and this unprecedented growth has brought genuine development. Production has been made more scientific: in agriculture, by the irrigation of large areas, and more recently by the increasing adoption of fertilizers and of high-yield varieties of wheat and rice; in industry, by the replacement of fatiguing and repetitive effort by rising levels of technology, specialization and skills. Consumption has also developed, in ways that at once use and underpin the development of production; poor countries now consume enormously expanded provisions of health and education, roads and electricity, radios and bicycles. Why, then, are so many of those involved in the development of the Third World— politicians and administrators, planners and scholars—miserable about the past and gloomy about the future? Why is the United Nations' "Development Decade" of the 1960s, in which poor countries as a whole exceeded the growth target,[1] generally written off as a failure? Why is aid, which demonstrably contributes to a development effort apparently so promising in global terms, in accelerating decline and threatened by a "crisis of will" in donor countries?[2]

The reason is that since 1945 growth and development, in most countries, have done so little to raise the living standards of the poorest people. It is scant comfort that today's mass-consumption economies, in Europe and North America, also featured near-stagnant mass welfare in the early phases of their economic modernization. Unlike today's poor countries, they carried in their early development the seeds of mass consumption later on. They were massively installing extra capacity to supply their people with simple goods: bread, cloth, and coal, not just luxury housing, poultry, and airports. Also the nineteenth-century "developing countries," including Russia, were developing not just market requirements but class structures that practically guaranteed subsequent "trickling down" of benefits. The workers even proved able to raise their share of political power and economic welfare. The very preconditions of such trends are absent in most of today's developing countries. The sincere egalitarian rhetoric of, say, Mrs. Indira Gandhi or Julius Nyerere was—allowing for differences of style and ideology—closely paralleled in Europe during early industrial development: in Britain, for example, by Henry Brougham and Lord Durham in the 1830s.[3] But the rural masses of India and Tanzania, unlike the urban masses of Melbourne's Britain, lack the power to organize the pressure that alone turns such rhetoric into distributive action against the pressure of the elite.

Some rather surprising people have taken alarm at the persistently unequal nature of recent development. Aid donors are substantially motivated by foreign-policy concerns for the stability of recipient governments; development banks, by the need to repay depositors and hence to ensure a good return on the projects they support. Both concerns coalesce in the World Bank, which raises and distributes some £3,000 million of aid each year. As a bank it has advocated—and financed—mostly "bankable" (that is, commercially profitable) projects. As a channel for aid donors, it has concentrated on poor countries that are relatively "open" to investment, trade and economic advice from those donors. Yet the effect of stagnant mass welfare in poor countries, on the well-intentioned and perceptive people who administer World Bank aid, has gradually overborne these traditional biases. Since 1971 the president of the World Bank, Robert McNamara, has in a series of speeches focused attention on the stagnant or worsening lives of the bottom 40 percent of people in poor countries.[4] Recently this has begun to affect the World Bank's projects, though its incomplete engagement with the problem of urban bias restricts the impact. For instance, an urban-biased government will prepare rural projects less well than urban projects, will manipulate prices to render rural projects less apparently profitable (and hence less "bankable"), and will tend to cut down its own effort if donors step up theirs. Nevertheless, the World Bank's new concern with the "bottom 40 percent" is significant.

These people—between one-quarter and one-fifth of the people of the world—are overwhelmingly rural: landless laborers, or farmers with no more than an acre or two, who must supplement their incomes by wage labor. Most of these countryfolk rely, as hitherto, on agriculture lacking irrigation or fertilizers or even iron tools. Hence they are so badly fed that they cannot work efficiently, and in many cases are unable to feed their infants well enough to prevent physical stunting and perhaps even brain damage. Apart from the rote-learning of religious texts, few of them receive any schooling. One of four dies before the age of ten. The rest live the same overworked, underfed, ignorant, and disease-ridden lives as thirty, or three hundred, or three thousand years ago. Often they borrow (at 40 percent or more yearly interest) from the same moneylender families as their ancestors, and surrender half their crops to the same families of landlords. Yet the last thirty years have been the age of unprecedented, accelerating growth and development! Naturally men of goodwill are puzzled and alarmed.

How can accelerated growth and development, in an era of rapidly improving communications and of "mass politics," produce so little for poor people? It is too simple to blame familiar scapegoats—foreign exploiters and domestic capitalists. Poor countries where they are relatively unimportant have experienced the paradox just as much as others. Nor, apparently, do the poorest families cause their own difficulties, whether by rapid population growth or by lack of drive. Poor families do tend to have more children than rich families, but principally because their higher death rates require it, if the aging parents are to be reasonably sure that a son will grow up, to support them if need be. And it is the structure of rewards and opportunities within poor countries that extracts, as if by force, the young man of ability and energy from his chronically stagnant rural background and lures him to serve, or even to join, the booming urban elite.

The disparity between urban and rural welfare is much greater in poor countries now than it was in rich countries during their early development. This huge welfare gap is demonstrably inefficient, as well as inequitable. It persists mainly because less than 20 percent of investment for development has gone to the agricultural sector (the situation has not changed much since 1965), although over 65 percent of the people of less-developed countries (LDCs), and over 80 percent of the really poor who live on $1 per week each or less, depend for a living on agriculture. The proportion of skilled people who support development—doctors, bankers, engineers—going to rural areas has been lower still; and the rural-urban imbalances have in general been even greater than those between agriculture and industry. Moreover, in most LDCs, governments have taken numerous measures with the unhappy side-effect of accentuating rural-urban disparities: their own allocation of public expenditure and taxation; measures raising the price of industrial production relative to farm production, thus encouraging private rural saving to flow into industrial investment because the value of industrial output has been artificially boosted; and educational facilities encouraging bright villagers to train in cities for urban jobs.

Such processes have been extremely inefficient. For instance, the impact on output of $1 of carefully selected investment is in most countries two to three times as high in agriculture as elsewhere, yet public policy and private market power have combined to push domestic savings and foreign aid into nonagricultural uses. The process has also been inequitable. Agriculture starts with about one-third the income per head as the rest of the economy, so that the people who depend on it should in equity receive special attention not special mulcting. Finally, the misallocation between sectors has created a needless and acute conflict between efficiency and equity. In agriculture the poor farmer with little land is usually efficient in his use of both land and capital, whereas power, construction, and industry often do best in big, capital-intensive units; and rural income and power, while far from equal, are less unequal than in the cities. So concentration on urban development and neglect of agriculture have pushed resources away from activities where they can help growth and benefit the poor, *and* toward activities where they do either of these, if at all, at the expense of the other.

Urban bias also increases inefficiency and inequity within the sectors. Poor farmers have little land and much underused family labor. Hence they tend to complement any extra developmental resources received—pumpsets, fertilizers, virgin land—with much more extra labor than do large farmers. Poor farmers thus tend to get most output from such extra resources (as well as needing the extra income most). But rich farmers (because they sell their extra output to the cities instead of eating it themselves, and because they are likely to use much of their extra income to support urban investment) are naturally favored by urban-biased policies; it is they, not the efficient small farmers, who get the cheap loans and the fertilizer subsidies. The patterns of allocation and distribution within the cities are damaged too. Farm inputs are produced inefficiently, instead of imported, and the farmer has to pay, even if the price is nominally "subsidized." The processing of farm outputs, notably grain milling, is shifted into big urban units and the profits are no longer reinvested in agriculture. And equalization between classes inside the cities becomes more risky, because the investment-starved farm sector might prove unable to deliver the food that a better-off urban mass would seek to buy.

Moreover, income in poor countries is usually more equally distributed within the rural sector than within the urban sector.[5] Since income creates the power to distribute extra income, therefore, a policy that concentrates on raising income in the urban sector will worsen inequalities in two ways: by transferring not only from poor to rich, but also from more equal to less equal. Concentration on urban enrichment is triply inequitable: because countryfolk start poorer; because such concentration allots rural resources largely to the rural rich (who sell food to the cities); and because the great inequality of power *within* the towns renders urban resources especially likely to go to the resident elites.

But am I not hammering at an open door? Certainly the persiflage of allocation has changed recently, under the impact of patently damaging deficiencies in rural output. Development plans are nowadays full of "top priority for agriculture."[6] This is reminiscent of the pseudo-egalitarian school where, at mealtimes, Class B children get priority, while Class A children get food.[7] We can see that the new agricultural priority is dubious from the abuse of the "green revolution" and of the oil crisis (despite its much greater impact on *industrial* costs) as pretexts for lack of emphasis on agriculture: "We don't need it," and "We can't afford it," respectively. And the 60 to 80 percent of people dependent on agriculture are still allocated barely 20 percent of public resources; even these small shares are seldom achieved; and they have, if anything, tended to diminish. So long as the elite's interests, background and sympathies remain predominantly urban, the countryside may get the "priority" but the city will get the resources. The farm sector will continue to be squeezed, both by transfers of resources from it by prices that are turned against it. Bogus justifications of urban bias will continue to earn the sincere, prestige-conferring, but misguided support of visiting "experts" from industrialized counties and international agencies. And development will be needlessly painful, inequitable and slow.

NOTES

1. The UN target was a 5 percent yearly rate of "real" growth (that is, allowing for inflation) of total output. The actual rate was slightly higher.
2. Net aid from the donor countries comprising the Development Assistance Committee (DAC) of the Organization for Economic Cooperation and Development (OECD) comprises over 95 percent of all net aid to less-developing countries (LDCs). It fell steadily from 0.54 percent of donors' GNP in 1961 to 0.30 percent in 1973. The real value of aid per person in recipient countries fell by over 20 percent over the period. M. Lipton, "Aid Allocation when Aid is Inadequate," in T. Byres, ed., *Foreign Resources and Economic Development*, Cass, 1972, p. 158; OECD (DAC), *Development Cooperation* (1974 Review), p. 116.
3. L. Cooper, *Radical Jack*, Cresset, 1969, esp. pp. 183–97; C. New, *Life of Henry Brougham to 1830*, Clarendon, 1961, Preface.
4. See the mounting emphasis in his *Addresses to the Board of Governors*, all published by the International Bank for Reconstruction and Development, Washington; at Copenhagen in 1970, p. 20; at Washington in 1971, pp. 6–19, and 1972, pp. 8–15; and at Nairobi in 1973, pp. 10–14, 19.
5. M. Ahluwalia, "The Dimensions of the Problem," in H. Chenery et al., *Redistribution with Growth*, Oxford, 1974.
6. See K. Rafferty, *Financial Times*, 10 April 1974, p. 35, col. 5; M. Lipton, "Urban Bias and Rural Planning," in P. Streeten and M. Lipton, eds., *The Crisis of Indian Planning*, Oxford, 1968, p. 85.
7. F. Muir and D. Norden, "Comonon Entrance," in P. Sellers, *Songs for Swinging Sellers*, Parlophone PMC 111, 1958.

27

· · · · · · ·

Urban Bias and Economic Growth
in Cross-National Perspective

· · · · · · ·

ERICH WEEDE

In Chapter 25 Erich Weede argued that the poor stay poor not because the rich make or keep them poor but because of a distributional struggle that the poor are ill-suited to wage. He considered the urban bias described by Michael Lipton in the previous chapter a result of rent-seeking but concluded that there was not sufficient cross-national evidence to confirm the argument. In this chapter, Weede presents the evidence from his own cross-national study of the impact of urban bias upon economic growth. He defines countries with a large disparity between agricultural and nonagricultural incomes as suffering from urban bias and finds that urban bias does indeed decrease growth rates.

According to Michael Lipton (1977, 1982 and 1984: 139), urban bias is "the main explanation of 'why poor people stay poor' in post-colonial LDCs." Since this is a rather strong claim, one should like to see a series of independent and thorough tests. Of course, Lipton (1977) himself supported his proposition by many pieces of evidence from diverse developing societies. Nevertheless, there remain reasons for doubt. If the evidence reported in "Why Poor People Stay Poor" (Lipton, 1977) inductively led Lipton to hypothesize that urban bias harms the growth prospects of nations, then it should *not* simultaneously be used in our evaluation of Lipton's claim. Since Lipton's account of events in LDCs inevitably is selective, since his explanatory preference might bias his

Reprinted with permission of the publishers, E. J. Brill Publishers, *International Journal of Comparative Sociology* 28, 1–2(1987):30–39.

sampling of events, we need systematic and independent tests of Lipton's proposition by others.

The intentions of my chapter are rather narrow and limited. I do *not* want to question the internal consistency, clarity or theoretical persuasiveness of Lipton's arguments. This has been done by Corbridge (1982) and others who have been quoted and rebutted by Lipton (1984). Whatever theoretical details deserve further elaboration and clarification, some aspects of Lipton s theory seem sufficiently clear to me to permit an empirical test. If urban bias keeps poor people poor, then the worse urban bias is, the more intractable and persistent the problem of poverty should be. So, the basic idea of this chapter is an attempt to estimate the cross-national relationship between urban bias on the one hand and the persistence of poverty on the other hand.

In principle, poverty may be reduced either by economic growth or by income redistribution or, of course, by some combination of both. While Lipton claims that urban bias is simultaneously unfair by redistributing away from the largest and poorest group in most LDCs and inefficient by retarding economic growth, I shall focus on the latter issue only. At least in the poorest LDCs, not even a perfectly egalitarian distribution of income would permit decent standards of living. For practical purposes, my concern in this chapter is limited to the issue of whether countries suffering from more urban bias simultaneously suffer from lower economic growth rates.

Urban poverty is more visible to Western visitors and native capital-based politicians and bureaucrats alike than rural poverty. Nevertheless, poverty affects many more rural than urban people in most LDCs. Rural poverty is both more widespread and more severe. An observable income disparity between rural and urban populations may reflect intersectoral differences in productivity. It is conceivable that urban people are better off than rural people because they work more productively. lt is conceivable that income disparities between city and countryside merely reflect productivity differentials without being generated or reinforced by price distortions. Then there might be much more rural than urban poverty in LDCs without there being any "urban bias."

In Lipton's view, however, the preponderance of rural over urban poverty doesn't simply occur. Instead it results from flawed political decisions and administrative processes which might similarly affect countries with rather different constitutions and political regimes. In almost all LDCs the ruling class is urban, although it might be allied to some rural elites. This urban ruling class prefers rural poverty over urban poverty, because it is less visible than squatters on the lawn in front of the presidential palace would be, because widely scattered poor people in the countryside find it very hard to give voice to their demands.[1] Therefore rural poverty is much less threatening to ruling elites than urban poverty and deprivations might be. In general, ruling elites favor urban over rural interests because urban interests are better organized and more capable of exercising political pressure than rural interests are.

In a conflict of interest between groups, an efficient strategy is to generate concentrated gains for a rather small group and to inflict diffused and preferably invisible losses on a much larger group. In most LDCs, the rural population tilling the land is by far the largest group. By rigging the urban-rural terms of trade, the ruling and largely urban coalition may exploit the rural masses. There are many different mechanisms by which governments may depress food prices or increase prices for urban products. Official monopolies or marketing agencies may offer less than competitive (or world) market prices to peasants. Overvalued LDC currencies decrease the international competitiveness of agricultural products and thereby inhibit exports. Of course, an overvalued currency simultaneously hurts the export prospects of largely urban industries. In a free market environment, LDC governments could not sustain overvalued currencies. But regulation of foreign trade and financial transactions—what an Indian newspaper once called "permit, licence, quota Raj"—enables governments to support overvalued currencies for protracted periods of time by rationing the access to convertible currencies and foreign goods. Thereafter, agriculture continues to suffer the consequences of overvaluation, i.e. in essence "negative protection." But non-competitive industries are positively protected from foreign producers by tariffs and other barriers to international trade. While peasants are forced to sell cheap, they have to buy rather expensive and often inferior domestic urban products. The discriminating treatment of the rural-agrarian and other economic sectors is exacerbated where governmental subsidies provide food for the *urban* poor at the expense of urgent rural investments, or where differential degrees of unionization create corresponding urban-rural wage differences. Moreover, peasants are the least likely group of people to obtain import licenses or convertible currencies from governmental agencies. They simply lack access. Big and well-connected urban entrepreneurs are much more likely to succeed in getting licenses and permits. Of course, the dispensing of import licenses provides opportunities for corruption and urban politicians and administrators may and often do enrich themselves. By and large, the ruling urban coalition distorts prices at the expense of rural producers and for the benefit of urban producers and civil servants.

While price distortions in general interfere with allocative efficiency and thereby reduce growth rates (World Bank, 1983:57–63; Weede, 1986a), urban bias also refers to a pattern of investment which is unfair and inefficient at the same time. According to Lipton (1977:180), "large disparities in labour productivity, with agriculture doing 'badly,' correspond to large differences in the productivity of 'everything else,' with agriculture doing 'well.'" While urban sectors outperform agriculture in labour productivity, because each unit of urban labour is combined with quite a bit of capital, agriculture outperforms urban sectors in capital productivity, because each unit of rural capital is combined with a lot of rural labour (Lipton, 1977:195). In most LDCs, in particular in the poorest and populous ones, capital is scarce, whereas unskilled labour is abundant. Therefore, it is more efficient to invest capital in agriculture where it may be combined with abundant unskilled labour than to invest capital in urban industries or services where it is combined with less labour or with less abundant skilled labour. Nevertheless, many LDCs prefer inefficient urban investment over more efficient rural investment. Since the rural population is usually poorer than the urban one, unfairness is also involved. The large and poor rural masses need investment even more than their relatively privileged urban compatriots, however poor the relatively privileged group may look from a rich country perspective.

Since the purpose of this chapter is not an elaboration or refinement of Lipton's (1977) theory, but a cross-national test of one of its implications, the crude and incomplete summary above may suffice. It is important, however, that readers keep in mind that income disparities between urban and rural sectors in LDCs do not just occur naturally. They result from political decisions, from misallocations of capital and resources and from governmental manipulations of urban-rural terms of trade. The larger urban-rural income disparities become, the more likely they are to reflect political pressures, misallocation and inefficient policies, i.e., urban bias. If Lipton's (1977, 1982, 1984) basic idea is true, we should expect the output-per-person disparity between urban sectors and agriculture to be correlated with economic growth rates. The higher the disparity, the slower economic growth rates should be. In Lipton's view, the correlation even deserves a causal interpretation. If Lipton's basic idea were false, however, there is *no* reason why the disparity should be systematically related to smaller growth rates.

DATA AND ANALYSIS

Lipton's proposition is to be tested by a cross-national and purely cross-sectional multiple regression analysis of data from the 1960s and 1970s. The dependent variables are economic growth rates as reported by the World Bank (1981:134–137) for the 1960–79 period. There are two alternative indicators of growth reported in this source: the growth rates of gross national product per capita, henceforth abbreviated GNPC, and of gross domestic product, henceforth GDP. While the conceptual difference between GNP and GDP matters little in cross-national analysis, the difference between per capita and other growth rates seems more important. GDP may grow and still average income may shrink, if the population grows even faster than GDP. I shall apply these two conceptually different economic growth rates, referring to GNPC or GDP, instead of a single measure, because I cannot see any reason why urban bias should affect the one and not the other. Empirically, such a difference in results remains conceivable and might point to unsolved problems. If, however, results turn out to be similar, irrespective of any particular operationalization of growth rates, then we may put some confidence in the robustness of our findings.

Lipton (1977:435–437) himself has published data on the urban-rural disparity in output-per-person ca. 1970 for 63 LDCs, i.e., ratios of nonagricultural to agricultural outputs or incomes per person. Lipton's data serve as one measure of urban bias. Since Lipton's compilation omits many LDCs, since it refers to a single time point in the middle of the growth period to be analyzed, it is desirable to add another measure of urban bias with broader national as well as temporal coverage. Following Bradshaw's (1985: 83) example, the disparity has been computed in the following way from World Handbook (Taylor and Jodice, 1983) data:

$$\text{Disparity} = \frac{\text{percent non - agricultural GDP} \; / \; \text{percent agricultural GDP}}{\text{percent non - agricultural labour} \; / \; \text{percent agricultural labour}}$$

Within a data set of 55 LDCs where both Lipton's disparities and the World Handbook–based measure of urban bias are available for 1970, the correlation is 0.83. In my view, this is evidence in favour of tolerable reliability in our measures of urban bias. Since the World Handbook–based measure has been computed for 1960, 1965, and 1970, we may even get some impression about its stability over time. *If* urban bias were very unstable, then one should not expect it to contribute much to the explanation of growth rates referring to the rather long twenty-year-period analyzed here.

Fortunately, urban bias seems fairly stable. 1960 estimates correlate 0.86 with 1965 estimates and 0.65 with 1970 estimates; 1965 estimates correlate 0.86 with 1970 estimates. Below I shall not rely on either one of the single-year estimates derived from the World Handbook, but apply an urban bias average of 1960, 1965 and 1970 data. The low correlation between any single year estimate and the averaged urban bias is 0.96.

The research design described so far includes some replication. There are two measures of economic growth rates, referring to GNPC and GDP. There are two measures of urban bias, derived from different sources of data, covering somewhat different sets of nations, and referring either to the midpoint of the growth period under observation (Lipton's disparity) or averaging three disparity measures from the first part of the two decades of growth observed. Since I see no theoretically compelling reason why some measure of either urban bias or growth should generate better results, I treat all regressions below as equivalent tests of the very same proposition. Only if all of them imply a similar verdict on the proposition, should we accept it.

Although Lipton (1984:139) has raised a rather strong claim by referring to urban bias as the "main explanation" of Third World poverty, I would not like to evaluate the effect of the conceivable "main" cause urban bias without controlling for the effects of at least some obvious background conditions which proved useful in previous research (Weede, 1984). The level of

economic development, as operationalized by logged GNP per capita, taken
from Taylor and Hudson (1972:314–320), has some curvilinear impact on
growth rates. Middle income nations grow faster than either poorer or richer
countries. Opportunities of backwardness provided by an ability to absorb
technology from more advanced nations might be focused on middle income
countries (Maddison, 1969:XXIII). Or, different weights of different sectors in
the economy at different levels of development coupled with sectorally
different growth rates (Horvat, 1971; Kuznets, 1976) might produce the
observable curvilinear relationship. Be that as it may, it seems best to
control for the level of economic development in any attempt to assess the
impact of urban bias on economic growth rates.

Among economists there seems to be widespread, if not general agreement, that capital formation is important in LDCs. That is why I shall control for the effects of gross domestic investment as a percentage of GDP,
taken from Ballmer-Cao and Scheidegger (1979:43–45). In addition to physical or capital investment, human capital formation might matter. Recently,
the World Bank (1980:96–97) reaffirmed the view that "the economic rate of
return to investment in schooling is high, frequently well above that of physical investment." Here, I shall control for the effects of primary and secondary
school enrolment ratios as reported by the World Bank (1979:170–171).

Growth rates refer to the 1963–79 period, school enrolment ratios to
1960, (logged) GNPC to 1965, urban bias either to 1970 (Lipton's measure)
or to average values between 1960 and 1970 (the World Handbook–based
measure). Gross domestic investment is the average of 1960, 1965, 1970 and
1973 values. This array of time periods and points is related to data
availability. Still, it might be meaningful.

My general idea is that independent variables should be typical of the
growth period, i.e., close to average values. Since the comparative level of
economic development (operationalized by GNPC) is rather stable over time,
almost any time point, preferably in the beginning or middle of the growth
period could do. I have chosen 1965 values. Since gross domestic
investment/GDP fluctuates somewhat over time, its value has been consolidated by averaging 1960, 1965, 1970 and 1973 values. For similar reasons,
the World Handbook–based measure of urban bias has been averaged over
1960, 1965 and 1970 values. Only primary and secondary school enrolment
ratios refer to the beginning of the growth period rather than to average
conditions in the growth period. Since there has to be *some* lag between
entering school and entering the workforce, this might be as it should be.

The data source for the dependent variables (World Bank, 1981:134–137)
reports growth rates for 124 countries. I excluded colonies or dependent territories, capital surplus oil exporters, centrally planned economies and industrialized countries (as defined by World Bank, 1979:127). Inevitably, some
nations had to be omitted because of missing values. Some of these omitted
cases suffered from prolonged international or civil war (e.g. Lebanon,

Indochinese states). The maximum number of cases in any regression below is 76; the minimum is 52.

Table 27.1 reports the results of four regressions of economic growth rates on the level of economic development: (operationally: logged GNPC), gross domestic investment, school enrolment ratios and urban bias. Despite the differences in sample size and composition, and despite the differences in the operationalization of economic growth, results are rather stable over equations. There is a curvilinear relationship between the level of economic development and growth rates. Countries at intermediate levels of economic development grow faster than the poorest nations or those LDCs which come close to joining the ranks of industrialized societies.[2] Investment matters; the higher investment ratios are, the faster economic growth is. Contrary to expectation and to my own previous results with an extremely similar data set (Weede, 1984: 302),[3] human capital formation hardly seems to matter Secondary school enrolment ratios never come even close to significance, while the size and significance of primary school enrolment depends on the equation considered. Urban bias effects are significant at the one percent level or better. Urban bias does decrease growth rates, as it should, if Lipton's (1977, 1982, 1984) theory is accepted as true.

One may question whether urban bias and gross domestic investment additively contribute to growth, or whether there are some interaction effects. Theoretically, it might make sense to argue that the growth enhancing effect of investment depends on the absence of urban bias. If investment effects were conditional effects of urban bias, then an interaction term should be added (see Friedrich, 1982, for technical details). While I have done it, results are disappointing. In three out of four equations corresponding to Table 27.1, the adjusted percentages of variance explained actually went down rather than up after the interaction term had been added. In the single equation where the adjusted percentage of variance increased at all, the difference was small (1%) and not significant. In another attempt to look for interaction effects I divided the entire sample into subgroups according to urban bias and looked for different investment and human capital effects in various subgroups. Again, this did not produce evidence in favour of some kind of interaction effect.

From a technical point of view the most worrisome aspect of the regressions reported above is the skewness of the urban bias variables and the corresponding weight of a few outlying cases. Although the negative effects of urban bias should be much stronger and worse, where it is practised with few constraints, than elsewhere, one should not make the demonstration of negative urban bias effects dependent on any small number of cases. That is why I have reduced the skewness of the urban bias variables by an ln-transformation.

While the weight of countries suffering from extreme urban bias is much smaller in Table 27.2 than it was in Table 27.1, results in both tables are broadly similar. In Table 27.2, there still is a curvilinear relationship

Table 27.1 Results of Regressions of Economic Growth 1960–79 on the Level of Economic Development, Gross Domestic Investment, Some Human Capital Variables, and Urban Bias (LDCs only)

	GNPC Growth		GDP Growth	
	(1)	(2)	(3)	(4)
LNGNPC	10.38	5.73	10.71	8.17
	00.01	0.07	00.01	0.02
LNGNPC^2	−1.07	−.62	−1.08	−.84
	00.01	0.04	00.01	0.01
Beta of b_1LNGNPC + b_2(LNGNPC)^2	00.43	0.33	00.38	0.35
	00.20	.014	00.18	0.13
Gross Domestic Investment	00.00	0.00	00.01	0.01
	00.48	0.36	00.43	0.35
	0.011	.018	0.022	.022
Primary School Enrollment	00.33	0.06	00.08	0.03
	00.16	0.29	00.32	0.35
	0.027	.042	−.021	F–level
Secondary School	00.36	0.13	00.52	insufficient
	00.15	0.24	−0.11	
	−0.10	−.081	−0.12	−.076
Urban Bias	00.01	0.01	00.00	0.01
	−0.37	−.29	−0.43	−.28
Constant	−25.94	−13.63	−24.59	−17.55
N	54	76	52	72
Adjusted Percentage of Variance Explained	38.1	42.4	35.2	30.5

Except for the third and the last three rows, first cell entries are unstandardized regression coefficients, second cell entries are significance levels of regression coefficients, and third cell entries are standardized regression coefficients. The standardized regression coefficients in the third row assess the curvilinear impact of the level of economic development on economic growth. For computation and interpretation of this coefficient, see Jagodzinski and Weede (1981). Urban bias data in columns (1) and (3) are taken from Lipton (1977:435–437); in columns (2) and (4) the index has been computed according to Bradshaw's (1985) formula from World Handbook data (Taylor and Jodice 1983).

between the level of economic development and growth rates, a positive relationship between gross domestic investment and growth and a negative relationship between urban bias and growth. The evidence on human capital effects is still mixed; primary school enrolment might help, secondary schooling almost certainly does not. The regressions in Table 27.2 have served their purpose, i.e, to demonstrate that negative urban bias effects are *not* artifacts of a few outlying and influential cases.

Table 27.2 Regressions of Economic Growth 1960–79 on the Level of Economic Development, Gross Domestic Investment, Some Human Capital Variables, and Logged Urban Bias (LDCs only)

	GNPC Growth		GDP Growth	
	(1)	(2)	(3)	(4)
LNGNPC	10.07	5.41	10.24	7.80
	00.01	0.08	00.02	0.03
$LNGNPC^2$	-1.02	-.59	-1.02	-.80
	00.01	0.05	00.02	0.02
Beta of b_1LNGNPC + b_2(LNGNPC)^2	00.39	0.33	00.33	0.34
Gross Domestic Investment	00.17	0.14	00.14	0.12
	00.01	0.00	00.05	0.02
	00.42	0.38	00.33	0.34
Primary School Enrollment	.0096	.018	0.020	.023
	00.40	0.06	00.11	0.04
	00.14	0.29	00.30	0.37
Secondary School Enrollment	0.025	.033	-.014	-.0051
	00.41	0.24	00.69	0.87
	00.14	0.19	-0.07	-.03
Logged Urban Bias	-1.05	-0.95	-0.97	-0.73
	00.01	0.01	00.02	0.05
	-0.35	-.33	-0.32	-.26
Constant	-23.89	-11.69	-22.32	-15.85
N	54	76	52	72
Adjusted Percentage of Variance Explained	37.4	42.8	28.2	27.6

For sources see Table 27.1.

CONCLUSION

This chapter reported the results of a cross-national test of Lipton's (1977, 1982, 1984) assertion that urban bias keeps poor people poor. But the research agenda of this chapter has been much more restricted than Lipton's. I have exclusively focused on the relationship between urban bias and economic growth rates. For the 1960s and 1970s it has been demonstrated that the growth performance of LDCs was reduced where there was urban bias, as operationalized by the income and output disparity between the agricultural and non-agricultural sector. Of course, results depend on the specification of the regression equations estimated, in particular on the list of control variables included. It is always conceivable that a longer and better list of control variables might enforce a revision of some of the results reported above. But the negative effect of urban bias seems to be fairly robust. It holds irrespective of one's focus on GDP or GNPC growth, of the weight of outlying cases, of the measurement of urban bias chosen and of sample size and composition insofar as these vary from equation to equation.

Despite the obvious importance of Lipton's claims there has been very little cross-national research on them in the past. Bradshaw's (1985, 1987) pioneering work is a lonely effort. It has stimulated my own work. While Bradshaw did produce some support for Lipton's views, his focus on the process of urbanization itself contrasts with my focus on the linkage between urban bias and economic growth rates.[4] But it is noteworthy that the only cross-national studies known to this author all seem to support some of Lipton's ideas.

Since Lipton's theory is rather controversial, the results of any empirical test are likely to be controversial, too. In addition to criticisms of particular technical details in data compilation and research design, critics may raise the following charge: Throughout this chapter I have merely *assumed rather than tested* the idea that urban-rural income disparities reflect biased political and administrative decision-making which interferes with allocative efficiency. This charge is admittedly true. There has been *no direct test* of Lipton's ideas about the causes and mechanisms of urban bias. Instead I simply accepted an indicator of urban bias suggested by Lipton himself. If Lipton's theory is true, then urban bias as reflected in urban-rural income disparities should be negatively related to economic growth rates. If Lipton's interpretation of the disparity *were* false, however, then there would be *no reason* at all to expect a negative relationship between it and economic growth. *Indirectly*, at least, my results support Lipton's interpretation of the urban-rural disparity as well as his claims about the relationship between urban bias and reduced growth rates.[5] If Lipton's measure of urban bias were not valid, why should it perform in a way corresponding to his theoretical expectations?

Lipton's (1977) theory about the impact of urban bias on economic performance should be put in a wider perspective. As can be seen from the following quotation, Lipton (1977:13) rejects Marxist class theories and neo-Marxist dependency or world-system theories by arguing: "The most important class conflict in the poor countries of the world today is not between labour and capital. Nor is it between foreign and national interests. It is between the rural classes and the urban classes. The rural sector contains most of the poverty, and most of the low-cost sources of potential advance; but the urban sector contains most of the articulateness, organisation and power. So the urban classes have been able to 'win' most of the rounds of struggle with the countryside; but in so doing they have made the development process needlessly slow and unfair."

Lipton's strong claims and his rejection of alternative explanatory approaches may seem exaggerated given the modest strength of the relationship between urban bias and less growth found in this study. But it is an item that fits well into a wider picture. Elsewhere (Weede 1985, 1986b) I have outlined two competing paradigms and the corresponding empirical evidence. Dependency and world-system approaches to LDC performance suffer from accumulating anomalies and lack of robust support. By contrast, rent-seeking[6] approaches do somewhat better. Urban bias is a specific instance of rent-seeking. Since urban bias consistently demonstrated the expected effect, this small empirical study vindicates and reinforces my earlier optimism (Weede 1985b) about the promise of the rent-seeking paradigm.

NOTES

1. Marx (1852) provides a classical analysis of this relationship.
2. The curvature in the relationship between logged GNPC and economic growth rates is much stronger in global samples including industrial democracies than it is in LDCs only samples.
3. Actually, the data set from Weede (1984:302) was the starting point of this analysis. But previous analyses did not control for urban bias and might have overestimated the impact of human capital formation.
4. Insofar as Bradshaw (1985, 1987) touches upon the urban bias–growth linkage, I am inclined to be critical of his panel regression design for technical reasons put forward by Jackman (1980).
5. An obvious expansion of the cross-national tests of Lipton's theory might be to relate the urban-rural disparity to income inequality. I consciously did not do it, because any relationship between the disparity and inequality is partly tautological. Sectoral inequality has to affect personal or household inequality, even where only an urban and a rural sector are distinguished.
6. Rent-seeking presupposes efforts to restrict and evade competition. It results in price distortions, less allocative efficiency, and less economic growth. According to the rent-seeking paradigm, state interference with the economy tends to generate rents, to reinforce political conflicts, and to result in economic stagnation.

REFERENCES

Ballmer-Cao, T.-H. and Scheidegger, J. 1979. *Compendium of Data for World System Analysis*. Zuerich: Soziologisches Institut.
Bradshaw, Y. W. 1985. "Overurbanization and Underdevelopment in Sub-Saharan Africa," *Studies in Comparative International Development*, vol. 20, no. 3:74–101.
Bradshaw, Y.W. 1987. "Urbanization and Underdevelopment: A Global Study of Modernization, Urban Bias, and Economic Dependency," *American Sociological Review*, vol. 52, no. 2:224–239.
Corbridge, S. 1982. "Urban Bias, Rural Bias, and Industrialization," in J. Harriss, (ed.), *Rural Development. Theories of Peasant Economy and Agrarian Change*. London: Hutchinson.
Friedrich, R. J. 1982. "The Workshop: In Defense of Multiplicative Terms in

Multiple Regression Equations," *American Journal of Political Science*, vol. 26, no. 4:797–833.

Horvat, B. 1974. "The Relationship Between Rate of Growth and Level of Development," *Journal of Development Studies*, vol. 10, no. 3 and 4:382–394.

Jackman, R. W. 1980. "A Note on the Measurement of Growth Rates in Cross-National Research," *American Journal of Sociology*, vol. 86, no. 3: 604–617.

Jagodzinski, W. and Weede, E. 1981. "Testing Curvilinear Propositions by Polynomial Regression with Particular Reference to the Interpretation of Standardized Solutions," *Quality and Quantity*, vol. 15, no. 5: 447–463.

Kuznets, S. 1976. *Modern Economic Growth*. New Haven, CT: Yale University Press (7th ed.)

Lipton, M. 1977. *Why Poor People Stay Poor: Urban Bias in World Development*. London: Temple Smith.

———. 1982. "Why Poor People Stay Poor," in J. Harriss (ed.) *Rural Development: Theories of Peasant Economy and Agrarian Change*. London: Hutchinson.

———. 1984. "Urban Bias Revisited," *Journal of Development Studies*, vol. 20, no. 3: 139–166.

Maddison, A. 1969. *Economic Growth in Japan and the USSR*. London: George Allen and Unwin.

Marx, K. 1852. *Der achtzehnte Brumaire des Louis Bonaparte*, reprinted in Marx-Engels-Studienausgabe, vol. 4 (Pp. 34–121). Frankfurt/Main (1966): Fischer.

Taylor, Ch. and Hudson, M. C. 1972. *World Handbook of Political and Social Indicators* (2nd ed.). New Haven, CT: Yale University Press.

Taylor, Ch. and Jodice, D. A. 1983. *World Handbook of Political and Social Indicators* (3rd ed.). New Haven, CT: Yale University Press.

Weede, E. 1984. "Political Democracy, State Strength, and Economic Growth in LDCs," *Review of International Studies*, vol. 10, no. 4:297–312.

———. 1985. *Entwicklungsländer in der Weltgesellschaft*. Opladen: Westdeutscher Verlag.

———. 1986a. "Rent-Seeking, Military Participation, and Economic Performance in LDCs," *Journal of Conflict Resolution*, vol. 30, no. 2:291–314.

———. 1986b. "Rent-Seeking or Dependency as Explanations of Why Poor People Stay Poor," *International Sociology*, vol. 1, no. 4:421–441.

World Bank. 1979. *World Development Report*. London: Oxford University Press.

———. 1980. *World Development Report*. London: Oxford University Press.

———. 1981. *World Development Report*. London: Oxford University Press.

———. 1983. *World Development Report*. London: Oxford University Press.

28

The Effects of Democracy on Economic Growth and Inequality

LARRY SIROWY & ALEX INKELES

In the best of all worlds, the political system that provided for the highest levels of civil and political freedom would also encourage high levels of economic growth and equality. In this chapter, Larry Sirowy and Alex Inkeles catalogue studies that analyze the relationship between democracy, economic growth, and inequality. Unfortunately, the authors do not find any consistent conclusions about democracy's impact, but they do offer suggestions for future research based on their analysis.

Over the last two decades many researchers have sought confirmation for hypotheses expressing systematic relations between characteristics of political regimes and patterns of national development. More specifically, do politics matter with respect to the pace and form of economic growth, and with respect to the distribution of income and social benefits? . . . .

Strikingly, the task of reexamining the development consequences of political democracy could not come at a more critical time in contemporary history. On the one hand, the presumption of a linkage between current democratic political reforms and future economic prosperity has come to inform much of the West's policy prescriptions for Eastern Europe and China. At the same time, numerous Latin American nations face critical

Reprinted with permission from the publishers, Transaction Books, "The Effects of Democracy on Economic Growth and Inequality: A Review," by Larry Sirowy and Alex Inkeles, in Alex Inkeles, ed., *On Measuring Democracy: Its Consequences and Concomitants* (New Brunswick, NJ: Transactions Books, 1991).

political tests in the near future because of the severe economic problems they are experiencing, problems which may or may not be contributed to by the democratic political organization of their polities. In the final analysis, such current events point out the urgent need to reexamine the issue of the development consequences of democracy.

THEORETICAL PERSPECTIVES

Effects of Political Democracy on Economic Growth

Since the early 1970s, a growing body of scholars and Third World officials have come to embrace the position that difficult, sometimes cruel, choices must be made among such development goals as economic growth, socioeconomic equality, and political democracy (for example, see the works of Hewlett 1979 and Huntington and Nelson 1976). As Huntington (1987) aptly describes it, there has emerged a strong tendency to perceive the relationships among such development goals as being conflictive, even to the point of incompatibility. With respect to the particular empirical questions of interest here, the implications of this position are clear: political democracy is a luxury that can be ill-afforded by Third World countries.

In general, proponents of this perspective suggest that developing countries in today's world cannot achieve rapid economic growth through a democratic framework. In other words, developing countries are considered to face the dilemma of choosing to pursue either economic growth or democratic development, but not both simultaneously.

This position stands in stark contrast to the earlier perspective that democratic institutions and political freedom are neither peculiarly limited to Europe nor relevant only to the nineteenth century, but rather that democratic institutions are meaningful, appropriate, and potentially very satisfying programs for organizing social and economic life in the currently less-developed countries. Moreover, proponents of this alternative perspective contend that the notion of conflict between democracy and development in Third World nations only serves to legitimate the denial of basic human rights and freedoms by repressive and exclusionary regimes, and so ultimately undermines democratic political change.

As Huntington (1987) notes, this older, alternative perspective, which appears to be receiving a groundswell of support in recent years, has its roots in such modernization theorists as Karl Deutsch, Daniel Lerner, and Cyril Black. For them, modernization was a systematic process, wherein such development goals as political democracy, economic growth, and equity were not only compatible with one another, but generally mutually reinforcing. All in all, it remains the case, as Huntington so perceptively points out, that this perspective continues to influence U.S. policy toward the Third World.

Following Huntington (1987) we adopt the terminological convention of labeling these theoretical positions as the "Conflict" and "Compatibility" perspectives, respectively. In the balance of this section these perspectives are more fully elaborated with respect to their implications for the effects of political democracy on economic growth and socioeconomic inequality. In addition, a third perspective, which we shall refer to as the "Skeptical" alternative, is presented. The hallmark of this latter alternative is the contention that no universal relationship exists between political democracy and the developmental outcomes under consideration here. Put simply, economic growth is held to be potentially compatible with both a more democratic framework and a more authoritarian framework.

The Conflict Perspective

Fundamental to the conflict perspective is the claim that economic growth is hindered by the democratic organization of the polity (see De Schweinitz 1964, Andreski 1968, Chirot 1977, and Rao 1985). In other words, democracy and economic growth are seen as being competing concerns; hence trade offs in the political realm are considered necessary. Moreover, in this view successful and rapid economic growth requires an authoritarian regime that suppresses or delays the extension of basic civil and political rights and the development of democratic procedures and institutions, because these latter would otherwise subvert the national development project. The reasons that have been offered in support of such a claim are basically threefold: 1) dysfunctional consequences of "premature" democracy act, in turn, to slow growth, 2) democratic regimes are largely unable to implement effectively the kinds of policies considered necessary to facilitate rapid growth, 3) the uniqueness of the present world-historical context requires pervasive state involvement in the development process, which is in turn unduly fettered by political democracy. . . .

The Compatibility Perspective

Proponents of the democratic model sharply object to the charges levied by proponents of the authoritarian model. Although the compatibility model concedes that economic development requires an authority to enforce contracts, ensure law and order, and so on, they strongly disagree with the assumption that development needs to be commanded in all respects by a central authority, an assumption that takes a heavy toll in terms of citizen rights and freedoms (see Holt and Turner, 1966). Moreover, even if one accepts the argument that latecomer nations in the post-World War II era need governmental structures that perform a wider range of functions and more heavily penetrate sectors of their societies than their Western counterparts did, we can still treat as analytically distinguishable the

scope of state involvement and the democratic character of political
institutions. . . .

Some proponents of the democratic model, however, do not stop at
simply taking issue with the assumptions of the authoritarian model.
Indeed, such theorists as McCord (1965), Goodin (1979), King (1981),
Goodell and Powelson (1982), and Kohli (1986) argue that it is a democratic
government in the Third World that is best suited to foster sustained and
equitable economic development. In their view, democratic processes and the
existence and exercise of fundamental civil liberties and political rights
generate the societal conditions most conducive to economic development. . . .

The Skeptical Perspective

Finally, we would like to briefly mention an alternative stance that some
theorists have taken toward the issue of the consequences of democracy for
economic growth. This alternative stance is skeptical that there is any
systematic relationship between democracy and economic development (see
Pye 1966). In other words, politics alone matter very little. Proponents of
this perspective note the variable nature of levels of economic performance
within groupings of more democratic and more authoritarian regimes and
suggest that this variability indicates that we need to concentrate instead on
the institutional structures that exist and the government strategies that are
embraced, factors that may vary independently of the democratic character of a
system, and how these can act to reconcile such development goals as
democracy and development. Such factors include, for example, the nature of
the political party system (two-party vs. multiparty), the level and form of
state intervention into the economy, the pattern of industrialization pursued
(labor-intensive vs. capital-intensive), and the cultural environment (see
Huntington, 1987). Hence, the skepticism in this perspective derives from
the contention that additional, often intervening, factors operate to confound
the direct link between democracy and development.

THE EFFECTS OF DEMOCRACY ON INEQUALITY

With respect to the consequences of political democracy for socioeconomic
inequality, we again find the positions of theorists divided. Regarding this
relationship, the source of that division, which is obviously very related to
that of the foregoing discussion, is the question of whether democracy
operates to reduce inequality, exacerbate inequality, or simply has no
systematic influence. In the following section these various positions are
referred to as the "Democratic Model," the "Authoritarian Model," and the
"Skeptical Model," respectively.

Democratic Model

Oddly enough, many proponents of either the conflict or the compatibility perspectives, as discussed in reference to the consequences of democracy for economic growth, converge on the position that political democracy operates to reduce distributional inequalities. The reasoning behind this convergence is essentially twofold. On the one hand, democracy is viewed to facilitate equality indirectly because economic development itself is argued to aggravate inequalities (Kuznets 1955), at least up to a point, and democracies are argued by proponents of the conflict perspective to be less able to achieve rapid economic growth.

On the other hand, proponents of the compatibility perspective emphasize the same outcome for different reasons. Democracies are conceived to tend to neither adopt economic growth policies that directly attempt to deprive specific social groups of their relative economic shares nor are they free to ignore the voices of mobilized sectors of the population due to their legitimacy needs. Because of electoral mechanisms and rights to opposition and participation, democracies are relatively open to battles over the distribution of societal resources (Lipset 1959). . . .

Authoritarian Model

The relatively popular democratic model just presented is not, however, uniformly accepted. Beitz (1982), for one, disagrees. For Beitz, authoritarian regimes are more likely to pursue egalitarian development policies than are democratic regimes. Central to his argument is the contention that authoritarian regimes may do a better job of protecting the interests of the poor and working classes in developing societies than democracies can. Why? Because the available political rights and their expression through electoral mechanisms cannot be taken advantage of by the more disadvantaged elements of society. In other words, inequalities in the distribution of material resources are reproduced in inequalities of political influence. Thus, although Beitz accepts the view that democracies are more receptive to claims made by societal members, he contends that democracies fail to respect their members equally as sources of claims. Moreover, the disadvantaged are unable to defend their interest through democratic processes. In contrast, authoritarian regimes are more capable of protecting interests unlikely to be protected by democracies.

Huntington and Nelson (1976), while supporting the logic of Beitz' argument to a degree, nevertheless qualify his reasoning by contending that since more privileged groups usually become politically active earlier than the less privileged, then it might well be the case that at most there is a curvilinear relationship between levels of participation and equality. Still, however, this pattern of relationship depends on how much, and how effectively, the less privileged strata exercise the opportunity to participate relative to participation by the "haves." Finally, Bollen and Jackman (1985) also question whether democracies tend to be better for equality. In particular, they question whether democracies adhere to majoritarianism, whether low-income voters demand redistribution—especially given the government intervention it requires—and whether inequality is even perceived as being unjust.

Skeptical Model

The two schools of thought most frequently cited as representatives of the skeptical model are functionalists and Marxists. As Marsh (1979) argued in his review of the "skeptical model," functionalism implies that the form of government does not affect the stratification systems, since any changes in the distributive outcomes are explained as a result of changes in the shape of the occupational structure brought on by the imperatives of industrialization. Any association between democracy and socioeconomic equality is spurious since both are determined by the level of a nation's economic development.

Alternatively, Marxists hold that the political system is largely of little importance. What is important is the particular configuration of the class structure, and, in particular, the economic power of the capitalist class. To understand the "why" of the distribution of inequalities and changes in distribution, one must understand the class structure and dynamics.

Finally, Nelson (1987) suggests that we should be skeptical in embracing any universal relationship between extended patterns of political participation, or democracy, and equality, since the pattern of participation may play an important intervening role. Particularly crucial may be the relative participation rates of urban versus rural populations in developing countries.

STATE OF EMPIRICAL RESEARCH

The Effects of Democracy on Economic Development

Thirteen cross-national, quantitative studies have been reviewed in the course of our work. Each of these studies explicitly attempted to evaluate the economic consequences of differences in the democratic character of national regimes. . . .

Out of these thirteen studies only three—Huntington and Dominguez (1975), Marsh (1979), and Landau (1986)—report findings suggesting an unqualified negative effect of democracy on rates of economic growth. Six studies—Feierabend and Feierabend (1972), Dick (1974), Russett and Monsen (1975), Meyer et al. (1979), Kohli (1986), and Marsh (1988)—report that there is no relationship between the democratic character of regimes and the pace of economic growth. Finally, each of the remaining four studies report some kind of qualified, or conditional, relationship. For example, Adelman and Morris (1967) report that democracy appears to inhibit growth, but not among the wealthier less-developed countries. Weede (1983) reports the existence of a negative relationship only when developed countries and less-developed countries are both included in the analysis (no effect when less-developed countries are examined alone), and also in those societies in which the role of the state in economic affairs is decidedly larger. Both Berg-Schlosser (1984) and Sloan and Tedin (1987), in contrast, report that the type of regime matters, that is, there are real differences among regime types, but the pattern of these differences depends on the particular measure of economic progress examined.

Hence, overall, these studies present a very mixed and confusing picture with regard to the effect of democracy on economic growth. The inconclusive results presented by these studies are further compounded by the fact that these studies are quite heterogeneous with respect to characteristics of measurement, coverage, design, and method of analysis.

One of the most systematic deficiencies to be found in these studies is the misspecification of the economic growth model. Only in the studies by Adelman and Morris (1967), Meyer et al. (1979), Weede (1983), Landau (1986), and Marsh (1988) is there any attempt to include as controls a number of factors known to affect economic growth. Indeed, clearly in seven of the studies: Feierabend and Feierabend, Dick, Huntington and Dominguez, Russett and Monsen, Marsh (1979), Kohli, and Sloan and Tedin, either no other factors were specified as influencing economic growth in the analysis or the analysis was badly underspecified. Such factors as initial level of development, the availability of human capital, the availability of internal investment, population growth, and so on must be properly specified in the analysis and thus controlled for in order for estimates of the effect of democracy to be at all meaningful. Nevertheless, even among the five studies identified as being the most adequate with respect to model specification, rather discrepant results were found.

A second feature that could account for the discrepancies in the results obtained is the set of countries examined. Besides substantial variation in the number of countries examined, some looked at a set including both developed and developing nations, some surveyed less-developed countries only, and several examined only a select group of less-developed countries. The exact composition of the set of countries analyzed in each study is presented in Table 28.1, along with a notation on the major result found in each study for the relationship between democracy and economic growth.

As Table 28.1 indicates, there has indeed been a substantial amount of variation in the number and set of countries examined. Moreover, an examination of the results reported by each of these studies indicates that there is no clear association between the population of countries observed and

Table 28.1

	Wide Survey of LDCs	
Adelman and Morris (1967)	Conditional	(N=74)
Dick (1974)	None	(N=72)
Huntington and Dominguez (1975)	Negative	(N=35)
Marsh (1979)	Negative	(N=80)
Meyer et al. (1979)	None	(N=23)
Weede (1983)	None	(N=74)
Landau (1986)	Negative	(N=65)
Marsh (1988)	None	(N=55)
	Survey of DCs and LDCs	
Feierabend and Feierabend (1972)	None	(N=84)
Russett and Monsen (1975)	None	(N=80)
Meyer et al. (1979)	None	(N=50)
Weede (1983)	Negative	(N=93)
	Survey of Select LDCs only	
Kohli (1986)	None	(N=10)
Sloan and Tedin (1987)	Conditional	(N=20, all L.A.)
Berg-Schlosser (1984)	Conditional	(N=38, all African)

the major finding. Unfortunately, there has been little effort to replicate studies and thereby enhance our knowledge in the area in a cumulative fashion.

A third factor that may account for the differences in findings is the period for which economic performance was assessed. Roughly speaking, three broad periods were investigated: studies assessing economic performance for a period beginning before 1960 and ending by 1965; studies assessing economic performance for a period roughly equivalent to the decade of the sixties; and, finally, studies assessing economic performance for a period beginning in the sixties and ending in the early eighties. . . .

If we categorize the twelve studies according to the appropriate period and then examine the findings reported, does any pattern emerge? Again the answer would have to be no. No systematic relationship appears between the period examined and the results. . . .

The Effects of Democracy on Inequality

Cross-national, quantitative research on the effect of democracy on societal inequality has come to form more of a research program than has research on the effects of democracy on economic growth. Surprisingly, however, the relevant studies are inconclusive. . . .

As can be seen in Table 28.2, seven of the studies present evidence indicating confirmation for the inverse relationship between democracy and societal inequality, where inequality is measured by the distribution of income. Their support, however, must be qualified. Cutright, after assigning nations to subgroups based upon level of economic development, found confirmation for the low and middle income subsets of nations, but not for the most advanced subset. Weede and Tiefenbach found confirmation of the inverse relationship for two measures of personal income inequality (using Paukert's data 1973), but not for four alternative measures of income inequality from two different sources. Hewitt found a negative correlation for his indicator of political democracy and income inequality, though he argues that it is social democracy (meaning the strength of Socialist parties or working-class politics within the lawmaking bodies), rather than political democracy, that is important. Finally, Muller presents results that would indicate it is the length of experience of democracy, rather than the level of political democracy as measured at one point in time, that facilitates reductions in inequality.

The five studies that indicate a disconfirmation of the proposed linkage report either that there is no significant relationship, in either a positive or negative direction, between political democracy and societal inequality or that the line of causation properly modeled actually runs in the opposite direction. The investigations of Jackman (1975) and Bollen and Grandjean (1981) each found nonsignificant effects of political democracy on societal inequality. Rubinson and Quinlan (1977) report that once the reciprocal effects between the two variables are explicitly taken into consideration, something that had not been examined before their study, the only significant direction of effects lies in the opposite direction (i.e., inequality affects democracy). In a more recent study, however, Bollen and Jackman (1985) reexamined the argument of Rubinson and Quinlan and found no significant effects between democracy or inequality in either direction. Muller (1988), however, reports that whereas length of democratic experience appears to facilitate significantly greater levels of income equality, he found no support for the "genesis" version of the causal impact of inequality on the inauguration of democracy.

Where do these studies leave us? It is clear that while no generalizable and robust confirmation of the thesis that democracy promotes greater

Table 28.2

Yes	No
Cutright (1967)	Jackman (1975)
Hewitt (1977)	Rubinson and Quinlan (1977)
Stack (1979)	Bollen and Grandjean (1981)
Stack (1980)	Kohli et al. (1984)
Weede and Tiefenbach (1981)	Bollen and Jackman (1985)
Weede (1982)	
Muller (1988)	

equality is forthcoming from this set of studies, the issue is by no means settled. Numerous differences in design, measurement, and model distinguish these studies, which alone or in combination might account for the kinds of results they have produced.

The first of these differences that can be considered is how social equality was measured. Each of these studies attempted to measure social equality by assessing the degree of concentration of the distribution of income, or some proxy for it. The difficulties in accurately measuring the distribution of income are widely known. Information on income distribution is confounded by global heterogeneity in its standards of collection, which makes international comparisons exceedingly difficult. Some of the sources of this heterogeneity include whether the income figures are pretax or posttax, whether the data are based on households or individuals (though the efforts of Bollen and Jackman (1985) and Muller (1988) attempt to control for this confounding factor in their analyses), and whether income figures are representative of the nation as a whole or refer only to certain regions or cities.

These data problems are yet further complicated by the fact that there are a number of data sources available (for example, Paukert, Ahluwalia, the World Bank), and these sources, although overlapping to some extent in the years reported and nations covered, are still distinguishable in terms of coverage and some of the figures reported. Hence it matters whose measure one happens to be using. This has been vividly demonstrated by Weede and Tiefenbach, who found confirmation using the data reported by Paukert (1973), but disconfirmation using the data of Ahluwalia (1976), though the two sources also differ somewhat in the nations covered.

Finally, one of the most serious obstacles to research on the link between democracy and income inequality continues to be the relative absence of data at more than one point in time. This forces research designs to be cross-sectional, which gives one very little leverage in addressing questions posed in dynamic terms. Efforts to piece together two points of inequality data, as only Kohli and associates attempted, to support at least a simple panel design are besieged by problems of comparability.

It is also important to remember that the dates the income inequality figures refer to in existing data banks vary across nations. Only Rubinson and Quinlan sought to explicitly match the dates for all of their variables in order to control for this possible weakness (they then included a control variable in their analysis, the value of which was the year the values were coded for). None of the other ten studies adopted this strategy. How much error is introduced in a cross-sectional design by having one variable measured in 1960 and another measured in 1965 is difficult to estimate, but it certainly would seem necessary in instances of discrepancies of a few years or more to make some effort to be reasonably sure that the discrepancy is not confounding the results.

In the set of twelve studies under review, only two, Cutright (1967) and Jackman (1975), did not use some measure of personal or household income distribution. Instead, these two investigators used a measure of the distribution of income across industrial sectors. As Bollen and Jackman (1985) point out, this latter measure is only an imperfect proxy for personal income distribution and may well be analytically and empirically distinguishable.

The remaining ten studies used some explicit measure of personal or household income distribution, but as a set they exhibit considerable variability with respect to the source of that data and with regard to which particular measures of income distribution they examined. . . .

In light of these weaknesses, a profitable area for future research is to investigate the construction of alternative indicators that have the virtue of being highly correlated with existing inequality measures, but which are available on a time-series basis and are based on information gathered according to standards that are much more comparable internationally. Such a measure might be along the lines of Morris' (1979) physical quality of life index. . . .

Beyond the factors already considered, what other factors might be affecting the discrepant findings evident in the set of a dozen studies under consideration? Three issues which have been noted in the literature (see Weede 1982; Bollen and Jackman 1985) are the model specification of the relationship between level of economic development and the measure of inequality, the possibility of reciprocal effects between democracy and inequality, and the composition of the sets of nations included in the respective data bases. We will turn briefly to each of these.

First both Kuznets (1955) and Lenski (1966) have argued that the relationship between economic development and inequality follows a nonlinear (inverted U) form. However, only five of the studies have specified this form of the relationship in the models they have tested (Bollen and Grandjean, Weede and Tiefenbach, Weede, Bollen and Jackman, and Muller). Though it is obviously important to include the correct specification, the presence or absence of a nonlinear relationship alone cannot explain the discrepant findings: two of the five studies that did specify a curvilinear relationship report a negative relationship between democracy and income inequality; two report no relationship; and one, Muller, reports a negative effect of democratic experience on inequality but no independent effect of the mere level of political democracy, as measured by Bollen's indicator, on inequality.

With regard to the possibility of reciprocal effects between democracy and inequality, only three studies, those by Rubinson and Quinlan, Bollen and Jackman, and Muller, have explicitly tested this possibility. In the kind of cross-section research being conducted on this issue, it is important to estimate a simultaneous-equations model in order to be relatively certain that a simple recursive model, where the only allowed effect is from democracy to inequality, is not yielding misleading results. Both of these studies found no effect of democracy on income inequality.

A third characteristic of these studies that must be considered in both interpreting the contradictory results of existing studies and developing an alternative indicator is that of sample composition. Because of the general scarcity of data on inequality, most of the studies examined here performed their analysis on an average of about a third of existing nations. The details of the composition of the sets of countries analyzed are presented in Table 28.3.

How far does the variation in composition of the sets of countries analyzed go toward explaining the pattern of results found? The answer is largely unknown. Obviously the differences in the sizes of the sets of countries analyzed could have had profound consequences for the results found. The sizes of many of these studies make them extremely sensitive to the inclusion or exclusion of just a few cases. Although Bollen and Jackman (1985) undertook the only effort to estimate whether their results would hold up under a check for outliers and replications with random subsamples, the fact remains that their sample was neither a random sample of all countries nor is its size large enough for us to place complete confidence in it. In addition, the issue remains as to whether the analysis should contain both developed countries and developing countries or only the latter.

A final feature of the studies being reviewed in this section that warrants attention is how democracy was measured in each. . . . Again . . . differences in the particular measure used cannot alone begin to explain the discrepancies on findings. . . .

Table 28.3   Sets of Countries Examined in the Studies

	DCs and LDCs	
Stack (1980)	Negative	(N=37)
Weede (1982)	Negative	(N=21)
Bollen and Jackman (1985)	None	(N=60)
Jackman (1975)	None	(N=60)
Bollen and Grandjean (1981)	None	(N=50)
Rubinson and Quinlan (1977)	None	(N=32)
Weede and Tiefenbach (1981)	Negative	(N=34–46)
Cutright (1967)	Negative	(N=44)
Muller (1988)	Negative	(N=50–55)
	DCs Only	
Stack (1979)	Negative	(N=18)
Hewitt (1977)	Negative	(N=25, 2 LDCs)
	LDCs Only	
Kohli et al. (1984)	None	(N=20)

Before leaving this topic, however, it must be noted that the use of voter turnout measures as an indicator of political democracy may well be quite unsatisfactory. Voter turnout data were used by both Stack and Weede in two of the studies above, and voter turnout is a component of Jackman's Democratic Performance Indicator which, in turn, was used in four studies. The problems with voter participation data are many-fold and are aptly described by Bollen (1980). Indeed, Bollen found that a measure of the percentage of the adult population who voted was either not related to or inversely related to a number of other dimensions of political democracy. Hence, its use probably only further confounds the results. . . .

CONCLUSION

In the final analysis, the worth of our review lies in its clarification of the theoretical issues at hand and in its careful scrutiny of the studies that have been performed so as to guide our evaluations of the theoretical implications and to inform future research with the hope that such efforts will not repeat past mistakes. . . .

In light of this state of affairs, a few remarks are in order. First, carefully designed replications of the kinds of studies reviewed are of utmost importance. In these studies special attention needs to be paid to the issues of sample composition, method of analysis, model specification, and measurement of the central variables. Moreover, assessments of robustness are crucial with respect to differences in subsamples of countries, measures, and periods examined.

Second, before this program of research can move forward in a fertile fashion, numerous measurement issues must be addressed. Of these, none is more central than the valid and reliable measurement of political democracy. Should political democracy be assessed on a point or period basis? Which dimensions of political procedures, practices, and institutions are relevant to our classification of national societies in terms of political democracy, and which are not? Should our measure of political democracy be continuous (ordinal) or discrete in form? All of these are critical issues that have only begun to be addressed (for a noteworthy exception, see Bollen, 1980). . . .

Third, with respect to information about the national political systems covered by these measures, the measures differ from one another with regard to whether information on system stability, extent of franchise, and degree of exercise of the franchise are included. Nonetheless, nearly all of the measures surveyed are anchored in the notion that distinguishing systems in terms of political democracy rests ultimately on the degree to which political elites are selected by citizens via elections that are regular and meaningful. Obviously, the meaningfulness of elections of political elites is a slippery concept to operationalize. Thus, how it is exactly observed and coded is of great interest and importance. Judging from the all-too-frequently brief and cryptic annotations associated with the existing measures, it would appear that evidence for making "meaningfulness" judgements rests most commonly on two pieces of information: 1) was the election conducted under circumstances that would have been conducive to the presentation of real electoral choice? and 2) were the elections in fact competitive or contested?

Relevant information examined to assess the first of these prerequisites of meaningfulness, while by no means universally examined, includes such factors as the status of press freedom, freedom from government acts to suppress opposition, and the health and vitality of intermediary interest groups such as parties and unions. The degree to which elections were indeed actually competitive is most frequently inferred from an examination of the outcomes of the elections observed, particularly those elections for positions in the national legislative body, namely in terms of the proportional representation of the party memberships of those in office. . . .

A [fourth] critical point is as follows. It is painfully clear that in order for the relevant theoretical debates to move forward, considerable attention must be allocated not just to evaluating the overall relationship between political democracy and development outcomes, but also to evaluating the relationships between political democracy and a host of intervening factors through which democracy is considered to have its ultimate effects on such development outcomes as rate of economic growth and inequality. For example, some speculate that democracy hinders growth because the former engenders higher levels of instability. Huntington (1987) notes, however, that this connection is less clear than we assume. In light of Hibbs's (1973) finding that there is little systematic relationship between mass political violence and economic growth, Huntington suggests that there is perhaps a threshold effect of political violence on economic growth. Couple this with Marsh's (1979) finding that among less-developed countries there is little difference in the level of conflict between those with democratic and those with authoritarian political institutions; then even a general negative relationship between democracy and rate of economic growth offers little support to a theory that is grounded in the linkages between democracy and political instability, and, in turn, instability and economic growth.

[Fifth], clearly more attention needs to be paid to specifying the conditions under which the relationships of interest hold and under which they do not. This point derives from the arguments of those who embrace what we have referred to as the "skeptical" perspectives. Clearly, even the conclusions put forth here—that democracy does not widely lead to rapid economic growth and that authoritarianism is not widely associated with lower levels of inequality—must be necessarily tempered in light of such obvious countercases as Taiwan, Republic of Korea, and Japan. Considering quantitative, cross-national research, Weede's (1983) investigation of the effects of political democracy on economic growth under different degrees of state involvement in the economy illustrates the kind of avenue that new research could pursue.

[Sixth] and last, we would wholeheartedly recommend that new outcome measures be pursued in future research. Along these lines it would be most worthwhile to move beyond simple measures of rate of economic growth and on to measures that indicate features of the type of economic growth and the pattern of industrialization. Income inequality, with its widely acknowledged shortcomings, needs to be supplemented by other indicators of the general social and economic welfare of the population, indicators that likewise tap into the issue of distribution. Such indicators exist in the form of measures of fulfillment of basic human needs and welfare provisions. But as of yet, and as briefly noted earlier, only a handful of studies have begun to look at such alternative indicators of development outcomes and their relation to democracy. Obviously, much work remains to be done.

REFERENCES

Adelman, I. and C. T. Morris. 1967. *Society, Politics, and Economic Development: A Quantitative Approach.* Baltimore: Johns Hopkins University Press.

Ahluwalia, M. S. 1976. "Inequality, Poverty, and Development." *Journal of Development Economics* 3:307–42.

Andreski, S. 1968. *Military Organization and Society.* Palo Alto: Stanford University Press.

Beitz, C. R. 1982. "Democracy in Developing Societies." In R. Gastil (ed.) *Freedom in the World: Political Rights and Civil Liberties,* pp. 145–66. New York: Freedom House.

Berg-Schlosser, Dirk. 1984. "African Political Systems: Typology and Performance," *Comparative Political Studies* 17:121–51.

Bollen, K. 1980. "Issues in the Comparative Measurement of Political Democracy," *American Sociological Review* 45:370–90.

——— and B. D. Grandjean. 1981. "The Dimension(s) of Democracy: Further Issues in the Measurement and Effects of Political Democracy," *American Sociological Review* 46:651–59.

Bollen, K. and R. W. Jackman. 1985. "Political Democracy and the Size Distribution of Income," *American Sociological Review* 50:438–57.

Chirot, D. 1977. *Social Change in the Twentieth Century.* New York: Harcourt Brace Jovanovich.

Cutright, P. 1967. "Inequality: A Cross-National Analysis." *American Sociological Review* 32:562–78.

De Schweinitz, K. 1964. *Industrialization and Democracy.* New York: Free Press.

Dick, G. W. 1974. "Authoritarian versus Nonauthoritarian Approaches to Economic Development," *Journal of Political Economy* 82:817–27.

Feierabend, I. K. and R. L. Feierabend. 1972. "Coerciveness and Change: Cross-National Trends," *American Behavioral Scientist* 15:911–28.

Goodell, G. and J. P. Powelson. 1982. "The Democratic Prerequisites of Development." In R. Gastil (ed.) *Freedom in the World: Political Rights and Civil Liberties,* pp. 167–76. New York: Freedom House.

Goodin, R. E. 1979. "The Development-Rights Trade-off: Some Unwarranted Economic and Political Assumptions," *Universal Human Rights* 1: 31–42.

Hewitt, C. 1977. "The Effect of Political Democracy and Social Democracy on Equality in Industrial Societies: A Cross-National Comparison," *American Sociological Review* 42:450–64.

Hewlett, S. A. 1979. "Human Rights and Economic Realities—Tradeoffs in Historical Perspective," *Political Science Quarterly* 94:453–73.

Hibbs, D. A. 1973. *Mass Political Violence*. New York: Wiley.

Holt, R. T. and J. E. Turner. 1966. *The Political Bases of Economic Development*. Princeton, NJ: Van Nostrand.

Huntington, S. P. 1987. *Understanding Political Development: An Analytic Study*. Boston: Little Brown.

——— and J. I. Dominguez. 1975. "Political Development," in F. I. Greenstein and N. W. Polsby (eds.), *Handbook of Political Science. Vol. 3. Macropolitical Theory*, 1–114. Reading, Mass.: Addison-Wesley.

Huntington, S. P. and J. M. Nelson, 1976. *No Easy Choice: Political Participation in Developing Countries*. Cambridge, Mass.: Harvard University Press.

Jackman, R. W., 1975. *Politics and Social Equality: A Comparative Analysis*. New York: John Wiley & Sons.

King, D. Y. 1981. "Regime Type and Performance," *Comparative Political Studies* 13:477–504.

Kohli, A. 1986. "Democracy and Development." In J. Lewis and V. Kallab (eds.) *Development Strategies Reconsidered*, pp. 153–82. New Brunswick: Transaction Books.

———, M. Altfeld, S. Lotfian, and R. Mordon. 1984. "Inequality in the Third World," *Comparative Political Studies* 17:283–318.

Kuznets, S. 1955. "Economic Growth and Income Inequality," *American Economic Review* 45:18–30.

Landau, D. 1986. "Government and Economic Growth in the LDCs: An Empirical Study for 1960–1980," *Economic Development and Cultural Change* 35:35–76.

Lenski, G. 1966. *Power and Privilege: A Theory of Social Stratification*. New York: McGraw-Hill.

Lipset, S. M. 1959. "Some Social Requisites of Democracy: Economic Development and Political Development," *American Political Science Review* 53:69–105.

Marsh, R. M. 1988. "Sociological Explanations of Economic Growth," *Studies in Comparative International Development* 23(4):41–77.

———. 1979. "Does Democracy Hinder Economic Development in the Latecomer Developing Nations?" *Comparative Social Research* 2:215–48.

McCord, W. 1965. *The Springtime of Freedom*. New York: Oxford University Press.

Meyer, J. W., M. T. Hannan, R. Rubinson, and G. Thomas. 1979. "National Economic Development, 1950–70: Social and Political Factors." In J. W Meyer and M. T. Hannan (eds.) *National Development and the World System: Educational, Economic and Political Change*. Chicago: Chicago University Press.

Morris, M. 1979. *Measuring the Condition of the World's Poor: The Physical Quality of Life Index*. New York: Pergamon Press.

Muller, E. N. 1988. "Democracy, Economic Development, and Income Inequality," *American Sociological Review* 53:50–68.

Nelson, J. 1987. "Political Participation," in M. Weiner and S. P. Huntington (eds.) *Understanding Political Development: An Analytic Study*, pp. 103–59. Boston: Little Brown.

Paukert, F. 1973. "Income Distribution at Different Levels of Development: A Survey of Evidence," *International Labour Review* 108:97–125.

Pye, Lucian. 1966. *Aspects of Political Development*. Boston: Little Brown.

Rao, Vaman. 1985. "Democracy and Economic Development," *Studies in Comparative International Development* 19(4):67–81.

Rubinson, R. and D. Quinlan. 1977. "Democracy and Social Inequality," *American Sociological Review* 42:611–623.

Russett, B. M. and R. J. Monsen. 1975. "Bureaucracy and Polyarchy as Predictors of Performance: A Cross-National Exam," *Comparative Political Studies* 8:5–31.

Sloan, J. and K. L. Tedin. 1987. "The Consequences of Regime Type for Public Policy Outputs," *Comparative Political Studies* 20:98–124.

Stack, S. 1980. "The Political Economy of Income Inequality: A Comparative Analysis," *Canadian Journal of Political Science* 13:273–86.

————. 1979. "The Effects of Political Participation and Socialist Party Strength on the Degree of Income Inequality," *American Sociological Review* 44:168–81.

Weede, E. 1983a. "The Impact of Democracy on Economic Growth," *Kyklos* 36(1):21–39.

Weede, E. 1982. "The Effects of Democracy and Socialist Strength on the Size Distribution of Income," *International Journal of Comparative Sociology* 23:151–65.

Weede, E. and H. Tiefenbach. 1981a. "Some Recent Explanations of Income Inequality," *International Studies Quarterly* 25(2):255–82.

29

. . . .

Big Business and the State: Latin America and East Asia Compared

. . . .

GARY GEREFFI

*In the late 1950s and early 1960s, Latin America seemed most likely to
be the next industrialized, developed region. Now attention has turned
to the East Asian countries. In this chapter, Gary Gereffi proposes that
different industrial structures have resulted in different paths to
industrialization. Industrial structure enables us to understand differences
not only between the Latin American and East Asian experiences but
within them as well.*

The Latin American and East Asian newly industrializing countries (NICs)
frequently have been taken to represent two contrasting development
orientations: Mexico, Brazil, and Argentina are seen as having given primacy
to an inward-oriented (import-substituting) mode of development, while
Taiwan, South Korea, Hong Kong, and Singapore are associated with an
outward-oriented (export-promoting) model. While these regional contrasts
help us to understand many features of Latin American and East Asian
development, national diversity among the NICs often overshadows regional
similarities.

One form of subregional variation that tends to have been ignored in
previous studies is industrial structure. There are two sets of indicators related
to industrial structure: (1) the characteristics of a country's leading firms and
(2) aggregate concentration measures that show how important big business
is within the national economy. At the firm level, the three main features of

industrial structure are: size, ownership, and industrial sector. At the aggregate level, the most convenient way to measure industrial concentration is to see what share of a country's gross domestic product (GDP) is accounted for by a certain number of the biggest firms. We will use both kinds of indicators in this chapter.

Taiwan and South Korea have sharply contrasting industrial structures in terms of the characteristics of their leading business enterprises. Taiwan has a predominance of small and medium-sized firms, often family owned, while Korean industry centers around huge economic conglomerates (*chaebols*). Although local private companies predominate in both East Asian countries, state-owned enterprises are still quite important in Taiwan. They are relatively insignificant in South Korea, however. Foreign-owned firms play a limited role in both economies, with a focus on select export industries. Even there, local companies account for the vast majority of export sales. Although both Taiwan and South Korea have strong textile and electronics industries, they differ in the prominence of their other leading sectors. Taiwan has given considerable emphasis to petrochemicals and plastics, while South Korea has emerged as a world power in heavier industries, such as steel, shipbuilding, and motor vehicles (see Haggard and Cheng, 1987).

The Latin American NICs, on the other hand, are extensively penetrated by transnational corporation (TNC) subsidiaries. Foreign firms and state-owned enterprises are clustered at the top of the industrial pyramid in each country. Mexico, to a greater extent than Brazil, has promoted joint ventures between foreign and local investors. As a result, local private capital has a somewhat larger role in the Mexican economy. The automobile complex has been central to the industrialization efforts of the Latin American NICs, but they differ in the relative importance of other leading industries. The capital goods sector in Brazil is the most advanced in Latin America. An export-oriented armaments industry and the local production of computers are top priorities for Brazil as well. Mexico's economy revolves around oil and petrochemicals, but a wide array of other industries from the booming labor-intensive *maquiladora* (bonded processing) export plants along the U.S. border to high-tech computer exports also are playing growing roles (see Gereffi, 1989a; 1989b). Whereas Mexican industries are becoming ever more tightly integrated to the U.S. market, Brazil is growing into a regional economic power with expanding investment and trade ties with Western Europe and Japan.

This chapter will explore the impact that these differences in industrial structures have on the *paths* of industrialization in the Latin American and East Asian NICs. The nature of each country's industrial structure also is a key determinant in understanding the choice, implementation, and consequences of the government's main economic *policies*.

Different industrial structures help us understand why the same broad industrial path may have distinctive characteristics within a region. Heavy and chemical industrialization (HCI) in South Korea and Taiwan in the 1970s, for example, had a contrasting pace and sectoral profile in each country. There is a similar contrast in the process of secondary import-substituting industrialization (ISI) in Mexico and Brazil, which began in the late 1950s. Industrial structure not only mediates the consequences of development trajectories, but it also helps to shape their design. In the 1980s South Korea has been pursuing a strategy that combines high value-added manufactured exports with aggressive (although still relatively limited) overseas investments and marketing efforts by the Korean *chaebol* groups in the United States and other developed country markets. This type of internationalization is beyond the capability of the smaller Taiwanese companies.

In the Latin American countries, foreign investors play a similar organizational role to the *chaebols* by utilizing their global networks to facilitate industrial integration across national boundaries. Transnational automobile companies in Mexico, relying on the country's proximity to the U.S. market and its plummeting labor costs due to recent peso devaluations, have converted Mexico into a major platform for automotive exports to the United States in the 1980s. A large proportion of these exports are intrafirm sales between related TNC units that directly link Mexican suppliers to their buyers in the United States and elsewhere. Japanese and American companies now are rushing to expand their manufacturing capacity in the Mexican industry. The Brazilian automobile industry is also strong and export-oriented, but the structure of its global integration is distinctive because of its geographical location and the relatively greater prominence of West German and Japanese auto firms there. Attention to industrial structure will allow us to better understand these and other national variations in development among the NICs.

BIG BUSINESS: NATIONAL VARIATIONS IN OWNERSHIP, SECTORAL DISTRIBUTION, AND SIZE

The ten largest industrial enterprises in Mexico, Brazil, South Korea, and Taiwan are listed in Table 29.1. This provides us with a glimpse into some of the most salient firm-level differences in industrial structure in the Latin American and East Asian NICs.

First, there are clear regional contrasts. The largest firms in Mexico and Brazil are state-owned enterprises or foreign subsidiaries of TNCs. Local private companies, on the other hand, are without question the dominant firms in South Korea, and together with state enterprises they share industrial leadership in Taiwan. A closer look, however, also reveals some important subregional differences in industrial structure.

There is a rather consistent division of labor in the roles played by

Table 29.1   The Ten Largest Companies in Mexico, Brazil, South Korea, and Taiwan, 1987

Rank/Company	Main Industry	Sales[a] (US$ millions)	Employees	Ownership[b]
Mexico				
1. Petróleos Mexicanos	Petroleum	13,115.7	210,157	State
2. Chrysler de México	Motor vehicles	1,216.6	15,412	Foreign
3. General Motors de México	Motor vehicles	1,129.6	9,793	Foreign
4. Teléfonos de México	Communications	1,081.1	44,700	State[c]
5. Ford Motor Company	Motor vehicles	1,054.4	5,344	Foreign
6. Altos Hornos de México	Iron and steel	816.1	24,963	State
7. Gigante	Commerce	681.1	20,680	Loc/priv
8. Volkswagen de México	Motor vehicles	644.9	12,855	Foreign
9. Cia. Mexicana de Aviación	Transportation	629.0	14,052	State[d]
10. Celanese Mexicana	Synthetic fibers/Resins	549.3	8,263	Loc/priv[e]
Brazil				
1. Petrobrás	Petroleum	12,492.4	50,000	State
2. Petrobrás Distribuidora	Petroleum	4,690.8	4,300	State
3. Shell Brasil	Petroleum	2,952.1	3,200	Foreign
4. Esso Brasil	Petroleum	1,877.3	1,350	Foreign
5. Eletropaulo	Electric power	1,755.3	20,600	State
6. Cia. Vale do Rio Doce	Minerals	1,736.4	23,673	State
7. Cia. Energetica São Paulo	Electric power	1,528.3	15,157	State
8. Texaco	Petroleum	1,464.9	1,313	Foreign
9. Cia.Brasileira Distribucão	Commerce	1,429.7	49,000	Loc/priv
10. Furnas Centrais Electricas	Electric power	1,385.3	9,101	State

(continues)

foreign, state, and local private capital in the Latin American NICs (see Gereffi and Evans, 1981; Newfarmer, 1985). Foreign firms have been central to the development of certain industries: electrical and nonelectrical machinery, motor vehicles, tires, rubber, chemicals, and pharmaceuticals, among others. State enterprises are concentrated in the natural resource industries, such as oil and minerals, transportation and communication, and steel production. Local private capital is quite diversified, but it is a more prominent actor in Mexico than Brazil. This has to do in part with Mexico's long-standing policy of promoting joint ventures in which domestic capitalists are involved.

We can see in Table 29.1, for example, that local private capital has a substantial minority share in two of the largest state firms in Mexico (Teléfonos de México and Compañía Mexicana de Aviación). Eleven of the top twenty-five industrial companies in the country are majority-owned by local private capital, compared with a total of seven foreign and seven state firms among the top twenty-five (*Expansión*, 1988). In Brazil, on the other hand, local private businesses account for only five of the top twenty-five industrial enterprises, while twelve state companies and eight TNC subsidiaries make up the remainder of the list (*Visão*, 1988). Although

Table 29.1 (*continued*)

Rank/Company	Main Industry	Sales[a] (U.S.$ millions)	Employees	Ownership[b]
	South Korea			
1. Samsung	Electronics	21,053.5	160,596	Loc/priv
2. Lucky-Goldstar	Electronics	14,422.3	88,403	Loc/priv
3. Daewoo	Electronics	13,437.9	94,888	Loc/priv
4. Sunkyong	Petroleum refining	6,781.6	17,985	Loc/priv
5. Ssangyong	Petroleum refining	4,582.7	16,870	Loc/priv
6. Korea Explosives	Chemicals	3,563.8	18,291	Loc/priv
7. Pohang Iron & Steel	Iron and steel	3,533.2	19,329	State
8. Hyundai Motor	Motor vehicles	3,437.4	29,000	Loc/priv
9. Hyosung	Textiles	3,257.8	24,000	Loc/priv
10. Hyundai Heavy Industries	Transportation equipment	2,964.5	48,200	Loc/priv
	Taiwan			
1. Chinese Petroleum	Petrochemicals and plastics	5,491.0	20,700	State
2. Taiwan Tobacco/Wine Monopoly Bureau	Food and beverages	2,277.1	13,495	State
3. Nan Ya Plastics	Petrochemicals and plastics	1,423.7	11,883	Loc/priv
4. China Steel	Steel	1,287.8	9,476	State
5. Formosa Plastics	Petrochemicals and plastics	946.8	5,352	Loc/priv
6. Ret-Ser Engineering	Construction	852.0	13,358	State
7. Tatung	Electronics	836.2	14,139	Loc/priv
8. Formosa Chemicals & Fiber	Textiles & dyeing	702.9	8,377	Loc/priv
9. Yue Loong Motor	Motor vehicles	687.4	3,782	Loc/priv
10. San Yang Industry	Motor vehicles	600.9	3,637	Loc/priv

Sources: Mexico: *Expansión* (1988); Brazil: *Visão* (1988); South Korea: *Fortune* (1988); and Taiwan: *CommonWealth* (1988).

a. The following annual average exchange rates for 1987 were used for converting company sales figures from the domestic currency into U.S. dollars: Mexico—1,378.2 pesos per $1.00 (IMF, 1988, p. 364); Brazil—39.229 cruzados per $1.00 (IMF, 1988, p. 132); and Taiwan—31.975 NT$ per $1.00 (calculated as an average of year-end exchange rates for 1986 and 1987, CEPD, 1988, p. 199). The sales totals for South Korean companies were initially given in U.S. dollars.

b. Ownership designations indicate a majority share. The classifications for Mexico, Brazil, and Taiwan come from the sources cited, while the ownership categories for South Korea have been supplied by the author using a variety of secondary sources.

c. Teléfonos de México; 51 percent state-owned, 49 percent local private capital.

d. Compañía Mexicana de Aviación: 56 percent state-owned, 44 percent local private capital.

e. Celanese Mexicana: 60 percent local private capital, 40 percent foreign capital.

foreign firms have a similar level of importance in the two Latin American NICs, the difference lies in the greater role for state enterprises in Brazil and for the local private sector in Mexico.

In the East Asian nations, local private firms are the main industrial actors. Nine of the ten largest companies in South Korea are privately held domestic conglomerates; the only exception is Pohang Iron and Steel, a state-owned enterprise that is ranked seventh (see Table 29.1). Each of the private South Korean conglomerates is involved in a wide range of industries and has a staggering number of affiliates. The Lucky-Goldstar group, for example, contained sixty-two companies in 1988; Samsung was made up of thirty-seven related firms, while Hyundai had thirty-four, and Daewoo twenty-eight (Clifford, 1988).

In Taiwan, as in South Korea, there are no TNCs among the top ten companies and only three foreign-owned firms in the top twenty-five. The upper level of Taiwan's industrial pyramid is relatively evenly divided between four state enterprises and six local private companies in the first ten, although four of the six biggest firms in Taiwan are government-owned (see Table 29.1). Fourteen of the top twenty-five companies in Taiwan and twenty-nine of the top fifty are local private businesses, while government and foreign-owned firms account for ten and eleven, respectively, of Taiwan's fifty biggest enterprises (*CommonWealth*, 1988). The state enterprise sector in Taiwan is more diversified than in the other NICs, with wide-ranging interests that include petrochemicals, plastics, steel, shipbuilding, construction, fertilizer, food, and beverages.

Just as significant as these regional and subregional variations in ownership and sectoral emphasis are differences among the NICs in the size of their leading industrial enterprises. South Korea's industrial structure is dominated by giant *chaebol* groups. The biggest Korean conglomerate, Samsung, had a sales total of $21 billion for 1987, which is nearly 40 percent larger than the sales of all of Taiwan's top ten companies in 1987 *combined*. Samsung's 160,000 employees exceed by more than 50 percent the total employment of the ten biggest companies in Taiwan.

The largest enterprises in Brazil and Mexico are their state-owned oil companies, Petrobrós and Pemex (Petróleos Mexicanos), with 1987 sales of $17.2 billion (including Petrobrás Distribuidora) and $13.1 billion, respectively. Once we move beyond these industrial leaders, however, the next largest Brazilian company is Shell Brasil, whose annual sales total of $2.95 billion for 1987 would place it just behind South Korea's tenth-ranking company (Hyundai Heavy Industries, with $2.96 billion in sales). Mexico's second largest firm, Chrysler de México, had a 1987 sales total of $1.2 billion, which is only two fifths that of Korea's tenth-ranking company, Hyundai Heavy Industries (see Table 29.1). South Korea had eleven companies in *Fortune*'s list of the five hundred largest non-U.S. industrial firms in 1987. There were six Brazilian companies on the list, three companies from Taiwan, and two from Mexico (*Fortune*, 1988).

The differing levels of industrial concentration in the Latin American and East Asian NICs are indicated by the share of the ten largest companies in

Table 29.2   GDP Shares of the Ten Largest Companies, 1987 (U.S.$ millions)

Country	Sales of the Top Ten Companies	Gross Domestic Product	Top Ten Companies/GDP (percent)
Mexico	20,917.8	141,940	14.7
Brazil	31,312.5	299,230	10.5
South Korea	77,034.7	121,310	63.5
Taiwan	15,105.8	105,750	14.3

Sources: Sales of the top ten companies for each country are from Table 29.1; gross domestic product figures for 1987 are from the World Bank (1989, p. 169) and CEPD (1988, pp. 23, 199).

the GDP of each country (see Table 29.2). South Korea's top ten firms accounted for 63.5 percent of the country's GDP in 1987, compared to concentration ratios of 14.7 percent for Mexico, 14.3 percent for Taiwan, and 10.5 percent for Brazil. The striking disparities that exist between the size of the largest companies in South Korea versus the other three NICs may be overstated somewhat because the listings for Taiwan, Mexico, and Brazil take firms rather than economic groups as the unit of analysis. The Korean *chaebol* that appear in *Fortune*'s "International 500" are in fact diversified enterprise groups, and similar kinds of economic groupings exist in each of the other countries as well.

A recent analysis of enterprise groups in East Asia compares six major intermarket groups (*kigyo shudan*) and ten large independent industrial groups (*keiretsu*) in Japan, the fifty biggest *chaebol* in Korea, and the top ninety-six business groups (*jituanqiye*) in Taiwan. The number and size of affiliated firms in each group vary markedly. Japan's business groups include the largest number of firms, with an average of over 112 companies for each of the six intermarket groups, and about thirty-three firms for each of the ten independent *keiretsu*. South Korea's *chaebol*, in contrast, are composed on average of about eleven firms each, while Taiwan's business groups are smaller still, typically having only about eight affiliated firms each. Overall sales also differ sharply, with Japanese business groups representing an extraordinary total of $871 billion (U.S.) in 1982, South Korea's fifty *chaebol* earning $68 billion in 1983, and Taiwan's ninety-six business groups selling $16.5 billion in 1983 (Hamilton et al., 1987, pp. 82–83). Thus even if we include business groups rather than individual firms as our unit of analysis for Taiwan, the gap between the two East Asian NICs is still very significant, with the average *chaebol* being eight times larger in terms of sales than the average Taiwanese business group.

THE POLITICAL IMPACT OF BIG BUSINESS

This analysis raises a key question about the political impact of these variations in industrial structure among the Latin American and East Asian NICs. How are the government's economic policies affected by the different character of big business in each country? The Latin American and East Asian NICs each have authoritarian states that have strongly supported industrial growth, often at the expense of the agricultural sector. The capitalist class in these countries plays a major role, not so much in formulating development strategies but, even more importantly, in implementing them. Development strategies must be carried out by a distinct constellation of big business interests in each nation, and this influences what can be achieved.

In the East Asian NICs, although the state actively participates in the public and private spheres of the economy, a good deal of this involvement is indirect (e.g., government-controlled credit, government regulation of the purchase of raw materials, energy, and foreign exchange, and price controls for selected commodities). In South Korea, the *chaebol* are crucially important in the implementation of the government's economic policies. This was especially true during the phase of HCI in the 1970s, when the steel, shipbuilding, automobile, petrochemical, and heavy machinery industries were the focus of the government's "big push" approach, which was predicated on an unprecedented concentration of capital in the *chaebol* groups. The normative or authority structure that underlies this pattern of interfirm relations is what might be called a principle of *corporate patriarchy*, in which "these huge industrial empires are the property of an authoritarian individual and his designees who manage them not by consensus, but by centralized command supported by the state" (Hamilton et al., 1987, p. 102).

The link between the government and business groups in South Korea is quite direct. These vertical pressures cannot be easily countered, because intermediate or independent local institutions are weak, repressed, or absent. A homogeneous and very nationalistic big business class thus is available in South Korea to carry out the government's objectives in terms of domestic and overseas investments and external trade.

Taiwan, in sharp contrast to South Korea, is characterized by a decentralized pattern of industrialization, a low level of firm concentration, and a predominance of small and medium-sized family businesses. Whereas there are strong pressures for vertical integration in Korea's *chaebols*, Taiwan's business groups resemble loosely knit agglomerations in which firms tend to be organizationally separate from other firms, with no unified management structure. Instead of a formal system of command, one finds a highly flexible management arrangement that relies on networks generated by personal relationships based on reciprocal trust, loyalty, and predictability (Hamilton and Kao, 1987). The underlying social principle here is that of the *patrilineal network*, since "the Taiwanese business groups do not express the will of a single patriarch but rather the interests of an extended family" (Hamilton et al., 1987, p. 102).

While South Korean patriarchs may direct their business empires even in the absence of a corporate position, Taiwanese business leaders simultaneously hold multiple executive posts to reinforce their authority. The strategy of expansion typically is to start new companies, even if it is in the same or a closely related product line, rather than enlarging the size of the original firm. This pattern of opportunistic diversification helps explain the existence of numerous small and medium-sized firms.

How does this configuration of interfirm relations in Taiwan affect state planning in the economy? Gary Hamilton and Nicole Biggart (1988) argue that while there is state planning in both South Korea and Taiwan, the difference in the role of the state resides in the fact that Taiwan's government has no real implementation procedures. Furthermore, in regard to the export business sector, the Taiwan government is said to promote "virtually free trade conditions," which leaves the export sector plenty of latitude to work out its own preferences.

This interpretation seems to ignore the fact that state enterprises continue to operate in a wide range of economic areas, and that they are disproportionately represented among Taiwan's biggest companies (see Table 29.1). The state, in fact, has tended to discourage the creation of large private firms. An alternative explanation for this pattern is that there is a strong ethnic cleavage in Taiwan between the Mainlander-dominated political elite that arrived on the island in the late 1940s (and which runs state enterprises) and the Taiwanese-based economic elite. This situation makes it very difficult for Taiwan's government to have an effective industrial policy, because the state cannot count on the unqualified support of a subordinate capitalist class to compete with the large, vertically integrated Japanese and South Korean conglomerates and general trading companies. This has led to Taiwan's "gradualist" approach in implementing large-scale projects like HCI and to its difficulty in penetrating external markets in capital- and technology-intensive industries associated with export-oriented industrialization (EOI), other than through short-term subcontracting relationships with big foreign buyers.

The Latin American NICs have very different industrial structures from their East Asian counterparts, as we have seen. Transnational corporations have been an integral part of the industrialization process in Mexico and Brazil, especially since the secondary ISI phase that began in the 1950s. In contrast to the familial basis of East Asia's leading businesses, which led to patrimonial and patrilineal interfirm networks, TNCs have tied the Latin American NICs to the rest of the world economy according to two very different principles of global economic organization: (1) during the ISI period of the 1950s and 1960s, TNCs, at the behest of national governments, followed a principle of *national segmentation*, in which the foreign companies set up parallel national industries to supply highly protected domestic markets; and (2) during the turn to diversified EOI in the 1970s and 1980s, TNCs followed the logic of *transnational integration* in reuniting the Latin American NICs to global markets through export promotion schemes that often were heavily subsidized by the host governments. While manufactured exports during the import-substitution phase were based on the utilization of existing excess capacity, new highly automated export-oriented plants began to be built at or above the minimum efficient scale in Mexico and Brazil during the 1970s and 1980s, with the export market increasingly seen as the main outlet for production.

Foreign firms in the postwar period typically came to establish new industries (like automobiles, petrochemicals, and electrical and nonelectrical machinery) to supply the domestic market, or they sought to modernize certain traditional industries (like textiles or food-processing), which resulted in the displacement of many of their domestic rivals. Family ties and personal networks play virtually no role in this setting. Foreign companies were authorized by the state to enter certain segments of the domestic market where local capital was relatively weak or absent. The subsequent bargaining that took place between TNCs and the host governments usually revolved around how to incorporate changing national priorities into the TNCs' global decision-making framework.

Mexico and Brazil enlisted foreign firms to help make the shift in the 1970s and 1980s from ISI to a diversified EOI strategy, while simultaneously restructuring domestically oriented industries by lifting the mantle of permanent protectionism and privatizing many public enterprises in order to push local companies to higher levels of competitiveness. The trend toward economic liberalization and a reduced governmental role in the Latin American NICs, when coupled with the relative weakness of their local private sectors and an overwhelming external debt burden, meant that foreign economic and political actors had increased leeway to shape development patterns in the region. Bargaining between TNCs and host governments during the EOI phase centered around renegotiating the form of insertion of the NICs in the world economy in response to new patterns of international production and trade that were redefining the spatial location of integrated global industries (see Gereffi, 1989a). As a *quid pro quo* for increased exports, the TNCs demanded and frequently got significant policy shifts from the Mexican and Brazilian governments with regard to the relaxation of local content requirements, reduced import tariffs on inputs, and very attractive packages of export incentives.

The presence of TNCs as major industrial actors in the Latin American NICs has posed both opportunities and constraints for the formulation and implementation of state development strategies. As long as the domestic market was expanding, the Mexican and Brazilian governments had a significant degree of bargaining power over foreign investors. Nonetheless,

TNCs inevitably are guided by a global rather than a national perspective, and their ability to shift their investments elsewhere meant that nationalistic governments had to be cautious in what they demanded. The financial controls that proved to be an effective lever of influence for East Asian governments in dealing with local private capital have little or no effect over TNCs since they have multiple sources of financing available to them. Since TNCs continue to be the major exporters in the Latin American NICs, their access to global markets through integrated production and export networks gives the TNCs the upper hand in their dealings with Latin American governments pursuing export-promotion strategies. Conversely, in the East Asian NICs, governments have the advantage as they induce their local private exporters to adopt a mercantilistic approach to global markets where overseas sales are equated with enhanced national security and prestige. . . .

CONCLUSIONS

Foreign capital, private and public, has played very different roles in the Latin American and East Asian NICs. The TNCs that came into Mexico and Brazil to help implement secondary ISI initially were satisfied to supply protected domestic markets, while some of these same firms entered the newly established export processing zones in Taiwan and South Korea in the late 1960s and early 1970s to produce manufactured items for export. The lesson here would seem to be that economically powerful TNCs, under the right conditions, can be induced to contribute to either ISI or EOI development objectives.

Brazil and Mexico had some success in the 1970s requiring foreign automobile manufacturers to generate increasing export revenues as a condition for continuing to supply their domestic markets (Gereffi and Evans, 1981). Transnational corporations substantially expanded their export efforts in the 1980s in response to the economic imperatives created by the reorganization of the global motor vehicle industry and the fiscal incentives offered by the Brazilian and Mexican governments to promote increased automotive exports. Brazil has made fewer concessions than Mexico in terms of reductions in local content requirements for car producers, which helps explain why Brazil has managed to run a sizable positive trade balance for its automotive industry since 1975, while Mexico has had an alarming growth in its trade deficit in this sector since the early 1970s (see Jenkins, 1987, p. 217).

In terms of the predominant role played by local private capital in East Asia, South Korea seems to have a key organizational edge over Taiwan. Both countries remain very dependent on the U.S. market for nearly half of their exports. Thus American protectionist pressures are a real threat to their continued economic prosperity. In South Korea's case, the *chaebols* have the capability to jump over these protectionist barriers by adopting an aggressive investment and marketing strategy overseas. In Taiwan, however, the main channel for exports (with the exception of the auto parts industry) has been OEM (original equipment manufacturer) procurement contracts with big foreign buyers, mainly in the United States. A relatively conservative estimate would place OEM sales at 60 to 70 percent of Taiwan's total exports, and this figure is probably higher in selected industries (like footwear). In the OEM market, Taiwan suppliers are basically selling components or generic finished goods to clients who put their own brand names on these products when they reach their final destination. If these buyers decide to shift their orders elsewhere (e.g., because of rising labor costs in Taiwan), Taiwanese producers may not have sufficient international marketing networks and skills to succeed on their own.

There are different levels at which one can compare national development experiences. One can emphasize commonalities among the NICs, or alternatively one can focus on interregional or intraregional differences. This chapter has focused on intraregional variations among the four main Latin American and East Asian NICs. Industrial structure has been our central concern. At this level, each one of the Latin American and East Asian NICs is quite distinctive. Although this variety in industrial structures does not allow easy generalizations applicable to all the NICs or even to the regional pairs, it is at the level of economic institutions that much of what is useful to other countries can be learned.

REFERENCES

CEPD (Council for Economic Planning and Development), 1988. *Taiwan Statistical Data Book*, 1988. Taipei.

Clifford, Mark. 1988. "Breaking Up is Hard to Do: South Korean *Chaebol* Still Thrive Despite Official Disapproval." *Far Eastern Economic Review*, September 29, p. 32.

CommonWealth. 1988. "The 1,000 Biggest Manufacturing Companies in Taiwan" (in Chinese). Taipei, July 1, pp. 111–12.

Expansión. 1988. "Las empresas individuales mas importantes de México." Mexico City. August 17, pp. 98–101.

Fortune. 1988. "The International 500." August 1, pp. D7–D31.

Gereffi, Gary. 1989a. "Development Strategies and the Global Factory." *Annals of the American Academy of Political and Social Science*, no. 505, pp. 92–104.

Gereffi, Gary. 1989b. "Rethinking Development Theory: Insights from East Asia and Latin America." *Sociological Forum*, 4, no. 4, pp. 505–33.

Gereffi, Gary and Peter Evans. 1981. "Development Strategies and the Global Factory." *Annals of the American Academy of Political and Social Science*, no. 505, pp. 92–104.

Haggard, Stephan, and Tun-jen Cheng. 1987. "State and Foreign Capital in East Asian NICs." In *The Political Economy of the New Asian Industrialism*, edited by Frederic C. Deyo. Ithaca, N.Y.: Cornell University Press.

Hamilton, Gary G., Marco Orrú and Nicole Woolsey Biggart. 1987. "Enterprise Groups in East Asia: An Organizational Analysis," *Financial Economic Review* (Tokyo), no. 161, pp. 78–106.

Hamilton Gary G., and Kao, Cheng-shu. 1987. "The Institutional Foundations of Chinese Business: The Family Firm in Taiwan." Unpublished manuscript.

Hamilton, Gary C., and Nicole Woolsey Biggart. 1988. "Market, Culture, and Authority: A Comparative Analysis of Management and Organization in the Far East." *American Journal of Sociology* 94, Supplement on Organizations and Institutions, pp. 52–94.

IMF. (International Monetary Fund). 1988. *International Financial Statistics.* Washington, D.C.: IMF. August.

Jenkins, Rhys. 1987. *Transnational Corporations and the Latin American Automobile Industry.* Pittsburgh, Pa.: University of Pittsburgh Press.

Newfarmer, Richard, ed. 1985. *Profits, Progress and Poverty: Case Studies of International Industries in Latin America.* Notre Dame, Ind.: University of Notre Dame Press.

Visao. 1988. "Quem é quem na economia brasileira—as 200 maiores." Sao Paulo, Brazil. August 31, pp. 54–59.

World Bank. 1989. *World Development Report 1989.* New York: Oxford University Press.

30

·······

The Rise and Crisis of
the Dragon Economies

·······

WALDEN BELLO & STEPHANIE ROSENFELD

The extremely rapid growth of the high-tech "miracle" economies of Asia has caused the developed countries to worry that they have lost their competitive edge in the international market. Those interested in development have often attributed the success of the newly industrializing countries (NICs) to what is characterized as their liberal economic policies focusing upon an export-led development model. In this chapter, Walden Bello and Stephanie Rosenfeld argue that the economies of South Korea, Taiwan, and Singapore are more aptly described as "command capitalism," and they contend that the NICs have grown at the expense of their own work forces. According to Bello and Rosenfeld, the NICs' success is attributable to the cold war policies of the United States and their own special relationship with Japan.

. . . At the very moment that the economists and technocrats have enshrined the NIC model as the new orthodoxy, that very strategy is running out of steam in Taiwan, Singapore, and South Korea. True, these economies continue to post 7 to 10 percent growth rates, but that is the glitter of half past high noon. The troublesome truth is that the external conditions that made the NICs' export successes possible are fast disappearing, while the long-suppressed costs of high-speed growth are catching up with these economies. It is the dangerous intersection of these trends that has led some

Reprinted with permission of the publishers, Food First Institute, *Dragons in Distress: Asia's Miracle Economies in Crisis*, by Walden Bello and Stephanie Rosenfeld, 1990, pp. 2–16. Food First, Institute for Food and Development Policy, 145 Ninth Street, San Francisco, CA 94103.

Korean technocrats to fear that the halving of the growth rate from 12.2 percent in 1988 to 6.5 percent in 1989 may be but the prelude to a severe structural crisis.

To be sure, these countries are at a different stage of economic transformation relative to the Third World. Their problem is not how to get out of the Third World but, having just left it, how to avoid being hurled back into the Third World.

The signals of distress are varied and often striking.

In Korea, workers launched over 7,000 strikes between the summer of 1987 and late 1989, or close to 10 per day—probably a world record for a labor force the size of that country's.

Farmers, formerly the mainstay of the ruling parties in both countries, fought pitched battles with police in Taipei and in Seoul as they protested policies opening the domestic market to a flood of U.S. agricultural imports. The technocrats have succumbed to American pressure, the farmers claim, and have boarded up the countryside. The farmers see resistance as the only alternative to extinction.

As aggressive protectionism limits the growth of exports to their main market, the United States, Korean exporters desperately scour the globe, from Siberia to Hungary, for new markets, but few hold real promise.

High-speed growth without environmental controls has converted Taiwan into a poisoned paradise of free-wheeling capitalism, leading increasing numbers of Taiwanese to a willingness to trade rapid growth for ecological equilibrium.

As wages rise in Taiwan and Korea, capital flees to sites in Southeast Asia, China, and the Caribbean that offer even lower wages.

Then there are the less visible symptoms of distress, like the quiet departure of increasing numbers of Singapore's educated work force, many of them to escape the pervasive authoritarian management of their lives that the ruling party says is necessary for their country's economic survival.

THE CONDITIONS OF GROWTH

[T]he conditions that enabled [the NICs] to emerge as important players in the world economy . . . also carried the seeds of their current distress. Three factors were especially critical: the NICs' "special relations" with the United States, their links with Japan, and the system of state-directed development that we shall call command capitalism.

The U.S. Connection

The East Asian NICs emerged as economies specializing in the export of labor-intensive manufactures during a particular period of the world economy that is now drawing to a close, a phase marked by the economic and political hegemony of the United States. In the early 1960s, following the example of Japan, the NICs tied their fortunes to the vigorously expanding U.S. market at a time when the United States was still the champion of a liberal international trading order.

The emergence of the United States as the guardian of the free market coincided with its assumption of the role of defender of the free world against communism. The place of South Korea and Taiwan at the frontlines of that global struggle had immense economic implications. For one, it entitled them to an Asian version of the Marshall Plan. Between 1951 and 1965, the United States pumped about $1.5 billion in economic aid to Taiwan—in addition, of course, to billions of dollars in military aid. U.S. aid financed 95 percent of Taiwan's trade deficit in the 1950s.[1] Economic aid to South Korea was even larger, coming to almost $6 billion between 1945 and 1978— almost as much as the total aid provided to all African countries during the same period.[2] More than 80 percent of Korean imports in the 1950s were financed by U.S. economic assistance.[3]

But an equally significant fallout from the status as frontline allies was that the U.S. blindly overlooked Taiwan and South Korea's protected markets and their tight regimes on foreign investment, even as the IMF, World Bank, and the General Agreement on Tariffs and Trade (GATT)—the institutions set up by the United States and its Western allies to safeguard free trade and the mobility of capital—were telling the rest of the Third World to end their restrictions on imports and foreign capital. In fact, Korea's foreign investment code was one of the world's most restrictive. This was a critical advantage, since Korea's protected domestic market provided a secure base from which its subsidized conglomerates, or *chaebol*, launched their drive for foreign markets in the late 1960s and 1970s.

U.S.-led containment strategy had another positive fallout for the NICs: Vietnam. War in East Asia served as an engine of prosperity. Just as the Korean War pulled the Japanese economy from post–World War II stagnation, so did Vietnam provide a vital stimulus for economic takeoff in Korea and Taiwan. The war provided what Taiwan expert Thomas Gold describes as an "incalculable boost" to the Taiwanese economy in the form of U.S. purchases of agricultural and industrial commodities, spending for "rest and recreation," and contract work for local firms in Vietnam.[4]

Like Taiwan, South Korea benefitted from U.S. purchases and recreational spending. But perhaps the most significant stimulus came in the form of the big Vietnam War–related construction contracts that firms like Hyundai were awarded as part of the offset arrangements under which the United States paid for the services of 50,000 Korean troops in Indochina. These arrangements are characterized as the "blood money" that "fueled the modernization and development of the country" by the main protagonist in *White Badge*, Ahn Jung-Hyo's acclaimed autobiographical novel about

Korean troops in Vietnam. "And owing to our contribution," he continues, "the Republic of Korea, or at least a higher echelon of it, made a gigantic stride into the world market. Lives for sale. National mercenaries."[5] By the end of the war in 1975, overseas work contracts had reached a total of $850 million[6]—accounting for almost 20 percent of Korea's exports of goods and services. Given their start by the U.S. military in Vietnam, Hyundai, Daewoo, and other Korean construction giants went on to conquer the Middle East in the late 1970s and early 1980s.

The Japan Factor

"Those Asian nations where the economy has been a success story, such as Korea, Taiwan, and Singapore were all, at one time or another, under Japanese administration," asserts the right-wing nationalist Shintaro Ishihara in the controversial book *The Japan That Can Say "No."* "We are aware that some negative changes happened under Japanese administration, but it cannot be denied that many positive changes were left behind."[7] While Koreans would probably take strong exception to this claim, there is an element of hard truth in it.

The proximity of the two countries to an expansionist Japan led to their being colonized in the first half of the twentieth century. Colonization meant repression, but it was also a period of vigorous economic development. Not only did the military-technocratic elite in Korea and the Kuomintang (KMT) elite in Taiwan inherit a relatively well-developed physical and educational infrastructure from the Japanese after World War II, but the old colonial economic and cultural ties became vital assets in the context of a revived and dynamic Japanese economy during the 1960s and 1970s.[8]

As Japanese firms sought to escape the rising cost of domestic labor, their first choice of location became their former colonies, Taiwan and South Korea. As the NICs sought to emulate Japan's export success, Japanese trading companies handled international trade for Taiwanese and Korean firms, with an estimated 50 to 70 percent of Taiwan's exports passing through them.[9] And as Taiwanese and Korean industrialization took off in the 1970s, Japan provided a significant portion of the machinery and components utilized by NIC enterprises to turn out toys, bicycles, radios, television sets, and PC monitors for export. Japan was more tightfisted when it came to technology transfers, but, especially as the United States lost its technological edge to Japan, the Koreans became dependent on licensing available Japanese technologies in finished form to achieve their export successes, particularly in consumer electronics, automobiles, and semiconductors. In the period 1962-80, Japan was the source of nearly 59 percent of approved technology licenses, while the United States accounted for only 23 percent.[10]

In the last three decades, a vigorous triangular trade in manufactured goods has developed, with the United States providing the market for the NICs, and the NICs depending on Japan for the critical technology, machinery, and component inputs. The dynamism of what political analyst Kent Calder calls the "emerging North Pacific political economy" stemmed from

> a highly unbalanced set of relationships through which South Korea and the other newly industrializing countries imported heavily from Japan to support their industrial development, and exported heavily to the U.S. to cover these imports. Japan compounded the imbalances by itself exporting heavily to the United States, and importing from the United States less than half of what it exported. These imbalances were supported financially through massive capital flows from Japan to the United States and, to a lesser degree, to South Korea and the other NICs as well. The system was kept in political as well as short-run economic equilibrium by huge U.S.-bound capital flows.[11]

By the mid-1980s, while the NICs were running multibillion dollar trade surpluses with the United States, they were running multibillion dollar trade deficits with Japan. The NICs export successes were undeniable, but they came at the price of extreme economic dependence on Japan. In 1988 Taiwan enjoyed a $10.4 billion surplus in its trade with the United States but suffered a $6 billion deficit in its commerce with Japan. In the case of Korea, the surplus with the United States in 1988 came to $8.6 billion, while the deficit with Japan amounted to nearly $4 billion. The Japanese connection, in short, was both an asset and a liability, and when Singapore, Taiwan, and Korea sought to move to a higher stage of development in the 1980s, the liabilities became all too prominent.

Command Capitalism

Among the myths surrounding the NICs is the idea that they are free market economies approximating the United States. And among those who casually pass along this "truth" was Ronald Reagan, who declared in his 1985 State of the Union address that "America's economic success . . . can be repeated a hundred times in a hundred nations. Many countries in East Asia and the Pacific have few resources other than the enterprise of their own people. But through free markets, they've soared ahead of centralized economies."[12]

Contrary to the views of Reagan and the neoclassical economists, however, the NICs, with the possible exception of Hong Kong, were hardly paragons of free trade. The laws of the market did operate in Singapore, Taiwan, and South Korea, but under the constraints or "guidance" imposed by state elites.

The technocratic state elite determined the direction of economic policy and did not hesitate to employ subsidies, preferential access to credit, investment incentives, and other market-violating administrative measures to achieve targets that they set. If these measures subverted the "efficient allocation of resources" that would be brought about in the short term by unrestrained market forces, so much the worse for the market. In a very real sense, development in the NICs depended on "getting relative prices wrong," to use Alice Amsden's phrase.[13]

Export success, not efficient resource allocation, was the over-riding goal of the technocrats. And to achieve export competitiveness, they were willing to distort the operation of market forces. Thus, the Korean state deployed credit resources and other subsidies to the *chaebol* to enable them to withstand short-term losses to achieve market share. In contrast, the Singaporean state's preferential treatment of foreign investors—its preferred export agents—via infrastructural subsidies and tax incentives ended up marginalizing the Singaporean business class. In all three countries, the state forcefully intervened in the labor market to press down workers' wages below market value in order to achieve competitiveness for NIC exports in the international market.[14]

Command capitalism, not free market capitalism, is the system that enabled the NICs to become major players in the world economy. True, the international market had the ultimate say. But the rigorous demands of international competition evoked in Singapore, South Korea, and Taiwan a system of forceful state intervention that distorted local markets and incurred short-term inefficiencies to win long-term effectiveness as exporters in a harsh world economy.

THE ONSET OF CRISIS

By the late 1980s, the NICs' external and internal environments had been radically transformed, and what had been key assets in the period of high-speed growth increasingly became liabilities.

Protectionism was preventing export expansion in the NICs' main markets, while the economic, environmental, and social costs of a strategy of industrialization imposed from above by an authoritarian elite spawned increasingly powerful opposition movements that directly challenged the NIC model. Moreover, in South Korea, Taiwan, and Singapore, the technocrats were forced to confront the same profound structural dilemma that was unraveling the NIC economy: rising wage costs were making the NICs unprofitable as sites for labor-intensive manufacturing at the same time that their continuing technological backwardness severely obstructed plans to create a more capital and skill-intensive, high-tech manufacturing base.

The Protectionist Threat

Once the guardian of the liberal trading order, the United States had been transformed by the late 1980s into an aggressively protectionist power.

Given the same label of unfair trader pinned on Japan, the NICs became prime targets of the protectionist offensive launched in the latter years of the Reagan administration to contain the massive U.S. trade deficit. Indeed, with the dramatic decline of the Soviet threat and the deepening technological crisis wracking U.S. industry, the NICs, together with Japan, became the leading candidates to replace the Soviet Union as America's new enemy.

Economic hostilities against the United States' staunchest cold war allies were formalized in what was tantamount to a declaration of war issued by senior Treasury official David Mulford in October 1987: "Although the NICs may be regarded as tigers because they are strong, ferocious traders, the analogy has a darker side. Tigers live in the jungle, and by the law of the jungle. They are a shrinking population."[15]

The U.S. trade offensive has had several prongs.

In January 1989 the United States revoked the tariff-free entry of selected NIC imports under the General System of Preferences (GSP). While elimination from GSP nominally affected only about 10 percent of NIC imports, its main intent was to warn the NICs that even more drastic measures would be taken if they did not cooperate by taking steps to radically reduce their trade surpluses.

Voluntary Export Restraints (VERs) on NIC products have drastically reduced their penetration of the U.S. market. Restrictive quotas placed on Korean textile imports drastically reduced their rate of growth from 43 percent per year in the 1970s to less than 1 percent per year in the early 1980s. Tough restrictions have also limited Korean steel to less than 2 percent of total U.S. steel imports.

To make the NICs' imports even more expensive and less appealing to consumers, Washington forced the appreciation of the New Taiwan dollar and the Korean won by 40 percent and 30 percent, respectively, between 1986 and 1989. Acknowledging the efficacy of currency warfare, a high executive of a leading Korean textile firm reported, "We can absorb wage increases, but we can't take any more appreciation."[16]

Protectionist measures were coupled with an aggressive drive to abolish import restrictions and lower tariff barriers for U.S. goods in the NIC markets. Threatened by the infamous Super 301—legislation that required the U.S. president to take retaliatory measures against those officially tagged as unfair traders—Korea and Taiwan have been forced to liberalize trade restrictions on thousands of services and commodities, from foreign banking operations to imports of cigarettes and beef.

Washington and U.S. corporations have teamed up to throttle unauthorized technology transfer to the NICs. While the government has sought to place restrictive covenants on intellectual property in the General Agreement on Tariffs and Trade, U.S. electronics companies have initiated technological warfare against Korean and Taiwanese clone makers, who have gained the reputation of turning out products even better and considerably cheaper than the originals. IBM, Texas Instruments, and Intel now stand to make hundreds of millions in royalty payments from Asian producers, who have no choice but to pay up, given their dependence on trouble-free entry to the U.S. market.

The techno-trade offensive has drastically curbed further expansion of exports from Taiwan and Korea to the U.S. market. Both countries' exports to the United States grew by only about 1 percent in 1988 over 1987, while imports from the United States rose sharply, by more than 75 percent in the case of Taiwan.[17] As the destination of NIC exports, the United States saw its share fall from 39 percent in 1987 to 32 percent in 1988 in the case of Korea and from 45 percent to 39 percent in the case of Taiwan. The American shock treatment has been quite effective.

Faced with a U.S. market that is becoming less hospitable, the NICs have been feverishly hunting for new markets. Efforts to export to Western Europe have intensified, but so have antidumping moves against NIC producers, especially the Koreans. In fact, many Taiwanese and Korean manufacturers assume that when the Economic Community becomes a unified market in 1992, their access to the continent will be severely limited.

NIC attempts to carve out a niche for their manufactured goods at the lower end of the Japanese market have had disappointing results. And the few NIC producers that have some success soon face a powerful protectionist alliance between bureaucracy and business. For instance, Korean knitwear manufacturers have been successfully intimidated by Japanese bureaucrats and garment makers to limit their exports to Japan—or else.

The prospect of markets in China, the Soviet Union, and Eastern Europe has received a lot of hype in the press, but recent developments have underlined the fact that these fragile postsocialist economies will generate no more than a fraction of the former U.S. demand. Moreover, the plans of the new market-oriented technocrats to shutdown inefficient factories, lay off surplus labor, and radically reduce social subsidies will depress popular purchasing power and eliminate Eastern Europe and the Soviet Union as significant mass markets, at least in the short and medium term.

The immense difficulties of diversifying from the U.S. market in an increasingly protectionist world are suggested by the following set of statistics. In 1988 Hyundai sold over 300,000 Excel subcompacts in the United States. In contrast, in the same year it was able to sell only 20,097 in the European Community and a minuscule 150 in neighboring Japan.[18]

The Internal Costs of the NIC Model

As the NICs' external environment worsened, so did their internal environment. Among the internal costs of the NIC model was the crisis of agriculture. The subordination of agriculture to export-oriented industrialization in Taiwan and South Korea led to the serious erosion of the agrarian base of these economies. This might come as a surprise to many, since Taiwan and Korea are often cited as examples of successful agrarian reform. True, decisive land reform was enacted in both countries in the 1950s, and certainly, in Taiwan at least, higher agricultural incomes contributed to a rise in domestic demand that sparked early industrialization efforts.

Since then, however, it was downhill for the agrarian sector in both countries, as a massive net transfer of resources from agriculture to industry was effected to fuel export manufacturing beginning in the late 1960s. Low grain-price policies translated into low wages for urban workers, which in turn translated into competitive prices for Taiwanese and Korean exports. Low grain prices had another, perhaps not unintended impact: as rural incomes fell relative to urban incomes, young people left the countryside for the cities, where they provided the work force for the growing industrial sector.

Half-hearted rural development efforts failed to stem the agrarian crisis in the 1970s, and in the 1980s, the erosion of agriculture was speeded up by intensified U.S. efforts to completely dismantle tariff and nontariff barriers to U.S. agricultural commodities. Liberalization of agricultural imports was the quid pro quo for continued access to the U.S. market for NIC manufactured exports. The ultimate price, farmers realized, was the extinction of wide swaths of the agrarian economy.

Taiwanese and Korean technocrats were no help to the farmers, for the U.S. effort to open up protected agricultural markets, in fact, dovetailed with their view on how to make agriculture more efficient—eliminate surplus labor in the countryside and concentrate land in larger units to take advantage of the economies of mechanization. Bereft of sympathy from the very governments that once valued them as a secure base of electoral support, farmers in both countries took to the streets with the same message: the countryside is no longer going to serve as the sacrificial lamb for export industry.

Like agriculture, the environment has been a prime victim of the NICs' high-speed industrial growth. With state technocrats assuming that some degree of ecological destabilization was the price of economic growth, export-oriented industrialization telescoped into three decades processes of environmental destruction that took many more years to unfold in earlier industrializing societies.

The dimensions of the environmental crisis in Korea are only now coming to light, but what is known indicates that the situation is grave: world-record levels of sulphur dioxide concentration in Seoul's air, rain with high acid content, tap water with heavy metals at many times the official tolerance level, and nuclear reactors plagued by malfunctions and accidents.

Taiwan, it appears, is in a more advanced state of environmental decay. Not only are crops overdosed with pesticides, but agricultural land has been heavily contaminated with heavy metals from unregulated waste dumping by thousands of manufacturing establishments that located in the countryside as a result of the government's rural industrialization policy. Levels of air pollution considered hazardous in the United States are normal in many of Taiwan's urban areas.

Rapid environmental deterioration has not only produced the ubiquitous motorcyclist with a surgical mask weaving in and out of Taipei's hellish traffic; it has also provoked the rise of a multi-class, grass roots environmental movement. This movement fills the role that the labor movement does in Korea—that of presenting the status quo with its most powerful challenge. Resorting to direct action like plant occupations, local residents have been able to stop the establishment of key petrochemical facilities and nuclear plants. But growth-oriented KMT technocrats fear not only the movement's impact on local investments but also its long-term philosophical impact on the people. Indeed, a 1985 survey showed that 59 percent of respondents favored environmental protection over economic growth.[19]

The crises in agriculture and the environment aggravated what was already a profound crisis in the legitimacy of the authoritarian political systems that had imposed high-speed, export-oriented growth.

The People's Action Party of Singapore had pushed export-oriented growth as a means to strengthen its political legitimacy, while in Korea and Taiwan the state elites had sought to use economic development to neutralize what was widely perceived to be their illegitimate assumption of power. Prosperity, it was hoped, would buy legitimacy and excuse the repressive policies imposed to achieve high-speed growth.

By the mid-1980s, however, it was clear that this strategy of purchasing legitimacy was not working. Instead, both the economic model and the power structure that imposed it were losing legitimacy. In Singapore, there was growing disaffection with the longstanding alliance between the authoritarian Lee Kwan-Yew regime and transnational capital, which had marginalized local business, emasculated labor, and subjected the population to pervasive political control. In Taiwan and Korea, decades of labor repression created working classes that were alienated from the paradigm of export-oriented growth. Indeed, in Korea, labor's attitude bordered on the insurrectionary, making nearly impossible the institutionalization of Western-style collective bargaining processes.

Rising opposition pressure from the social groups that had been marginalized by the NIC strategy of growth forced a gradual democratization of the political process. But precisely because labor and other groups had been so strongly repressed in the pursuit of high-speed development, political decompression did not lead to the creation of a new consensus around the traditional strategy of growth but to a politics of polarized struggle over the distribution of income, sectoral priorities, the trade-off between environmental and economic priorities, and the direction of development itself. Late industrialization, followed by late democratization, promoted not consensus but divergent views on economic priorities. As one report on Korea aptly put it, "the country's new-found democratic politics are putting wage push, labor unrest and demands for welfare expenditure in the way of continued super-growth."[20]

But clearly there was no alternative to democratization, whatever limitations and however late it might be. For example, in Singapore, the one East Asian NIC that resisted democratization, opposition nevertheless expressed itself in a way that threatened the viability of the old economic model, as the very middle class that the Lee Kwan-Yew regime had envisioned as the base of a future high-tech economy expressed its discontent by emigrating in large numbers.

One of the key lessons of the NIC experience is that there is no alternative to democratic participation in the making of economic policy, and the longer democracy is postponed, the more difficult will it be to create the necessary social consensus to underpin a strategy of economic development.

The Structural Squeeze

Coinciding with the rise of protectionism and the eroding legitimacy of the model of export-oriented growth was the worsening structural squeeze on the economy. Throughout the 1960s and early 1970s, cheap labor was the chief asset that provided NIC exports with their competitive edge. But by the late 1970s and 1980s, the drying up of labor reserves from the countryside and militant labor organizing created strong upward pressures on wages that raised labor costs in the NICs significantly above those in other Third World countries that were moving fast to adopt export-oriented growth policies. In 1988, for instance, the average monthly wage stood at $643 in Taiwan, $558 in Hong Kong, $401 in Singapore, and $610 in Korea. In contrast, the figure was $132 in Thailand, $129 in Malaysia, and $209 in Indonesia.[21]

In the view of NIC technocrats, the solution was to move their economies away from dependence on labor-intensive manufacturing processes to more skilled, higher-value-added production. Singapore's technocrats took the boldest step along this path in 1979, when they decreed a wage correction policy that raised unit labor costs by 40 percent over the following six years. Contrary to expectations, however, most transnational corporations refused to automate their production processes or shift to producing high-tech commodities, preferring to move their investments to other low-wage sites. The onset of a deep recession in 1985–86 forced the Singaporean technocrats to retreat and return to the old strategy of attracting multinationals with the promise of a cheap labor force, a policy that was increasingly dependent on bringing in more low-wage foreign workers from Thailand, Malaysia, and other neighboring countries.

In rhetoric, Taiwan's technocrats also committed themselves to a high-tech future. In practice, however, their strategy was to back only a few high-tech projects, especially in electronics, while the island's manufacturers continued to concentrate on low-tech, labor-intensive investments. To slow the inevitable loss of competitiveness, Taiwan's capitalists either transferred their manufacturing operations to China and other low-wage countries or, following Singapore's example, began importing foreign workers who were paid from a third to half the average wage of the Taiwanese worker. In Taiwan, this rear-guard strategy has led to the emergence of a two-tier labor force, composed of poorly paid foreign workers and better paid local workers—a sure-fire formula for social and political conflicts in the near future.

South Korea was, for a time, buffered from the consequences of rising wages by its ability to organize its labor force into an efficient manufacturing system that could take advantage of economies of scale. But a 60 percent rise in wage costs between 1986 and 1989 pushed the technocrats toward the two-pronged policy of transferring low-tech, labor-intensive manufacturing to Southeast Asia, China, and other low-wage countries, while moving domestic production toward high-tech manufacturing.

The government laid out ambitious plans to develop the ultra-advanced 64 megabit DRAM (dynamic random access memory) chip, artificial intelligence computers, videodisc players, and even a Korean rocket to launch satellites. But the Koreans were soon up against the moment of truth: their complex of basic and intermediate industries was still inadequate to sustain significant high-tech manufacturing, and they did not have adequate numbers of trained technical personnel to support self-sustaining technological innovation. Skilled personnel were not as easy to clone as VCRs and IBM personal computers. And it was the pool of scientists and engineers that would make the difference in the vicious competition with Japan and the United States in the frontiers of high technology.

The coming together of protectionism in Western markets, the internal political crisis of the NIC model, and the structural squeeze in the economy posed a formidable threat to the strategy of high-speed export-oriented industrialization. To surmount the developing crisis meant more than just macroeconomic adjustments in the basic paradigm. Continued economic transformation demanded fundamental changes in the strategy, direction, and quality of growth, but this could only come about with a profound change in the very structure of political and economic power. . . .

In 1984, at a time that the East Asian NICs were the star performers in the world economy, a confidential study by the Central Intelligence Agency's Office of Global Issues predicted that "the change in the composition of the NICs will more likely be the result of a country falling from its [sic] ranks rather than advancing to the status of an industrial country."[22] Accurate forecasting is not the CIA's forte, but recent developments have rendered this particular prediction credible. . . .

NOTES

1. Ramon Myers, "The Economic Development of the Republic of China on Taiwan, 1965–81," in Lawrence Lau and Lawrence Klein, eds., *Models of Development: A Comparative Study of Economic Growth in South Korea and Taiwan* (San Francisco: Institute for Contemporary Studies, 1986), p. 47.

2. Jon Halliday, "The Economies of North and South Korea,: in John Sullivan and Roberta Foss, eds., *Two Koreas—One Future?* (Lanham, MD: University Press of America, 1987), p. 36.

3. *Ibid.*

4. Thomas Gold, *State and Society in the Taiwanese Miracle* (Armonk, NY: M. E. Sharpe, 1986), pp. 86–87.

5. Ahn Junghyo, *White Badge* (New York: Soho Press, 1989), p. 40.

6. Gavan McCormack, "The South Korean Economy: GNP versus the People," in Gavan McCormack and Mark Selden, eds., *Korea North and South: The Deepening Crisis* (New York: Monthly Review Press, 1978), p. 101.

7. Akio Morita and Shintaro Ishihara, *The Japan That Can Say "No"* (Tokyo: Kobunsha Kappa-Holmes, 1989), unauthorized translation by Japanese-American Joint Leadership Foundation, p. 73.

8. See, among others, Bruce Cumings, "The Origins and Development of the Northeast Asian Political Economy: Industrial Sectors, Product Cycles, and Political Consequences," *International Organization* 38, no. 1 (Winter 1984), pp. 1–40.

9. Huang Chi, "The State and Foreign Capital: A Case Study of Taiwan," Ph.D. Dissertation, Department of Political Science, Indiana University, February 1986, p. 189; Denis Simon, "Taiwan, Technology Transfer, and Transnationals: The Political Management of Dependency," Ph.D. Dissertation, University of California at Berkeley, 1980, p. 350.

10. Kim Kwang-Doo and Lee Sang-Ho, "The Role of the Korean Government in Technology Import," in Lee C. H. and Ippei Yamazawa, eds., *The Economic Development of Japan and Korea* (New York: Praeger, 1990), p. 93.

11. Kent Calder, "The North Pacific Triangle: Sources of Economic and Political Transformation," *Journal of Northeast Asian Studies*, 7, no. 2 (Summer 1989), p. 5.

12. Quoted in Foreign Policy Association, "Third World Development: Old Problems, New Strategies," *Great Decisions '86.*

13. Alice Amsden, "Late Industrialization in South Korea: The General Properties of Expansion Through Learning," Manuscript, Boston, 1988, p. 62. This excellent manuscript has since been published as *Asia's Next Giant: South Korea and Late Industrialization* (New York: Oxford University Press, 1989).

14. The influential role of the Singaporean state in depressing wages below their market value was openly admitted in the late 1970s, when the government issued the "corrective wage policy. . . ." What is important to note here is that the government "argued that the policy has been necessary to restore wages to their market value." As Gary Rodan has commented, "The very notion of a 'corrective' wage policy is an indictment on the freedom of labor as a factor of production. It is an open admission of the government's control over a key aspect of the economy. For this reason alone, it is hard to accept uncritically the notion of comparative advantage in labor costs as having any meaning in isolation from . . . the state's role in helping to define these costs. The 'advantage' is thus anything but natural or given." "Industrialization and the Singapore state in the Context of the New International Division of Labor," in Richard Higgott and

Richard Robison, eds., *Southeast Asia: Essays in the Political Economy of Structural Change* (London: Routledge and Kegan Paul, 1985), p. 179.

15. David Mulford, "Remarks before the Asia-Pacific Capital Markets Conference," San Francisco, November 17, 1987.

16. Interview with Y. C. Park, senior manager, Tae Heung, Ltd., by Walden Bello, Seoul, May 23, 1988.

17. So threatened was Taiwan by the American offensive that in 1988 it took to importing large quantities of gold from the United States to reduce the trade surplus, which it did again in 1989. Even without the gold imports, however, the impact of the American pressure on Taiwan is seen in the fact that the surplus fell by 30 percent between 1987 and 1989, from $16 billion to $12 billion. See "Annoying Big Brother," *Economist*, January 13, 1990, p. 68.

18. Peter Montagnon, "Wanted: A Truly Free Market," *Financial Times*, April 2, 1990, sec. 3, p. v.

19. "Most People Here Put Environmental Protection Before Economic Growth," *China News* (Taipei), May 5, 1985. See also Michael Hsiao and Lester Milbrath, "The Environmental Movement in Taiwan," Paper prepared for the Sino-U.S. Binational Conference on Environmental Protection and Social Development, Taipei, August 20–23, 1989, table 7, p. 23.

20. "Sympathy for South Korea," *Financial Times*, March 22, 1990.

21. Kim Sam-O, "Better Labor Conditions Creep into NICs," *Electronic Korea*, December 1989, p.38.

22. Gregory Moulton, "Future Newly Industrializing Countries: More Competition," *Confidential*, Office of Global Issues, Central Intelligence Agency, Washington, D.C., March 1984, p. 8.

PART 6

. . . .

Conclusion

. . . .

31

. . . .

Inequality in a Global Perspective:
Directions for Further Research

. . . .

MITCHELL A. SELIGSON

That there is a vast gap between the world's rich and its poor is beyond dispute. The causes and dynamics of the gap, however, are the subject of considerable debate. Fortunately, this debate differs considerably from the pattern normally encountered in the social sciences, where discussion all too often does not lead to the development of a cumulative body of knowledge. Indeed, it can be said that research in this area provides one of the best illustrations of a cumulative social science that continually deepens its understanding of a complex problem. In this concluding chapter, I will suggest some directions for future research so that continued rapid progress can be made in our understanding of the problem.

EVOLUTION OF RESEARCH ON THE GAPS

Once it became clear that the post–World War II hopes for rapid, universal development in the Third World were not going to be fulfilled, social scientists set their minds to determining why that was the case. It was obvious, then as now, that unless development in the Third World were to surge ahead, the gap between these economies and those of the increasingly prosperous developed countries would inevitably widen. The serious implications of this situation for world peace were too great to be ignored.

Early thinking focused on the cultural distinctiveness of the Third World. The observation that these cultures were indeed different from those of industrial, capitalist countries convinced a generation of social scientists to offer cultural barriers as the principal explanation for underdevelopment. Much of this work was extraordinarily intriguing, showed creative scholarship, and seemed to make a good deal of sense. As research proceeded, however, disenchantment with this perspective began to set in. The more that was known about the Third World, the less that cultural factors seemed able to account for its underdevelopment. Many researchers found the explanation ethnocentric at best and insulting at worst. Studies also revealed many instances of a single "underdeveloped culture" producing vastly different developmental outcomes; wide variation was observed within supposedly monolithic cultures. In addition, people proved highly capable of tailoring their cultures to conform to more "modern" ways of doing things; cultures proved to be far more malleable and responsive than had been originally believed. Finally, despite putative cultural limitations, some Third World nations made rapid strides in economic growth; some middle-income countries, for example, have been able to achieve higher growth rates in recent years than many industrialized countries. The debate on the impact of culture on development continues to be quite lively, as the reviews of Lawrence Harrison's book, excerpted in Chapter 14 of this volume, has shown. Indeed, as this chapter is being written, Harrison (1992) has published a new book entitled *Who Prospers?: How Cultural Values Shape Economic and Political Success.* The discussion has become more technical, as a series of quantitative studies have attempted to reinvigorate the study of culture (Inglehart 1988, 1990) and others have challenged this approach (Booth and Seligson, 1984; Seligson and Booth, forthcoming).

Whatever their explanatory power, cultural explanations no longer dominate the field, and other theories have emerged. Increasingly, thinking about development has become "globalized." The very nature of the income gap probably forced such thinking to emerge. After all, in order to study the gap, one must adopt some sort of comparative perspective. Studies can focus on the absolute or relative gap, but these terms have no meaning unless they are situated within a comparative framework; poor people are poor only with respect to rich people.

In this book extensive consideration has been given to the "inverted U curve" of development. In global terms, according to Kuznets and other proponents of this thesis, developing nations are likely to experience a widening internal gap before they see the gap narrow in the later phases of industrialization. Dependency and world-system thinkers agree that the gaps are widening but do not believe that they will ultimately narrow as industrialization matures. These schools regard the widening internal and external gaps between rich and poor as functions of the world capitalist economic system.

The studies by Morawetz (Chapter 2) and Passé-Smith (Chapter 3) suggest strongly that the gaps are very large and growing larger with each passing decade. Yet the controversy presented in Part 2 of this book between those who argue that the economies of the world are converging and those who argue that the gaps are widening shows that the issue has still not been resolved. This disagreement has led some to examine more closely key cases of dependency and development. O'Hearn (Chapter 22) points out that the neoliberal policies that presumably have done so much to spur the development of East Asian nations have not worked in Ireland. Gereffi (Chapter 29) makes an explicit comparison between East Asia and Latin America and comes up with numerous differences that make drawing definitive conclusions quite difficult.

Considerable data has been brought to bear on the various theories seeking to explain these dual gaps, and it is in the analysis and interpretation of this data that we see the clearest example of cumulative social science in the making. This book presents some of the best examples of rigorous testing of theory with data. Some of those examples provide strong support for dependency/world-system explanations; others refute those explanations just as strongly. It is too early to predict the outcome of the debate or even to say which side seems to have the edge. A pessimistic interpretation is that both sides are locked into their respective positions and that future research will be stalemated. The vital importance of the problem, not only to the world's poor but also to those trying to secure peace, requires that such a stalemate be avoided. It is therefore appropriate to assess where research has taken us and where it ought to go. The contributions in this volume trace the intellectual history of the debate over the gaps; the remainder of this chapter is devoted to outlining the directions in which fruitful future research might proceed.

THE INTERNATIONAL GAP

In GNP per capita terms, a small group of oil exporting nations already enjoy incomes higher than the average income found among industrial market economies. In 1981, Saudi Arabia had a GNP per capita of $12,600; Kuwait; $20,900; and the United Arab Emirates, $24,660; while the mean income of the industrial market economies was $11,120. None of the industrialized countries came even close to exceeding the income of Kuwait and the United Arab Emirates; Switzerland had $17,430, the highest GNP per capita of the industrial countries. The United States, not long ago the world's GNP per capita leader, was far behind at $12,820. Oil-rich Libya was moving up rapidly, with its per capita GNP reaching $8,450, only slightly behind that of the United Kingdom ($9,110).[1]

Much of the dramatic increase in the GNP of the oil states was a short-term phenomenon owing to the sharp price rises of petroleum in the 1970s. By 1990, the World Bank was reporting that Saudi Arabia had a GNP per capita of only $7,050, compared to the U.S., with $21,790. Kuwait, still a very rich country, was recovering from the Gulf War and much of its economy was in ruins. And the United Arab Emirates had declined to $19,860.

The rapid growth and equally rapid decline of the oil states, however, is the exception to the rule. As Passé-Smith has shown, there is very little movement over the long term, from rich to poor and vice-versa. While South Korea, Taiwan, and Malaysia, for example, are rapidly growing, they have incomes that are are still only a fraction of those found in the industrialized countries. Thus, it seems clear that there is a near-universal widening gap between rich and poor.

This conclusion, however, is based upon a single indicator, namely GNP/pc. The use of a single indicator to explain any social phenomenon has long fallen into disrepute in the social sciences. Why then base conclusions about such an important subject entirely upon GNP/pc data? The response from those who use this statistic as a sole indicator of income is that it is by far the most widely accepted indicator. The principal problem emerges not because of the unreliability of data collected on each nation, but because of validity problems associated with expressing local currency values in U.S. dollars.

In order to standardize income data involving the multitude of currencies used around the world, it has long been common practice for researchers to convert all figures into dollar amounts using international exchange rates. This appeared for a long time to be the only reasonable way to compare the value of different currencies. In fact, however, it is now known that such conversions introduce considerable distortion into the data: The exchange rate comparisons do not accurately measure differences in the relative domestic purchasing power of currencies. The net result is that the exchange rate GNP measures *can* greatly exaggerate the gap between rich and poor countries. This exaggeration occurs in part because international exchange rates are susceptible to fluctuations in equilibrium value. In addition, according to the "law of one price," the cost of goods and services that are traded among countries tends to equalize. For a developing country in which most of the production does not enter the world trade market, the exchange rate–converted GNP figures will underestimate true income.

In order to correct for this bias, the United Nations has undertaken the International Comparisons Project which has provided some revealing findings.[2] Using purchasing power rather than exchange rates, Passé-Smith (Chapter 9) finds the gap to be less expansive but still considerable. For some countries, the change was large. For example, Sri Lanka exhibits a gap nearly four times as large when the traditional measure is used as when the purchasing power index is applied. Countries such as Colombia and Mexico also reveal considerable differences, although not as great as in the case of Sri Lanka.

It would seem appropriate to suggest that future research on the international gap employ the purchasing power index rather than the exchange rate–based data in order to obtain a truer picture of income comparisons. When measured with purchasing power–converted GNPs, the gap remains, albeit slightly smaller. Even with the dramatic narrowing of the international gap in the case of Sri Lanka, as noted above, that country's income per capita is only 9.3 percent of that of the United States. Kenya, in which the GNP/pc almost doubles with the new index, still confronts an income level only 6.6 percent the size of that of the United States. The revised measure, therefore, does not eliminate the gap between rich and poor. It does, however, provide what appears to be a more appropriate standard of comparison. The mere fact that the gap narrows through the use of the new index does not necessarily imply that there is an overall trend toward a narrowing of the international gap.

Another way of looking at the gap question is to shift the focus away from per capita income measures and look at human needs and human development instead. Using this criterion, one obtains a rather different perspective on the international gap question. According to studies conducted by the World Bank (1980:32–45), the proportion of people around the world living in absolute poverty has declined significantly since the close of World War II. In addition, there has been a worldwide increase in literacy levels, such that over the past thirty years literacy in developing countries has increased from 30 percent to over 50 percent of the population. Even more dramatic improvements have been made in the area of health: Infant mortality rates have dropped considerably, and life expectancy has been extended. For example, citizens of low-income countries in 1950 had a life expectancy of only 35.2 years, whereas by 1990 it had risen to 62 years (World Bank, 1980:34; 1983:192; 1992). The World Bank (1980:35) states that "the gaps in education and health have narrowed—by 15 percentage points in adult literacy and five years in life expectancy" between the industrial countries and the middle-income countries.

Research more consciously directed at these indicators of basic human needs may provide a clearer picture of the impact of the gap than that presented by income figures alone. But before one leaps to the conclusion that the human-needs approach can demonstrate that the gap is narrowing, some additional context needs to be added to the discussion. Although it is true that the *proportion* of people experiencing improved education, health and life expectancy has increased, the *absolute number* of poor people in the world has risen dramatically because of high birth rates in the developing world. Hence, the World Bank (1980:35) estimates that despite the increases in the levels of literacy, the number of illiterate people has grown by some 100 million since 1950. And in 1990, in the low-income countries of the world alone, there remained some 1.2 billion illiterate adults (World Bank, 1992:218). Moreover, there is mounting evidence that the quality of education in the developing world lags far behind that found in the industrialized countries. The quality gap is especially acute in secondary and higher education, where technical advances are very rapid and the cost of obtaining modern training equipment ever more expensive. It is increasingly difficult for developing countries to adequately train their young people for the skills they need to compete in the high technology world of today.

The education gap has two particularly pernicious implications. First, the frustration that the brightest youngsters in developing countries face as a result of antiquated equipment and poorly prepared teachers results in a tendency for them to migrate to the industrialized nations. Hence, the "brain drain" is a worsening problem that promises to continue to adversely affect the ability of poor nations to develop. Second, the technological nature of contemporary society seems to be creating a higher and more impenetrable barrier between rich and poor countries. The efficiency of modern manufacturing techniques, along with the requirement of exceptional precision in manufacturing, makes it more and more difficult for developing nations to compete with the industrialized nations. The price advantage that developing nations have as a result of their considerably lower labor costs remains an advantage only for those items that require relatively low technical inputs. Hence, the proliferation of in-bond industries in the Far East and Latin America, where consumer goods are assembled for reexport, only highlights the gap in technology—nearly all of the machinery and a good deal of the managerial skill used in those factories are imported from the industrialized nations. Even without tariff barriers, the Third World faces a growing gap in technology, which is serving to reinforce the income gap.

In sum, improved income measures and basic needs data provide important avenues of research for those who wish to study the international income gap. A look at some of these data gives reason for optimism that conditions in poor countries are improving. At the same time, however, there is little reason to believe that the international income gap is narrowing. In fact, it would appear that each passing day finds the world inhabited by a larger number of people who live in absolute poverty, even though the proportion of the world's population in absolute poverty may be declining. This gap, then, seems to remain the single most serious problem confronting the family of nations, one that cries out for the attention of policymakers.

THE INTERNAL GAP

However problematic the reliability, validity, and availability of data on the international gap, even more formidable problems hinder the study of the internal gap. Empirical testing of dependency/world-system explanations for the internal gap has produced widely varying results. Any reader of the major social science journals today would be rightly confused by the varied findings reported in the increasingly frequent articles on this subject. In reviewing this growing body of research in Chapter 21, Muller points out a number of the weaknesses of those articles and goes a long way toward correcting many of them. Beyond the flaws reported by Muller, however, it appears that there are at least four chronic problems that beset macrolevel empirical tests of internal gap theories and that may ultimately lead us down a blind alley of inconclusive findings even after the "best" methodology has been applied.

The first difficulty plaguing these macroanalytic investigations concerns sample skewing. Income inequality data are difficult to obtain because many nations do not collect them (or at least do not publicly acknowledge that they do), a problem noted in several of the articles included in this volume. In spite of the availability problem, researchers have proceeded with the data that are available, following the time-honored tradition in the social sciences of making do with what one finds rather than postponing research indefinitely. Although such a procedure is appropriate in many research situations, one wonders if it is justifiable in this one. The principal reason for expressing this cautionary note is that the countries that do report income distribution data are probably not a random sample of all nations. One suspects that there are at least two factors that tend to skew the sample. First, the poorest, least developed nations often do not have the resources (financial and technical) to conduct such studies; indeed, there may not even arise the need for such data to be collected in some of these nations. Second, nations in which income distribution is very badly skewed are probably reluctant to authorize the collection of such data, and even if the data are collected, governments may not make them publicly available. Hence, the data we do have may include fewer cases of the poorest nations and fewer cases of highly unequal distribution than one might expect if the sample were random. It is impossible to prove the second assertion because one cannot know the extent of inequality until the data are actually collected, but even a superficial glance at the list of nations included in the various studies reveals the incompleteness of data from the world's poorest nations.

The second major problem with macroanalytical investigations is a direct outgrowth of the first. I call this problem the "Mauritania effect"—that is, the dramatic differences in results that can be produced by the inclusion or exclusion of as few as one or two countries. In one investigation, for example, the inclusion of Mauritania, with a population of only 1.5 million, had a major impact on the results of a key regression equation. The findings tend not to be robust when minor variations in sample design occur; one's confidence in the results is therefore shaken. An unusually frank comment by a proponent of macroanalytic investigations of this type is contained in an article coauthored by Erich Weede, who contributed two chapters to this volume: "It seems impossible to predict with any confidence what would happen if inequality data on all or about twice as many countries were to become available" (Weede and Tiefenbach, 1981).

The third problem concerns the general lack of cross-time data. However limited the sample of countries may be for the present period, even less reliable information exists on developing countries for the pre–World War II period. This is a particularly serious problem because both dependency/world-system analysis and the traditional developmental approach propose longitudinal hypotheses, whereas data limitations generally impose cross-sectional designs. Although cross-sectional designs can sometimes be useful surrogates for longitudinal studies, the problem of skewed samples reduces the value of these cross-sectional studies.

One serious manifestation of the lack of longitudinal data emerges in studies that include Latin America. As a region, Latin America is more developed than most Third World nations and not surprisingly has somewhat more income distribution data available. It is also the case that Latin American nations have been found to exhibit comparatively high levels of both dependency and income inequality. One might leap to the conclusion, as some have, that inequality is therefore a function of dependency. However, there is another, equally appealing thesis suggesting that inequality in Latin America is part of a corporatist bureaucratic/authoritarian political culture considered to be characteristic of the region (Chapter 14). One does not know, therefore, if Latin America's comparatively high level of inequality is a function of its intermediate level of development (as Kuznets would suggest), its dependency (as the dependency/world-system proponents would suggest), or its political culture. Determining which of these hypotheses is correct would require longitudinal data to explore the dynamics of dependency, development, and inequality.

A final difficulty with the macroanalytical research is that there is no meeting of the minds as to suitable standards of verifiability. For example, there is a wide gulf separating many dependency/world-system theorists on the one hand and researchers who seek to test their hypotheses with quantitative data on the other. Cardoso and Faletto (1979), authors of one of the most influential and highly respected works on Latin American dependency (see Pakenham, 1982: 131-132), argue that empirical tests of dependency theory have largely missed the target. Cardoso (1977:23, n. 12) explains that the tests have been "ahistorical." Although not rejecting empirical verification as useful, he questions the validity of many of these studies, even those sustaining the dependency approach. Finally, in the preface to the new English edition of their book, Cardoso and Faletto argue that "statistical information and demonstrations are useful and necessary. But the crucial questions for demonstration are of a different nature" (Cardoso and Faletto, 1979:xiii). The demonstrations proposed would be heavily grounded in historical detail, highlighting all the more the problem of the lack of longitudinal income distribution data.

In the coming years, it is likely that many more macroanalytical empirical investigations will be published and will continue to add to our understanding. However, it is difficult to imagine how the four major problems enumerated above will be overcome entirely. Given the difficulties apparently inherent in the macroanalytical studies conducted to date, more attention needs to be paid to methodologies that will examine from a microanalytic perspective the question of the origin of domestic inequality. In concluding an extensive review of the dependency/world-system literature, Palma (1981:413) argues for microstudies of "specific situations in concrete terms." And the study by Bornschier, Chase-Dunn, and Rubinson (1978) concludes by arguing for microsociological studies that would "clarify the specific mechanisms by which these processes operate."

Problems of data availability need not cause the abandonment of future studies of the internal gap. Rather, a series of microanalytical studies would seem to offer a promising alternative. Such investigations would make it possible to trace how inequality is stimulated in developing countries. The emphasis needs to be placed on drawing the explicit links, if they exist, between income distribution and factors such as culture, dependency, rent-seeking, urban bias, and so on. Indeed, it can be argued that even if the data problems were not as serious as they are and if macroanalytical empirical research were to demonstrate unequivocally the existence of a connection between, for example, culture and domestic inequality, one would still need to understand how one affects the other, something that cannot be known from the macrostudies.

Some research has already been published that opens the door to this type of analysis. Studies of transnational corporations in Colombia (Chudnowsky, 1974) and Brazil (Evans, 1979; Newfarmer, 1980) reveal much about the internal dynamics of dependency. An even more recent microstudy, however, has demonstrated that imperialist penetration in one African state, Yorubaland, at the end of the nineteenth century produced a "vibrant and creative" reaction on the part of Yoruba traders in response to new opportunities in the international market (Laitin, 1982:702).

These microanalytical studies, helpful though they are in beginning to penetrate the "black box," reflect weaknesses that would need to be overcome by those seeking to test the various explanations of income inequality proposed in this volume. First, these detailed case studies, although providing a wealth of rich, descriptive material, betray all of the limitations of generalizability inherent in the case study method. It is to be hoped, of course, that the accumulation of these various cases ultimately will lead to a synthesis; but given the widely divergent methods, time periods, and data bases employed in these studies, it is unclear if such optimism is warranted. What is clear is that if a cumulative social science is to continue to emerge in this field, future research will need to be not only microanalytic but also self-consciously comparative. Only by applying the comparative method at the outset of a study of the internal causes of inequality will the data generated allow immediate comparisons and subsequent theory testing.

In sum, an appropriate study ought to be (1) microanalytic, (2) comparative, and (3) capable of testing the relative merits of competing paradigms. That certainly is a tall order for any researcher, but one way to achieve this goal and still plan a project of manageable proportions is to focus on key institutions through which dependency mechanisms are thought to operate. In an effort to accomplish this task, one study analyzed exchange rate policies as the "linchpin" that helps "uncover the mechanisms through which these various [dependency] effects occur" (Moon, 1982:716). A major advance of this study over previous work was the explicit linkage of dependency effects to particular policies of Third World governments. Hence, the analysis went far beyond most dependency literature, which typically makes frequent reference to the so-called internal colonialist *comprador* elite without revealing precisely how such elites affect income distribution. Studies such as Moon's that examine the impact of other crucial linchpins through which dependency is thought to operate, are to be encouraged.

Two efforts, therefore, need to be made for the debate to advance beyond its present state. First, historians need to assist those working in this field to develop measures of income distribution for prior epochs. Creative use of historical records (e.g., tax rolls, property registers, census data, etc.) might permit the reconstruction of such information, providing the longitudinal data that are so sadly lacking at this time. Second, once the historical data have been gathered, social scientists need to direct their attention to the various linchpins of the causes of growth and inequality and study them in a comparative context. Perhaps with these two efforts underway, significant advances are possible in a relatively short period of time.

CONCLUSIONS

The research presented in this volume was not conducted in a vacuum. Investigators study problems such as the gap between rich and poor because they are concerned, and the great majority of them hope that their findings ultimately will be translated into public policy. Even though definitive findings are still far from our grasp, as has been made clear by the debate presented in this volume, many world leaders already have sought to implement policies to correct the problem.

As the gaps between rich and poor grow wider throughout the world, the debate grows more heated. Discussions in international forums today are characterized by increasing intolerance. More distressing, perhaps, is that the academic debate has also taken on a shrillness that only serves to dilute its credibility. It is hoped that this collection of studies along with the suggestions made in this concluding chapter will help in some small way to moderate tempers and guide thinking and research toward more productive answers to this important question.

NOTES

1. The data are from the World Bank (1983).
2. See Kravis et al. (1975) and Kravis et al. (1982).

REFERENCES

Booth, J. A., and M. A. Seligson. 1984. "The Political Culture of Authoritarianism in Mexico: A Reexamination." *Latin American Research Review* (no. 1):106–124.

Bornschier, V., C. Chase-Dunn, and R. Rubinson. 1978. "Cross-National Evidence of the Effects of Foreign Investment and Aid on Economic Growth and Inequality: A Survey of Findings and a Reanalysis." *American Journal of Sociology*, vol. 84 (November).

Cardoso, F. H. 1977. "The Consumption of Dependency Theory in the United States." *Latin American Research Review* 12 (3):7–24.

Cordoso, F. H., and E. Faletto. 1979. *Dependency and Development in Latin America*. Berkeley: University of California Press.

Chudnowsky, D. 1974. *Empresas multinacionales y ganancias monopolicias en una economía latinoamericana*. Buenos Aires: Siglo XXI Editores.

Collier, D., ed. 1979. *The New Authoritarianism in Latin America*. Princeton: Princeton University Press.

Evans, P. 1979. *Dependent Development: The Alliance of Multinational, State and Local Capital in Brazil*. Princeton: Princeton University Press.

Jackman, R. W. 1982. "Dependency on Foreign Investment and Economic Growth in the Third World." *World Politics* 34 (January):175–197.

Harrison, L. E. 1992. *Who Prospers? How Cultural Values Shape Economic and Political Success*. New York: Basic Books.

Inglehart, R. 1988. "The Renaissance of Political Culture." *American Political Science Review* 82 (December):1203–1230.

———. 1990. *Culture Shift in Advanced Industrial Societies*. Princeton: Princeton University Press.

Kravis, I. et al. 1975. *A System of International Comparisons of Gross Product and Purchasing Power*. Baltimore: Johns Hopkins University Press.

———. 1982. *World Product and Income: International Comparisons of Real GDP*. Baltimore: Johns Hopkins University Press.

Laitin, D. D. 1982. "Capitalism and Hegemony: Yorubaland and the International Economy." *International Organization* 36 (Autumn):687–714.

Malloy, J. M.. ed. 1977. *Authoritarianism and Corporatism in Latin America*. Pittsburgh: University of Pittsburgh Press.

Moon, B. E. 1982. "Exchange Rate System, Policy Distortions, and the Maintenance of Trade Dependence." *International Organization* 36 (Autumn): 715–740.

Newfarmer, R. 1980. *Transnational Conglomerates and the Economics of Dependent Development: A Case Study of the International Electrical Oligopoly and Brazil's Electrical Industry*. Greenwich, Conn.: JAI Press.

O'Donnell, G. 1973. *Modernization and Bureaucratic Authoritarianism: Studies in South American Politics*. Berkeley: Institute of International Studies of the University of California, Politics of Modernization Series No. 9.

Packenham, R. A. 1982. "Plus ça change . . .: The English Edition of Cardoso and Faletto's Dependencia y Desarrollo en América Latina." *Latin American Research Review* 17 (1):131–151.

Palma, G. 1981. "Dependency: A Formal Theory of Underdevelopment or a Methodology for the Analysis of Concrete Situations." In Paul Streetin and Richard Jolly, eds., *Recent Issues in World Development*. New York: Pergamon.

Ray, J. L., and T. Webster. 1978. "Dependency and Economic Growth in Latin America." *International Studies Quarterly* 22 (September):409–434.

Seligson, M. A., and J. A. Booth. Forthcoming. "Political Culture and Regime Type: Evidence from Nicaragua and Costa Rica." *Journal of Politics*.

Weede, E., and H. Tiefenbach. 1981. "Some Recent Explanations of Income Inequality." *International Studies Quarterly* 25 (June):255–282.

World Bank. 1980. *World Development Report 1980*. New York: Oxford University Press.

World Bank. 1982. *World Development Report 1983*. New York: Oxford University Press.

World Bank. 1992. *World Development Report 1983*. New York: Oxford University Press.

Index

Abramovitz, M., 12, 74(n3), 75(n13), 79, 81, 84, 85, 99(n2)
absolute gap, 3, 10–12, 19, 21, 22, 24, 27,28
achievement, need for, 5, 141, 143–148, 150–157, 184, 185, 187, 188, 212, 270; in basic needs, 121, 126–135. *See also n* achievement
Adelman, I., 99, 122, 359, 395–396
Africa, 6, 70, 105, 111, 207, 221, 253, 255, 263(n24), 264(n29), 271, 275, 289, 291, 345, 350, 363(n3), 423, 445; aid to, 423; dependency in, 207, 350, 363(n3); economic growth in, 17, 19, 52, 116, 244, 245, 247–249; gap in, 10, 28; maldistribution, 55(n4); marketing boards in, 333–344; mobility, 27, 28; power motive, 150; underdevelopment in, 52
agriculture, 46, 61, 66, 71, 122, 214, 227, 230(n4), 232, 317, 318, 320, 321, 324, 325, 327(n12, n14), 333–346, 356, 357, 365, 372–375, 379, 380, 428–430
agro-export, 315, 319, 320
Ahluwalia, M., 273, 276, 348, 376(n5), 398
Algeria, 105, 229
alienation, 214
Alschuler, L., 244, 351
Amin, S., 214(n5), 220, 300
Andreski, S., 359, 364(n11), 391

Angola, 229
Arbenz, J., 319
Argentina, 27, 32, 89(n6), 93, 94, 96, 98, 99(n6), 100(n10), 159, 209, 210, 253, 261, 271, 276, 286, 407
"Arielismo," 212
army, 99, 100, 171, 176
Asturias, 94
Athenian, 141, 145
austerity, 122
Australia, 12(n1), 51, 74(n8), 75(n9), 80, 81, 94, 98–100, 105, 262, 279, 287, 350
Austria, 12(n1), 74(n8), 96, 100(n10), 262, 276, 278, 364(n4)
The Authoritarian Personality, 166(n1)
authoritarianism, 155, 402; and economic growth, 178

Bagú, S., 204, 207, 214(n6), 215(n12)
Bairoch, P., 94
Ballmer-Cao, T., 248, 249, 261(n14), 262(n19), 263(n26), 270, 272–276, 283, 288, 291(n6), 296, 304, 306, 349, 351, 352, 382
Bangladesh (formerly East Pakistan), 12, 13(n4), 105, 111, 159, 225
Baran, P., 220, 295
basic needs, 16, 113, 117, 119–136, 442
Bates, R., 6, 333, 345(n12), 346(n13, n14)
Bauer, P., 120, 122, 361, 363

Baumol, W., 75(n12), 77, 91–94, 99(n1)
Becker, G., 360
Belgium, 12, 74, 75, 100, 262(n18), 278
Belize, 27
Bello, W., 295, 421
Benin, 111, 276
Bhagwati, J., 13(n3)
BID. *See* Inter-American Development Bank
Biersteker, T., 124, 296
Bolivia, 208, 209, 286; output per capita, 81
Booth, J., 315, 327(n8, n13, n17); challenge to cultural approach, 438
Bornschier, V., 124, 239, 240, 248, 253, 260(n8), 262(n17, n19), 263(n21, n23, n26), 278, 290(n1), 295, 304, 349, 351, 352, 353, 361, 445; measure of TNC penetration, 244, 249, 250, 274; TNC penetration and economic growth, 268, 269; TNC penetration and external debt, 285; TNCs and internal inequality, 270, 272, 273, 275, 287, 288, 289, 296, 306
Botswana, 26, 28, 29(n3), 103; economic growth of, 19, 23
bourgeoisie, 79, 160, 296; in Central America, 321; and inequality, 269; strengthening of, 208; TNCs' impact on, 268
Bradburn, N., 154
Brazil, 104, 196, 204, 209, 210, 216(n19), 260–

449

261(n9), 301, 302, 310, 363–364(n4), 445; compared with East Asia, 407–413, 415–417; and convergence, 99(n5); dependent development of, 206, 209, 210, 272, 445; economic growth, 15, 130, 209; poverty and inequality in, 32, 268; TNC penetration, 276, 286, 290, 310

Britain, 67, 68, 96, 225, 305, 308, 360, 373; and Central America, 319; and convergence, 98, 99(n6); developmental stages, 219–223; economic growth, 71; investment, 94, 95; occupation of Ireland, 297, 305, 311(n5)

Bulgaria, 89(n6)

Burkina Faso (Myanmar), 103

Burma, 224, 275, 276

Burundi, 253

CACM. *See* Central American Common Market

Calvinist doctrine, 100(n11), 143–144, 177

campesinos. See peasants

Canada, 12(n1), 74(n8), 222, 223, 225, 262(n18), 270, 295, 350; and convergence, 93–94, 98; and inequality, 51, 270; protestant ethic in, 100(n10); TNC penetration in, 276, 279, 287

Cantril, H., 13

capital formation, 48–49, 54, 63, 250, 254, 382; in Ireland, 302; TNCs and, 240, 241

Cardoso, F., 204, 206, 209, 213(n4), 214(n7, n8), 215(n9, n11, n15, n16), 216(n19), 268, 272, 290, 327(n9), 444

Caribbean, 196, 247; low wages in, 422

cartel, 262(n19); industrial, 67; and modernization, 164; and rent-seeking, 353–355

Castro, F., 320

Catholicism, 100(n10); in Costa Rica, 325; and development, 97, 178, 181(n7); and Ireland, 311; parents instilling values, 154

Central American Common

Market, 318–321, 323, 324, 326

Central Intelligence Agency, 432, 434(n22)

Ceylon, 43, 49, 50. *See also* Sri Lanka

Chad, 275, 276

chaebol, 408, 409, 412–414, 417, 423, 426

Chase-Dunn, C., 7(n3), 124, 213(n5), 239, 244, 261(n15), 262(n17), 269, 272, 273, 295, 296, 352, 361, 445

Chenery, H., 122, 124, 348

Chile, 159, 208, 209, 214(n6), 215–216(n19), 276; and convergence, 94, 96, 98, 100(n10)

China, 4, 9, 10, 21, 22, 81, 89(n6), 155, 171, 184, 230(n2), 347, 348, 389; and the collapse of the Soviet Union, 6, 224, 428; environmental concerns, 434(n19); wages in, 422, 432,

CIA. *See* Central Intelligence Agency

Clark, C., 55(n1), 79, 148

Colombia, 440; export-oriented elites, 209; TNC penetration in, 261, 445

colonialism, 52, 164, 195, 204, 207, 224, 229, 297, 311(n5), 319, 327(n12); and Asian NICs, 271, 275, 296, 424; and convergence, 98; economic advantage of colonial power, 174, 195, 205, 342–343, 350; economic distortion of dependent state, 196, 200, 208, 214(n6); and inequality, 377, 446; and TNCs, 291(n5)

communism, 220, 319, 423

The Communist Manifesto, 79

communists, 148, 220, 222, 225, 281, 289, 291(n7), 316

"Confucian Ethic," 5, 7, 169–171

consumer price index (CPI), 116, 322

consumer prices, 320, 321; agricultural goods, 6

consumption, 33, 38(n5), 54, 121, 123, 186, 187–188, 297, 311(n1), 317, 333, 372; calorie intake, 32, 260(n7); and convergence, 61; and dependency, 195, 196, 205, 232,

240, 242, 287; energy, 251, 253, 274; and the poor, 125–126, 135(n1); and production, 13, 372

core countries, 6, 213–214(n5), 226–229, 232–235, 240, 245, 251, 253, 254, 260(n7), 262(n18), 267–271, 274, 276, 278, 279, 281, 283–285, 287–289, 296, 360

Cornia, G., 121, 122

Costa Rica, 209, 316, 319, 325, 327; inequality and wages, 322–324; unemployment, 323

Côte d'Ivoire (Ivory Coast), 105, 276, 345(n4)

coup. *See golpe de estado*

CPI. *See* consumer price index

Cuba, 197, 320; convergence, 94, 99(n5); revolution, 225, 319

Cutright, P., 397, 399

Czechoslovakia, 89(n6), 96, 223, 363–364(n4)

DAC (Development Assistance Countries). *See* development assistance

Deane, P., 79

debt, 289, 291(n9), 310, 344; crisis, 15, 17, 121, 209; debt dependence, 272, 285; and domestic policymaking, 268, 416; and economic growth, 272, 285–286; and inequality, 305

decapitalization, 198, 285, 295, 351

deindustrialization, 77, 223

Delacroix, J., 351, 352, 363–364(n4)

De Long, J., 91

democracy, 16, 67, 180, 185, 218, 331, 341, 389–405, 431; and civil liberties, 358; and convergence, 91, 96, 97, 100(n11); democratization, 430–431; and economic growth, 7, 155, 358, 359; and inequality, 7, 47, 179, 360, 362, 364(n10, n11), 365(n13); peoples', 225; and rent-seeking, 358, 359; and unionization, 47, 67

Denmark, 12(n1), 74(n8), 100(n10), 262(n18), 271, 275, 276

dependency, 6, 193–197, 203–216, 220, 230, 240,

263(n21), 267, 268, 272–
274, 276, 278, 285, 348,
349, 352; debt depen-
dence, 285–286; defini-
tion of, 194–195; and
economic growth, 174,
202, 204, 205, 246, 254,
262(n17), 273, 349–352;
forms of, 195–199; and
income inequality, 200–
201, 268, 270, 272, 273,
274, 276–279, 287–290,
349–352; in Ireland, 295–
313; mindset created by,
178; origins of theory,
203–216; and TNCs, 195,
196–199, 268, 272
determinism, economic, 148,
288, 290; pyschological,
148, 164
development assistance, 4,
15, 166, 198, 199, 200,
271, 278, 285, 297, 319,
361, 372, 373, 374,
376(n2), 423;
Development Assistance
Countries (DAC), 120,
260(n9), 278, 376(n2); investment aid, 7(n3)
Diamond, L., 253, 261(n15),
263(n26), 352
Dixon, W., 119, 123, 135(n3,
n5), 136(n8)
Dolan, M., 245, 247, 248,
253, 263(n26)
Domar, E., 241, 260(n1)
dos Santos, T., 189, 193, 204,
205, 209, 213(n3),
215(n16, n19), 220, 268,
272, 85
"Dragon economies," 117–
118(n5), 421. See also
newly industrializing
countries
Dreze, J., 119
dualism, 300, 308
Dube, S., 15
Dudley, D., 54–55(n1), 220
Durning, A., 15

East Asia, 9, 10, 24, 28,
29(n2), 105, 111, 423,
425, 431, 432; big busi-
ness in, 407–419; depen-
dency in, 296, 309–310,
438–439; and economic
growth, 17, 114, 300, 303,
432; and income inequal-
ity, 308, 309–310; U.S.
policy toward, 423–425
Easterlin, R., 12, 99(n2)
ECLA. See Economic
Commission for Latin
America
ecology, 226, 422, 429
Economic Commission for

Latin America, 195, 197,
202, 203, 207, 208,
214(n8), 268
Ecuador, 276
education, 59, 60, 65, 66, 67,
72, 73, 75(n18), 87, 122,
125, 126, 127, 160, 165,
170, 171, 173, 175, 176,
178, 180, 218, 219, 228,
270, 287, 308, 320, 372,
374, 422, 424, 441, 442
Egypt, 81, 99(n6), 118(n6),
263(n24)
Eisenstadt, S., 224, 230(n5)
El Salvador, 315–325,
327(n18)
employment, 64, 69, 84,
135(n2), 156, 260(n4),
297, 304, 308, 318, 319,
321, 323, 326, 327(n12),
357, 364(n11), 412
England, 44, 151, 155, 307,
311(n5); and economic
growth, 80, 146; inequal-
ity in, 48, 79; and Ireland,
305–306; and Latin
America, 207. See also
Britain, Great Britain, and
United Kingdom
entrepreneurs, 46, 80, 84,
119, 143, 146, 148, 151–
153, 154, 155, 156, 175,
177, 178, 180, 185, 186,
187, 205, 206, 207, 209,
212, 237, 327(n10), 354,
356, 364(n9), 379
EOI (export-oriented industrialization). See export-
led development
ethnocentrism, 365(n16),
438
Europe, 6, 66, 71, 74, 84, 94,
105, 111, 116, 144, 151,
171, 207, 214(n6), 220,
222, 232, 262(n18), 264,
296, 302, 310, 372, 373,
390, 408, 428; aid to, 4,
297; and colonization,
204, 207, 223–224,
230(n4); 297, 305; con-
vergence, 67–70, 84, 94,
98, 99–100(n8); Eastern
economic growth, 66,
389; Eastern Europe, 6,
66, 69, 389, 428; and
Latin America, 176;
Western economic
growth, 28, 60, 311(n3);
Western Europe, 4, 15,
54, 55, 98, 311, 408, 428;
Western inequality, 51,
54, 55, 73, 302, 305, 310,
372, 373
European Community, 54,
55, 67, 68, 70, 71, 94, 151,
171, 204, 207, 214, 217,

220, 222, 224, 230, 281,
305, 428; European
Economic Community,
296, 297, 302, 303
Evans, P., 124, 245, 247,
272, 288, 296, 306, 410,
417, 445
export-led development
(export-oriented indus-
trialization), 124, 195,
196, 207, 208, 209, 297,
299, 310, 321, 407, 408,
409, 415–417, 418, 421–
434

Faletto, E., 209, 213(n4),
214(n8), 215(n11, n15,
n16), 216(n19), 444
fascism, 202, 213(n3),
215(n19)
FDI. See foreign direct investment
Fei, J., 123
Feinstein, C., 75(n17), 79,
81, 87(n1)
Feis, H., 94
feudalism, 184, 214(n6),
219, 220, 222, 290, 349,
350
Fields, G., 130
Figueroa, A., 271, 272
Finland, 12(n1), 74(n8), 94,
100(n10), 262(n18), 268,
279, 281, 289
Fishlow, A., 38(n2), 130
foreign direct investment
(FDI), 7(n3), 38(n5), 54,
58, 61, 66, 84, 94, 95,
99(n5), 124, 195, 196,
198, 199, 209, 210, 239–
266, 269, 270, 271, 272,
273, 274, 281, 283,
291(n5, n8), 295, 296,
300, 302, 303, 304, 308,
310, 320, 349, 351, 352,
357, 372–375, 408, 409,
414, 423, 425, 431
France, 12(n1), 71, 74–
75(n8, n16), 80, 94, 95,
96, 103, 225, 226, 229,
262(n18), 268, 350, 360;
colonialism, 350; conver-
gence, 96, 100(n10); eco-
nomic growth and devel-
opment of, 71, 80, 207;
inequality in, 268;
Revolution, 218, 219
Franco, F., 150, 271
Frank, A., 214(n8), 220, 231,
295, 443
Freud, S., 142, 157
Fromm, E., 166(n1)
Furtado, C., 220, 268, 272

Galtung, J., 263(n21), 349–
351, 363(n3, n4)

Gandhi, I., 373
GATT. *See* General Agreement on Tariffs and Trade
GDP. *See* gross domestic product
General Agreement on Tariffs and Trade, 423, 427
Gereffi, G., 7, 407, 408, 410, 416, 417, 439
Germany, 12(n1), 43, 44, 45, 48, 54–55(n1), 68, 78, 88, 96, 143, 147, 150, 153, 207, 222; Berlin, 55; East, 89(n6), 94, 100(n10), 363–364(n4); West, 74–75(n8, n18), 80, 100, 262(n18), 360, 409
Gerschenkron, A., 81
Ghana, 338, 339, 342, 345(n4, n5, n6), 346(n14)
GINI, 39(n8), 86, 276
GNP. *See* gross national product
Gobalet, G., 253, 261(n15), 263(n26), 352
golpe de estado, 290, 339
Great Britain, 181(n6), 219–223, 225
Great Depression, 45, 65, 66, 78, 206, 208
Greece, 12(n1), 144, 145, 154, 275, 276
Green Revolution, 345(n9), 375
gross domestic product, 62, 63, 77, 81–83, 84, 86–89, 104, 105, 111, 113, 114, 117, 126, 127, 130, 134, 136, 246, 250, 251, 261, 320, 351, 358, 359, 380–382, 386, 408, 413
gross national product, 3, 10, 11, 13, 15, 16, 19, 21–29, 35, 78, 83, 99, 103–105, 111, 113, 114, 116–120, 123–126, 130, 135, 160, 166, 180, 244, 246, 250, 251, 253, 256, 261, 285, 302, 303, 310, 350, 351, 376, 380, 382, 433, 439–441
Guatemala, 209, 315–318, 319, 320–325; counterinsurgency, 315; economic growth, 320, 321; inequality in, 316, 321, 322, 323, 324; revolutionary coalitions in, 317, 318, 325
guerrillas, 4, 316
Guinea, 117–118(n5), 339
Gurr, T., 356
Guyana, 26, 27

Habib, I., 220, 230(n1)
hacendados, 327(n10)
haciendas, 196, 319
Hagen, E., 175, 181(n2, n3), 184, 185, 212
Haiti, 111, 258
Harrison, L., 173, 181(n4), 438
Hayek, F., 354
HDI. *See* Human Development Index
healthcare, 122, 125, 127, 173, 175, 176, 180, 195, 287, 307, 308, 372, 441
hegemon, 195, 196, 197, 198, 200, 221, 222, 423
Hesiod, 144
Heston, A., 13(n3), 80, 86, 87(n2), 103, 104, 117(n3), 126, 135(n6)
Hewitt, C., 397
Hirschman, A., 274, 300
Hitler, A., 150
Hoadley, J., 120
Homer, 144
Honduras, 81, 276, 320–325, 327(n10, n12); economic growth in, 319; inequality in, 322, 323, 324; political violence in, 316
Hong Kong, 171, 262(n19), 296, 311, 407, 425, 431; development strategy, 296, 407, 425; economic growth in, 122, 171; state intervention in economy, 311(n2)
human capital, 121, 122, 127, 134, 135(n2), 233, 349, 352, 359, 363(n4), 364(n5), 382–384, 387(n3), 395
Human Development Index (HDI), 111
Hungary, 89(n6), 422
Hyundai, 412, 423, 424, 428

IBM, 428, 432
IBRD (International Bank for Reconstruction and Redevelopment). *See* World Bank
Iceland, 12(n1), 89(n6), 105
ICP. *See* International Comparisons Project
illiteracy, 176, 177, 441
ILO. *See* International Labor Organization
IMF. *See* International Monetary Fund
imperialism, 100(n12), 173, 174, 194, 198(n3), 200, 204, 207, 220, 225, 232, 270–272, 288, 349, 350, 351, 445
import substitution industrial-

ization, 6, 68, 204, 209, 215(n19), 297, 299, 409, 415–417
income distribution, 5, 7, 12, 13, 31, 32–35, 39, 43–53, 54, 55(n1), 77(n1), 113, 121, 123, 124, 180, 193, 233, 242, 260, 267, 270–283, 287–290, 295, 303–311(n4), 324, 348, 349, 350–352, 358, 398, 397–400, 443, 444, 445, 446
India, 43, 103, 105, 111, 147, 159, 220, 223, 230(n1), 253, 257, 283, 291(n7), 357, 360, 373, 376(n6), 379; economic growth in, 13(n4), 105; foreign investment in, 283; income inequality, 32, 43, 49–51
Indonesia, 171, 224, 257, 431
industrial revolution, 47, 68, 80, 83, 92, 99(n2), 146, 223
inflation, 45, 54, 103, 122, 126, 204, 318, 320, 322, 324, 326, 358, 376(n1)
infrastructure, 71, 120, 122, 125, 285, 299, 300, 358, 424, 426
Inkeles, A., 7, 166–167(n2), 184, 185, 389
Intel, 428
Inter-American Development Bank, 202
Inter-American Economic and Social Council, 198
International Comparisons Project (ICP), 104, 105, 111, 113, 117(n3), 440
International Labor Organization (ILO), 122
International Monetary Fund (IMF), 16, 29(n2), 104, 105, 113, 116, 121, 197, 310, 423
Iran, 100(n11), 223
Iraq, 276
Ireland, 12(n1), 96, 100(n10), 253, 291(n7), 439; and convergence, 93, 94, 98; dependence, 295–313; economic growth in, 68
irrigation, 336, 338, 372, 373
ISI. *See* import substitution industrialization
Israel, 118(n6), 159, 262(n19), 363–364(n4)
Italy, 12(n1), 25, 74–75(n8, n16), 91, 93, 98, 100(n10), 141, 142, 147, 176, 223, 363–364(n4); Rome, 55, 79, 141

Ivory Coast. *See* Côte
d'Ivoire

Jackman, R., 16, 17, 29(n1),
117(n4), 245–247, 352,
387(n4), 394, 397–401
Jain, S., 39(n9), 271
Jamaica, 27, 276
Jameson, K., 120, 125
Japan, 12(n1), 25, 29, 60,
74–75(n8), 87, 91, 97–99,
150, 171, 188, 224,
262(n18), 276, 295, 296,
361, 363–364(n4), 402,
408, 409, 428, 432,
433(n7, n10); and the
Asian NICs, 413–425;
"Confucian ethic," 169–
171; convergence, 60, 67,
68, 71, 78, 80, 81, 94, 98,
99(n1, n6); economic
growth in, 7, 29, 60,
74(n2), 94, 97, 413, 415;
imperialism, 225, 271; inequality in, 276, 296;
political culture in, 144,
147, 161, 224; women's
role, 155
Jordan, 262(n19)
Judaism, 177, 178, 181(n7)

Kahn, H., 7, 19, 169
Kaufman, R., 213(n5), 214–
215(n8), 244, 247,
261(n10)
Kenessey, Z., 117(n3)
Kenya, 111, 276, 338, 339,
345(n4, n8), 441; coup in,
339; inequality, 50,
55(n4), 276; marketing
boards, 335, 336
Keynes, J., 78, 241
Kim Il Sung, 225
Kindleberger, C., 71, 73,
76(n19)
Kirkpatrick, C., 300, 326(n5)
Krauss, 360–362, 365(n15)
Kravis, I., 13(n3), 61, 62,
74(n5), 86, 103, 117(n3),
446(n2)
Kriesberg, L., 317
Kuo, S., 123
Kuwait, 29(n4), 94, 439
Kuznets, S., 5, 9, 16, 19, 27,
29(n4), 32, 34, 38, 43,
55(n1), 79, 103, 104,
117(n2), 290, 382, 393,
399, 438, 444

Lal, D., 120, 122
land ownership and reform,
64, 123, 196, 204, 208,
227, 270, 297, 306, 318,
319, 320, 326, 327(n10,
n16), 338, 349, 373, 374,
375, 379, 429

Landes, D., 80
Latin America, 27, 66, 169,
173, 179, 189, 244, 245,
247, 261, 271, 315; con-
vergence, 66, 70; culture
and development, 179;
dependence, 52, 174, 189,
193–202, 203–216, 220,
221, 268, 271; develop-
ment strategy, 407–419,
442; economic growth
and crisis, 10, 261(n10),
389; foreign investment,
99(n5); inequality, 444;
political violence (Central
America), 315–330
Lebanon, 382
Lenin, V., 174, 204, 222
Lenski, G., 399
Leontief model, 13(n5)
Lesotho, 19, 27
Levin, I., 195
liberalism (neo), 6, 15, 121,
125, 207, 218, 219, 220,
221, 223, 225, 233, 310,
319, 372, 421, 423, 439
liberalization, 6, 120, 122,
310, 416, 427, 429
Liberia, 339
Libya, 9, 10, 263(n24), 439
Lorenz curve 39(n8)
Luxembourg, 12(n1),
89(n6), 105

Madagascar, 111, 276
Maddison, A., 62, 75(n9,
n10, n16), 79, 80, 81, 82,
84, 86, 87–88(n3), 89, 92,
93, 94, 96, 99(n3), 382
Malawi, 276, 286, 335
Malaysia, 171, 431, 440
Mali, 257
Malta, 19
Marshall Plan, 4, 5, 174, 297,
423
Marx, K., 151, 160, 214,
222, 230(n3), 355,
387(n1)
Marxism, 194, 218, 219, 221,
272
Marxist, 157, 174, 204, 210,
213–214(n5, n6, n8), 218,
220, 223, 225, 230(n1,
n3), 233, 268, 269, 360,
386, 394
"Matthew effect," 17
Mauritania, 105; effect, 443
McClelland, D., 141, 159,
179(n8), 181, 184, 185,
212
McGowan, P., 244, 248
McNamara, R., 120, 373
mercantilist, 83, 207, 417
metropole, 295
Mexico, 94, 208, 209, 223,
224, 302, 319, 360, 440;

agriculture, 208, 209;
convergence, 94; depen-
dence, 213(n2, n3, n4),
214(n7), 301, 310; eco-
nomic growth and devel-
opment strategy, 209,
407–419; foreign invest-
ment, 99(n5), 301–302;
inequality, 32
Middle Ages, 79
Middle East, 9, 10, 17–19,
28, 105, 111, 118(n6), 424
military, 141, 150, 187, 202,
209, 228, 272, 290, 319,
352, 364, 423, 424; mili-
tary aid, 423
mobility, 26–27, 52, 178,
186, 251
mobilization, 188, 316–318,
324–326
modernization, 5, 59, 71,
159, 160–166, 169, 171,
185, 203, 204, 206, 207,
210–213, 224, 231–232,
235, 236, 269, 278, 296,
302, 305, 309–311, 372,
390, 423
monopoly, 164, 195, 197,
198, 201, 242, 337, 347,
353, 354, 355, 356, 362,
364(n6), 379
Moon, B., 119, 123, 127,
135(n3, n4, n5), 136(n8),
446
Morawetz, D., 4, 13(n7), 15,
19, 21, 22, 23, 27, 28, 438
Morocco, 275, 276
Mozambique, 111
Muller, E., 123, 295, 352,
397–399, 442
Myanmar. *See* Burma
Myint, H., 300, 308
Myrdal, G., 178, 179,
181(n10)

n achievement, 141, 143–
150, 152–157, 159, 169,
184, 185, 187
Nakane, C., 170, 171(n2)
NAMBoard (Zambian Food
Marketing Board), 335
national liberation, 229, 230,
307
nationalism, 179, 225, 227,
414, 417
Nepal, 105
Netherlands, 12(n1), 75(n9),
100(n10), 223, 262(n18),
276
New International Economic
Order (NIEO), 4
New Zealand, 12(n1), 51,
89(n6), 94, 100(n10),
262(n18)
newly industrializing countries (NICs), 17, 19, 28,

122, 295, 407–418, 421–
   432, 434(n20)
Nicaragua, 26, 27, 176–177,
   315, 316, 317, 318, 319,
   320, 321, 322, 323, 324,
   325, 327(n11)
NICs. *See* newly industrializing countries
NIEO. *See* New Inter-
   national Economic Order
Niger, 275, 276
Nigeria, 89(n6), 159, 226,
   275, 276, 334, 335, 336,
   338, 345(n2), 346(n14)
Norway, 12(n1), 75(n8), 93,
   100(n10), 262(n18), 271,
   276
Nyerere, J., 373

O'Brien, P., 213(n1), 268,
   287
O'Hearn, D., 295, 297, 300,
   303, 305, 307, 438
Ohkawa, K., 59
oligopoly, 240, 291(n5), 353
Olson, M., 60, 66, 72(n4),
   75(n14), 76(n21), 353,
   354, 355, 362
OM syndrome, 161
OPEC, 321, 350
other-directedness, 150
overurbanisation, 365(n12)

Packenham, R., 214
Paige, J., 317
Pakistan, 15, 105, 111, 224,
   291, 345(n9)
Palma, O., 445
Panama, 276, 279, 319
Papua New Guinea, 118
Passé-Smith, J., 438, 439,
   440
Paukert, F., 273, 275, 276,
   397, 398
Pearson, P., 219, 345
peasants, 297, 317, 339, 345,
   357, 379
periphery, 6, 195, 205, 206,
   209, 210, 213, 214(n5,
   n6), 226–228, 229, 232–
   234, 235, 240, 241, 245,
   247–249, 251, 253–256,
   257, 258, 259–260(n7,
   n9), 261(n10), 263(n24),
   267–272, 273, 274, 276,
   278, 279, 281, 283–285,
   287, 288, 289, 290, 295,
   302, 310, 317, 364(n4)
Peru, 27, 167(n3), 208, 276,
   310
pharmaceuticals, 307, 308,
   410
Philippines, 81, 171
pluralistism, 100, 179, 180,
   340, 341
Poland, 89(n4), 364(n6)

political control, 341, 430
political violence, 315, 316,
   319, 402
Portes, A., 186, 268, 287
Portugal, 12, 94, 96, 98, 100,
   147, 150, 207, 229
protectionism, 69, 200, 362,
   365, 416, 417, 422, 426–
   428, 431, 432
"Protestant ethic," 5, 91, 97,
   98, 100, 141, 143, 144,
   146, 154, 157, 169, 170,
   171, 177, 178, 181, 183,
   184, 311
Prussia, 44, 55
public good, 82–85, 87, 88,
   92, 98
Puerto Rico, 29(n4), 32, 43,
   49, 50
purchasing power parity, 62,
   89, 103–105, 111, 114,
   116, 117, 126, 147, 148,
   201, 227, 322, 323, 336,
   428, 440; benchmark
   countries, 34, 75, 99,
   104

Ranis, G., 29(n4), 123
Ray, J., 244, 247, 261(n10),
   351, 352
Reagan, R., 425, 427
real gross domestic product
   (RGDP), 77, 103, 104,
   105, 111, 113, 114, 116–
   118
Red Army, 99, 100
Redfield, R., 160
redistribution, 121–123, 125,
   190, 268, 287, 290, 306,
   324, 356, 360, 361,
   376(n5), 378, 394
relative gap, 3, 9, 10, 12, 23–
   25, 28, 438
rent-seeking, 6, 7, 347–349,
   352–355, 357–360, 361,
   362, 363(n1, n2),
   365(n12), 377, 387(n6),
   445
RGDP. *See* real gross domestic product
Romania, 89(n6), 261(n11),
   263(n22)
Rosenfeld, S., 7, 295, 421
Rostow, W., 219, 220
Rubinson, R., 7(n3), 272,
   273, 288, 304, 306, 349–
   352, 361, 363(n2), 397,
   398, 399, 445
Rwanda, 257

Sandinistas, 316
Saudi Arabia, 261–262(n15),
   262–263(n20), 439
Saxony, 45, 55(n1)
Scheidegger, J., 249,
   261(n14), 270, 273, 275,

276, 283, 288, 291(n6),
   382
Schumpeter, J., 83, 151, 174,
   175, 364(n6)
Seers, D., 54–55(n1), 119,
   272
Seligson, M., 3, 437, 438
semiperiphery, 6, 226, 229,
   232, 233, 251, 253,
   263(n27), 302
Senegal, 276
Sierra Leone, 111, 276
Singapore, 29, 122, 171,
   262(n19), 296, 300, 308,
   310, 311(n2), 407, 421,
   422, 424–426, 430–
   433(n14)
Singh, R., 359, 361
Sirowy, L., 7, 389
Skocpol, T., 231, 317
Somoza, A., 315, 316
South Africa, 150, 223, 286,
   361
South Asia, 10, 178
South Korea, 23, 26, 28, 122,
   169, 171, 296, 309, 310,
   364(n4), 421–434, 440;
   "Confucian ethic," 169;
   development strategy,
   296, 300, 309, 310, 407–
   419; economic growth in,
   4, 7, 10, 11, 19, 122, 309,
   440; inequality, 283, 402
Soviet Union, 6, 171,
   214(n6), 220, 222, 363–
   364(n4), 427, 428
Spain, 12(n1), 93, 94, 96, 98,
   100(n10), 146, 150,
   157(n6), 181(n16, n17),
   207, 271, 276, 283, 286
Sri Lanka, 43, 105, 111, 116,
   440
Stack, S., 401
stages of development, 32,
   164
*The Stages of Economic
   Growth*, 219
state-owned industry, 122,
   334, 408, 409, 412
Stevenson, P., 244
Stoneman, C., 244, 245, 247,
   248, 249, 260(n5)
Stonequist, E., 160
Streeten, P., 119, 122, 125,
   126, 376(n6)
subsidies, 198, 200, 333, 338,
   341–343, 345, 355, 356,
   357, 375, 379, 425, 426,
   428
Sunkel, O., 204, 206, 209,
   213(n1, n2, n4), 215(n9,
   n11, n15, n16), 216(n20),
   268, 272, 290(n3)
Sweden, 12(n1), 75(n8,
   n16), 94, 100(n10), 105,
   155, 262(n18), 271, 276

Switzerland, 12(n1), 74–75(n8, n16), 100(n10), 103, 105, 262(n18), 439
Syria, 118(n6), 262(n19)
Szymanski, A., 244, 247, 261(n10), 262(n17)

Taiwan, 10, 169, 267, 276, 291(n7), 296, 402, 440; "Confucian ethic," 171; development strategy, 296, 300, 309, 310, 407–419, 421–434; economic growth in, 4, 7; foreign investment in, 78, 271; in-equality in, 122, 271
Tanzania, 276, 335, 336, 373
tariffs, 103, 197, 199, 297, 305, 310, 311(n1), 337, 354, 359, 379, 416, 417, 423, 427, 429, 442
Thailand, 19, 171, 431
Tilly, C., 231, 317
tribe, 144, 146, 154, 164, 179
"trickle down," 121, 125, 128, 129, 130, 132, 133, 134, 291(n8), 310
Trinidad and Tobago, 276
Tullock, G., 352, 354, 360, 362, 365(n17)
Tunisia, 286
Turkey, 12(n1), 99(n6), 154, 157(n10), 224, 363–364(n4)

Uganda, 89(n6)
UNCTAD. See United Nations Conference on Trade and Development
underdeveloped, 31, 32, 34, 35, 38, 49–55, 148, 155, 156, 166, 186, 188, 189, 194, 195, 197, 198, 200, 201, 205, 212, 213, 355, 438
underdevelopment, 159, 163, 164, 167(n3), 173, 174, 183, 194, 203–206, 210, 212, 213–214(n5, n6), 220, 287, 295, 437, 438
unemployment, 15, 69, 78, 124, 213(n5), 304, 305, 308, 309, 311(n5), 320, 321, 323, 324, 327(n18), 354
unions and unionization, 67, 72, 74, 125, 161, 170, 208, 210, 307–309, 317, 354, 355, 356, 357, 361, 365(n15), 379, 402
United Kingdom, 12(n1), 43–46, 49, 50, 54–55(n1), 62, 74–75(n8, n9, n16),

78, 80, 81, 87(n1), 88(n4), 100, 262(n17), 271, 439
United Nations (UN), 4, 13(n5), 15, 55(n4), 104, 197, 215, 261(n10, n11), 290(n9), 345, 372, 376(n1), 440
United Nations Conference on Trade and Development (UNCTAD), 197, 202
United States, 4, 12, 13, 27, 29, 35, 43–46, 48–51, 54(n1), 57, 62, 64–68, 69, 71–75, 77, 78, 80, 81, 84, 91–94, 96, 98, 100(n10), 105, 126, 127, 129, 131, 134, 136, 142, 143, 147, 150, 154, 155, 160, 163, 164, 169, 173, 174, 180, 184, 194, 207, 216(n19), 219, 222, 224–226, 233, 241, 247, 251, 255, 260–261(n9), 261(n10, n13), 262(n18), 263, 270, 271, 276(n2), 301, 302, 308, 319, 326(n5), 327, 345(n9), 350, 353, 360, 364(n11), 390, 397, 400, 407–409, 417, 422–428, 429, 430, 432, 434(n17, 19), 439, 441; colonial background, 51, 98; con-sumerism in, 72; conver-gence with, 64–68, 92–94, 96, 98; democracy as factor in development of, 96, 219; foreign aid, 271, 423; foreign investment, 174, 199, 270, 299, 301–302, 308, 408; inequality in, 43–46, 48–51; and Mexico, 360, 408–409; military intervention, 319, 423–424; "n achieve-ment" in, 147, 150, 154, 155; productivity levels, 62, 65–69, 72, 77–78, 80, 81, 84, 92, 98; protection-ism, 417, 422–423, 427–432; technological superi-ority, 57, 67, 84, 92, 432; trade, 418, 425, 427; unions, 74; Washington, D.C., 54, 74, 76, 261, 345, 376, 427, 434; welfare in, 73
urban bias, 7, 331, 345(n9), 357, 365(n12), 371–373, 375, 376(n6), 377–386, 387(n3, n4), 445
urbanization, 46–49, 228, 365, 386

Uruguay, 176
USAID (United States Agency for International Development), 173, 261
USSR (former Union of Soviet Socialist Republics), 89(n5), 155, 219–221, 224, 225. See also Soviet Union

Veblen, T., 71, 81
Venezuela, 89(n5), 99(n6), 197, 208, 209, 247, 261(n9), 263(n24), 276, 286
Vernon, R., 69, 166
Vietnam, 229, 262, 423, 424

wages, 35, 38, 68, 69, 79, 84, 88, 124, 207, 306, 308, 318, 321, 322, 324, 326, 327, 339, 340, 344, 354, 357, 360, 422, 426, 429, 431–433
Wallerstein, I., 6, 184, 210, 214, 215, 217, 231–237, 263, 349–352, 361, 362, 363
Weber, M., 5, 100, 141, 143, 144, 152, 157, 169, 171, 177–179, 181, 183, 184
Weede, E., 6, 7, 246, 247, 273, 274, 347, 351, 352, 358, 359, 361, 364, 365, 377, 379, 381, 383, 387, 395, 397–399, 401, 402, 443
Weiner, M., 183
World Bank, 7(n1, n2), 9, 15, 16, 19(n2), 29, 89(n5), 104, 105, 111, 113, 116, 117(n3, n5), 120, 122, 126, 174, 250, 261(n10, n11, n13), 267, 276, 281, 283, 285, 288, 291(n7, n8), 345(n9), 347, 348, 358, 364–365(n12), 373, 379, 380, 382, 398, 423, 439, 441, 446(n1); World Development Report, 7(n1, n2), 16, 21, 28–29(n1, n3), 29, 111, 113, 117(n4), 174, 267, 311(n1)

Yorubaland, 445
Yugoslavia, 89(n6), 224, 261(n11), 263(n22), 268, 279, 281, 283, 286, 289

Zambia, 26, 276, 335, 340, 342, 344–345(n1), 346(n13)

About the Book and Editors

Why have some countries succeeded at the task of economic development, while others have failed dismally? Designed to address this question—to explain the persistence and even widening of the gap between both rich and poor countries and rich and poor within poor countries—this anthology draws upon classic as well as current literature.

Students will find conventional explanations based on theories of modernization and culture, revisionist explanations focusing on dependency and world-systems analysis, and the most recent literature on rent-seeking, markets, and states. Empirical evidence evaluates the success of the contending theories presented; case studies are also included. The final chapter draws conclusions about where development theory has been and where it is going.

Mitchell A. Seligson is UCIS Research Professor and professor of political science at the University of Pittsburgh. His most recent books include *Elections and Democracy in Central America* and *Authoritarians and Democrats: Regime Transition in Latin America. John T Passé-Smith* is assistant professor of political science at the University of Central Arkansas. He is coauthor of *Unionization of the Maquiladora Industry* and is completing a book on growth and world inequality in the post–World War II era.